OXFORD

Nazism

Neil Gregor is Lecturer in Modern German History at the University
of Southampton. He is the author of *Daimler-Benz in the Third Reich*
(1998) and of articles on the history and memory of National
Socialism.

OXFORD **READERS**

....

The Oxford Readers series represents a unique resource which brings together extracts of texts from a wide variety of sources, primary and secondary, on a wide range of interdisciplinary topics.

Available

Aesthetics
Edited by Patrick Maynard and Susan Feagin

Class
Edited by Patrick Joyce

Classical Philosophy
Edited by Terence Irwin

Ethics
Edited by Peter Singer

Ethnicity
Edited by John Hutchinson and Anthony D. Smith

Evolution
Edited by Mark Ridley

Faith and Reason
Edited by Paul Helm

Fascism
Edited by Roger Griffin

Feminisms
Edited by Sandra Kemp and Judith Squires

The Mind
Edited by Daniel Robinson

Nationalism
Edited by John Hutchinson and Anthony D. Smith

Nazism
Edited by Neil Gregor

Political Thought
Edited by Michael Rosen and Jonathan Wolff

Racism
Edited by Martin Bulmer and John Solomos

Sexuality
Edited by Robert A. Nye

War
Edited by Lawrence Freedman

Forthcoming

Anti-Semitism
Edited by Paul Lawrence Rose

The British Empire
Edited by Jane Samson

Consciousness
Edited by Geoffrey Underwood

Revolution
Edited by Jack Goldstone

Slavery
Edited by Stanley Engermann, Seymour Drescher, and Robert Paquette

OXFORD **READERS**

Nazism

Edited by Neil Gregor

OXFORD
UNIVERSITY PRESS

OXFORD

UNIVERSITY PRESS

Great Clarendon Street, Oxford OX2 6DP

Oxford University Press is a department of the University of Oxford.
It furthers the University's objective of excellence in research, scholarship,
and education by publishing worldwide in

Oxford New York

Athens Auckland Bangkok Bogotá Buenos Aires Calcutta
Cape Town Chennai Dar es Salaam Delhi Florence Hong Kong Istanbul
Karachi Kuala Lumpur Madrid Melbourne Mexico City Mumbai
Nairobi Paris São Paulo Shanghai Singapore Taipei Tokyo Toronto Warsaw

with associated companies in Berlin Ibadan

Oxford is a registered trade mark of Oxford University Press
in the UK and in certain other countries

Published in the United States
by Oxford University Press Inc., New York

British Library Cataloguing in Publication Data

Data available

Library of Congress Cataloging in Publication Data

Data available

ISBN 0-19-289281-9

1 3 5 7 9 10 8 6 4 2

Typeset in Dante
by RefineCatch Limited, Bungay, Suffolk
Printed in Great Britain by
Biddles Ltd., Guildford, Surrey

Preface

I should like to thank Joan Tumblety, Tony Kushner (whose work on old Eastleigh continues to be a source of inspiration), David Cesarani, Jo Reilly, Kendrick Oliver, Edgar Feuchtwanger, Rodney Livingstone, Alan Bance, Tim Reuter, and many other colleagues in the Faculty of Arts at the University of Southampton, not only for their various suggestions for this volume, but also for providing such a stimulating environment for thinking about the history and memory of European fascism; thanks are also due to Jeremy Noakes, both for his many suggestions and comments on this volume, and for his continued support and encouragement. George Miller, Fiona Kinnear, Lesley Wilson, and Jackie Pritchard provided excellent editorial support at OUP. To John Want, Judith Hayward, Sue Young, Beth Linklater, Bella Millet, and most 'Germanist' colleagues in the School of Modern Languages here at Southampton I owe gratitude for their help with some of the translation work. I also benefited greatly from the expertise and helpfulness of librarians at the Wiener Library in London, the Parkes Library at the University of Southampton, the German Historical Institute in London, the Ural State University of Ekaterinburg, the British Library, and Cambridge University Library. In Helen Cope I had a tireless and endlessly helpful research assistant for whose hard labours I am also grateful. Last, but by no means least, I should like very much to reaffirm my gratitude to all of my colleagues in the Department of History at the University of Southampton for their collegiality and good humour, and for the stimulus which their own scholarship provides. In an age in which most of what is valuable about British higher education is being vandalized, their support and the intellectual stimulus of their work are particularly important.

As I worked on this volume the University of Southampton was hit by the tragic loss of three students in an outbreak of meningitis. One of them, Charlotte Simpkin, was a first-year student in the Department of History. Although she was only with us for a very short time, she impressed all who taught her with her ability, commitment, and enthusiasm, and her loss affected us all deeply. Like so many undergraduates, she had a particular interest in the history of Nazi Germany and had intended to specialize in this field. It thus seems fitting to dedicate this volume to her memory.

N.G.

Contents

C. The National Socialist Regime

D. The 'Seductive Surface' of National Socialism

E. National Socialism and German Society

F. The Impact of National Socialism

G. The Legacy of National Socialism

General Introduction

The ideological origins of National Socialism, the development of a political culture in which it could prosper, and the social formation of its potential constituency all go back to the late nineteenth century. Very rapid and uneven industrialization had created deep social fissures which formed the basis for increasing political conflict. Most importantly, the speed of German industrialization, and the failure of either the state or existing political parties to respond to the challenge of integrating the growing industrial working classes into the existing political framework, had led to the rapid emergence of Social Democracy, which represented a new, radical threat to the propertied classes. Not least as a result of the early introduction of universal male suffrage in 1867 and then in the Reich constitution of 1871, Germany became a highly politicized society. However, the weakness of Germany's parliamentary institutions was simultaneously such that the Reichstag did not provide the means for the mediation and resolution of political conflict, and all pressure to reform the constitution was vigorously resisted by the landowning conservative classes, whose entrenched power in the Prussian parliament gave them an effective veto over reform.

The weakness of Germany's parliamentary institutions may be seen as having contributed in the last decade of the century to the growth of extra-parliamentary pressure and protest groups whose ideological goals and interests partly coincided with those of the establishment, but whose autonomy and style of populist mobilization and activism represented an additional challenge to the status quo nonetheless. It would be easy to overstate the significance and influence of these groups, but it is worth noting that there were clear lines of continuity in the style of populist agitation, the aims, and the constituencies which they mobilized between groups such as the Pan-German League or the Agrarian League of the pre-1914 period and the radical nationalist and rural protest movements of the 1920s. Further, we should note that the late nineteenth century witnessed the consolidation within both the political elites and broad sectors of society of a definition of nationhood expressed in the polarized language of inclusion and exclusion, in which marginal or minority political, ethnic, or cultural groups—Socialists, Catholics, Poles or Jews—were stigmatized as 'enemies of the Reich'. The official sanctioning and popular consolidation of such political, cultural, and ethnic resentments helped to create a climate which, under extreme conditions of crisis and disorientation, could provide fertile ground for a radicalized ideology of community in which the language of exclusion could easily evolve into the rhetoric of eradication.

This was particularly ominous when extreme variants of nationalism began to merge with new biological-racial theories of social development which provided pseudo-intellectual underpinning for growing popular anti-Semitism in the late nineteenth century. If we wish to find German peculiarities in the late nineteenth century which help to explain the long-term origins of National Socialism we should undoubtedly focus on the emergence of the mixture of ideas of Social Darwinism, nationalism, 'race science' and eugenics, and *völkisch* thinking during that period. Such ideas were not confined to a few cranks, but began to inform the thinking of many in professions such as medicine, psychiatry, and academia. However, it remains hard to define the precise relationship between ideas within specific professional communities, the formation of broader cultural ideologies, and the world of high politics, and it should be noted that many of these ideas were in no sense the preserve of the nineteenth-century radical Right. Darwinist theories could be ideologically allied to *laissez-faire* liberalism; organicist notions of community could be pressed into the service of internationalist or social-liberal political visions; eugenics and 'race hygiene' could be adopted by progressive forces on the Left.

Most of all, such ideas were far from peculiar to Germany. Although the political polarization of German society was as great as that of most other European societies immediately prior to the First World War, and although there are grounds for believing that liberal values and liberal politics were facing particular challenges in Germany, Nazism, or a variant of it, was no more likely in Germany at this point than it was elsewhere. What made Nazism possible in Germany was, above all, the experience of the First World War, of defeat, and of national humiliation in the subsequent peace.

The hardships imposed on German society by four years of wartime mobilization exacerbated the already deep-seated social and political conflicts which had come to a head in the elections of 1912 and which had been only momentarily submerged by the *Burgfrieden* (peace at the fortress) of 1914. Although the Social Democratic Party had initially supported the war, the consensus behind it began to break down as the war aims of the Army High Command became more and more expansionist and annexationist. As the war began to place increasing burdens on the German working classes, criticisms of the war grew from the Left, which started to demand 'peace without annexations'. Eventually the Left split, leading to the formation of the more left-wing and pacifist Independent Social Democratic Party in 1917; this was followed by a further moment of fracture and radicalization on the Left in 1918 with the formation of the Communist Party. Social Democratic support for the war also became increasingly tied up with demands for constitutional reform, which was resisted by the conservative landowning classes since their constitutionally guaranteed effective veto enabled them to enforce the financing of the war by loans, rather than by taxation of their property. This refusal to accept reform, and the ensuing reliance of the government on successive loans, laid the foundations for the subsequent inflation which was to do so much to destroy the fragile legitimacy of the Weimar Republic; in the short term it was instrumental in undermining the fragile consensus behind the war and in fostering growing domestic political polarization.

Within the middle classes and on the Right, the war also led to a further moment of populist mobilization and nationalist radicalization, in the shape of the Fatherland Party, which was formed in 1917 to generate support for the military's annexationist aims. The Bolshevik Revolution of 1917 also greatly intensified middle-class fears of the spectre of the radical Left. Above all, however, the war, the subsequent defeat, and the terms of the Treaty of Versailles provided the Right with a powerful set of memories and nationalist mythologies which were to become central to Nazism both in its attacks on the Weimar Republic and in its practices and actions once in power. More important than the reality of popular reactions to the outbreak of war, which were in fact mixed, was the myth of the 'spirit of 1914'—of a moment of national unity in which class divisions were transcended by patriotic fervour as young men rushed to enlist in the defence of the Fatherland. The trench experience itself, the experience of mass slaughter and violence, gave rise to hundreds of thousands of men who found it impossible to readjust to civilian life—many of whom joined the various right-wing paramilitary leagues which contributed so strongly to the culture of violence which bedevilled the Weimar Republic. The first generation of National Socialists, the so-called 'old fighters' (*Alte Kämpfer*) from whom the secondary leadership of *Gauleiters* was heavily drawn, was the generation which had fought in the First World War. But just as important, especially when we bear in mind that most members of the Nazi party or SA were too young to have fought in the First World War, was its subsequent mythologization: just as important were the masculine myths of camaraderie and of a classless community forged in the blood of the trenches which were to form a central part of National Socialism's self-understanding and of its rhetorical arsenal against democracy. Most important of all, the circumstances of defeat, revolution, and humiliation of 1918–19 laid the foundation for the potent nationalist myth of the 'stab in the back'—the idea that the German army had been let down by a collapse in the home front treacherously orchestrated by the internal enemies of the people, above all Marxists and Jews. For the radical Right, the German nation at war had been infiltrated and undermined by parasitic enemies who were now in charge of a Republic which represented everything un-German: regenerating and renewing the health of the 'national body' would mean above all the eradication of these enemies.

The multiple negative legacies of the First World War and the impact of successive crises of capitalism proved too much for a fledgling democracy struggling to establish its legitimacy. Saddled with the burdens of defeat and the peace treaty, weakened by distributional conflicts born of successive economic crises whose origins—in the case of the hyperinflation—pre-dated it, and the object of hostility from powerful economic and functional elites who continued to sustain a culture of deep-seated anti-democratic sentiment shared by significant sectors of the population, the Weimar Republic singularly failed to establish a Republican political culture. The militarization of political activism and rhetoric, itself a legacy of the First World War, rendered the formation of a democratic political culture difficult; the Republic itself never managed to create a set of Republican symbols or images which inspired popular support. The polarization of Left and Right and the disintegration of the pro-Republican middle-class constituency made the formation of governing coalitions increasingly difficult. The progressive recentering of political debate onto the agenda of the nationalist Right—embodied in the campaign against reparations—meant that the forces of moderacy and political realism were constantly on the defensive.

The deep political and ideological divisions which ran through German society were held in check to some extent in the initial years of the Republic by the need to manufacture domestic unity in the face of external pressures, particularly with regard to Germany's diplomatic position, and by perceived internal threats, particularly that of Communism. The accelerating erosion of the value of Germany's currency during the inflation also served to take the edge off distributional conflicts and to mask the real costs of the First World War for the German economy. Once the immediate threat of revolution had receded, however, the elites felt able to seek to renege on the compromises of 1918–20 with increasing self-confidence, while the stabilization of Germany's currency in 1923–4 brought home to German industry the real costs of the concessions made to labour in the revolutionary period. The German military establishment regarded the restoration of authoritarian government as a precondition for rearmament and a more overtly revisionist foreign policy. Although Weimar's economic problems and welfare commitments were overwhelmingly legacies of the lost war and not of the supposed excessive powers of organized labour, industrialists used the growing unemployment bill caused by the high unemployment of the mid–late 1920s as a stick with which to beat a Republic which they blamed for their elusive profitability. Increasingly, and especially during the Depression, they saw in the Republic a barrier to industrial peace and sustained profitability, and agitated actively for its replacement.

Nazism emerged in the context of this crisis of legitimacy of liberal parliamentary democracy in the aftermath of the First World War. It developed by stages over the 1920s and 1930s to fill the vacuum created by the Republic's failure. As with other fascist ideologies and movements it subscribed to an ideology of national renewal, rebirth, and rejuvenation, manifesting itself in extreme populist radical nationalism, militarism, and—in contradistinction to many other forms of fascism—extreme biological racism, directed above all against the Jews. The movement understood itself to be, and indeed was, a new form of political movement, held together by charismatic leadership and engaging in a new form of revolutionary political activism, central to which was paramilitary mobilization and street violence. The glorification of violence and militarism was particularly evident in the ritual and symbolic practices of Nazism, with their emphasis on rallies, uniforms, and paramilitary display, and with their appropriation of military heroes, military values, and events in the construction of a legitimizing symbolic system. Once in power, violence was used to terrifying effect on the regime's perceived internal and external enemies, political and ideological. At first this manifested itself in the incarceration of many tens of thousands of political opponents (overwhelmingly supporters of the Left) in concentration camps, alongside growing categories of loosely defined 'enemies of the people' such as homosexuals, members of minority sects, or 'hereditary criminals'. In the case of these latter groups National Socialist ideology provided a rationalization for the brutalization, and often murder, of groups who were socially stigmatized and marginalized by 'healthy popular opinion'. Later, Nazi aggression was directed outwards as it sought to implement its imperialist goals. Finally, it reached a climax in the 'euthanasia' programme, in the murder squads in Poland and on the eastern front, and in the mass extermination of European Jewry. In short, the ritualized martial imagery of the *Kampfzeit* (time of struggle) and of the party rallies after 1933 was not a superficial end in itself but an expression of Nazism's fundamental nature and intentions.

The Nazi movement drew its support from broad sectors of the population, from all socio-cultural milieux, and could claim with some justification to be genuinely transclass in nature. Nonetheless, the social basis of Nazism's support was still primarily in the middle class, both before and after the seizure of power, and in small-town and rural milieux rather than in the large industrial centres. The anti-Socialist, anti-liberal, and radical nationalist tenets of Nazi ideology appealed particularly to the sentiments of a middle class disorientated by the domestic and international upheavals in the inter-war period. The radical anti-Semitism of the party's activists was not the prime motive for most people's support for the party, but neither did it prevent most voters from supporting it. The party appealed particularly to the young, for whom its new style of politics was attractive, and succeeded at key moments in mobilizing large numbers of those who had previously not voted. In rural areas, especially in Protestant north Germany, Nazism's ideology of renewal mobilized often diffuse cultures of protest in communities where the hostile forces of modernity, embodied in the Weimar Republic, combined with the debilitating impact of the agricultural Depression, appeared to be threatening the rural way of life in its entirety. As the Depression deepened, the movement grew radically in membership and support, emerging from fringe splinter group to largest party in the Reichstag in a few short years.

Once in power, it was also able to manufacture a high degree of popular consensus among all social classes, including, to a somewhat lesser extent, among workers. Far from duping a population whose sense of disorientation opened it to being misled, National Socialist propaganda spoke to deep-seated social resentments within broad sectors of the population; the mobilization of these contributed much to the underlying dynamism of the regime. Especially from 1936, when unemployment was overcome and the Rhineland was reoccupied, to 1940-1, when Germany's armies occupied almost the entire continent, Hitler enjoyed huge support. Success upon success contributed to the enhancement of Hitler's charismatic authority; at the same time, the nature of this charisma demanded ongoing success and thus eventually encouraged the regime to overextend itself. The general climate of popular consent also ensured that resistance to the Nazi regime was very limited in extent and effect. Although resistance came from all sectors of society, it was only from a small minority of each community in each case, and for every individual willing to resist there was another willing to denounce his or her neighbour to the Gestapo for even the most minor of transgressions. Even the apparatus of coercion was underpinned by popular participation.

The Nazi movement also attracted considerable support from the conservative economic and functional elites—landowners, industrialists, the army, and the civil service—and relied on the support of sectors of these elites to achieve power. While only a minority of the elites offered direct support, and while Hitler's appointment as Chancellor was regarded as the outcome of first choice by only a few, the widespread predilection of the conservative elites for authoritarian forms of rule and their unwillingness to compromise within the confines of constitutional Republican politics were crucial preconditions for Hitler's achievement of power. The partial programmatic and ideological affinities between German conservatism and Nazism were also crucial to the stabilization of Hitler's power and to the functioning of the regime in the early years, during which period it took the form of a compromise between the two. Despite some differences of emphasis, for example over policy towards Poland, the military establishment and the Foreign Office and diplomatic corps shared Hitler's goals in relation to overcoming the Treaty of Versailles and embarking upon rearmament. Similarly, the destruction of the organized Left in 1933, the erosion of collective bargaining, and the counter-cyclical stimulation of economic expansion generated widespread consensus within industry which outweighed occasional concern over trade policy or the balance of payments. In 1934 the marginalization of those elements of the NSDAP, above all the SA, who wished to confront too openly the conservative establishment further cemented stable relations between the conservative and Nazi Right.

However, National Socialism was far from being a conservative force, in that the commitment to its core ideology derived from its desire to restructure society in such a way that the traditional order upon which conservative claims to political power rested would itself be destroyed. The anti-conservative nature of National Socialism was evident above all in the processes of social engineering, 'positive' and 'negative' eugenics, and physical eradication through which it sought to fulfil its programme of racial renewal. This entailed the division of German society into 'national comrades' on the one hand, and 'community aliens' on the other. For members of the 'national community' (*Volksgemeinschaft*), comprehensive programmes of 'regeneration' (*Aufartung*) were developed, including marriage loans, mother and child welfare clinics, and so on, backed up by massive propaganda espousing the virtues of women pursuing their feminine destiny in motherhood. In many ways, these programmes, and the blend of eugenicist and technocratic mentalities which underpinned them, were similar to programmes developed in other European countries in response to the demographic impact of the First World War. For those deemed to be outside the 'national community', however, the Nazis pursued a programme of 'eradication' (*Ausmerze*), the dimensions of whose impact were out of all proportion to the 'positive' programmes, and at the end of which stood the concentration and extermination camps. Imagining the 'nation' as a 'body', the Nazis sought metaphorically and literally to purge society of all those elements it regarded as 'unhealthy', 'degenerate', 'asocial', or 'alien' and to foster the growth of a racially homogeneous and 'pure' society in which status would be defined not by old patterns of deference or authority but by *Leistung* (achievement), breeding, and commitment to the 'national community'. The external corollary of this programme of internal racial engineering was the pursuit of 'living space' in the east and the creation of a European 'New Order' based on racial reordering, expulsion, and extermination, culminating in Auschwitz.

As has often been pointed out, Nazi policy evolved in an ad hoc way. Decisions were often taken on a very short-term and opportunistic basis, and under circumstances which were sometimes different from those which Hitler or the Nazi leadership had expected. However, it is important not to lose sight of the wood for the trees. The Third Reich was driven by an ideological imperative. It is impossible to understand the introduction of rearmament, the announcement of conscription, the reoccupation of the Rhineland, the union with Austria, the destruction of Czechoslovakia, and the invasion of Poland, western Europe, and the Soviet Union without recognizing that Hitler was pursuing, in broad terms, a programme. The processes of economic exclusion, social discrimination, sexual segregation, brutalization, ghettoization, expulsion, and mass murder of the Jews can also not be understood as anything other than the product of an ideological drive which was, at least implicitly, genocidal. To give one example, the Law for the Prevention of Hereditarily Diseased Offspring (the so-called Sterilization Law) of July 1933 is clearly announced by unambiguous passages in Hitler's *Mein Kampf*. Although Hitler's statements were turned into law by a complex process of drafting and redrafting by officials, and although such laws often bear the traces of the specific moment at which they were introduced, the stipulations of the Nuremberg racial laws of September 1935 (to give a further infamous example) represent the implementation of measures clearly derived from core aspects of Nazi ideology which can be read in Hitler's pre-1933 writings.

Nonetheless, if we are to understand how the 'cumulative radicalization' of persecution, violence, and aggression spiralled out of control so quickly and with such little resistance, why it was that at particular moments Hitler felt it either necessary or possible to embark on further initiatives in pursuit of his goals, how it was that under the peculiar conditions of war, discrimination and expropriation escalated so rapidly into systematic genocide, and how it was that the apparatus of government, the institutions of civil society, and large sectors of the population came to be co-opted into the machinery of genocide with such apparent ease, we need to consider how it was that the political, institutional, and above all moral barriers to the realization of a process of mass murder which few can have envisaged, let alone hoped for, in 1933, were removed.

As a huge and persuasive body of research has shown, the Nazi polity was far from monolithic and was anything but stable. Although the early years of Hitler's rule were characterized by a substantial degree of cooperation between the Nazis and the conservative establishment which, as suggested, did much to stabilize the regime in the initial period, Hitler did not envisage the creation of a stable, authoritarian regime within the existing structures of the state. Unlike in Italy, where the radical dynamism of the Fascist movement was dissipated once Mussolini had achieved power, as Mussolini moved into an essentially stable relationship with the forces of conservatism and built his regime within the pre-existing institutions of state, the revolutionary radicalism of National Socialism was sustained in power. Unlike Mussolini, Hitler gradually dispensed with the cooperation of the traditional elites, removing power from the traditional organs of state, whose bureaucratic routines and sense of administrative order Hitler regarded as an impediment to the drive and dynamism of the 'politics of the will'. In the sphere of foreign policy, for example, the Foreign Office and the military were gradually marginalized as independent centres of power and decision-making. A turning point here came with the removal of Generals Blomberg and Fritsch and the conservative Foreign Minister Neurath during the winter of 1937–8, but this was an ongoing process. Similarly, control over policing and security functions was gradually removed from the Interior Ministry, and concentrated in the hands of Himmler and Heydrich's SS, which grew into a huge terror and murder apparatus independent of the traditional institutions of state.

Not only did Hitler gradually allow responsibility for policy to pass into the hands of party radicals, he also tended to foster the creation of a large number of organizations and institutions, whose status in relation to party and state differed from case to case, but which typically took on the role of a 'special authority' under an individual charged with finding the 'solution' to a particular 'problem' which pre-existing institutions had failed to overcome. As a result, the internal development of the Third Reich was characterized by the proliferation of organs which operated in similar areas of policy with loosely defined jurisdictional boundaries and which competed for control of that area of policy against their rivals. In the field of labour policy, for example, the jurisdiction of the Reich Labour Ministry was challenged by the German Labour Front under Robert Ley, and the Ministry then lost control over significant fields of policy during the war to the office of the General Plenipotentiary for Labour Deployment under *Gauleiter* Fritz Sauckel. Similarly, the Reich Economics Ministry found itself sidelined in important areas of policy by the creation in 1936 of the offices of the Four Year Plan under Göring, which sat alongside existing civilian and military bodies in the economic sphere; their failure to resolve the so-called 'munitions crisis' in 1940 led to the creation of the Ministry for Weapons and Munitions under Fritz Todt, which was expanded in 1942 and 1943 under Albert Speer to become the Reich Ministry for Armaments and War Production and which in turn marginalized the Four Year Plan offices.

The growing personalization of power and authority under the National Socialist regime, a product of Hitler's view that politics was a matter of will and that problems would be solved by dynamic individuals unencumbered by bureaucratic or legal restraint, encouraged the emergence of more radical leaders in each field of policy. In order to gain Hitler's support and prove themselves most able to carry out Hitler's ideas, these individuals and organizations tended to outdo each other in proposing ever more radical solutions than their rivals, which in itself tended to encourage a permanent radicalization of policy. These individuals saw themselves as implementing the 'Führer's will', as translating the 'Führer's wishes' into action. Hitler became the sole point of integration in an increasingly chaotic regime. The peculiarly unstable nature of his charismatic leadership, combined with the unfettered radicalism of the Nazi movement, resulted in a progressive decomposition of the rational, bureaucratic state, the radical erosion of legal norms and barriers, and the increasing transfer of power into the hands of party radicals. The period after 1939, in particular, witnessed a major process of transfer of power away from the state and into party and SS hands, as new institutions of colonial exploitation were created at the moment of ideological self-realization marked by the outbreak of war and the invasion of the Soviet Union. This created space for the unleashing of the movement's destructive impulses at the same time as the process of expansion presented the regime with ever-greater 'problems'—most obviously in the form of the growing numbers of Jews under its control—which rendered previous 'solutions' inadequate.

We neither explain the Holocaust nor do justice to its terrifying reality, however, if we seek to explain its evolution solely in terms of abstract structures or systems of rule. The complexity of the decision-making process or of Hitler's position within the National Socialist regime is one thing; the processes of implementation of Nazi racial policy and genocide are another. In addition to the enormous apparatus of mobilization and repression represented by the party, its subordinate institutions, and the SS, the Nazis relied upon the huge and complex substructures of a state which fulfilled multiple functions on every level, right down to the local—in administration, in welfare, in education, in medicine, in public order, etc. These apparatuses were populated by thousands upon thousands of bureaucrats and professionals—the sterilization and euthanasia programmes, for example, relied upon thousands of ordinary psychiatrists, doctors, nurses, social workers, and administrators for their implementation. Similarly, the administration of Nazi 'justice' could not have functioned without thousands of ordinary policemen, prison officers, lawyers, and judges who, whatever the occasional misgivings or scruples of a few of their members, colluded in and sustained the machinery of persecution, repression, and murder. Further, although the implementation of genocide was driven primarily by the SS, it relied upon the participation of thousands of policemen and ordinary soldiers who participated directly in the killing process. As many historians have stressed recently, the crimes of National Socialism were mass crimes not only in the sense that they claimed mass numbers of victims, but also in the sense that they were committed by a mass of perpetrators. The millions of ordinary people murdered under the National Socialist regime were not murdered by impersonal structures, but by many hundreds of thousands of other ordinary people.

Although, as outlined above, those institutions which had hitherto represented bastions of conservative reaction rather than National Socialist ideological zeal had been progressively marginalized or downgraded to the status of executive organs, the National Socialist regime still relied upon them to pursue and implement its goals. That it was able to do so was a product, in part at least, of the progressive dissipation of conservative influence and values in institutions such as the armed forces under the pressure of ideological penetration and generational change. Initially, there were enough generals with National Socialist sympathies for the regime to rely on to

inculcate its values into the army; the rapid expansion of the military hierarchy under the impact of rearmament created new opportunities for promotion for younger officers whose generally more pro-Nazi proclivities further
undermined the homogeneity of the old officer corps with its more 'Prussian' *esprit de corps*. The desire to prove their reliability to their new political
masters in the face of rivalry from first the SA and then the SS also ensured
that the armed forces 'coordinated' themselves and promoted National
Socialist values within their own ranks. By the time of the invasion of the
Soviet Union in 1941, the officer corps had become a deeply nazified institution, sharing the Nazi leadership's hatred of the 'Jewish-Bolshevik' Soviet
Union and, some individuals aside, fully committed to the racial war of
annihilation in the East. Significantly, whereas some generals had protested at
the murderous activities of the SS in Poland in 1939, such protests were
conspicuous by their absence following the attack on the Soviet Union—
indeed, the army leadership helped to draw up the orders for the campaign of
barbarism and supplied units of regular soldiers to augment the killing
squads of the SS. Most of all, the armed forces were directly responsible for
the deaths of millions of Soviet prisoners of war. Although only a minority
of army units participated actively in the mass killings of Soviet Jews, it is
notable that there are few indications that those units who were faced with
this task had any real qualms about fulfilling it—an indicator of the extent to
which Nazi ideology, propaganda, and images of the enemy had penetrated
the rank and file of the military too.

Similarly, although the SS and police apparatus were the leading agents of
radicalization in the administration of terror, the judiciary continued to play
a key role. For all its insistence on the maintenance of a degree of legalistic
order, the legal system became infused with National Socialist spirit and
ideology as the judiciary internalized and acted upon Nazi legal philosophy.
The inherently authoritarian sensitivities of a profession which saw its duty to
the rule of law in terms of serving the state rather than protecting individuals
facilitated its initial co-option. The wish to prove its reliability as an institution within the system was augmented by the ideological commitment of a
younger generation of pro-Nazi lawyers and judges which came to the fore
during the war, at precisely the point when the need to maintain the strength
of the home front and to prevent another 'November 1918' demanded the
ruthless persecution of 'enemies of the people'. The war witnessed a spiralling of terroristic justice as thousands were sent to prison, work education
camps, or concentration camps for allegedly 'undermining military morale'
(*Wehrkraftzersetzung*), for example by listening to foreign radio broadcasts or
spreading rumours. Likewise, supposed 'sabotage' of production or failure to
turn up to work in the factory could result in transfer to a concentration
camp, even if it had resulted from simple exhaustion or the need to make
basic repairs following air raid damage. Even more brutal and arbitrary,

especially in the final months of the war, was the treatment meted out by the justice authorities to the hapless and starving foreign forced workers, who could be condemned to summary execution if caught trying to escape or even trying to still their hunger by procuring a little food.

The implementation of genocide and racist social policy did not just rely upon the professional elites, however, but depended upon the mobilization of hundreds of thousands of ordinary Germans from all walks of life. Individuals who had been socialized in subcultures which had maintained a greater distance from Nazism, or in which there were no strong traditions of anti-Semitism, could, once placed in a different context, become mass killers. Workers might have regarded themselves as members of an oppositional culture; once in a soldier's uniform, however, they could participate in mass shootings of Jews. Some scholars have argued that this can only be explained in terms of a deep-seated, peculiarly German variant of anti-Semitism which was deeply ingrained in German culture. However, we only need give consideration to the thousands of Ukrainian or Lithuanian auxiliaries who participated in the genocide process in the east, or to the collaboration of the French *Milice*, to recognize that ethnic resentments or ideological commitment could, especially in the context of war, be mobilized among many non-German groups. Further, as many other scholars have emphasized, National Socialist mass murder did not begin with or confine itself to the Jews—the transition to mass murder began with the killing of the mentally ill, and millions of Soviet citizens and up to half a million gypsies were also the victims of killing processes closely linked to the murder of the Jews. Finally, although resistance in Germany was isolated when viewed in the context of the climate of overall consent and participation, the fact that many thousands of people did resist for a variety of moral and political motives shows that there were subcultures in Germany in which non-racist and non-nationalist mentalities survived. The reliance of the regime on cultures of authority and subservience within certain organizations, such as in the armed forces, or on the routinization of discrimination as an administrative principle, such as in the bureaucracy, was such that it may be possible to speak of institutional cultures which helped to facilitate genocide, but generalizations about uniquely racist national culture are unpersuasive.

The mentalities, pressures, and decisions which led to individuals or organizations becoming complicit in the implementation of Nazi racial and social policy differ from case to case. Insofar as ideology was concerned, the majority of Germans did not share the extreme anti-Semitism of the party leadership or activists, but a general culture of racial arrogance and pervasiveness of negative racial stereotypes did inform the attitudes of broad sectors of the population. Beyond this, a mixture of self-interest, commitment, sense of obligation, professional ambition, routinization, and peer pressure in contexts which differed radically and demand individual examination was usually involved. Although in one sense individuals had free choice over whether or not to participate, directly or indirectly, in the crimes of the regime—and many, indeed, exercised it—in practice they were exposed to situational pressures in each case which circumscribed from the outset the likely range of individual responses. In any case, individuals were rarely simply presented with a clear-cut choice of shifting from non-involvement to active participation in immoral acts of brutality, sadism, and murder. We can illustrate this briefly with two examples, neither of which involved primarily Jewish victims.

In the case of forced workers, for example, a mixture of impersonal imperatives and human discrimination was involved. Given the massive demand for armaments and the shortages of workers caused by call-ups to the army, companies willingly deployed large numbers of prisoners of war, foreign deportees, and concentration camp inmates under conditions which were at best extremely harsh and at worst brutally exploitative and murderous. The desire to generate profit, combined at a factory level with the daily pressure to maintain continuous production under increasingly difficult conditions, provided the underlying capitalist institutional rationale behind industry's cooperation with the forced labour programme. However, we cannot explain how managers who would have regarded themselves as civilized employers came to participate in such barbaric practices without recognizing the extent to which the shifting moral terrain from 1933 onwards eased their co-option into behaviour which they would have found unthinkable only a few years before. Long-standing traditions of paternalism and belief in their right to be 'masters in their own house', combined with deep hostility to Socialism and Communism, ensured their support for the destruction of the organized Left in 1933 and the institutionalization of an authoritarian shop-floor culture which was backed up by state terror; this authoritarian factory culture and collusion in Nazi terror made it correspondingly 'natural' to collude in the harsh treatment of west European prisoners of war and deportees. By 1942 it was only logical to extend this process further to collude in the exploitation of Soviet prisoners of war and civilian deportees under dreadful conditions, and, as this source of labour dried up, it was only a small further step to participating unquestioningly and willingly in the exploitation of concentration camp inmates. The descent into barbaric practices did not occur overnight, but was an incremental process.

Furthermore, we cannot explain the appalling experience of forced workers solely in terms of the infiltration of racist indifference into managerial culture. The system of forced labour relied upon hundreds of thousands of German skilled workers and foremen for it to operate on a shop-floor level, and upon many tens of thousands more to staff the primitive barracks in which the forced workers were housed—as guards, cooks, or administrators. The daily experience of degradation, hostility, and violence encountered by the foreign workers in the factories and barracks is evidence of the brutality of ordinary German workers towards the foreigners whom the former regarded mostly with a mixture of racial arrogance and indifference. Soviet prisoners of war in the factory could embody in person the enemy against whom other family members or colleagues were fighting on the eastern front, while their presence offered German workers the chance of promotion, upward mobility, and enhanced status as a member of the racially select within the factory environment. Although there were many individual acts of solidarity and support for foreign workers, their experience at the hands of ordinary Germans was mostly dreadful.

The medical profession serves as an example of how professional cultures could adapt with relative ease to National Socialist policies which often spoke, at least partially, to pre-existing beliefs within some sectors of the profession concerned. In the case of doctors and psychiatrists, the general climate of disregard for the rights of socially marginal and physically or mentally weak individuals was reinforced by the widely held view that such 'ballast existences' were an unnecessary and unaffordable burden on the state. A medical profession which had already come to accept certain more 'moderate' brands of eugenicist social thinking could rationalize its behaviour by the knowledge that it was doing the state's bidding. Within this climate, ambitious young professionals could find plenty of opportunities for promotion and self-advancement if they proved themselves dynamic and capable. In this field as elsewhere, the pervasive climate of indifference facilitated successive shifts in the boundaries of what was deemed to be not only acceptable but normal. The Sterilization Law of 1933 established the principle of wide-scale state-sanctioned intervention in the reproductive life of individuals, defining medical decisions in terms of the needs of the state—or rather the *Volk*—and not the patient, while the ongoing neglect and mistreatment of patients in hospitals and asylums from 1933 onwards further fostered a climate in which human sympathies for the weak gave way to the widespread acceptance of the desirability of 'mercy killing'. By the time mobile vans were travelling from institution to institution delivering the mentally ill to be murdered in large numbers, the killing process was being discussed only in terms of finding the best technical solution to what was seen by now as a purely practical problem.

In twelve short years, the National Socialist regime incarcerated many hundreds of thousands of political and ideological opponents in concentration camps, prisons, and labour camps in Germany and all over Europe, of whom hundreds of thousands died—workers, homosexuals, the socially marginal, priests, Jehovah's Witnesses, Jews. Some 350,000 German women and men fell victim to the programme of forcible sterilization. Over 70,000 mentally ill, handicapped, or fragile children and adults were murdered in hospitals and asylums in the name of so-called euthanasia. Millions of prisoners of war, above all from the Soviet Union, were left to die of starvation, disease, and exposure during the war in the east. Millions more prisoners of war, civilian deportees, and concentration camp inmates suffered appallingly as forced labour in factories in Germany and the occupied territories, their fate dictated by their position in the Nazi racial hierarchy. Up to half a million Sinti and Roma fell victim to Nazi genocide. Above all, over 6 million Jews were murdered in ghettos, expulsions, labour camps, mass-killing actions, and extermination camps. Taken in isolation, some of these acts may find parallels in the barbaric acts of twentieth-century regimes both in Europe and elsewhere. Taken together, seeing each within the context provided by the sum of the others, and recognizing that the bulk of these acts of inhumanity were implemented during a five-year war of ideologically motivated annihilation towards which National Socialism had been working from the moment of its inception, it is difficult not to see the immensity of National Socialist destruction as unique. Whatever similarities it exhibited to other regimes, the singularity of National Socialism lies in its unique destructiveness.

Few historical subjects have generated as much scholarly literature; few historical subjects occupy as central a place in the contemporary consciousness. From the 'totalitarianism theory' of the 1950s to the 'fascism debate' of the 1960s, through the 'intentionalist-structuralist' debates of the 1970s and 1980s to the emergence in the 1980s and 1990s of theories of charismatic authority and the primacy of the 'racial paradigm', changing emphases in the scholarly literature have reflected both the findings of ongoing empirical enquiry and changes in the contexts in which the scholarship has been occurring. As many have observed, western writings of the 1950s betray the concerns of liberal democracy fighting the Cold War. In the 'fascism debate' which took place in West Germany in the 1960s we can detect a set of concerns rooted in a critique of capitalism which placed emphasis on the need to combat perceived fascist potential in the society in which that debate was taking place—there was clear intellectual and political cross-fertilization between academic discussions of fascism taking place in the 1960s and the critiques of the Federal Republic being articulated by the West German students' movement at the time. Scholars of a later generation will no doubt detect contemporary concerns in the writings of historians in the 1990s.

Yet, for all these shifts, the key point about ongoing discussion of the Nazi past is that it is occurring in a democratic culture and that the past which it is discussing remains contested. The proliferation of scholarship, and the diversity of it, refines our knowledge in many ways and yet makes it harder to retain a sense of the overall trends in the historiography at the same time. At least two competing overall narratives of the emergence of National Socialism seem to exist—one a modified version of the *Sonderweg* (Special Path) thesis, which continues to stress the authoritarian legacies of the imperial era, the other a history which emphasizes more the massive rupture of the First World War. On the one hand, the 1990s have witnessed a welcome rediscovery of the concept of 'fascism' (the work of Roger Griffin, editor of the companion volume on *Fascism* in this series, is both symptom and cause of this trend), and scholars have rediscovered interest in those aspects of National Socialism which allow us to relate it to similar movements which emerged at the time; on the other hand, and in apparent contradiction to this, the 1990s have seen proper emphasis for the first time on the centrality of racism and racial politics to all spheres of National Socialist policy, serving only to underline its uniqueness.

This reader is designed to introduce students to some of the key writings of the last seventy years which have sought to explain the origins, nature, consequences, and legacy of this unique destructiveness. It is not the intention to survey and reproduce in detail historiographical developments relating to specific aspects of the Third Reich. Many excellent anthologies of recent secondary literature exist to introduce students to the most important interpretative debates on, for example, the origins of the Second World War or the Nazi rise to power. On an ongoing basis, scholars collaborate in the production of research-based volumes enhancing the state of knowledge in particular areas of enquiry, and, within a reasonable period of time, those works of scholarship, individual or collective, which find their way into the canon usually begin to inform more general texts offered to students. The volume focuses, rather, on a broader set of questions relating to the nature of Nazism, the reasons why it took root in Germany, the sources of its peculiar radicalism and dynamism, the extent and nature of its destructive actions, and the peculiar legacy it left to post-war Germany and the world. The texts offered are indicative, I hope, of a broad set of historical, political, and moral concerns, tempered, I also hope, with a healthy element of eclecticism.

Proceeding from the assumption that the causes of Nazism and the roots of its peculiar impulsiveness are to be explained in terms of the depth and multi-dimensionality of the crises which began with the First World War, the emphasis in the section on the Origins of Nazism is on studies which discuss aspects of the immediate crisis of Weimar and the emergence of the movement. The belief that the key to understanding the unprecedented spiral of radicalization once the movement had achieved power lies initially in comprehending the specific relationship of the institutions of conservative power to the Nazi movement after 1933 and the progressive emergence of the prerogative 'Führer State' underlies the inclusion of a substantial body of texts discussing the role of the army, the civil service, industry, and the judiciary in the Nazi 'state'; their progressive marginalization within the increasingly chaotic and disintegrating body-politic is discussed by a further set of texts which focus on the nature of the Nazi polycracy. Since the Third Reich is to be understood, at least for a very substantial proportion of ordinary Germans, as primarily a voluntarist regime underpinned by popular acclamation, a further group of texts deals with the 'seductive surface'—the rituals, rallies, and symbols which characterized Nazism's self-understanding and a significant aspect of most ordinary Germans' daily experiences during the Third Reich. This voluntarist mobilization, and its success in marginalizing the potential for opposition, is explored in texts examining the limits of dissent and the ability of the regime to co-opt large numbers of Germans into implementing its goals. The consequences of this are explored in texts examining the impact of Nazism, and above all the impact of its racial policies. Finally, the reader contains a set of texts discussing aspects of the legacy of Nazism and genocide for the post-war world.

The possibilities and limitations of a reader of secondary extracts are to some extent defined by the conventions of the genre. I have consciously chosen not to organize the book around a central narrative of the Third Reich on the grounds that other formats lend themselves much better to this (the volume might most usefully be used by students in conjunction with the admirable series of primary source readers produced by Jeremy Noakes). For every text used there are many which have had to be excluded—many scholars whose work I admire are not represented here solely because it was difficult to find passages which lent themselves to being reproduced as internally coherent short extracts.

For reasons of space there was also much which I had to omit. Lest the Germanocentricity of this collection be taken to imply a set of assumptions about the relationship of Nazi Germany to other regimes of the far Right, I should emphasize that I believe firmly that Nazism should be analysed within the context of inter-war European fascism in general—here, I can only refer readers to the 'sister' volume in this series on fascism, by Roger Griffin, whose work formed one important starting point for the planning of this volume. I have been unable to include sections on the relationship of Nazism to modernity, sections representing the rich strand of western, non-dogmatic Marxist theories of Nazism, or sections discussing the nature of 'everyday life' under Nazism. Perhaps most regrettably, I felt unable to do justice to the even richer range of writing on the Third Reich written from the perspective of gender history, and elected therefore not to include a separate section. Feminist history and theory, in particular, has produced some of the most useful insights into the nature of power and the possibilities of its contestation—themes of obvious relevance to the study of Nazism. But there is more than one way to skin a cat, and there is more than one legitimate way of organizing a reader on Nazism, and I hope that the organizing principles of this volume offer a useful starting point for examining at least some aspects of the historiography of the period. Colleagues in the field will doubtless have their own 'favourites' which they feel I have unfairly or unwisely excluded, but given the tens of thousands of texts produced on the subject over the decades I should be surprised indeed if we all came up with the same 100 passages.

Given the impossibility of including all the material which I find stimulating and helpful, I make no apologies for excluding texts which, in my view, are ultimately unhelpful to those seeking to arrive at a better understanding of the Third Reich. To take an obvious example, I have opted to exclude the work of Daniel Jonah Goldhagen. He may or may not have something beyond the obvious to tell us about Nazis (I am sceptical). He certainly has nothing to tell us about ordinary Germans. Neither have I made reference to those who argue, for example, that Nazism was an intentionally modernizing force, or to those whose apparent interest in comparing Nazi Germany to other regimes is not motivated by the desire to understand but is pursued, it seems to me, for pernicious ends.

On the positive side, the genre offers the possibility not only of introducing to students some of the findings of the richly varied and nuanced body of scholarship to which they might not otherwise have access—including much work not available to an English-speaking readership—but also the possibility of underlining the contingent and contested nature of historical knowledge and the ways in which historians' perspectives on the past are not fixed but are constantly evolving. Partly for this reason, this volume contains a substantial proportion of older texts, many of which date back to the 1930s and 1940s. The balance between older and newer texts in individual sections is naturally partly conditioned by the fact that different issues have been the subject of intense research at different times. This aside, I have tried to maintain a balance between the older historiography and newer work. On the one hand, the reification of a canon poses the threat of a failure to rethink and reappraise. On the other hand, however, a crucial part of rethinking involves constant critical rereading. In a day and age in which scholars are forced to publish more than is necessary or healthy, we need to remind ourselves that there is much excellent older scholarship that still stands up to critical scrutiny. The selection of texts written at the time which preface this volume remind not only of the innately fascinating insights which many contemporaries had to offer, but also of the fact that many of the positions adopted by subsequent historians are foreshadowed in earlier writings.

At the same time, the very welcome development of the multitude of historical sub-disciplines over the three decades—of social history, gender history, minority history—and of new methodologies such as oral history, combined with a continued fascination with the crimes of the Third Reich which seems to be growing rather than fading as the Nazi regime recedes into the past, have led to a growing body of meticulous and subtle scholarship on aspects of the Third Reich which were long considered marginal. The questions which we ask of the past after 1989 are often different from those we were asking in the context of the Cold War. Seen from the perspective of the present, it is hard to comprehend that the Holocaust was only marginal in most early historical works on the Third Reich, and that it only became properly integrated into more general narratives of Nazi criminality from the 1970s onwards. The availability of new archives in eastern Europe, and especially in the former Soviet Union, is enabling scholars to explore aspects of the Third Reich's practices in the east about which we still know very little. As the crimes of Nazism fade into the past, it is only to be hoped that the growing scholarly output on the horrors of the Third Reich continues to connect with the concerns of a critically engaged public, and that Nazi genocide remains not merely a yardstick by which other crimes against humanity are judged, but an active stimulus to the creation of a world in which such crimes are less likely to recur.

Section A

Contemporary Characterizations of National Socialism

INTRODUCTION

Politicians, academics, journalists, and commentators of all political and ideological persuasions offered analyses of National Socialism from the early 1920s onwards. They were often oversimplified and often one-dimensional; they could blend insight with distortion in equal measure and, infused as they were with assumptions that reflected the ideological positions of their authors, they often tell us as much about the politics of the commentator concerned as they do about the nature of National Socialism. And yet, these often forgotten or obscure writings have, sometimes, a great deal to tell us about National Socialism. The questions they ask are often similar to those that subsequent scholars have posed: was National Socialism unique, or was it to be understood as a manifestation of a more general European phenomenon? Was it primarily a reactionary force, intended to restore the political dominance of the old elites in the face of the forces of democracy, and to protect an increasingly crisis-prone capitalism against the growing threat to private property posed by the Left? Or was it a new, revolutionary force, with a genuine transformative agenda that sought to remould society according to a vision which conservatives would regard as anathema? Was it an ideological force, or a blind, impulsive movement with no concrete programme or goals? Was its propaganda—and particularly its anti-Semitism—merely a means of diverting the attention of the masses from their real material interests and conflicts, or did it speak to pre-existing mentalities and aspirations deeply embedded in broad sectors of the population?

Above all, the Reichstag electoral results of September 1930, which saw the National Socialists move from fringe splinter party to second-largest party in the Reichstag, marked the onset of a burgeoning critical literature on the movement, its leader, and its aims. The years immediately before Hitler's seizure of power produced a mass of rich commentary that has a great deal to offer the careful reader. In particular, commentaries of the early 1930s gain in immediacy through the sense of urgency they convey, written as they were at the height of the fascist onslaught in Germany. They were 'analyses for action' (Ayçoberry), designed to warn and to galvanize resistance to the movement; at the same time, they bear powerful witness to the uncertainty with which commentators of all political persuasions reacted to a complex, novel movement that did not fit easily into pre-existing theoretical frameworks or lend itself to easy comparison.

Liberal commentators recognized in the National Socialist movement above all a rejection of the values of the Enlightenment—of reason, individual liberty, and equality. However, the universalist notions of humanity subscribed to by liberals meant that they often underestimated the extent to which hatred of its ideologically defined enemies, and particularly of the Jews, was at the core of National Socialism. Most writers on the Left (a very broad position that encompassed many different shades of opinion) saw National Socialism as a product of capitalism in crisis. They also recognized that it enjoyed powerful support from sectors of the military, business, the landowners, and the bureaucracy. Beneath the propagandistic rhetoric of transformation they perceived a movement designed to reinforce existing power relations and, specifically, to protect the interests of the propertied classes. In other words, they saw the revolutionary rhetoric of the movement as masking reactionary goals. The most perceptive, however, could combine this with thoughtful analyses of the cultural impact of the First World War and of the legacy of embittered nationalism created by the Treaty of Versailles. The Marxist Left tended to proceed from more or less crude assumptions about the relationship between politics and material interests. In particular, those who thought of Hitler as an 'agent' of the 'ruling classes' often overstated the homogeneity of the dominant forces whose interests he was supposedly serving. They were also generally unpersuasive when trying to understand the movement's ideology, particular its anti-Semitism. Nonetheless, when they moved beyond crude theories of instrumentalization and gave serious thought to the sources and causes of Hitler's mass support they too could offer highly penetrating insights.

On the Right—also a diverse group encompassing a variety of positions from liberal-conservative to conservative-nationalist—perceptive commentators recognized that, despite its anti-parliamentary, anti-Socialist, and nationalist rhetoric, and despite its attempts to gain respectability by pursuing a 'legal path' to power, the movement was pursuing anything but a restorative agenda. Beneath the slogans of law and order they perceived an impulsive, aggressive, and ultimately destructive force that had only superficial affinities with the conservative traditions of the nineteenth and early twentieth centuries. The patrician and elitist instincts of many of these writers, however, led them to be often all too eager to castigate National Socialist 'demagoguery' as a product of the 'age of the masses' and, in situating its ideological attractiveness in a general cultural crisis caused by the secularizing impulses of modernity, they were often (willingly or unwillingly) blind to the fact that concrete forces within the establishment, with substantial political and ideological sympathy for National Socialism, were undermining the Weimar

Republic and often directly supporting Hitler. The ambivalence within conservative institutions was reflected in the stance of the Christian churches. While hostile to National Socialist racial theory and above all to the movement's claims to supplant Christianity as an alternative belief system, the movement's anti-liberal and nationalist tendencies spoke to an institution whose own culture was not immune from patriotic and authoritarian values. However, as the writings of Alfons Wild and the courageous partnership of Fritz Gerlich and Ingbert Naab show, there were many whose Christian convictions led them to recognize the National Socialist threat and to speak bravely against it.

The aspect of most contemporary analyses that stands the test of time least well is their treatment of the issue of anti-Semitism. Many recognized in National Socialism an ideology of hatred but did not adequately understand the centrality of the Jews to Hitler's world view; others tended to see in National Socialism a revival of traditional anti-Semitism and failed to recognize its novel, unique qualities or the implications of its pseudo-scientific biological-eugenicist underpinnings. In part, this is explicable by the fact that during the early 1930s, when most of these extracts were produced, the National Socialists consciously toned down their anti-Semitic propaganda in an effort to gain respectability among middle-class voters. More to the point, however, these commentators did not have the 'benefit' of hindsight when writing about the intentions of the National Socialist movement towards the Jews. However much they recognized the ceaseless dynamism and capacity for radicalization of the Nazi movement, they were unable to imagine how appalling its consequences would be.

HERMANN RAUSCHNING

1 Germany's Revolution of Destruction

Hermann Rauschning was a conservative nationalist who initially supported the National Socialists, became disaffected, and then went into
exile, where he wrote books aimed at rallying conservative opposition
to Hitler. Emphasizing its revolutionary dynamism and destructive will,
he sought to warn against the consequences of a Nazi victory.

What must come of this revolution, in which the present leaders of the
nation continue staunchly to profess their faith? And there is a yet more
fundamental question: what *is* this revolution, what is its nature? A national
'awakening,' with the unmistakable features of a radical, all-embracing revolution; surface discipline and order, beneath which the destruction of all
elements of order in the nation is plainly visible; a vast display of energy and
achievement, which cannot hide the wasteful and destructive exploitation of
irreplaceable resources, material, mental, and moral, accumulated through
generations of fruitful labour; a boundless activity that can no longer conceal
the ebbing of energies—what is this Third Reich in reality, a new order in the
making or a holocaust, a national re-birth through the historic energies of the
nation or a progressive, permanent revolution of sheer destruction, by means
of which a dictatorship of brute force maintains itself in power? What in all
this is make-believe and what is reality? What is deceit or delusion, and what
is genuine in this movement? This is the vital question for the nation, a
question not to be evaded with careful euphemisms or soothing self-
deception. [. . .]

Those of us who played a responsible part in what is still busily celebrated
as the 'rebirth of the nation' are in duty bound to protest against the most
tremendous betrayal that perhaps was ever committed in all history. I am
entitled to make this denunciation of the revolutionary development in the
Reich in the name of a growing number of those who shared my conviction
of the nation's need for a fundamental change of policy. For the very reason
that we acknowledge the eternal values of the nation and of a political order
rooted in the nation, we are bound to turn against this revolution, whose
subversive course involves the utter destruction of all traditional spiritual
standards, utter nihilism. These values are the product of the intellectual and
historical unity of Western civilization, of historic intellectual and moral
forces. Without these, Nationalism is not a conservative principle, but the
implement of a destructive revolution; and similarly Socialism ceases to be a
regulative idea of justice and equity when it sheds the Western principles of
legality and of the liberty of the person. [. . .]

The shortcomings of the present time cannot be made good by the muz-
zling of criticism; nor can they by patient waiting. 'Let things take their

course! In five years' time nobody will want to know about them'—so an important member of the Cabinet of the Reich, not a National Socialist, exclaimed to me in 1934, with Olympian short-sightedness, when I expressed my concern about the nature of the new German policy. No less out of place was the talk of 'preservation of continuity.' Only a fundamental change in Germany's course, only the restoration of equal justice for all and of personal freedom and security, can assure Germany's future. Yet there is no possibility of evolution in the direction of legality; those who harbour the idea are shutting their eyes to the essential feature of the 'dynamic' revolution, that its course is in the very opposite direction of all legality, in the direction of the destruction of everything of value that the past held, a course of total nihilism. [. . .]

There are many who will contend that National Socialism reveals a broadly conceived, dogmatically defined philosophy, possessing absolutely definite doctrines in regard to all human relations which must be unreservedly accepted by every loyal citizen. Nevertheless, we must ask: is National Socialism doctrinaire? It is, of course, beyond question that it is the product of doctrinaire ideas and that doctrinaire personages play a part in it to this day. Of much more importance is the question of the connexion of what was regarded as National Socialist doctrine with the two elements that characterize the movement, the irrational passions that undoubtedly play an important part, and its leading personalities. A sharp distinction must be drawn in National Socialism between this genuinely irrational revolutionary passion, affecting not only the mass of followers but the leaders themselves, and the very deliberate, utterly cold and calculating pursuit of power and dominance by the controlling group. We may generalize: The doctrine is meant for the masses. It is *not* a part of the real motive forces of the revolution. It is an instrument for the control of the masses. The élite, the leaders, stand above the doctrine. They make use of it in furtherance of their purposes.

What, then, are the aims of National Socialism which are being achieved one after another? Certainly not the various points of its programme; even if some of these are carried out, this is not the thing that matters. The aim of National Socialism is the complete revolutionizing of the technique of government, and complete dominance over the country by the leaders of the movement. The two things are inseparably connected: the revolution cannot be carried out without an élite ruling with absolute power, and this élite can maintain itself in power only through a process of continual intensification of the process of revolutionary disintegration. National Socialism is an unquestionably genuine revolutionary movement in the sense of a final achievement on a vaster scale of the 'mass rising' dreamed of by Anarchists and Communists. But modern revolutions do not take place through fighting across improvised barricades, but in disciplined acts of destruction. They follow irrational impulses, but they remain under rational guidance and command. Their perilousness lies in their ordered destructiveness—it is a misuse on a vast scale of the human desire for order—and in the irrationality and incalculability of their pressure for the 'victory of the revolutionary new order.' This pressure is completely uncalculated, unconsidered, the pressure of men with no programme but action, instinctive in the case of the best troops of the movement; but the part played in it by its controlling élite is most carefully and coolly considered down to the smallest detail. There was and is no aim that National Socialism has not been ready for the sake of the movement to abandon or to proclaim at any time.

The National Socialist revolution, at the outset a nationalist seizure of power, is viewed much too much in the light of historic precedents. There are no criteria and no precedents for the new revolutions of the twentieth century. The revolutionary dictatorship is a new type, in its cynical, unprincipled policy of violence. The outsider overlooks above all the essential distinction between the mass and the élite in the new revolutions. This distinction is vital in every field. That which is intended for the mass is not applicable to the élite. Programme and official philosophy, allegiance and faith, are for the mass. Nothing commits the élite—no philosophy, no ethical standard. It has but one obligation, that of absolute loyalty to comrades, to fellow-members of the initiated élite. This fundamental distinction between élite and mass does not seem to have been sufficiently clearly realized, but it is just this that explains many inconsistencies, many things done, that leave the outsider dumbfounded. [. . .]

[The philosophy] is of functional importance only, a means and nothing more. It is the main element in propaganda. The question to be asked of it is not its meaning but its purpose. It serves mainly for the propagation, in a form assimilable by the masses, of revolutionary aims which can be harboured at first hand only by a small élite. The function of the philosophy is to keep alive the fighting character of the movement. 'Train them in the philosophy,' 'constantly impress on the men the fighting character of our movement,' 'when we have won, our real fight will be only beginning'—these were the instructions given over and over again to the National Socialist propagandists during the so-called *Kampfzeit*, the 'period of struggle' (for power). 'Dynamism' is kept alive in the masses only in the form of permanent pugnacity. The masses tend all the time to grow slack, and need constant stimulating. Nothing is of more importance to National Socialism than the possession of 'enemies,' objects on which this pugnacity can sharpen its claws. This is the root explanation of such senseless and horrible myths as that of the totally evil character of the Jews. If there is no other enemy available there is always the Jew, whose despised figure can be made to serve as fuel for the fighting spirit, and at the same time to keep alive the happy feeling of belonging to the company of the elect. Whenever during the 'period of struggle' the attention of the masses had to be turned away from existing problems, or simply when it was

desirable to rouse the fighting spirit of the followers of the movement, the
Jew-Freemason record was regularly set going.

All these elements, so primitive and threadbare in their psychology, are
nevertheless thoroughly effective in practice. It would be a great mistake to
suppose that so cunning an individual as the German Minister of Propaganda
is not perfectly well aware that the atrocity propaganda against the Jews,
including the 'Protocols of the Elders of Zion,' is preposterous nonsense, that
he does not see through the racial swindle just as clearly as those compatriots
of his whom it has driven out of their country. It would be simply foolish to
imagine that any member of the élite truly and sincerely believes in the bases
of the 'philosophy.' They have been deliberately concocted for their demagogic effectiveness and for the furtherance of the party's political aims. They
have also been chosen with a cunning realization of the needs of the masses
and particularly of the German masses. Other representations of good and
evil, of hero and weakling, may 'work' in other countries; the selection for
Germany was already indicated by the experience of the pan-Germans and
the anti-Semitic 'racial' parties. They had proved already the effectiveness of
anti-Semitism and of racial mystification with the masses. The popular
attractiveness of nationalist ideas of expansion by conquest had also been
revealed even before the War. All that National Socialism did was to work up
these ideas, already propagated among the middle classes under the past
regime, into yet more demagogically effective shape.

[*Germany's Revolution of Destruction* (London: Heinemann, 1939), pp. xi–xiv, 19–21, 55–7.]

EWALD VON KLEIST-SCHMENZIN

2 National Socialism: A Menace

Ewald von Kleist-Schmenzin was a conservative nationalist of deeply
undemocratic persuasion who, unlike Rauschning, opposed National
Socialism from the start. Rejecting the DNVP's willingness to entertain
the notion of bringing Hitler into a coalition in order to 'tame' him,
Kleist-Schmenzin realized that National Socialism was a fundamentally
anti-conservative force with a dynamism far more powerful than anything the conservatives would be able to harness. His own deeply conservative convictions are evident in his stress on the anti-religious, anti-
monarchical elements of the movement, while his comments on the
populist dynamism and the centrality of racism to National Socialism
reveal him to have been a better judge of the movement than those
conservatives who believed that Hitler could be incorporated into a
stable authoritarian regime.

The impact of National Socialism is assuming dimensions that threaten our
future. National Socialism has caused a complete change of attitude among a

large number of people, particularly workers, who were originally just rationalistically minded. These people, who were unmoved by the socialistic demands and slogans of the Social Democrats, have adopted these same demands and slogans when they were offered in nationalistic wrappings. Now they are firmly convinced of their truth, and most of them turn with hatred against any kind of personal property. The ideal of nationalism pales into a slogan. The party is made an equivalent of the nation, and loyalty to the fatherland is transferred to the party. The intuitive contradiction between religion and fanatic hatred of private property is gradually leading to disdain and even fervent rejection of religion. The same is· true of their attitudes toward monarchy, reverence, tradition, obedience outside of the party discipline, and so on. Mere mention of the word *religion* has caused eruptions of animalistic rage among the National Socialists. Basically dependable workers neglect their duties under the influence of National Socialism. It appears that this anti-establishment attitude is being passed on to children as well, in a way previously known only in the Communist districts of large cities. The discipline of the SA should not divert us from this fact. The indoctrinated belief in the unique salvation and redeeming qualities of National Socialism, and in Hitler personally, fosters an incredible intolerance. In villages where conservative Nationalists and Social Democrats once lived together tolerably, those Nationalists and National Socialists now often oppose each other like enemy nations. Similar destructive effects are evident among National Socialist farmers, notably the younger ones. Laborers, artisans, lesser job holders, and others might go Social Democratic in the foreseeable future, but they are more likely to join the Communists. Declining Marxism is reviving because of Hitler; that is the harvest of his dragon's seed.

The devastating effects of National Socialism are making themselves felt in every aspect of life. The fanatic Nazi followers are loyal only to their party. They undercut proper decision-making, even in nonpolitical organizations, and employees neglect their work. In short, everywhere the conditions for living together in human and governmental association are being destroyed.

The youth and educated classes who have succumbed to National Socialism are uprooted and constitute a threat to the future. In general it is no longer true except in isolated cases that National Socialism makes nationalism attractive to Marxists. Those Marxists whom the Nazis converted had already recognized the inadequacy of Marxism in the face of economic distress and would have abandoned it sooner or later. Some of these converts hope to foster the class struggle more successfully with nationalist slogans than with international ones. Others were ready for a genuine inner conversion and, attracted by nationalist slogans, are now hooked by the National Socialist ideology that forces them back to socialistic thinking.

These circumstances cannot necessarily be ascribed to all National Socialists, but generally things are developing thus and in fact have accelerated in the last few weeks. The National Socialist assault on the very foundation of human and political life is even more dangerous than that of the Social Democrats. Because of its misleading name and the deliberate duplicity of its leadership, people who would normally resist an open attack on their way of life succumb to National Socialism. Public National Socialist agitation is unprincipled and thorough, especially in small gatherings; but the propaganda on a personal level is even more ruthless. Even in this region, where the National Socialists still pretend to support conservative national views and behave somewhat peaceably, their agitation consists of an alarming amount of purely communistic hatemongering. This incitement to destruction persists and engulfs all the other professed national aspirations. One is constantly amazed how few people see, or want to see, this danger. [. . .]

The flow of followers to Hitler is largely a movement of fear and desperation. In fear of what may yet come, people flock to the National Socialist Party in senseless despair because they hope that the mass of voters, by casting like ballots, can avert the troubles threatening us and can above all spare the individual from personal involvement. Many of them put all their hopes in Hitler and do not want to see the shortcomings of National Socialism. Those who stick with the German National People's Party only do so because they believe that a counterbalance is still somehow necessary. No wonder there is such confusion of thought. If political action is to be successful for Germany's future, [. . .] our struggle against the aberrations of National Socialism must be waged promptly with dignity and earnestness, but with rigorous determination.

Religious attitudes are crucial in separating conservative thinking from National Socialism. The foundation of conservative policy is that obedience to God, and faith in Him, must determine the whole of public life. National Socialism is based on a fundamentally different point of view in which questions of faith must of course be dropped as irrelevant. Hitler actually recognizes race and its demands as the highest law of governmental action; if at times he says otherwise, that does not make any difference. His materialism cannot be reconciled with Christianity. According to Hitler, the state does not have the responsibility to foster creativity but only to guard the racial heritage! [. . .] Hitler is primarily interested in breeding healthy bodies; he stresses emphatically that building character is only of secondary importance. This conviction is unacceptable [. . .] Inseparably connected with National Socialism are a superficial search for happiness and a streak of liberal rationalism that is expressed in its motto, group welfare has priority over individual desire. National Socialism leans increasingly toward the liberal conception of the greatest good of the greatest number. For us, the nation per se is not the ultimate measure but rather the will of God which obligates us to live for the nation. That is a fundamental difference.

It is difficult to tell how National Socialism officially views marriage and the family, but it is evident from numerous comments of well-known Nazis that they accept many views which we must resolutely reject.

It is certain that National Socialism does not favor monarchism and is definitely republican in conviction. The core of its domestic political program is synonymous with Social Democracy on economic, social, and tax policy, and largely also in agrarian proposals. Hitler is demanding continuation of the socialist policy that contributed to our economic collapse and harmed the workers as well. His excessive agitation against property and capital and his unscrupulous provocation of people to militancy, threaten to destroy every possibility of reconstruction by arousing instincts of envy that will not easily be controlled. [. . .]

A glance at National Socialist newspapers, pamphlets, and other propaganda should convince anyone (who is still willing to look) of the unscrupulous dishonesty of the movement and its leaders. Their arguments can be cited both for and against almost any position. Since people are not aware of this duplicity, it is no wonder that they succumb to National Socialism in their ignorance. We can no longer tolerate the pretense that National Socialism is the one movement that can save the nation. This delusion must be destroyed together with the totally false image that the people have of Hitler. In light of the foregoing, I ask: have we conservatives anything left in common with National Socialism? Surely we must recognize that its essential assumptions are a menace to the nation and to unselfish patriotic convictions. The many respectable groups presently cooperating with National Socialism will progressively have less power to influence the nature of the movement. In the French Revolution, with its appeal to national striving for freedom and socialism, a vanguard of selfless and confused visionaries prepared the way for destruction; similarly under National Socialism the nationalist elements will involuntarily set the stage for a national disaster. A National Socialist government will inevitably end in chaos. Their rulers would soon be swept away by the unmanageable tide of upheaval they created. We conservative nationalists should no longer abet the destruction caused by Nazi slogans of national interest and by Hitler's romantic image.

[*Der Nationalsozialismus: Eine Gefahr* (Berlin: Verlag Neue Gesellschaft, 1932); this translation from Anton Kaes et al. (eds.), *The Weimar Republic Sourcebook* (Berkeley and Los Angeles: University of California Press, 1994), 172–5.]

THOMAS MANN

3 German Address: A Call to Reason

The novelist and essayist Thomas Mann was one of Nazism's most penetrating critics. Delivered as an address following the success of the National Socialists at the September 1930 elections, Mann's critique of both the movement and its origins bears all the hallmarks of his self-confessed nineteenth-century bourgeois origins and outlook. An ardent critic of the Treaty of Versailles, Mann nonetheless distinguished himself from most other conservative intellectuals by his public defence of the Republic, which he regarded as best able to safeguard what he saw as traditional German bourgeois and patriotic values against the philistine irrationality of National Socialism.

The results of the elections . . . cannot be explained solely by economics [. . .] It would not be intelligent to explain them thus to the outside world, nor would it be a true account of the facts were one to present things in such a one-sided manner. The German people are not naturally given to radicalism, and, if the current wave of radicalization which has momentarily surfaced were merely a consequence of economic depression, this would explain an increase in support for Communism, but not the massive growth of support for a party which appears to join the national idea with the social in the most militant and aggressively strident way. It is wrong to represent the political purely as a product of the economic. Rather, in order to understand such an incredible psychological state as that with which our people is currently astonishing the world, it is necessary to draw in political passions, or, put better, political sufferings; if it would not be clever or dignified to be proud of the results of 14 September or to shout their merits abroad, one can still quietly leave them to take their effect in the outside world as a storm warning, as a reminder that a country which has as much right to self-esteem as any other cannot be expected in the long run to endure that which the German people has indeed had to endure, without its psychological state developing into a danger to the world [. . .]

The Versailles Treaty was an instrument intended to suppress permanently the vitality of one of the main peoples of Europe, and to see this instrument as the Magna Carta of Europe, upon which future history could be built, ran counter to life and nature, and already today represents a viewpoint which hardly appears to have any supporters anywhere. Life and reason themselves have already disproved the inviolability of this treaty, and, if one hears French nationalists complaining that it is already as full of holes as a sieve, then this just proves precisely the impossibility of the impossible and speaks in favour of the means which have been deployed by the Germans to prove this natural impossibility. The fact that it is not yet remotely full enough of holes for the stability of the world is also tacitly accepted by all reasonable people outside Germany; however, the German people are not aware of this reasonableness and necessarily judge things on the basis of the factual situation around them, and feel themselves to be the main victims of its absurdity. It seems almost pointless to say, and yet necessary to repeat: it is not an acceptable situation for Germany to stand defencelessly in the middle of nations armed and full of military prowess, so that everyone, the Pole in Poznań, the Czech on the

Wendelsplatz, can unashamedly vent his anger on her; so that the fulfilment of the promise that German disarmament should be only the beginning of a general disarmament is always postponed *ad calendas graecas** and that every expression of displeasure on the part of the German people against this situation is taken as a threat to be met by further rearmament. This is the first injustice which one has to mention if one is to explain the German people's current frame of mind, but it is only too easy to list five or six others which darken their mood, such as the absurd border settlements in the east; a mindless reparations system based on *vae victis*;† the complete lack of under-standing of the Jacobin conception of the state for German popular sens-ibilities in the minorities question; the problem, which need not be one, of the Saar region; and so on.

Those are the diplomatic woes and sufferings which determine the Ger-man state of mind. To these one must add deep, but also vague and uncertain, doubts of a domestic kind, i.e. doubts over whether a parlia-mentary constitution according to the western system, such as that which Germany took after the collapse of the feudal system simply because it was the ready-made historical example on offer, is fully suited to her character, or if it does not to some extent distort and harm her political ethic. These worries concerning our national political ethos are all the more tormenting for the fact that no one has concrete suggestions for something better and more suitable, and for the present there can be no conclusion other than that as long as the Germans do not manage to invent something new and original from their innermost nature *in politicis*,‡ it will be necessary to take the most personally amenable elements and thus make the best out of the historical precedents on offer, since no observer of Germany can doubt that the previ-ous attempts to supplant parliamentary democracy—the east and south European models, i.e. the dictatorship of one class and the democratically created caesarist adventurer—are even more alien to the German people than that against which a part made its gesture on 14 September.

One does not need great psychological insight [. . .] to recognize in these external and internal woes the causes which, alongside the poor economic situation, led to the sensational voting demonstration of the German people. The people responded to the so-called National Socialist garish placards as a way of expressing their feelings. But National Socialism would not have had the powers of mass emotion and persuasion which it now shows if it had not, unbeknown to the majority of its supporters, been able to draw succour from an emotional force which, as with everything born of the spirit of the age, possesses a subjective truth, legitimacy, and logical necessity with which it

---

* To the Greek calends, i.e. indefinitely.
† Woe to the vanquished.
‡ In political matters.

endows the popular reality of the movement. The economic downfall of the middle class was combined with sentiments which first appeared as intellectual prophecy and critique of the age: the sense of an end of an era, announcing the end of the bourgeois epoch and its moral universe dating back to the French Revolution. A new spiritual disposition of humanity, which wished to have nothing to do with the bourgeois and its principles—freedom, justice, culture, optimism, belief in progress—was proclaimed, and expressed itself artistically in the expressionist cries of the soul, philosophically as the rejection of the doctrine of reason and of the mechanistic and ideological world view of decades gone by; it expressed itself as an irrationalist relapse placing the concept of life at the centre of all thought; as raising to a pedestal the uniquely life-giving force of the unconscious, the dynamic, the creative-mysterious; as rejecting the mind, by which it meant merely the intellectual, as destructive of life and contrasting it with the darkness of the soul, the Mother-Chthonic, the sacred, creative underworld, which it celebrated as the real truth of life. Much of this religion of nature, which by its very nature tends to the orgiastic, to bacchic excess, has found its way into the neo-nationalism of our age, which represents a contrast to the far different, balanced bourgeois nationalism of the nineteenth century, which was characterized by its strong cosmopolitan and humanitarian elements. It distinguishes itself from the latter precisely by its orgiastic cult of nature, its radically anti-humanitarian, intoxicatingly dynamic, absolutely unrestrained character.

['Deutsche Ansprache: ein Appell an die Vernunft' (1930), in Thomas Mann, *Gesammelte Werke*, vol. xiii (Frankfurt am Main: S. Fischer Verlag, 1960), 873–7.]

THEODOR HEUSS

4   The Party

Theodor Heuss, a liberal member of the Reichstag from 1924 to 1928 and again from September 1930 onwards, provided an interesting critique of the rise of the NSDAP from a pro-Republican bourgeois perspective (although his writing is also indicative of the disillusionment with the Republic felt within the liberal intelligentsia by this point). Criticized at the time and since for his gently ironizing tone and his lack of polemic, Heuss's observations on the nature of the movement in comparison to other parties remain instructive, as do many other aspects of his book.

When the 'National Socialist German Workers' Party' submitted its list of candidates for the elections of 1930, it added to the names, in brackets, the label 'Hitler Movement'. This was not just for those stupid people who might not be able to find their way through the multitude of labels, but had a deeper meaning, was a residue from that time when participation in

parliament meant nothing and the 'movement' in the country meant everything. And occasionally one hears in debate the opinion that this is indeed not
a 'party as such', but precisely a 'movement'.

This juxtaposition is more than a play on words. It is indicative of the fact
that concealed within the NSDAP are two very different tendencies: a completely irrational one and a highly rationalistic one. Both have their roots in
Hitler's personality, and they accommodate the ambiguities of the German
character. One might speak of bureaucratized romanticism. The romantic
element is in the Führer myth, the devotion of the followers, the belief in the
man, in the *one* man, in the willingness to make sacrifices for him alone (and
not for a paper programme), the enthusiastic will for one person, not for a
'thing' [. . .]. He dominates them with incomparable virtuosity—at the
moment he can still speak of his martyrdom and life of persecuted sacrifice,
if he does not choose the other means of self-projection, that of the triumphant or soon-to-be-triumphant victor. Both are masterly: he courts sympathy
and he confers a sense of pride in taking part in history if one declares
oneself for him. He relieves them all of the burden of thought, of the burden
of decision, and yet lets them know that without their faith he cannot think,
he cannot decide. This bond is consummated firmly in the realm of the
irrational, in the effect of an ecstatic (not demonic) possession, which understands how to combine pedagogic technique with the passion of spiritual
overpowering. Or—used to understand. The martyr motif has also be taken
over by other leaders. Even the very robust Otto Strasser makes use of it
occasionally. Goebbels was roused by its usefulness to tell of a history of
mistreatment in Belgian dungeons—he let the subject drop, however, when
pressed hard about the detailed circumstances.

Into this world of feelings, of strong words, of intense sentiment, of
emotion and devotion, is inserted quite another: the apparatus, the party
machinery, the organization, the card file, the telephone exchange, the office,
the sales organization, the textiles concern (quartermasters), accident and life
assurance, treasurers, press officers, and in addition the militant group of the
party, the SA and the SS. All these things are completely unromantic, very
sober, very businesslike—the members are registered, trained, controlled.
There are prescribed channels of authority, but they go from top to bottom as
much as the other way round. And Hitler holds these in his hands. Of course,
he is aided by a 'chancellery', he has to delegate decisions, he cannot do
everything, but in the last resort he *can* do everything, as he makes the final
decisions and gives the final decrees. This, we know, he does in very determined fashion, when it is a question of interpreting the party programme, or
of organizational directives, or of the adjudication of personnel issues; the
solemn, severe tone usually appears somewhat laughable to outsiders, but he
can afford to be indifferent to this, as he knows that it has its effect on the
insiders. He appeared a little monstrous as he reacted against the rebellion of

Captain Stennes in the spring of 1931*—here, he mixed sentimentality and brutality. But he remained triumphant. For he controls the apparatus. And claims, demands, that nothing happens without him.

This is sometimes underestimated. Of course, one would not be doing justice to Hitler's achievements were one to see him merely as the great, tireless organizer. He has also set souls in motion and created enthusiastic willingness to sacrifice and submission through his appearance. This fact is occasionally used propagandistically to claim uniqueness: this idealism which burns for the Führer and the idea supposedly represents the novel, the unique element of this mass movement. This is naturally exaggerated nonsense. For virtually the entire existence of the political associations is based on the voluntarism and the belief of countless individuals: National Socialism has not created a new ethos here, it just says the obvious more loudly, and perhaps more effectively, than the other groups. The noise of these powerful demonstrations drowns out the constant hum of the actual party machine. The information given in the *National Socialist Yearbook* gives only a superficial picture of its form and structure, because essentially only the main subdivisions are shown, but not the extraordinarily intensive organizational expansion that the party has undergone. The number of local offices, often involved with administering the party membership books (in a manner reminiscent also of the early days of the Social Democratic movement), has become almost uncountable. The precondition and consequence of this development is that, already today, thousands are working full-time for the party, and at the same time derive their living from it. This comment is not meant to sound derogatory: modern party life cannot exist without the professional political functionary. Within the NSDAP this type has expanded incredibly quickly; it is unlikely that a political movement has ever encouraged such a rapid growth of the 'professional politician' as a mass phenomenon. One should not comment on their quality: Hitler gives this systematic consideration and works to remove any weaknesses through specific education. This development is of great importance for the structural side of the party: it gives rise to 'functionaries', but they are not the organs of the party membership—rather, they are the organs of the party leader, bound to him, dependent upon him. This extends, via these bonds, into the other groups. Herein lies the absolutist strength of the party leadership, which is able to install and depose *Gauleiters* and functionaries, dissolve local groups, and even impose candidates' lists in the manner of a centralized bureaucracy; this power is also, however, bound up with immense responsibility. For the leader cannot personally know everyone who is subordinated to his will. He experiences the difficulty with which all parties find themselves confronted sooner or later when faced with the

---

* Stennes was leader of the Berlin SA until 1931, when he was dismissed for resisting Hitler's 'path of legality'.

impulsive elements of their followers—that of having to dispense patronage. This is competed for by a small circle of people, the early followers, who point to services and sacrifices in the early years, who fought in the days when the National Socialist faith still demanded a little inner conviction and was not yet the latest fashion in salons or clubs, nor in student residences or bowling associations. The 'old soldiers' are in a somewhat embarrassing situation— they welcome the deluge of new members, but are also mistrustful, fearing that too many of them are just attracted to success itself [. . .]. Hitler does not have an easy job, negotiating these tensions—it is reliably told that he himself is shocked at the composition of his parliamentary party and would very much like to distance himself from some of them. But the call to loyalty, which he naturally needs, binds him himself—along with the rationalistic task of being leader of a large-scale, multi-branched political organization comes the mutually reinforcing duty of obligation underpinned by literary-romantic conceptions. Modern vassalage, if one wishes to call it that, is not just one-sided right of disposal, it involves obligation on both parts. Splits, which may be the result of personal issues or differences of opinion, are therefore treated in the Nazi press (only, of course, when referring to their own party) in a moralizing tone, as 'treachery', almost as 'felony'.

[*Hitlers Weg* (1932; repr. Stuttgart: Union Verlag, 1968), 117–21.]

FRITZ GERLICH

5   The Impossibility of Constructive Achievement

Fritz Gerlich, editor of the *Münchner Neueste Nachrichten* in the 1920s, was one of the most prominent of Catholic activists against Nazism. He continually warned against the notion that Hitler could be tamed by being brought into a coalition. The following extract, published in February 1932 in a Catholic journal, is representative of his argument. Gerlich was murdered during the 'Night of the Long Knives' of 30 June 1934.

[S]howing accommodation towards demagogic arousers of mass hysteria and their followers only leads to the opposite of that which accommodation towards normal, decent people brings. Making concessions towards the Hitler party only increases the megalomania of its leadership. It also agitates the party insofar as it exposes it to the danger that it might have to abandon its irresponsible attitude towards the policies of the fatherland. This, however, is precisely the secret but also greatest desire of all political rabble-rousing and swindling: to avoid every situation which might force it to show positively what it can do.

That is also to say that the widespread suggestion of 'educating' the National Socialist movement in the ways of practical politics by incorporating it into the responsibilities of statesmanship is fundamentally false. This suggestion is predicted upon the false notion that the leadership of the Hitler movement is comprised of honest fanatics who, once their ideas collide with reality, i.e. once they are forced to implement their ideas responsibly, will, precisely because they are honest, be ready to correct them as soon as they are forced to accept the error of their ways.

It is possible that such honest fanatics are present in the Hitler movement in declining numbers. We have yet to see anything of them. They play no role there. Beginning with Hitler, the National Socialist leadership is an association of mass hysteria-inducing agitators. As a result, the entirety of National Socialist politics knows only one thing, the tactics of struggling for power, but not the necessity to think through the needs of the situation of the moment and how to improve it.

Insofar as the Hitler propaganda and press machine concerns itself with the needs of the age, it uses them as a basis for the rousing of the people against those who shoulder the burden of responsibility for government. It knows only 'the guilty', whether they be guilty through malice or through stupidity. Its own positive contributions to alleviating need consist of promises! This malicious rabble-rousing promises every estate and profession that which each wants to hear, without being remotely concerned that the individual promises are self-contradictory in their practical effects. Thus the Hitler agitators promise town-dwellers *cheap* bread and peasants *high* grain prices, to name but one of the self-contradictory manœuvres of the party.

We mentioned the suggestion [. . .] that normal people react with an almost helpless sense of fury and horror to the uninhibited claims of the rabble-rousers because they have the feeling that these are people speaking whose brains are no longer receptive to logical thought and reason. This viewpoint [. . .] largely conforms to our own. It must, however, be added that in one specific sphere the mass agitators are capable of thinking highly logically and acting with a cleverness bordering on genius. This sphere comprises all those issues which are of importance for their one sole real, secret goal: the goal of increasing their own power and establishing a dictatorship.

For the mass agitators, or, better put, the leaders of the Hitler party have, in reality, no interest in the fatherland, Germans, or humanity in general. All turns of phrase uttered in this respect have just one *goal*, namely to confuse their contemporaries and make them enthralled to them.

The leadership of the Hitler party has absolutely no convictions. Neither in the field of foreign policy and reparations nor in the national, social, or economic fields. It has only one single conviction and this it seeks to achieve with all means, namely the achievement of power.

People were surprised in Germany when Hitler chose to negotiate directly with abroad in order to offer himself over the heads of the legal German government—i.e. using the stab-in-the-back tactic—as a future, amenable master of Germany. People were amazed at how willing Hitler was in this to recognize the private debts of Germany abroad. People asked how this willingness could be squared with the nationalistic ranting on the 'breaking of interest slavery' and the struggle against 'international finance capitalism'.

People thus grew suspicious of this self-contradictory stance of Hitler because people thought that the ideas he acquired from Feder formed part of his political conviction. Were one clear that Hitler has absolutely no convictions of any sort and strives only after coming to power as quickly as possible, one would not have found this declaration of his so surprising.

['Hetzer, Verbrecher und Geistesverwirrte', *Der Gerade Weg, 14 Feb. 1932; repr. in Prophetien wider das Dritte Reich: Aus den Schriften des Dr Fritz Gerlich und des Paters Ingbert Naab*, ed. Johannes Steiner (Munich: Verlag Dr Schnell & Dr Steiner, 1946), 226–8.]

INGBERT NAAB

6   The Third Reich is Here!

Fritz Gerlich's close collaborator Ingbert Naab similarly warned against cooperation with Hitler. Like Gerlich, Naab appreciated the difference between the Nazis and the Nationalists; in contrast to Gerlich, he placed more emphasis on the significance of Nazi ideology. Note also his emphasis on the nature of authority within the movement.

When the new government* took office it declared that it did not represent a simple change of cabinet, as is otherwise usually the case, but a new conception of the state. Most of the population of Germany find it hard to imagine a revision of the concept of the state. The many who simply subscribe to the notion 'it can't go on like this; things have to change' also do not give a second thought to the restructuring of the state. It has always been characteristic of the purely bourgeois mentality, even when it is deeply unsatisfied, to justify a change of circumstances on the grounds that in future one will have to pay less tax and that existence will be less troubled. The great mass thinks no differently today, including the great mass of the tendency which most want a restructuring of the state, the great majority of the National Socialists. [. . .]

We are living in a revolutionary age. The current struggle for power truly does not, as the government rightly sensed, merely signify a change of cabinet, but a fundamentally new conception of the nature of the state. The Schleicher–Hitler–Papen government (the order reflects the actual relative influence of each) has begun its work. For the time being it does not seek a direct collapse, but rather an accelerated restructuring. But the collapse will nonetheless precede the restructuring.

---

* Naab is referring to the appointment of the Papen government on 1 June 1932.

Hitler and his committed supporters speak in favour of a completely new house. Our bourgeois politicians still fail to recognize this sufficiently. They have still not recognized the true nature of the Hitler movement, even the gentlemen in Berlin. Hitler, however, always speaks of the new National Socialist *world view*, and wishes to infuse all the veins of the future state with the blood of this world view. He does not seek to make a few changes to the Reich constitution, but rather seeks a completely new constitution embodying the ideas expressed in his book *Mein Kampf*. It would be completely wrong to believe that this book is simply the product of the need to idle away time. Anyone who follows the National Socialist movement will always notice how intent Hitler is on hammering into the masses the ideas expressed in it more and more. Of course, he does not remain faithful to all of the principles contained therein, however much he repeatedly emphasizes his trueness and constancy, but the essential goals remain the same.

The voices of complacency insist that Hitler can easily be negotiated with in the same way as other party leaders. The result would amount to the incorporation of one or two useful ideas of the National Socialists. But this is absolutely not the case. This is precisely why Hitler has always avoided responsibility hitherto. He wants power for himself and wishes to shape the new state solely according to his own ideas, without regard for previous developments and without regard for possible other preferences within the German people.

The issue is not that in a future parliament Hitler's people will be in the majority and will be able to outvote the others, with whom their deputies have done long battle in debate. The issue is that there will be no parliament at all, that no Centre Party, no German Nationalists, and no Socialists will exist. The point is that no votes will take place at all, merely consultations within the corporate state. Everything will be decided by one responsible person, who is responsible only to those above. From the highest leader down to the lowest block office everything is completely organized. Votes will no longer be necessary. Every responsible office will choose its own people within its sphere of responsibility.

The current government may have some features in common with such plans, but Hitler nonetheless wants something very different to the government. The current government seeks more a return to earlier forms, corresponding to the traditions of the elements of which it is comprised; Hitler has nothing to do with the old forms. The two will only tolerate each other as long as the government helps smooth the path for Hitler and as long as it helps him on his way. But the government does not intend to step aside. Essentially it would like to exclude Hitler entirely, by taking the wind out of his sails through fulfilling his demands. This is where Herr von Papen is mistaken, of course. The 'cabinet of the barons' is in essence something much different from that which the largely revolutionary supporters of Hitler imagine a future Reich government to be. And the SA will fight, in its new guise, for other ideals; it will not accept having to follow the path of legality and new conception of the state offered by Herr von Papen.

['Das Dritte Reich ist da!' *Der Gerade Weg,* 19 June 1932; repr. in *Prophetien wider das Dritte Reich: Aus den Schriften des Dr Fritz Gerlich und des Paters Ingbert Naab,* ed. Johannes Steiner (Munich: Verlag Dr Schnell & Dr Steiner, 1946), 386–9.]

ALFONS WILD

7 Hitler and Christianity

Many Christian commentators, especially Roman Catholic ones, were moved by Hitler's claim that National Socialism embodied 'positive Christianity' to offer analyses of the movement and its goals. These often highly exegetical critiques, of which Wild represents a good example, sought to contrast statements from *Mein Kampf* with passages from the Bible or from papal pronouncements to prove that National Socialism was anything but a Christian doctrine.

Hitler's theory of the *rights* of the Aryan race is closely associated with his racial theory, which regards the members of the Aryan race as the real human beings whilst seeing the members of other human races as sub-humans, 'half-apes', and so on.

According to *Catholic* doctrine war is not a legitimate normal means for the resolution of conflict between states. War is only allowed in self-defence. This viewpoint conforms to human reason too. It is not for nothing that statesmen always place great emphasis on representing their wars as 'defensive wars'. In this way, they wish to accord with the general population's sense of right and wrong. Of course, conflicts can emerge. Of course, each people has the right, even the duty, to provide the means of life for the members of that people, but every other people has just that same right! And when the rights of two people stand in opposition to one another, war is not the normal means acceptable under natural law by which the conflict should be resolved. Every people has the duty to defend its rights, but it does not have the right to steal the property of neighbouring people. The same moral codes apply to *peoples* as do to *individual human beings!*

Hitler, however, is of the view that the Aryan race is of a higher value and thus has a higher right to life than other races! It thus corresponds to his racial theory when he ascribes to the German people the right to expand their living space by the violence of the sword. [. . .]

It is correct that the borders of states are 'accidental', in the philosophical sense which contrasts 'accidental' to 'necessary'. The borders could, after all, just as easily follow along different lines. In this sense, borders are 'accidental', i.e. not set in stone. But this is far from meaning that they are *arbitrary*, and is far from meaning that they can be *arbitrarily* altered. When Hitler compares the current situation, i.e. the currently existing borders, with a moment of pause in the development of nature, he is thereby denying the existence of any state of law. The state of law is precisely there to contain the blind, unfettered urges of human nature and to create order between individuals and peoples. Mankind must distinguish itself, through its capacity for reason, from animals, which know no state of law but only instincts. [. . .]

The principle that 'might is right', as Hitler clearly believes is true, is a principle which he should do better to keep to himself as things stand today. Otherwise the Poles and the Czechs might just decide that they need German land for themselves, and we would appeal to the rule of law in vain.

What, after all, is the purpose of *treaties*, if wars are as natural as real natural catastrophes? What is their purpose if borders just represent a pause in development, i.e. in the struggle between great powers, as does the state of the world in general?

Are not Hitler's thoughts an incitement to the Poles and Czechs to engage in wide-scale expropriation in their lands and to drive Germans from house and home? [. . .]

[O]bservations on Hitler's position in relation to Christianity have shown that the entire thought of the National Socialist leader is dominated by racial ideology. National Socialism is therefore heathen through and through. It is not the case that the heathen world view is just a secondary element, a mere cliché in the National Socialist programme which could simply be jettisoned without further ado. To the contrary, it is the source of the many errors and distorts the few truths to be found in Hitler's thinking. Thus love of the fatherland is transformed into idolization of one's own nation. Internally, however, the National Socialist world view tears the people apart. It recognizes only *one part of the German people*, namely the famous 'racial core element', as truly German. Valuable sectors of the population are abused as being not nationally orientated. The party is declared to be the fatherland: instead of love for the fatherland one gets party fanaticism. Anyone of a different opinion is labelled 'enemy of the German freedom movement'. A few superficial characteristics are borrowed from Christianity: the immutability of the dogmas born of the innermost core of divine truth is transposed in completely miscomprehending fashion to the programme of the party, a thoroughly earthly and temporal phenomenon. Otherwise everything—humanity, ethics, education, marriage, the life of the state—is subordinate to the principle of race.

Hitler's ideology is no Christianity but the gospel of race, a gospel which proclaims not peace and justice, but violence and hate.

[*Hitler und das Christentum* (Augsburg: Verlag Kaas & Grabherr, 1931), 17, 19–20, 46.]

8 **The Psychology of Nazism**

> The German-born popular psychologist Erich Fromm began life as a
> disciple of Freud, but became more and more interested in the social
> and cultural determinants of personality. His analysis attempts to bal-
> ance discussion of the material factors leading to the establishment of
> the regime with awareness of the psychological and cultural factors, in
> which connection his discussion of the impact of the First World War is
> particularly interesting.

In contrast to the negative or resigned attitude of the working class and of
the liberal and Catholic bourgeoisie, the Nazi ideology was ardently greeted
by the lower strata of the middle class, composed of small shopkeepers,
artisans, and white-collar workers.[1]

Members of the older generation among this class formed the more passive mass basis; their sons and daughters were the more active fighters. For
them the Nazi ideology—its spirit of blind obedience to a leader and of
hatred against racial and political minorities, its craving for conquest and
domination, its exaltation of the German people and the 'Nordic Race'—had
a tremendous emotional appeal, and it was this appeal which won them over
and made them into ardent believers in and fighters for the Nazi cause. The
answer to the question why the Nazi ideology was so appealing to the lower
middle class has to be sought for in the social character of the lower middle
class. Their social character was markedly different from that of the working
class, of the higher strata of the middle class, and of the nobility before the
war of 1914. [. . .]

Although it is true that the social character of the lower middle class had
been the same long before the war of 1914, it is also true that the events after
the war intensified the very traits to which the Nazi ideology had its strong
appeal: its craving for submission and its lust for power.

In the period before the German Revolution of 1918, the economic
position of the lower strata of the old middle class, the small independent business man and artisan, was already on the decline; but it was not
desperate and there were a number of factors which made for its stability.
[. . .]

The post-war period changed this situation considerably. In the first place,
the economic decline of the old middle class went at a faster pace; this
decline was accelerated by the inflation, culminating in 1923, which wiped out
almost completely the savings of many years' work.

While the years between 1924 and 1928 brought economic improvement
and new hopes to the lower middle class, these gains were wiped out by the
depression after 1929. As in the period of inflation, the middle class, squeezed

in between the workers and the upper classes, was the most defenceless group and therefore the hardest hit.[2]

But besides these economic factors there were psychological considerations that aggravated the situation. The defeat in the war and the downfall of the monarchy was one. While the monarchy and the state had been the solid rock on which, psychologically speaking, the petty bourgeois had built his existence, their failure and defeat shattered the basis of his own life. [. . .]

The inflation, too, played both an economic and a psychological rôle. It was a deadly blow against the principle of thrift as well as against the authority of the state. If the savings of many years, for which one had sacrificed so many little pleasures, could be lost through no fault of one's own, what was the point in saving, anyway? If the state could break its promises printed on its bank notes and loans, whose promises could one trust any longer?

It was not only the economic position of the lower middle class that declined more rapidly after the war, but its social prestige as well. Before the war one could feel himself as something better than a worker. After the revolution the social prestige of the working class rose considerably and in consequence the prestige of the lower middle class fell in relative terms. There was nobody to look down upon any more, a privilege that had always been one of the strongest assets in the life of small shopkeepers and their like. [. . .]

The increasing social frustration led to a projection which became an important source for National Socialism; instead of being aware of the economic and social fate of the old middle class, its members consciously thought of their fate in terms of the nation. The national defeat and the Treaty of Versailles became the symbols to which the actual frustration—the social one—was shifted.

It has often been said that the treatment of Germany by the victors in 1918 was one of the chief reasons for the rise of Nazism. This statement needs qualification. The majority of Germans felt that the peace treaty was unjust: but while the middle class reacted with intense bitterness, there was much less bitterness at the Versailles Treaty among the working class. They had been opposed to the old régime and the loss of the war for them meant defeat of that régime. They felt that they had fought bravely and that they had no reason to be ashamed of themselves. On the other hand the victory of the revolution which had only been possible by the defeat of the monarchy had brought them economic, political, and human gains. The resentment against Versailles had its basis in the lower middle class; the nationalistic resentment was a rationalization, projecting social inferiority to national inferiority. [. . .]

The old middle class's feeling of powerlessness, anxiety, and isolation from the social whole and the destructiveness springing from this situation was not the only psychological source of Nazism. The peasants felt resentful against the urban creditors to whom they were in debt, while the workers felt deeply disappointed and discouraged by the constant political retreat after their first victories in 1918 under a leadership which had lost all strategic initiative. The vast majority of the population was seized with the feeling of individual insignificance and powerlessness which we have described as typical for monopolistic capitalism in general.

Those psychological conditions were not the 'cause' of Nazism. They constituted its human basis without which it could not have developed, but any analysis of the whole phenomenon of the rise and victory of Nazism must deal with the strictly economic and political, as well as with the psychological, conditions. [. . .] The reader may be reminded [. . .] of the rôle which the representatives of big industry and the half-bankrupt Junkers played in the establishment of Nazism. Without their support Hitler could never have won, and their support was rooted in their understanding of their economic interests much more than in psychological factors.

This property-owning class was confronted with a parliament in which 40 per cent of the deputies were Socialists and Communists representing groups which were dissatisfied with the existing social system, and in which were an increasing number of Nazi deputies who also represented a class that was in bitter opposition to the most powerful representatives of German capitalism. A parliament which thus in its majority represented tendencies directed against their economic interest deemed them dangerous. They said democracy did not work. Actually one might say democracy worked too well. The parliament was a rather adequate representation of the respective interests of the different classes of the German population, and for this very reason the parliamentary system could not any longer be reconciled with the need to preserve the privileges of big industry and half-feudal landowners. The representatives of these privileged groups expected that Nazism would shift the emotional resentment which threatened them into other channels and at the same time harness the nation into the service of their own economic interests. On the whole they were not disappointed. To be sure, in minor details they were mistaken. Hitler and his bureaucracy were not tools to be ordered around by the Thyssens and Krupps, who had to share their power with the Nazi bureaucracy and often to submit to them. But although Nazism proved to be economically detrimental to all other classes, it fostered the interests of the most powerful groups of German industry. The Nazi system is the 'streamlined' version of German pre-war imperialism and it continued where the monarchy had failed. (The Republic, however, did not really interrupt the development of German monopolistic capitalism but furthered it with the means at her disposal.) [. . .]

How can one reconcile the statement that the psychological basis of Nazism was the old middle class with the statement that Nazism functions in the interests of German imperialism? The answer to this question is in principle the same as that which was given to the question concerning the rôle of the urban middle class during the period of the rise of capitalism. In the post-war period it was the middle class, particularly the lower middle class, that was threatened by monopolistic capitalism. Its anxiety and thereby its hatred were aroused; it moved into a state of panic and was filled with a craving for submission to as well as for domination over those who were powerless. These feelings were used by an entirely different class for a régime which was to work for their own interests. Hitler proved to be such an efficient tool because he combined the characteristics of a resentful, hating, petty bourgeois, with whom the lower middle class could identify themselves, emotionally and socially, with those of an opportunist who was ready to serve the interests of the German industrialists and Junkers. Originally he posed as the Messiah of the old middle class, promised the destruction of department stores, the breaking of the domination of banking capital, and so on. The record is clear enough. These promises were never fulfilled. However, that did not matter. Nazism never had any genuine political or economic principles. It is essential to understand that the very principle of Nazism is its radical opportunism. What mattered was that hundreds of thousands of petty bourgeois, who in the normal course of development had little chance to gain money or power, as members of the Nazi bureaucracy now got a large slice of the wealth and prestige they forced the upper classes to share with them. Others who were not members of the Nazi machine were given the jobs taken away from Jews and political enemies; and as for the rest, although they did not get more bread, they got 'circuses'. The emotional satisfaction afforded by these sadistic spectacles and by an ideology which gave them a feeling of superiority over the rest of mankind was able to compensate them—for a time at least—for the fact that their lives had been impoverished, economically and culturally.

[*The Fear of Freedom* (London: Routledge & Kegan Paul, 1942), 182–90.]

CARL MIERENDORFF

9 Overcoming National Socialism

Carl Mierendorff, a young Social Democrat (SPD) member of the Reichstag and later member of the Resistance, wrote regular discussions of National Socialism for the journal *Sozialistische Monatshefte* during the years 1930 to 1933. Critical both of the SPD's policy of 'toleration' of Chancellor Brüning, which he regarded as overly passive, and of calls for a 'Popular Front', which he believed were based on an illusory belief in the potential for cooperation between the SPD and the Communists, Mierendorff argued that the only way to defeat Hitler was for the Republic to register political successes itself. This was rooted in his

perceptive recognition that National Socialism's success was not merely
a product of economic protest votes, but was made possible as a result
of a deeper-seated political crisis of democracy itself.

One of the few pleasing consequences of 14 September 1930 is the great
increase in activity which has been noticeable in the last months in the ranks
of the republican organizations, namely within the Social Democrats and the
Reichsbanner.* A great defensive movement is in motion. Its aim is to confront the National Socialist wave with a defensive will, in order at the same
time to overcome the extraparliamentary pressure which gives the 107
National Socialist deputies their particular strength and which has temporarily made them into a crucial axis of domestic politics. No one will underestimate the significance of this defensive action. But it would be a mistake to
believe that these means will suffice. The National Socialist movement cannot
be overcome by propaganda and agitation, and it will not be defeated by
raising one's own organizational strength. This is clear from the character of
this movement. If it is to be overcome, it has to be seized at the roots. If
agitation, education of the voters, and all our work on public opinion, whose
significance should in no way be disputed, are not to remain mere imploring
gestures, they must be complemented by positive politics. Only then are there
prospects for a lasting success.

Where lie these roots of the swastika movement? Before 14 September 1930
people made the mistake of explaining it simply as a resurgence of anti-
Semitism. People thought that it could be explained away like this. Today
people explain it primarily in economic terms, as a product of the economic
crisis. This is nearer the truth, but still in no way adequate. Nothing would be
more dangerous than to overlook the other two components present in this
movement and which give it its particular character: the nationalist and the
anti-parliamentarian elements. Careful sociological analysis of the movement
shows, in fact, what a great role is played precisely by these two tendencies.
Were they not linked to these, economic events would hardly have attained
their significance. They are so strong that with the passing of time even the
anti-Semitic element has been noticeably driven to the background in their
agitation. That does not change the fact that this remains a characteristic
element of the National Socialist ideology, typical of its whole lack of productive capacity for positive input. Feelings of hate cannot give rise to creative achievement. In this connection the stark contrast to Italian Fascism is
notable, formulated strikingly by Mussolini on the occasion of the reception
of foreign journalists in Rome in 1927: 'Anti-Semitism equals destruction and
division. Anti-Semitic Fascism is therefore a crass absurdity. We find it highly
amusing in Italy when we hear that in Germany the anti-Semites are trying

---

* The Reichsbanner was the paramilitary wing of the SPD.

their luck with Fascism . . . we reject emphatically the notion that Fascism is thereby being 'exposed'. Anti-Semitism is a product of barbarism, while Fascism stands at the highest level of civilization and is thus diametrically opposed to anti-Semitism.'

National Socialism is a social movement of the old- and new *Mittelstand* (white-collar workers and public employees) and of the peasantry. At the same time it is also a nationalist movement of 'liberation', and, finally, it is the political formation of all anti-democratic and anti-parliamentary forces which stem from these and other constituencies (a movement of internal 'liberation'). If one bears this in mind one can see that overcoming the economic crisis is indeed important, but that this can only have a limited impact on the National Socialist movement. (Aside from this, it is still questionable when and to what extent unemployment will be overcome.) The other driving impulses are in no way reduced; in some ways they possess their own life, which will remain highly significant after the economic crisis has receded and once their organizational and ideological consolidation has occurred. If socialism and democracy therefore wish to emerge victorious from the struggle against the National Socialist tide, the struggle must be pursued with a positive set of goals, which not only removes the economic causes of German pseudo-Fascism but also takes the ground from under the feet of the goals pursued by its other components.

Not only the physical, but also the psychological pressure points which have led to this deep inflammation of the social organism must be removed. The physical pressure points include unemployment, especially in strata such as the white-collar workers, who are experiencing unemployment for the first time (in contrast to the working class, which as a class is, so to speak, 'used to it'); further, they include the impoverishment and proletarianization of the *Mittelstand* and the distress of agriculture. The psychological pressure points include the wounds to inflamed national self-consciousness, which are most painful when they are linked with physical pressure points (payment obligations, the corridor question, etc.). Why the second type of wound is felt to be so painful almost solely by the old and new-style bourgeoisie will not be gone into here. However, the oversensitivity with which the bourgeoisie, in the broadest sense, reacts to the whole complex of the collapse of 1918 ('stab in the back', 'November criminals') is largely explicable by the memories of its own failure, of the loss of social pre-eminence for which it was itself partly to blame.

If these conditions had been observed more carefully at the right time, and taken into account when developing policies, then it would hardly have come to the elemental eruption which we experienced on that 14 September. But what has Social Democracy in particular, which naturally should be taking the lead in this, done to counteract nationalist distortions of national tendencies in good time? Nationalism cannot be trumped by hypernationalism, and if anything is dangerous it is the urge, visible in Social Democratic circles, to take away the National Socialists' nationalist arguments by competing with them. [. . .]

To National Socialism the Treaty of Versailles is the source of all social, national, and economic evil. Its central demand is: down with Versailles! But this policy is nationalist and reactionary, because its goal lies in the past. It leads down a dead end. The slogan of Social Democracy, by contrast, must be: Overcoming Versailles through Europe! In concrete terms, it demands a German-French entente as the essential element of such an approach. This path leads to freedom. [. . .]

The pursuit of positive goals in order to fight against National Socialism has to extend equally to the overcoming of the anti-parliamentary tendencies. The motto here can only be: reform of democracy. However much one hears of the struggle against the 'system', a closer examination shows that this hostility is based on phenomena which are in no way intrinsic features of democracy and parliamentarianism *per se*, but which are primarily failings of their German manifestation. [. . .]

Closing the sources from which National Socialism is fed: this is the problem of overcoming it. This cannot occur through a mechanical driving back of the movement, but must become a process of organic integration of its followers into the democratic way of life. Otherwise the danger remains, a constant threat, a volcano which can become active at any time.

['Überwindung des Nationalsozialismus', *Sozialistische Monatshefte* Mar. 1931), 225–6, 229.]

KARL KAUTSKY

10   Some Causes and Consequences of National Socialism

> The Austrian Marxist and leading theoretician of the Second International Karl Kautsky shared Mierendorff's pessimistic assessment of the strength of the Left in the face of the National Socialist onslaught. In this piece, written shortly after Hitler's seizure of power, Kautsky is dismissive of National Socialist ideology, characterizing the movement's electoral success as the product of general disorientation born of the crisis; however, he also stresses the limits to which the movement should be seen solely as a product of the Depression. In particular, he draws attention to the cultural legacy of the First World War and to the climate of embittered nationalism which it engendered.

But where did this irresistibility stem from? From the superiority of the National Socialist programme? From the higher morality or intelligence of its leadership? From the greater bravery and willingness to sacrifice of its followers? In all these issues it is way behind the 'Marxists'.

If one wishes to locate the cause of their irresistibility, one only has to look at the date from which point onwards they began to grow. Until the crisis they were of no importance in the Reich. At the Reichstag elections of 1928 they still only won 12 seats. Just two years later they were able to increase their number of seats almost tenfold, from 12 to 107. The onset of the *world crisis* fell precisely in these two years. This has had revolutionary consequences everywhere. Not, admittedly, in the sense that it favoured socialist-revolutionary parties, but in the sense that it created incredible masses of desperate existences who blamed the existing governments or political systems for their misery and believed that salvation would come through their overthrow. Whoever pursued this overthrow most impetuously and successfully was their man, the one from whom they hoped for deliverance, regardless of what his programme was. The politically and economically uneducated sectors of the population, many of whom were mobilized politically for the first time by the war and its consequences, thought entirely militaristically, not economically. They believed that one only needed the right will and the necessary power to be able to achieve everything that they wanted. [. . .]

All other parties had worn themselves down in parliament, either in opposition or in government. This was not yet true of the National Socialists. Their attraction lay in their novelty. They were young, and appeared thus to many superficial observers as good.

And, as soon as this situation had begun to take effect, the attractions of novelty were compounded by a second attraction: that of success. Here, too, one could say: success breeds success. [. . .]

To the superiority of the National Socialists over the German Nationalists, which was born of the fact that the former represented, in comparison to the latter, a new party, unspent in parliament, was added the magic of success, the belief in their strength.

This made the National Socialists irresistible—not a particular programme, which they do not even have and which they are totally incapable of producing. But precisely this incapability helps them too—as long as they are in opposition. It forces them to keep their plans vague, in order that they may make the most contradictory promises, to promise everything to everyone, to capitalists and proletarians alike.

Those comments which they do, however, make about the future correspond fully to the thoughts of those circles from which they draw their main strength, who are sunk in need and misery and yet abhor or fear the proletarian class struggle. It is the peasants, small shopkeepers, and craftsmen, along with white-collar workers and wage-workers, who lose faith; finally, it is those intellectuals (and the same can be said of artists) for whom knowledge is not a means to self-improvement but the provider of their daily bread. Their socialism is not directed at industrial capital. On this they remain silent. They merely want to break 'interest slavery', on which topic they are incapable of distinguishing between profiteering and credit. They rage against the warehouses and the Jews: not against the functions which they perform, but only against Jewish competition, and not only in trade, but also in science and art. Similarly, they wish to eliminate the competition of women. They are supposed to confine themselves to the family.

This striving does not distinguish itself in its great originality. An anti-Semitic programme emerged as long as half a century ago [. . .] It is suited to the intellectual horizons of the philistines of every class. But only now is the political situation so favourable to it that sheer lack of understanding about everything which has occurred through over a century of social development can be victorious over all knowledge to the contrary. At the moment it has great propagandistic power. This is even more the case as since the world war narrow-minded military thinking is prevailing over economic thinking. A far-sighted man of war is capable of recognizing the economic factors. But the bigoted soldier believes in the all-embracing power of violence. The war and all its consequences has drummed this ignorant belief into some sections of the population. Now the dullest ignorant philistinism is gaining the courage to give directions for the shaping of state and society, not from a position of knowledge but merely to satisfy its most immediate needs.

These are the factors which have led National Socialism to achieve such a great propagandistic strength among the German people today. The final cause is represented by the impact of the world crisis under the conditions created for the German people by the world war and the peace treaties. To this must be added, in an age in which energetic intervention in the economy is desperately needed, the paralysis of parliament caused by a situation of equilibrium between the classes and parties, the wearing out of the old parties, the desperation not only of the workers but also of the middle classes and the intellectuals; further, the belief in the omnipotence of violence, and, since the war and not least as a product of the war, an ignorance among large parts of the population, namely among young people, of economic and social affairs.

Those were the conditions which inspired belief in dictatorship as a means of salvation. The fact that the National Socialists have thus far been prevented from wearing themselves down in parliament, combined with their narrow intellectual horizons—which even the most stupid could grasp—and their subsequent electoral success have created the spiritual epidemic of the brown plague from which we suffer today.

National Socialism has the situation outlined above to thank primarily for its current rapidly growing popularity. But this only enables us to understand one side of its nature. There is another, very important side. It relates not to the world crisis, but directly to the Versailles peace. It forced the German Reich to disarm, and to reduce its standing army down to the little

Reichswehr. This could have been the starting point for a general disarmament and thus a regeneration of the European economy. [. . .]

The victors have acted differently—blinded by war rage, limited by nationalist mentalities, or cowardly in the face of popular opinion, they have sacrificed better judgement to the short-sighted momentary whims of influential circles.

Under these circumstances national differences which had surfaced in the war did not cease, the victors continued the arms race, and the world did not find peace. And the German people, hit so hard by the peace treaties, namely by reparations, found peace least of all.

This had the effect that Germany's forced disarmament in no way brought all the advantages which it would have achieved had it been part of a negotiated peace. It saved Germany from the worst, for without it Germany would have collapsed completely under the burden of reparations. But it has also created a new source of discontent in Germany.

It led to the dismissal of numerous officers and soldiers who often refused to accept the dictated peace and to revert to civilian life. These rebellious elements kept trying to join into illegal armed formations, which was greatly encouraged by the insecure states of east Prussia and its neighbouring territories, and later also by the Ruhr occupation.

These elements were also seeking political expression. The most diverse range of extreme nationalist groups joined together under their leadership. Finally, since 1925, they have all joined together under Hitler's leadership. From their ranks came the cadres, the commandants, the masters of the most active elements of the National Socialist party, the staunchly militaristic Storm Troopers (SA) who represent a separate army within the state. In purely military terms they posed no threat to the *Reichswehr* and the state police. But they became powerful once they knew that the mass of the population, as well as large parts of the state apparatus, was behind them. Even if the government was opposed to them, many civil servants, judges, and others showed themselves to be well disposed. Initially a few thousand strong, they infiltrated ever-greater parts of a youth which was streaming towards the National Socialists with their spirit—or rather their ill spirit: the spirit of violence and brutality, indeed of cruelty towards everyone who did not support them. They also infiltrated them, however, with the mentality of the mercenary, who will sell himself to anyone who will pay him, and in whose service he baulks at no bloody acts of violence or arson. [. . .]

We can see that Hitlerism is a complicated phenomenon. One source of its strength is the economic crisis. Because of it parliament, unable to overcome the crisis, becomes unpopular among the middle classes who are sinking into poverty and among the uneducated, unorganized workers—the same parliament which is hated by the capitalists because it gives the socialists a room for manœuvre which is too dangerous to the capitalists. The opposite of parliament—dictatorship—becomes attractive to all of them.

But to this is added the gang movement born of the Versailles peace, which places itself at the service of the emerging dictatorship, becomes its strongest source of power, and gives its techniques of rule their appalling character.

If to these two elements are added possession of the authority of the state, a force is created which no single party is able to resist.

['Einige Ursachen und Wirkungen des deutschen Nationalsozialismus', *Der Kampf: Sozialdemokratische Monatschrift*, 26/6 (June 1933).]

HAROLD LASKI

11   The Meaning of Fascism

Harold Laski, a Jewish socialist intellectual closely associated with the British Labour Party, argued that there was a strong relationship between big business interests and the establishment of the Nazi dictatorship, and saw that business derived great benefit, initially at least, from the Nazi seizure of power. However, he argued against seeing the regime as a puppet of big business, recognizing that the regime enjoyed far more autonomy on the political plane than most Marxist contemporaries believed. Characterizing Fascism as a movement of 'doctrineless nihilism', he argues in this passage that the nature of the Nazi system itself contained contradictions which could only be resolved by recourse to war; while recognizing that the militaristic side of Nazism was one of innate destructiveness, his dismissal of the significance of ideology led Laski himself to understate the importance of anti-Semitism to the Nazi regime.

While it is true, as I have said, that its rise to power has been associated with a partnership, revealed only after the event, between its leaders and the ruling elements in the capitalist democracy they destroyed, its use of power has made it more than a simple tool in the hands of monopoly-capitalism.

For it has been driven by its own inner logic to the destruction of capitalism in its historic liberal form. Granted the problems Fascism confronted, this was, I think, inevitable if, as an organized movement, its leaders, whether in Italy or in Germany, were to retain power. For they had to do two things. On the one hand, they had to grapple with the problem of unemployment; on the other, they had to renew the national tradition, to dissipate the deep sense of frustration that had been brought by the post-war years. They could not do the first according to the classic formulae of capitalism; Dr. Brüning's experience in Germany had made that clear. They could not, either, do it by inflation; the memories of the crisis after the French invasion of the Ruhr were still too vivid. They therefore required a programme of public works which yet permitted the pursuit of a spirited foreign policy. The first would absorb the unemployed; the second would draw attention away from domestic grievance.

But a spirited foreign policy, if it is to have any prospect of success, must be built on rearmament; the statesman who makes large demands must have the material power with which to back his demands. A disarmed Germany, a weak Italy, could argue and plead and cajole; they could not insist. A policy of large-scale rearmament therefore presented obvious advantages. It acted as a programme of public works; and it enabled the Fascist leaders to pitch their demands ever higher as their strength in armament proceeded. It was obvious that the major European powers would do much, at least, to avoid war; concessions, thereby, could be obtained by threat which would restore the national prestige. Rearmament would absorb the unemployed; and this would not only appease the discontent the previous régime was unable to overcome, but would, also, to the degree of its achievement, enhance the reputation of Fascism among the workers, would even act, to some extent, as a compensation for their lost liberties. We must not forget—as the Fascist leaders have not forgotten—the magic appeal of the Soviet Union to the workers as the land from which unemployment has been abolished.

But a programme of this character could not, under a capitalist economy, be carried out on any considerable scale. It required the control of investment by the state; it required the control of imports by the state; it required the limitation of profit by the state to promote continually the extension of rearmament by investment in the manufacture of arms of surplus profits. More than this. As rearmament proceeded, there were the twin dangers that approximation to full employment necessarily brings—a rise in wages and therewith a rise in prices; and the related danger, also, of the movement of labour into the industries, and the firms within each industry, which paid best. It was therefore necessary for the government to limit the possibility of wage-increases; this involved, in order to prevent discontent, the fixation of prices, and this, in its turn, especially in the context of the devotion of profits to investment in armaments, to the rationing of consumption. Germany, by 1939, and in a less degree Italy, had abandoned every characteristic symptom of a liberal capitalist economy.

This development had further consequences. If it was facilitated by the abolition of the trade unions, which made any struggle for a higher standard of life impossible, its scope resulted in a rapid decline in mass-consumption. This in its turn did grave damage to the small shopkeeping class; they found themselves unable to maintain their position and were driven into the ranks of the wage-earners. From this angle, Fascism has undoubtedly strengthened the power of the large industrial units. But it has also weakened them because their authority, being subordinated to the requirements of the rearmament programme, is limited by the purposes of that programme, namely, the recovery of national prestige. But as the political system of Fascism is the dictatorship of the party, it follows that the definition of what national prestige requires is a matter for the party leaders. And since their object, like that of all *condottiere*, is simply to remain in power, that definition is made in terms of what they judge is most likely to keep them in power.

Granted this is, that they had (i) to deal with unemployment in a spectacular way, and (ii) that they had to restore the national prestige, they were compelled to rearmament and thence, inescapably, to a complete control of the productive system. In the light of the past, they had to avoid inflation. They had, therefore, to prevent, at the least, a rise in the standard of life at the same time that they were increasing productivity. Aware that any continued depression of that standard over any long period was bound to result in discontent, they had to do two further things. They had to control profits, lest the workers contrast their own situation with that of their employers; and this was necessary, also, in order that the necessary capital for rearmament could be attained. But the limitation of profit was not enough. It might prevent the rise of anger and envy; it had a negatively beneficent effect psychologically. It did not, however, create hope; and a régime which seeks for permanence and stability must be able to create hope. The Fascist leaders, therefore, were bound to make rearmament the foundation of an imperialist policy of conquest. They had to be able to promise great future benefits in return for present sacrifice. Unless conquest was possible which presented the prospect of an exploitation from which the nation, whether Germany or Italy, would benefit, they could not satisfy either the workers, on the one hand, or the owning class on the other. The first would be impossible by reason of that proportion of production devoted to rearmament; the second because the removal of the limitation on profit would exacerbate working-class opinion. And they could not escape from the necessity of rearmament, because, if they did so, they would have to abandon that spirited foreign policy which enabled them to claim that they were renewing the national tradition; and they would have to find some substitute for rearmament as public works if immense unemployment was not to recur. Caught in that dilemma, both in Italy and in Germany, conquest became the inevitable end of their policy; and it was, of course, certain that, at some stage, conquest was bound to lead to war.

This is, of course, an excessive simplification of the complicated economic processes of which Fascism has disposed. What I am here concerned to emphasize is that the leaders of the Fascist parties have in each instance used the power of the state to make themselves the masters alike of the working classes and of the capitalist class in the interest of perpetuating their own authority. They have won some approval from the first by solving the problem of unemployment and by limiting profits; they have won the approval of the second by abolishing the organs of working-class advance and by making the industrial machine work at full pressure. They have won approval from all by making their respective nations feared by other nations; and this has been equated with a revival of national prestige. And that fear has led to the extension of the territories of each nation; with the prospect of continuous profit as the result of the extension. Profit offered the hope that, at some stage, there would be an increase in the standard of life; as that came, it would ensure security for the masses and stability for the régime.

The weakness of the scheme is apparent. It was dependent upon conquest without in order to maintain its conquests within. Its terror at home was matched by its threats abroad; and those threats impelled those whom it menaced to arm against their possible implications. I do not need here to summarize the history of international relations in the post-war period. The effort of the capitalist powers to 'appease' Fascism is too well known to need detailed analysis. What is clear now from the history of that effort is that the purpose of 'appeasement' could not possibly have been fulfilled. For the price that Fascism would have exacted would have left Great Britain and France with problems fatal to the maintenance of their own economic well-being; and there is no evidence that the surrender would have enabled the Fascist powers to accept a policy of peace. For that policy would have meant a threat to the authority of their leaders which would have been rapidly fatal to them. Peace would have meant that attention was withdrawn from foreign adventure to domestic grievance. It would have been necessary for them to confront the problem of the workers' standard of life, of the transformation of a war-economy to a peace-economy, and of the claims of the capitalist class for a return to less rigid controls. They were bound, therefore, as in the case of Germany with a rapidly increasing tempo, to make ever more demands, to convince their neighbours, that is, that a settled Europe was impossible while they remained in power. [. . .]

Hitler came to destroy; he did not come to fulfil. There have been dictators in the past, like Napoleon, who were the residuary legatees of a revolution; they made war, they used terror, but they were the missionaries of an idea. Hitler had no idea to propagate except his hate of a civilization in which he failed; his genius was that he organized into the service of its destruction every element which had complaint to make of the social order it established. Having used those elements to become its master in Germany, there was nothing he could do with his power except to gain more power. First, therefore, he had to destroy all opposition within. That accomplished, he had to extend his power without for two reasons. First, by so doing, he could secure a factitious glory at home; this would prevent or, at least, postpone the rise of a new opposition. Secondly, the very nature of the régime was a threat to the settled arrangements of the outside world. He had to be powerful because, sooner or later, he would have to render account to it. To grow in power meant that he would become the apostle of militarism. That, again, temporarily strengthened his power. It provided work for the unemployed, and it satisfied the German tradition that the army was the primary element in the state. Since, moreover, he was dealing with a world which had grown into the hatred of war, he found that his first steps in the international adventure were unopposed. This served at once to feed his own ambitions, and to prove to his own subjects that the period of servitude to Versailles was over; by the methods of the bully Hitler reawakened in Germany a kind of parvenu national pride. And he harnessed to that pride all the skill in organization and power of work for which the German people is deservedly famous. He built the most massive war-machine in the history of the world. But, having built it, he became, inescapably, its prisoner.

For either he had to stop its operations; in which case he would have found himself confronted with the mass-unemployment grievance about which was a vital cause of his rise to power. Or, he had to use it, in which case, at some point, war was certain since, even if the smaller powers capitulated, like Austria, to his threats, it was certain that the great powers would refuse to accept his mastery of Europe. But if he stopped his operations, he had to have some principle upon which to organize the internal life of Germany; and it was grimly clear, both from his own utterances and those of his chief lieutenants, that he had no such principle to employ. He had, therefore, to continue the operations of his war-machine since peace would have been fatal to his retention of authority.

[*Reflections on the Revolution of Our Time* (London: George Allen & Unwin, 1944), 91–5, 102–3.]

ERNST TOLLER

12 On the German Situation

The German-Jewish dramatist and essayist Ernst Toller was a perceptive critic of fascism from the perspective of the Left. As with many Jewish intellectuals on the Left, his socialist convictions led him to understate the anti-Semitic nature of National Socialism; unlike many, he recognized, however, its violent and destructive potential. Tragically, it took the victory of National Socialism for the 'popular front' which he proposed to come into existence.

An evil spirit dominates in Germany. Violence and hollow words triumph, characters are replaced by flags, understanding by music and noise, action by parades. Hardly anyone speaks any more of sound convictions or of conscious political action. No one distinguishes anymore between causes and effects. The diplomatic situation, economic and sociological problems are marginalized by domestic political sloganeering, and discussion occurs by means of rubber truncheons, stink bombs, and revolvers.

The Reichstag is becoming a fiction. Mostly it stands empty, and, when it convenes, it is only to agree the hour of its adjournment.

According to the Weimar constitution there is no censorship. 'Every German', so it says there, 'has the right to express freely his opinion in word, text, print or image.' But, in reality, books are being banned, newspapers suppressed, editors sent to prison, film screenings prevented, radio broadcasts forbidden, and all by means of the freest constitution in the world.

The power of the dominant classes can unfold unrestrainedly, because Germany has become 'the best equipped poorhouse in the world' and the mass of its inhabitants have become starving, stirred-up, mistrustful people. Economic difficulties grow from day to day. More and more factories are being shut down, bankruptcies are piling up, no section of the workforce, no type of profession is safe from being endangered by unemployment. The number of unemployed doctors, engineers, and senior teachers has risen from 10,000 to 30,000 from 1928 to 1931. At the same time the graduate population grows each year by about 24,000 students who leave the universities and by about 40,000 students starting university. Schools are being closed, teachers' freedoms curbed, and school meals cut.

The set levels for all benefit categories are reduced; payments for the ill, for pregnant women, and for weak children are cut. They threaten to merge unemployment insurance, crisis care, and welfare benefits into one, and thereby to reduce 6 million citizens to charity recipients. Whilst every tenth adult desperately seeks in vain for work, we see child labour in the private sector on the increase. In the Thuringian forest, in the *Erzgebirge*, and in the *Oberpfalz* children regularly work into the late evening, but one can also find children working after midnight. In the pencil factory in Steinach the casing of 1,000 pencils by children's hands is paid with 20 pf; in Erfurt 100–200 children are employed for an hourly wage of 10 pf. In most rural areas of Germany 20 per cent of children get up at 5 o'clock, work in the house and in the stable before they go to school, and in the field or with the cattle after school. The children's food has to be sparse and cheap. Thirty per cent of all Berlin schoolchildren are undernourished, are thus easily worn out, and are tired and completely incapable of work by lunchtime. But what can a child get to eat when its unemployed parents get 51 Marks per month in benefits and when after unavoidable expenditure on rent, heat, and light is taken into account 18.50 Marks are left with which to feed three people? Let us be clear what this means.

The child receives two-thirds of a litre of milk a day; beyond this, for three people there is half a pound of bread—representing five average slices per day—a pound of potatoes, i.e. six potatoes, a small portion of cabbage, 16 cm³ of margarine, and one herring per person three times a month.

The accommodation situation is just as bad as the food situation. We speak not of the luxurious new buildings 'with all comforts' but of the workers' apartments. In the Prenzlauer Berg district of Berlin eight or ten people live in a single room with kitchen, while 47 per cent of all Berlin schoolchildren do not have their own bed. Social misery only functions as a stimulus to fight up to a certain point. If it becomes a mass everyday phenomenon it has a retarding effect, reducing the willingness to fight of the old and creating willingness to enter into rural servitude on the part of the young unemployed.

In this situation the fascist storm threatens, which the disorientated, ignorant petit bourgeoisie sees as its last hope. If fascism comes to power it will, in possession of the administrative apparatus, the armed forces, and the police, use all modern military means to revoke the remains of the constitution by means of the constitution. The first major victim will be the trade unions. The workers, robbed of their one strong, unifying organization, will wear themselves down in desperate struggles. The days in which isolated barricade struggles and rebellions had a chance of success are gone—only revolutionary romantics can place their faith in them. With poison gas, machine guns, and tanks tens of thousands of workers can be held in check by a few hundred soldiers. We have reached the point where the opponent decides the hour of reckoning. Only one means of preventing the victory of fascism remains: the creation of a unified organization of the entire working class with clearly defined, concrete goals.

If this fighting bloc is not created, the way is clear for fascism; we are facing a period of fascism which will last for *years* and at the end of which war threatens not against France, but against the Soviet Union. It is in the interest both of the German working class and of all the peaceful and unblinded citizens of Europe to prevent this development.

['Zur Deutschen Situation' (1932), in *Gesammelte Werke*, i; *Kritische Schriften, Reden und Reportagen* (Munich: Carl Hanser Verlag, 1978), 73–6.]

Section B

The Emergence of National Socialism

INTRODUCTION

Perhaps understandably, immediate post-war writings on the origins of Nazism took the form of either radical anti-German polemic which depicted Nazi aggression as the product of the German national character or of centuries-old traditions, or conservative apologetics arguing that Nazism had been a short-term aberration in an otherwise healthy national history hijacked by 'demonic forces'. As might be expected, the former tended to appear in the victorious nations rather than in Germany. A. J. P. Taylor's *The Course of German History* is a prime example—published in 1945, it spoke of 'certain permanent factors' which could be traced back a thousand years. Of the latter, there was no shortage of texts published in Germany insisting that Nazism had been a product of the 'age of the masses' or of 'demagogic politics' which, far from being peculiarly German, had entered European politics with the French Revolution; similarly, pointing to the fact that Hitler himself had been Austrian helped found the exculpatory myth that Germany had been the 'first country occupied by Nazism', as if the millions of people who had voted for and joined the Nazi party had been anything other than Germans.

The first serious debate on the place of Nazism within the broader context of modern German history was stimulated by the controversial work of Fritz Fischer on Germany's war aims during the First World War. Fischer's work, first published in 1961, sought to suggest lines of continuity between an aggressively imperialist and annexationist foreign policy pursued by Wilhelmine Germany and the foreign policy of the Nazi era. The relationship between authoritarian political continuities and a continuous tradition of aggression came to form the core of the 'Special Path' thesis, advocated by a younger generation of more critical German historians following in Fischer's wake in the 1970s. Turning the pre-1945 thesis of a positive German 'Special Path' on its head, these scholars argued that in contrast to other western industrial nations, whose development had been characterized by a more-or-less standard process of industrialization, 'bourgeois revolution', democratization, and the establishment of a political culture based on liberal values and norms, Germany took an abnormal path, the result of which was the tragedy of National Socialism. According to this view National Socialism was the product of a weak liberal tradition in Germany, the middle classes having 'capitulated' to the forces of pre-industrial Prussian authoritarianism whose power had been cemented in the Reich constitution of 1871. These pre-industrial elites, it was argued, sought to divert the growing social and political antagonisms arising from the pressures of accelerated industrialization by pursuing an imperialist and expansionist foreign policy, which culminated inevitably in the conflagration of 1914–18. Despite the collapse of the *Kaiserreich* and the revolution of 1918/19, these pre-industrial elites retained much of their power and were instrumental in undermining the Weimar Republic and contriving the Nazi seizure of power, thereby facilitating the renewed pursuit of traditional expansionist aims.

The assertion of basic continuities in German political and social structures between 1871 and 1933, and of a concomitant continuity in militarism and imperialist aggression, was challenged in the 1980s (not least by several British scholars) for not recognizing the extent to which Germany did indeed experience her own 'bourgeois revolution' in the nineteenth century. These historians argue that the differences between nineteenth-century Germany on the one hand and Britain or France on the other have been greatly overstated, and that neither German liberalism nor the German middle classes were as weak or supine as their critics have suggested. To them, the causes of National Socialism tend to be found more in the short term, and more specifically in the successive crises which occurred in the aftermath of the First World War. They are inclined at least to modify arguments about continuities from the pre-1914 era, regarding the emergence of a dynamic, populist radical Right as representing at least a partial break from traditional conservatism, a break reflected in the fact that the destructiveness of Nazi foreign policy and above all racial policy was of a qualitatively different dimension to that which came before.

Although the particular problems faced by German liberalism and the emergence of new forms of radical populist mobilization and protest from around 1890 onwards remain important to most scholars' understanding of the roots of Nazism, recent work has tended, indeed, to emphasize more the short-term causes of Nazism. In particular, the multiple negative legacies of the First World War and the impact of successive crises of capitalism on a fledgling democracy struggling to cope with these negative legacies have gained more in emphasis. The climate of embittered nationalism created by the war, defeat, and the peace treaties, the entry of the rhetoric and culture of violence into the political life of Germany, the impact of hyperinflation, agricultural depression, and the radical economic downturn of 1929–32 on the Republic's ability to establish its legitimacy and consolidate a positive Republican culture have all been the subject of increasingly nuanced research. In this polarizing and disorientating context, National Socialism's simplistic and emotive diagnoses of the ills of the nation, which it saw as being undermined by the international forces of Marxism, the Jews, and global finance capitalism, appealed to broad sectors of the population; the representation of the national community as an organism whose regeneration demanded the eradication of those parasitic elements which were undermining it may have been implicitly rather than explicitly genocidal, but, for all the vagueness of its rhetoric of renewal and revival, the German public could be in little doubt that this was a movement of aggressive activism which would wreak extreme violence on those it castigated as Germany's enemies. With the awareness that the popular basis of Nazism's support was substantially more heterogeneous than was hitherto supposed has come the tendency to concentrate less on explanations relying upon the assumption that particular groups—above all the lower middle class or the middle class—were historically susceptible to authoritarian politics or nationalist and racist ideologies, and more on examining how and under what local conditions the Nazis came to penetrate particular social and cultural milieux so successfully. As well as continuing to stress the role of Nazi propaganda and activism in mobilizing often diffuse forms of social resentment and anti-Republican and nationalist protest, recent work has done much to illuminate the ways in which the movement infiltrated the local public sphere.

Nazism's appeal as a charismatic movement of populist radical protest and national regeneration would have counted for little, however, had it not been for the presence of powerful anti-Republican forces within the economic and functional elites. One does not have to subscribe to an unmodified 'Special Path' thesis to recognize that the German conservative elites bear crucial responsibility for the failure of the Republic and the Nazis' achievement of power; recognition of the fact that Germany after the First World War experienced an extreme crisis of civil society as a whole should not lead us to forget that there were concrete institutional and political interests working to undermine the Republic and to restore authoritarian government of the Right. Since Karl-Dietrich Bracher's monumental study this has been confirmed by numerous studies—despite occasional attempts to represent the failure of the Republic as the product of its inherent constitutional weaknesses or of tactical failings on the part of its supporters, it remains the case that the Republic was defeated by its enemies, and that its enemies were firmly on the Right. A military establishment which refused to recognize the loss of the First World War as a product of the bankruptcy of an authoritarian system it had helped to sustain saw in the right-wing mythologies of a 'stab in the back' confirmation that rearmament and national regeneration would only be possible in the context of a reversion to non-democratic rule; likewise unwilling or unable to accept that high welfare costs and problems of capital formation were the legacy of a war and inflationary spiral for which the Imperial regime and not the Republic was to blame, industry came to regard the exclusion of the political Left, the reversal of the gains of organized labour, and the dismantling of Weimar's progressive welfare apparatus as preconditions for the restoration of profitability. The transition to increasingly authoritarian rule by presidential decree under first Brüning, then Papen and Schleicher, represented the achievement of the long-held goal of the elites to marginalize permanently the Reichstag and exclude the Left; the protracted attempts to find a basis for authoritarian rule without Hitler show nonetheless that Hitler was not the first choice for the majority of the elites. However, the growing strength of the Communists during the Depression perpetuated the sense of crisis within the elites. Their irresponsible unwillingness to respect the values of the democratic constitution ensured that, when all other alternatives had failed, they were willing to entrust Hitler with the reins of power.

i. A Special Path?

HANS-ULRICH WEHLER

13   **The German Empire 1871–1918**

In the concluding passages to one of the classic texts advocating the *Sonderweg* thesis, Hans-Ulrich Wehler argues for the need to understand National Socialism through analysis of authoritarian structures and culture going back to the 'configuration of 1871'.

The unbroken tradition of government by pre-industrial power-élites, the prolongation of absolutism among the military, the weakness of liberalism and the very early appearance of deliberalising measures suggest on the surface a depoliticising of society, but one which deep down favoured a continuation of the *status quo*. The same can be said of the barriers to social mobility, the holding over of differences and various norms between separate estates, which is such a revealing aspect of Imperial Germany, and the essentially élitist character of education. Much of this resulted from the political weakness and defeats suffered by the bourgeoisie in the nineteenth century, and all these factors, which are given here only as examples, had assumed their importance during a phase of historical development which was uninterrupted by a successful revolution. They were further strengthened by the success of Bismarck's policies for legitimising the *status quo*. [. . .]

There is no denying that the system of connections between the nobility, the ministerial bureaucracy, the provincial authorities and the district administrators—who were a veritable pillar of stability east of the river Elbe—created political tensions. But the myth of the bureaucracy's neutrality and the patina of inherited traditions, together with the preference shown to powerful interests, kept these below the danger-mark for a considerable time. Without doubt, the combination of compulsory military service with a social militarism in everyday life, in school subjects and in various organisations, created areas of friction. But the gains made in terms of the stability which these elements helped to achieve more than made up for this friction throughout the period up to and including the first years of the war. In both cases, it was not until November 1918 that the true extent of the population's strong dislike of the bureaucracy and the military could be seen.

Most effective of all, perhaps, were those strategies which, also depending on the ruling élites' capacity to learn, combined an ability to adapt to modern forms of politics and propaganda with, at the same time, a stubborn defence

of their inherited positions of power. The unholy trinity of social imperialism, social protectionism and social militarism provides more than sufficient
examples of this. In the case of social imperialism, the ruling élites' reaction
to industrialisation was closely linked to its usefulness in stabilising the social
and political hierarchy of privilege. In the case of social protectionist measures, institutional arrangements of future import, such as state legislation on
social insurance, were combined with welfare measures and rights which
were not essentially liberal, but reactionary, so long as they led to an increase
in the numbers of 'friends of the Empire'. In the case of social militarism,
which was intensively encouraged, privileges of social status handed down
from the past were defended by means of modern techniques of political
campaigning pursuing carefully thought-out aims. The same is true of the
early forms of state interventionism. Even a modern-style pressure group like
the Agrarian League reveals quite clearly how this ability to adapt to modern
methods of organisation and propaganda was entirely compatible with the
continued promotion of traditional interests. All in all the entire process,
which Hans Rosenberg has described as 'the pseudo-democratisation' of the
old agrarian elite,[1] showed an often astonishingly flexible readiness on the
part of the ruling élites to move with the times while all the more ruthlessly
defending their traditional positions behind the façade.

All these strategies, measures and processes of pathological and ingenuous
learning were interwoven. Together with a combination of traditionalism
and partial modernisation, they were able, on the one hand, to preserve the
stability of an historically outdated power structure over a surprisingly long
period. Time and time again they achieved the necessary social cohesion. On
the other hand, they added, especially in the long run, to an unmistakably
increasing burden. The various interests and traditions thus protected
became all the more difficult to reconcile with the growing demands for
equality, a share of power and liberation from an increasingly intolerable
legacy. Just as the economic successes of German industrialisation threw up
enormous social and political problems, so the successful defence of traditional political, social and economic power relationships exacted its price.
The costs were all the greater and more numerous as a result. The accumulation of unsolved problems which eventually had to be faced, the petrification
of institutions which had outlived their usefulness and were in need of
reform and the obstinate insistence on prerogatives which should no longer
have been the sole property of the privileged few, pronounce their own
judgement on the extent to which the ruling élites were prepared to adapt. So
do the continual recourse to evasive strategies and attempts to divert attention from the need for internal reforms, as well as the decision to accept
the risk of war rather than be forced into making concessions. In practice, the
ruling élites showed themselves to be neither willing nor able to initiate the
transition towards modern social and political conditions when this had

become necessary. This is not a judgement based on theoretical speculation but on processes which culminated in the breakdown of the German Empire in revolution and the end of the old regime. This hiatus now belongs among the undisputed facts of history and cannot be explained away. It represented the bill that had to be paid for the inability of the German Empire to adapt positively to change.

The fact that this break with the past did not go deep enough and that the consequences of the successful preservation of outworn traditions remained everywhere visible after 1918, accounts for the acute nature of the problem of continuity in twentieth-century German history. Instead of bewailing 'the distortion of judgement caused by the category of continuity',[2] in arguments which patently seek to defend the German Empire's record, we should, in keeping with the essential requirements of an historical social science, face up to the problems of continuity and seek to analyse them further, rather than encourage an escapist attitude. This does not, of course, mean we should offer superficial explanations based on the 'great men' approach to history (from Bismarck to Hitler via Wilhelm II and Hindenburg); rather we should investigate the social, economic, political and psychic structures which, acting as matrices, were able to produce the same, or similar, configurations over a long period of time. Conversely, we should also analyse those factors which gave rise to anomalies and discontinuity. The question as to whether, in fact, certain conditions favoured the emergence of charismatic political leaders in Germany should be re-examined against the background of these structures.

In the years before 1945, and indeed in some respects beyond this, the fatal successes of Imperial Germany's ruling élites, assisted by older historical traditions and new experiences, continued to exert an influence. In the widespread susceptibility towards authoritarian policies, in the hostility towards democracy in education and political life, in the continuing influence of the pre-industrial ruling élites, there begins a long inventory of serious historical problems. To this list we must add the tenacity of the German ideology of the state, its myth of the bureaucracy, the superimposition of class differences on those between the traditional late-feudal estates and the manipulation of political antisemitism. It is because of all these factors that a knowledge of the history of the German Empire between 1871 and 1918 remains absolutely indispensable for an understanding of German history over the past decades.

[*The German Empire 1871–1918* (1973; new edn. Oxford: Berg, 1985), 242–6.]

14 The Causes of National Socialism

> Whilst accepting the significance of the short-term crisis of capitalism
> in bringing National Socialism to power, Kocka argues that the real
> peculiarity of German development is still to be found in the survival
> of pre-industrial and pre-modern traditions and structures.

'Whoever is unwilling to talk about capitalism should also keep silent about fascism.'[1] Max Horkheimer's dictum of 1939 has—in many different variations—played a major part in the discussions of recent years. This hypothesis, that German fascism too was a fruit of the crisis of the capitalist economic and bourgeois social system and emerged from this with a certain necessity, has been supported in many relevant publications, particularly from the Marxist side.[2] Roughly summarized, there are in particular three factors which indicate that such a hypothesis has a certain justification:

1. There can be no doubt that the rise of National Socialism was promoted by the economic crisis around 1930, which itself can be explained by the internal contradictions of the private economic system. The slowdown in economic growth, and the reduction in company profits at the end of the 1920s, intensified distributional conflict and made the already difficult distributional compromise even harder. It is symptomatic that the last parliamentary government in 1930 had collapsed over a socio-political conflict.[3] The structurally determined (i.e. already before the economic turndown) relatively high unemployment level (1929: 9 per cent) which reached the figure of almost 6 million or 30 per cent in 1932, the deterioration in wages and salaries accelerated by Brüning's deflationary policy since 1930, which was ultimately harsher than the general decline in prices—all this was a product of the crisis of the private economic system, and at the same time a major condition for the rise of National Socialism. [. . .]

2. A second piece of evidence of the connection between capitalist crisis and fascism can be seen in the political behaviour of the owners of capital and industrialists. Undoubtedly only a minority of employers had identified themselves even to some extent with the Weimar system. Rather, most of them were sceptical towards parliamentarianism and democratic suffrage: they criticized the expansion of social policy, and they rejected the strong growth of trade union influence since the Imperial period. Their lack of support for the first German republic was, then, also their most important contribution to the rise of National Socialism. Against this, direct support of the NSDAP by industrialists and business groups was extremely limited up to 1932.

If we leave out individuals such as Adolf Kirdorf and Fritz Thyssen, there was little sympathy within 'business' for the social-radical small party, which did not call itself 'National Socialist' completely without reason. Financial assistance was still very much limited after 1930, particularly when one considers that the large companies and trade associations mostly supported several parties (apart from the KPD) financially, so as to have several lines of influence at the same time. Nevertheless, donations of funds increased after 1930, and in the last month before the seizure of power, heavy-industry groups in particular, but also bank representatives, appear increasingly to have brought their influence to bear on behalf of Hitler. [. . .]

3. Thirdly, the hypothesis of the connection between capitalism and fascism is supported, if one looks at certain important outcomes of National Socialist policy from 1933 to 1939. The total state which was in the process of establishing itself hit the organized body of labour with full force. It was broken up or incorporated into sections of the NSDAP. The old leaders were deprived of power, persecuted, in some cases annihilated: in any event they were replaced. The ideology of the labour movement was combated: if different fascist movements have something in common, it is their anti-Socialist, anti-Marxist, anti-Communist agenda and their anti-Bolshevik ideology of struggle. Hitherto no fascist system has tolerated independent free trade unions, collective bargaining, and the freedom to strike. In comparison to this, the industrialist organizations were treated with kid gloves. It is true that there were also organizational changes here; in cases of conflict the new political leaders had no doubt who was boss. But if one disregards the so-called 'Aryanization', the ousting of the Jews from economic life, there was little change in personnel: the larger industrialists and their organizations retained remarkable independence (compared with other groups). By and large, the growth of an economy gearing up early for a later war was of very much greater benefit to the companies than to the employees. [. . .]

Nevertheless, an explanation which analyses German fascism as a necessary retarded birth of capitalism in crisis does not go far enough. At best it represents half of the truth, i.e. it is wrong if it is claims to be the entire truth. This is also—very briefly—for three reasons:

1. There is a whole series of central elements of National Socialist policy, including economic policy, which cannot be explained adequately as the consequence of capitalist interests or of imperatives towards preserving the capitalist bourgeois system. For example, the stepping up of rearmament after 1936 led to the first signs of a state-administered economy, and to the overstretching of the labour market to such an extent that it was in no way acceptable even to powerful representatives of industrial interests and provoked their opposition. Another example: Hitler's foreign policy, with its nothing short of obsessive striving for 'Lebensraum' in the east, cannot be

explained adequately by economic interests or by the self-reproductive impulses of the capitalist economic system. Rather, the expansionist and aggressive impulses in the policy of the time gained a certain priority and economic and interest-based considerations were subordinated to them. Finally, a third remark: precisely the most inhumane features of the NS dictatorship, particularly its extermination policy towards the Jews, can in no way be explained in terms of the interests of those who owned capital, or by the logic of the capitalist system.[4]

2. In the ideology and, less so, in the practice of National Socialism, there was—more before 1933 than afterwards—a series of elements which must be described quintessentially as anti-capitalist and anti-bourgeois; as anti-hierarchical and anti-conservative. It would not be too difficult to list the class struggle-populist elements in the programme of the National Socialists and in the policy of the National Socialist rank and file. Even the corporatist-restorative elements in the NS programme—reagrarianization, 'blood and soil' myth, *mittelständisch* anti-capitalism, etc.—were in stark contrast to the basic principles and values of a modern capitalist-bourgeois order.[5]

3. Most importantly and most conclusively there is the fact that fascist movements triumphed in Germany and Italy, but not in England and the USA, and hence precisely not in those nations in which industrial capitalism was most developed, and where bourgeois society was most clearly established. Nevertheless, the economic crisis also hit England and the USA, and, incidentally, even harder and for longer in the USA than in Germany. Above all, therefore, it is not possible to explain fascism adequately as the consequence of the capitalist-bourgeois crisis, because there was one like it in other western countries, which nonetheless did not fall prey to fascism. To explain these factors, we must therefore look for factors which were present in Germany, but not in the USA and Great Britain.

If one searches for such German peculiarities, the first thought is of the lost First World War and its consequences. Had it not been for the First World War, which came closer to being a total war than any previous one, and which set the social structure and social consciousness literally in turmoil, German and Italian fascism would not have come about. [. . .]

But it would be problematic to overemphasize the period since the First World War in the prehistory of National Socialism. Long before 1914 special features of German social history existed which were absent in other, comparable countries, and which favoured the later rise of National Socialism. [. . .]

The question of the causes of the *mittelständisch* basis of National Socialism raises the issue of the great importance to its rise of the dual-pronged ideological imperative of National Socialism. What drew precisely younger clerical employees of the great German National White-Collar Workers'

Association and many other white-collar workers straight to the Hitler movement was that in response to their dissatisfaction for the first time a truly radical opportunity for protest against the prevailing conditions was being offered, without incorporating them into the Socialist-orientated united workers' front. National Socialism offered the possibility of being radical and anti-elitist, against capitalists and 'bigwigs', *on the one hand*, and *on the other hand* of appearing strongly anti-Socialist, national, and of acting in accordance with their social status. This Janus-faced character of the NS movement—ideologically reactionary and revolutionary at the same time— made it—so it seems—attractive to large parts of the growing group of white-collar workers. The leaning of many members of the 'old (independent) *Mittelstand*' towards National Socialism can be similarly explained. The NSDAP responded skilfully to the anti-capitalism of the small craftsmen and traders, it spoke to them, but of course not in Marxist terms. To the small self-employed the NSDAP offered an ideological framework in which they could be militant and conservative, anti-capitalist and anti-Socialist at one and the same time.[6]

But what, in terms of social history, was the cause of this dissatisfaction and protest potential, which under particular conditions could become the social basis of a right-radical mass movement? [. . .]

If we wish to explain the mass basis and thus the possibility of the advancement of German fascism in social-historical terms, we must certainly not forget that it was the crisis-like manifestions of, or even simply the ever progressing development of, the industrial-capitalist economic and bourgeois social system which led to tensions and conflicts, and which—under specific conditions—nurtured the right-radical protest movement. But just as important is this: the socio-economic crisis phenomena and consequences of modernization would only become the source of such vehement protests because they collided with continuing traditions of pre-capitalist and pre-bourgeois origin. In Germany, the crisis of the private economy and the middle-class social system ended in catastrophe, because—thanks to a specific path of German modernization—pre-capitalist and pre-bourgeois, authoritarian, feudal and corporatist residues had survived more than in the other western countries. One might almost say: because German society had never truly been a bourgeois society, its crisis produced the post-bourgeois, anti-bourgeois system of fascism when it emerged in the 1920s. The hermaphrodite character of German National Socialism—both anti-modern and dynamic, anti-capitalist and anti-socialist, reactionary and revolutionary at the same time—can be explained in conjunction with this.[7] Horkheimer's dictum, cited at the start, is not wrong. But by the same right one can say: 'whoever is unwilling to talk about pre-industrial, pre-capitalist, and pre-bourgeois traditions should also keep silent about fascism.' [. . .]

It is indeed generally known that the seizure of power first became possible when the new National Socialist Right succeeded in joining forces with the old Right—parts of the conservative elites in industry, large-scale agriculture, the army, and the bureaucracy.

Visible stations on the route to this alliance were the 1929 collaboration of the NSDAP and conservative groups (such as the *Stahlhelm* and *Landbund*) on the common platform of the 'national opposition' against the acceptance of the Young Plan, which revised the reparations question, and which the government supported for lack of better alternatives; the 'Harzburg Front' of 1931; the support of Hitler's candidacy as chancellor since the last months of 1932 on the part of conservative party and of interest-group representatives, higher officers, and civil servants; and finally the first Hitler–Hugenberg cabinet, of which as is known only three National Socialists, but eight conservatives with close connections to major industry, large-scale farming, the DNVP, and the *Reichswehr*, were members. A clear demonstration of this alliance, in which Hitler then certainly outmanœuvred his conservative partners, was the 'Day of Potsdam' of 21 March 1933. This important role of major parts of the conservative ruling classes in Hitler's 'seizure of power'— there was nothing comparable on the side of the workers' movement up to the seizure of power—must not be relativized by emphasis on the middle-class mass basis of National Socialism. The '*Mittelstand* theory' must not be allowed to have an exculpatory function.

The diverse reasons and motives behind the initially very hesitant but finally decisive support for Hitler amongst parts of the German ruling classes have been mentioned briefly above; they were varied. In the context of the argument advanced here, however, it is particularly important that a peculiar mixture between modernity and backwardness had been preserved in parts of the German ruling classes: the product of a development in which the most rapid economic modernization into an industrial state had taken place without socio-political radical reform at the same time. The great power of the Junkers in industrial Germany, the feudalization tendencies in the upper bourgeoisie; the extraordinary power of the bureaucracy and military in a state which had never experienced a successful bourgeois revolution and which had been unified from above; the social and political alliance of the rising middle class and a still extant agrarian nobility against a proletariat which was thereby strictly excluded; the anti-parliamentary, anti-democratic, and anti-liberal orientation of large parts of the German ruling classes caused through this—all became fatally crucial in the economic and social crisis around 1930. The great role of the landowners in the final phase of the Weimar Republic is particularly instructive in this connection. The German path of economic modernization without thorough social liberalization and political democratization now took its revenge.[8]

['Ursachen des Nationalsozialismus', *Aus Politik und Zeitgeschichte* (June 1980), 3–7, 9–12.]

15 What Produces Fascism: Pre-industrial Traditions or a Crisis of Capitalism?

One of the most sophisticated critics of the *Sonderweg* thesis, Geoff Eley, has consistently argued that this view overstates the importance of long-term origins and places too much emphasis on 'pre-industrial traditions'. In this piece, he argues that fascist potential was rooted not so much in pre-industrial classes as in social groups which were pre-cisely a product of Germany's emergence as a mature industrial soci-ety, and that the causes of National Socialism are to be located more within a short-term crisis of capitalism itself, combined with a crisis of political legitimacy, from the First World War onwards.

My suggestion is that we can explain the attractions of radical nationalism (and by extension those of fascism) without recourse to the cultural and economic 'despair' of threatened 'traditional' strata, to concepts of 'anti-modernism', or to the persistence of Kocka's 'pre-industrial traditions'. Those attractions may be grasped partly from the ideology itself, which was self-confident, optimistic and affirming. It contained an aggressive belief in the authenticity of a German/Italian national mission, in the unifying poten-tial of the nationalist panacea, and in the popular resonance of the national idea for the struggle against the left. Radical nationalism was a vision of the future, not of the past. In this sense it harnessed the cultural aspirations of many who were comfortably placed in the emerging bourgeois society, the successful beneficiaries of the new urban-industrial civilization, whose polit-ical sensibilities were offended by the seeming incapacitation of the estab-lishment before the left-wing challenge. While [. . .] this outlook possessed a definite appeal to a certain type of patriotic intellectual or activist, it is also likely that in times of relative social and political stability the ideology in itself could achieve only a limited popular appeal. But in times of crisis, which brought the domestic unity, foreign mission and territorial integrity of the nation all into question, this might easily change. The dramatic con-juncture of war and revolution between 1914 and 1923 produced exactly a crisis of this kind.

Given the operation of certain recognized social determinations (like the status distinctions between white-collar and manual work, or the deliberate fostering of white-collar consciousness by employers and the state), we should concede a certain effectivity to this specifically political factor when trying to explain the radical right-wing preferences of large sections of the new petty bourgeoisie. There is no space to develop this argument more fully here, and in some ways the knowledge to do so is not yet assembled, given the general paucity of research in the area. Though we are well equipped with data concerning the voting patterns in Weimar elections, for instance, or the relative prominence of different occupations amongst the Nazi Party members, we are still very ignorant about the social histories of the particular professions and categories of white-collar employment. What we *do* know certainly suggests that the avenue of inquiry is worth pursuing. The presence of professionals, managers and administrators amongst Nazi activists is now well attested, and the Nazi state provided plenty of scope for the technocratic imagination—in industrial organization, public works, social administration and the bureaucracy of terror.[1] This sort of evidence moves securely with the direction of the above remarks. At the very least the grievances of the 'traditional' petty bourgeoisie co-existed in the fascist movements with other aspirations of a more 'forward-looking' and 'modernist' kind. [. . .]

The promiscuous adaptability of Nazi propaganda has often been noted, and it was certainly adept at tapping manifold popular resentments, promising all and nothing in the same breath. But this remarkable diversity of social appeal can easily mislead. Though both cynical and opportunist, Nazi eclecticism was also a major constructive achievement. The Nazis rallied a disparate assortment of social and political elements who lacked strong traditions of co-operation or effective solidarity in the political sphere, and often surveyed long histories of hostility and mutual suspicion. From September 1930 to January 1933 the NSDAP was a popular political formation without precedent in the German political system. It not only subsumed the organizational fragmentation of the right. It also united a broadly based coalition of the subordinate classes, centered on the peasantry and petty bourgeoisie, but stretching deep into the wage-earning population.

It did so on the terrain of ideology, by unifying an otherwise disjointed ensemble of discontents within a totalizing populist framework—namely, the radicalized ideological community of the German people-race. The resulting combination was extraordinarily potent—activist, communitarian, anti-plutocratic and popular, but at the same time virulently anti-socialist, anti-semitic, intolerant of diversity and aggressively nationalist. [. . .]

This line of argument reinstates the importance of ideology for our understanding of fascism. In particular, it directs us to the contested terrain of popular-democratic aspirations, where the socialist left proved most deficient, the fascist right most telling in their mode of political intervention. Where the left, in both Italy and Germany, kept aggressively to a class-corporate practice of proletarian independence, the fascists erupted into the arena and appropriated the larger popular potential.[2] Of course, putting it like this presupposes an expanded definition of ideology, where it means something more than what happens inside a few literati's heads and is then committed to paper and published for wider consumption. In other words, I mean something more than the well-tried intellectual history so popular with many

Germanists during the 1950s and 1960s—that is, not just ideas and attitudes, but also types of behaviour, institutions and social relations, so that ideology becomes materially embodied as well as just thought about (for example, not only the fascist movement's formal aims, but its style of activism, modes of organization and forms of public display). On this basis fascism becomes primarily a specific type of politics, involving radical authoritarianism, militarized activism and the drive for a centralist repressive state, with a radical-nationalist, communalist and frequently racialist creed, and a violent antipathy for both liberal democracy and socialism. Providing these elements are treated not as some revealed unity, but as a set of potentials whose concrete substance may be unevenly and partially realized in 'real' (particular, historical) fascisms, a definition of this kind could be quite serviceable. [. . .]

[Fascism] registered a qualitative departure from previous conservative practice, substituting corporatist notions of social place for older hierarchical ones, and ideas of race community for those of clerical, aristocratic and bureaucratic authority. These and other aspects of fascist ideology are intimately linked to its broadly based popular appeal. Fascism is an aggressively plebeian movement, espousing a crude and violent egalitarianism. Above all, fascism stands for activism and popular mobilization, embracing everything from para-military display, street-fighting and straightforward terror, to more conventional forms of political activity, new propagandist forms and a general invasion of the cultural sphere. It is negatively defined against liberalism, social democracy and communism, or any creed which seems to elevate difference, division and conflict over the essential unity of the race-people as the organizing principle of political life.

At the same time, fascism was not a universal phenomenon, and appeared in strength only in a specific range of societies. In explaining this variation there are two main emphases. One is the deep historical perspective discussed in relation to Jürgen Kocka. At some level of explanation the structural factors stressed by the latter are clearly important and might be summarized as follows: accelerated capitalist transformation, in a dual context of simultaneous national state formation and heightened competition in the imperialist world economy; the coexistence in a highly advanced capitalist economy of large 'traditional' sectors, including a smallholding peasantry and an industrial-trading petty bourgeoisie, 'deeply marked by the contradictions of capitalist development';[3] and, finally the emergence of a precocious socialist movement publicly committed to a revolutionary programme. This complex over-determination (the 'contemporaneity of the uncontemporary', or 'uneven and combined development') characterized both German and Italian history before the First World War, articulated through the interpenetration of national and social problems. [. . .]

However, German historians have given this structural argument an additional formulation, which is far more problematic. Evaluating German development (or 'misdevelopment', as they call it) by an external and linear model of 'modernization', which postulates an ultimate complementarity between economic growth and political democratization (which in Germany, for peculiar reasons, was obstructed), such historians stress the dominance in German public life of 'pre-industrial' ideological traditions. The absence of a liberal political culture is thought to have permitted the survival of traditional authoritarian mentalities which enjoyed strong institutional power bases, and which could then be radicalized under the future circumstances of an economic or political crisis. Thus a 'reactionary protest potential' is created.[4] Fascism draws its support either directly from 'traditional social strata', or from newer strata (like white-collar employees) supposedly beholden to 'traditional' ideas. This essentially is Jürgen Kocka's argument.

Though not incompatible with a modified version of the above, the second approach stresses the immediate circumstances under which the fascists came to power. Here we need to mention the impact of the First World War, the nature of the postwar crisis in the European revolutionary conjuncture of 1917–23, the unprecedented gains of the left (both reformist and revolutionary), and the collapse of parliamentary institutions. Together these brought a fundamental crisis in the unity and popular credibility of the dominant classes, which opened the space for radical speculations. Here again, although one was the major defeated party and the other a nominal victor in the First World War, the German and Italian experiences were remarkably similar in these respects. In both cases the radical right defined itself against the double experience of thwarted imperialist ambitions and domestic political retreat, each feeding the other. In both cases the postwar situation was dominated by the public accommodation of labour, whose political and trade union aspirations appeared to be in the ascendant: trade unions acquired a new corporative legitimacy; socialists attained a commanding presence in large areas of local government; the national leaderships of the SPD and PSI occupied the centre of the political stage; and substantial movements to their left (first syndicalist and then communist) added an element of popular insurgency. In both cases, too, liberal or parliamentary methods of political containment were shown to have exhausted their potential, guaranteeing neither the political representation of the dominant classes, nor the mobilization of popular consent. In such circumstances fascism successfully presented itself as a radical populist solution.

In other words, fascism prospered under conditions of general political crisis, in societies which were already dynamically capitalist (or at least, which possessed a dynamic capitalist sector), but where the state proved incapable of dispatching its organizing functions for the maintenance of social cohesion. The political unity of the dominant classes and their major economic fractions could no longer be organized successfully within the existing forms of parliamentary representation and party government. Simultaneously the

popular legitimacy of the same institutional framework also went into crisis.
[. . .]

In the context of the Weimar crisis, adjustments within the existing institutional arrangements looked increasingly untenable, and more radical solutions beyond the boundaries of the existing political system consequently
became more attractive.

The problem of defining fascism is therefore not exhausted by describing
its ideology, even in the expanded sense of the latter intimated above. Fascism
was not just a particular style of politics, it was also inscribed in a specific
combination of political conditions (themselves the structured, mediate effect
of complex socio-economic determinations), namely the kind of dual crisis
of the state just referred to. Now, that kind of crisis is normally associated
with the Great Depression after 1929, but the postwar crisis of political order
between 1917 and 1923 was equally important. The global ideological context
of the Bolshevik Revolution and its international political legacy gave enormous impetus to the radicalization of the right, and the more vigorous fascist
movements generally arose in societies which experienced serious left-wing
insurgencies after 1917–18. As well as Italy and Germany, Hungary, Austria,
Finland and Spain are all good examples. [. . .]

The operative circumstances were ones which made it possible for the
dominant classes to take extreme or exceptional solutions seriously, though
never without well-founded hestitation. One such circumstance was obviously the very emergence of the fascists as a credible mass movement, for
without the popular materials an 'extra-systemic solution' [. . .] was clearly a
non-starter.[5] But, as a generalization, recourse to the fascist option was politically most likely where the left had achieved significant inroads into the
administration of state power and the limitation of private capitalist prerogative, or where combinations of entrenched left reformism and concurrent
revolutionary activity seemed to obstruct the resolution of economic crisis
and the restoration of order. For example, the most persuasive reading of
the crisis of Weimar stresses the importance of a kind of social democratic corporatism (embodied in trade union legislation, a Ministry of
Labour, compulsory arbitration procedures, unemployment insurance,
other welfare legislation, and so on), whose defensive strengths could not
be dismantled within the existing constitutional framework of parliamentary decision-making. The structural necessity of fascist remedies
(given certain inflexible commitments and requirements among the most
powerful fractions of the dominant classes) can then be located in the
labour movement's ability to defend the institutional advances of the 1918
Revolution (or more accurately, of the political settlement of 1918–23)[6]
When we add the SPD's strong position in provincial and local government, the impressive militancy of the Reichsbanner militia, and the continued vitality of a strategic Marxist-reformist vision amongst the party

intelligentsia, the appeal of a radical authoritarian solution becomes all the more intelligible.[7]

This idea of a defensive social democratic corporatism, which within the limits of this essay has to remain theoretically underdeveloped, may well be a fruitful one for the discussion of fascism. It lends a formal unity to the political crisis of Weimar, between the foundering of the Grand Coalition in March 1930 on the issue of insurance legislation, and the precipitation of the Papen–Hitler manœuvre in December 1932–January 1933 by Schleicher's renewed corporatist exploration. *Mutatis mutandis*, the argument also works for the Italian situation in 1918–22, where the presence of a mass socialist party publicly committed to a revolutionary programme (however rhetorically) had effectively thrown the state into paralysis. Here the growing popular strength of the left, its aggressive use of the workers' councils in Milan and Turin, its commanding position in northern local government, and its massive concentrations of regional support, provoked a massive counter-revolutionary backlash, organized through Mussolini's Fascists. In both Germany (1918–33) and Italy (1918–22), and for that matter Spain too (1931–6), we are dealing in effect with limited socialist enclaves (some of them physical, some institutional, some merely attitudinal or ideological) within the existing state, which constituted intolerable obstructions to the kind of stabilization which a powerful coalition within the dominant classes was increasingly pursuing. [. . .]

Fascism may be best understood, therefore, as primarily a counter-revolutionary ideological project, constituting a new kind of popular coalition, in the specific circumstances of an interwar crisis. As such it provided the motivational impetus for specific categories of radicalized political actors in the immediate aftermath of the First World War, embittered by national humiliation, enraged by the advance of the left. As working-class insurgency defined the capacities of the existing liberal polities to achieve the necessary stabilization, this radical-nationalist cadre became an important pole of attraction for larger circles of the dominant classes and others who felt threatened by the reigning social turbulence. In Italy, where the socialist movement was generally further to the left than in Germany, and where no equivalent of the SPD functioned as a vital factor of order, this process of right-wing concentration around the redemptive potential of a radical-nationalist anti-socialist terror was far more advanced. But later, in the renewed but differently structured crisis of 1929–34, a recognizable pattern recurred. Elsewhere a similar scenario was scripted, but indifferently played out. [. . .]

In the end both perspectives are necessary—the deep historical or long-term structural one *and* the stress on the immediate crisis. But we have to be clear about what exactly each of them may reasonably explain. In particular, the causal primacy of 'pre-industrial traditions' threatens to become both teleological and heavily determinist, locating the origins of fascism somewhere in the middle third of the nineteenth century, when Germany (and Italy) failed to take the 'long hard road to modernity', in Dahrendorf's phrase. Much of this would be perfectly acceptable and in the most rounded of analyses should be complemetary to the other type of approach rather than antithetical. Yet in the works of Jürgen Kocka and other German historians the explanatory claims are far more aggressive than this. The 'pre-industrial traditions' are given a privileged place in the causal repertoire in a way which specifically displaces certain other approaches, those which begin with the interior dynamics of the immediate fascism-producing crisis.

['What produces Fascism: Pre-Industrial Traditions or a Crisis of Capitalism', in G. Eley, *From Unification to Nazism* (London: Allen & Unwin, 1986), 266–7, 269–73, 276.]

DIETER GROH

16   The Special Path of German History: Myth or Reality?

Dieter Groh's article on the *Sonderweg* debate from which these passages are taken examines the arguments for and against the thesis. While accepting the criticisms of Blackbourn and Eley, he suggests that they have been more successful in undermining a pre-existing explanatory model than they have been in offering a new one.

Where the history of West Germany is concerned, the positive image of the *Sonderweg* disappeared once and for all in the late 1960s and early 1970s with the widening of the historiographical perspective resulting from the 'Fischer controversy'. This controversy was sparked off by the work carried out by Fritz Fischer, a historian at Hamburg University; since 1958 he had been trying with his students to prove empirically the overwhelming culpability of the German Empire in triggering the First World War. The debate first used the traditional methods of narrative history, but soon moved away, as regards both content and method, from its immediate purpose. The history of the Second Reich in all its aspects, above all its social and economic history, became the number one theme of historiography in the German Federal Republic. The time-scale also widened, ultimately including the whole 1848–1945 period. The zeal of some historians took them even further back into the German past. Finally a consensus of opinion was arrived at within a group of historians and political economists, ranging from liberals to social democrats, though they were in the minority. By then the original topic of study, the triggering of the First World War, played only a secondary role: the whole previous century of German history was seen as leading more or less directly to National Socialism. To paraphrase the Marxist formula: 'Those who do not wish to speak of capitalism should also remain silent on fascism'; one might even say: 'those who do not wish to speak of the

German *Sonderweg* should also remain silent on German fascism.' The *Sonderweg* found its way into every field, and especially into social history and foreign policy, while advocates of the explicit *Sonderweg* theory asserted the primacy of domestic policy. This theory could be resumed in the following formula: industrialization without social innovations and without the corresponding politics [. . .]

It would be possible to follow Blackbourn and Eley and set the following hypothesis against the *Sonderweg* theory from the beginning of the nineteenth century, or from 1848, at latest: just as the constitutional German monarchy of the nineteenth century formed a 'constitutional type *sui generis*' (E. R. Huber) and not a transient or intermediate stage of development, the state and society in pre-1914 Prussian Germany unquestionably manifested the typical features of bourgeois domination, both in the economic field and where fundamental social values (zeal, profitability, sobriety, rationality, efficiency) are concerned. Is it possible to talk of a sin by omission, or a weakness of some kind in the bourgeois spirit—meaning it was easily led astray— during the history of pre-1914 Germany, when the aspirations of the bourgeoisie were fulfilled as much as, if not more than, those of its neighbours? The answer to this question requires more persuasive and detailed arguments than those so far put forward by the advocates of the *Sonderweg*. The dominant bourgeoisie in Germany were not cast in the same *mould* as in France or Britain: that point should be accepted by any historian without seeking any further explanation. Instead of applying Ranke's famous maxim and looking for 'what really happened', many historians studying the history of pre-1914 Germany endeavour to show 'how it didn't happen', to use David Blackbourn's phrase.

Advocates and defenders of the *Sonderweg* put forward two main arguments in reply to criticism. On the one hand they cannot see how National Socialism can be explained other than by the *Sonderweg*. On the other, following a Marxist perspective they claim the bourgeoisie of every nation merges into the fog of capitalism. I will formulate this theory more trenchantly: even if we concede both the following two points, first that the economic and political system in Prussian Germany ran counter to the interests of the bourgeoisie, and secondly that manipulation and integration strategies could have an effect only because they answered the needs of the different social strata existing as a result of the objective conditions, then a Marxist analysis must be able to explain why fascism came to power only in one single advanced capitalist industrial country, i.e. Germany, and not in countries like France, Great Britain, and the United States. [. . .]

Even leaving the politico-moral aspect aside, adherents of the *Sonderweg* are right with regard to the following points: reference to (and possibly also proof of) the normality of the development of the German bourgeoisie and German capitalism considerably complicates the solution of *the* problem of

German contemporary history: how did Hitler-style fascism come about? Marxists—of whatever tendency—who dispute the *Sonderweg* model have to recognize their own failure, given that all Marxist interpretations of fascism so far have been less satisfactory than the explanatory model based on the *Sonderweg*. If the *Sonderweg* theory is wrong, or according to Blackbourn and Eley far less correct than has hitherto been claimed, the only remaining alternatives are these: either the history of Germany between 1914 and 1933 developed in such a way as to enable us to explain fascism in Germany through that development, or there is another explanatory model for the 1848–1945 period which it should be possible to verify empirically.

Eley explicitly rejects the second solution. Where both he and Blackbourn are concerned it is a question of rethinking established ideas regarding the continuity of German history and of considering the *Kaiserreich* as a thing in itself: neither as the scene where all the 'pre-industrial continuities' were played out, nor as a prelude for what lay ahead—Weimar and the 1930s—but as a fertile period endowed with original characteristics. 'The structure of the imperial state and its problems at the onset of the First World War . . . are not a heritage resulting from being politically "backwards" (hence from "abnormal" conditions which "should" have been overcome by "moderniza-tion") but from a series of cyclical contradictions.'[1] [. . .] [O]ne could carry on along the same lines and say: the causes of the rise of Hitler-style fascism have to be sought in combinations of circumstances of medium-term dur-ation rather than in long-term structures, for example in the consequences of the war or in the post-war period, in the civil war of the 1920s and the economic crisis that started in 1929. Blackbourn and Eley should have com-mented on this crucial element in the German history of the last 150 years by means of a small explanatory note. Similarly, if emphasis is placed on the importance of an accumulation of *cyclical* contradictions to explain the his-tory of the German *Kaiserreich* as well as the rise of the system of National Socialist domination, account has to be taken of two permanent aspects of the *social structure*: on the one hand the continuity of elite power in the economy, the army and politics as well as the ideological hegemony which was exercised with the cooperation of the conservative bourgeois majority; on the other hand the constancy of the specific form of the class struggle, from the pre-war period to the war and the Revolution.[2] Nobody would expect a music critic to able to conduct the orchestra better than the con-ductor he criticizes; but we can expect him to say how the performance of the piece could be improved. From this point of view the two authors have made their own task somewhat easier. [. . .]

[It] is too soon to give verdict on the value of the model based on the German *Sonderweg* as an explanation for National Socialism; that will be possible only when another 'theory' comes to rival it, and the pros and cons of each can be weighed against one another. As regards empirical verification of the *Sonderweg* for the period 1848–1945 its main advocate, Hans-Ulrich Wehler, has declared expressly on several occasions 'that the question of the "Sonderweg" is still first and foremost a topic for discussion'[3]

['Le "Sonderweg" de l'histoire Allemande: mythe ou réalité', *Annales*, 38 (1983), 1168–9, 1174–8.]

ii. The National Socialist Movement

MARTIN BROSZAT

17 The Social Motivation and Führer Bond in National Socialism

Broszat seeks to combine analysis of the mass dynamism of the National Socialist movement with emphasis on the peculiar signifi-cance of Hitler, problematizing the relationship of the vague agenda of protest and renewal which drove the movement to the central elements of Hitler's ideology, i.e. his anti-Semitism and anti-Bolshevism. In doing so he emphasizes the extent to which National Socialism mobilized existing social and national resentments. His emphasis on the nature of the movement and the dynamism under-lying it can be seen as evidence of the way in which the shift away from the 'totalitarianism' paradigm and the revival of interest in gen-eric fascism was resulting in new perspectives.

Given the mass basis which the National Socialists achieved even before the takeover of state power, especially among the middle classes of German society, the issues of the ideological disposition of these sectors towards National Socialism or the manipulative power of National Socialist propa-ganda are not the only questions which arise. Just as important is the ques-tion of the real social motivation of National Socialism. For all the skill and suggestiveness of their propaganda Hitler and his party could not invent the conditions for their mass effectiveness. And, given the panic induced by the economic crisis, the traditional anti-democratic ideology and propaganda of the German-national opposition was insufficient to foster the emergence of a radical national mass movement. If to the surprise of many contemporaries the economic crisis, which objectively meant impoverishment and prole-tarianization to broad sectors of the population, benefited Marxist Socialism little, or not at all, and produced National Socialists far more than it led directly to class fighters or Communists, then this was obviously a product of the fact that the Hitler movement seemed to satisfy most the simul-taneous desire for continuity *and* change which filled broad sectors of the population.

Marxist theory, which diagnosed National Socialism as the last resort of dying capitalism in the face of the threatening proletarian revolution, and thus as a force in the service of social reaction, has not been accepted by non-Marxist scholarship in this exaggerated form. But there is still sufficiently far-reaching consensus behind the fundamentally socially reactionary character of National Socialism that the real social dynamic of change which (fused with the equally utopian restorative ambitions) stood behind National Socialism and which greatly facilitated its emergence as a mass party in the first place is rarely given adequate consideration. The illusory and contradictory character of the social propaganda and ideology of the NSDAP, and above all the fact that neither the programme of the Socialist Strasser wing, nor that of the National Socialist Factory Cell Organization (NSBO), and neither Darré's nor Himmler's visions of reagrarianization nor the aims of the National Socialist proponents of a *Mittelstand*-orientated policy were fulfilled, but that rather after the seizure of power the opportunist arrangement with big business and the conservative forces of the Reichswehr and bureaucracy came foremost, appear to confirm the thesis of the socially reactionary character of National Socialism. But the illogicality and mendaciousness of the social promises of the NSDAP do not undermine the significance of the social dynamism which provided the actual basis for the mass success of the party and which was kept in motion by the National Socialist regime. And the non-realization of the Socialist points of the NSDAP's programme articulated before 1933 does not mean that this regime did not still have strong social consequences and legacies. [. . .]

The lack of a rational analysis of social and political conditions by the NSDAP, already noted by contemporary critics, and its unclear and ambivalent intentions were hardly seen as a disadvantage by most Hitler voters: in contrast, it appeared to many as flexibility and liveliness, encouraging the hopes of individuals and of particular groups that National Socialism could be influenced in accordance with their own views and would revolutionize things in their interests. The irrational faith of which this was an expression can certainly be characterized as hysterical aberration, as irresponsible self-abandonment, or as unpolitical expectations of salvation, but the motive power of the social dynamism behind this mass phenomenon cannot be explained away by this. Precisely the irrationality and blindness of the will for change speaks for the pent-up pressure of social tensions, which erupted in the form of the Hitler-movement and which are an indicator of the fact that the dismantling of authoritarian, bureaucratic, feudal, and upper-middle-class structures and barriers was also regarded as an overdue desideratum by the mass of the anti-Marxist middle-class population. [. . .]

Hitler, with the image of decisiveness which he offered, knew how to articulate and to celebrate that which the audience semi-consciously wished for and felt. He gave voice to that which they secretly wished, thought, and wanted, strengthened their as yet uncertain longings and prejudices, and in doing so provided them with a deeply satisfying self-confirmation, with the feeling of being party to a new truth; he awoke their equally selfless and self-forgetting commitment to community and action. Such rousing

Führer-oratory could not be achieved by an at-ease, mature individual and personality, but needed—similar to the leaders of other fascist or similar agitational movements—a psychological and mental state which itself was so extremely marked by the crisis and panic mood of its time and social stratum that it was able to express itself instinctively; it needed a person like Hitler, who, with the growing self-confidence of the successful mass agitator, found his mission more and more, along with grandiose personal fulfilment which his hitherto eccentric pursuits had failed to achieve.

Hitler's sudden rise from intellectual and social mediocrity and anonymity to the stage of politics underlines that his leadership could only unfold in the fluid state of a certain crisis atmosphere and collective psychological state. The unusual passion with which Hitler succumbed to the general pathology, and the absoluteness with which he concentrated on giving it expression and translating it into action, enabled him to become 'Führer'. Against a background of general exaltation he was able to experience his own neuroses as a general truth and to use the collective neurosis as the sounding board for his own fanaticism. Hitler's leadership was thus from the outset the pivotal point of a paradoxical situation: on the one hand, merely the exponent of a broad nationalistic psychosis, on the other hand the integrative figure of this 'movement' which, without such integration, could not make its political breakthrough.

It thus becomes clear that Hitler as an individual cannot be bracketed out from the history of National Socialism, but, equally, Hitler's historical potential for exerting influence was, much more than with other politicians and statesmen, and down to the level of psychology, dependent upon quite specific, pre-existing conditions. Thus one also needs to ask with reference to Hitler's ideological fixed points what objective factors there were which led specifically to these elements establishing themselves in Hitler's thinking and alone being pursued consistently in practice.

As suggested, part of Hitler's objective function as leader was to unify a vague ideology which tended towards factional splintering. This meant that the Führer stood above the ideology and was not constrained by concrete, practical points of the programme. Nonetheless, a dynamic, committed mass following was unthinkable without a dominant 'idea', i.e. without a direction-giving set of objectives, however vaguely expressed, in which social needs and expectations found their reflection; and it was not possible without the naming of irreconcilable enemies, which had to be fought fanatically against. It corresponded to the political reasoning of the party which he led, when Hitler avoided making specific programme commitments over and again, and this kept the movement open and flexible. On the other hand, it was psychological necessity which led him passionately to promote certain fanatically supported positive and negative ideological goals. The leader of the National Socialist movement had to be able to present some unalterable 'ideas', which in positive and negative implication expressed the utopia of national and social renewal, the aim of self-liberation from internal and external obligations and enemies, but these had to be formulated in such a way that the diversity of objective interests among the supporters and partners of National Socialism was not brought to the surface and that a corresponding fragmentation was avoided.

These criteria were satisfied by the fixed points in the personal world view of Hitler. Anti-Semitism, anti-Bolshevism, and the goal of acquisition of ethnic living space in the east, as the negative and positive poles of the Hitlerian theory of history as the merciless struggle of races and peoples, played for Hitler personally the function of highest articles of faith. Without these his entire agitation and political action would be revealed as a nihilistic struggle for struggle's sake. However, they also fulfilled the objective function of acting simultaneously as a focal point for the vague urge for social and national renewal and as a diversion of this urge from real and concrete plans for reordering: anti-Semitism and anti-Bolshevism mobilized the social and national resentments of the middle classes against alleged conspirers or exploiters and against feared cultural-social proletarianization; the living space utopia appeared as a redemptive vision of racial-social regeneration, and as the projection of a future of a fully independent, self-sufficient land power, promising a return to a healthy, vital racial life and social elite status for the whole nation. These ideological goals (or rather directions for action) had on the other hand, however, so little to do with actual social reality that they were hardly exposed to correction through real pressures or opposing aims. In this way they could be consistently held on to, and in this way Hitler was forced more and more to return to them and to keep the movement in motion, the more others of the party's visions of reordering proved themselves to be illusory.

['Soziale Motivation und Führerbindung des Nationalsozialismus', *Vierteljahrshefte für Zeitgeschichte*, 18 (1970), 393, 395, 401–3.]

JEREMY NOAKES

18   The Nazi Party in Lower Saxony

In the conclusion to one of the most important of a number of regional studies of the rise to power which appeared in the early 1970s, Jeremy Noakes categorizes the movement as a 'quasi-*Volkspartei*', emphasizing the importance of its ability to integrate a fragmented middle-class milieu in the Depression. While recent more sophisticated electoral analysis has emphasized the slightly more diverse nature of Nazism's mass support, and the slightly more complex routes via which some groups of voter transferred their allegiances to

the party, Noakes's assertion that the core support of the movement—
the *propaganda* of national and social community notwithstanding—
consisted of middle-class people, and, moreover, that these defined the
essential nature and values of the movement, remains convincing.

The sense of disorientation created by [the] crisis, which found expression in
the protest movement of 1928, provided a political vacuum into which the
NSDAP could move. Through its propaganda, it appealed to the ideals and
interests of the *Mittelstand* groups. It was not burdened by the limitations
created by historical experiences and commitments; it offered an ideology
which reaffirmed the traditional status, symbols and values of the 'old' *Mittelstand*; it provided the 'new' *Mittelstand* with an ideology which was nationalist without being reactionary and socialist without being Marxist; through its
exploitation of the reparations issue and the evils of 'international finance
capitalism' it provided an easily comprehensible explanation for the economic
crisis, while its programme of autarky provided an apparently simple solution. Finally, its propaganda hammered away at the weakness of any political
representation, such as the Economic Party, which was limited to one specific
group. Through its organization the NSDAP provided a solution to this
weakness of the interest parties, by creating an integrative framework in
which all social and economic groups could find individual representation
and expression in their own department or *Fachgruppe*. The problem of conflicting interests, which had bedevilled other parties, was avoided by its tight
discipline, by its refusal to participate in a Reich government of which Hitler
was not the head, and by its vague vision of the Third Reich in which all were
encouraged to expect the fulfilment of their demands. In the meantime these
demands could simply be fed into the propaganda machine where they were
processed into effective slogans; meanwhile the various professional organizations were infiltrated and taken over, thereby facilitating the process of
Gleichschaltung after 1933.

Above all, however, the NSDAP offered an all-embracing *Weltanschauung*
with which to fill the vacuum left by a discredited liberalism. Nazi propaganda successfully portrayed liberalism as the ideology of selfish individuals
and selfish parties which, by undermining the unity of the nation, had
already helped destroy the Second Empire and was now responsible for the
present crisis. In the place of liberalism and the 'divisive' party system, the
Nazis promised to substitute the *Volksgemeinschaft* in which the common weal
would take precedence over individual gain, and in which the class barriers of
the old society would be overcome. In a situation in which capitalism had
clearly broken down and in which the individualism which was the basis of
liberalism had been simplified to the point of catch-as-catch-can, a creed
which condemned such a system as selfish and emphasized the importance of
community values had a great attraction, particularly to a society which had

never really absorbed the liberal ethos, but remained attached to archaic *Gemeinschaft* values.

There was, however, a second aspect to this process of integration. Although in its propaganda, the NSDAP portrayed itself as the party best able to overcome the divisions within German society, one of its most effective techniques for integrating the *Mittelstand* was to emphasize and exploit the division in Germany between the politically organized working class and the bourgeoisie. This was particularly effective in local government. The problem originated, of course, in the Bismarckian era or even earlier. By excluding the working class from effective political influence and by appropriating the idea of patriotism for an extreme form of nationalism, the authorities and the great majority of the middle class in the second Reich had themselves helped to ensure that the German working class would be 'Vaterlandslose Gesellen'* bitterly opposed to the ideology and symbols of that society and forced to establish what was virtually a separate SPD community. This division was then exacerbated by the revolution of 1918. Significantly, immediately after 1918, the bourgeoisie was successful in uniting for a political purpose by creating *Bürgerblöcke*† in local government with which to resist the SPD.[1] In a similar way, the Nazis exploited the fear and resentment of the Left which increased in intensity as the economic crisis deepened and social conflict sharpened. They created a sense of obligation in the minds of the bourgeoisie by continual emphasis on the sacrifice which young SA men were making on their behalf in the front line.[2] After 1929 the NSDAP succeeded in convincing the middle class of its indispensability and in creating what was virtually another *Bürgerblöck*.

Yet, there was an important difference between the *Bürgerblöck* created by the NSDAP and those formed after the revolution. The latter were clearly counter-revolutionary. The NSDAP, however, although the reactionary aspects of its ideology and its opposition to the political results of the revolution conveniently disguised the fact, was a revolutionary movement. It was revolutionary in two senses: in the first place, the cadres which it created contained 'new' men from the lower middle class who wished to overthrow the *status quo*. In the second place, its organization and *Weltanschauung* were totalitarian, and would not only transform the political structure, but would also disrupt the traditional patterns of German social life.[3]

One key to this revolutionary aspect of the party was the way the NSDAP was able to exploit the deep rift which existed between the generations in the Weimar period.[4] During its first years, the party succeeded in creating a political style which could appeal to the younger generation, its desire for charismatic leadership, personal commitment, and a sense of *Gemeinschaft*

---

* 'Vaterlandslose Gesellen': fellows with no fatherland.
† *Bürgerblöcke*: bourgeois blocs, i.e. coalitions of middle-class parties.

through a quasi-military organization; its contempt for the institutions and processes of the Weimar political system; its desire to escape from social convention—*Spiessertum*—and the rigidities of the class structure. Above all, the organization of the NSDAP provided an effective instrument for exploiting the energies of this group while retaining control in the hands of the leadership. Young activists could make it to a considerable extent *their* party as opposed to the other parties which, with the significant exception of the KPD, were staffed with ageing functionaries who treated politics in purely 'rational' terms and who viewed experiments with undisguised suspicion.[5] Promotion was rapid for those who proved effective; communications between the local leadership and *Gau* head-quarters were good—a stream of directives from the *Reichsleitung* were passed on by the *Gauleitung* to local leaders, keeping them informed of party tactics and propaganda techniques; and, above all, every member was provided with an active role in the party's work.

The organization in some ways was tightly disciplined. Through its use of the *Führerprinzip* and bureaucratic rules such as speakers' passes and signed declarations of loyalty by their deputies, the party leadership kept a close control over all important aspects of party activity—the content of propaganda, appointments, relations with outside groups and individuals. Yet the party's discipline was subject to permanent strain. The lines of jurisdiction within the party often overlapped, and conflict was continually breaking out between individuals and sections of the party at different levels within the organization. This tension was the reverse side of the remarkable activism of the party. Conflict, however, tended to reinforce the position of Hitler. For, by 1927, he had established his absolute authority and, from then on, the charge of disloyalty to Hitler was an important weapon in the internecine rivalries which continued; no member or leader, therefore, dared question that authority. This authority could, in turn, be used to support the *Gauleiter* and other leaders in their struggles with rival groups and individuals. In short, recognition and promotion within the NSDAP depended first, on absolute loyalty to the *Führer*, and secondly, on performance, as measured by the degree of activism shown by the member or functionary. Members were, therefore, obliged to compete with one another both in loyalty and activism. This competition, which was encouraged by Hitler's refusal to define clearer lines of jurisdiction between its organizations, helped to sustain the dynamic of the Party.

Through its authoritarian structure, then, of which the charismatic *Führerprinzip* was the core, the NSDAP maintained the discipline which, given the heterogeneous and radical nature of the membership, was essential to its effectiveness, particularly in the crisis months after July 1932. In the period of the Nazi electoral successes, however, it was the skill of the party in retaining and exploiting the radical commitment of its members and cadres for the purposes of propaganda which was decisive. For, the youth and commitment of the party's membership created that *élan* and sense of destiny—expressed, for example, through the sheer number of party meetings and in the SA marches—which proved such a magnetic attraction to a society which had lost its sense of direction. It was this impression of representing the future— the chiliastic vision—which the party was able to project, with Hitler as its prophet, which was perhaps, in the last analysis, crucial to the success of Nazism.[6] In this sense, the revolutionary style and organization of the NSDAP provided the final impetus to integration; and it is in this context that the pre-1927 period in the party's development, during which its style and structure had been formed, and the leadership of Hitler established, acquires its real significance.

[*The Nazi Party in Lower Saxony 1921–1933* (Oxford: Oxford University Press, 1971), 248–51.]

ALBRECHT TYRELL

19   The NSDAP as Party and Movement

> Tyrell, like many scholars, sees the characteristics which the move-
> ment developed during the 'time of struggle' as crucial to understand-
> ing the development of the regime after 1933 and its internal dynamic.
> In this passage, he examines the permeation of the 'leadership prin-
> ciple' through the movement following its second foundation in 1925,
> and the combination of absolute authority on the one hand with the
> existence of extensive space for the pursuit of individual initiatives on
> the other, a combination which gave the movement its peculiar
> dynamism.

In fact, during the years after its second foundation in February 1925, the NSDAP took on the organizational form of the 'Führer Party', in which policy-making was in principle to take place from the top to the bottom via the various levels of the organization without any direct involvement of the party members. The principle of 'authority to those below and responsibility to those above', as the National Socialists put it, was not completely accepted even after 1933, but it applied unreservedly to those at the top. Hitler was superior to all party offices, and this position became more and more self-evident and secure as a result of the growth and increasing integration which the party achieved under his leadership. The NSDAP, which at the end of 1928 had some 80,000 members and which in the Reichstag election in May of that year won 810,000 votes and twelve seats, acquired in this period a cadre of sub-leaders and followers who were devoted to Hitler almost without reservation. Under these circumstances the party could also cope with the strong fluctuation in membership, which occurred particularly when it expanded into a mass party that, by January 1933, nominally contained 1.4 million members. The subordination of these functionaries was based not only on a widespread concept of organization on hierarchical and authoritarian lines, which—in the eyes of many Germans—had only recently been confirmed by the model of the army of the First World War. The position of Führer was underpinned by a readiness to follow and a willingness to believe, which in part took even pseudo-religious forms, among a majority of party members. To a large extent they surrendered their independence of judgement and pinned their hopes on Hitler. The fact that many saw the political objectives of National Socialism personified in him soon made Hitler the object of spontaneous worship, which shortly widened into a Führer cult that could be and indeed was systematically used for propaganda purposes. The greeting 'Heil Hitler!' gradually became established among party members from as far back as 1923/4.

There were other factors involved. During this period developments occurred in the leadership structure of the party, in Hitler's style of leadership, and in respect of the binding character of programmatic demands which shaped some of the essential elements of the subsequent system of rule. Partly from calculation, partly from an unwillingness to take decisions, Hitler rarely used his power as the party leader. The members of the Reich party leadership responsible for particular political or organizational areas, the *Gauleiters* as the regional leaders also directly subject to Hitler, as well as the leaders of special organizations generally representing specific occupational groups operating within the framework of the NSDAP, all had considerable scope to pursue their own initiatives. Personal failures and mistakes, which unavoidably occurred as a result, were initially tolerated by Hitler, and this often had the effect of reinforcing the personal loyalty towards him of the functionary concerned. Only those cases where the damage caused by an individual, particularly in terms of its external impact, obviously exceeded his usefulness to the party, and especially those rare cases which directly affected Hitler's own position within the party or his personal reputation, could cause him to intervene. The one-sided orientation of party activity towards propaganda work, in which most functionaries and members found both a sphere of action and personal satisfaction, and the division of the organization into units which were isolated from each other and subordinated to the Reich party leadership, helped to limit the negative effects of special interests as well as those of Hitler's often irresolute decision-making.

The organizational structure of the party, the willing subordination of most of his supporters, and Hitler's style of leadership contributed to the fact that the conflicts over programme and strategy which naturally broke out on occasion could be resolved without major convulsions or, as a result of the aggressive focus on external opponents, could be marginalized or covered up.

The non-committal vagueness, indeed manipulability, of individual political and social demands which can be seen in National Socialist propaganda was already part of Hitler's original political plan. While its ideological basis and its long-term goal were firmly fixed, it was also geared to ensure that all appropriate means which improved the prospects of its realization could be employed. Individual demands in the programme were considered first and foremost in terms of their propaganda effectiveness as well as their integrative power. This proved advantageous under the prevailing political and social conditions. The openness of the National Socialist movement of renewal, held together as it was by a Führer figure integrating the various ideological expectations of its followers, enabled individuals as well as social groups not only to find their different ideological preferences and material interests represented in the NSDAP, but also to have the opportunity to develop them further within fairly wide limits.

['Die NSDAP als Partei und Bewegung: Strategie und Taktik der Machtergreifung', in Volker Rittberger (ed.), *1933: wie die Republik der Diktatur erlag* (Stuttgart: Kohlhammer, 1983), 109–11.]

ROGER GRIFFIN

20   The Rise of German Fascism

In one of the key works of the renewed wave of interest in the concept of 'fascism' in the 1990s, Griffin argues that Nazism, like other forms of fascism, represented a revolutionary ultra-nationalist force driven by a vision of national renewal and rebirth after a period of decay or decline associated with liberalism and democracy. This passage emphasizes the extent to which the ability of Nazism to portray itself as something radically new and different was bound up with its new style of politics and activism. As with much other recent work, Griffin stresses the diffuse nature of Nazism's mass support; arguably, as with much other recent work too, he understates the middle-class nature of Nazism's core support.

What enabled the NSDAP to eclipse all other ultra-right formations after 1925, however, was not just the ideological appeal of its policies to ultra-right activists and intellectuals who, after all, represented a small percentage of the population. Far more important in the long run was its impact on the increasing number of 'ordinary' Germans who became convinced that Nazism really was *different*, that it could break the mould of the Weimar 'system', that the NSDAP was the nucleus of a national revolution which was already under way, no matter how many seats it held in the despised Reichstag. For those who came under its spell, the Hitler movement alchemically transformed a generalized despair at the present order of society, a sense of being a foreigner in one's own country, into hope for the future, a sense of belonging. This, rather than anti-Semitism or middle-class reaction as such accounts for the steady build-up of the party and the SA before 1928, despite the pathetic showing at the ballot box. The ethos of paramilitary discipline and hierarchy, the omnipresence of the SA, the demagogic techniques used by the speakers, the carefully timed emotional crescendo leading up to the climax of Hitler's appearance on the podium, the theatrical effects produced by lighting effects and banners deliberately transformed the superbly organized mass meetings, rallies and congresses into initiatic rites for those who longed for Germany's rebirth.

It was when the depression started biting deep into German society that the NSDAP finally began to harvest the rich crop of mythic energies which countless publicists and activists of integral nationalism had been sowing since the late nineteenth century. A guru of the Conservative Revolutionaries, Edgar Jung was prompted to observe ruefully that 'the spiritual preconditions for the German revolution were created *outside* National Socialism' and that thinkers like himself had carried out the 'meticulous preparatory work' which provided each Nazi candidate with his votes.[1] Though convinced Catholics, socialists and Communists generally, and Jews universally, were inoculated against the fascination of the brave new world Nazism was promising, those who did succumb were not just former DNVP voters or frightened bourgeois, but came from a wide spectrum of social milieux and walks of life. This explains the profound heterogeneity of the party's social base after its 1929 'take-off'.[2] That about one-third of the NSDAP's 850,000 members were classified in the *Partei-Statistik* of 1935 as workers does not reflect the desire of a middle-class movement (*Mittelstandsbewegung*) to have the public image of a mass movement (*Massenbewegung*), as generations of Marxist scholars have tried to make out, but the fact that it exerted a genuine trans-class and trans-generational appeal.

Against the background of the sustained crisis of confidence in liberal democracy unleashed by economic collapse, the new converts were lured by the cumulative effect of Nazism's demagogic, paramilitary and terroristic style of campaigning. For millions who after 1929 despaired of the 'old' system and rejected the communist alternative, it generated a powerful subjective impression that the Germans were being transformed before their eyes from a degenerate and anarchic mass to a majestically co-ordinated new nation. This was the subliminal message of the numerous ceremonies and special days invented by the party, one of which even turned the failed putsch of 9 November 1923 into a Nazi holy day.[3] In the carefully contrived climate of hysteria whipped up by party meetings and congresses, the slogan 'Germany awake', the omnipresent Swastika with its connotations of mystic regeneration and the appearance of Hitler as the embodiment of a new order could symbolize the hopes and certainties which the Weimar state could no longer provide.

[*The Nature of Fascism* (London: Routledge, 1991), 98–9.]

JÜRGEN FALTER

21   The NSDAP: A 'People's Protest Party'

> One of the most sophisticated of recent analyses of electoral behaviour in the 1920s and 1930s has been provided by Jürgen Falter. His conclusions, in line with the tenor of much recent research, suggest that the NSDAP was much more than just a middle-class party; nonetheless, attention must also be drawn to his assertion that voters tended to move politically within broad milieux rather than across or between them, the implication being that the core of the industrial working class remained faithful to the SPD and the KPD. His characterization of the NSDAP as a 'People's Party with a Middle-Class Belly' strikes a balance between recognizing that some workers were not immune from the attractions of National Socialism and resisting the attempt to engage in revisionism for revisionism's sake, as some recent writing has tended to do.

We can conclude by confirming that in the Weimar Republic voting within blocs indeed occurred much more often than the transfer of votes between blocs. Within a very short period of time after 1924 the liberal sector was almost completely destroyed, as was the German national-conservative sub-culture to a considerable extent. The majority of their supporters moved, in part via newly formed interest groups, to the new collective movement of the bourgeois-Protestant camp, the NSDAP. From the voting perspective it was above all the fragmentation of the bourgeois-Protestant camp, and thus the absence of an explicit, socially binding voting norm, which facilitated the onward march of National Socialism. [. . .]

If one combines the old and new middle class, approximately 60 per cent of the NSDAP's votes came from the middle class overall, a proportion which remained remarkably stable throughout the five Reichstag elections which are of central interest. Voters from the working class or from working-class households, on the other hand, provided up to 40 per cent of the NSDAP electorate. Even if we take into account the fact that the category 'worker' in the German census and work records includes not only industrial workers, but also a high proportion of rural workers, craft workers, and workers in other trades, this proportion seems far too high for us to continue to be able to refer to the NSDAP as a purely, or at least very predominantly, middle-class movement. In terms of the social composition of its votes it was most of all a people's party of protest, or, as one might also call it in view of the still higher-than-average, although not overwhelming, proportion from the middle class—and in allusion to the resulting distribution curve—a 'people's party with a middle-class belly'.

This finding is not contradicted by the observation that within the electorate of the NSDAP the petit-bourgeois and lower-class elements—irrespective of the classification of social groups according to insurance law—probably predominated. This assertion in no way implies a much higher-than-average susceptibility of this group of the population towards National Socialism, as the various versions of the 'middle-class' theory suggested. For, given their concrete material situation, not only most white-collar workers and public employees, but also many self-employed and 'atypical' workers led a petit-bourgeois or lower-class existence in the Weimar Republic. A party of mass integration such as the NSDAP, whose electorate was not comprised primarily of the industrial proletariat, to a certain extent automatically therefore recruited above all from petit-bourgeois and lower-class circles. [. . .]

In terms of the susceptibility of the different social strata it is [. . .] unmistakable that the theories of a class party, a mass party, or a confessional party each only captures a partial aspect of the phenomenon, but not the National Socialist voting patterns in their entirety. Of the formulae referred to, above all the first two approaches represent interpretations whose premisses are mostly wrong or questionable, and whose hypotheses are sometimes correct but sometimes do not concur with the evidence. By raising to absolute status in each case one correctly recognized aspect, which they then overemphasize, other complementary aspects of the same phenomenon are correspondingly overshadowed. Both theoretical approaches are thus unsuited in their current form to explaining the electoral successes of the NSDAP before 1933.

Common to all three explanatory approaches is the admittedly only general reference to the significance of crises to which the Weimar Republic was repeatedly exposed in its short history. Above all the world economic crisis with its long-lasting mass unemployment, its immiseration of broad sectors, and the corresponding general air of uncertainty is cited as a catalyst for the process of political radicalization. However, electoral analysis shows that unemployment did not directly strengthen the NSDAP, but primarily the KPD. In districts and localities with high unemployment the NSDAP fared less well overall than in regions with lower unemployment. The unemployed voted overwhelmingly for the extremism of the left, not for that of the right or centre, as an instrument of political protest. According to our results only the unemployed white-collared minority appear to have voted somewhat more often for the National Socialists. The almost perfect coincidence of unemployment levels and NSDAP electoral success must therefore be explained by other factors than that of the behaviour of the unemployed themselves. Clearly it was precisely also voters who were not directly threatened by unemployment themselves who lost faith in the ability of those parties sustaining the system to solve the economic and social problems of the early 1930s; this developed into a loss of confidence in the problem-solving capacity of the Weimar system in general, which led them to strengthen their support for the NSDAP.

[*Hitlers Wähler* (Munich: C. H. Beck, 1991), 369–73.]

iii. The Failure of Weimar and the Crisis of 1933

KARL-DIETRICH BRACHER

22 Stages of the Seizure of Power

The first serious post-war scholarly study of the failure of Weimar was produced by Karl-Dietrich Bracher in 1955 (*Die Auflösung der Weimarer Republik*). This magisterial study, with its emphasis on political structures and tangible forces and agendas emanating from the parties, the *Reichswehr*, the bureaucracy, etc., remains a crucial work. Bracher followed this with a contribution to a jointly authored volume on the Nazi seizure of power, from which this extract discussing developments from mid-1932 onwards is taken. Note the emphasis on personalities, and the argument that other alternatives were available down to the wire.

The specific impact of the confusing events which sent the dramatically accelerated immediate prehistory of 30 January 1933 in the decisive direction is disputed even today. Amidst the wealth of fast and furious events the most important point to recognize is that this final phase was determined far more than the preceding stages by individual preferences and decisions. They could certainly only unfold within a situation which had been brought about through general political conditions, through a problematic development encompassing the entire history and prehistory of the Weimar Republic, by which it was also predetermined to some degree. But, even now, the course of events was not preprogrammed: more than ever before it was dependent upon the actions of a small circle of people. For, in accordance with both the constitutional reality and the general development towards the authoritarian state, the lever for the decisive about-turn lay with Hindenburg. The way things were, it could be set in motion only by persons who belonged to the innermost circle of the Reich presidential palace, and who had already been pushing forward their authoritarian reform plans for years. [. . .]

The fact is that an NSDAP crippled by the dilemma of the power vacuum and weakened by electoral losses, internal conflicts, and finance problems suddenly—and surprisingly for the party itself—was brought into the political frame again, and was thereby rescued from the threat of Schleicher's counter-plans and included in power—and all this at the moment when the economic crisis finally began to recede. The appointment to power and subsequent seizure of power by a party already threatened visibly by decline could now also benefit from the new upswing in the world economic cycle—as previously the deterioration of general conditions had favoured the rise of National Socialism as a destructive opposition. This may be understood as a fatal interaction of circumstances; it was no less, however a direct consequence of the Papen initiative of January 1933 and of the authoritarian restructuring plans, on which it was hoped agreement could be reached with Hitler, and which they hoped to realize with National Socialist help but on their own terms. [. . .]

The influence of personal initiatives had in fact become historically decisive in these closing months of the Republic. As with the crisis surrounding the SA ban, the overthrow of Brüning and Hindenburg's abandonment of the democratic version of presidential government, and finally Papen's *coup d'état* in Prussia and his rash experiments in dictatorship, they finally also brought about the unexpected appointment of Hitler as Reich chancellor at a moment when the depths of the economic crisis had been gone through and the NSDAP had already suffered perceptible setbacks. It would certainly be an unobjective simplification were one to try to reduce the dramatically complicated events and interrelationships of these months between June 1932 and January 1933 to a *single* common denominator. And certainly the worsening of the structural problems of the Republic in the apparently hopeless 'power vacuum' of 1932 (with the mutual blocking of the democratic parties, totalitarian revolutionary movements, and authoritarian rulers) had made the rise of the National Socialists possible in the first place. But equally indisputable against this historical background is the ultimately decisive role played by the high-handed games of intrigue of a tiny minority around the only remaining power centre, the Reich President, who was now devoid of political understanding. That this was possible in the first place, and now met with so little resistance, confirms that the parliamentary Republic, having distanced itself too much through its authoritarian experiments, was now no longer capable of functioning. But this was precisely the fatal drawback of the presidential regime. [. . .]

Thus misfortunes and errors, consequences and coincidences, combined to create an almost inextricable tangle of causes of the National Socialist seizure of power. But 'necessity' remained, even *in extremis*, subordinate to choice—a freedom of choice, admittedly, which both the majority of the population and the political and intellectual ruling class had finally abandoned, partly out of tired resignation, partly having been carelessly seduced, and partly out of conscious destructiveness. The circumstances of this event also confirm that in the early moves towards attempts at an authoritarian solution outside of the unfamiliar democracy many determining factors developed which substantially facilitated 30 January 1933 and its consequences. And alternatives, themselves hardly less historically legitimate, still existed under Schleicher, almost up to the final moment. The decisive

factor was the careless playing with further-reaching projects and the associated activity of the Papen–Hugenberg–Hindenburg group. Believing with
ambitious self-assurance that it was capable of taming and exploiting the
totalitarian mass movement, this tiny minority in actual fact helped the
National Socialist leadership into positions of power they had not been able
to achieve of their own accord.

['Stufen der Machtergreifung', in K.-D. Bracher, W. Sauer, and G. Schulz, *Die*
nationalsozialistische Machtergreifung: Studien zur Errichtung des Totalitären Herrschaftssystems
in Deutschland 1933/4 (2nd edn., Cologne: Westdeutscher Verlag, 1962), 42–4.]

HANS MOMMSEN
....

23 The National Socialist Seizure of Power and German Society

Mommsen's article represents an attempt to place the cabbalistic
machinations of 1932 to 1933 within the broader context of the period
of presidential politics since 1930. Whilst placing blame firmly at the
door of the conservative elites, rather than on the mass constituency
of the Nazi movement, he rejects the notion that Hitler's appointment
can be seen solely as the product of a 'backstairs intrigue'. The intri-
guers of 1932–3 are seen very much as representatives of broader social
forces and lobbies—above all of the army and of sectors of business.
The Nazi seizure of power thus appears as a compromise between the
various interests and lobbies exerting influence during the early 1930s,
all other attempts to find a basis for an authoritarian regime of the
Right with mass support having failed.

It would be wrong to make responsible for the development towards fascist
dictatorship those millions who, out of desperation at their material situation, out of disappointment at the established parties, and out of rejection
of an increasingly ossified political system which measured itself by the
standards of the pre-war era, temporarily gave their votes to Hitler. In elections before the seizure of power the NSDAP never gained as much support
as the two parties of the Left combined. The crisis of the parliamentary
system was not triggered by Hitler's electoral successes; rather, it was the
crisis of the parliamentary system itself which made the breakthrough of the
NSDAP as a mass movement possible in the first place.

The political responsibility for the National Socialist seizure of power lies
primarily with the traditional elites, who regarded it as acceptable to exclude
one-third of the population from a share of political co-responsibility. Certainly, the crisis of the parliamentary system was a general continental European phenomenon, and only the diplomatic dependency of the Reich on the
western parliamentary democracies thwarted earlier authoritarian plans for
an overthrowal. The dissolution of the existing power system under the

pressure of the world economic crisis gave the conservative elites the starting signal to seize political power for themselves and to make the transition to an active policy of revisionism as long demanded by them. [. . .]

The complex and opaque processes which led to the formation of Hitler's cabinet give the appearance of a palace coup, but they occurred within a broader social context. They were made possible through the vigorously forced elimination of democratic parliamentarianism by the majority of the bourgeois parties and their related associations. This was often equated with social policy and relabelled with the slogan 'trade union state'; this was true insofar as a parliamentary system is predicated upon social compromise.[1] It is misleading for the period after March 1930 to speak of a lack of willingness on the part of the parties to take responsibility, which prevented them from entering stable coalitions. By 1932 at the latest the only remaining alternative was between an authoritarian system supported by the military, and a fascist dictatorship.

A decisive role was played by the interests of the *Reichswehr*, which since the end of the 1920s had been abandoning the political neutrality ordered by Seeckt,* in order to create the diplomatic and domestic political preconditions for German rearmament and an active policy of revisionism. It appeared essential to the *Reichswehr* leadership to exclude the internationalist and pacifist forces within the SPD and to eliminate the KPD, whose political importance was greatly overestimated. The concept initially pursued by Schleicher, of isolating Hitler from the radical forces in his own movement and of dividing the 'healthy national elements' from the radical leftist National Socialists, was the common property of the conservative elites. This explains why the bourgeois Right made no efforts to oppose Hitler, and at the same time undermined similar attempts by the Social Democrat-led government in Prussia by all possible means.

It is difficult to imagine today the extent of the mistrust, contempt, and disparagement with which otherwise quite honourable circles on the Right, but also the vast majority of the German intelligentsia, regarded the Social Democrats and all those who sympathized with them. The right-wing nationalist paper *Germany's Renewal* spoke in early 1932 of the 'Subhumanity united in the Iron Front'[2]—the political instrumentalization of this concept was not an invention of the NSDAP. The causes are to be found on the one hand in the hysterical reaction of broad sectors of the German elites to the endangerment of their traditional social privileges. On the other hand they are rooted in the trauma of defeat in war, November Revolution, and 'Stab in the Back', in the refusal to accept political realities, and in the myth that precisely from defeat the 'national revolution' of a nation no longer torn apart by class barriers would emerge.[3] [. . .]

* Seeckt was Head of the German Army until 1926.

As far as big business and heavy industry are concerned, since 1928 those forces were becoming dominant who rejected the idea of genuine cooperation with the organized Left, and who at most thought of tolerating a trade union movement robbed of its support from the political representatives of the working class, but on the condition that the social welfare apparatus would be further dismantled and that the existing wage legislation would be largely abolished.[4] Certainly, industry did not actively support the rise of the National Socialists, one or two of its representatives apart, and it was far more inclined to support the line of Franz von Papen, which largely corresponded to industrial interests. However, the forces of industry were willing to come to terms with the National Socialists if this was the only way political stability could be achieved. Leading representatives of industry such as Paul Reusch and Hjalmar Schacht succumbed to the illusion that the NSDAP could be tamed in the economic sphere and used to serve their purposes.[5]

Nevertheless, only a minority of industry advocated a Hitler chancellorship in the autumn of 1932, and the influential representatives of heavy industry were surprised by the formation of the 'cabinet of national concentration'.[6] But it is also noticeable that determined resistance to the taking of the National Socialists into government responsibility was a rare exception to the rule, not to mention the connections formed by the chemical industry with the NSDAP, whose autarky programme appeared to chime with their interests. Influential heavy industrial circles also supported Gregor Strasser, because they wanted to prevent a coalition of the Centre Party and NSDAP giving new strength to the Christian trade unions and thus ruining their plans for a total overhaul of social policy.[7] Von Schleicher's policy of the trade union axis was therefore also perceived by them as extremely dangerous. The power of veto which the German economic associations exercised within the political system thus decisively favoured the foisting of the fascist dictatorship, even if only a few groups within industry and big business were prepared to stand directly behind Hitler. The susceptibility of mittelständisch interests to the NSDAP, especially under the impact of the world economic crisis, has often been described. They played a significant role in the rise of the NSDAP as a mass movement but not, however, in the processes which led to the formation of Hitler's cabinet.[8]

Nonetheless, economic interests were not on their own the decisive factor in ensuring that, by Brüning's fall at the latest, German politics would land on the downward path which would have to end with the passing of political power to Hitler; what was crucial, however, was that the unwillingness of the leading industrial associations to seek social compromise with the Social Democrats and with the free trade unions prevented any regeneration of the parliamentary system, even in the limited form ascribed to it under the first Brüning cabinet, from the start. It was the chronic crisis situation created by this, and not by the unrealistic and extremely contradictory policy of the KPD, whose significance was and is usually overestimated,[9] which made possible the chain of wrong decisions, breaking of laws, and manipulations, without which Hitler would never have come to power. Weimar democracy did not fail because of Hitler. Rather, Hitler was the final consequence of its failure.

['Die nationalsozialistische Machtergreifung und die deutsche Gesellschaft', in Wolfgang Michalka (ed.), *Die Nationalsozialistische Machtergreifung* (Paderborn: Ferdinand Schöningh, 1984), 35–6, 40–2.]

RICHARD BESSEL

24   Why Did the Weimar Republic Collapse?

Richard Bessel here relates the failure of the Republic to establish its legitimacy to the legacy of the First World War—a legacy which was clearly huge in both economic and political terms, but also in cultural terms. Above all, as Bessel emphasizes in this passage, German society in the 1920s suffered from a collective unwillingness to accept the fact of Germany's defeat in the war. Its refusal to accept the realities of Germany's economic and political situation after the war encouraged a false sense of what government could achieve in the 1920s, measured against which the Republican system would inevitably be found wanting.

The costs of the War and the subsequent readjustment to a peacetime economy cast a shadow over German government finance for the whole of the Weimar period. The problem of the huge debts and reparations bill arising from the War was one aspect of this; the costs of the demobilization, in particular the determination of the Reich Government to ease the transition to peacetime production and provide work for the millions of returning soldiers, formed another—making it necessary for state and national government to continue their dependence upon massive deficit spending into the post-war period.[1] Considering the position in which they found themselves, it is hardly surprising that postwar governments opted for inflationary fiscal policies rather than measures which would contract economic activity, increase unemployment and raise taxation sufficiently to stabilize the currency in the aftermath of the War. According to Heinz Haller, the amount of taxation required to meet the costs of reparations, social-welfare programmes and the normal running of government without inflationary consequences would have involved trebling the prewar tax levels relative to national income—at a time when living standards were considerably below those of 1913; to accomplish this, it would have been necessary to have 'a strong government that had the entire population behind it and was thus in a position to demand great sacrifices'.[2]

However, after the First World War, and indeed for the whole of the Weimar period, 'a strong government that had the entire population behind it' was precisely what was absent from German politics. Weimar governments lacked the basis of support, and popular legitimacy, to push through unpleasant but necessary measures on a basis of democratic politics; and the failure to push through these policies—a failure which led to the hyperinflation of 1922–3—then further undermined the legitimacy of Weimar governments. It is hardly coincidental that the painful measures taken by the Stresemann cabinets in late 1923 to halt passive resistance in the Ruhr (which had made impossible any stabilization of German finances, currency or foreign relations) and to introduce a stable currency rested on emergency measures which bypassed the Reichstag. It should be remembered that the famous Article 48 of the Weimar Constitution was used not just by the Republic's enemies during the early 1930s but also provided a necessary tool of its defenders—Ebert and Stresemann—during 1923. There was, it appeared, an insufficient democratic basis for democratic politics. [. . .]

Thus the First World War left Germany a much poorer place than it had been in 1913, and the social and economic costs of the War formed one of the heaviest burdens of the past which confronted the new democratic political system. The problem, however, was not just that the German economy had suffered a body blow, but that few Germans fully appreciated how much poorer their country had become. Paradoxically, part of the difficulty may have been that the seemingly overwhelming problems of the demobilization and the immediate postwar transition were overcome with too much apparent ease, and that as a result Germans still measured their situation during the 1920s against (a largely mythical image of) conditions in 1913. The thrust of the demobilization efforts was in large measure to return to 'peacetime' conditions, i.e. conditions as people perceived them to have been before the War. Indeed, it was common during the War and even in late 1918 for economic projections to be made on the assumption that the end of the conflict would be followed by a return to 'peacetime' prices.[3] The extent to which '1913' was regarded during the 1920s as somehow 'normal' (and, by implication, conditions during the Weimar period as 'abnormal' and therefore blameworthy and illegitimate) is striking. Economic statistics during the 1920s and early 1930s invariably measured things against figures from 1913; and the disorder of Weimar could be juxtaposed with a rosy picture of the 'good old days' before the War. It is revealing in more ways than one that the success of the currency stabilization rested partly on the psychological benefits of pegging the value of the new currency at the level of the old, prewar gold Mark.[4]

All this reinforced two dangerous illusions in Weimar Germany: that it was possible to return to prewar conditions, and that the War had not really circumscribed the possibilities for German power politics or economic development. This may sound surprising, especially when considered against the chorus of protest about the allegedly harsh terms of the 'Diktat' of Versailles, the 'intolerable' levels of 'unjust' reparations payments, the dwelling on the sacrifice made by Germany's soldiers during the War and the legacy of the 'front spirit' for German politics. But that was precisely the problem. The idea of a 'front generation' was at least partly a myth.[5] The incessant din about the injustices heaped upon a defeated Germany, allegedly undefeated on the field and stabbed in the back at home, in effect served to re-enforce an idea that things would be normal if only the external burdens, imposed by the Allies, could be lifted. That is to say, the constant—indeed ritual—complaints about Versailles in effect served to disguise the extent to which the War really had impoverished Germany, that Germany was a poorer place not just because she had lost the War but because she had fought it.

These illusions were dangerous not least because they helped fix the political agenda of the Weimar Republic so as to favour certain parties and disadvantage others. In order to function, a democratic political system needs a certain responsible consensus recognizing the parameters of policy making. That is to say, if politics is the 'art of the possible', successful democratic politics must be based upon a clear recognition of what in fact is possible. As long as the truth about the War, its causes and consequences, remained excluded from mainstream public political discussion, it was impossible fully to face harsh economic and political realities. The popular rejection of the peace settlement did provide a basis for consensus, but the anti-Versailles consensus was essentially negative, serving to undermine policies which took account of these realities. Responsible politics remained a hostage to myths about the First World War, and Weimar democracy eventually had to pay the price.

['Why did the Weimar Republic Collapse?', in Ian Kershaw (ed.), *Weimar: Why Did German Democracy Fail?* (London: Weidenfeld & Nicolson, 1990), 123–7.]

DETLEV PEUKERT

25   The Crisis of Classical Modernity

In one of the most original interventions on the Weimar Republic for many years, Peukert emphasized the fact that the Nazi seizure of power took place in a 'classically modern' state, characterized by rational industrial production and high technology, bureaucratic management and administration, urbanism and mass culture. Furthermore, the deep crisis experienced at the end of the 1920s was one experienced by other modern societies—the United States and Great Britain included. Here, he suggests reasons why the Weimar Republic failed to ride this crisis and why specifically Germany resorted to National Socialism instead.

As the economic crisis was a world-wide structural phenomenon, so the crisis of liberal democracy affected all the countries of Europe. The anxieties and the challenges to traditional ideas and practices that had been generated by modernization were evident across the continent. Why, then, was it only in Germany that the mass exodus from reality into the promised land of totalitarianism took place?

There is no single answer to this question. Several distinct factors combined to shape the situation in which Germany found herself at the start of the 1930s.

Germany was more badly hit by the economic crisis than were most other countries. In France, for example, the crisis did not arrive until 1931, and its impact was less severe. The Germans therefore became more despairing about the ability of the system to right itself and placed their faith in a totally new political departure. This explanation, however, is not a sufficient one, since the United States, for example, despite very severe economic setbacks, found a solution that did not involve abandoning constitutional democracy. A further contributory factor in the German case was that the country, as contemporaries saw it, had been in a state of crisis since 1918 and there seemed less and less likelihood that this crisis was ever going to be overcome. The German people, in other words, had seen the whole course of their lives undermined and all their hopes for the future thrown into question.

Furthermore, before the end of the century the process of modernization in Germany had already begun to accelerate at a pace and with a dynamism that clearly outstripped the social changes in other European countries. Until the First World War the transformation of German society had been viewed with a mixture of bombastic, imperialistic enthusiasm and submerged unease. With the traumatic events of the war and the post-war period, the whole process of modernization began to be seen in a darker light, and during the twenties people became very sharply aware of the drawbacks that came with modern life. The chronic economic and social weaknesses and recurrent acute crises of the twenties and early thirties led to a questioning of, and a retreat from, many of the achievements of modernization. With the deepening of the crisis, the mirage of radical 'renewal' and a re-created 'national community' became increasingly attractive: an image that was the more lustrous for being ill-focused. Similar processes were at work in other countries, but change there was less rapid and it was not accompanied by the additional factors that jointly led to catastrophe in Germany.

A further ingredient in the German situation was the decisive breach of political continuity that took place in 1918 and became allied, in the popular imagination, with the decline in social morality that occurred in the war years and during the inflation. A crisis of political legitimacy had, in fact, already begun to build up in the years before the war, but the dramatic upheavals of the decade 1914–24 caused people to forget this challenge to the late-Wilhelmine system of authority. Certainly, nostalgia for the pre-war era was not so profound as to tempt a majority of Germans to wish for a return to the Wilhelmine order. The crucial new feature of the counter-revolution against the Weimar Republic was that it was itself subversive and revolutionary and was not an attempt to restore the past.

The Weimar Republic had failed to build on the fundamental compromises achieved in 1918 and to use them to create a deep-rooted legitimacy of its own: it had lost the struggle for the hearts and minds of the people. This vacuum of political authority was the vital factor that caused a growing section of the population to seek its salvation in the promises of the National Socialists. What undermined the Republic was not, primarily, the resistance to modernization put up by the old élites who wanted to cling to traditional attitudes and practices: it was the peculiarly crisis-prone nature of the process of modernization itself. Yet the dynamism of modernization did impel the old élites into making a head-on assault on the fundamental compromises of 1918, an assault that was to help destroy themselves as well as the Republic. And the same experience of crisis drove the mass of the population into the arms of the National Socialist movement. [. . .]

The end of Weimar did not happen overnight and was not the product of any single set of causes. We can distinguish four separate processes which together destroyed the Republic and which led in three separate chronological phases to the events of 1933.

In the first place, the Republic was badly weakened by the chronic economic and social crisis. The scope for building on the fundamental compromises of 1918–19 gradually diminished. This *destabilization* placed a severe strain on the Republic, though it was not sufficient to destroy it, as the crisis of 1923 proved.

Secondly, in the course of the 1920s the popular legitimacy of the Republic, never secure at the best of times, underwent a steady decline. The Republic's *loss of legitimacy* reflected the collapse of the fundamental compromises of 1918; it was the expression of a widespread lack of faith in the future, in both a personal and societal sense; and it was symbolized, notably, by the electoral attrition of the moderate liberal and conservative parties, though the split in the labour movement also prevented the left from functioning as an effective political force. The loss of legitimacy was already alarmingly far advanced by 1930, when the international economic crisis set in: the Weimar constitution had become unworkable and unwanted. Nevertheless, this process too was insufficient in itself to bring about the Republic's downfall.

A third necessary condition, then, was the avowed determination of the old anti-republican élites to destroy Weimar's already battered parliamentary and democratic institutions. The *reversion to authoritarianism*, the policy pursued by the presidential cabinets of the years 1930–32, finally brought the political and social order of Weimar to an end. Moves towards a conservative and authoritarian system were, of course, a common response in Europe to the crises of the 1930s, but the German version of this response was distinctive in two ways. Nowhere else in Europe had both traditional values and new political and social reforming ideas been so called into question as they had been in post-war Germany; and nowhere else had public life become so politicized and polarized. The one phenomenon reduced the chances of an accommodation between liberals and conservatives and threatened the very survival of the fundamental compromises of 1918. The other deprived the old élites of the mass support they needed in their search for a return to authoritarianism, while at the same time ruling out the possibility of any authoritarian solution that did not rest on such support. Finding themselves in an impasse of their own making, the old élites plumped for an alliance with Hitler.

Fourthly, even Hitler's broad-based *totalitarian movement* was not capable of toppling the Republic on its own, despite the fact that it had attained an astonishing level of political dynamism and had become the voice for the anxieties of a good one-third of Germans as the crisis deepened. By the end of 1932 the NSDAP had plainly reached the limits of its electoral potential and was showing signs of falling back once again. It was only thanks to the consortium of élite representatives which became the new government on 30 January 1933 that Hitler was given the chance of translating the destructive dynamism of the National Socialist movement into the *Machtergreifung*, the seizure of power.

Freedom died, if not by inches, then in three main chronological phases. In the years leading up to 1930 an increasing number of republicans disavowed the Republic, and the fundamental compromises of 1918 evaporated. This was the end of 'Weimar' proper. After 1930 the presidential regimes destroyed what was left of the republican constitution and created a power vacuum which their own moves towards authoritarianism proved unable to fill. Any feasible alternative to the Weimar 'system' was thereby also extinguished. In 1933, finally, the new governing élite consortium, in partnership with the National Socialist movement, released the destructive energies of the 'Third Reich'. The German crisis had become the German catastrophe; its ultimate result was to be the devastation of Europe.

[*The Weimar Republic: The Crisis of Classical Modernity* (London: Penguin, 1991), 243–5, 266–7.]

26   30 January 1933

> Kershaw argues, pessimistically but persuasively, that Weimar was unsaveable from an early point in the crisis of 1930–3, and that, even had it had any realistic alternatives to its strategy of toleration, the SPD was not in a position to restore the fortunes of the Republic. Rejecting the notion that the Republic 'capitulated' of its own accord, he also stresses the limits of the extent to which Hitler's appointment as chancellor was the product of consensus—still less conspiracy— amongst the elites, who were operating from a position of weakness, having exhausted all other possibilities of finding an authoritarian solution to the crisis.

The events of 30 January 1933 marked the unnecessary, completely avoidable end of a state crisis which was unusual in the history of highly developed, pluralistic state systems and industrial societies in its depth and multi-dimensionality. A central element of the state crisis was an especially deep-seated and extensive crisis of legitimacy—both among the elites and 'below'—which excluded the possibility of a *democratic* resolution as early as 1930, in my view by 1931 at the latest, but which at the same time showed even more clearly how little the traditional power elites were capable of finding an *authoritarian* solution which corresponded to their wishes and interests.

Of prime importance for the character of the way out of the crisis was the combination of crisis situations: economic crisis, government crisis, crisis of the party system, social crisis, far-reaching crisis of legitimacy among the elites and 'below'.[1] The fragmentation and political weakness of the elites corresponded to the inability 'below' of each political camp to come to power on the back of its own strength. For its part, the crisis of legitimacy 'below' created the heterogeneous but dynamic protest potential of the National Socialist movement. Through the exclusion of all alternative traditional authoritarian solutions the crisis among the elites opened the door to by far the worst conclusion—a National Socialist dictatorship.

If one of the preconditions of Hitler's seizure of power was not the strength, but the weakness—and, even more importantly, the fragmentation—of the traditional elites, then in my view one cannot really speak of a genuine conspiracy, in the normal sense of the word, as a cause. Hitler was the last chance, not the first choice or the preferred solution for the overwhelming majority of the traditional elites. Despite their anti-democratic consensus the elites themselves were too fragmented and too diverse in their alternative visions to be able to mount a deliberate conspiracy, although of course the circumstances of Brüning's fall and the intrigues among the camarilla around Hindenburg in the last weeks of the Republic cannot be ignored.

In fact the willingness of the elites to embark upon the risk of 30 January 1933 represents the bankruptcy of their strategies and of the goal of an essentially traditional, typically reactionary 'counter-revolution'.[2] The behaviour of the different power groups was characterized by an over-estimation of their own strength and an underestimation of the modalities of the new mass politics. The *destructive* capacity to play a key role in undermining and destroying democracy was doubtless there. But, with the failure of the various semi-authoritarian experiments under Brüning, Papen, and Schleicher, the elites had proven themselves incapable of establishing a viable authoritarian alternative of the old type and without mass support. After Papen's cabinet had failed miserably, and Schleicher's attempts either to 'tame' Hitler by integrating him into the government or to marginalize him by including Gregor Strasser in government had also run aground, the transferral of power to Hitler on 30 January 1933 can be seen not only in retrospect as an extremely risky undertaking from the point of view of the power interests of the traditional elites, as a 'leap in the dark', as one Bavarian daily newspaper put it on the following day.[3]

The 'pact' between the elites and the National Socialist leadership may have brought a way out of the state crisis, the closure of the power vacuum, and, potentially, the re-establishment of the old power structures on a new authoritarian basis. However, the basic conditions of Hitler's assumption of power, born of the weaknesses, the fragmentation, and the political failure of the elites, meant that—for all the willingness to collaborate on the part of the traditional elites—the rapid progress of the consolidation of the regime's power in the next months witnessed a progressive shift in the balance of power within the 'power cartel' of the Third Reich—a shift from the traditional elites to the National Socialist forces.[4] Given the key positions in the Reich cabinet not only of Hitler himself but also especially of Göring as Prussian Minister of the Interior, the actual initiative passed into the hands of the National Socialists from the beginning. What was decisive was the fact that the representatives of the traditional elites had neither the will nor the strength to prevent the destruction, which was already occurring during the 'coordination' phase, of the norms of civilized behaviour, which mostly are retained even under 'normal' authoritarian regimes.[5] This marked the beginning of a development which by 1938 had led to the transformation of the former power elites to purely 'functional elites'.[6] Even more seriously: it was the beginning of a breach of civilization which radicalized even more in the next years and which reached its culmination in Auschwitz.

The events of 30 January 1933 marked the end of a particular variety of comprehensive crisis of legitimacy which influenced the contours of the new form of state in important ways. The total loss of legitimacy of the pluralist party system in the final phase of the Weimar Republic was accompanied by the total discrediting of the *impersonal* bureaucratic-functionalist administrative state among broad sectors of the population. The attraction of Hitler and the National Socialist movement lay not least in the willingness of more than 13 million Germans to believe in this crisis of legitimacy that salvation could come only through a leader who would practise *personal*, unbureaucratic rule and would take *personal* responsibility for his policies.[7] For their part, the dominant military and economic forces were also willing, given the lack of alternatives, to entrust the protection of their own interests to a new, extremely unusual, purely *populist* political force, which based its own claims to power in the *personal* 'mission' of its leader.

One should not, however, necessarily speak of a 'capitulation' of democracy. The concept would appear to overemphasize the role of free political will in the downfall of German democracy. For, long before the admission of Hitler to power, the only forces among the political parties who still advocated democracy were more or less the SPD, who were so weakened and bereft of almost any political room for manoeuvre that a possibility of defending a democracy which was widely unpopular and diminished, even in SPD circles, against the powerful anti-democratic forces both in the populist mass movements and within the elites was, in reality, not available. Those democratic forces which still existed had long since been outmanoeuvred and excluded by the time Hitler came to power.

The events of 30 January were not only an end, but also a beginning. Although Hitler's assumption of power ended the Weimar state crisis and crisis of legitimacy, it marked the beginning of a different, much greater, and comprehensive state crisis, which led to the total ruin and finally to the total collapse of the German state.

['Der 30. Januar 1933: Ausweg aus der Krise und Anfang des Staatsverfalls', in
H. A. Winkler (ed.), *Die deutsche Staatskrise 1930–1933* (Munich: Oldenbourg-Verlag,
1993), 277–80.]

iv National Socialism, Civil Society, and the Seizure of Power 1929–1933

WILLIAM SHERIDAN ALLEN

27   **The Nazi Seizure of Power**

> One of the first major studies of the seizure of power on the local
> level was William Sheridan Allen's study of Northeim (fictionalized in
> his book as Thalburg). Allen stresses the importance of local initiatives
> and party dynamism; prefiguring more recent research, he also
> stresses how local peculiarities and traditions influenced the manner
> in which the seizure of power took place locally, and suggests that
> the ways in which the movement fitted into the town from 1933
> onwards were conditioned by similar factors.

Thalburg is not now, and never was, a 'typical' German town. The composition of Thalburg in Weimar and Nazi days was not the same as the rest of
Germany. There was an inordinate number of civil servants and the town
was dominated economically by the railroad. Few places in Germany began
the Third Reich with a two-thirds vote for the NSDAP, the national average
being on the order of two-fifths. On the other hand, there were many places
in Germany that saw more violence than Thalburg in the early days of the
Third Reich.[1]

What, then, is to be learned from Thalburg's experience in the years 1930
to 1935, the years of the Nazi seizure of power?

In the first place, it is clear that an essential arena in the Nazi electoral
surge and the seizure of power was on the local level. Thalburg's Nazis
created their own image by their own initiative, vigor, and propaganda. They
knew exactly what needed to be done to effect the transfer of power to
themselves in the spring of 1933, and they did it apparently without more than
generalized directives from above. [. . .]

Hitler, Goebbels, and the other Nazi leaders provided the political
decisions, ideology, national propaganda, and, later, the control over the
government which made the revolution possible. But it was in the hundreds
of localities like Thalburg all over Germany that the revolution was made
actual. They formed the foundation of the Third Reich.

As for the reasons behind the particular experience in Thalburg, the most
important factor in the victory of Nazism was the active division of the town
along class lines. Though there was cohesion in Thalburg before the Nazis

began their campaigns leading to the seizure of power, the cohesion existed within the middle class or within the working class and did not extend to the town as a whole. The victory of Nazism can be explained to a large extent by the desire on the part of Thalburg's middle class to suppress the lower class and especially its political representatives, the Social Democratic party.

This is why Thalburgers rejoiced in the gains of the Nazis, and this is why they applauded the institution of the dictatorship. The antipathy of the middle class was not directed toward individual members of the SPD, but only toward the organization itself; not toward the working class as such, but only toward its political and social aspirations; not, finally, toward the reality of the SPD but mainly toward a myth which they nurtured about the SPD. For a variety of reasons, Thalburg's middle class was so intent on dealing a blow to the Social Democrats that it could not see that the instrument it chose would one day be turned against itself. [. . .]

Perhaps the behavior of the good burghers of Thalburg becomes more understandable when one realizes the extent to which they were committed to nationalism. The excess of patriotic feeling in the town during the pre-Hitler period was the great moral wedge for Nazism. In many ways the actions and beliefs of Thalburgers during the last years of the Weimar era were the same as if World War I had never ended. It was in this sort of atmosphere that the SPD might seem treasonable and the Nazi reasonable.

A similar effect was wrought by the depression. While Thalburg's middle class was not decisively affected by the economic crisis, the burghers were made desperate through fear and through an obsession with the effects of the depression, especially the sight of the unemployed. As for the effect of the depression upon the lower classes, it was equally large. There is no doubt that the progressive despair of the jobless, as reflected in the longer and longer periods of unemployment, weakened the forces of democracy in the town. It may be that this sapped the SPD's will to fight and led it into ritualistic responses to Nazism. It was hard for Socialists to bend all their efforts to combating Nazism when this involved defending a system which could produce this sort of economic misery. Had the SPD seriously undertaken to introduce democratic socialism in response to the depression, it seems likely they would have found new sources of strength among their own followers, and very likely might have won the votes of the many Thalburgers who cast ballots for the NSDAP simply because the Nazis promised to end the depression.

The depression weakened Thalburg's Socialists in other ways, too. The use of economic pressure at the sugar factory and at the railroad deprived the SPD of much of its prestige and power. If it could not even defend its own people when the chips were down, how could it defend democracy, and how could it bring about the socialist society? The success of [an] action at the railroad yards no doubt opened up several possibilities for the Nazis. It was there that they learned how economically vulnerable the workers were; it was there that they learned essentially that the SPD would not fight.

But the main effect of the depression was to radicalize the town. In the face of the mounting economic crisis, Thalburgers were willing to tolerate approaches that would have left them indignant or indifferent under other circumstances. Thus the disgusting and debilitating party acrimony and violence mushroomed in the years before the dictatorship. The extent of the violence in Thalburg was an expression of the radical situation, but it also added to it by making violence normal and acceptable. With the growing nationalism and increasing impatience over the depression, violence and political tension were significant factors in preparing the town for the Nazi takeover.

All these factors were exploited with considerable astuteness by Nazi propaganda. In the face of the senseless round of political squabbling and fecklessness, the Nazis presented the appearance of a unified, purposeful, and vigorous alternative. Their propaganda played upon all the needs and fears of the town and directed itself to almost every potential group of adherents. By their own efforts the Nazis captured the allegiance of the confused and troubled middle class.

This set the stage for the actual seizure of power, but the revolution itself was also conducted in such a way as to insure success. The fact that this was, in the words of Konrad Heiden, a 'coup d'état by installments' kept the Reichsbanner from responding decisively at any one point. By the time the SPD had been broken, the terror system had been inaugurated, largely through social reinforcement.

The single biggest factor in this process was the destruction of society in Thalburg. What social cohesion there was in the town existed in the club life, and this was destroyed in the early months of Nazi rule. With their social organizations gone and with terror a reality, Thalburgers were isolated from one another. This was true of the middle class but even more true of the workers, since by the destruction of the SPD and the unions the whole complex of social ties created by this super-club was effaced. By reducing the people of Thalburg to unconnected social atoms, the Nazis could move the resulting mass in whatever direction they wished. The process was probably easier in Thalburg than in most other places, since the town contained so many government employees. By virtue of their dependence on the government the civil servants were in an exposed position and had no choice but to work with the Nazis if they valued their livelihood. Especially Thalburg's teachers—who formed the social and cultural elite of the town—found themselves drawn into support of the NSDAP almost immediately. As other

Thalburgers flocked to the Nazi bandwagon in the spring of 1933, and as terror and distrust became apparent, there was practically no possibility of resistance to Hitler. [. . .]

Thus many factors combined to make Nazism a possibility for Thalburg. At the same time the town itself influenced the nature of Nazism as it manifested itself locally. It seems probable, for example, that the general lack of violence during the first months of the Third Reich was due to the nature of Thalburg as a small town. Much as the Nazis hated all that the Socialists stood for, both sides knew each other too well for cold and systematic violence to occur. The SA might be willing to pummel their neighbors in a street fight, but they seemed to shrink from attacking the Socialists when they were defenseless. [. . .]

The smallness of Thalburg, the fact that many families had known each other for generations undoubtedly modified the nature of the mature dictatorship. The Nazis could come and go but the 'Club for the Defense of Old Thalburg Privileges'—composed of old city dwellers of every hue in the political spectrum—continued to meet and work together to make sure they would receive their annual ration of free beer, their 18 marks' worth of wood from the town forest. [. . .]

[*The Nazi Seizure of Power: The Experience of a Single German Town 1930–1935* (London, Eyre & Spottiswood, 1966), 274–9.]

ZDENEK ZOFKA

28   The Growth of National Socialism in the Countryside

As with many relatively early studies of the rise to power on a regional basis, Zdenek Zofka's study of the predominantly Catholic rural community of Günzberg placed emphasis on statistical evidence of electoral behaviour and party membership; however, in addition, Zofka offered thoughtful discussion of the ways in and extent to which Nazism was able to penetrate the local public sphere and co-opt local elites which prefigured much more recent research.

Its miserable election propaganda alone would hardly have been enough for the NSDAP to succeed in portraying itself as a party of rebuilding, of constructive reordering, and to succeed in winning the trust and confidence which is needed by a 'programme party' as a prerequisite for a stable, lasting commitment to the party—in contrast to the pure, mood-dependent protest movements without deeper party commitment. Even the written programme of the NSDAP (party programme and agricultural programme) was not finally decisive to the success of the party. The written or spoken word alone cannot generate confidence: what is far more decisive is *who* says something, who represents the party and the programme. In this respect, a meteoric development took place in the years 1931/2, an enormous expansion of the regional and local party, of the 'movement'—through the winning over of members, sympathizers, local advocates, and agitators. Because of its radical image, it was difficult for the NSDAP to win for itself the caste of rural local notables in its entirety, yet still it succeeded in breaking through, and in winning over an entire rank of important opinion leaders in local communities, and above all in the agricultural and middle-class lobbying and self-administration associations and organizations. Not the statements, but these persons embodied the programme of the NSDAP; for the voters, they offered the assurance of an NSDAP policy that would be friendly to the farming community and the middle class.[1] It is not possible to subsume this process of winning over opinion leaders who had proven their ability to represent local interests under the term 'infiltration' of the rural middle-class interest organizations by the Nazis—because it was not the penetration from outside (of unimportant, unknown, or even outside party members)[2] into the interest organizations, but the conversion of key opinion leaders *in* the organizations, which created the starting point from which the party was able to build up its basis of trust.[3]

Terms such as 'infiltration' or 'occupation of the interest-based political substructures of the bourgeois parties'[4] make clear the tendency amongst historians (even those who write about fascism as a social movement) to emphasize the instrumental character of the party (as an apparatus for seducing the masses, as an extended office of the Führer), instead of properly and consistently perceiving the NSDAP as a true social movement. From the overall historical point of view, from the experience of the use of the party and the misuse of this instrument for Hitler's takeover of power, this is only too understandable. It is nevertheless too one-sided a view of the real existence and development of the NSDAP as a social movement, the independent impetus 'from below' of which must neither be overlooked nor underestimated, if one is to understand its dynamism and also its noteworthy stability.

[S]ystematic investigation of this process of winning over the opinion leaders shows [. . .] that the Nazis had enormous difficulties in getting the rural notable caste onto their side. Here they had only limited success (in individual communities) and then too the involvement of the notables did not go beyond expressions of sympathy. It was not decisive for the development of the NSDAP to win over the stratum of notables in its entirety or in large number. Instead, what was decisive was that it was successful in winning over to its side quite specific 'important' persons (i.e. particularly respected and trust-inspiring persons) from the previous elites—both in the previously dominant parties and in the interest organizations (generally in personal union). They did not then restrict themselves to openly proclaiming their sympathy for the party, but took up leading positions in it, thereby representing the party in public in the particular role of guarantors of a specific interest-based political influence on the party. [. . .]

Prerequisite for the switch of opinion leaders and voters to National Socialism was the softening and elimination of existing party orientations, such as the [. . .] great uncertainty and resignation of the Peasant League's voters, and the growing doubt (given the crisis) in the strength of this party to represent and push through the interests of the peasants, which led finally to the search for a new and more effective representation of their interests. The new party had therefore to 'guarantee' both the continuity of the representation of their interests as well as greater effectiveness in push-ing through these interests, and both appeared to be guaranteed by the NSDAP. The middle-class origin of the movement in this region, its militant anti-socialism (and the fundamental anti-trade union stance, important also in terms of interest politics), the party and agricultural programme, and the organizationally safeguarded offer of the representation of interests within the party (herein lies above all the importance of the 'agrarian political apparatus', as an instrument which should conspicuously guarantee the influence of rural representatives at all levels of the party's politics) appeared to guarantee the continuity of the representation of interests by the new party. The size of the NSDAP, resulting from its election success as a protest party (1930), had become one of the main criteria of its attractive-ness: here was the starting point for the expectation of a greater efficiency in the implementation of its political objectives. Equally important here however was the convincingly militant public appearance of the NSDAP, its demonstration of energy and vigour—the trend towards the militarization of politics obviously corresponded to a situationally caused need of broad strata of voters, to which all large parties attempted to respond as far as they could—most intensively and most successfully, however, the NSDAP. [. . .]

The NS movement did not revolutionize the political culture of this region. It had managed to adapt itself, to latch onto the existing traditions and prevail-ing political mentalities. This was also something which could not have been otherwise: after all the NS movement was being carried to an increasing extent by representatives of the old political traditions. The political culture was not changed by the NS movement: had they really wished to achieve this they would not have had the strength. It was changed by the changed histor-ical situation, by the economic crisis—for example in the spread of a sense of the need for a 'total solution', or in the trend towards the militarization of politics. But [. . .] the economic crisis did not, after all, turn the human value system completely upside down, as one would have to assume had been the case were one to believe that the transition to National Socialism should be equated with a wave of extreme nationalism.

[*Die Ausbreitung des Nationalsozialismus auf dem Lande: eine regionale Fallstudie zur politischen Einstellung der Landbevölkerung in der Zeit des Aufstiegs und der Machtergreifung der NSDAP 1928–1936* (Munich: Neue Schriftenreihe des Stadtarchivs. München, 1979), 343–6, 348–9.]

RUDY KOSHAR
....

29   Toward the Mass Party

In his study of the rise of National Socialism in the Protestant university town of Marburg, in Hesse, Rudy Koshar portrays the local middle class—economically diverse but unified as an anti-Socialist 'community of sentiment'—as enforcing its social hegemony locally through a vibrant 'apolitical' associational life which enabled it to eschew participation in bourgeois party politics. The relative homogeneity of this 'moral community' made it relatively easy, under conditions of political and economic crisis, for National Socialism to mobilize it as a political movement once the party had successfully penetrated the local social networks. The penetration of local associational life was, according to Koshar, as important in this case as the impact of the Depression; significantly, indeed, National Socialism made early breakthroughs in Marburg although the town was only moderately affected by the Depression.

In these passages he discusses the initial electoral breakthroughs after 1930.

How can these initial successes be explained? We should first discuss what seems to be the most obvious factor, namely, the Depression of 1929. The Depression was not a direct factor in either electoral victory, but it created a broad backdrop for other more important processes. Unemployment, the main tracer of the deteriorating economic situation, was still too low in the city in September 1930 to influence Reichstag elections. What is more, not sudden and drastic unemployment but chronic joblessness and underemployment were the most severe problems in the city and country.[1] In 1930 there was heightened concern in occupational associations about economic hardships, but most economic demands, such as those supporting independent trade and artisanry, had been on the agenda of local organizations since the beginning of the Republic. In the countryside the economic situation had been deteriorating since well before September 1930, and the Depression was not a sudden shock.[2] Among university students, debates before the AMSt* elections indicated that economic issues were either secondary or only one of a number of concerns. The NSDStB† treated

---

* Allgemeiner Marburger Studentenschaft (General Marburg Student Government).
† Nationalsozialistischer Deutscher Studentenbund (Nazi Student League).

economic issues perfunctorily before the 1931 elections.[3] Clearly, after Hitler benefited from the 1930 protest vote, the worsening Depression caused Nazi party electoral and membership increases to be far greater than they would have been otherwise, and the NSDAP could never have been the mass movement it became without the hardships of the economic crisis. But in the Hessian town the economic disaster was less important to the rise of Nazism in 1930 and the first half of 1931 than were other considerations.

More crucial were two sociopolitical factors. The first had to do with the interplay of organizational life and the Nazi party. The town bourgeoisie became more organized in the Weimar Republic, as [. . .] evidence on organization formation and density suggests. More nonelite *Bürger* were gaining organizational skills and social contacts. Additionally, bourgeois social organizations gained members or remained stubbornly resilient while working-class organizational life faltered. There was also a general mobilization away from the bourgeois parties, a trajectory vividly demonstrated in the appearance of economic interest coalitions in city politics in 1924–29. But other organizations contributed to this process even more. Social clubs adopted a number of mechanisms—from older practices of muffling political tension to aggressive domination of nationalist festivals—to encourage popular apoliticism. At the university the Stahlhelm, NSD-StB, Hochschulring* and other organizations became more lively; students took a greater interest in politics by late 1929, although they advocated nonpartisanship. These trends coalesced in a moralistic and nationalist consensus driven primarily by bourgeois nonparty organizations. Before September 1930 the NSDAP was politically marginal compared with the bourgeois parties, more dependent than the bourgeois parties on social ties, and willing to present itself as the culmination of efforts to build an apolitical and antisocialist community of sentiment. The NSDAP had an opportunity to be the political head of this mobilized tangle of social organizations.

The second factor was Nazi dynamism. Though bourgeois elites began the apolitical mobilization of the 1920s, numerous weaknesses—a failed referendum against the Young Plan and ineffectiveness of the AMSt and Hochschulring among them—exposed the limits of their mobilization efforts. Bourgeois elites lost control over popular apoliticism, bourgeois parties fumbled away still more support, and Nazi party activists successfully grasped for the resources that were now available, showing more dynamism than liberal or conservative competitors. But Nazi dynamism was necessary in an underfinanced and marginal organization seeking a path out of political impotence. Political activism was a matter of survival, not a result of

* The *Hochschulring* was a nationalist university students' association.

extraordinary brilliance or perspicacity. In a very real sense Nazi agitators exploited the advantage of political 'backwardness.' [. . .]

The 1930–31 electoral victories were more lasting than expected, because the NSDAP was gaining control over a field of social organizations wider than that supporting bourgeois parties. Beginning before September 1930, this process—fueled more strongly than before by mounting economic difficulties—gained momentum after the first Reichstag successes. It was partly a result of Nazi infiltration of voluntary organizations. By the summer of 1928, von Eltz* claimed that the NSDStB had 'representatives' in at least five major Marburg student organizations.[4] Later, the Nazi Student League attended regular discussion evenings of fraternity and non-fraternity student groups. In late 1931 the national NSDStB leader von Schirach ordered all local leagues to establish 'contact organizations' consisting of trustworthy members in the fraternities. The goal was to monitor fraternity actions, stir up conflict, and 'disarm' fraternity leaders. The process worked well in the Christian-conservative fraternity Marburger Wingolf, an organization with thirty-eight active members in summer 1930. By 1933 thirteen *Wingolfisten* had joined the Nazi movement. Additionally, members of the Association of German Students, Turnerschaft Philippina, Studentenverbindung Chattia, Burschenschaft Germania, the Students' Gymnastics Club of Kurhessen, Corps Teutonia, and many other student groups joined the NSDAP. Parallel processes of cross-affiliation occurred for town organizations. Nazi non-student party members could be found in bourgeois occupational associations, sports clubs, municipal nonparty coalitions, and many other groups.[5] Through infiltration, the NSDAP gained moral authority over organizations in which it also established a material base. It was becoming the political hub, the focus of legitimacy and material power, that bourgeois constituencies had lacked.

But it would be wrong to see infiltration as something planned in great detail by party tacticians. Nazi occupation of bourgeois networks also occurred through parallel and independent actions that escaped full party control. Some party members, such as DHV† chair (since the early 1920s) and Gymnastics Club member (since before World War I) Emil Wißner, achieved positions of power in local organizational life before entering the NSDAP (as Wißner did in 1929). Wißner used his influence in both organizations, but especially in the DHV, to recruit members for the Nazi cause. His authority also extended to neighborhood life, as Wißner got DHV members who lived in his apartment building to join the NSDAP. Other party members also employed their affiliations with the NSDAP to achieve influence in non-Nazi

---

* Kuno von Eltz-Rübenach, head of the local SA and NSDStB.
† Deutschnationaler Handlungsgehilfenverband (German National Commercial Employees' Association).

organizations. The baker and member of the local County Artisans' Association Ludwig Schweinsberger, who joined an independent nonparty slate in the 1929 city elections to protest association policies, joined the Nazi party in June 1931. The following October he gained a seat on the board of directors of the County Artisans' Association. In this case, Schweinsberger joined the Nazi party to force the Artisans' Association to defend artisanal interests more effectively. Kurt Hübner, a member of Corps Teutonia in 1925–28 and 1930–31, joined the NSDAP in late 1930 and then gained the AMSt presidency.[6] In these and other cases, the NSDAP conceded much power to party members, partly because it could not monitor everything, and partly because their actions necessarily furthered Nazi occupation of social networks. Indeed, because social penetration was often the result of independent activity by party joiners, the NSDAP's capacity to hegemonize the population increased; Nazi joiners' ostensible distance from centralized party control enhanced the legitimacy of their message. Unpredictable and chaotic, such unauthorized grass roots activity promoted Nazi social conquests just as effectively as did approved, stamped, and standardized party propaganda.

[*Social Life, Local Politics and Nazism: Marburg 1880–1935* (Chapel Hill: University of North Carolina Press, 1986), 199–203.]

ODED HEILBRONNER

30   The Abandoned Regulars' Table

> Oded Heilbronner's study of the relationship of bourgeois associational life to the rise of National Socialism in the Catholic Black Forest area argues that it was the dissolution of the bourgeois social infrastructure under the impact of the Depression, rather than its successful penetration by the National Socialists, which created a vacuum into which the latter could move; in this case, according to Heilbronner, National Socialism did not so much infiltrate bourgeois associational networks as supplant them.

Why did the bourgeois camp turn to the NSDAP? Was there a connection between the work and structure of the bourgeois cultural associations and the Nazi party? Did the party try to penetrate these important power positions and subject them to its domination as had previously occurred with other organizations? Were the association members also members of the NSDAP, as in Marburg and other small places?[1] It must first be noted that on the basis of the available data no clear conclusions can be drawn with regard to the composition of the membership of the local groups of the NSDAP in the Black Forest and its connections to the bourgeois associations as the data are contradictory, and unreliable in terms of the identity of individual local group members. Undoubtedly there were among the association members also some who were members of the NSDAP at the same time, but the ban on taking political stances within the associations, the relatively modest importance of ordinary members (of whom some were maybe only passive members), and the impossibility of identifying the association members among the party members and of understanding clearly their significance for the association make an answer to the question of the connection between the association members and the members and sympathizers of the NSDAP impossible.

Compared to this the question of the presence of party members on the association committees and among the prominent figures in the associations is more important. Members who held influence within the association and were simultaneously members or sympathizers of the NSDAP could have a decisive influence on the behaviour of the associations and their relationship to the NSDAP. But only few sources point to there having been chairmen of the highly regarded cultural associations who were at the same time sympathizers or members of the NSDAP. [. . .]

In contrast to the accounts of associational life in Marburg or Günzburg the connection between the bourgeois associations, with their cultural and social goals, and the NSDAP was exceptionally loose in the Black Forest.[2]

We are faced with the question of why many voters from the bourgeois camp supported the NSDAP and of whether there was a connection between this support and their membership in the associations. Along with the adequately understood causes there are grounds to suppose that a significant proportion of the NSDAP's votes in 1932 belonged to the group who had just left the associations, or who found themselves in a process of detachment from the associational culture. A proportion of this group stood outside local social life and sought refuge in an organization which was willing to accept them into its ranks.[3] This group—as did a part of the organized bourgeoisie overall—regarded the NSDAP as a further association,[4] albeit one whose character was distinct from the usual pattern, it being more politically orientated, with, however, the administrative structure of an association (local group, chairman, treasurer, secretary, agenda, sporting and singing events). The political ideology and language of the party was similar to the language of the association and of bourgeois society: anticlerical traits, resistance to political Catholicism, political populism, and primarily the struggle against Socialism and Bolshevism. Rather than participating in the events of the cultural associations, people now attended the evenings of National Socialist culture, the so-called 'German evenings', the contents of whose programmes were similar to the associations' evenings. [. . .]

In contrast to the expositions of other studies of the rise of the NSDAP in various localities in Germany neither the local leading figures who supported the NSDAP and led the population towards the party, nor the local bourgeois press, nor the chairmen or members of the associations who persuaded the other association members to support the NSDAP are at the centre of our discussion of circumstances in the Black Forest; neither is the NSDAP itself, with its dynamic character, which revealed itself above all in propaganda, with its young image of striving for a new situation, with its new methods of recruitment, its charismatic leadership and its especially attractive ideology, which appealed to the local bourgeoisie.[5] The organizational-social vacuum which emerged in bourgeois society in the Black Forest and which was caused among other things by the mass resignations from the associations, the disintegration of local cultural and social life, must be regarded as a decisive (if also not exclusive) explanation for the success of the NSDAP. [. . .]

The strengthening of the NSDAP should not be explained solely in terms of its party activity, organization, and propaganda. Rather, more attention needs to be paid to the crisis and the organizational-social vacuum which was the field of agitation of the party; for the processes of dissolution of the bourgeois infrastructure made it easier for the NSDAP to enter the organizational vacuum without great effort.

The most powerful expression of the crisis in which bourgeois society in the Black Forest found itself was the fear of the Bolshevik danger which had grasped the bourgeoisie—a danger which found its concrete expression in the rise in activity of the KPD. The local press, which reported incessantly on events in Bolshevik Russia, warned at the same time of a precedent for the bourgeois Catholic population in the Black Forest. Fear of hated Bolshevism and the inability of the bourgeoisie to combine into a political and social bloc in order to find an answer to the threat are visible in all areas. On a national level the situation is known. On a local level, however, especially in Catholic areas, in small towns and villages, where the political development may have differed strongly from the national level, research on the fear of Bolshevism is still in its initial stages.[6] The consequences and impact of the First World War, in connection with the economic crises which set in after the war, caused the self-confidence of the bourgeoisie, which in any case had been shaken before the war, finally to falter, and also attacked the 'crown jewel' of the bourgeois—the association. With the outbreak of the great economic crisis the association structure also collapsed. The members who left the associations were the NSDAP's voters of 1932. They still felt themselves to be members of bourgeois society. But their withdrawal from the most respected of bourgeois institutions hit their self-confidence in a sensitive spot. The unjustified sense of feeling threatened by the forces of Socialism and Catholicism, the justified fear of Communism, the feeling of isolation and of being threatened as a result of the 'betrayal' of their social environment—all this drove those who stood on the margins of bourgeois society into the arms of the NSDAP. Is it possible to see this support for National Socialism as revenge on the bourgeois establishment which had expelled them from its ranks? If the *Donaubote*** interpreted the membership of members of the middle class in the NSDAP as the funeral of the bourgeoisie then its diagnosis was correct.[7] The abandoned regulars' table at the gathering of the soldiers' and military association on the Titisee contrasted to the brimming rooms of the adjacent guesthouse in which a National Socialist propaganda meeting was being held,[8] and made easier for National Socialism the process of 'coordination' visited on the disintegrated infrastructure of the German bourgeoisie after 1933.

['Der verlassene Stammtisch: vom Verfall der bürgerlichen Infrastruktur und dem Aufstieg der NSDAP am Beispiel der Region Schwarzwald', *Geschichte und Gesellschaft*, 19 (1993), 194–201.]

WOLFRAM PYTA

31   Protestant Rural Milieu and National Socialism prior to 1933

Analysing the success of the National Socialists in mobilizing support within the Protestant rural milieu, Wolfram Pyta notes the success with which the Nazis were able to co-opt the support of local village elites, who played an important role in giving political leads to the community. The relatively closed and homogeneous community lent itself to rapid penetration once this co-option had occurred, especially given the conditions of agrarian crisis prevailing at this time.

Above all, the Protestant village of the 1920s and 1930s offers rich illustrative material of the behaviour-regulating effects of firm anchorship in a social milieu.[1] For, in the rural villages—far away from the lively hustle and bustle of the big cities, and with only inadequate transport connections to the different environment of the cities—a form of social coexistence had been preserved which sought, with noteworthy doggedness, to defy the tangible trends in the towns towards social pluralization and individualization. This form was: the village community. The village of this period can be regarded as a habitat, largely cordoned off socially, where people were intensely rooted within the milieu. This also had a profound impact on political life. Because, in the network of social relationships within the village, a collective way of life usually flourished particularly well. [. . .]

Since politics, insofar as it broke apart the purely *Heimat*-centred framework, appeared as a foreign body in village life, it was 'delegated' to the few villagers who, because of their occupation and education, were considered best prepared to deal with those forces which came from outside the village.

---

* A Black Forest newspaper.

Politics in the country were consequently neither an affair of the heart of local persons hungry for political engagement nor did they fall under the responsibility of professional politicians from outside the village. The political process proceeded in the villages rather more along the existing authority structures of the rural social structure:[2] the task fell to the dominant figures in society to translate, as it were, 'high politics' for village consumption. This conversion of social standing into leadership of political opinion underlines the extent to which the German village of the 1920s and early 1930s was still a pre-modern, pre-urban social body.

For specific political behaviour to be able to grow out of the rural social milieu an intermediate station therefore had to be introduced: the village authorities formed the connecting link between milieu and politics, they deciphered political messages and fed them into rural everyday life. Recognizing this paves the way to understanding the recipe for success which enabled a political party to occupy the rural social milieu.

The success of parties therefore depended quite decisively on how far they managed to bring as many such mentors as possible onto their side and to convert their social status into political recommendation. Accordingly, the breakthrough of the NSDAP in the country could be achieved only *with* the support of a large number of high-ranking local villagers, and in no way *against* their closed opposition.

First and foremost amongst the ranks of these tone-setting authorities were lords of the manor (in the manorial villages mainly to be found in *Ostelbien*), large-scale peasants, village parsons, and country teachers. What has to be considered therefore is the political dispositions of this rural ruling caste: did it show political tendencies which made it particularly susceptible to the message of the Hitler party?

It is difficult at first sight to bring the political ideas of peasants and squires, teachers and clergymen to a common denominator. Was the internal relationship of these unequal pairs not clouded by rivalry and competitive jealousy? Had not so much social conflict potential accumulated, particularly in the tension-charged relationship between village teacher and country parson, that political parties were always able to win over only one of the two adversaries, but never both together?

A multitude of very different interests was also gathered together within German agriculture, and this stood in the way of a closed corporate representation. Not only the size of farm separated the smallest farm of under 5 hectares from the noble estate comprising more than 100 hectares:[3] the different types of agricultural organization of the farm also ensured internal tensions in the 'Green Front', which was united only in its outward appearance. [. . .]

Only under the influence of the ever greater agricultural crises since 1928/9 did the internal conflicts in German agriculture gradually begin to melt, and a true corporate awareness emerge. For most farmers it took a considerable leap of the imagination before they could come to the view that their own well-being was inseparably linked with the destiny of the entire occupational community. It required first the lasting experience of a threat to their very existence to bring together the solitary farmers of all size classes into a cooperative front. They had quickly agreed on a guilty party for their misery: the state in general (with its exaggerated tax demands) and the hated Weimar Republic in particular had driven German agriculture to ruin. [. . .]

At the end of the 1920s however, the initial spark for the agrarian revolt came from the ranks of the rural peasantry. The parochial passivity and obsequiousness towards the noble estate gradually gave way to a growing peasant consciousness: parallel to this came an increasing emancipation from previously preferred political orientations. Without giving up their conservative fundamental beliefs, directed at the preservation of 'community', more and more farmers moved away from the 'old Right' and turned towards the 'new Right' in which they thought they perceived a more socially open version of agrarian conservatism.

Thus a new party of the Right which had no fear of dealing with the politically aroused rural masses and which skilfully gave attention to such political yearnings was presented with the unique opportunity to inherit the traditional parties of the Right in Protestant rural areas. The NSDAP pushed skilfully into this gap in the market, because it knew how to present itself as a modern agrarian party, and very painstakingly avoided the impression of wishing to shake the foundations of the rural social order. [. . .]

All in all, the NSDAP presented itself in Protestant rural areas as a national-conservative party, and at the same time consciously downplayed its racist views. Its programmatical offering was skilfully tailored to winning the rural multipliers. It created a conservative image for itself by speaking up for the preservation of the rural way of life. It promised to raise the status of farming above that of industry and trade; it raised the status of the peasantry to that of the most important pillar of German creativity. It promised rural priests that it would combat the political representatives of secularism. This originally conservative message was enhanced by the Führer party, however—and this is what gave it its own profile—thanks to the national invocation of a 'People's Community' transcending the classes, which awoke a multitude of expectations, particularly amongst parish priests and teachers. Many of the rural clergy hoped for a Christian reformation of the negative side of village community life if the sense of 'People's Community' expanded parochial local horizons. Not a few rural teachers felt that they were being taken seriously as important cultural agents who could finally gain the social recognition due to them for their education work amongst the people, work which they had previously performed without recognition.

Thus the NSDAP, as the only party operating throughout the Reich, was able to present an attractive offering to *all* village authorities. Because of their class-struggle slogans, the parties of the Left as always had difficulties gaining the recognition of the rural milieu. The conservative parties—above all the DNVP—had lost so much of the trust of the political mentors of the rural population that they increasingly had to abandon the field to a party whose programme they imitated, but which had the starting advantage of being new. [. . .]

Overall it must be emphasized that the NSDAP's infiltration of the Protestant-rural milieu was not least also the work of a political professionalization which did not appear artificial because it employed methods suited to the milieu. The Hitler party, however, was not just the political executor of the will of the rural social milieu. For, with it, a new quality of politics made its entry in the village: its political agitation did not even omit remote hamlets; even in intact village communities there was hardly an escape from the impact of party politics on rural social life.

This politicizing thrust, itself alien to the village, was not (and this was the formula for success of the NSDAP) rejected as an unwanted intrusion into the rural world, because the political openings of National Socialism were normally synonymous with the familiar village authorities. The Hitler party therefore set its foot *in* rural life with the help of proven political mentors, whose function for their part changed to purveyors of their slogans, to an extent which was previously unknown. Even if they experimented with new political mechanisms, and also previously sought to co-opt for political leadership tasks groups who had hitherto stood on the outside—in the final analysis, the NSDAP stuck mainly to the well-worn rule of the game: to pursue politics in the country in conjunction with the traditional rural elite.[4] [. . .]

['Ländlich-evangelisches Milieu und Nationalsozialismus bis 1933', in H. Moeller et al. (eds.), *Nationalsozialismus in der Region* (Munich: Oldenbourg, 1996), 202–5, 207, 210–11.]

Section C

The National Socialist Regime

INTRODUCTION

Since the period of the Third Reich itself, political scientists and historians have sought to explain the peculiar destructiveness of the National Socialist regime by analysing the relationship between its ideology and its power structures. Taking the regime's own pretensions to total control and its own self-representation largely at face value, many scholars have sought in particular to discuss the regime using the language of 'totalitarianism'. Emphasizing its anti-liberal characteristics, its elevation of the state over civil society, its strong reliance upon terroristic forms of rule, and the role of the dictatorial leader, these scholars have used the concept of totalitarianism to relate the National Socialist regime to other forms of twentieth-century dictatorship.

The label has tended (although not exclusively) to be used by scholars of liberal or conservative persuasion, and many have pointed to the fact that it was most in vogue in the 1950s as evidence that it sought primarily to equate the Soviet Union and National Socialist Germany as the twin enemies of liberty and democracy and was thus a product of Cold War politics rather than historical scholarship. There is more to the term than this. Its usage pre-dates the Cold War, and numerous respected scholars continue to make use of the term in the post-Cold War era. However, it does have serious weaknesses, and is of limited value beyond the level of the generally descriptive and evocative. It tends to imply a static model of a regime which, in the case of National Socialism, was characterized above all by dynamic internal processes of change. On an empirical level, the notion fails to do justice both to the internal complexities of the regime itself and to fundamental differences between National Socialism and the Soviet Union. While its advocates (rightly) asserted that each was underpinned by a mass movement, for example, they rarely engaged with the problems presented by the fact that support for each was located in very different social groups. In particular, the failure to discuss adequately the specific nature of fascism's mass support enabled the avoidance of any confrontation with the fact that it arose out of a series of crises of capitalism and a concomitant crisis of bourgeois liberalism, albeit one conditioned strongly by the specific cultural impact of the First World War. It therefore provided an interpretative framework which, by virtue of the fact that it did not demand the critical articulation of questions about capitalism itself, was conducive to the relegitimization not only of liberal democracy but of capitalism itself in the post-war era.

From completely the opposite end of the ideological spectrum, orthodox Marxist historians, and especially the Marxist-Leninist historians of the German Democratic Republic, argued that the National Socialist regime had represented the 'dictatorship of monopoly capitalism' in Germany. Focusing on its anti-Socialist and anti-Marxist elements, its destruction of the organized Left in 1933, its role (initially, at least) in stabilizing German capitalism after the crisis of 1929–33, and the complicity of German big business in crimes such as the exploitation of the occupied territories and the brutal abuse of forced labour, they argued with varying degrees of crudeness that the regime had been established by powerful reactionary business interests and was pursuing goals dictated by the needs of business itself. Imperialism, as Lenin had argued, represented the highest form of capitalism—since National Socialism was an aggressive imperialist regime it therefore had to represent capitalism at a particular stage of development.

The scholarship of the German Democratic Republic did much to uncover the close relationship between the regime and German big business, and was instrumental in revealing the existence of strong continuities in personnel between the regime and the elites of the post-war Federal Republic, but its overall contentions have found little support among western scholars. In particular, its utter failure to integrate an analysis of National Socialist racial policy and genocide into its interpretations has rendered it highly problematic in most historians' eyes. As far as the National Socialist political system is specifically concerned, neither theories of monopoly capitalism nor those of totalitarianism have stood up effectively to the careful empirical scholarship published from the 1960s onwards.

From the mid- to late 1960s especially, increasing numbers of historians began to produce work which suggested that far from being a stable monolithic regime, with clearly defined structures of authority implementing a detailed, well-defined plan, the Third Reich had represented a far more complex structure comprising numerous, often conflicting power blocs. Taking their cue from the analyses of wartime émigré writers such as Ernst Fraenkel and Franz Neumann, they developed a far more nuanced picture of the National Socialist 'system', producing a picture of an inherently unstable, increasingly chaotic regime in which internal personal and institutional rivalries propelled a broad process of radicalization of policies which, in terms of their detail, emerged in an extremely arbitrary and ad hoc fashion. In particular, scholars such as Martin Broszat and Hans Mommsen argued that National Socialist ideology offered not a clear programme but a set of 'metaphors' for a far vaguer drive towards expansion and persecution.

Such often controversial arguments did not go unchallenged by those who continued to argue that such systemic pressures were at most secondary and that the Third Reich still had to be understood primarily in terms of the programmatic pursuit of an ideological agenda by Hitler and the National Socialist leadership. From the 1970s to the mid-1980s scholarship on the Third Reich thus came to be dominated by what was labelled the 'structuralist' vs. 'intentionalist' debate. On the one hand, 'intentionalists' focused primarily on the implementation of Hitler's ideological intentions, usually emphasizing the personal role of Hitler and the systematic pursuit of foreign policy and social-racial policy goals, which they believed could be read into Hitler's pre-1933 statements; any diversion from these they ascribed to Hitler's tactical flexibility or to an opportunism which even most ardent 'intentionalists' were willing to admit characterized the regime's policies. On the other hand, increasing numbers of scholars both in Germany and abroad sought to explain the radicalization of National Socialist policy as a product of the evolving structures of the regime or in terms of the ways in which it functioned. Within the 'structuralist' school of thought there was considerable diversity and the label contains what should be understood as a variety of positions on several key issues. Some saw the proliferation of agencies under Hitler's rule as a transfer of the principles of Social Darwinism to the practice of government; others saw in it a process of 'divide and rule' by which Hitler consolidated his position over potential rivals within the system; others saw it in terms of Hitler's innate mistrust of bureaucratic regularity and procedure. Some saw Hitler as an all-powerful figure setting strong lines of policy and intervening directly in core spheres of decision-making; others regarded him as remote and distant, intervening only rarely to resolve the disputes which inevitably emerged between his satraps; it was even suggested that his vacillation and unwillingness to intervene was such that he could be seen as a 'weak dictator'. Some 'structuralist' scholars saw the functioning of the regime in terms of a fundamental dualism between party and state; others saw more far-reaching processes of institutional proliferation within and between both party and state and characterized the system as multi-centred, or 'polycratic'. All, however, were agreed that the evolving internal structures of the regime held the key to explaining its dynamism and impulsiveness.

The 'intentionalist' vs. 'structuralist' debate informed the historiography of almost every aspect of the history of the Third Reich in the 1970s and 1980s. In particular, the 'structuralist' school helped greatly to enhance understanding of National Socialist policy towards the Jews, offering thoughtful interpretations of the relationship between internal political development, territorial expansion, and the radicalization of racial policy. Above all, in underlining how the regime's uncoordinated policy towards the Jews initially centred on economic marginalization, social discrimination, and emigration, and only under the specific changing conditions of territorial expansion and war escalated so radically into genocide, it drew out central weaknesses of an explanation based too heavily on detailed programmatic analysis. Further, in helping to develop a broader understanding of the range of institutions involved in the implementation of the regime's policies, the 'structuralist' approach encouraged research on wider aspects of racial policy which had hitherto been largely ignored by historians in the field. On the back of a growing body of research on the genocide of the Jews, which itself only began to occupy a central position in scholarly concerns in the 1970s, work began to appear on issues such as the experiences of Soviet prisoners of war, of forced deported labour and concentration camp labour, or on sterilization and euthanasia, which, taken together, emphasized the extent to which racial policy informed social policy at every level.

By the 1990s, indeed, the centrality of race to all areas of National Socialist policy and practice had been established. With this, however, came a renewed assertion of the importance of ideology to any understanding of the National Socialist regime, calling into question some of the more extreme 'structuralist' positions and resulting in attempts to offer a new synthesis of the arguments of 'intentionalists' and 'structuralists'. Most notably, the Third Reich has been characterized in the 1990s using the language of 'charismatic authority'. Defining 'charisma' less in terms of personal attributes than as a relationship of power and authority, such analyses combine discussion of the role of Hitler as leader and arbiter with emphasis on the dynamism of a system which, for all its chaotic characteristics, was held together by a broad ideological belief which was understood by everybody and which Hitler was seen as embodying. Scholars have used the term to examine not only the interplay between party and state institutions at the level of high politics, but also the mutually reinforcing impulses emanating from centre and periphery in the implementation of racial policy on the ground. Such analyses have the advantage that, rather than suggesting a conflict between personally held ideological motives and blind institutional-bureaucratic impulses, they reveal the extent to which the entire system became infused with a broad ideological imperative which enabled local initiatives from low-ranking figures deep in the occupied territories to interact with directives issued at the centre to generate a self-perpetuating spiral of destruction which needed only occasional direct involvement from the leadership in Berlin.

i. The National Socialist Regime as a Monolith: Theories of Totalitarianism

CARLTON J. H. HAYES

32 | The Novelty of Totalitarianism

> In 1939, the American Philosophical Society organized a symposium on the nature of totalitarianism, at which Carlton J. H. Hayes presented the lecture from which these extracts are taken. In a lecture which prefigured much post-war writing on the subject, Hayes was at pains to suggest the modern nature of the dictatorships under discussion, which in his view distinguished themselves from earlier forms of despotism and tyranny through their relationship to the masses.

In contrast with the quality and training of earlier dictators, note who and what the present ones are. There is Benito Mussolini, whose father was a blacksmith, whose education was obtained in a minor normal school, whose career was that of an unsuccessful elementary-school teacher and a second- or third-rate journalist, and whose military service was brief and inconspicuous. There is Joseph Stalin, generated by a peasant shoemaker, dismissed from a seminary and further schooling at the age of seventeen for irregularity in conduct and discipline, self-trained in the strong-arm arts of highway robbery and factory disorder, and as a convicted criminal relieved of any military service in the World War. There is Adolf Hitler, son of a minor Austrian customs-official, with a minimum of formal schooling and a maximum of frustrated efforts at hack work in painting and drawing, and with a curious record of having fought for four years in the German army without rising above the rank of corporal. In fine, not one of these world-shaking despots of our day comes of what we would deem distinguished antecedents; not one of them has been well educated or gained military repute.

How has it happened that such persons could become dictators? It is, I submit, precisely because they have come from the masses rather than from the classes and could therefore more readily get the ear of the masses. For the masses count nowadays as never before, and this is the first and most fundamental of the novelties which distinguish contemporary dictatorship and the totalitarianism accompanying it. [. . .]

There is another novel trend of our age which affects the masses and forwards dictatorship—and totalitarianism. It is a decline of traditional religion and an obscuring of religious values. In the past every civilization has been built upon a particular religious profession and upon the popular *mores* emanating from it; and to this generalization our occidental civilization is no exception. [. . .]

In the present crisis, when the historic Christian faith of the Western masses grows cold, a kind of religious void is created for them. But inasmuch as any such void is unnatural and eventually unendurable, the masses promptly seek to fill it with some new faith. This they hardly find in 'humanity' or 'science,' which are too abstract and intellectual and nowadays a bit stale. They find it rather in materialistic communism or in nationalistic deification of blood and soil. Indeed, we miss a main point about the nature of contemporary communism and nationalism and their relationship to contemporary dictatorship if we overlook the essentially religious element in them and the essentially religious appeal they make. It is as high priests of novel and fervent religions that the dictators of today appeal to the masses. It is as recent converts that the masses respond enthusiastically and fanatically to the appeals of dictators. [. . .]

[I] may summarize what I believe to be the specific novelties of dictatorial totalitarianism.

First, it is really totalitarian. It monopolizes all powers and directs all activities of individuals and groups. It subordinates to itself all economic, religious, and educational institutions and policies. It levels classes and restricts or suppresses the liberty of family and person. It leaves no room for the free play of individual wills and recognizes no utility in free inquiry. On the contrary, it has a passion for making everyone conform to the will and thought of the governing party and dictator. Alike to Communists and to Fascists, the state is omniscient and infallible as well as omnipotent. In all these respects the Russia of Stalin is totalitarian as the Russia of the Tsars never was, the Germany of Hitler as no divine-right monarchy of Hohenzollerns or Habsburgs ever was.

Second, it commands and rests upon mass-support. It is no affair of an aristocratic class or a military caste. It is frankly for and by the half-educated and half-propertied lower middle class and upper proletariat. It springs from and returns to the great median of what are truly the masses, and everyone above or below who is not sycophantic is suspect and liable to liquidation. Previous régimes may have been aristocratic or plutocratic, but at least they had a tolerance for the masses which these, under the new dictatorship, seldom evince for the classes. And despite past apologies for Fascism in Italy and National Socialism in Germany on the ground that they were last-ditch defenses against the anti-capitalist Communism of Russia, time has already shown that their real defense has been piece-meal capitulation to the same socializing of goods and the same levelling of persons, which latter is a levelling down and not a levelling up.

Third, totalitarian dictatorship is maintained, and its overthrow rendered unusually difficult, by novel and marvellously effective agencies of popular education and propaganda. The radio and amplifier only date from after the World War; the cinema, from just before that war. The production of wood-pulp paper and large-scale cheap journalism arose in the 1890's, and compulsory school attendance began only in the 1880's and then only in a very few countries. Now all these agencies are perfected, and ready to be seized and used by a dictator. [. . .]

Again, totalitarianism has an almost irresistible allure—it moves people—by reason of the emotional and essentially religious spirit which its leading apostles have infused into it. Communist Russia and Nazi Germany are churches as well as states, and they are churches not old and conventional but pristine and full of missionary zeal. Their mythologies (that is, their ideologies) are new; their banners and rituals and slogans are new. No wonder that the number of their first-generation converts is incomparable. [. . .]

Furthermore, totalitarian dictatorship has evolved a new pattern of methods and techniques. Behind a mask of plebiscites, popular elections, and occasional assemblings of a so-called parliament—which listens and applauds but doesn't really parley—the government actually functions through and with a single political party which comprises a minority, usually a small minority, of the nation, but which is more or less hand-picked, severely disciplined, and equipped with a monopoly of the means of influencing public opinion and enforcing the will of the dictator. [. . .]

Still another novelty of totalitarianism is its exalting of might and force, not only as means to an end—there is precedent aplenty in Western history for that—but as an end in itself. In earlier and less totalitarian days, a despot who got rid of a foe or appropriated some neighbour's land went to considerable trouble, as a rule, to justify his action on conventional moral grounds. Now the totalitarian despot is hardly expected to offer any explanation at all, and when he does, it bears no trace of the Decalogue or the Sermon on the Mount. It suffices to echo the more up-to-date Nietzschean and pseudo-Darwinian principles that patience is a vice and that progress depends on a struggle for existence and *Lebensraum* for the fittest. Or it may suffice to recite the Marxian creed that proletarians have to fight for what they get and they are always right. The fact remains that brute force is boastfully invoked alike in the internal affairs and foreign policies of the totalitarian state. Force against Jews and Christians! Force against domestic critics! Force against Czechs and Albanians, Poles and Finns! The exalting of force and terrorism does not signify merely the immoral doctrine that the end justifies the means. It signifies an utter denial of any moral law superior to the might of dictators.

['The Novelty of Totalitarianism in the History of Western Civilisation', *Proceedings of the American Philosophical Society*, 82/1 (Feb. 1940), 92–3, 95–6, 98–101.]

33 | Ideology and Terror

Hannah Arendt's work was one of the most widely disseminated treatises on totalitarianism during the 1950s and 1960s. Her focus is very much on the centrality of terror to totalitarian regimes. She sees totalitarian regimes as using terror to accelerate what they see as the laws of nature or history—for Nazi Germany, laws based on racial-biological theory; for the Soviet Union, laws based on class and economic development—as a result, terror is visited inevitably upon those who are deemed by the laws of nature or history to be unacceptable to the totalitarian regime.

By lawful government we understand a body politic in which positive laws are needed to translate and realize the immutable *ius naturale** or the eternal commandments of God into standards of right and wrong. Only in these standards, in the body of positive laws of each country, do the *ius naturale* or the Commandments of God achieve their political reality. In the body politic of totalitarian government, this place of positive laws is taken by total terror, which is designed to translate into reality the law of movement of history or nature. Just as positive laws, though they define transgressions, are independent of them—the absence of crimes in any society does not render laws superfluous but, on the contrary, signifies their most perfect rule—so terror in totalitarian government has ceased to be a mere means for the suppression of opposition, though it is also used for such purposes. Terror becomes total when it becomes independent of all opposition; it rules supreme when nobody any longer stands in its way. If lawfulness is the essence of non-tyrannical government and lawlessness is the essence of tyranny, then terror is the essence of totalitarian domination. [. . .]

Total terror, the essence of totalitarian government, exists neither for nor against men. It is supposed to provide the forces of nature or history with an incomparable instrument to accelerate their movement. This movement, proceeding according to its own law, cannot in the long run be hindered; eventually its force will always prove more powerful than the most powerful forces engendered by the actions and the will of men. But it can be slowed down and is slowed down almost inevitably by the freedom of man, which even totalitarian rulers cannot deny, for this freedom—irrelevant and arbitrary as they may deem it—is identical with the fact that men are being born and that therefore each of them *is* a new beginning, begins, in a sense, the world anew. From the totalitarian point of view, the fact that men are born and die can be only regarded as an annoying interference with higher forces.

---

* Natural law.

Terror, therefore, as the obedient servant of natural or historical movement has to eliminate from the process not only freedom in any specific sense, but the very source of freedom which is given with the fact of the birth of man and resides in his capacity to make a new beginning. In the iron band of terror, which destroys the plurality of men and makes out of many the One who unfailingly will act as though he himself were part of the course of history or nature, a device has been found not only to liberate the historical and natural forces, but to accelerate them to a speed they never would reach if left to themselves. Practically speaking, this means that terror executes on the spot the death sentences which Nature is supposed to have pronounced on races or individuals who are 'unfit to live,' or History on 'dying classes,' without waiting for the slower and less efficient processes of nature or history themselves. [. . .]

Under conditions of total terror not even fear can any longer serve as an advisor of how to behave, because terror chooses its victims without reference to individual actions or thoughts, exclusively in accordance with the objective necessity of the natural or historical process. Under totalitarian conditions, fear probably is more widespread than ever before; but fear has lost its practical usefulness when actions guided by it can no longer help to avoid the dangers man fears. The same is true for sympathy or support of the regime; for total terror not only selects its victims according to objective standards; it chooses its executioners with as complete a disregard as possible for the candidate's conviction and sympathies. The consistent elimination of conviction as a motive for action has become a matter of record since the great purges in Soviet Russia and the satellite countries. The aim of totalitarian education has never been to instill convictions but to destroy the capacity to form any. The introduction of purely objective criteria into the selective system of the SS troops was Himmler's great organizational invention; he selected the candidates from photographs according to purely racial criteria. Nature itself decided, not only who was to be eliminated, but also who was to be trained as an executioner.

No guiding principle of behavior, taken itself from the realm of human action, such as virtue, honor, fear, is necessary or can be useful to set into motion a body politic which no longer uses terror as a means of intimidation, but whose essence *is* terror. In its stead, it has introduced an entirely new principle into public affairs that dispenses with human will to action altogether and appeals to the craving need for some insight into the law of movement according to which the terror functions and upon which, therefore, all private destinies depend.

The inhabitants of a totalitarian country are thrown into and caught in the process of nature or history for the sake of accelerating its movement; as such, they can only be executioners or victims of its inherent law. The process may decide that those who today eliminate races and individuals or the members of dying classes and decadent peoples are tomorrow those who must be sacrificed. What totalitarian rule needs to guide the behavior of its subjects is a preparation to fit each of them equally well for the role of executioner and the role of victim. This two-sided preparation, the substitute for a principle of action, is the ideology.

[*Origins of Totalitarianism* (London: Secker & Warburg, 1958), 464, 466–8.]

KARL-DIETRICH BRACHER

34   Totalitarianism as Concept and Reality

Despite the critical responses to the concept over the last thirty years, many influential and highly regarded scholars continue to see value in the term. Amongst these is the political scientist Karl-Dietrich Bracher, who regards the conflict between totalitarianism and democracy as the key characteristic of the twentieth century. While his analysis implicitly addresses some of the concerns raised by critics of the concept, his emphasis on terror and propaganda arguably betrays one of the fundamental weaknesses of the idea of totalitarianism—namely its underestimation of the genuinely voluntarist aspects of National Socialist rule.

Let us begin by examining the nature of these new, totalitarian regimes. They can no longer be grasped using the classical types of despotism and autocracy, nor are they mere throwbacks to traditional predemocratic forms of rule. Instead, as apparently total-democratic dictatorships, they constitute something quite new.

The authoritarian wave of the interwar period, the call for a 'strong man,' the great leader, was one precondition for the rise of these regimes. The other was the increased possibility, created by the technicalized age of the masses, for encompassing and making uniform the life *and* thought of all citizens. For in contrast to the older, conventional (so to speak) dictatorships and military regimes, these regimes now laid claim to all-embracing rule and total submission, indeed to a perfect *identity* of leadership and party movement, of the nation and the individual, of the general and the individual will. This claim can be implemented and enforced only if extremely harsh political controls and terror are legitimated by the fiction of such a system of complete identification, and if the belief in *one* absolute ideology is made obligatory—supposedly as 'voluntary' consent but in fact on penalty of death. The Marxist-Leninist dogma of class warfare, or the Fascist-National Socialist friend-foe doctrine of a war between peoples and races, were such totalitarian ideologies. They justified all acts by the government, even mass crimes and genocide, regardless of whether they were committed in the name of the will of the people, the party, the leader, or whether they were given a pseudodemocratic and pseudolegal or revolutionary and messianic-chiliastic cast, as in the myths of a future classless 'workers' paradise' or a 'Thousand-Year Reich.' Also of importance was the role of pseudoreligious needs and manipulations in a period that saw the decay of and a vacuum in religious values: thus the fervent belief in Adolf Hitler or Stalin, and also in symbols and rituals of mass events that were intended to convey the emotional experience of community.

Totalitarianism aimed at the elimination of all rights of liberty that were personal and prior to the state, and at the obliteration of the individual. To be sure, it was nowhere fully realized, but it was implemented to such a degree that it could ask normal citizens to perpetrate the most horrible crimes. At the same time, however, these regimes created the impression that they could realize the true destiny of humankind, indeed true democracy and the perfect welfare state, far more effectively than all previous forms of state and society. This power of seduction was spread better than ever before through the means of modern communication technology and propaganda. All the differences between Communism, Fascism, and National Socialism aside, each case shows three great, characteristic tendencies.

1. Fundamental is the striving for the greatest possible degree of total control of power by a single party (organized in a totalitarian fashion) and its leadership, the leadership being endowed with the attributes of infallibility and the claim to pseudoreligious veneration from the masses. Our century has taught us that power can be seized by such a totalitarian party not only in the 'classic' way, through the revolutionary putsch of a militant minority (as in the Russian October Revolution in 1917). It can also be seized through the undermining, abuse, and pseudolegal manipulation of democratic institutions (as in the pseudolegal seizure of power by National Socialism in 1933). All other parties and groups that represent political and social life are subsequently either destroyed through the use of bans or terrorism, or they are coerced into line through deception and threats of violence. In other words, they are reduced to a hollow existence in phony elections and sham parliaments, as in the Communist 'people's democracies,' with their single ticket of a 'national front'.

2. The total one-party state bases itself on a militant ideology. As an ersatz religion, a doctrine of salvation with a claim to political exclusivity, this ideology seeks to justify the suppression of all opposition and the total *Gleichschaltung* of the citizenry in historical terms as well as with reference to a future utopia. The historical background, political designs, and ideological doctrines of the various totalitarian systems might be very different, yet Russian Bolshevism, Italian Fascism, and German National Socialism have in common the techniques of omnipresent surveillance (secret police),

persecution (concentration camps), and massive influencing or monopolizing of public opinion. The unconditional consent of the masses is manipulated using every available tool of propaganda and advertising. According to findings of recent work in mass psychology, the goal is the creation of a permanent war mood directed against an enemy that is defined in absolute terms. In this process both the 'positive' needs of the masses for protection and feelings of enthusiasm and their 'negative' fears and obsessions are mobilized and used to consolidate power. The tightly controlled need for movement, excitement, and entertainment is satisfied with rallies and parades. The one-dimensional organizing of all spheres of life conveys at the same time a feeling of security, compelling the submission of the individual to the community, the collective. The state replaces constitutional legitimation with a system of pseudolegal consent and pluralistic elections with acclamatory plebiscites. With its claim to complete control over the life and beliefs of its citizens, the total state denies any right to freedom, any final meaning and purpose outside itself; it thinks of itself as the only, binding 'totality of all purposes'.

3. They all shared an essential component of the ideology of totalitarian rule: the myth that a total command state is much more effective than the complex democratic state based on the rule of law and limited by numerous controls and checks. The totalitarian ideology invokes the possibility of total economic and social planning (Four- and Five-Year Plans), the capacity for quicker political and military reaction, and the *Gleichschaltung* of political-administrative processes and increased stability by means of a dictatorial running of the state. However, the reality of totalitarian governing bears only a very qualified resemblance to this widely held notion. Constant rivalries within the totalitarian party and its controlling bodies, an unresolvable dualism of party and state, and the arbitrary actions of an uncontrolled central agency overloaded with authority—all this counteracts the perfecting of a command state constructed after the model of the military command structure. In this coercive system, partial improvements are bought at the expense of a tremendous loss of freedom of movement, legal order, and humanistic substance. In the final analysis this also reduces the professed ideals of security and truth to absurdity. The failure of Fascism and National Socialism, and the political and economic problems of modernization within post-Stalinist Communism, reveal that totalitarian systems of rule by no means guarantee a higher resistance to crisis and a more effective 'order'. Instead, a coercive system not subject to any control renders the exercise and consequences of concentrated political power immeasurably more costly in the long run than the seemingly cumbersome process of separating powers and striking compromises in a democratic state governed by the rule of law. [. . .]

All justifications for getting rid of the concept of totalitarianism are inadequate, so long as we do not come up with a better word for this phenomenon: to call it authoritarian or fascist does not quite capture it and is even more vague and general.

The rejection of the concept comes primarily from those to whom it may very well apply—just as, conversely, we hear talk of 'democracy' especially where no such thing exists.

The intensification of power occurs through the removal of all dividing lines between state and society and through the highest possible degree of total politicization of society—in the sense of Trotsky's statement that Stalin could say with every right, *'La société c'est moi'*.

One could raise the objection that totalitarianism is more of a tendency, a temptation or seduction, rather than a definitive form of government, and that, semantically, the word tends to be evocative rather than descriptive. This, indeed, is the reason for the difficulties of classification: totalitarianism as a nightmare, a syndrome instead of a clearly defined system. But for all that, it is no less effective and oppressive to those affected by it.

['Totalitarianism as Concept and Reality', in K.-D. Bracher, *Turning Points in Modern Times: Essays in German and European History* (Cambridge, Mass.: Harvard University Press, 1995), 145–7, 151.]

ii. Marxist Theories of National Socialism

WALTER ULBRICHT

35 The Nature of Hitler Fascism

> Originally issued immediately following the war and itself clearly owing much to orthodox Comintern statements from before the war, Ulbricht's statement set a tone for the scholarship of the German Democratic Republic, characterizing National Socialism as a tool of reactionary capitalism whose destructive foreign policy was driven by the need of big business to capture raw materials, markets, and labour abroad and to subjugate the working class at home. Interestingly, Ulbricht mentions gas chambers as an extreme form of destruction, but neglects to mention the racial-ideological motive behind this— again setting the tone for subsequent GDR writing, which systematic- ally understated the significance of racial ideology and the peculiar position of the Jews in the hierarchy of suffering experienced under Nazism.

The twelve years of the rule of Hitler fascism plunged Germany into the deepest catastrophe. Hated throughout the world and isolated from the democratic countries, Germany stands alone. *Nazism has thus shown itself to be the deadly enemy of the German nation.*

Fascist rule, which called itself 'national' and 'socialist', was neither one nor the other.

It was the open terroristic dictatorship of the most reactionary, chauvinist, and imperialist elements of German finance capital.

The Hitler party, the war party of the German armaments plutocracy, has carried its programme through to the end—to the catastrophe of Germany. It operated according to two principles which Hitler had already established in 1925 in *Mein Kampf*:

1. Transition from the trade policy of the past to the territorial policy of the future through the conquest of territory in the east, meaning war and the unleashing of racial hatred for a struggle of destruction against other peoples.

2. Abolition of all democratic popular rights, cruellest terror against all progressive popular forces, and introduction of the leadership principle, the rule of the most rapacious, war-mongering company and bank chiefs and parvenu Nazi bureaucrats.

'National Socialism' claimed to be beginning a new epoch of German history. In reality it was the regime of German monopoly capital in its declining phase. Nazism was the expression of the inability of the ruling class and its bourgeois parties to solve the crises and to secure the existence of the people. In face of the danger of being swept away by the German working people the armaments industrialists and bankers saw only one way of prolonging their rule: the total enslavement of their own people and the pillaging of the other peoples. [. . .]

Hitler began with hate propaganda against Versailles, although already at that time no more reparations were being paid. He solemnly announced that after the incorporation of the Saar region he had no more territorial demands. Hardly did the Saar region belong to Germany than Hitler demanded the unifying of all Germans, i.e. the conquest of those European countries anywhere in which groups of Germans live. He had Austria 'occupied militarily' as a strategic position for a further offensive towards the Balkans. German troops then fell upon the Sudetenland, accompanied by the declaration that Germany did not want to have Czechs. The military attack on Czechoslovakia followed on its heels. Hitler then 'terminated' his Non-Aggression Pact with Poland and occupied Poland in order to secure his rear for the planned attack on France and to extend forwards the assembly area for the planned war against the Soviet Union. Having declared that he had no claims on the Balkan countries, Hitler transformed the Balkan states into an assembly area against the Soviet Union. As Hitler finally treacherously attacked the Soviet Union, he explained this not with the proclamation in *Mein Kampf* on the 'conquest of territory in the East', but with the alleged 'threat of Bolshevism'. Only following the occupation of the Ukraine did Hitler and Goebbels speak openly of their war goal of suppressing and pillaging the Soviet Union and the other countries of Europe. And only in 1942 did the main interests behind the war, Röchling, Krupp, Vögler,* and their associates, come openly to the fore as members of the Armaments Council.

In attacking the Soviet Union militarily Hitler had provoked the strongest state power in the world and made possible the formation of the great anti-Hitler coalition. With the transgression of the borders of the Soviet Union began the path to catastrophe of the German army. Hitler had to lose the war, because he was fighting an unjust, imperialistic war of conquest against the Soviet Union and the other freedom-loving peoples.

Hitler Imperialism proved itself to be the darkest reaction. The people were degraded to being the retinue of the most reactionary circles of heavy industry and banking capital. A massive police and bureaucratic apparatus was erected to keep down the people. *For Hitler and his backers war against other peoples was simultaneously a weapon for the complete enslavement of the German*

* Leading industrialists.

workers and the German people. To a proportion of the working people he gave crumbs from the table of those riches robbed from other countries, in order to make the workers compliant for his war policy.

Fascist German imperialism hindered economic development in that it one-sidedly stimulated the armaments industry and limited the consumer goods industry to the detriment of the people.

Fascist German imperialism turned the state into a state of robbers and profiteers, in which the owners of large-scale capital and their Nazi support lived primarily from the plundering of foreign countries and the enslavement of other peoples.

Fascist German imperialism led to the deepest cultural decay, insofar as it made everything reactionary and anti-democratic in our history into the German way and suppressed all progressive aspects.

The bestiality and putrefaction of German imperialism found their expression in the destructive rage with which foreign countries were destroyed, in the cold-blooded destruction of the German homeland, in the eradication of members of other peoples, and in the destruction of the progressive forces within its own people. Destruction of humans in torturous dens and gas vans, through raping murder and in gas ovens—this characterizes decaying German imperialism.

[*Der faschistische deutsche Imperialismus* (East Berlin: Dietz, 1956), 99–100, 108–10.]

E. PATERNA, W. FISCHER, K. GOSSWEILER, G. MARKUS, AND K. PÄTZOLD

36   The Beginning of a New Stage of State Monopoly Development

> These passages are typical of the orthodox Marxist-Leninist scholarship produced in the former German Democratic Republic, above all in their insistence that the National Socialist regime represented the interests of 'monopoly capitalism'.

With the incipient consolidation of the dictatorship and the transition to the fascist one-party state, German finance capital acquired new conditions for the control and exploitation of the state apparatus which favoured them to a hitherto unknown extent. Following the elimination of parliament, the democratic and bourgeois parties and organizations, together with their press, the objectives and interests of the exploiter class, which were hostile to the masses, could be implemented far more effectively than had ever been possible under the bourgeois Republic—even in its final phase. The deep satisfaction at the elimination of democracy and the establishment of tyranny was shown by the declarations of greetings and allegiance which local and central organizations of capital addressed to the Hitler government. [. . .]

The general programme towards rearmament and war of the new rulers lay in the general interest of all monopolistic groupings and at the same time demanded their active cooperation. This fact formed the strongest driving force for the rapid and multiple building up of links between the economic and political hierarchy in Germany, which grew more and more. This basic situation was not contradicted by the fact that even the powerful figures in the German economy had to adapt to the new situation which they had desired and which had been brought about with their active support. Traditional methods of lobbying, old structures for influencing policy which had been developed and had proved effective in the years of the Weimar Republic were no longer suitable. Hitherto valuable links to bourgeois parties, groups of members of the Reichstag, and individual parliamentarians, contacts with civil servants in the state bureaucracy and in the party apparatuses had lost their previous usefulness. Into the foreground came now the exploitation of those relationships to fascist leaders and organizations which all factions of monopoly capital possessed. Hence with 30 January 1933 the bitter hidden struggle for dominant influence on the leading figures in the National Socialist party and regime intensified. Because the driving forces behind these conflicts remained hidden from the public, the rivalry struggles of the groupings of finance capitalism often appeared to be merely the jockeying for lucrative state posts of the 'old fighters'. In fact in 1933 and in the following years, the financial powers of the German Reich—usually unified but sometimes bitterly fighting on individual questions, triumphing and succumbing at the same time—controlled the economic policy decisions of the Hitler government. During informal discussions, in concerted deliberations, by memoranda and petitions, the bosses of the German economy prompted the legislative and executive bodies. Thus Gustav Krupp, chairman of the Reich Association of German Industry, was in continuous contact with the key people in the Berlin government quarter and the Munich 'Brown House'. The influence of the monopolies extended not only to decisions on questions of economic and finance policy, to the organization of the apparatus of the monopoly fascist state and appointments to its key positions, to the shaping of the fascist organizational structure, to repressing and containing social revolutionary endeavours, and to other domestic and foreign trade policy matters. Already in 1933, the strongest groups of finance capital were also trying to influence fundamental diplomatic decisions—right down to the details—in such a way that they would conform completely with their economic and political interests. [. . .]

However, many Germans, and particularly the adherents of National Socialism, saw Hitler and his subordinates as the sovereign rulers in Germany. West German historiography continues to foster this illusion, in which it is argued that a dictatorship of the National Socialist leaders had been established in the Third Reich over the economy too, and that the economy's powerful figures had fallen from being commanders to the commanded. In reality, state force as practised in the economy as in all other areas of society was directed towards consolidating the power of the big figures who had helped the National Socialists into government. The first legislative acts and practical measures in the area of economic policy prove this, unsystematic as they were overall, as provisional, experimental, and dilettantist as were their features. The traditional ruling economic powers acquired decisive influence over all economic regulatory bodies—the old as well as the newly created— such as the Reich Commissariat for Air Travel, the General Inspectorate of the Roads, the Reich Agency for Foreign Exchange Control, the Board of Foreign Trade, and even the Reich Committee for Foreign Travel. At the same time, as with every change of government and particularly with every change in a form of state into an exploiter state, individual shifts in power could occur. This also happened in 1933. Such shifts were determined by burdens from the so-called 'period of struggle', by the nature of the relation-ships with the now elevated NS leaders, by greater or lesser skill in intrigue and bribery. All in all, however, the traditional hierarchy in the economy was retained. This applied to industry and banks as well as to agriculture. Despite their rivalry, the monopoly groups were also brought together in the initial phase of the fascist dictatorship by a temporary factor: they joined forces in common defence against pressures within the fascist following which wanted to proceed from anti-capitalist propaganda to action against 'acquisitive capital'.

[*Deutschland 1933–1939* (East Berlin: Verlag der Wissenschafften, 1969), 47–50.]

ERNST GOTTSCHLING

37   The Fascist State: The German Example

Ernst Gottschling's treatment of the fascist state is indicative of a move towards a more differentiated analysis in the late years of the GDR. In place of a completely deterministic reading of the develop-ment of capitalism and its impact upon politics more emphasis was placed upon historical contingency, as scholars asked why this particu-lar crisis of capitalism, occurring in this particular context, led to this specific form of fascist regime. They also started to problematize, in their own language, the polycratic and charismatic aspects of the National Socialist regime. Nonetheless, the continued emphasis on the centrality of the 'monopoly bourgeoisie', and the marginality of the genocide of the Jews in their discussion, remained key weaknesses in GDR historiography until the end.

We can distinguish between two main forms of the bourgeois state of the twentieth century: the bourgeois democracy and the fascist regime. In this sense, Dimitroff named the coming to power of fascism as 'the *replacement* of one form of state of the class domination of the bourgeoisie—bourgeois democracy—by another: the open terrorist dictatorship'.[1] The bourgeois democracy and the fascist regime therefore possess common general features, but differ from one another at the same time. [. . .]

Moreover the fascist regime as one of the two main forms of the modern bourgeois state has emerged directly out of capitalist society. It is a product of its general crisis. Capitalist society is the soil on which the fascist state was able to come into being. It had provided it with the conditions for growth. As a result, the fascist state has major features in common with bourgeois democracy. Like bourgeois democracy, it is destined to serve the safeguarding of the positions of power of the last remaining exploiter class. However, the aggressive and misanthropic nature of the imperialist power system, the denial of any democratic conditions, finds its most visible expression in it. In accordance with the concrete power constellation after the First World War, the 'change from democracy to political reaction'[2] as a general trend of imperialism made it possible in the 1920s and 1930s for fascism to raise its head in Europe in a series of states.

The establishment of fascist dictatorships is not a historical inevitability. The only immutable law is the striving of the imperialist bourgeoisie towards the negation of democracy. This is why, after the First World War, fascism was far from coming to power in all European capitalist states. For example, a powerful anti-fascist popular front movement in the middle of the 1930s prevented it from establishing itself in France. Wherever the working-class movement was split in itself, the movement was no match for the onslaught of the forces of reaction, and despite self-sacrificing struggles—particularly of the Communists—it was not possible to avert the new form of bourgeois tyranny which had been set up in some way or another.

This most brutal form of the dictatorship of the monopoly bourgeoisie was therefore an expression of the weakness of the working class. At the same time it was an expression of the weakness of the bourgeoisie insofar as it showed itself incapable of further pursuing its economic and political objectives using the conventional methods of bourgeois democracy, and therefore took refuge in the methods of violence.

The main characteristics of fascist regimes in terms of the laws of state:

- abolition of bourgeois-democratic rights and freedoms; abrogation of the principles of formal equality and the inviolability of the individual;
- abolition or substantial erosion of the elected representative institutions;
- concentration and bureaucratic centralization of the entire executive power of the state into a few hands;

- far-reaching destruction of bourgeois legality; expansion of lawless despotism, use of organized terror;
- banning and ruthless persecution of the parties and other class organizations of the workers' movement (and also perhaps of the bourgeois parties other than the fascist ones) up to and including annihilation.

These most important features of fascist rule do not manifest themselves always and everywhere in the same way and to their full extent. However, in this combination they develop a new quality which distinguishes the fascist regime qualitatively from bourgeois democracy—within the framework of the uniform bourgeois type of state. [. . .]

The comment by Frick that 'the NSDAP had become the sole pillar of the state' reflects the characteristic tendency—particularly for fascist regimes—to 'unify' all socio-political forms of organization of the ruling class. As it is, the legal organization of their interests remains denied to the exploited classes and strata. The economic power of the most reactionary forces of monopoly capital is to be converted without frictional losses, and without allowing serious conflict within its own ranks. Nevertheless, this collides with the laws of the class struggle, so that this line can never be realized completely. Contradictions break out continually between its highly heterogeneous constituent elements and these run counter to the intended purpose. Nevertheless, in the process of converting the will of the economically powerful into the will of the state, this uniting of the spectrum of the socio-political organizational forms can, in the corresponding constellation, bring about a temporary and stronger 'alignment' in the interests of monopoly capitalism. Italy, Germany, and Spain provided examples of this during their fascist stages. [. . .]

Of particular importance was the 'unity' of fascist party and state in the practice of terror against political opponents in the establishment of the overall apparatus of suppression. From the very beginning of the Nazi dictatorship, the actions of the SA and SS against the working class and their organizations were not just accepted: murders were not only tolerated, but SA and SS were officially used in the first six months as 'auxiliary police'. The first concentration camp was set up by the SA and later taken over by the SS. The tendency towards amalgamation of fascist terror organizations with the state mechanisms of suppression led to the police apparatus gradually growing together completely with the SS.

The term 'SS state', which is used more and more frequently in this connection by historians and political scientists of the Federal Republic to characterize the fascist German state overall, must be subjected to critical assessment. With this, false ideas can be created which are suitable for distracting from the class-based underlying principles of the fascist power system. It is no longer German imperialism or German monopoly capital which is responsible for war and million-fold genocide, not capitalism as the social system, but only 'the SS'. For example, Broszat says of the armed SS units that they were 'the typical example of a special authority which was founded on party and state, but which had been detached from, and become independent of, both of these'.[3] This hypothesis favours the impression that the monopoly-capitalist relationships of power and rule had very little or nothing at all to do with Broszat's apostrophized 'special authority'. The theoretical error in this type of argument lies in the fact that the relative autonomy which the state like any other component of the imperialist political system possesses, within the confines of the specific functions of government which it fulfils, is exaggeratedly made absolute. The consequences of isolating a part of the superstructure, and its separation from the superstructure, are also that the mutual dependencies between its numerous parts, and the character of the superstructure as a system, and its complexity, can be lost.

['Der faschistische Staat: das deutsche Beispiel', in Dietrich Eichholtz and
Kurt Gossweiler (eds.), *Faschismusforschung: Positionen, Probleme, Polemik* (East Berlin:
Akademie Verlag, 1980), 73, 76–7, 89, 91.]

iii. The Regime as a Polycratic State

a. Wartime Émigré Writers

ERNST FRAENKEL

38   The Dual State

> Fraenkel sees the Nazi polity as a combination of the normative state,
> by which he means a rational state governed in accordance with
> clearly defined legal norms, and the prerogative state, by which he
> means a state which exercises power arbitrarily. The normative state is
> maintained as a precondition for the stability of capitalism, while the
> scope for arbitrary violence provided by the prerogative state enables
> the state to persecute its enemies. The escalation of the persecution of
> the Jews is particularly related to the growth of the prerogative state.
> However, for Fraenkel the ideology of community, and the pursuit
> of the perfect ethnic community via the persecution of the Jews,
> exists and occurs in order to obscure the reality of National Social-
> ism's role in restabilizing capitalism and reasserting class relations. It
> is Fraenkel's emphasis on the nature of Nazi polity as an evolving
> system whose pursuit of ideological goals was a product of the
> increasing erosion of legal norms and their replacement with a state
> of growing lawlessness which makes his work central to subsequent
> discussions.

By the Prerogative State we mean that governmental system which exercises
unlimited arbitrariness and violence unchecked by any legal guarantees, and
by the Normative State an administrative body endowed with elaborate
powers for safeguarding the legal order as expressed in statutes, decisions of
the courts, and activities of the administrative agencies. [. . .] In studying the
development of judicial practice as it is embodied in decisions, we learn that
there is a constant friction between the traditional judicial bodies which
represent the Normative State and the instruments of dictatorship, the agents
of the Prerogative State. By the beginning of 1936 the resistance of the
traditional law-enforcing bodies was weakened; thus the decisions of the
courts are an impressive illustration of the progress of political radicalism in
Germany. [. . .]

The National-Socialist state is remarkable not only for its supreme arbitrary powers but also for the way in which it has succeeded in combining
arbitrary powers with a capitalistic economic organization. One of the basic

propositions of Max Weber's works is that a rational legal system is indispensable for the operation of a capitalistic economic order. The German reformist labor movement took this proposition for granted. But we must then resolve the paradox of a capitalistic order continuing within a system under which there is no possibility of rationally calculating social chances. Rational calculation is not consistent with the rule of arbitrary police power which is characteristic of the Third Reich.

It may be argued, both by those who are sympathetic with and by those who are opposed to National Socialism, that the problem of the Dual State has no fundamental or permanent significance, that it is merely a transitory phenomenon. To those who think the Prerogative State transitory we point to the records of judicial proceedings in the Third Reich, which show that it is gaining rather than losing importance. And we would remind those who think that the Normative State has already disappeared or that, if it exists, it is a mere remnant of the old state and therefore doomed to oblivion, that a nation of 80 million people can be controlled by a plan only if certain definite rules exist and are enforced according to which the relations between the state and its members, as well as the relations between the citizens themselves, are regulated. [. . .]

Inasmuch as the legal protection of the Normative State is reserved only for the 'constructive forces of the nation' (Best), and inasmuch as the Jews are not considered a part of the German nation but rather are regarded as enemies, all questions in which Jews are involved fall within the jurisdiction of the Prerogative State. Although this was at first only a theoretical principle of National Socialism, it has now become the regular practice of the Third Reich. The completion of the subjugation of the Jews to the Prerogative State was realized at the moment it was resolved to extirpate the Jews from economic life.

As long as the Jews were allowed to operate small and middle-sized shops and to carry on certain types of industrial production, a contradiction existed in the National Socialist policy towards the Jews. Since the Jews at that time were more or less integrated into the capitalistic system of the Third Reich,[1] a strict application of the procedures of the Prerogative State would have disturbed the normal course of economic life. Therefore it was the task of the judiciary to guard the economy against disruption, even when that necessitated a certain protection of Jews. [. . .]

Once Jews had been eliminated from the economic life, it was possible to deprive them of all legal protection without adversely affecting the economic system. Thus, the progress of anti-Semitism forced the Jews beyond the outer limits of the Normative State. A decision in the field of commercial law may serve to illustrate this. A half-Aryan and half-Jewish partnership owned a cigar and cigarette store for sailors whose ships were docked in the free port of Hamburg. Although the Jewish partner had fought in the Great War and was by far the more efficient of the two partners, the Aryan partner applied for an immediate dissolution of the partnership. He gave as a reason that the district leader of the National-Socialist Party had threatened to confiscate the store licence because the 'economic activities of a non-Aryan firm caused unrest among the seamen.'[2] The application was successful. The behavior of the district leader conflicted directly with two orders issued by the Ministry of Economics. These 'orders did not influence the district leader,' as was demonstrated by his testimony. Even though the pressure brought by the district leader was in violation of the law, it had a legal bearing on the Jewish question. For according to the court 'the plaintiff cannot be expected to oppose the wish of the district leader . . . If he were to do so he would be opposing the general sentiment of the people and also the National-Socialist Party which rules the state.'[3] This decision marked the defeat of Dr. Schacht's policy and the triumph of his opponents among the party authorities. Since 1937, the situation discussed in the foregoing decision has frequently recurred. The party authorities, as agents of the Prerogative State, have used their power to exclude the Jews from all economic activities. [. . .]

German capitalism today requires state aid in two respects:

(a) against the social enemies in order to guarantee its existence, and (b) in its role as guarantor of that legal order which is the pre-condition of exact calculability without which capitalist enterprise cannot exist. German capitalism requires for its salvation a dual, not a unitary state, based on arbitrariness in the political sphere and on rational law in the economic sphere. Contemporary German capitalism is dependent on the Dual State for its existence. [. . .]

The legal order of the Reich is thoroughly rationalized in a functional sense for the regulation of production and exchange in accordance with capitalistic methods. But late capitalistic economic activity is not substantially rational. For this reason, it has had recourse to political methods, while giving to these methods the contentlessness of irrational activity. Capitalism at its best was a system of substantial rationality which, relying on the pre-established harmony which guided its destinies, exerted itself to remove irrational obstacles. When the belief in the substantial rationality of capitalism disappeared its highly rationalized functional organizations still remained. What is the character of the tension which arises out of the juxtaposition of disappearing substantial rationality and an overdeveloped functional rationality? [. . .]

Faced with the choice between substantial rationality and substantial irrationality, German capitalism casts its vote for the latter. It will accommodate itself to any substantial irrationality if only the necessary pre-requisites for its technically rational order are preserved. German capitalism has preferred an irrational ideology, which maintains the existing conditions of technical rationality, but at the same time destroys all forms of substantial rationality.[4]

If such substantially irrational ideology is useful to capitalism, the latter is ready to accept the programmatic aims of this ideology. This symbiosis of capitalism and National-Socialism finds its institutional form in the Dual State. The conflict within society is expressed in the dual nature of the state. The Dual State is the necessary political outgrowth of a transitional period wrought with tension.

[*The Dual State* (New York: Oxford University Press, 1941), pp. xiii–xv, 89–91, 205–8.]

FRANZ NEUMANN

39 Behemoth

The émigré Franz Neumann's rich and detailed study of the Nazi regime drew on the intellectual inspirations of both Marx and Weber; in addition, elements of the thought of left-wing inter-war commentators on fascism such as Otto Bauer and August Thalheimer are visible. Eschewing the model of the totalitarian monolith, Neumann's was the first influential attempt to analyse the structures of the regime in terms of a multitude of power blocs. Of particular interest are his attempts to analyse the autonomy of the political sphere and his discussion of the 'statelessness' of the Nazi 'state', both of which prefigure post-war discussions. In these passages he discusses the relationship of what he sees as the four key groups—party, army, bureaucracy, industry—but also reveals his interest in the charismatic function of Hitler as Leader.

These various strata are not held together by a common loyalty. To whom could they give it, after all? Not to the state, for it has been abolished ideologically and even to a certain extent in reality. The ideological basis on which the army and bureaucracy formerly rested has been destroyed. Adoration of the Leader is no adequate substitute, because the Leader's charisma will be completely deflated if he does not prove his worth, that is, if he is not successful. Furthermore, leadership adoration is so deeply contradictory to the process of bureaucratization and depersonalization that a mere postulation of a community integrated by a Leader is insufficient. Racial proletarianism is similarly dependent on final victory. As for such concepts as freedom and equality, it is doubtful if they were ever the basis for common loyalty, certainly not now. [. . .]

Nothing remains but profits, power, prestige, and above all, fear. Devoid of any common loyalty and concerned solely with the preservation of their own interests, the ruling groups will break apart as soon as the miracle-producing Leader meets a worthy opponent. At present, each section needs the others. The army needs the party because the war is totalitarian. The army cannot organize society 'totally'; that is left to the party. The party, on the other hand, needs the army to win the war and thus to stabilize and even aggrandize its own power. Both need monopolistic industry to guarantee continuous expansion. And all three need the bureaucracy to achieve the technical rationality without which the system could not operate. Each group is sovereign and authoritarian; each is equipped with legislative, administrative, and judicial power of its own; each is thus capable of carrying out swiftly and ruthlessly the necessary compromises among the four. [. . .]

But if National Socialism has no political theory, is its political system a state? If a state is characterized by the rule of law, our answer to this question will be negative, since we deny that law exists in Germany. It may be argued that state and law are not identical, and there can be states without law. States, however, as they have arisen in Italy, are conceived as rationally operating machineries disposing of the monopoly of coercive power. A state is ideologically characterized by the unity of the political power that it wields.

I doubt whether a state even in this restricted sense exists in Germany. It has been maintained that National Socialism is a dual state, that is, in fact, one state within which two systems are operating, one under normative law, the other under individual measures, one rational, the other the realm of prerogative.[1] We do not share this view because we believe that there is no realm of law in Germany, although there are thousands of technical rules that are calculable. We believe that the monopolists in dealing with non-monopolists rely on individual measures, and in their relations with the state and with competitors, on compromises which are determined by expedience and not by law. Moreover, it is doubtful whether National Socialism possesses a unified coercive machinery, unless we accept the leadership theory as a true doctrine. The party is independent of the state in matters pertaining to the police and youth, but everywhere else the state stands above the party. The army is sovereign in many fields; the bureaucracy is uncontrolled; and industry has managed to conquer many positions. One might say that such antagonisms are as characteristic of democracy as they are of National Socialism. Granting that, there is still one decisive difference. In a democracy and in any other constitutional system, such antagonisms within the ruling groups must be settled in a universally binding manner. The absolutistic king is the real legislator; in his person, legislation, administration, and the judiciary are actually unified. When his absolutistic claim comes into conflict with reality, the state disintegrates, as France before the Revolution of 1789 when the king was absolutistic in name only, while the power was exercised by the bureaucracy, the feudals, the courts, the high bourgeoisie, all of them bitterly fighting each other. In an absolute monarchy, in a constitutional system, and in a democracy, the compromises between various groups claim and have universal validity. If it is necessary for the state to co-ordinate and integrate hundreds and thousands of individual and group conflicts, the process must be accomplished in a universally binding manner, that is, through abstract rational law or at least through a rationally operating bureaucracy. Under National Socialism, however, the whole of the society is organized in four solid, centralized groups, each operating under the leadership principle, each with a legislative, administrative, and judicial power of its own. Neither universal law nor a rationally operating bureaucracy is necessary for integration. Compromises among the four authoritarian bodies need not be expressed in a legal document nor must they be institutionalized (like the 'gentlemen's agreements' between monopolistic industries). It is quite sufficient that the leadership of the four wings agree informally on a certain policy. The four totalitarian bodies will then enforce it with the machinery at their disposal. There is no need for a state standing above all groups; the state may even be a hindrance to the compromises and to domination over the ruled classes. The decisions of the Leader are merely the result of the compromises among the four leaderships. The ministerial council for the defence of the realm has no executive apparatus different from that of the four wings of the ruling class.

It is thus impossible to detect in the framework of the National Socialist political system any one organ which monopolizes political power.

The most advanced National Socialist lawyers, Reinhard Höhn[2] and Gottfried Neesse[3] reject the very concept of the state, and their ideas are widely approved.[4] Both reject the notion of the state's personality as a mere liberal construction, for if the concept of the state is accepted, they argue, those exercising its power are merely its organs. According to them, Germany's political power rests in the Leader, who is not the organ of the state but who *is* the community, not acting as its organ but as its personification. Neesse distinguishes three independent powers of equal rank, the party, the army, and the state (by which he means the bureaucracy); above them is the Leader 'acting not only for the people and in its place but as the people'.[5] He utilizes the party, the army, and the state as his tools only because he cannot do everything personally. We are not concerned with the sophistry of this new theory of transubstantiation implied by the identification of the Leader and the people, but rather with the consequences that derive from such theory. This advanced National Socialist constitutional theory, although attacked even by Carl Schmitt,[6] clearly admits that it is not the state which unifies political power but that there are three (in our view, four) co-existent political powers, the unification of which is not institutionalized but only personalized. It may be readily admitted that in constitutional law, as in any other field, the theories of the people's community and leadership are a mere shield covering the powers of the enormously swollen bureaucratic machines. But at least a grain of truth may be contained in these theories; to wit, that it is difficult to give the name state to four groups entering into a bargain. In fact, except for the charismatic power of the Leader, there is no authority that co-ordinates the four powers, no place where the compromise between them can be put on a universal valid basis.

But if the National Socialist structure is not a state, what is it? I venture to suggest that we are confronted with a form of society in which the ruling groups control the rest of the population directly, without the mediation of that rational though coercive apparatus hitherto known as the state. This new social form is not yet fully realized, but the trend exists which defines the very essence of the regime.

[*Behemoth: The Structure and Practice of National Socialism, 1933–1944* (London: Gollancz, 1942), 323–4, 382–4.]

b. The Regime and the Conservative Establishment

TIM MASON

40 The Primacy of Politics

Tim Mason combined the political commitment and theoretical underpinning of Marxism with the traditions of less explicitly theorized anglophone empiricism to produce a stimulating set of arguments concerning the ways in which an ideologically driven rearmament programme altered the relationship of the state to business and thus of politics to economics as Marxists would see it. Mason's writings remain central to any engagement with the history of the Third Reich.

One of the main concerns of Marxist historiography is the question of the relationship between economics and politics in the capitalist epoch. Its central thesis can perhaps be outlined as follows: the sphere of politics represents, by and large, a superstructure of the specific economic and social system, and has the function of perpetuating that system. The existence of an autonomous political realm with its own self-determining laws is usually denied by Marxist historians, and passing tendencies toward the development of such an autonomous political realm are ascribed to a temporary balance between the various social and economic forces. Politics as such are held to remain incomprehensible until those forces of economic and social development are elucidated which determine the forms and substance of political life. [. . .] But the overwhelming majority of works on the history of National Socialism which have appeared in the West are characterized precisely by a

rejection of this approach; they are all too quick to apostrophize the economy as just one more sphere of public life alongside many others, all of
which are supposed to have been subjected in like measure to the draconian
coercion of an uninhibited political dictatorship.[1]

On the other hand, modern historical research in East Germany is still
conducted in the light of Dimitroff's definition of fascism as 'the openly
terroristic dictatorship of the most reactionary, most chauvinistic and most
imperialistic elements of Finance-Capital'.[2] No doubt this definition had a
function and a degree of plausibility in 1935, but today, in view of the later
development of Nazi Germany, it can have only very limited use as a starting
point for an investigation, and can certainly not be regarded as an answer to
the problem of the relationship between politics and economics under
National Socialism.

It is not that the truth lies somewhere in the middle, between these two
interpretations (here almost caricatured). To anticipate the conclusion of this
still very provisional study: it was apparently the case that both the domestic
and the foreign policy of the National Socialist government became, from
1936 onward, increasingly independent of the influence of the economic
ruling classes, and even in some essential aspects ran contrary to their collective interests. *This relationship is, however, unique in the history of modern bourgeois
society and its governments; it is precisely this that must be explained.*[3] [. . .]

The seizure of power by the National Socialists would hardly have been
possible without the support of considerable circles in heavy industry during
the years of crisis. But in 1936 a great change in the structure of the German
economy became apparent, which, although inherent in the system, was not
apparently foreseen by any of the ruling groups. Whereas under the Weimar
Republic industrial expansion had been inhibited by a lack of liquid capital,
now, as a result of the rearmament boom, more tangible limits on production
became apparent—shortages of raw materials from abroad, and of labor.
These became the two decisive factors in the German arms and war economy and resulted in a far-reaching transformation of the economic power
structure; and hence in a change in the relationship between economics and
politics, industry and the state.

First, the lack of foreign exchange: rearmament demanded increasingly
large imports of raw materials but did not contribute to a corresponding
increase in exports,[4] added to this was the necessity of importing increased
quantities of foodstuffs for a population whose overall purchasing power
slowly rose with the disappearance of unemployment. If rearmament was
not to be scaled down, the only way to avoid a repetition of the foreign trade
crisis of 1936 was to bring about an immense increase in the domestic production of raw materials.[5] But to curtail rearmament was a *political* impossibility
for National Socialism. Schacht vainly urged this course of action, and the
leaders of the iron and steel industries gave him objective if not deliberate

support by opposing the exploitation of low-grade German iron ores. The chemical industry (i.e. IG Farben) became the new economic pillar of the Third Reich; it urged the large-scale synthetic production of vital raw materials such as rubber and petrol. The decision in its favor by the state leadership and the announcement of the second Four Year Plan in September 1936—in its final phase a personal decision by Hitler—finally broke the economic and political supremacy of heavy industry. At the same time this meant an end to the formation of any general and unified political will or representation of interests on the part of German capital, such as the Industrial Association (*Reichsverband*) had achieved under the Weimar Republic. In the forced rearmament of the last years before the war, the top industrial organizations lost their overall vision and control of the general economic development—all that was left were the special interests of individual firms, at most of certain branches of the economy. Heavy industry could no longer maintain that its interests were identical with those of German imperialism in general, let alone make good this claim. As a result of technological developments, rearmament, for which heavy industry had fought so bitterly and doggedly since 1919, marked the start of its own downfall. Heavy industry became the victim of its own expansionism. The direction and the dynamic of National Socialist economic and foreign policy after 1936 rested upon the domestic production of raw materials. Without the accelerated expansion of the chemical industry a European war could never have been risked in 1939.[6]

These structural changes were strengthened and speeded up by developments in the labor market. In this period of rapidly advancing rearmament, the public purse became the decisive factor in the shaping of the German economy. In 1939 the share of Reich expenditure in the gross social product was 34 to 35 percent, of which two-thirds went toward preparation for war. Armaments expenditure had increased fifteenfold in seven years.[7] Up to January 1939, public contracts were not subject to the price-freeze—on the contrary, most were calculated on a 'costs plus' basis. To increase his own profits, every contractor tried to obtain these orders and to fulfil them as punctually as possible, so that he would be taken into consideration when contracts were next distributed. In conjunction with the shortage of labor and raw materials brought about by the rearmament drive, this led to ruthless competition between firms, not for markets, which were well-nigh unlimited for the industries concerned, but for the basic factors of production. The firms which produced goods needed in the armaments drive had an advantageous position in the struggle for raw materials, and were, by virtue of the generously calculated estimates, able to attract workers by increased wages, to poach them from other firms. So a second rift was added to the division in the economy caused by the rise of the chemical industry: that between firms primarily engaged in the armaments drive and those working mainly for civilian or export markets. Although the coal mines, for example, were indispensable to the war economy as a whole, this industry exported about one-sixth of its production and did not deliver direct to the armed forces; consequently, wages remained low and miners left in increasing numbers for other branches of industry; the per capita productivity of the miners decreased and, at the outbreak of war, there was a shortage of coal which presented a severe threat to the army's rail transport program. The same factors threatened agricultural production too, whereas the building, chemical, and engineering industries enjoyed an unprecedented prosperity.[8]

This intensification and change in the character of capitalist competition contributed further to the disintegration of the political power of industry. Once freed by the terrorist methods of the Gestapo from the necessity of defending themselves against an organized working class, and relieved by the armaments boom from the necessity of planning and limiting production on a cartel basis, the propertied classes lost their sense of common interest. The collective interest of the capitalistic economic system dissolved progressively from 1936 to 1939 into a mere agglomeration of the short-term interests of individual firms, which, to reverse a dictum of Lenin, marched separately and fell together. It is not a gross oversimplification to say that they were bought by the government.[9] [. . .]

The historically typical behavior-patterns of capitalist economic policy and management had, thanks to the forced rearmament drive, become largely irrelevant; all that was left were the primitive and short-term interests of each and every firm.

In these conditions the large firms became larger still. For various reasons rearmament necessarily accelerated the process of concentration in the German economy. This tendency was particularly obvious in the electrical industry (Siemens), in the chemical industry (IG Farben), and in the iron and metal industries (Reichswerke Hermann Göring). By virtue of their position as monopolies and of the importance of their products for the war economy, these firms maintained close and direct contacts with the machinery of state and with the military; sometimes they even achieved through their personnel the equation of the interests of the state with those of their firms—leading managers were seconded to public economic agencies.[10] But rearmament also meant that the *direct* relationships with the agencies distributing contracts became more important for most big firms than *collective* dealings with the state through the channels of the economic and industrial organizations. Once the problem of the allocation of raw materials and labor had become crucial, this traditional form of collaboration between industry and the state became secondary. For all these reasons, which were inherent in the political and economic system, the capitalist economic structure largely disintegrated into its component parts. It was easy for the huge armaments firms to prosecute their immediate material interests, but, in the process, the responsibility for the overall economic system was left to a political leadership whose final arbiter, Hitler, saw in the economy merely a means for attaining certain vaguely outlined, yet in principle quite unattainable, political goals—goals which, though certainly of great incidental benefit to German industry, were not determined by economic considerations. Even the fact that Speer called in 'Leaders of the Economy' in 1942–1944, to help with the distribution of public contracts and raw materials, did little to alter this situation. The 'rings' and committees in his system of the 'self-government of German industry' were indeed run by industrialists, but they were responsible, in accordance with the *Führerprinzip*, only for ensuring that the rulings and plans made by Speer's ministry were carried out. They were given considerable freedom of action in this sphere, but on decisive questions of strategy, foreign policy, and war aims their opinion was not sought. Their competence was limited entirely to the question of *how* things were done." [. . .]

From 1936 onward the framework of economic action in Germany was increasingly defined by the political leadership. The needs of the economy were determined by political decisions, principally by decisions in foreign policy, and the satisfaction of these needs was provided for by military victories. The fact that numerous industrialists not only passively cooperated in the 'Aryanization' of the economy, in the confiscation of firms in occupied territory, in the enslavement of many million people from eastern Europe, and in the employment of concentration camp prisoners, but indeed often took the initiative in these actions, constitutes a damning judgment on the economic system whose essential organizing principle (competition) gave rise to such conduct. But it cannot be maintained that even these actions had an important formative influence on the history of the Third Reich; rather, they filled out in a barbaric manner a framework which was already given. The large firms identified themselves with National Socialism for the sake of their own further economic development. Their desire for profit and expansion, which was fully met by the political system, together with the stubborn nationalism of their leaders did, however, bind them to a government on whose aims, inasmuch as they were subject to control at all, they had virtually no influence.

['The Primacy of Politics', in H. A. Turner (ed.), *Nazism and the Third Reich* (New York: Quadrangle Books, 1972), 175–7, 184–7, 189–90, 192–3.]

41 The Nazi Empire 1938–1944

The giant chemicals combine IG Farben has often been cited both as evidence of the extent to which Nazi expansionism was strongly influenced by the interests of big business, and as an example of the complicity of industry in some of the Nazi regime's most appalling crimes—IG Farben not only exploited slave labour in the war, as did all other German companies, it even established production at Auschwitz-Monowitz, exploiting the labour of Jews under the most inhumane conditions imaginable. Here, Peter Hayes takes issue with the idea that IG Farben's business interests were served by an aggressive war of expansion eastwards, but suggests that pragmatic defence of business positions led the company to adapt to the evolving conditions of the 'New Order' as they emerged. The same pragmatism, combined with blinkered professional—rather than moral—concerns, led managers to collude unquestioningly in the deployment of slave labour.

There is little reason to suppose that IG Farben sought, encouraged, or directed the Nazi conquest of Europe.[1] If German expansionism was the lowest common denominator to which differences between industrial interests and Nazi ideology could be reduced during the 1930s, as much recent writing hypothesizes, Farben's leaders do not appear to have thought so.[2] To be sure, the combine's financial situation did mirror the overloading of the Reich's economic resources in 1938–9, an overloading that some scholars see as a precipitant of Nazi aggression.[3] But in partial contrast to the situation of German heavy industry, IG's stakes in autarky or military production were neither so complete nor so compelling as to have created the national crisis or militated in favor of conflict as a means of solving it.[4] [. . .]

For Farben, though perhaps not for Hitler, R. J. Overy's conclusion holds: 'Economic pressure was all for postponing general war in 1939, not for speeding it up'.[5]

Arguments to the contrary with regard to IG generally rely on cui bono logic, which deduces the combine's wishes from what it allegedly stood to gain by Nazi expansionism or ultimately did acquire.[6] Although the Nazi empire did offer IG chances to revise international cartel agreements in its favor and to cut into undesirable competition within Europe, the foreseeable net cash value of either change has usually been assumed and exaggerated. Even critical commentators have acknowledged that the firm's commercial interests did not require the seizure of foreign enterprises or sources of raw materials.[7] When pressed, IG had merely to begin production abroad. Though less lucrative than exporting, this policy was also less costly than war. [. . .]

German bellicosity entailed weighty risks and costs for the concern. Defeat meant, at minimum, a repetition of the reparations and loss of foreign subsidiaries and markets experienced after World War I; at most, the destruction of the firm's plants from the air and even of the corporation by the victors.[8] Nothing in IG's commercial position in 1939 suggested the need to play *va banque*. Even peaceful accretions to the Reich's territories or a successful war posed dangers for an enterprise already bothered by fragmentation and with ample reason to feel mistrusted in Berlin. In the event of conflict, Germany's gains would have to be very great, indeed, if they were to compensate for the export markets lost to competitors during the fighting or to new producers called into being by the interdiction of supplies from the concern. Meanwhile, each international flare-up rekindled demands that IG transfer its main plants from the Rhineland to the German interior, demands the firm resisted vigorously.[9] [. . .]

Once confronted with a series of territorial faits accomplis, however, IG Farben felt compelled to protect its interests within the new context. From the concern's standpoint, Nazi Germany's European conquests fell into two categories: those annexed to the Reich or clearly foredoomed to a semi-colonial status within a German imperium, and those to be vouchsafed a degree of independence, within the reorganized European economy, the so-called New Order.[10] Austria, the Sudetenland, the Czech Protectorate, Poland, Alsace-Lorraine, the Baltic states, and Russia made up the first group, The second group of nations consisted of France, the Benelux states, Norway, Denmark, and the Balkan lands. In neither area did the concern engage in indiscriminate aggrandizement or plunder. There was no 'rape of the European chemical industry.'[11] Only in Austria and Czechoslovakia did IG's takeovers account for more than 5% of any subject country's chemical output. So far as was politic, Farben refused involvement in fields that did not bear on its central interests, even when prodded by the Reich or presented with obvious opportunities for profit.[12] [. . .]

With regard to both acquisitions and plant closings, IG compiled a mixed record in occupied Europe. No more than in domestic policy making did the combine's motives and needs naturally coincide with those of Nazi planners; no more than at home did the concern's ability to extract advantages from the government's actions necessarily bespeak a preference for them; no more than within Germany could Farben consistently bend the authorities to its will or vice versa. Nazi planning for the Greater German Economic Sphere (Grossraumwirtschaft), like Hitler's foreign policy, was an unstable compound of ideological visions, political interests, and strategic requirements.[13] Though the firm's desires were sometimes compatible with Nazi policy, they also frequently conflicted with the Reich's fluctuating priorities, especially the short-range needs to cultivate loyalty in the occupied and allied states and to maximize their contributions to the German war effort. Not only German political interests, but also adroit actions by the subject nations, as well as astute lobbying by competing German and foreign firms, stymied Farben's already limited ambitions almost as often as not. Because IG learned to clothe its objectives in appeals to military necessity or the Party's goals, this ambiguous pattern has been easy to mistake or distort. [. . .]

There is no gainsaying Farben's disregard for the property interests of foreign nationals in occupied Europe. Nor, although IG usually achieved its successes without recourse to direct pressure from German authorities, can one deny that the concern occasionally took advantage of German military preponderance. These offenses against the victims and international law do not, however, add up to the conclusion that IG conspired to capture and exploit the chemical and related industries of Europe for German military purposes. [. . .] The combine reacted opportunistically and defensively to the regime's diplomatic and military triumphs, but IG did not foment them. Ironically, responding in this manner not only placed IG Farben on a criminal path, but also reinforced that mistrust of large corporations among Party and state functionaries that repeatedly attended the concern's efforts in the subjugated areas.

[*Industry and Ideology: IG Farben in the Nazi Era* (Cambridge: Cambridge University Press, 1987), 213–18.]

HANS MOMMSEN

42 The Civil Service in the Third Reich

> Hans Mommsen was one of the first post-war scholars to lay emphasis on the evolutionary and fluid nature of the National Socialist body-politic; his discussion of the relationship between the civil service and the regime shows that, from the outset, 'structuralist' historians conceived of the regime as being something more complex than just a fusion of rational state apparatus with irrational movement.

The question of the political role of the civil service in the Third Reich is most closely connected to the problem of the inner structure of the National Socialist regime and its changes [. . .] The inner structure of the National Socialist system [. . .] cannot be grasped if one wishes to see in it a power structure which was fixed for good or consolidated into a particular form. The constant reshaping of social and state institutions, and the continual new formation of bearers of authority with their own arbitrarily defined fields of jurisdiction not properly distinct from older state organizations, make it impossible to give general answers to the question of what the 'state' was in the National Socialist period, or to what extent the typical characteristics of the modern institutional state were lost in the disorderly pluralism of newly created or reformed state and political offices. One of the significant defining features of the Third Reich appears to us to lie precisely in the fact that its development was founded on a progressive parasitic decomposition of a pre-existing authoritarian state, and that it must logically decay within in the same way that the overextension of its diplomatic goals towards a great European empire of the 'German nation' simultaneously led to external catastrophe.

In such a context the question of the position of the civil service in and towards the National Socialist state is of particular interest. The state administration is a fundamental element of historical continuity and—this is also true for the Third Reich—the precondition for every long-term domestic and foreign display of power. The considerable initial successes of the Third Reich and its relatively high internal stability would not be explicable without the service and fulfilment of duty of a civil service loyal to the state. Alongside the armed forces the civil service represented the strongest traditional and stabilizing factor in the power structure of the Third Reich. From an overall point of view it was not really changed by the purging measures; there was indeed a comprehensive change of personnel in the senior positions of the state and communal administration, but its impact should not be overestimated. The homogeneity of the Reich ministerial bureaucracy remained essentially intact, the newly created ministries aside. The systematic exclusion of potential political opponents and Jewish civil servants in the subordinate administrative apparatus was limited in the main to reversing the steps towards 'republicanizing' the civil service, insofar as this had not already occurred under the presidential cabinet of von Papen.[1] A new formation of a National Socialist civil service corps from the bottom up did not get beyond the stage of individual consideration; personnel losses and the increased demand for personnel caused by the annexation of new territories and the administration of the occupied territories[2] set natural limits to such plans; at the same time, the period of National Socialist rule was too short for such a reformation to have been possible.

The National Socialist leadership was thus constantly obliged to work with the greater part of the old civil service apparatus. Fears of passivity or, as Hitler expressed it, 'sabotage' on the part of the administration proved themselves to be unjustified, however. Rather, the willingness of the mass of civil servants to serve the regime loyally cannot be doubted. The fact that the civil service offered no serious resistance to their 'coordination' was not only a consequence of the pseudo-legal takeover of state power;[3] the cabinet of 'national concentration', like the Prussian commissioner government before it, consciously used the German civil service tradition to eliminate parliamentarianism. The promised 'restoration of a national professional civil service' conformed to the wishes of the civil servants; the overwhelming majority of them welcomed the national 'uprising' because they hoped that it would lead to the liberation of state activity from the confusing influences of political parties and interest groups and a return to objective decision-making—a tendency which had already been suggested in Brüning's concept of the 'policy of objectivity'.[4] The civil service expected from the new government that they would regain the central position in the life of the state which they had occupied under the *Kaiserreich*. The majority of the civil service was therefore willing to accept short-term losses of rights which in the context of the reconstruction of the professional civil service appeared to them as a necessary evil.[5]

The path taken by the civil service from the situation of hopeful expectation in 1932–3 down to the last years of the war, during which it became the executor of increasingly irrelevant 'Führer orders' and downgraded to the role of a mere 'apparatus', was accompanied by the build-up of disappointment and embitterment over the lack of recognition for its achievements and the mistrust of its loyalty. The development of the professional civil service is closely connected to that process which led from the initial tightening of state authority to an increasing erosion of the jurisdiction, responsibility, and effective power of the general and domestic administration and thus to a diminution of the reputation and political role expectations of the civil servants in all departments. The history of the civil service in the Third Reich—whether it expressly supported National Socialism or served the state led by it out of an 'unpolitical' mentality—is overwhelmingly the history of its internal and external self-defence. On the one hand the aim of the civil service had to be to defend its monopoly as the executive organ of the government, and to resist the attempts emanating from the NSDAP and its organizations to take over the functions of state authority. On the other hand the civil service attempted to guarantee the legality of state activity against individual arbitrariness and the momentary whims of its leadership, in a system which impatiently piled on directives which were contradictory and all too often incompatible with the orderly activity of the state. Increasingly it saw its task in 'rescuing the chaos while it is still organized'.[6]

The civil service was thus in equal measure antagonist of the National Socialist leadership and executor of its wishes, which it was able to translate into laws and orderly administrative decrees and thus make them implementable and effective in the first place. The relationship between the political leadership and the ministerial bureaucracy thus depended less on the personal attitudes of the civil servants responsible than on the contradiction between the inherent imperatives characteristic of all modern administration and the decisions coming from Hitler and those around him which were taken in many cases without consideration for the state organism. Precisely among National Socialist state secretaries there emerged in some departments a resistance to excessive domestic radicalization, and there was a silent faction of senior civil servants, reaching into the legal department of the staff of the Deputy of the Führer, which opposed the progressive disintegration of the state apparatus and made not inconsiderable cuts in the legislative plans of the government.[7]

The role of the bureaucracy, conditioned by tradition and function, of being guardians of the substance of the state became even more clear under the conditions of the Third Reich, compared to which the interventions of social forces in the administrative apparatus under the Weimar Republic were child's play.[8] The fundamental precondition for this role was the maintenance of an expert, disciplined, and regular civil service. The civil service policy of the National Socialist period must thus be regarded from a dual perspective. On the one hand the question emerges of to what extent and with what means the system managed to gain the loyalty and trust of the civil service and to infuse it 'with National Socialist spirit', as was said at the time; on the other hand it needs to be clarified how far the personal and institutional integrity of the administration was maintained against the personnel and external interventions of the NSDAP and the apparatuses which had grown from their organisations. [. . .]

Following the takeover of power the NSDAP was faced with the problem—in both principle and practice—of fulfilling the assurances which had been made to the professional civil service and which Hitler had repeated on the occasion of the Enabling Act in the Reichstag. Two essentially heterogeneous political directions immediately emerged whose fundamental incompatibility was a key cause of the fact that the Third Reich— far from developing a rigid apparatus, in accordance with National Socialism's self-understanding—fell into a situation of institutional degeneration which in the long run reduced the effectiveness of the state apparatus and the system overall to a minimum.[9] The dualism from which the departmental and institutional pluralism of the National Socialist regime emerged is not adequately described by juxtaposing the terms 'party' and 'state' or 'movement' and 'state', as the party with its organizations and 'associated formations' which operated largely independently—above all the SA, SS, DAF, and the professional organizations—was already by 1933 no longer a closed, unitedly led overall organization. Further, it would be an inadmissible simplification not to describe as exponents of the party those National Socialists who, following the assumption of state offices on the level of *Oberpräsident* and *Reichsstatthalter*—consistently in 'personal union' with party offices—are to be seen as advocates of state interests. The comment made by the State Secretary in the Reich Chancellery, Kritzinger, on his colleague from the Party Chancellery, Klopfer, that 'he had a feeling for state order'[10] describes precisely the point at which the civil service, above all the ministerial bureaucracy, and not least Frick and at the outset Göring too, attempted to counteract the dynamism of the 'movement', which amounted to permanent revolution and the dissipation of the substance of the state.

[*Beamtentum in Dritten Reich* (Stuttgart: Deutsche Verlags-Anstalt, 1966), 13–16, 31.]

JANE CAPLAN
....

43 State Formation and Political Representation in Nazi Germany

> In this extract from one of the most perceptive studies of the evolu-
> tion of the internal structures of the state under National Socialism,
> Jane Caplan questions the extent to which the language used by vari-
> ous institutions within the polity to describe the system—and particu-
> larly their representations of each other—can be taken at face value,
> suggesting that the rhetorical strategies being deployed were them-
> selves reflections of the process of conflict within the system.

No one who has studied the intricacies and contradictions of policy in the Third Reich can doubt that this was a period of profound assault on the personnel and principles of the German administration. At one level, the fragmentation of the apparatus of government, the chronic conflicts in policy-making and execution, and the persistent violation of procedural norms resulted from the destructive impact of National Socialist rule on the standards of administrative practice previously developed in Germany. This was not because the Nazi leadership had adopted a deliberate strategy of displacing the existing structures of administration and substituting a set of newly legitimated institutions. The subversion of the civil service was piece-meal and *ad hoc*, the effect of incompetence, impatience, and neglect rather than the pursuit of a clear alternative vision. In what Hans Mommsen has described as a 'parasitic' process, the Nazi regime dissolved the institutional apparatuses it had inherited, and consumed the sources of its own survival as a functioning political system.[1] If this was an example of Nazi social Darwin-ism in practice, its effect was one of negative selection, the survival of the unfittest.

The image of a functionally rational state under assault by a dynamic and undisciplined party has become widely accepted in the historical literature, and it appears to be solidly confirmed by the archival evidence. [. . .] Yet it is questionable whether the character of Nazi administration can be best explained as the effect of a collision between the principles of bureaucratic rationalism on the one hand, and the elemental dynamism of the Nazi movement on the other. In acknowledging the existence of a party-state dichotomy in Nazi Germany, we need also to avoid confusing the func-tional rationality of the bureaucratic process with the substantive quality of bureaucratic rule as a political system.[2] The latter was at least as great an object of contention as the former; the defence of the civil service as a privileged institution in the structure of government was a political rather than an administrative issue. Moreover, the evidence from which historians have assembled the dualist construct, documents conflict not only between 'party' and 'state' as such, but also between rival representations of what was rational in administrative terms and what was chaotic. It was as part of this strategy of representation that particular interests depicted themselves and their actions as rational, and those of others as the opposite, irrespective of their real character and effects. It can be argued, in other words, that the dualism of state and party was over-determined by this partisan battle of representation, in which the two institutions figured respectively and polemically as embodiments of stability and dynamism, even when they were not. For it is perfectly clear to any outside observer that the Nazi party was quite as bureaucratic as the civil administration, and that, similarly, the civil administration was itself responsible for a good deal of the confusions and complexities of the Nazi state.[3] The assignation of the bureaucracy to the category of administration and order, and of the Nazi party to that of politics and disorder, needs, therefore, to be stripped of its rhetorical associations in the documentary representations from which the historical narrative is drawn. Of course there were real clashes between bureaucracy and party, administration and politics; but there were also powerful motives among the protagonists for perpetrating and exaggerating this very set of contrasts, and for suppressing or ignoring contrary evidence. Partisans of bureaucratic rule could legitimate their own status and press their arguments home by magnifying the degree of external pressure on the bureaucratic process; conversely, a party mired in its own bureaucratic apparatuses and procedures had good reason to divert criticism elsewhere. [. . .]

Two rhetorics dominated the official discourse about governmental structure and civil-service policy in Nazi Germany: the rhetoric of unity, concentration, and rationalization, and the rhetoric of crisis. These represented the polarities of administrative experience: on the one hand, an aspiration for clarity of structure, decision-making, and policy execution; on the other, a recognition that this had entirely eluded policy-makers, and that the ostensible bearers of the structure were themselves in equal disarray. Men like Frick, Schulenburg, Pfundtner, Lammers, and Killy, along with many of their lesser colleagues like Seel or Fabricius, looked to the Prussian tradition for their models of the administration and its personnel. At the same time, they saw National Socialism as the bearer of a revived national unity that would also necessarily require and rebuild the authority of the civil service. Other senior officials, among them ministers like Popitz, Krosigk, and Gürtner, were perhaps always more sceptical of the promises of National Socialism, but they could nevertheless accept this vision of national recovery, even if they preferred to keep their distance from the party in whose name it was to be achieved. Yet between them, these representatives of Germany's politico-administrative elite presided over the disintegration of their own ideals, in so far as these were embodied in the institutions and practices of the civil administration. Schulenburg had been right to argue that the National Socialist state could not dispense with the help of the bureaucracy in 1933. But what he saw as a principled and collaborative effort of renewal, in which a political division of labour assigned one set of tasks to the party and another to the civil administration, fast collapsed into a morass of mutual rivalries and suspicions. The conflicts this engendered were evidence not only of the *differences* between the two institutions, but also of their *shared* characteristics as bureaucratic apparatuses. They also demonstrated the practical impossibility of differentiating between 'leadership' and 'administration' in a political system which vigorously rejected the separation of powers.

[*Government without Administration* (Oxford: Oxford University Press, 1988), 322–4, 325.]

DIETER REBENTISCH AND KARL TEPPE

44 Administration versus Human Leadership

The following summary of the main processes of internal change within the National Socialist polity and their impact upon the bureaucracy represents a judicious and balanced summary of the state of research in the mid-1980s, by which point the structuralist-intentionalist debate had reached its heights (and its limits).

Both those interpretations which emphasize the totalitarian character of the Führer State and those which prefer to speak of a polycratic power structure with the tendency towards cumulative radicalization agree that a high degree of bureaucratization and, in the police and SS sphere at least, a bureaucratic perfectionism was characteristic of the way in which the regime functioned. There is also no fundamental dispute over the fact that the traditional bureaucratic and military elites entered into a partial and temporary alliance with National Socialism.[1] Indeed, during the period of the Third Reich there was a great upsurge in bureaucratization, while at the same time the exponents of the regime, first and foremost Hitler, never tired of subjecting the bureaucracy, and its claims to regulate, to derogatory criticism and mockery over and over again. The regulation of the individual via procedures and directives took on totalitarian forms without one being able to say that National Socialism had been a bureaucratic form of rule. The bureaucracy, with its claims to regulate and mentor, proved itself to be an excellent instrument of rule because it functioned smoothly as an administrative executive authority but could also be used for political purposes.

If it has now become commonplace in recent literature to speak of the ministerial bureaucracy with a certain amount of generalization and to see in it a compliant and inventive agent of the National Socialists,[2] then such formulations show that the task of a differentiated analysis of the history of the administration still remains. The work of precision will first have to be undertaken in relation to the different stages of development. The administrative history of the Third Reich cannot avoid careful periodization. The toleration, which was rooted in the orientation towards authoritarian presidential regimes, of the National Socialist ideological movement by the conservative ministerial bureaucracy[3]—which for its part hoped for the eventual establishment of etatist-bureaucratic structures—during the seizure of power experienced its first shock with the murder of the SA leadership, the death of Hindenburg, and the creation of the constitutional basis of Hitler's dictatorship in the late summer of 1934. The following phase of relative stability, in which the constitutional status quo of 1934 appeared to be consolidated by rationalization, the creation of norms, and bureaucratic perfectionism, and during which the NSDAP allowed only the partial erosion of administrative order, ended with the unleashing of the war. Its beginning marked a deep caesura for the constitutional structure of the Führer State.

The self-image of the NSDAP as a community of struggle, and the ideological dogma that the 'eternal law' of struggle determined the rise and fall of peoples and thus simultaneously the biological value and historic position of its racial core, meant that the conditions of total engagement in war appeared as those political conditions in which National Socialism could realize itself more than in any other way of life. If National Socialism was a system of rule in permanent motion, and if ever more office-holders with arbitrarily defined jurisdictions overlayered the pre-existing administration, then it was unavoidable that additional impulses for the reformation of the administration would be unleashed by the war. The intensified line of domestic policy following the outbreak of war, characterized by the exclusion of those 'harmful to the *Volk*', by the 'consolidation of Germandom', by the murder of the mentally ill, and by the deportation and destruction of the Jews, makes it clear that this war did not only have an expansionist military dimension. The National Socialist leadership grasped the opportunity at the same time to carry out domestically a racial-*völkisch* and ideological war, a simultaneous 'second stage of the National socialist revolution'.[4] It can be shown clearly that the dismantling of the traditional bureaucracy began, significantly, in the annexed areas, and to a certain extent in the colonized areas, and then worked back into the territory of the Reich. [. . .]

Abolition of the parliamentary organs in the Third Reich created free space for the administration, i.e. liberation from public control. However, this element of autonomy was in turn absorbed by the claims to political organization and leadership on the part of the new leaders. At the same time the competing effects of diverse party organs on the administration also opened for the latter the chance to manoeuvre, to seek allies, and to play one against the other. To the extent that the political leadership loosened the reins, i.e showed weaknesses in its powers of political integration, organizational possibilities opened up for the administration. The ostensibly centralist organization of the administration in the Third Reich was in reality punctured by varying forms of partial authorities, regionalisms, and the satrap politics of the National Socialist *Gauleiters*. Under these structural conditions an observation of the actors as individuals reveals easily that some of the conflicts of jurisdiction which are usually cited as evidence for the dualism of party and state were in reality conflicts between rival National Socialist functionaries. On the other hand, it is also clear that new office-holders who came from the party and now became mayors or county prefects, *Regierungspräsidenten* or *Oberpräsidenten*, could be the best defenders of ordered administration against the activist National Socialist offices. Even within the NSDAP, if one thinks for example of the State Secretary in the Party Chancellery, Gerhard Klopfer, young, qualified, professional civil servants rose to top positions and would have been equal to all demands in the analogous jobs in the state administration.

The following must finally be considered when judging the role of the bureaucracy in the National Socialist state. If the thesis is true that bureaucrats are inclined to conserve inherited power structures, then just in terms of its self-image the administration must have had a distanced relationship to the National Socialist system and above all to the competing apparatuses of the party. On the other hand preservation is only possible via a more or less flexible accommodation to the change of overall circumstances. The ambivalence arising from these considerations make it necessary to examine closely in each case how far this accommodation went and how strong the conservationist tendencies were. The reaction was obviously very different in the individual ministries.[5] Sometimes this depended upon the leadership of the ministry. While the State Secretary in the Reich Finance Ministry, Fritz Reinhardt,[6] who was at the same time the relevant official for the Reich finances in the Party Chancellery, protected the ministry from influence from within the ranks of the NSDAP, Wilhelm Stuckart, as head of the Department for Constitution and Administration in the Reich Ministry of the Interior, appears to have been far more open to the policy of the NSDAP towards civil servants. At the same time he left the civil servants of the 'old school' considerable conceptual room for manoeuvre. Pure revolutionary ministries, on the other hand, such as Goebbels' Ministry for Popular Enlightenment and Propaganda, were completely and utterly a domain of the Party. [. . .]

[*Verwaltung contra Menschenführung im Staat Hitlers: Studien zum politisch-administrativen System* (Göttingen: Vandenhoeck & Rupprecht, 1986), 15–19.]

45 The Army and the Third Reich

> The army had been a key institution in the Nazi seizure of power and had had high expectations of the regime. However, during the Third Reich its experience was one of progressive marginalization as a separate power centre within the regime—by the outbreak of the war at the latest it had become merely the executor of Hitler's orders. In the article from which the following passages are taken, Klaus-Jürgen Müller surveys the reduction of the army from a political elite to a functional elite, examining in particular the 'turning point' of 1938.

Hitler's government was formed in 1933 on the basis of an *entente* between elements of the traditional elite and the leadership of the Hitler movement. Within this *entente* the Reichswehr had a unique position and carried special weight.

Each of the parties to it saw particular advantages for themselves and their specific interests. The old elites were no longer capable of maintaining their traditional position alone or of realising their political objectives inside or outside Germany. They lacked the necessary social base. And Hitler—or so it seemed to the advocates of an alliance with the National Socialists—could bring them that essential mass base, thereby solving the problem of integration for them. For his part, Hitler was forced to the realisation that he could never achieve power on the strength of his own support. 9 November 1923 had proved the impossibility of a *coup d'état*. The elections of November 1932 demonstrated the impossibility of obtaining power through a parliamentary majority. The mass movement had brought him to the threshold of power: but only the old power elites, which still held a decisive position in the power apparatus, could help him cross this threshold. Only they could help him to a share in power. [. . .]

Thus, the army appeared at the time to be not merely a strong bulwark, not merely a political counterweight to the mass populism of the Hitler movement. It appeared to be once more an autonomous political factor. Precisely for this reason the overwhelming majority of the officer corps—or so it appears—were in agreement with the so-called 'National Coalition', despite minor reservations. The new regime appeared to promise what the old elites no longer felt capable of achieving alone: the nationalist integration of the overwhelming majority of the nation and the suppression of the rest. In the first place, the Reichswehr thus escaped the struggle for power within Germany which was feared: it could once again regard its position, which had become increasingly precarious, as secure. Secondly, the integration of the nation under Hitler's government seemed to grant the preconditions for a comprehensive solution to the problems posed by mechanised industrial war-fare. Thirdly, there was a desire to believe that the leadership role of the army had been secured by the supposed re-establishment of its quasi-autonomous political power. The domestic political conditions for the realisation of the foreign policy objectives of a great power appeared to have been met.

It was for these reasons that the leaders of the new Reichswehr supported Hitler in the consolidation of the new regime.[1] They looked on 'neutrally', i.e. supportively, as he first suppressed the left, then eliminated the bourgeois parties, centralised the political and administrative structure of the Reich and so appeared to realise the political ideal of an authoritarian, centralised state. The politically privileged position of the army seemed assured, but it was relieved of the task, which was in any case beyond it, of giving that position a social and political foundation. [. . .]

In historical perspective it was not 1933 but 1938 which proved to be the decisive break in the relationship between the military and politics in Germany. Despite altercations between representatives of the party and the military and despite the increasingly totalitarian character of the regime there had been until then a clear continuity in the political demands of the military elite. [. . .]

In the spring of 1938, however, Hitler did away with the last vestiges, institutional and in personnel, of traditional Prusso-German dualism. He removed the War Minister and the commander-in-chief of the army, together with a large number of generals, from their posts and from active service in what came to be known as the Blomberg-Fritsch crisis. A few months later he banished the chief of the army general staff, General Beck, to the wilderness. In this way the personnel who embodied the army's political perspective and its traditional view of itself were eliminated.[2] The institutions which embodied these perspectives were emasculated too in 1938, when Hitler assumed direct supreme command of the armed forces. From then on he exercised control by using the supreme command of the armed forces as his personal military staff—his 'Maison militaire'—and by granting his immediate subordinate, the Chief of the Supreme Command of the Armed Forces, many of the functions of the Minister of Defence. From that point it was impossible for the military elite, bereft of representatives at the top, to play an independent, politically meaningful role even as an institution. The break in the historical development of the dualist principle of Prusso-German military history is evident. [. . .]

The leading figures of both the army and the armed forces supreme command now had neither the will nor the ability to represent or apply the concept of an independent role for the army in the state. They no longer aspired to participate in fundamental decision-making or consequently in the power of the state. They confined themselves strictly to professional military matters and to executive functions on the instructions of the head of state and supreme commander of the armed forces—Hitler—who alone issued political directives and assumed responsibility, and who had become their immediate, highest superior. [. . .]

Within the framework of German military history the process we have outlined whereby what had once been a *political* elite was transformed into a merely *functional* elite can be termed 'revolutionary' in the sense that it brought about a fundamental break with historical tradition. In the Third Reich the Prusso-German officer corps became for the first time a purely executive agent of the state under political control. Such would certainly be its normal role under a liberal democratic constitution, whatever one might add as regards problems of the business state and the garrison state.[3] But this 'normality' had never existed in the Prusso-German empire or in the Weimar Republic. Prusso-German dualism had remained the hallmark of relations between the politicised armed forces and civilian politics throughout the changes of the time. At first glance it seems a paradox of history, that it should have been the Führer of a totalitarian regime who effected such a transformation in the relationship between the two forces as to correspond with liberal democratic constitutional principles. One could scarcely claim that constitutional normality had been achieved, however. It was rather a case of a bringing to heel of a totalitarian subjugation, to which the traditional military elite succumbed in its co-operation and collaboration with the leader of the National Socialist mass movement. The profound changes that had been wrought in the state, in society and in the economy from the onset of industrialisation, through the world war and the great inflation, up to the international economic crisis, may well have paved the way for this radical change in the history of the Prusso-German military elite, but they had not brought it about on their own.

Once he had achieved power it became possible for Hitler to establish an effective counterweight to the old leadership elites by virtue of the gravitational pull of his mass movement and the occasional consolidation of his rule by plebiscite. The old leadership elites were to a large extent mentally paralysed in their reaction by the apparent ability of Hitler's regime to enable them to realise their political aims at home and abroad; with eyes fixed on the supposed identity of their objectives they were blind to the fact that this identity was at best only partial and that Hitler's wider aims were inevitably destructive not only of their position but also of the state itself. The expectation of the military elite that, in alliance with Hitler, they could regain their lost power base among the people and solve long-standing problems of integration and mobilisation was bound to be disappointed. In fact the opposite occurred. Hitler represented for many Germans, at least for a time, the great alternative to traditional class society. He seemed able to fulfil the political and social desires of a large part of a nation that had been led for so long by entrenched power elites. He was capable, it seemed, of bringing about effective equality in the face of traditional privilege, and setting free the dynamic forces of modernisation, while at the same time offering protection against the frustrating consequences of that modernisation as well as securing property and authority.[4] In the face of these expectations, held by wide sections of the population, and the faith reposed in the promises of the Nazi regime, the old leadership elites did not have a chance, even if the expectation and the faith turned out to be a dreadful illusion.

[*The Army, Politics and Society in Germany 1933–1945* (Manchester: Manchester University Press, 1987), 29–31, 35–7, 40–1.]

WILHELM DEIST

46   The *Gleichschaltung* of the Armed Forces

Those officers of the *Reichswehr* who had supported Hitler's succession to power had done so partly out of the hope that the *Reichswehr* would be able to regain its traditional position 'above politics'. However, as this passage argues, the logic of a one-party state with totalitarian claims demanded the opposite—the subordination of the armed forces to the political leadership. The Blomberg–Fritsch crisis of February 1938 marked the completion of this process of subordination; nonetheless, although the army was keen to protect its autonomy *vis-à-vis* the SA and SS, its leadership was itself responsible for some of the subordination process. Indeed, as Wilhelm Deist argues, the fact that the armed forces' leadership shared many of the aims of the National Socialist regime led it to active complicity in the transformation of the military into a 'National Socialist *Wehrmacht*'.

At the beginning of February 1933 Blomberg had summed up his intentions in a talk to Reichswehr commanders. He considered it his task to maintain the Reichswehr as an 'instrument of power above party politics, to underpin the Wehrmacht by making the population fit to fight (*wehrhaft*)', and 'to build up the Wehrmacht with all possible means to make it a usable instrument for preserving national security'.[1] The idea of the army being 'above politics', which Blomberg deliberately emphasized in the changing situation of February 1933, not only reflected a traditional position but was also intended, in conjunction with the aim of making the population battle-ready, to express the attitude of the military leaders towards the new political forces outside the executive. The army's duty to remain 'above politics' also implied maintaining a clearly reserved attitude towards the dominant political party, the NSDAP. In Blomberg's opinion, abandoning this position would mean a 'decline to the level of a party army (*Parteitruppe*)' and destroy the foundations on which the Reichswehr had been built up. This ingrained attitude became difficult for the military leaders to maintain when, in the summer of 1933, it became clear that in future the state would be controlled not by several but by only one, totalitarian party. Remaining above politics in a one-party state was not only a logical, but also a political impossibility. For this reason Blomberg abandoned his earlier attitude as early as the beginning of March 1933 and called upon his commanders to 'support the national revolution' without reservation.[2] Moreover, he lost no opportunity to point out that the leaders of the NSDAP deserved the confidence of the Reichswehr, as they represented the best traditions of Germany's past and took those traditions as guide-lines for their actions.[3] The domestic and foreign-policy decisions of Hitler's government in 1933 supported Blomberg's assertions. In spite of their sceptical attitude towards the party and their criticism of NSDAP political forms and methods, the officer corps could not maintain the reserve implied by the principle of remaining 'above politics' towards a movement whose domestic and foreign-policy goals largely agreed with the national traditions embodied in the Reichswehr itself. The 'partial identity of aims'[4] required a new definition of the relationship between the armed forces and the state.

In his speech on the anniversary of his coming to power, Hitler himself coined the expression that the state was 'supported by two pillars', politically by the 'national community' (*Volksgemeinschaft*) organized in the National Socialist movement, and militarily by the Wehrmacht.[5] This two-pillar theory, whereby Hitler also declared the Wehrmacht to be the 'sole bearer of arms' in the state, agreed completely with the ideas of the Reichswehr leaders and the officer corps in general. It implied the recognition of the independence of the armed forces within the state, and also seemed to accept the military's claim to a decisive influence in political matters. But the symbolism of the two pillars also expressed the competitive element in the relationship between the military and the Party and its organizations as the 'sole embodiment of the political will of the nation'. As Hitler was not only the head of state but also the undisputed leader of a totalitarian political movement, it was inevitable that sooner or later the armed forces would come to be regarded no longer as part of the foundation of the state but rather as merely its instrument, and would thus forfeit the special degree of influence and independence on which the two-pillar theory was based. This point was reached in 1938. Thereafter, the armed forces constituted a 'National Socialist Wehrmacht' with Adolf Hitler as its commander-in-chief.

The political history of the Wehrmacht in 1933–9 is usually described against the background of the important political role played by the Reichswehr in the Weimar Republic. But it should not be overlooked that the special circumstances under which the Reichswehr had been an important factor in German domestic politics disappeared more or less rapidly after 1933. Above all, within little more than two years the military leaders and the entire officer corps were freed from all the domestic- and foreign-policy restrictions that had prevented them from performing their military functions before 30 January 1933. Concentration on a rapidly increasing number of military tasks led to a decline in political activity within the Reichswehr and also in its domestic political influence.

In January 1934, when Hitler formulated his two-pillar theory, the Reichswehr was still an important factor in domestic politics and even necessary for the stability of the regime, as Röhm's SA threatened not only the position of the military but also, implicitly, that of the party itself. In the eyes of the Reichswehr developments from the 'seizure of power' until the Röhm affair at the end of June and the beginning of July 1934 confirmed the wisdom and success of the political course pursued by Blomberg and especially Reichenau. The Reichswehr's ideological acceptance of the new regime— which the officer corps generally found quite easy, since it emphasized their own strongly national and military traditions and convictions—had been rewarded, as they saw it, with the elimination of their dangerous rival for the position of 'sole bearer of arms' within the state.

Blomberg had not only vigorously promoted the 'opening' of the Reichswehr towards the National Socialist regime[6] in speeches and articles; he had also taken appropriate measures, ranging from permission for the Reichswehr music corps to play hallowed National Socialist tunes to acceptance of the 'Aryan clause' for the Reichswehr.[7] To this last measure may be added the Reichswehr's active participation in the elimination of its rival Röhm and his SA, its unprotesting acceptance of the murders on that occasion of Generals Schleicher and Bredow, the constantly intensified 'national political indoctrination courses' at all levels, and above all the administering of the Wehrmacht oath of loyalty to the person of Adolf Hitler, the 'Führer of the German Reich and nation', on the day of Hindenburg's death—a measure taken on the initiative of Blomberg and Reichenau.[8] With all these developments, the process of 'adjustment' and 'opening up' amounted to an almost complete ideological integration of the Wehrmacht into the National Socialist regime. Blomberg consistently promoted what he called 'this *Gleichschaltung* with the National Socialist philosophy'[9] until his dismissal at the end of January 1938. He refused to be deterred either by frequent conflicts with individual groups within the party or by the end of the Wehrmacht's status as 'sole bearer of arms' when Hitler sanctioned the creation of three armed SS regiments.[10]

['The Rearmament of the Wehrmacht', in Militärgeschichtliches Forschungsamt (ed.),
Germany and the Second World War, i: *The Build-up of German Aggression* (Oxford:
Clarendon, 1990), 520–2.]

47 The *Wehrmacht* in the National Socialist State

The theme of complicity in the ideological penetration of the armed forces is developed further by Manfred Messerschmidt, who examines the infusion of the army's personnel policy and propaganda with National Socialist ideology. Application of National Socialist ideology may have been partly motivated by the desire to prove the army's reliability and to sustain its position against the SA and the SS, but it was at least partially a product of conviction among the leadership of the armed forces. In any case, as Messerschmidt argues, far from enabling the army to retain its independence, it led to ever deeper complicity in the translation of Hitler's goals into reality.

The armed forces and the National Socialist state underwent considerable changes between 1933 and 1945. This is also true of the relationship between the two. This process can be traced in important areas of politics; it can be traced most revealingly in foreign, domestic, and armaments policy, the areas of prime interest for the armed forces. More important for the military elite, however, became their relationship to Hitler, especially during the war. It was characterized by the constantly declining influence of the military leadership, even in military and strategic questions, by accommodation to the will of the Führer, and by cooperation all the way to catastrophe.

Such a catastrophe cannot be understood by starting at the end. From the perspective of 1933 the coming opportunities of armed power and the associated political prospects for the German Reich represented something thoroughly positive for the leadership of the armed forces. For years, its political efforts had focused on overthrowing the armaments restrictions imposed by the Versailles Peace Treaty and thus of attaining equality of rights in the field of armaments and of implementing the 'lessons of the World War'. The fact that this could be pursued more resolutely and energetically under Hitler was a key and cementing precondition for the alliance between the military and National Socialism which was not to disappoint Hitler. [. . .]

When the leadership of the armed forces entered its alliance with Hitler under allegedly reliable preconditions, the issue of its official attitude to the 'Jewish question', to 'International Jewry', and to the treatment of the few Jewish officers and soldiers in the armed forces could only be a matter of time. The armed forces were aware of the determinedly malevolent agitation of the NSDAP towards the Jews and of the pronounced intention of the party to remove them from public life. Senior military personalities such as General von Fritsch, head of the Army Staff from 1934 to 1938 and finally commander-in-chief of the army, were themselves convinced anti-Semites, in the tradition perhaps of General Erich Ludendorff. This name can be taken as a symbol for the transition within the military from traditional to modern, racially motivated anti-Semitism.

If we examine the early years of cooperation between the armed forces and NSDAP, then we must recognize that, despite the numerous points of political convergence—which cannot be discussed out of existence by pointing out that the coarse manners and the language of National Socialist functionaries were not very congenial to the officer corps—the path to the Holocaust was neither open nor recognizable. On the other hand, these early years also reveal something of the inability of the armed forces to influence, still less to change, Hitler's political will. Their political and social values offered no starting points for achieving this, and the strategy of gaining influence through participation created impetus on National Socialism's terms. Numerous relevant statements exist in orders and decrees of the armed forces' leadership which confirm this, such as, for example, a decree of Blomberg to the officers' corps of 24 May 1934[1] which relates to the exclusion of Jewish soldiers. There it says: 'National Socialism bases the law of its action on the vital needs of the entire people and on the duty of communal work for the entirety of the nation. It is based on the idea of the community of blood and fate of all German people. It is also incontrovertible that this law is and remains the basis for the service work of the German soldier.'

In the field of education, everything led in the direction of the political soldier. As early as summer 1933 an article appeared in the *Militär-Wochenblatt**entitled 'The Soldier and the National Revolution',[2] which spoke of the 'insoluble bond between People-Race-State, and thus of the necessity of higher human breeding and therefore of the combating of those who are alien and harmful to the race'. The author, who can be supposed to have come from close to the Armed Forces Office, saw as the goal the 'total state', as the highest form of racially and therefore ideologically kindred people.[3] The head of this office, von Reichenau, had already declared upon assumption of office that the armed forces had never been 'more identified with the state' than at that time.[4] And of the things which this state set in motion—the boycott of the Jews, the Nuremberg Laws,[5] the pogrom of 9 November 1938—nothing caused the armed forces to reconsider their political stance. To the contrary, anti-Semitic and racial-biological themes were provided for in national-political education. In 1937 two issues of the 'Directives for Instruction in Political Current Affairs' were devoted to racial policy and to the 'Jewish Question'.[6] They presented the official position of the Armed Forces Office and thus of the Supreme Commander of the Armed Forces, and cannot therefore be dismissed as the scribblings of individual officers. They are to be seen in the context of the attitude of the armed forces to the 'Jewish

* A weekly military news-sheet.

Question', in whose 'solution' they later played a cooperative role in Russia and Serbia with brutal consequences. These official armed forces' teaching guidelines had the following to say on the 'Jewish Question': 'during the time of struggle there were many people's comrades—and there still are some today—who were of the view that the treatment of this question represented an injustice towards a particular class of people, and who said that the Jews were after all people too, that just as with Aryans there were good, decent Jews and bad, indecent ones . . . The education work of the last decade has led to a reduction of the number of advocates of such views.' The aim of education on National Socialist racial policy was 'to create the preconditions for the eternal life of Germany'. [. . .]

Before the war, finally, the armed forces still felt obliged to expand on Hitler's declaration of 30 January 1939,[7] which stated that the consequence of a new world war would be 'the destruction of the Jewish race in Europe', with its own comments. In 1939 an article entitled 'The Jew in German History' appeared in the new series 'Education Pamphlets for Schooling in National Socialist Ideology and National Political Goals'[8] in which it stated that the defensive struggle against Jewry would still continue when the last Jew had left Germany: 'For there remain two great and important tasks: 1. The eradication of all after-effects of the Jews' influence, above all in the economy and in intellectual life. 2. The struggle against World Jewry, which is striving to incite all the peoples of the world against Germany.' The solidarity with the most extreme racist slogans of the party is visible in the sentences: 'Today we Germans are waging a dual struggle. Against the non-Jewish peoples we wish only to assert our vital interests. We respect them and engage in a chivalrous dispute with them. We fight against World Jewry, however, as one must fight against a poisonous parasite; in it we confront not only an enemy of our people, but a plague of all peoples. The struggle against Jewry is a moral struggle for the purity and health of the race as created by God and for a new, more just order in the world.'

With an armed forces leadership engaged in such political education work it would not be a problem for Hitler to plan and carry out his war of ideology and annihilation shortly thereafter. The beginning of the accommodation and self-coordination process was marked by tactical considerations, under-pinned by acceptance of core elements of the National Socialist ideology. The consequence was the loss of distance to the political immorality of the system. [. . .]

['Die Wehrmacht in NS-Staat', in K.-D. Bracher, M. Funke, and H.-A. Jacobsen (eds.), *Deutschland 1933–1945: neue Studien zur nationalsozialistischen Herrschaft* (2nd edn., Düsseldorf: Droste Verlag, 1993), 377, 384–7.]

> In his monumental study of the legal system in the Third Reich during the Gürtner era, Gruchmann stresses the extent to which the commitment of the highly conservative legal establishment to creating an authoritarian justice system led it to collaborate in the undermining of the inherited liberal legal system during the Nazi era. However, despite its collusion in the erosion of the liberal legal system, it was permanently on the defensive, as more and more of the juridical and policing functions of the Justice Ministry and Interior Ministry were usurped by the more radical SS-police system under Himmler. Moreover, having done so much to facilitate the descent into lawlessness of the Third Reich by successive retroactive legalization of illegal acts of terror and barbarism, the Justice Ministry found itself unable then to fall back on institutional and legal safeguards to defend its position. As a result, it was powerless to prevent the ongoing expansion of the concentration camp apparatus and the concomitant radicalization of terror in the war in particular.

The competing, corrective activity of the police also had an impact on the administration of justice: to avoid being reproached by the political leadership for having 'failed', and so exposing the judiciary to further exclusion in favour of the police, the Reich Ministry of Justice acted to secure the imposition of more severe penalties in certain fields and the use of judicial preventive detention in appropriate cases. Judges found themselves forced into a position of either imposing a more severe penalty than a conscientious judgement would recognize as appropriate to the degree of guilt, even if it came within the boundaries of penal law, or of provoking correction by the police—which undermined the authority of the judiciary and justified the police's claim to an expanded role in criminal prosecution. As the transfer to a concentration camp of an acquitted defendant or a person convicted 'correctly' could under some circumstances mean death for the person concerned, judges even had to act unjustly in such cases if they wanted to extricate such people from the unjust measures of the police state. This shows the perversion to which penal justice was subject in the 'dual state'.

While the Reich Ministry of Justice accepted substantial intrusions by the police into its sphere of competence from 1933 on, its potential for intervening in Himmler's field of activity was constantly reduced. If the attempt to control preventive custody by the introduction of judicial review of the Gestapo's measures failed, endeavours to intervene to counteract the illegal treatment of prisoners in the concentration camps also foundered. The exercise of their ongoing legal responsibility to bring proceedings against killings and instances of ill treatment by SS guards in the concentration camps was made *de facto* impossible for the Ministry of Justice by the sabotage of investigations and the quashing of proceedings by Hitler. Gürtner's efforts to make disciplinary and supervisory provisions more humane and to bring them closer to the regulations prevailing in state prisons so as to prevent cruel punishments that were at variance with penal law, and to prevent the ruthless use of firearms, foundered because of the diminution of the Reich Ministry of the Interior's jurisdiction and because of the opposition of Himmler. [. . .]

Gürtner and the leading officials of his ministry had involuntarily promoted the stripping away of power from the Ministry of Justice in favour of the SS when in 1933 they approved without contradiction the decision to entrust the police with powers unrestricted by law to combat opponents of the 'national' state in—as they believed—a temporary and exceptional situation. By the time they realized the consequences of this politically motivated infringement of constitutional principles, the powerful position of those in charge of the SS and the police had become so entrenched that they were no longer able to stop the development. [. . .]

With the intention of creating procedural law that would make a strict, rapid 'authoritarian' criminal justice possible—through a relaxation of the strict observance of rules and the extension of the judges' and prosecutors' powers of discretion—Gürtner and the representatives of anti-liberal penal law in the Reich Ministry of Justice had embarked upon a path which led to the dismantling of protective constitutional guarantees and to the restriction of the legal security and possibilities of defence of the accused, a path which, through further legislative measures from 1942 onwards, ended with a system of punishment that, while certainly ensuring a 'National Socialist' application of the law, no longer afforded any kind of protection against unjust judgements.

Despite the installation of a centrally run, strict Reich Justice administration, despite new regulations regarding the training and selection of the up-and-coming generation in accordance with National Socialist principles, despite the intrusion into judges' personal independence made possible by civil service law, despite meddling by the party in personnel policy, despite the pressure the police exerted with their corrections of the work carried out by the Ministry of Justice, and despite the equipping of the judiciary with appropriate legal instruments in the fields of material law, court law, and procedural law: despite all of this, the political leadership reproached the Ministry of Justice with only carrying out its task inadequately and ordered that it must consequently submit to corrective actions and to the removal of responsibilities. [. . .]

Given the Reich Ministry of Justice's previous preparatory actions described above, taken on 'national' grounds in 1933, there was little prospect of success for its endeavours in the following period to shield the sphere of activity of the Ministry of Justice against outside interference, to prevent itself from being excluded from prosecuting illegal acts, and to prevent the final removal of some of its responsibilities. These efforts should not be seen solely as a struggle for power motivated by a selfish desire on the part of the judicial system, at least during Gürtner's period of office, to guard its sphere of competence, as was the order of the day between party and state institutions and organizations in the formless structure of the 'Führer State'. In discussions relating to the curbing of the 'revolutionary' use of power by party bodies and the restriction of the arbitrary activity of the police with regard to preventive measures, Gürtner was concerned, even in the 'Führer State', with upholding or re-establishing a legal system—one with an authoritarian stamp—that guaranteed legal security to the individual, and with preventing a further decline into the arbitrariness of a police state. Although on occasion he made no secret of his ethical and legal motives in doing so, as a rule Gürtner had to speak to those in power in their own language and use arguments of expediency in order to pursue his objective. However, an important precondition for the successful defence of its sphere of responsibility against the police, who were competing to take it over—and snapping at the Ministry of Justice's heels with the threat of removing more of its powers—was that the Ministry for its part should adapt to the demands of the political leadership, which could not be done without sacrificing legal principles. In putting these demands into forms that were in conformity with the legal system, Gürtner's authority was successful in arriving at compromises that were tolerable for the Ministry of Justice and able to ensure that a legal system—though not an inviolable one—was upheld. [. . .]

But, even under Gürtner, the Reich Ministry of Justice was already forced onto the path of injustice through the process of accommodation. Accommodation meant not simply passively accepting the regime's criminal practices, which were contrary to the traditional civil service ethos of the Ministry of Justice, but actively underpinning them and giving them the status of legal norms, and hence participating in injustice. Every compromise whereby the Ministry sought to contain the measures or demands of the political leadership and to bring them into harmony with the legal system was another step along that path. The idea that by being acquiescent the Ministry would be able to preserve a sphere of untrammelled legal activity proved to be an illusion. The path towards injustice runs like a constant thread through the activity of the Reich Ministry of Justice between 1933 and 1940, and after Gürtner it led to a situation where 'in the end what was achieved looked almost as bad as what it had prevented',[1] to the point where, after August 1942, Thierack had no juristic scruples against proceeding to fulfil Hitler's instructions and 'building a National Socialist judicature'.[2] At the start of this development was the fatal mistake of Gürtner and the dominant conservative forces within the Reich Ministry of Justice: their belief that the prosperity of the nation could best be ensured by an authoritarian, i.e. anti-democratic, anti-liberal, and anti-parliamentarian state, such as Hitler and the National Socialists promised to bring about in 1933, and that to achieve this goal the inviolability of the rule of law could 'temporarily' be disregarded without destroying law and justice in the long term.

[*Justiz im Dritten Reich 1933–1940: Anpassung und Unterwerfung in der Ära Gürtner* (Munich: Oldenbourg, 1990), 1126–8, 1137–8, 1144–6.]

RALPH ANGERMUND

49   Jews on Trial

The terroristic nature of the Nazi regime naturally created a prominent role for the judiciary in general. Beyond this, moreover, they played an important role in reinterpreting existing laws in line with the new state ideology, and thus in infusing the legal system with National Socialist values. Not only pressure from the party, but also substantial sympathy with the anti-Semitism of the regime on the part of the judiciary, meant that the legal establishment proved more than amenable to facilitating ever greater discrimination against the Jewish population. This was despite the fact that the party had relatively little success in influencing the personnel policy of the legal authorities.

In January 1933 Hitler assumed government of Germany with the declared intention of leading Germany to a 'new age' and of changing politics and society from the bottom upwards. From the legal point of view, this included in particular the suspension of the Weimar constitution, with its catalogue of individual and political basic rights, and the creation of a legal system which was to serve the enforcement of the interests of the 'people' as opposed to the interests of the individual. 'Communal interest' should take precedence over 'self-interest'. A 'racial system of law' was to replace the individualistic, abstract, and 'alien' legal system of liberalism.[1]

Numerous laws and decrees which undermined the Weimar constitution and created the legal basis for brutal political and racial persecution thus also followed the 'seizure of power'. Thus, by the 'Decree of the Reich President for the Protection of People and State' of 28 February 1933 and similar laws,[2] fundamental political rights were suspended, and the doctrine of racial inequality was anchored into German law by the 'Law for the Restoration of the Professional Civil Service' of 7 April 1933. Even legislation which at first sight appeared to be unpolitical such as that for 'amending penal provisions' of 26 May 1933[3] which, amongst other things, greatly intensified the punishments for those committing treason and high treason as well as for 'notorious' criminals, were of great importance to the 'National Socialist struggle' against 'enemies of the state' and 'criminality'.

However, despite the determination with which the National Socialists dispensed with those provisions which stood in the way of their totalitarian claims to power and the unrestrained persecution of their opponents, it soon became obvious that their plans for a new 'racial legal order' were not very precise. Much of the new legislation was extremely dilettantist in its conception and formulation. The above-mentioned law amending penal provisions listed, for example—with no internal logic—provisions for crimes as diverse as high treason and cruelty to animals; as to the definition of the contents of the new legal system, NS legal political experts did not initially go beyond general phrases such as 'law is what is of service to the people'. [. . .]

The National Socialist legislators did not answer central legal questions such as what form the new 'racial' system of legal norms should adopt, and how the 'racial' re-evaluation of the existing legal principles from pre-National Socialist times should be carried out. They restricted themselves essentially to extremely serious, but in no way comprehensive, 'corrections' of what already existed.[4] [. . .]

Particularly in the initial phase of National Socialist rule, and quite contrary to the National Socialist 'Führerprinzip', according to which the political leadership or Hitler himself should have determined the concrete contents of National Socialist law, the task of 're-evaluating' pre-National Socialist legislation was carried out to a considerable extent by the justice administration. Paradoxically, the legislative incompetence of the National Socialist government made this professional group, which time and time again had been attacked by the NSDAP before 1933 as 'reactionary', into interpreters of National Socialist legal matters. [. . .]

In 1933–4 National Socialist jurists gave legitimacy to the 're-evaluation' of pre-National Socialist legislation by the courts by appealing to the judicial right of review, which the judiciary had already reclaimed for itself as a means of judicial 'self-help' against 'illegitimate' parliamentary laws. The positivistic notion of the unity of right and state legislation was abolished, distinctions were made between (National Socialist) law and (pre-National Socialist) legislation, and the judge was granted the right to review pre-National Socialist laws in respect of their compatibility with 'racial' legal ideas and if need be to endow them with new contents. In the view of various authors, in dealing with pre-National Socialist laws the judge should even proceed as if he were the legislator.[5] He should follow National Socialist legislation strictly, on the other hand.[6] [. . .]

The administration of justice against Jews cannot be explained by a positivistic, uncritical obedience towards the laws of state. Likewise, the reference to the 'removed impact' of anti-Semitic legislation and to the National Socialist 'spirit of the age'—hence the hypothesis that the judiciary in fact only acted on ideas that were generally socially accepted—does not wash.[7] Both the legal context and the 'spirit of the age' were doubtless anti-Semitic, but they were nevertheless both unclear and contradictory in the practical questions of the legal treatment of the Jews. In consequence, the judiciary not only implemented laws imposed by the legislator and by its social environment, but was also significantly involved in the formulation of 'race law' legal concepts. The courts filled significant gaps in National Socialist racial law with their judgements, in which the judges often sought to outdo each other with regard to their anti-Semitism, despite the availability of more moderate courses of action, and they extended the existing legislation—building on a pre-existing anti-Semitic stance already in existence before 1933—to the detriment of the Jews. The judges thus bore substantial responsibility for the 'civil death' of the Jews in National Socialist Germany.[8]

The behaviour of the German judiciary is not just characterized by a broad interpretation of the law in the areas of 'racial law' in which the National Socialist regime initially was silent. Rather, where the National Socialist legislator prescribed discrimination against the Jews, it is also possible to discern a gradual intensification in the anti-Semitic judgements. This is shown especially by the handling of the 'Law for the Protection of German Blood and German Honour' of 15 September 1935'.[9] [. . .]

The question remains of why, between 1935 and 1937, the courts often delivered relatively mild judgements, and why a harsher judgement practice only gradually emerged in matters concerning 'miscegenation'. The 'pinprick' tactic,[10] with which the German Ministry of Justice, various chief presidents as well as the NSDAP and Gestapo pressed for harsher punishment of perpetrators of 'miscegenation', may have had an effect on many of the judges. However, the 'pinprick' tactic alone was probably not decisive, because it did not ultimately seriously endanger judicial discretion.[11] The pronouncements of the Reich Court were probably more important. From December 1936 onwards it used ever-increasing opportunities to facilitate extremely far-reaching and harsh sentencing in cases of Jews involved in 'miscegenation'.

It should also be noted that in the middle of the 1930s to an increasing extent the strongly racist-nationalist and anti-Semitically inclined generation of 30- and 40-year-olds, who had been appointed to office and status by the Third Reich after the long 'sufferings of the probationers', were moving up into the criminal courts dealing with 'miscegenation'.[12] According to a contemporary observer, these judges were generally far more open to National Socialist ideology than their elder colleagues[13] and not least of all were driven by the desire for rapid promotion. In their dealings with Jewish lawyers,[14] and particularly in the handling of penal law towards the Jews, they exhibited a hitherto unknown harshness in many cases.[15]

[*Deutsche Richterschaft 1919–1945* (Frankfurt am Main: Fischer, 1990), 104–7, 124–5, 131–2.]

....

c. *Charismatic Authority and the Erosion of Rational-Bureaucratic Government*

....

ROBERT KOEHL

50 **Feudal Aspects of National Socialism**

Koehl's essay represents an early post-war attempt to analyse the irrational aspects of the National Socialist political system. Taking the two key aspects of feudalism—'vassalship' and 'fiefdom'—he argues that the National Socialist system of government can be seen in these terms. In picking up on the similarities between the charismatic elements of medieval monarchy and Hitler's style of rule, Koehl was pre-empting later discussions which sought to apply Weberian theories of charismatic domination to the Third Reich, although most recent scholarship would be disinclined to accept Koehl's suggestion that the adoption of feudal power relationships was a product of National Socialism's allegedly atavistic ideology.

In spite of its pretentiousness, National Socialist talk of man-to-man loyalty and of the leader-and-his-following really expressed their deepest convictions. This is revealed in both the formal systems they created to run Germany and in the informal structure of their internal politics. It is sometimes said that National Socialism lacked a real ideology. Insofar as a rational and systematic philosophy is meant, this is true. Yet no elaborate semantics are necessary to find consistency in the Nazi *Weltanschauung*.

Above all, they believed in a modern version of elective kingship. The Führer replaced a figurehead president and a prime minister responsible to a parliamentary assembly. He was elected for life by acclamation, but was in reality chosen and maintained in power by his paladins. They chose him for his personal qualities. In the form in which political battles are fought in the twentieth century, his prowess was supposed to outshine that of the fighters grouped around him.[1]

The Nazis tried to do away with the Germans' instinctive loyalty to abstract law and order, to 'the state' and to tradition. They instituted an oath of personal loyalty to the Führer Adolf Hitler and sanctioned an almost ludicrous series of subinfeudations via oaths extorted by 'little Führers.' In legislation, in jurisprudence, police practice, and administrative policy they tried to substitute men for laws, personal judgment and responsibility for the rule-book and anonymity. They did away with the power of the old consti-tutional organs like the cabinet and the Reichstag and erected a system of

Reichsleiter and *Gauleiter* whose positions depended, of course, on the Führer's good will and loyalty *to them*, but also on their ability to get things done and to command the loyalty and respect of their underlings and of the German people entrusted to their care.[2]

It was the aim of the Nazis to develop both the institutions and the political atmosphere conducive to furthering the exercise of power. Rejecting the modern bureaucratic state with its elaborate channels, they wished to simplify the exercise of power, to pin down the responsibility for decisions, and to encourage independence and aggressive problem-solving. Not strangely, the military analogy seemed to offer a substitute for the bureaucratic state. At least the soldier could always be brought to account by his superior. But here, too, lay a danger that 'artificial hierarchies' and 'paper structures' would get in the way of on-the-spot action.[3] The solution? *Führerprinzip!* But the doctrine that a leader must be allowed full freedom to solve a problem meant in effect a neo-feudal system.

According to this *Weltanschauung*, the nation's leader had total power, received from the *Volk*, and revocable by it, though not through legalistic processes so much as through withdrawal of confidence expressed in his failure to carry them with him in his exploits.[4] This total power he parceled out among proven followers. The long battle for control over the streets and the parliament, followed by the battle for the total support of the German people after 1933, afforded a maximum testing ground for these sub-leaders. It never ended. A *Reichsleiter* or a *Gauleiter* was continuously being weighed in the balance and not a few were found wanting between 1933 and 1945, not to mention the years 1923–1933.[5] As a consequence the Nazi political scene was filled with ever-changing groups and clusters of protagonists. Their relationship to each other was only semi-hierarchical. The student of Nazi administration has difficulty even with the formal structures because of their fluid character.

One of the most amazing similarities to the feudal system in Nazi administration is the nominal subordinate who acquired power to give his superior orders through appointment by a still higher superior as his 'personal agent.' Of course the universal example of this is the party member in the line organization, such as the Foreign Office. However, it is more striking when we realize that full-fledged *Altkämpfer* (party veterans) like Darré, Ley, Rosenberg and Hans Frank found themselves in a position similar to Foreign Office career diplomats, forced to take orders from subordinates like Herbert Backe, Fritz Sauckel, Erich Koch, and F. W. Krüger.[6] The effect of this Nazi habit was an ever-modified network of personal loyalties. At any given moment a German with an axe to grind (and the modern student) had to ask, not 'what is the chain of command,' but who has the actual 'connections'—the nominal boss, or someone else?

Equally characteristic was the practice among National Socialist bigwigs of appointing each other as 'deputies.' Thus a man like Himmler was a Supreme Reich Authority as *Reichsführer SS*, though technically subordinate to the Ministry of the Interior, and also the deputy of Hermann Göring for the management of confiscated Polish agricultural properties. Himmler, in turn, as Reich Commissar for the Strengthening of Germandom, named as his deputies the Minister of Agriculture (Darré), the Minister of Labor (Ley), the Reich Health Leader (Conti), the chief of the Foreign Section of the NSDAP (Bohle), and the *Reichsstatthalter* of the annexed Polish territories.[7] A delicate hierarchy can be discovered: men like Göring and Goebbels spurned nomination as anyone's deputy save Hitler's. They were *Reichsunmittelbar* (direct vassals). Himmler and Ribbentrop were powers in their own right, but they could not do without the added authority of responsibilities assigned by their colleagues. Lesser lights collected deputyships the way Göring collected medals: mere symbols of status. Darré, Frank and many of the *Gauleiter* fall in this third group. Finally we come to those Nazi officials glad to have one great connection (often with Hitler) or lacking even that: men such as Otto Dietrich, the Press Chief; Arthur Seyss-Inquart, handyman and trouble-shooter; and Baldur von Schirach, the Youth Leader.[8]

A third aspect of National Socialist political life which may be likened to the feudal nexus was the 'private war' with its rule of neutrality, peace treaties, and its schemes of mediation and arbitration by higher authority and by peers. Göring, Goebbels, Hess, Himmler, Ribbentrop and Rosenberg were the principals in such encounters, though often the combatants were lesser figures chosen by one or another. Needless to say, such wars were the result of the criss-crossing ambitions of rival empire-builders. [. . .]

Numerous eyewitnesses have reported that Hitler held his power not as an absolute monarch but through his ability to operate a delicate system of checks and balances.[9] He was a unifying factor for the disparate and competing elements of National Socialism, possessed of a considerable power of his own over the masses and over many leading Nazis which has been termed 'charismatic'. These characteristics are precisely those of the successful feudal monarch like St. Louis. Without precisely encouraging strife among his cohorts, Hitler was capable of remarkable neutrality—an ability to remain above the battle. Thus he could intervene when he had discovered where lay the advantage to his own power and to the Reich as he saw it. He also had the habit of so 'impartially' deciding an issue that aggressor and victim were treated equally, with the result that there was an advantage to activist policy.[10] Since he could not be everywhere, especially in the continuous crisis of wartime, Hitler had to encourage self-reliance and independence, both in his paladins and in the regional chieftains, the *Gauleiter*.

In the last years of the Nazi era there is the most striking evolution along feudal lines. The *Gauleiter* became so fully identified with the interests of their bailiwicks that we find them behaving more like ancient stem dukes in their refusal to recognize the authority of the central government than like *missi dominici*.* Hitler had to inveigh against the idea of hereditary Gauleitership, though he did not dare transfer recalcitrant *Gauleiter* where they had personally won the *Gau* for National Socialism.[11] As for the paladins, Göring, Goebbels, Himmler, and the newcomers, Speer and Bormann, had constructed virtually impregnable appanages. The more dependent Hitler became upon their empires for German victory, the more easily they looted the power of rivals like Rosenberg and Ribbentrop, Sauckel and Keitel. They made their systems independent of the central authorities and even of the Führer's support by absorbing some vehicle of power, usually economic, though Goebbels also used the mass media and Himmler the secret police.[12]

['Feudal Aspects of National Socialism', *American Political Science Review*, 54 (1960), 921–33; repr. in H. A. Turner (ed.), *Nazism and the Third Reich* (New York: Quadrangle Books, 1972), 158–62.]

MARTIN BROSZAT

51   The Hitler State

Martin Broszat's study of the 'Hitler State', which originally appeared in Germany in 1969, was the first influential attempt at a synthesizing analysis which sought to emphasize the relationship between the evolution of policy and structural developments within the regime. Broszat argued that the 'coordination' of the state and public sphere which occurred in 1933–4 resulted in a regime which combined authoritarian and fascist elements and which lasted until 1936–7; thereafter, the increasing fragmentation of government reduced institutional and bureaucratic restraints upon the exercise of arbitrary power. These systemic pressures, rather than fixed ideological goals which Broszat characterizes as being 'of a very general nature', led to the destruction of the Jews.

[The] mingling of official, semi-official and Party political institutions and responsibilities, which also tended to mix the state bureaucratic organization and the structures of the associations of private business with the Führer principle derived from the National Socialist movement, made the boundaries between the state, society and the Party fluid, and created, as it were, a totalitarian partnership between them. The complex institutional traits of the regime which arose in 1933/4 reflected the pluralism of forces and centres of action which were trying during this phase to establish their own spheres of influence and power, their own particular interests and their own views on

* Envoys of the King.

the nature and direction of the new regime. Just as the NSDAP's mass movement had already begun to infiltrate broad sectors of society and public life by setting up numerous auxiliary organizations, offices and associations and through its entry to the parliaments, Land and municipal governments, so the process of co-ordination in 1933 constituted a new, still more intensive form of fusion and confrontation between the National Socialist movement and the old leadership forces in state and society. The speed and smoothness with which this co-ordination generally took place, provided certain 'essentials' of National Socialism were acknowledged and the corresponding conclusions were drawn (the elimination of democratic procedures, and of Jewish, Marxist, and left-liberal forces of leadership), show that very often it was more a matter of readjustment than a revolutionary upheaval. But this also resulted in a significant proportion of the National Socialist movement being incorporated in the nominally co-ordinated, new centralized associations. Co-ordination signified that the social forces were contained but very often at the price of a simultaneous dilution and a further softening and splitting up of the National Socialist movement.

There was both necessity and method in this development in so far as only confrontation and collaboration with the powerful specialists and experienced established forces of leadership could bring about the transformation from propaganda movement to a governing organization. There was pressure on both sides for collaboration and this was also decisive not least in the Ministries and the state administrations. Collaboration offered those nominally co-ordinated and established leadership forces and specialists who were prepared to 'co-operate loyally' the possibility of recommending themselves to their new masters through their particular ability and activity, of contributing their own ideas in order to fill the vacuum left by the National Socialist programme, or else of carrying out their proposals for reform with the help of National Socialism. At the same time this collaboration provoked an expert screening and replacement of National Socialist functionaries and filtered from the vague aims of the National Socialist ideology those elements which were attainable and practicable in the given circumstances. The tactic of allowing individual scope and experiment, which Hitler had already successfully adopted towards the Party before 1933 in order to encourage initiative, spontaneity and activity, was now applied over and over again but chiefly in the realm of practical government measures, of technical and economic management and organization. The relatively generous nature of the process of co-ordination for the liberal middle class and conservative groups in state and society was a precondition for a successful National Socialist take-over of power. Because it was only with the aid of those 'co-ordinated forces' that demagogic activity could successfully be transformed to practical control. Terrorist intimidation on the one hand, to demonstrate unmistakably the new masters' claim to leadership, and halting the revolution on the other hand to prove the determination to govern effectively even at the cost of the 'old fighters'—the seizure of power swung between these two inter-dependent poles and in so doing helped the Hitler regime to succeed. [. . .]

As long as the organizational coherence of the various branches of the National Socialist regime was to some extent preserved, as long as the Führer's will was not completely remote from the state and the government and there was a minimum of all-round readiness to co-operate and com-promise between the rival authorities, leadership groups and apparatuses, a certain degree of rationality, control and self-regulation was guaranteed. But the growing decline of the regime's centralized character and its progres-sive splintering into new centres of activity that tended to devour neighbour-ing authorities and make themselves indispensable according to the law of motion underlying the leadership principle, increasingly disrupted any rational over-all organization of government and reinforced the particularist egocentricity of the respective departmental values and ideologies.

The prevailing tendency to resort to expediency constantly extended the regime's institutional jungle after 1938. As time passed the Third Reich was more and more burdened with the elements and relics of *ad hoc* authorities and with their offices and organizations, which owed their existence to con-siderations of expediency that no longer applied. Improvisation led to Nem-esis. Because of the multiplicity of conflicting forces the Führer's will (even when Hitler had something different in mind) was ultimately only able to influence events in this or that direction in an uncoordinated and abrupt fashion, and it was certainly not in a position to watch over and to curb the new organizations, authorities and ambitions which developed as a result. The institutional and legal results of the intermittent orders and decrees of the Führer became increasingly unfathomable and clashed with later authori-zations granted by him. Even as organizational shells devoid of political importance they threatened the uniformity and orderliness of the exercise of power and the organization of government. This is why it would also be impossible and illusory to provide a diagrammatic sketch of the organization of the National Socialist regime in the form of a chart for the period after 1938. Unless, that is, it were possible to discover a means of showing how on a chart of such nominal institutions the real source of power and the actual decision-making changed from case to case.

But the more the organizational jungle of the National Socialist regime spread out the less chance there was of restoring any rationally organized and consistent policy-making and governmental process. The mushrooming of institutions, special powers and specific legal arrangements, which caused an increasingly bitter struggle for protection and favour as well as a steeper decline in rational policy-making and allocation of responsibilities, led to the establishment in each case of different techniques of organization and this, in turn, contributed to a speeding up of the 'movement' and a radicalization of measures. To suggest that the development of National Socialist policy only consisted in steering towards and carrying out prefabricated long-term ideological aims in small doses is an over simplification. Like the mass terror in spring and early summer 1933, the growing anarchy and resort to violence backed up by secret orders and special authorizations during the War was not based on a regime where power was totally controlled either. On the contrary it took place amidst a progressive division of power, an increasingly fragmentary process whereby particularist power apparatuses made themselves independent and where any over-all co-ordination and regularity was missing. The disruption of the unified bureaucratic state order, the growing formlessness and arbitrariness of legislation and of decision-making, and of transmitting decisions, played a part in speeding up the process of radicalization which was every bit as important as any ideological fixity of purpose.

Admittedly Hitler's obsessive preoccupation with specific ideological and political principles proved to be a decisive driving force behind National Socialist policy. But the Führer was not in the least able to decide entirely for himself on the whether, when and how of specific measures. His 'spontaneous' decisions were invariably the reflection and expression of the internal constitutional order and the external position of the regime. The practicability of carrying out, as well as the actual significance of, ideological aims which had been hitherto of a very general nature was only decided once certain patterns of power and responsibility had changed.

> [*The Hitler State: The Foundation and Development of the Internal Structure of the Third Reich* (London: Longman, 1981), 348–9, 358–9.]

PETER DIEHL-THIELE

52 Party and State in the Third Reich

> The work from which this extract is taken is representative of a growing body of work which emerged in the 1970s developing the 'structuralist' interpretation further. Note the characterization of the proliferation of offices as a product of Hitler's 'divide and rule' tactics, and the emphasis on Hitler's desire for a regime of 'permanent movement'.

The coexistence, additional existence, and conflicting existence of *Ortsgruppenleiter* [local leaders], *Kreisleiter* [district leaders], *Gauleiters* [regional leaders], and Führer's Deputy[1] as representatives of the party on the one hand and the town mayors, county prefects, *Regierungspräsidenten* and *Oberpräsidenten* [district governers], state governments, and Reich ministries on the other is only one part of the dualism between 'movement' and state which led to the progressive undermining of binding legal norms and thus to the 'dissipation of the substance of the state'.[2] The relationship of 'party and state'[3] became a constitutional problem because the NSDAP, which after the abolition of the parliamentary system had essentially lost its function, was neither moved 'into the state' by Hitler—for example as the 'substructure' of the Propaganda Ministry—nor fused with the state through a process of thorough 'personal union' of the relevant offices.

There was also no party forum of which it could be said in constitutional terms that it gave orders to the state. The party 'commanded' the state 'only' indirectly and unofficially, e.g. with the force of moral pressure, to which the civil servants in the so-called 'political offices'[4] were naturally more exposed than those in the technical agencies or in the Reich financial administration.[5] However, the party—and the other organizations of the movement—also exerted pressure on the state through the existence of its parallel organizations. The *Kreisleiter*, who was aware of his greater powerfulness *vis-à-vis* the county prefect, only accepted his role as 'watchdog' with great reluctance, and pressed for all those issues which were brought to the county prefect for decision to be decided by himself. As this was officially not permitted—the *Kreisleiter* was to embody the permanent threat that in case of insufficient radicalism on the part of the county prefect and his staff the replacements stood waiting; this changing of guard was not, however, supposed to occur through the county prefect being reduced to receiving the *Kreisleiter*'s orders and thus being 'deactivated'!—he tried to gain control of some of the functions of the office of the county prefect and to have them dealt with by his staff. Such efforts, which were regularly kept in check 'from above', but were never explicitly forbidden, were in principle likely to succeed as the 'leading role of the party' was repeatedly emphasized to the population while the civil servants were often only spoken of in disparaging tones. Thus on the level of the rural district as on all other levels a permanent conflict of jurisdiction existed, as Hitler was not willing to establish orderly conditions free of general power struggles even on the subordinate level of the administration.

By the time the party cadres had actually become highly superfluous as far as stabilizing Hitler's authority among the German people and within the German state was concerned, they still retained sufficient influence and power for them to be able to intervene in the state governed by Hitler. A permanent state of tension thus emerged, a fractious dualism. Ultimately the party saw the state as 'the enemy'.[6] [. . .]

Had Hitler's revolutionary goal merely been the conquest of state power and the establishment of an authoritarian state structure organized according to the military model, he would have achieved this goal by the end of March 1933. However, since Hitler saw the 'seizure of power' only as the starting point for a quite different revolution, the establishment of a strong state which in the short or long term would only moderate and dilute the revolutionary élan of the movement could only be a hindrance to him. Aside from the 'racial revolution', which through the mission of permanent 'higher breeding' also signified a permanent revolution (and to which ever greater groups of 'less valuable' people would have fallen victim in the event of a victorious war on the basis of an inexhaustible population reservoir and ever-stricter selection criteria), Hitler intended a type of regime which no state and no mere apparatus of authority is suited to establish, but only a 'movement' kept in constant movement: the complete and all-encompassing domination of each individual person and total disposal over them.

In order to establish this state of affairs—or at least an optimal approximation—it was necessary to avoid the establishment of a hierarchical state structure in which authority and power are necessarily distributed more or less in planned fashion and according to rules. For a hierarchically ordered transmission of orders makes the power of the commander dependent upon the hierarchical chain of command. Any hierarchy, however authoritarian its leadership, and every chain of command, however high-handed and dictatorial the giving of orders, would stabilize and thus restrict the total power of the leader of a totalitarian movement. The *Führerprinzip*, expressed by Hitler in the formula 'authority to those below and responsibility to those above',[7] was never implemented in the Third Reich, as the 'sub-leaders' named from 'above' were not given genuine, independent authority; rather, because of dual responsibilities and parallel organizations none of them could be sure which position he actually occupied in a power hierarchy determined solely by the prevailing favour of the leader. With his divide-and-rule tactics Hitler constantly attempted to prevent the formation of stable intermediary ranks of power-wielders and thus to secure his position against potential 'palace coups'. [. . .]

[*Partei und Staat im Dritten Reich: Untersuchungen zum Verhältnis zwischen NSDAP und allgemeiner innerer Staatsverwaltung 1933–1945* (Munich: C. H. Beck, 1971), 2–4, 6–7.]

HANS MOMMSEN

53 Cumulative Radicalization and Self-Destruction of the Nazi Regime

In another defining statement of the 'structuralist' position, Mommsen argues that specific or concrete ideological imperatives played only a very subordinate role in the formulation of policy in the 'Third Reich', the dynamic of whose internal development was responsible for what he characterizes as the 'cumulative radicalization' of the regime. Note his insistence that orders or decrees from Hitler often only gave retroactive sanction to initiatives which had been embarked upon 'from below'.

The National Socialist system of rule is characterized by the interplay between a constant overstretching of its own political and economic resources, and an increasing inner disintegration of the social and state institutions on whose usurpation its power-political opportunities were based. Similar to the fascist system of Benito Mussolini, the National Socialist dictatorship had come into existence on the basis of an alliance between the fascist leadership elites and the conservative power elites. However, while Mussolini managed for a long time to maintain a certain equilibrium between the representatives of the fascist movement and the leaderships of the bureaucracy and army, and only came to overextend fascism's potential in the course of the Second World War, and under pressure from the Third Reich and in rivalry to Hitler, the development of the National Socialist regime was determined by a step-by-step erosion of the pre-existing state apparatus and the ongoing exclusion of the former alliance partners and of the moderating influence of the traditional leading circles within army, bureaucracy, and economy. In connection to this there occurred a process of cumulative radicalization of the dominant groupings of the regime and its virtual inner dissolution into a multitude of bitterly feuding power groups. The united political will evoked to the outside encouraged the partly coordinated, partly newly created organs of party and state to rival each other for the expansion of their competencies and the extension of their jurisdiction. The fiction of the unity-endowing dictator, who remained the common reference point, and a constant activism, which focussed towards war and towards constantly expanding annexationist and imperialist plans, held the system together. [. . .]

One of the characteristics of the political decision-making process in the Third Reich was that as a result of uncoordinated individual initiatives from the rival apparatuses problem situations arose which appeared insoluble with the means of the notionally responsible state institutions and which were transferred to special task groups for an 'unbureaucratic' solution, i.e. one unconstrained by law, having been declared an unavoidable and temporary exceptional measure. Precisely the fact that the extermination actions of the regime were represented to the outside as unavoidable, exceptional acts mostly forced on the regime by its enemies, and did not primarily emerge from long-term, rational planning, serves to explain—the conscious suppression of communication between the relevant power groups aside—why the elites in army and ministerial bureaucracy, who stood at a certain inner distance to the terror methods of the regime, found no means of united protest and limited themselves to avoiding possible legal culpability of their own. The apostrophic 'higher orders' repeatedly referred to in the context of the subsequent prosecution of National Socialist war crimes were only present on exceptional occasions; the subsequent invocation of them is part of an exculpatory ideology which had its roots in the regime, and which was combined with the tendency to suppress information on actual or alleged crimes of the regime.

Using the examples of the Night of the Glass, the Commissar Decree, the Final Solution of the Jewish Question, the foreign worker problem, the treatment of Soviet prisoners of war, and the crimes against the civilian population in the occupied east, one can construct an ideal type for the mechanism which led to a maximization of terrorism and criminality in a political system otherwise moulded by petit-bourgeois values. Irresponsibility and political and administrative inability of the relevant offices lead to the emergence of irresolvable situations, which are created by the impulses of particularist power-figures in the power structures of party and state—impulses which are nurtured by rivalry and the desire for political 'proving of oneself'—to which the system adapts out of convenience and given the impossibility of reaching stable compromises. Under normal circumstances this should have led to resounding political failure. In individual cases, such as for example the murder of the Austrian Chancellor Engelbert Dollfuss, the regime saw itself forced to repudiate clearly its party functionaries who were pushing for radicalization. With entry into the Second World War considerations of neutral powers fell by the wayside; in addition, the invocation of national unity in war led to the extensive isolation of potential domestic sources of resistance. In contrast, the secondary bureaucratic apparatus which had now established itself in the intermediary zone between party and state—above all the Reich Security Main Office and the associated apparatus, which extended far beyond the borders of the Reich—lent itself to solving such 'emergency situations', which had been wilfully conjured up but not consciously pre-planned, with terroristic means, thereby bypassing the offices responsible. It was only this which gave the directionless and contradictory criminal dynamism which the regime unleashed, without giving it anything other than destructive goals, the character of bureaucratically administered methodicality; in this, ideological factors had much less significance than the desire to justify its existence through bureaucratic effectiveness and to expand its power. The main actors in the eradication of the Jews, Adolf Eichmann and Rudolf Höss, were not marked anti-Semites. Final Solution and euthanasia programme were implemented with meticulous secrecy—an indicator that the extent of the ideological indoctrination of the population was not adjudged to be exactly great.

In many cases these far-reaching actions did not need the initiating role of the 'Führer decree', which often only sanctioned that which was long since under way. Only in this fashion could utopian speculations such as the eradication of European Jewry be translated into political reality. The precondition for the criminal policies of the National Socialist regime was the skilful usage of the willingness to show solidarity on the part of broad sectors of the population, which was rooted in the Prusso-German authoritarian tradition, but above all the collaboration of the higher bureaucracy and the officer corps. The latter had the ultimately dubious effect of confining the radical and overtly illegal measures demanded by the leading circles of the NSDAP to a sustainable level and thus of temporarily securing the functionability of the system. The far-reaching exclusion from power of the Political Organization of the NSDAP did not, however, prevent the appropriation of the influence of the pre-existing state institutions, the erosion of the rationality of the administration, and the corruption of the judicial system along the lines of the regime via the emergence of a multitude of special authorities. The neo-feudalism in the occupied eastern areas, which represents in exemplary fashion the behaviour of the territorial commissars, reminiscent as they were of early modern territorial princes and their corrupt Byzantine practices, and which was independent of the Reich administration, fed back into the territory of the Reich itself and finished in a partly virtual, partly real dissolution of the domestic and general administration. Political blindness and the cynical glorification of violence turned against the representatives of the National Socialist system of rule themselves, as the struggles for the succession of the last few weeks of the regime show. Never in history has a political movement driven itself *ad absurdum* as National Socialism did.

['Der Nationalsozialismus: Kumulative Radikalisierung und Selbstzerstörung des Regimes', in *Meyers enzyklopaedisches Lexikon* (Mannheim: Lexikonverlag, 1976), 786, 789–90.]

PETER HÜTTENBERGER

54   National Socialist Polycracy

> Hüttenberger's analysis takes Franz Neumann's central assumptions regarding the National Socialist 'cartel' as his broad starting point,* but places greater emphasis on the dynamics of the changing relationship between each power bloc over time, developing a picture of a system of rule in which each institution existed in a state of interdependency and of a system which was held together only by the authority of Hitler.

The relationships between the power blocs in the year of the seizure of power, 1933, can be defined as a 'pact'[1] between big business,[2] armed forces and National Socialism. It is noticeable that the state is not named. The state

---

* See extract 42 above.

bureaucracy of the Reich and the states had clearly contributed to the promotion of National Socialism before 1933, but during the process of the seizure of power it gradually lost its original status,[3] a loss which probably can be traced back on the one hand to internal divergences within the context of federalism, on the other to the separation of the armed forces from the interior administration, and finally to the lack of a homogeneous social grouping as the basis for the personnel structure of the bureaucracy. [. . .]

The character of the National Socialist bureaucracy does not, however, lie in the consolidation of the situation as established in 1933, but in the constantly changing relationships and constellations. In the abstract these changes can be defined with the concepts of differentiation, dissociation, and penetration. The process of penetration did not occur through competition for proportions of the population in the manner of parliamentary elections, but in sporadic encroachments and mutual seizure of political tasks and jurisdictions, linked with a strategy of the formation of 'personal unions' and the accumulation of offices on the part of the relevant leaders, and in the occupation and creation of fields of action which had not hitherto been filled by any power centre.

The most dynamic element within the overall set of power relationships was represented by the NSDAP itself after the seizure of power. Hitherto specializing in electoral propaganda, street terror, and the formation of cadres, it lost its original tasks after the March elections of 1933 and the 'ending' of the revolution. Since its strength did not lie in the ownership of means of production or in the disciplined deployment of weapons, since it also had no general, permanent socially significant tasks, e.g. in the distribution of goods and services, and since its potencies consisted purely in the organized power of socially frustrated individuals, it found itself in a politically precarious situation at the end of 1933.[4] Its organizations would inevitably collapse if it did not manage to satisfy the economic needs of its members and to convey to them the feeling of participating in the regime. This dangerous situation appears to have surfaced before 1933 occasionally in the SA, which, during periods of relative calm, was forced to keep its units together with fictitious rumours of putsches and actions. The complicated situation forced the NSDAP not only to occupy the relevant leadership positions as with a normal takeover of power, but also to penetrate those sectors of politics and society vacated by the other power blocs or left empty by the destruction of political opponents. These included above all the inner administration and the societies and associations. [. . .]

Significant for the development of the polycracy in this phase, however, is the fact that as a result of the internal conflicts associated with its own thrusts, the NSDAP itself became caught in a complicated process of differentiation through which above all two power centres emerged: the

NSDAP/PO complex including the administrative apparatus which it occu-pied and a series of divisions and associations, and the SS/SD/Gestapo complex. The SA likewise attempted to lift itself to the status of power centre, through for example the establishment of a 'people's army' or through the propaganda of the 'second revolution', but failed in 1934 against the resistance of the armed forces, the SS/SD/Gestapo complex, and the NSDAP/PO.[5] Finally, the DAF undertook numerous initiatives aimed at expanding its position—which was circumscribed from the outset by Hitler—such as through a broadly conceived DAF law shortly before the war which met with the resistance of business and the NSDAP/PO, and finally during the war, as Ley attempted to gain the post of General Plenipotentiary for Labour Deployment, which Speer prevented. [. . .]

Overall this process of differentiation caused a growing dissociation between the power centres originally of National Socialist provenance. The mistrust of the NSDAP/PO of the secret service activities of the SD and the Gestapo or its dislike of the Reich Food Estate were striking. The conflicts become clear for example in the attempts to have National Socialist elites trained in National Political Education Centres or Adolf-Hitler-Schools, which became embroiled in the intrigues of the power centres.

On the other hand, the unregulated penetration of the party into the administration had the effect that a power centre that was traditionally influential in Germany, the civil service, particularly since the civil service before 1933 and more so before 1918 was closely interlinked with the aris-tocracy, the churches, and the military, gradually dissolved politically despite its resistance. The state thus disintegrated into fragments which were only held together on the surface by administrative law. This political loss of status is clear for example in the case of the judiciary, which had maintained its almost secular continuity and which now, despite its attempts at accommoda-tion, had on an ongoing basis to give up its important jurisdictions to the SS/SD/Gestapo-complex[6] or to the Honorary Courts of the Professional Cor-porations [Ehrengerichtsbarkeit der Berufsstände].[7] During the war it was even forced to come to terms with a new legal dogma derived from National Socialism, which caused it numerous difficulties. The open attacks on the judiciary by the party or even by Hitler were only symptoms of an inner loss of prestige. [. . .]

The power centres emanating out from the NSDAP and those parts of the state dependent upon them were from 1935 essentially held together by the person of Hitler and—to a more limited extent—those of Göring and Goebbels. This cohesion-giving function of Hitler was probably rooted less in his abilities as a statesman than in the awareness of the functionaries that their own conflicts generated by the process of dissociation rendered their positions unstable. They had to stylize Hitler as a symbolic figure, which also suited his demagogic skills. A complicated relationship of mutual dependencies of a sometimes almost ganglike mentality existed between Hitler and the individual political centres of National Socialism. The National Socialist leadership groups were thus each in themselves dependent upon Hitler as the 'Führer'; on the other hand they were also able to function as autonomous political units in all those spheres in which he paid them no attention. Without that substructure Hitler himself would similarly have hardly been able to maintain his position despite his tactical skills *vis-à-vis* big business and the armed forces. National Socialist ideology thus emphasized 'loyalty' as the basis of its internal politics in notably pronounced fashion. However, this covered over its internal tensions. [. . .]

The division of National Socialism into two power complexes, the NSDAP/PO and the SS/SD/Gestapo complex, and two unsatisfied organizations, the DAF and the Reich Food Estate, along with the fragmentation of the state bureaucracy, changed the original three-sided relationship of 1933 around the middle of the 1930s into an unstable four-sided relationship, during which the emphases in the alliance necessarily shifted. A formal expression of these emerging new forms of polycracy is the gradual development of spheres of law tailored to each individual power centre. One can thus discern a sphere of law for big business, which crystallized into corporation law, one for the SS/SD/Gestapo, one for the armed forces, and one for the NSDAP/PO, each, however, closely related to the still valid laws of state. For a normal citizen it could have very different consequences depending on in which sphere of law he found himself.

The power relationships within the new 'quadrangle' were not stable but developed dynamically with a tendency towards the further expansion of the SS/SD/Gestapo complex and towards the weakening of the armed forces, which may possibly be explained by the fact that Hitler was able to bar the military from any involvement in foreign policy and the party to block their access to the population. Between the SS/SD/Gestapo complex and big business there prevailed—as far as can be seen today—a distanced relationship, although Himmler attempted to bind industrialists to him. On the other hand, precisely because of the emergent economic crisis of 1936 the Gestapo stabilized the position of big business through its policy of terror towards the population. The NSDAP/PO likewise had no politically decisive links to big business—there were occasional attempts by Schacht to incorporate the party as an ally for himself; at regional level however rivalries or commonalities between industrialists and functionaries could develop in turn, which have not yet been analysed case by case. Either way, the NSDAP/PO had no influence on big business, which for its part paid the NSDAP only limited attention. [. . .]

To summarize, one can say:

1. The polycratic character of the Third Reich developed out of the overall constellation of the regime at the time of the seizure of power.

2. The polycratic regime consisted of numerous oligarchies which differed in ideology, interests, personnel structure, and style of working, of which big business was organized—depending upon the situation—according to the principles of competition or collegiality, the armed forces were organized according to bureaucratic-hierarchical principles, and National Socialism according to the principle of leadership and cliques.

3. The most dynamic element of the polycracy was represented by National Socialism, necessarily so from its perspective since its position during the period of the seizure of power was precarious. The precondition for the possibility of its expansion lay in the fear of the other two power centres that they would not be able to prevail over the revolutionary forces in Germany during the economic crisis.

4. The confusion of jurisdiction in the Third Reich cannot be explained purely in terms of a hyper-Machiavellian policy on the part of Hitler, but through the permanent attempts at penetration, through the process of differentiation and the compromises of the individual power centres. This fact also cannot be reduced to an ideal type conceptual pairing such as improvisation vs. political planning, as Hitler and the National Socialists pursued single-mindedly and using all available space—if often also with tactical improvisation—the goal of securing their political position, whereby however they often came up against resistance and thus against their limits.

5. The Third Reich did not reach a stable constitution peculiar to itself, within which politics would occur according to constant, universally accepted, transpersonal rules. One should thus avoid the concept of pluralism and the theoretical conception underlying it, but one should also avoid the concept of 'anarchy', since, after all, National Socialism had no inclination to abolish authority.

6 The individual members of the polycracy were reliant upon one another, for which reason they reached internal accommodation and for which reason the impression could be gained from the outside that this was a monolithic regime.

['Nationalsozialistische Polykratie', *Geschichte und Gesellschaft* (1976), 423–4, 427–32, 442.]

TIM MASON

55   Intention and Explanation

The tendency of 'functionalist' scholars to downplay the role of Hitler as an individual led to charges of historical trivialization (which were returned in kind). In this seminal piece, Mason defends the 'functionalist' approach of scholars such as Hans Mommsen and Martin Broszat against the charge of trivialization, but suggests the need to incorpor-

ate it into a Marxist reading which relates developments within the
'superstructure' to social and economic pressures and conflicts.

The historians under attack for offering an unwitting apologia for National
Socialism have been called functionalists.[1] The label is not strictly appropriate
since, unlike the schematic writings of self-consciously functionalist authors,
those of Hans Mommsen and Martin Broszat do not pass over human agency
in politics and do not assign historical and moral responsibility for Nazi
policies to blind forces and pressures.[2] However, the label is worth retaining
as a rough form of shorthand: it indicates the emphasis which these historians have placed on the machinery of government and its effect upon
decision-making in the Third Reich, on the dynamic interaction of the different component institutions of the regime and of the different forms of
political power on the structure of Nazi politics. The 'cumulative radicalization' of Nazi policies which ended in total war and genocide, the progressive
selection for implementation of only the destructive elements within the
regime's *Weltanschauung*, are portrayed not as the work of a deliberate dictatorial will, but rather as the consequences of the way in which the Nazi
leadership conceived of political power and of the way in which political
power was organised in the Third Reich: the dominant tendency was a striving towards 'politics without administration', or towards the substitution of
propaganda for administration.[3] The traits of systematization, regularity,
calculability inherent in the construction of a comprehensive administrative
base for the dictatorship, were perceived, particularly by Hitler, Himmler and
Goebbels, as limiting factors, as constraints, actual or potential, on their
power as they understood it. The regime thus characteristically produced
both non-policies or evasions which were of great political consequence at a
later date (civil service policy; economic policy in the late 1930s; treatment of
the Jews 1939–40), or sudden and drastic decisions which had not been prepared in the governmental machine and thus both disrupted existing policies
and practices and had quite unforeseen administrative and political results,
which latter in turn called for further ill-considered decisions (Reichskristallnacht, occupation policies in Poland). These characteristics of the political
system were enhanced in the late 1930s by the consequences of earlier
decisions to establish special new agencies and jurisdictions directly responsible to Hitler, whenever political tasks of especial urgency or interest arose
(Himmler's career to 1936, DAF, Ribbentrop's Office, Todt (autobahns), Four
Year Plan, Speer (cities)). This trend was symptomatic of the disintegration of
government into an aggregation of increasingly ill-coordinated special task-
forces; it also reinforced the fragmentation of decision-making processes,
since lines of political responsibility became increasingly blurred as ministerial and party jurisdictions expanded, were fractured, eroded and contested. That ministers learned of important decisions from the newspapers is

significant less of their personal (or collective) dispensability, than of fundamental changes which were taking place in the processes and procedures of
government and administration. There was less and less co-ordination. [. . .]

The central point in this 'functionalist' position is an insistence upon the
fact that the way in which decisions are reached in modern politics is vital to
their specific outcomes, and thus vital to the historian for an understanding
of their meaning. Only in retrospect and without consideration of decision-
making do policies appear to *unfold* over the years with a necessity which is
coherent. Nor, given the high degree of interdependence between all sectors
of public life, can this be a matter of individual decisions to be taken as 'case
studies' or 'models': uncoordinated, unprepared and arbitrary decisions,
decisions taken with regard only to a single project or goal (e.g. the Siegfried
Line 1938; the battle fleet 1939) had without reference either to side-effects or
to their impact upon other imperative projects, always further fragmented
the processes of policy-making, making them cumulatively more arbitrary in
their character, more violent and radical in their implementation, more conducive to competitive struggle among the executive organs of the regime.
Policy-making on this analysis is simply not comprehensible as the enforcement of consistent acts of dictatorial will—the view that it can be so com-
prehended is superficial and does not do justice to the available evidence on
the conduct of politics in the Third Reich. [. . .]

It is true that there are pitfalls in this type of analysis: in the study of
decision-making processes it is possible to get entrapped within the fascination of that subject, and to fail to place the results in a wider context of
interpretation; and, more importantly, if the debate about polycracy is
reduced to a discussion of how polycratic or monocratic the Third Reich was,
if polycracy is understood as a *static* concept which will help only to produce
a cross-section of the complex layer-cake of power structures, then this concept will indeed be of little use to historians. But the work of those attacked
for trivializing National Socialism has *not* fallen into these pits. Hans Mommsen has moved the discussion about polycracy into its proper dynamic
political context. He has shown, though not yet in an extended historical
account, how this discussion illuminates the formulation of policy and the
selection of goals in the Third Reich—and not just the regime's secondary
goals.

If this point is correct, it must be concluded that the study of institutions
and decision-making processes and enquiry into the polycratic nature of
National Socialist rule form an essential part of a liberal/moral history of the
regime and its crimes. They are not in themselves alien considerations or
factors, nor are they morally neutral. To introduce them into a moral historical enquiry is simply to insist that the responsibility of political leaders needs
to be and can be more widely defined than reference to their policy intentions
alone will allow, defined to include the workings of institutions. From this it

follows that the moral responsibility of the historian can be more widely defined too. The monstrous will and administrative dilettantism were, at the very least, necessary to each other. It seems trivial to resist this line of enquiry. [. . .]

What was permitted by conditions, or was possible, must be analysed, and it is here that marxism offers a more comprehensive framework than an approach which concentrates heavily upon political institutions and decision-making processes. We need to understand how it is decided what the available options are, which political leaders can choose among. Which alternative possibilities in the Third Reich were never even entertained as such by the leadership? Which got lost in the lower ranks of the bureaucracy or party and were thus never presented as policy options?[4] These non-decisions are an important part of any system of power. They define the parameters of possible intentions at the top of the system, which are almost always narrow at that level. It is in this analytically difficult area that the economy and the state need to be taken as a whole in the study of the Third Reich, for the dynamic of economic development played a primary role in the filtering out of impossible options, in determining what it was that could be decided in terms of policy. [. . .]

But then the will and the intention still have to be specified. It may be helpful here if we can find ordering concepts for the analysis of National Socialism, which *both* capture objective processes (capital accumulation, institutional darwinism, expansionism) *and* also relate clearly to the self-consciousness of the political actors. One such bridging concept is 'struggle', which incorporates notions of both competition and war. Competition and struggle were of the essence of economic and institutional processes, and they furnished one context of social life in general—the individual struggle for advancement and advantage, social mobility. In war too struggle appeared as an inexorable process. Struggle was also for the Nazi leaders a basic intention, the title of Hitler's book. Struggle was, in a distinctive and extreme manner, what their politics was all about, struggle against certain enemies but not struggle for any clearly perceived ends. Politics is struggle, as Hitler says in *Mein Kampf*. That one remark *does* perhaps have to be taken literally. But from this distance in time it can legitimately be, must be, related back to wider contexts than its author had in mind—to the highly competitive economic, social and institutional order over which he came to preside and which went under his leadership to destruction.

It might be suggested that just beneath the surface the Nazi leadership sensed that their particular struggle was a hopeless one. The enemies were too numerous, and, in the case of 'the Jews', they were by Hitler's definition too clever and too powerful *ever* to be beaten, even by the Third Reich. The crucial problem for National Socialist politics was to destroy as many enemies as possible while going down fighting to the very bitter end. Genocide was the most distinctively Nazi, the most terrible part of an over-arching politics of struggle. And these were the politics of a whole capitalist epoch.

This suggests in conclusion the need for a materialist history of social darwinism, a history which sees that subject in terms of economic forces and institutional power, in terms of social and economic practice and individual behaviour (intentions), and not just as a peculiar set of ideas which were influential around the turn of the century. It was that too, but it was also capitalist economic competition, economic and territorial competition between states, ethnic, national and cultural conflict, the struggle for eugenic improvement, the struggle on a group and individual basis for material advantage, respectability, virtue and God's grace. Only then in Germany did it become struggle as war and race war. In this broader sense of an interlocking pattern of structures, forces, ideologies and motives social darwinism was, of course, not peculiar to Germany. There are British, American and French versions; liberal conservative, fascist and Nazi versions. Maybe there is the framework for an enquiry here which is both structural and dynamic, and within which the specifically distinctive features and force of the National Socialist political will can be precisely identified.

The precision of the identification matters. Contrary to the implication in the charge that 'functionalists' or marxists trivialize National Socialism, it is logically and morally possible to hold a system responsible for terrible crimes, as well as those persons who exercised power within the system. While systems of domination and exploitation cannot be represented as individual moral actors can, it can be demonstrated that they generate barbarism. The demonstration of exactly how they have done so is often complex, but complex historical arguments are not indifferent to moral issues just because they are complex. If historians do have a public responsibility, if hating is part of their method and warning part of their task, it is necessary that they should hate precisely.

['Intention and Explanation: A Current Controversy about the Interpretation of National Socialism', in T. W. Mason, *Nazism, Fascism and the Working Class* (Cambridge: Cambridge University Press, 1996), 213–14, 216–17, 224, 227, 229–30; originally published in G. Hirschfeld and L. Kettenacker, *Der Führerstaat: Mythos und Realität* (Stuttgart, 1981).]

MICHAEL GEYER

56 The State in National Socialist Germany

Geyer argues that what was becoming a new orthodoxy concerning the fragmentation of the National Socialist system was in itself problematic. He argues that the fragmentation and conflict between autonomous power centres in themselves explain nothing, since the state in the twentieth century is characterized precisely by a decentring of state power and its fragmentation into dispersed entities operating—sometimes in conflict with other manifestations of itself— in numerous spheres of public life. Simply pointing out that the National Socialist state was incohesive explains nothing of the dynamism of the regime. The key to explaining this, according to Geyer, is to be found on the level of ideology.

The majority of studies on the German state still focus on the classical instruments of that state and their use, that is, domestic and foreign administration, the military, fiscal bureaucracies, and the police. They tend to juxtapose state and society, though they may—in the tradition of Max Weber—postulate a universalization of bureaucratic domination in both state and society.[1] Studies on the Third Reich have taken up this tradition. Hence, it is not surprising that conflicts between the 'state' or its parts like the army or the bureaucracy and the National Socialist party or 'movement' are seen as one of those elements that constituted and shaped the Third Reich. However, despite such conflicts, the Third Reich was always a state of both highly bureaucratized domination and of a social-ideological movement in power. The nature and the actions of the state in the Third Reich cannot be understood by merely analyzing conflicts between separate spheres of a bureaucratic state—i.e., the military, domestic, or fiscal bureaucracies—on the one hand and the National Socialist party or Hitler on the other.[2] Neither are they as separate as one might think, if one follows a still predominant trend in the historical literature; nor was conflict the only or even the most prominent form of relations between those spheres; nor, finally, do their frictions sufficiently explain the dynamics of the development of the state in the Third Reich. It is, indeed, necessary to reconsider the convenient notion of such separate spheres and entities and their interrelations from scratch. [. . .]

National Socialist rule did not create a neat division of labor among bureaucracies, but furthered a burgeoning system of bureaucratic domination composed of shapeless and ill-defined institutions. The state in the Third Reich was omnipresent in the sense that almost every organization and association had a statelike quality, that is, gained the quality of bureaucratic domination which is traditionally associated with the state. Some became more statelike than others while a number of institutions quite consciously opposed this tradition. Centralization of power in a contradictory and crisis-prone process on the one hand and extreme dilution of domination into a seemingly endless series of partial statelike organizations on the other hand is the major paradox of the Third Reich. If we want to study the state in the Third Reich, we have to deal with both tendencies.

Focusing on social classes and power in interwar Germany, the concept of a 'hegemonic bloc,' however, seems rather artificial. If anything, the striking element that urgently needs explanation is the lack of a serious alliance of dominant forces and the lack of cohesion among the subordinated groups in Germany. [. . .]

If we assume that a not so well ordered state and a not so cohesive society must be a weak or even self-destructive one, we just continue to extrapolate from our traditional assumptions about the Third Reich. This argument has certain emotional attractions: it denies the Third Reich the ability to survive on its own or, more fashionably, to reproduce itself, but it underestimates the National Socialist party and the state in the Third Reich. The National Socialists formed a genuine social movement and the Third Reich survived for twelve long years, six of which saw the bloodiest war in the history of the twentieth century so far. The not so well ordered state of the Third Reich must have been quite strong after all, and the not so cohesive German society must have been held together somehow. [. . .] What is it that held this confusion together and gave it focus and direction to take on the rest of the world deliberately and for such a long time? [. . .]

(1) It was distance among power holders that counted and that needed to be maintained, not cooperation and consensus. (2) The setting free of autonomous institutions led to a system of value-oriented—or, as we shall call it, ideological—politics that guaranteed this distance by ascribing status in a competitive field of political values and goals, rather than simply regulating ways and means of 'getting something.' Hence, the political procedure or process of regulating access to power became meaningless, while statelike spheres sprang up everywhere. (3) Politics melted into permanent conflicts over guiding values and priorities which shaped the parameters of the autonomous units. The 'state' as apparatus was omnipresent, yet it only existed in endless variations of more or less powerful autonomous units.

Once the postliberal and postauthoritarian quality of the political realm of the Third Reich becomes transparent, the fortunes of the National Socialist cadres and of Hitler are more easily comprehensible. The National Socialist party underwent most dramatic changes in the remaking of the state after 1933. It cut loose from its social-counterrevolutionary clienteles, culminating in the bloody purge of the SA in summer 1934. This could have been fatal for the party, especially for the middle echelon party functionaries—the 'facilitators'—had they not entrenched themselves in state and local administrations and converted the social power of the movement into control over administrations and organizations which were rigorously and brutally nazified. The former clientele-politics were thus carried into the state apparatus, with hair-raising results. The traditional bureaucracies grew larger and larger, new ones were added under the onslaught of National Socialist would-be bureaucrats, and administrative work was parochialized on all levels. The old bureaucracies which had held together the German state on a federal, state, and local level in the past became the targets for predatory polities, losing in this process of co-optation their character of rationally organized producers of state control. These administrations continued, of course, to discharge bureaucratic services, but their main purpose consisted in providing National Socialist patronage. Whole institutions expanded as a means of granting protection and security to party functionaries and of conferring status and paying salaries to individuals, rather than of rationally administering the state. The old authoritarian bureaucratic state was dissolved by the Nazi compradors.[3]

We have to be very careful not to confuse this anarchic struggle for positions—clientele politics—with National Socialist cadre politics. The top cadre of the National Socialist party had to struggle like everybody else,[4] but they set out from the beginning to enforce control in specific domains. They reshaped, partly created, and partly centralized the repressive and ideological state apparatuses. Control of the police, centralization of the ideological apparatuses, and penetration of the military structure, primarily with the help of Himmler's SS, and control over labor through the newly created German Labor Force were rigorously pursued. These domains became the base of National Socialist cadre power in the state.

What did this mean in the emerging Third Reich? We might be inclined to speak of a new division of labor, in which the National Socialists took over the realm of social control much like industry took over the organization of production, or the army the system of war preparations. Indeed, this is the role which some in army and industry envisaged for the National Socialists, but it is not the role which the National Socialists accepted. From the very beginning the National Socialists attempted to control the making of politics. The National Socialists cadre were not ordinary power holders, even though they attempted to control access to power and aspects of domination, much like every other power holder in the Third Reich. The National Socialists distinguished themselves by steadily assuming control over the political directions and values—the priorities that guided the relations among the autonomous institutions. They began to set the rules for ascribing status and rank to the various other power centers and to regulate the relations and the distance between them by defining political values and goals. They controlled the ideological domain whose essence was not the accumulation of power as such, but the guarantee of the political and social distance, which regulated and only made possible accumulation of power. Rather than simply controlling people, they began to control the process of reproduction of the state in the Third Reich. The National Socialist cadres achieved this position only slowly, but they set out to acquire it from the very beginning. The dynamics of this conquest, which ultimately led to a National Socialist monopoly over political directions and values, increasingly shaped the development of the Third Reich after 1934.

In this context, Hitler's role becomes more apparent. Standing beyond the 'extreme diffusion and dislocation of authority' and beyond the 'highly disordered proliferation of agencies and hierarchies'[5] he was the 'leader' (*Führer*) from the very beginning, though not at all in the totalitarian sense of defining the actions of each individual center of power. We would underestimate Hitler and his powers if we described his role as simple arbiter or mediator in the organizational jungle of the Third Reich. At times, he did exactly that, though more often he failed to mediate, letting conflicts run their disruptive course and bringing upon himself the epithet of being a weak dictator.[6] In fact, however, he eventually occupied the nodal points between the partial fields of power, defining ever more precisely what the conditions for domination were and how they were to be achieved.

The more the National Socialist regime approached war, the more it was anchored in one person alone, Hitler. His unique position neither implies that the dominant groups found a convenient figurehead, nor does it mean that Hitler was there despite them. Hitler occupied an ever more crucial position because the formation of a coherent alliance or a hegemonic power bloc was preempted by the way in which the state in the Third Reich was organized. Hitler increasingly managed to control the conditions that shaped distance and status of autonomous power holders, and he did so by relentlessly driving the Third Reich toward war. [. . .]

What was the ideology of the Third Reich and what was its role in National Socialist statemaking? We know that the Third Reich did not work in the way we traditionally assume that states work. It did not routinize access to power, but formed fields of autonomous units whose parameters and whose relations to each other were defined by a few 'political' priorities or guidelines such as armaments and war preparedness. The emerging system may look like anarchy to us, and it certainly looked like chaos to all the old civil servants in Germany. In reality the reference to anarchy conceals a number of concurrent historical processes: the rise of new centers of power, their competitive expansion, and the embattled formation of political priorities or, as we call it, ideological politics that regulated the competitive expansion.

['The State in National Socialist Germany', in C. Bright and S. Harding (eds.), *State-Making and Social Movements: Essays in History and Theory* (Ann Arbor: University of Michigan Press, 1984), 194, 196–7, 208–11.]

IAN KERSHAW

57 Working towards the Führer

Kershaw uses Max Weber's theory of charismatic domination to analyse a regime which he, rather like Franz Neumann, sees as characterized by an essential 'systemlessness'.

[Where] Soviet communism in the Stalin era, despite the dictator's brutal
destabilisation, remained recognisable as a *system* of rule, the Hitler regime
was inimical to a rational order of government and administration. Its hallmark was *systemlessness*, administrative and governmental disorder, the erosion of clear patterns of government, however despotic.

This was already plain within Germany in the pre-war years as institutions
and structures of government and administration atrophied, were eroded or
merely bypassed, and faded into oblivion. It was not simply a matter of the
unresolved Party–State dualism. The proliferation of 'special authorities' and
plenipotentiaries for specific tasks, delegated by the Führer and responsible
directly to him, reflected the predatory character and improvised techniques
immanent in Nazi domination.[1] Lack of coherent planning related to attainable middle-range goals; absence of any forum for collective decision-
making; the arbitrary exercise of power embedded in the 'leadership
principle' at all levels; the Darwinian principle of unchecked struggle and
competition until the winner emerged; and the simplistic belief in the 'triumph of the will', whatever the complexities to be overcome: all these
reinforced each other and interacted to guarantee a jungle of competing and
overlapping agencies of rule.

During the war, the disintegration of anything resembling a state *system*
rapidly accelerated.[2] In the occupied territories, the so-called Nazi 'new order'
drove the replacement of clearly defined structures of domination by the
untramelled and unco-ordinated force of competing power groups to
unheard of levels. By the time Goebbels was writing in his diary, in March
1943, of a 'leadership crisis'[3]—and speaking privately of a 'leader crisis'[4]—the
'system' of rule was unrescuable. Hitler's leadership was at the same time
absolutely pivotal to the regime but utterly incompatible with either a
rational decision-making process or a coherent, unified administration and
the attainment of limited goals. Its self-destructive capacity was unmistake-
able, its eventual demise certain. [. . .]

It was not in itself simply the undermining of 'rational' structures of
government and proliferation of chaotic, 'polycratic' agencies that mattered.
It was that this process accompanied and promoted a gradual realisation
of ideological aims which were inextricably bound up in the 'mission' of
the 'charismatic' Leader as the 'idea' of Nazism, located in the person of

the Führer, became translated between 1938 and 1942 from utopian 'vision' into practical reality. There was, in other words, a symbiotic relationship between the structural disorder of the Nazi state and the radicalisation of policy.

The key development was unquestionably the growth in autonomy of the authority of the Führer to a position where it was unrestrained in practice as well as theory by any governmental institutions or alternative organs of power, a stage reached at the latest by 1938.[5] After the Blomberg–Fritsch affair of February 1938 it is difficult to see where the structures or the individuals capable of applying the brakes to Hitler remained. By this date, the pressures unleashed in part by the dictator's own actions, but even more so by diplomatic and economic developments beyond his control, encouraged and even conditioned the high-risk approach which was in any case Hitler's second nature.

Meanwhile, in conjunction with the expansion into Austria and the Sudetenland in 1938, race policy, too, shifted up a gear. The *Reichskristallnacht* pogrom in November, instigated by Goebbels, not Hitler—though carried out with the latter's express approval[6] was the culmination of the radicalisation of the previous year or so, and ended by handing over effective centralised co-ordination of the 'Jewish Question' to Heydrich.

Territorial expansion and 'removal of the Jews', the two central features of Hitler's *Weltanschauung*, had thus come together in 1938 into sharp focus in the foreground of the picture. The shift from utopian 'vision' to practical policy options was taking shape.'

It would be mistaken to look exclusively, or even mainly, to Hitler's own actions as the source of the continuing radicalisation of the regime. Hitler was the linchpin of the entire 'system', the only common link between its various component parts. But by and large he was not directly needed to spur on the radicalisation. What seems crucial, therefore, is the way in which 'charismatic authority' functioned in practice to dissolve any framework of 'rational' government which might have acted as a constraint and to stimulate the radicalisation largely brought about by others, without Hitler's clear direction.

The function of Hitler's 'charismatic' Führer position could be said to have been threefold: that of unifier, of activator, and of enabler in the Third Reich.

As *unifier*, the 'idea' incorporated in the quasi-deified Führer figure was sufficiently indistinct but dynamic to act as a bond not only for otherwise warring factions of the Nazi Movement but also, until it was too late to extricate themselves from the fateful development, for non-Nazi national-conservative élites in army, economy and state bureaucracy. It also offered the main prop of popular support for the regime (repeatedly giving Hitler a plebiscitary basis for his actions) and a common denominator around which an underlying consensus in Nazi policy could be focused.[7]

As *activator*, the 'vision' embodied by Hitler served as a stimulant to action in the different agencies of the Nazi Movement itself, where pent-up energies and unfulfilled social expectations could be met by activism carried out in Hitler's name to bring about the aims of Leader and Party. But beyond the movement, it also spurred initiatives within the state bureaucracy, industry and the armed forces, and among the professionals such as teachers, doctors or lawyers where the motif of 'national redemption' could offer an open door to the push for realisation of long-cherished ambitions felt to have been held back or damaged by the Weimar 'system'.[8] In all these ways, the utopian 'vision' bound up with the Führer—undefined and largely undefinable— provided 'guidelines for action'[9] which were given concrete meaning and specific content by the voluntary 'push' of a wide variety of often competing agencies of the regime. The most important, most vigorous and most closely related to Hitler's ideological imperatives of these was of course, the SS, where the 'idea' or 'vision' offered the scope for ever new initiatives in a ceaseless dynamic of discrimination, repression and persecution.

Perhaps most important of all, as *enabler* Hitler's authority gave implicit backing and sanction to those whose actions, however inhumane, however radical, fell within the general and vague ideological remit of furthering the aims of the Führer. Building a 'national community', preparing for the show-down with Bolshevism, purifying the Reich of its political and biological or racial enemies, and removing Jews from Germany, offered free licence to initiatives which, unless inopportune or counter-productive, were more or less guaranteed sanction from above. The collapse in civilised standards which began in the spring of 1933, and the spiralling radicalisation of dis-crimination and persecution that followed, were not only unobstructed but invariably found legitimation in the highest authority in the land. [. . .]

Time after time, Hitler set the barbaric tone, whether in hate-filled public speeches giving a green light to discriminatory action against Jews and other 'enemies of the state', or in closed addresses to Nazi functionaries or military leaders where he laid down, for example, the brutal guidelines for the occu-pation of Poland and for 'Operation Barbarossa'. But there was never any shortage of willing helpers, far from being confined to party activists, ready to 'work towards the Führer' to put the mandate into operation. Once the war—intrinsic to Nazism and Hitler's 'vision'—had begun, the barbarism inspired by that 'vision' and now unchecked by any remnants of legal con-straint or concern for public sensitivities plumbed unimaginable depths. But there was no prospect, nor could there have been, of the 'New Order' settling into a 'system' of government. Competing fiefdoms, not structured govern-ment, formed the grim face of Nazi rule in the occupied territories. The rapaciousness and destructiveness present from the start within Germany now became hugely magnified and intensified with the conquered peoples rather than the Germans themselves as the main victims. [. . .]

The model of 'charismatic authority', which I have suggested is applicable to the Hitlerian but not to the Stalinist dictatorship, not only helps to characterise the appeal of a quasi-messianic personalised form of rule embodying national unity and rebirth in the context of the collapse of legitimation of the democratic system of Weimar. It also, given the irreconcilable tension between 'charismatic authority' and bureaucratic rule in the Third Reich, offers insights into the inexorable erosion of anything resembling a *system* of domination capable of reproducing itself. Within this 'Behemoth' of governmental disorder,[10] 'working towards the Führer' amounted to a selective push for the radicalisation and implementation of those ideological lines most closely associated with Hitler's known broad aims, which could gradually take shape as policy objectives rather than distant goals.

Above all, the 'charismatic' model fits a form of domination which could never settle down into 'normality' or routine, draw a line under its achievements and come to rest as conservative authoritarianism, but was compelled instead to sustain the dynamism and to push ceaselessly and relentlessly for new attainments in the quest to fulfil its chimeric goal. The longer the Hitler regime lasted, the more megalomaniacal the aims, the more boundless the destructiveness became. But the longer the regime went on, the less it resembled a governmental *system* with the capacity to reproduce itself.

The inherent instability of 'charismatic authority' in this manifestation— where the specific content of the 'charismatic claim' was rooted in the utopian goal of national redemption through racial purification, war and conquest—implied, then, not only destructiveness but also self-destructiveness. Hitler's own suicidal tendencies could in this sense be said to reflect the inbuilt incapacity of his form of authoritarian rule to survive and reproduce itself.

['Working towards the Führer: Reflections on the Nature of the Hitler Dictatorship', *Contemporary European History*, 2 (1993), 109–10, 113–14, 117–18.]

Section D

The 'Seductive Surface' of National Socialism

INTRODUCTION

The names mostly closely associated with the National Socialist regime—Dachau and Buchenwald, Treblinka and Auschwitz—themselves underline the extent to which the regime relied upon repression and existed to destroy. Yet momentary reflection upon the associations connected with the city of Nuremberg also reminds that, for all the conformity demanded by the regime, most Germans did not experience the years 1933 to 1945 solely as years of terror, repression, and fear, but also—until the military setbacks from the middle of the war onwards—as years of renewal, revival, and integration within the 'national community'. Of the victims of National Socialism, 95 per cent were foreign, and, apart from political opponents, the socially marginal, and the racially stigmatized, relatively few ordinary Germans saw the inside of a concentration camp. Far more important in terms of the everyday experience of ordinary Germans, and in its own way equally important to the regime in terms of maintaining popular consensus behind itself, was the 'seductive surface' of National Socialism. The annual Nuremberg rallies, with their invocation of the unity of people, movement, and Führer, were only the central point of a comprehensive calendar of rallies, rituals, and sacred events which sought to generate a process of perpetual integration and mobilization which extended into every sphere of life. Celebrations of the Munich Putsch of 1923, of the fallen heroes of the First World War, of inductions into the Hitler Youth, or of the annual harvest were, in turn, reinforced by National Socialist propaganda through every possible medium—architecture, art, film, radio, newspapers, posters, advertising, postage stamps, and paper money—which ensured that everyday life was comprehensively infused with a single symbolic system propagating both the integrative and exclusive dimensions of the vision of community which the National Socialist regime espoused.

Some of the most perceptive of contemporary observers of National Socialism in the 1930s and 1940s recognized in the regime's politicization of aesthetics and its aestheticization of politics both its most novel and its most threatening aspects. Far from seeing propaganda merely as a means to dupe the masses—as many crude Marxists were inclined to do—independent left-wing critics such as Ernst Bloch and Walter Benjamin produced what remain highly stimulating analyses of the self-representation of the regime and of the mass production and mass consumption of National Socialist images and symbols. In the post-war era, however, under the influence of the dominant 'totalitarianism' paradigm, such issues of fascist integration and mobilization did not receive adequate attention from most scholars. Most writing contented itself with reinforcing the exculpatory myth that the ordinary population had been led astray by the propaganda genius of Hitler and Goebbels. Even as this model of interpretation gave way under the 'fascism debate' of the 1960s, commentators were reluctant to see in either National Socialist ideology or ritual anything other than a means to divert the masses from the real nature of power under the regime; the rallies and celebrations of community were often held to be merely a means of papering over the continued divisions of industrial class society and of masking the failure of the regime to overcome class barriers as it had promised.

On one level this interpretation is true, but on another it runs the risk of failing to take fascist self-representation and self-understanding seriously enough. Anthropological analysis of the rallies and rituals shows that they were anything but diversionary invocations of an illusionary community, but rather embodiments of the core values of the movement and the regime and, in very general terms, expressions of political intent. It is not difficult to see in the endless columns of marching soldiers the militarist and imperialist values which were to result in the invasion of Europe; it is not difficult to recognize in the celebrations of conformity and community represented by the mass ranks of uniformed party members an ideology whose translation into practice manifested itself in the construction of the concentration camps; the corollary of the de-individualized ranks of 'people's comrades' at the rally sites was the piles of dehumanized corpses at Auschwitz. The rallies did not only represent National Socialism's 'will to power'—they also revealed its will to destroy. In this sense, Nuremberg and Auschwitz were two sides of the same coin.

As scholars have moved their focus away from the overtly terroristic aspects of National Socialist rule and examined the nature and extent of popular consent under the Third Reich, they have increasingly suggested that the propaganda and everyday symbolic practices of the regime had a genuine and not-to-be-underestimated role in mobilizing and integrating large sectors of the community behind the regime. It was particularly effective given that the regime's total control of the public sphere precluded the contestation of its propaganda by competing symbols and rhetorics. Although, for example, many workers were cynical about the 'Beauty of Labour' schemes fostered by the German Labour Front, there is evidence to suggest that such campaigns to improve the working environment of factory workers—which went very much with the grain of modern factory management—were not without positive resonances; similarly, although in reality modern sports facilities for industrial workers were built by already overworked workers performing unpaid overtime, the multitude of leisure and travel activities developed by the Labour Front's 'Strength through Joy' schemes were among the most popular achievements of the regime. As Alf Lüdtke's work has also shown, the National Socialists' glorification of the 'honour of labour' might have been rejected by some, but for others it had sufficient overlaps with pre-existing notions of the 'dignity of labour' prevalent among workers themselves that the regime could genuinely appear to be raising the status of workers in German society. Although such integration on the level of everyday life does not in itself explain the extreme collapse in values represented by the Holocaust, it does help to explain the nature and extent of popular acquiescence in the policies of the regime and why it was that, outside of small closed groups of ideologically committed opponents, resistance was so limited in scope and effect.

58   Inventory of Revolutionary Appearance

> The unorthodox Marxist philosopher Ernst Bloch stressed how the appropriation of elements of the political activism and ritual of the Left was aimed at creating the illusion of Nazism's revolutionary nature and disguising what he saw as its reactionary goals.

When two do the same thing, they do not do the same thing. Especially when one copies what the other is doing, in order to deceive. So it is today, when the Nazi cannot yet reveal the way he really looks and what he really wants, and thus disguises himself. He pretends to be rebellious, as we know; the most dreadful white terror against populace and socialism which history has ever seen camouflages itself as socialist. To this end its propaganda must develop sheer revolutionary appearance, garnished with thefts from the commune. The business of deception could not be done more cheaply any more; for even the slogan of master-race nationalism would not go down well unless—apparently meeting the real need of the people—it first poses as an anti-capitalist one. [. . .]

1. First they stole the colour red, stirred things up with it. The first declarations of the Nazis were printed on red, this colour was enormously extended on the fraudulent flag. The posters gradually grew paler and paler so that they no longer frightened the financial backer. The flag itself bore its crookedly coiled, slantingly distorted symbol from the beginning anyway, and it is named after it, not after the colour. But when an efficient worker cut the swastika out of it, there still remained metres of red appearance on the cloth. Only with a hole in the middle, gaping like a mouth and totally empty.

2. Then they stole the street, the pressure it exerts. The procession, the dangerous songs which had been sung. What the red front-line soldiers had begun, the forest of flags, the marching entry into the hall, precisely this was copied by the Nazis. The Parliament day of Potsdam, on 21 March 1933,[1] steered the would-be revolutionary image more into the usual, military channel again, but 1 May 1933 made up ground with stolen magic all the more shamelessly. In Offenbach they erected the maypole, the old Jacobin symbol of liberty, and danced around it like members of the White Guard, indeed Hindenburg in person celebrated the world holiday of the proletariat. And the business concerns advertised for the first of May in the newspaper that nothing but 'workers of the brow and fist' were employed in them, and shared in the celebrations in honour of the day. The life of profit even stole his festive day from the worker too, laid down derision as its trump card.

All in all they pretended to be merely workers and nothing else, thus distorting boundlessly. Took the word in the wishy-washiest sense, and so spread a nebulousness in which nobody knows who is the guest and who the waiter any more. So the 'Völkische Beobachter'[2] writes about the pimp Horst Wessel:[3] 'He was a worker in the truest sense of the word, a worker on himself, a fighter with his self, and thus he gained inner firmness and strength.' With such a truest sense of the word there are of course no exploiters, class struggles, let alone exploited people; unless one is not a worker on oneself, but one for others, like all proletarians up to now, unfortunately. Only the word proletarian is not adopted by the Nazi, any more than the word crisis, for which even in the Weimar Republic the image 'undulation of economic life' was substituted and in the Third Reich, with even better speculation in human stupidity, they simply say 'November crime'.[4] The 'workforce' at any rate becomes an extraordinarily cordial mush, the basic contradiction between capital and work, which the petite bourgeoisie has not understood anyway, is totally blurred with it, and the fraudulent monster is nevertheless, or for this very reason, called a 'Workers' Party', causes the murderers and their victims to greet one another as comrades and even poses, by practising Marx's resolving of the proletariat with shootings and concentration camps, as the real stuff of socialism. [. . .] Thus in the fraudulent Nazi world from the Thyssens to the lowest donkey-worker there is only a single classless 'work-front', and the 'Reich Peasants' Day' in Goslar likewise recognizes no differences any longer between big landowner and little peasant, apart from the insignificant ones which are denoted by acre and hectare and are of no consequence before the Father of all at harvest festival. Whatever constitutes village poverty and urban proletariat is merely described by Hitler as faint-heartedness, which can be removed by operation in purely psychological terms, precisely through inner elevation out of 'the depths of the people'. [. . .]

3. And finally they pretend to think of nothing except what will change things. This sounds almost formally Marxist, recognizes no intellect in itself, but places it instead in the service of politics. Goebbels expressly declared the film 'Battleship Potemkin' to be a model for the German film, so far does the formal consent go, as the crook and thieving perverter imagines it.[5] What is important, according to the latest dramatic guidelines of these shabbily cunning plagiarists, is not how good or bad the performed play was but the mood in which the spectator leaves the theatre. The pleasure in theatrical performance for its own sake, the problems of the private sphere and the ivory tower, the development of unpolitical themes, are all rejected; Goebbels desires no romanticism, unless it is 'steely' (an admittedly strange alloy); he wants tendency in the theatre instead of l'art pour l'art. All this seems, undoubtedly, as deceptively anti-contemplative as a forgery can only be which confuses the Marxist application of theory to practise with the patter of a con-man.

['Inventory of Revolutionary Appearance' (1933), in *Heritage of our Times* (Cambridge: Polity Press, 1991), 64–7; originally published Frankfurt, 1962.]

59 Magic and Manipulation

In an important early post-war treatment of the subject, Vondung analyses how the National Socialists appropriated and reworked a range of pre-existing genres in their development of a legitimizing set of rites, rituals, and ceremonies. Arguing that National Socialism relied particularly heavily on Christian ritual practices and liturgical forms for its inspiration, he characterizes the movement as a 'political religion'; he also argues that the 'revolutionary transformation' achieved by the regime was not one of transformed social reality but one of transformed perception and representation. In drawing attention to rituals as embodying ideological beliefs which both contained and represented reality for their participants, Vondung rejects both totalitarian theories of ideology as manipulation and the more instrumentalist readings of fascism prevalent in the late 1960s, which also tended to downplay the significance of ideology as a belief system.

The National Socialist cult embraced a wide spectrum of celebrations. These ranged from spectacular 'consecration hours' (*Weihestunden*) at national and party ceremonies, via National Socialist 'celebrations of life' at birth, marriage, and death, up to simple Sunday 'morning ceremonies' of the party organizations. Party offices created specially for the purpose oversaw the structuring of the ceremonies as if they were ritual congregations, and issued guidelines and sample programmes. They tried to develop 'forms of ceremony of liturgical character', and consciously sought to give the National Socialist ceremony the 'character of a cultic event'.[1]

As well as words of the Führer and songs, literary works of a particular type—so-called 'choral poems'—were used as liturgical texts. Such 'celebratory poems' and 'cantatas' were used exclusively for the structuring of National Socialist ceremonies: many were commissioned by the relevant official. Special ceremonial locations, ritual events, and solemn props increased the formality of the cult.

The existence of a cult in the Third Reich gives grounds for believing that National Socialism was in certain respects religious in character. [. . .]

It could at first sight be argued that the ridiculous nature of, for example, the 'celebrations of life' and the guidelines for their arrangement are additional evidence of their irrelevance and lack of importance. Against this it must be emphasized that the term 'ridiculous' has been coined for the analysis of the phenomena under discussion for the purpose of its critical characterization. It must further be emphasized that the characterization of a phenomenon as 'ridiculous' does not necessarily make it harmless: a matter can appear completely ridiculous to those who are not divorced from reality, but can be dangerous in its concrete impact despite this. This is possible when the ideologues—as happened here—take themselves and their ideology so seriously that they lose contact with reality, and are no longer in a position to recognize the ridiculous nature of their undertakings. They then pursue their opinions with such deadly earnestness that they do not shy away from the appropriate measures for implementing their objectives. If, however, the power and social effectiveness of the ideologues who take themselves seriously becomes great enough, then they can only be prevented from pursuing their activities by their being rendered physically harmless. This happened in the case of National Socialism and of the cultic projects of the National Socialist Führer through the military defeat of Germany. [. . .]

Analogous to sacred vocabulary, the significance of most ritual acts of the National Socialist cult was preordained. This means that from the outset and generally they were understood to be solemn, because they were known (in identical or similar form) from the Christian cult. Of course such acts are also to be found as typical cult rituals in other religions, but the conspicuous and sole model for the imitations of the National Socialist ritual stage managers was unquestionably the Christian cult in this case, as was the case with the imitations of the liturgical structure of the ceremonies, the liturgical form of the responses, and the sacred vocabulary. [. . .]

The most obvious imitation was that of the form of the procession, as is customary in the Roman Catholic Church—particularly in the Corpus Christi procession—by the traditional march of the 'old fighters' from the *Bürgerbrau* to the *Feldherrnhalle* on 9 November. As with a normal parading of the colours, the consecration took place reciprocally. The solemn character of the procession—due to its form, due to its origin in the Christian cult of procession—was heightened still further by the meaning of this procession. This meaning lay in the myth into which the historical event had been transformed [. . .] A further heightening of the solemn character was achieved by carrying a 'Holy of Holies', the blood flag, and by the destination of the procession, the 'holy' location of the *Feldherrnhalle*. On the other hand, the procession itself had a consecrating function. The consecration of the contents and objects of the ceremony was promoted and supported considerably with the aid of the solemn ritual: the transfiguration of the historical event into a myth with the consecration of all moments connected to it. The most manifest was the consecration of the objects which appeared physically in the procession: the 'blood flag' which was carried in the procession, and the *Feldherrnhalle*, to which the procession moved; likewise the consecration of the 'old fighters with blood decorations' marching at the front of the procession as a type of living 'martyr' and into 'apostles' of the idea.[2]

Not only the procession on 9 November showed the solemn function of the ritual parade: marching in general, this most beloved form of National Socialist demonstration, was interpreted as a ritual parade. This became clear particularly at the ceremonial marches or march-pasts in the various events at Reich party rallies, and also in the *Thingspiel* with its 'mass choirs streaming to the stage' from within the rows of spectators.[3] [. . .]

Like the procession, the marching of the brown columns meant that the 'sacred' wished to conquer the world, by which are to be understood the contents of National Socialist ideology in this case. For, thanks to the consecration of most of its contents, the ideology acquired a 'sacred' aura and assumed a religious character. However, the marching also fulfilled the other functions of the procession: it acted as 'mass crystal' and awoke, in those who were not repelled from the outset, the inclination to follow this vital procession striding obviously into a happy future. And, finally, the marching columns, in hundreds and thousands, and particularly in the impressive manner in which they appeared at Reich party rallies, were the most conspicuous, powerful, and impressive self-portrayal of the regime and its ideology. [. . .]

The syncretic National Socialist symbolic apparatus is not appropriate to reality: mankind and society in the modern technological world cannot be interpreted by the myths and symbols described. On the other hand these speak to the consciousness of persons whose mental needs ran counter to the realities and requirements of the external world. Two further facts give great importance to the symbolic world of the ideological myth and to the fact that they were articulated through cult. First the symbol could be made visual in the cult: the central symbols—blood, people, Reich, and Führer were manifest in the liturgical performance within the celebrative community, and in the person of Hitler. The borrowed revelatory symbols as expression of historical-speculative projections occupied a special position; however, the dominant cosmological symbols, which surrounded or substituted for the centre of the symbol, could likewise and still more obviously be represented. Because the symbols were acted out concretely, the contents of the consciousness experienced an affirmation and ostensible confirmation in reality. Secondly, these symbols were especially suited, when articulated within the ritual, to changing the view of the external world of those participating in the celebrations, to switching off their intellect, and to releasing their emotions. A state emphasizing feeling, a state of ecstasy, even, of the type described above lent itself exceptionally to influencing people. [. . .]

The basic objective of the manipulation, that of converting members of society into submissive followers of National Socialism, attains particular importance with regard to the war for which Hitler had striven since the beginning of his political career. Not by chance were the vital forces celebrated in the cult, and obedience, heroism, and readiness to make sacrifices promoted to the rank of central virtues, these qualities incidentally always being determined vitalistically. It is moreover characteristic that the organizing of celebrations was not only continued during the war, but that there was also an expansion and intensification of the activity in this area, even though the celebrations were less successful than the impressive mass events of the pre-war years. At least they tried with all their might—particularly for instance by the ceremonies honouring heroes—to keep the population in the 'correct' frame of mind, i.e. in readiness to conduct the war with full commitment and to make the appropriate sacrifices, even after defeat had become certain for all clear-sighted people. The National Socialist *Volksgemeinschaft* was to be formed into a collective which submitted unconditionally to the will of its Führer and followed blindly wherever it was led. [. . .]

The question occurs of whether the National Socialist cult was capable, in view of its social function, of overcoming reality. Undoubtedly it served the aims of manipulation adequately: in the pre-war period quite successfully but during the war less effectively. In this respect, it had concrete effects on reality: as an instrument of the attempt to construct a social order by means of magic, to integrate the members of society into this order, and to activate them for the goals of the manipulators. If it is possible in respect of such influences to speak generally of 'overcoming' reality then this would be only in the limited and instrumental sense. The actual social, economic, and political problems could not be overcome adequately, because the protagonists refused to apperceive them as they were or to transform reality into an imaginative image of reality itself. Because reality did not therefore change, confrontation between the actualities and demands of reality on one hand and the magical attempt to influence them on the other hand was unavoidable, the latter having of necessity to give way. In fact the artificially stimulated Führer, Hitler, could prosecute the war to the bitter end: but he could not avoid defeat.

[*Magie und Manipulation: Ideologischer Kult und politische Religion des Nationalsozialismus* (Göttingen: Vandenhoeck & Rupprecht, 1971), 8–9, 111–12, 155, 157–8, 197–9.]

ANSON G. RABINBACH

60 The Aesthetics of Production in the Third Reich

The 'aestheticization of politics' in National Socialist Germany reproduced itself in all spheres of society, including in the factory environment and industrial relations, where improvements to work conditions and symbolic assertions of the notion of 'community' within the workplace served as compensation for the political emasculation of the working class. These methods simultaneously embodied capitalist strategies of management and control and a eugenics-orientated programme of hygiene and health improvement. Rabinbach argues that the growing emphasis on productivity and technology in Nazi aesthetics is indicative of the problems faced by the German economy in the late 1930s as a result of accelerated rearmament. Whether or not this superseded pre-industrial and more romantic *völkisch* imagery, the eugenics-inspired agenda itself remained central to DAF programmes into the war.

The attempt to legitimize political rule through aesthetic symbolization is perhaps the decisive characteristic distinguishing twentieth century fascist regimes from other forms of authoritarian domination. Under National Socialism, aesthetics and politics were integrated not only in mass festivals and public architecture, but in the sphere of production as well.

Under the slogan—'the German everyday shall be beautiful,'—the Bureau of Beauty of Labour (*Amt Schönheit der Arbeit*) attempted to radically transform both the interior and exterior landscape of the German industrial plant. After 1934, intensive efforts to persuade management to remodel and renovate the work-place became a central focus of the German Labour Front. According to Robert Ley, head of the Labour Front, prior to National Socialism workers had been systematically convinced that their activities served no higher purpose, that their labour was only a commodity, that they were proletarians.[1] Beauty of Labour would return to the worker 'the feeling for the worth and importance of his labour.'[2] Albert Speer, the bureau's director, envisioned the emergence of 'a new face of the German workplace' and a new epoch that no longer considered factory architecture inferior.[3] In the past degraded to a 'joyless compulsion', labour itself would now give way to 'a new spirit', manifested in the 'new formation of the environment.'[4]

Beauty of Labour combined social policy with cultural policy in a single administrative unity. Its function, the creation of social harmony, was to be achieved through aestheticization of labour relations. Aesthetic illusion was integrated into concrete social forms, motivated by political goals. As such, Beauty of Labour is a paradigm of the aestheticized politics characteristic of National Socialism. Moreover, factories were not simply beautified by improvements in their external appearance; the subordination of human subjectivity to industrial processes was itself expressed in an aesthetic form. If Nazism had brought about the political subordination of labour, it returned to it a cultural image that 'would liberate physical labour from the curse of damnation and feelings of inferiority which had imprisoned it for hundreds of years.'[5]

Beauty of Labour's ideological function was underscored by the limitations which the National Law of Labour, adopted in January 1934, placed on the Labour Front by establishing the absolute hegemony of management within the industrial enterprise.[6] The resulting dual structure of authority separated possession of the means of production from the instruments of political control and legitimation.[7] Through Beauty of Labour the control of management over labour could be furthered, while still maintaining the appearance of Labour Front activity in the interests of labour. The aesthetic transformation of the workers' environment was to result in a political transformation of the German worker.

Beyond its specific ideological function within the Labour Front, the development of Beauty of Labour reflects the profound change in Nazi culture and ideology that emerged after the seizure of power. Increasingly, Nazism was forced to reconcile its earlier programme and ideology to the demands of an industrial society in crisis.[8] Especially after 1936, when the Four-Year Plan and 'war economy in peacetime' became the *ultima ratio* of Nazi policy, and when full productive capacity and the labour shortage brought about a greater effort to raise industrial output and efficiency through rationalization and the intensification of labour, Beauty of Labour embodied a reversal in the traditional ideological substance of Nazi cultural policy. By combining industrial psychology with a technocratic aesthetic that glorified machinery and the efficiency of the modern plant, Beauty of Labour signified the emergence of a new dimension in Nazi ideology. In its image of technology and design, its architectural principles, and above all in its growing functionalism in all areas, Beauty of Labour is a striking example of the Nazi modernism and cult of productivity and efficiency which eclipsed the traditionalism of earlier Nazi ideology in the late 1930s. [. . .]

After 1939 the bureau was severely limited by reductions in its operating budget brought on by the war. Its activities of the previous half decade were largely abandoned in the interest of contributing to the war effort, mostly by providing technical information on the construction of shelters, troop entertainment centres, methods of improving blackout techniques, and energy saving measures.[9] But in its six years of activity almost 80,000 factories were transformed by the bureau's projects.[10] Lighting, ventilation and noise levels were improved, wardrobes, washrooms and gymnasiums provided or remodelled, lawns and parks built surrounding the plant. Flowers, decorations and new coats of paint appeared. Factories and canteens were provided, and 'community rooms' and 'comradeship houses' were constructed in numerous plants. Architectural modernism and contemporary design were furthered in industrial construction. The German factory had indeed received a new face.

In Beauty of Labour the utopian promise of an industrial society where work was beautiful and the class struggle abolished was given political and administrative form. Its goal was the domestication of labour, to be achieved by treating the plant as a 'sphere of life', detached from the social relations that enclose the world of work and removed from the spectres of working class culture and autonomous organization. Beauty of Labour was to integrate the German worker, deprived of political and economic representation into the 'facade' socialism of the Labour Front. As objectified ideology it signified a critique of liberalism, in which concern for hygiene and aesthetics in the environment restored the value and meaning of work. But if Beauty of

Labour presented itself as a radical break with the aesthetic deficiencies of industrialization in the liberal epoch, it solidified and strengthened its political-economic basis: management was supreme, the bureau had no power to enforce its policies—its ultimate goal was the depoliticization of industrial relations. As industrial psychology, Beauty of Labour extended the domination of material nature to the nature of the worker, whose consciousness was reduced to an environmental 'factor', to be transformed in the interest of productivity and habituation. As social policy Beauty of Labour subjected labour to the intervention of techniques derived from the politicized science of industrial relations of the 1920s and 1930s on an unprecedented scale.

Perhaps most important, Beauty of Labour not only integrated aesthetics into the world of production, but derived from production a technocratic aesthetic which dissolved the *völkisch* and pre-industrial imagery of pre-1933 Nazism into a new legitimation based on the autonomy of technical rationality. If Nazism did not display the generation of machinery that characterized Italian fascism in the early 1920s, or the Soviet Union in the early 1930s, this was true only before 1936, when Germany's condition could be attributed to the ills of modernity, and the support of the *Mittelstand* could be secured by the image of its dissolution.

As early as 1935 Ernst Bloch contrasted the widespread rejection of contemporary society by a German middle strata which 'sought transcendence in the past', with an exaggerated faith in the power of 'neutral cleanliness, new architecture and its comforts, manufactured goods, technical functionalism and the standardization of products', as a dialectic of 'non-contemporaneity and contemporaneity', specific to Germany's historical development.[11] The shift from one extreme of this dialectic to the other took place once Nazism could no longer rely on the simple legitimacy of *völkisch* ideology and an agrarian utopia. Policies directed at the *Mittelstand* were abandoned. The expansion of technical rationality to all aspects of the production process in the Four-Year Plan was extended to ideology as well. The goal of full employment, an end to the economic crisis, and industrial supremacy and military expansion, led Nazism to abandon its 'utopian anti-modernism' to the institutional and ideological requirements of war production.[12] If Nazism's mass support was rooted in its promise of a Germany free from the discontents of capitalism, rationalization and the eclipse of traditional values, its historical function was to exorcize the traditional patterns of culture which conflicted with modern modes of production. In Beauty of Labour this shift in cultural values was objectified ideologically and administratively. Its emphasis on production and the glorification of technology as ends in themselves was affirmed by persons and principles derived from the *Neue Sachlichkeit* that swept Germany in the mid 1920s. The aestheticization of machine technology, Taylorized work-processes and efficiency provided the new requirements of the regime with a cultural *raison d'être*.

It is the image of the worker, however, that most clearly illuminates the unity that binds the extensive range of Beauty of Labour's efforts between 1934 and 1939. The worker, like all the subjects of National Socialism, becomes an ornament of technically preconceived and constructed environments. As objects of management and production they are subordinated to the tempo of machines: 'At machine four stands a punch operator, she activates the mechanism, moves to and fro, places plate after plate in the devouring jaws of the monster.'[13] The small geometric roof gardens organize workers into prescribed patterns during rest pauses; sports areas organize their physical activity; newly cleaned machines organize them for greater productivity; neat rows of washing facilities order their cleanliness. The image culminates in the neat rows of happily producing workers which adorn the factory itself.

['The Aesthetics of Production in the Third Reich', *Journal of Contemporary History*, 11 (1976), 43–4, 66–7.]

HANS DIETER SCHÄFER

61   Split Consciousness

Hans Dieter Schäfer argued that the experience of everyday life in the Third Reich, and the memory of that daily experience, was and is characterized by split consciousness. While propaganda, indoctrination, and terror formed an important part of the equation, they existed co-terminously with the integrative experience of the regime's stimulation of consumerism, a consumerism which did not necessarily have to be matched by a growth in actual *consumption*. The ability of the regime to create the *illusion* that it could satisfy the demands of an increasingly consumerist culture played an important role, according to Schäfer, in the stabilization of the regime in the eyes of workers and the middle classes alike.

It has become customary to draw statistical comparison between real wages in the Third Reich and payments made in the Weimar Republic: for the most part, attainment of the previous level can be seen, or—as in the case of the above-scale remuneration in 1938/9 at companies central to war preparations—a modest increase above the 1928 level. This perspective takes no account of the shock triggered by the 1929–32 crisis. Unlike during the Weimar Republic, the stability achieved during the rearmament boom mobilized powerful influences which held the system together. Part of the workforce felt it was being wooed, because of the overheating of the economy at the end of the 1930s: 'the experience that individual achievement paid off through exploitation of the rearmament economy, whereas the model of trade union-based representation of interests had failed in the world economic crisis' supported the decline in class-war thinking:[1] the labour shortage, which in 1939 led to the recruitment of 200,000 foreign workers,[2] created a socio-psychological climate which was closer to the economic miracle of the Adenauer 'restoration' than the conflicts under the Republic. The symbolic payments of the state, special contributions of industry, as well as 'Strength through Joy' trips and events stabilized relations to the Hitler State to a not inconsiderable degree. In 1938, every third worker took part in 'Strength through Joy' holidays.[3] The regime skilfully nurtured the yearning of the labour force for embourgeoisification. In weekly programmes, the district office in Munich was offering not only holidays but also theatre and concert visits plus courses in such sports as riding, sailing, tennis, and skiing—which earlier had been the exclusive preserve of the higher social strata. Political problems were mostly ignored in the lecture events. Topics included the crossing of the Atlantic in a sailing boat (29 Mar. 1939), carcinogenic illnesses (17 May 1939), colour photography (15 Feb. 1940), Chinese wisdom (17 Apr. 1940), the child with learning difficulties (16 June 1941), and new research from the Inca Empire (26 Mar. 1941). It has long been overlooked that social advancement in the Third Reich did not only occur symbolically. [. . .] The fact that during the last years of the Third Reich the 'workers showed a closer solidarity with the rest of German society than in the final stages of the German Empire or the Weimar Republic'[4] is *inter alia* an expression of the integration effectively promoted during the war.

Whereas the dictatorship convinced the workforce above all by security and opportunities for upward mobility, it also bound the middle and higher classes through the production of a wide range of consumer goods. Those values which were propagated in the rearmament economy with things such as 'home ownership', 'car/caravan', 'radio/television', 'camera', 'kitchen appliance', 'washing powder', 'hygiene/cosmetics', etc. were those which our consciousness assigns almost exclusively to the 1920s or to the Adenauer period. Advertising addressed both National Socialist concepts and—particularly—private aspirations. Thus there was advertising for the radio using the words 'Germany is marching in Nuremberg! Join in the experience! Become a radio listener'[5] or which showed the 'people's receiver' suspended above a large crowd. On the other hand, the individual radio listener was depicted as someone who—withdrawn from the masses—was listening to his Blaupunkt-Super. The cigarette manufacturers Sturm-Zigaretten GmbH, Dresden, sought to mobilize the 'old Fighter' for its products using the brands 'Trommler' (Drummer), 'Alarm', 'Sturm' (Assault), and 'Neue Front' (New Front), and individual facial features were deliberately toned down, appearing on the placard as shadows or objectified, as in the marching columns of the Reich party rally filmed by Leni Riefenstahl. The Coca-Cola advertising has a quite different feel: the smiling face appears in close-up; the purchaser is attracted by the subjective, warm expression which was omitted in the 'Trommler' advertising. The formula 'the likes of us in particular need a break now and then, best of all with ice-cold Coca-Cola' underpins the sense of the politics-free sphere. A Coca-Cola advertisement in the periodical *Die Wehrmacht* published by the Armed Forces High Command in the second half of October 1938, in which the occupation of the Sudetenland was celebrated, has a quite different character. A hand holds the Coca-Cola bottle up high in front of a world map: 'Yes! Coca-Cola has a world-wide reputation'; the adjacent text emphasizes that 'to an ever increasing extent, highest concentration and sharpest exertion of all senses' would be needed by the 40 million vehicle drivers from all corners of the earth, who therefore treasure the 'refreshing break with ice-cold Coca-Cola'. The advertisement, which was to appeal to German soldiers, mixed cosmopolitan and technological-sporting elements—which from the outset stood in successful competition with the racial-national ideals, and which attracted the majority. [. . .]

Whereas the presence of Coca-Cola in the Third Reich has almost been forgotten, our consciousness links the Volkswagen, as a further symbol of the West German economic miracle, with the Hitler State even today. Presumably the recollection of it has become easier because the National Socialists did not keep their promise to produce more than 100,000 cars for the market in 1940. Hitler initiated the development of the VW himself and had taken part personally in shaping it. At the opening of the International Automobile Exhibition in 1936, he called for the manufacture of inexpensive motor vehicles because 'the German people have exactly the same need as [. . .] the American people'. Hitler promoted the Beetle shape ('it should look like a beetle. One only needs [. . .] consider Nature and how it copes with streamlining')[6] and drafted proposals for the bodywork.[7] The foundation stone of the Volkswagen factory was laid in May 1938: the prototypes developed by Porsche were exhibited in Munich and Vienna at the autumn trade fair, and then driven in columns through several major cities.[8] Confidence in the NS regime was so great that 300,000 purchasers had acquired savings certificates for these cars by November 1940. From the beginning, Hitler had declared that the 'motorization of Germany' was to be the objective of National Socialist policy: the automobile exhibitions were integrated into the annual ritual calendar above all in order to bind Youth to the system.[9] Special trains and buses brought visitors to Berlin: the press printed detailed photographic reports and 'racing cars with numbers' dominated the picture even in toyshops. 'Tanks, caterpillar tractors, motorcycles, open cross-country vehicles . . . lorries' and 'the black limousine of the Führer copied true to life and often with working headlamps' could be seen in the shop windows. According to a retrospective of the automobile show of 1935, one could argue without exaggeration that 'the car has become popular first with the Führer and—thanks to him—with the German people'.[10] In fact the number of car owners increased somewhat more rapidly in the Third Reich than in Great

Britain although a comparison with the USA shows that Germany was still far removed from the stage of a modern consumer society.[11] Here too, the statistical data should be given less consideration than the expectations fostered by the regime. [. . .]

As today, the car cult of the 1930s was an expression of the growing attraction which mechanical inanimate objects exert on human beings in industrial society, but 'in a world of uncertainty', the car appeared then as 'the only thing reliable, precise, and never disappointing'. According to one of the contemporary manifestos, youth showed its solidarity with technology in the economic crisis, because technology 'could show unequivocal, measurable results'.[12]

When Peter Suhrkamp enthused about the 'strong and simple unity of each engine' and speculated that out of this bond 'came about something akin to race for the human',[13] he endowed both the paramilitary and the private love of the car with a mythical aura which released humans from their isolation. The publicity spoke of the 'systematic mercilessness of Opel's planning' and blended the technology with the power of uncontrollable natural events: '*blitzschnell* in acceleration—from walking pace to that of an express train in a few seconds, with temperament on the hill, and completely safe in the bend—this is the Hanomag "Sturm".' The advertising style—which concentrated on hardness and objectivity—anticipated changes with which Göring was to characterize Hitler's war strategy in 1940: 'With lightening speed, the Führer changes the marching plans of the armies and divisions wherever necessary and concentrates them where he proposes to wield the powerful blow.' 'Ice-cold' and '*blitzschnell*' characterize not only set phrases from Coca-Cola and car advertising but also the mental coldness of Hitler, who also readily used both attributes to connote his actions. This materialization exerted a powerful attraction on the people and imbued political events with a technical character, and technical events often with a political character.

[*Das gespaltene Bewusstsein: deutsche Kultur und Lebenswirklichkeit 1933–1945* (Munich: Carl Hanser Verlag, 1981), 116–20.]

PETER REICHEL

62   The 'Seductive Surface' of the Third Reich

In common with other scholars who seek to place National Socialist mass culture within a broader chronological continuum, Peter Reichel characterizes the cultural policies and practices of the Third Reich as 'Reactionary Modernism', in the sense that they sought to harmonize pre-modern national traditions with an industrial economy, modern technology, and uniform mass culture. In arguing that the production of culture under National Socialism cannot be evaluated using purely aesthetic judgement, but should also be examined for its political and instrumental intent, Reichel suggests that the aestheticization of polit-ics in the Third Reich be seen within the broader development of the modern culture industry, with its role in enforcing authority and order in advanced industrial society generally.

To a great extent, and perhaps more than any other regime of the modern period, the National Socialist regime attempted to define and legitimize itself by means of its art and popular culture.[1] National Socialist leaders and large parts of the population regarded 'major cultural achievements'—including technological progress—rather than economic achievements as the real 'supreme achievements of community life'.[2] At least until the war began. Hitler is known to have seen himself as a frustrated architect. For him, the boundary between a work of art and the art of political leadership was a fluid one. Raised in a Catholic society, strongly influenced by the exceptional circumstances of war, an actor, artist, and politician inspired by Wagner, Hitler regarded politics as a form of 'total work of art'. Cultural issues played a major part in his many speeches.[3] The National Socialist regime expended considerable organizational, financial, and human resources on trying to con-trol and promote cultural development in Germany. And even the core of National Socialist ideology, the racial doctrine, was also an element of a 'concept of society' geared to visualization and 'confirmed in the image'.[4] Its biological, social, and Darwinist foundations were aesthetically exaggerated. Thus in the racist vision of the 'nordic' race; thus in the model of the 'national body' whose concepts of superiority, purity, and harmony character-ized the ideology of the 'people's community' and were to justify exclusion followed by liquidation of those 'alien to the nation'.

In the Third Reich the political function of aestheticization was therefore as necessary to the internal integration of society as it was to the regime's self-image and to the state crimes perpetrated in its name and on its behalf. To this extent, there appears to be some justification for the emphatic state-ment that the aesthetic phenomena and action plans themselves tended to become 'an independent form of fascist rule', 'although originally intended only to help aestheticize it'.[5] In concrete but superficial terms, Hitler under-stood aestheticization as 'beautification of life', as producing a virtual reality that would influence the perceptions and image of reality of millions of people, and would allow them, visually and symbolically, something that was denied to them in reality. Those directing this virtual reality wanted to make the masses believe in a view of things that deviated from empirical reality in ideological terms. The fact that they themselves lived in a world full of myths and fictions made it all the easier for them to do this. And they probably also succeeded in creating a seductive surface at least until well into the war years, because they were capable of using the technical resources available in a sophisticated and professional manner. To this extent, one must at the very least describe this as instrumental rationality. Moreover, the National Socialist directors were dealing with a public that preferred to be entertained or edified—depending on taste and education—rather than politicized or even indoctrinated. In this, it was deceiving itself in two ways, not only by believing in the autonomy of the fine arts, but also and above all with regard to Hitler's political programme. The willingness of the masses to deceive themselves corresponded to the policy of his regime, which was geared to deception. The reason why his regime put so much effort into pursuing aestheticization was that the old elite of the new National Socialist leadership had left behind two major unresolved questions, which Hitler's supporters now expected him to resolve:

1. One was the social question. The solution to it involved overcoming the class-based division of society of the Weimar period, or at least forgetting it or simply making it invisible. This was the objective of the suppression of the organized labour movement on the one hand and, on the other, the model of the 'people's community'. This model, with its many welfare state facilities and popular events in the modern culture of leisure and mass entertainment of the time, was designed to give German society a fake air of Socialism.

2. The other was the national question. In the stylized and mythologized models of the Führer and the Reich, the solution to it took on symbolic form, and with all the window-dressing and stage-managing of power, Germany's longed-for national greatness, unity, and international political influence became an apparent and auspicious reality.

The reason why aestheticization appeared to be so essential in dealing with the national and social questions was that achievement of these goals was either possible only by repressive means or by complete illusion. This strategy served not so much to alter reality as to change the perception of it or to conceal the regime's true intentions. The Nazis used a variety of instruments and techniques for this purpose, the great majority of which they found in the basic ways in which bourgeois and proletarian political players portrayed themselves. They perfected and at the same time perverted these self-portrayals, which did not, incidentally, simply perish with the Third Reich.

The following four concepts were particularly important to implementation of the aestheticization strategy. At the same time, however, one reservation must be expressed, namely that when one later attempts to describe the situation in a discriminating and systematic way, there is inevitably a tendency to ascribe too high a level of rationality and intentionality to the players involved and to their actions.

1. The personification of politics, i.e. the reduction of complex, anonymous political structures to one name, one idol, one model with whom to

identify personally, and to the stylization of him in the heroic/religious mode of the times into the 'redeemer/emperor', into the Führer who stood out from the crowd, but who at the same time came from the masses and was, 'for better for worse', bound up with them.

2. The mythologization of politics by the conjuring up of older worlds and ways of life (Führer, Reich, community), but also via mythologically exaggerated modern models (nation, revolution, technology). This gave expression in particular to the desire to supplant a political process based on a system of abstract rationality. In other words, the desire for emotionalism, spontaneity, and authenticity, away from a world in which the conflicting social interests are resolved through compromise, which was experienced as being unsatisfactory, and also away from a world of confused but formally regulated procedures. With the myth, sacred enchantment appeared to return to a world that had almost completely 'lost its magic' (M. Weber).

3. The stage management, window-dressing, and ritualization of politics to overcome its shabbiness and to satisfy the needs of the masses for identification, for community, entertainment, and beauty. The choreography of the mass events sought to satisfy these needs, as did architecture and the fine arts, or the programming of mass media and a representative style for the elite that was at the same time folksy and monumental. A variety of traditions were taken up and used as instruments in the process: the inheritance of romanticism and the wars of liberation, Prussian classicism and militarism, the Christian liturgies and elements of the culture of the labour movement, and, last but not least, the symbolism and mystique of old and new German nationalism with fire and banners, blood and songs.

4. Standardization of the individual, i.e. shaping of the individual (into a 'national comrade' and a member of the 'people's community') via the attentions of KdF (Strength through Joy), aesthetic products, and the culture industry. This process of an expanding, rationalized working environment, a public culture of consumption and technical elegance, began in Germany in the 1920s and continued in the 1930s, before coming to fruition in the 1950s. In it, the individual was increasingly subjected to technical and industrial functionalism. At the same time, he had absolutely no awareness of a democratic modernity geared to emancipation and the autonomy of the individual. Instead, he seeks happiness or at least compensation in the form of what is on offer and the facilities available in the audio-visual mass media, leisure, travel, sport, and technology. As long as the individual tends to merge into the crowd and allows himself to be overwhelmed by a reality that is superficially attractive, the deception of society and deception of the self constantly mesh with one another, and beauty and violence cease to be perceived as contradictions.[6]

[*Der Schöne Schein des Dritten Reiches: Faszination und Gewalt des Faschismus* (Munich: Carl Hanser Verlag, 1991), 371–5.]

63 The Honour of Labour: Industrial Workers and the Power of Symbols under National Socialism

> Alf Lüdtke argues that the Nazis' emphasis on 'the honour of labour' found a receptive audience among a working-class population whose own beliefs in the 'dignity of labour' represented a central part of a working-class culture which the traditional parties of the Left had failed to tap into. In doing so, the Nazis were able to elicit the cooperation of key sectors of the working class in the pursuit of the goals of the *Volksgemeinschaft*.

The forms of acceptance were not restricted only to an 'aestheticization of politics' staged 'from above.' This thesis of Walter Benjamin, formulated in 1935–6 in the very face of fascism, grasps only the one, spectacular side of symbolic practice.[1] Benjamin insistently drew attention to the 'enormous festive processions,' 'monster meetings; mass sports events,' and, above all, the war. According to Benjamin, these mass movements made it possible for the participants 'to express themselves' but 'certainly not to exercise their own rights.' In two respects Benjamin fell victim here to the exaggeration of the isolation imposed upon the persecuted exile. On the one hand, he failed to see the continuation of previous ways of constructing meaning (*Deutungsweisen*). At the same time, the variety of unspectacular everyday practices eluded him, in which in the work-place, in the neighborhood, in the family, but also in the 'mass organizations' the participants themselves produced and experienced the fascination with and the utilization of the 'new times.'

The National Socialist leaders and offices certainly did include the 'great' gestures and scenes. Marches and mass performances were not just staged on 1 May 1933. Ley's attempt from the autumn of 1933, in countless 'Houses of German Labor' to give permanent significance to his organization, the German Labor Front, can be understood as an attempt to 'eternalize' the mass movement.[2] Here it stayed at the level of the gigantic; yet at the same time vague plans, starting in 1934, with the opening of the annual Reich Professional Contest (*Reichsberufswettkampf*), brought the appearance of leading Nazi 'big-wigs' on to a large stage with considerable media effect.[3] And in 1937 the Reich Party conference of the NSDAP took place under the motto 'The Party Day of Labor.' The usual marches and speeches, the usual fanfare and flag dedication were supposed to embody 'the triumph of labor', so too was a 'monumental well installation' which the city of Nuremberg provided as a gift at the opening of the party meeting. [. . .]

The mass rituals were, however, not everything by a long shot. The everyday connection of material achievements with sensual, tangible symbols became decisive, even when they remained limited to certain occasions. In every instance, experiences, anxieties and hopes could be seen to be addressed, which the labor movement of the Weimar Republic had scarcely even noticed. The recognition of the materiality of the work-place, with its hardships and unwholesomeness during work, made reference to key points of proletarian life and survival experiences. Brighter lighting or bigger windows, more spacious machine placement, the expansion of washing facilities or cloakrooms, or, indeed, their provision for the first time, places to sit during breaks set apart from the machines—such symbolic announcements promised a new quality of recognition and practical welfare. And individual examples produced a striking reinforcement (of the message). Above all, who previously had publicly even conceded the importance of this side of everyday reality or even made an attempt at change? In this context of experience the symbolic references meant real improvements. [. . .]

The 'honor of labor' alluded to 'community' (*Gemeinschaft*), but at the same time turned to the individual. The picture language makes this concrete. Picture icons of muscular labor, toil and sweat reflected real-life experiences. They were intensively deployed in the Nazi picture press. However, photographs in illustrated newspapers, mainly in the factory newspapers of the 1930s, increasingly displayed bodies and faces that, despite all of the stylization of steeled corporality, not infrequently bore traces of the individual.[4] This, too, was not a complete novelty. The working-class press of the 1920s had, however, projected personal goals much more emphatically upon the symbols of the masses and the collective. By contrast, the individualizing work-symbols of the 1930s carried multiple meanings in a special way; they cited the picture of the worker, secure in his experience, who controlled the tool and the machine and thus referred to pride in work and the pride of the worker. But at the same time—and this was new—the half-length portraits and pictures of the worker's naked chest placed individual faces at their center-point. These pictures of individuals and of small groups seldom emphasized demonstratively heroicizing gestures. Much more often they carried a restrained documentary signature. To this extent it was perhaps possible for the first time to see openly addressed that 'unhappy consciousness' about the worker's existence, that only a few workers put on display, but which certainly worried many more. [. . .]

The field of force in which men and women workers and working-class wives found themselves in Nazi Germany was transformed. Silent as well as open violence increased perceptibly. But at the same time, a multitude of symbolic practices and presentations facilitated an altered self-perception. Equally decisive were concrete sensual, as well as general-rhetorical, reinforcements of the 'honor of labor.' The diffuse rhetoric of the sense of 'community' in the factories gave individual survival interests in the work-places—and in fact the self-assertiveness of the 'quality worker'—increased legitimacy and opportunities. In this way, in an unprecedented fashion, hopes for a 'good life' could be sensually experienced and felt to be justifiable. Naturally in the process a certain ambivalence was unavoidable; individual survival, especially the exploitation of the new chances, required continuous acquiescence and, not infrequently, active participation in the fascist mobilization of the economy for war. Survival and enjoyment of the 'honor of labor' thus also meant becoming an accomplice to criminal policies.

['The Honour of Labour: Industrial Workers and the Power of Symbols under National Socialism', trans. and repr. in D. Crew (ed.), *Nazism and German Society 1933–1945* (London: Routledge, 1994), 95–8.]

JOST DÜLFFER

64   The Matrix of Totalitarian Imagery: Public Space, the National Socialist Year, and the Generational Cycle

In the following discussion of National Socialist efforts to remodel the public sphere, Jost Dülffer offers a cautious assessment of the extent to which the regime succeeded in using architecture, public ceremony, and education to mobilize the 'people's community' behind war.

Hitler's position within the system was based not least on the faith of others in him as the Führer. As that faith had its limits, not only among the victims of National Socialism, the claim that Germany was one national community was not completely accepted. But in the stereotyped phrases of Nazi propaganda the Führer and the nation constituted a unity, and this was expressed in many ways. The organization of public space, the calendar of events and celebrations during the year, and the teaching that every German was simply a biological link in a long succession of generations reflected the claim to totalitarian inclusiveness. [. . .]

In Berlin, Hitler, who himself would have liked to have become an architect, soon ignored existing authorities and simply began, with a staff sworn to carry out his plans, to construct monumental buildings in the centre of the city. For Hitler, Berlin had remained a city of Hohenzollern palaces. But he was interested in creating the capital, to be named Germania, of a future world empire. The centre of that capital would be the intersection of two gigantic streets in a north-south and an east-west direction, with imposing buildings for ministries and other state and party agencies. The intersection would be dominated by an enormous triumphal arch twice as high as the Arc de Triomphe in Paris. In the north of a bend formed by the Spree a domed hall with space for 180,000 people was planned, whose volume was to have been seventeen times that of Saint Peter's Cathedral in Rome. In Munich, at the Königsplatz, the National Socialists were able to realize their first plans as early as 1933–4. The main features of their plans for Munich involved the construction in Pasing of a gigantic new railway station, whose domed hall would have a diameter of 285 metres, and the building of an impressive boulevard where the tracks of the previous station had been. The old main railway station was to be replaced by a monument to the 'Movement' reminiscent of the Washington Monument, but with a height of 189 metres, crowned by an eagle with outspread wings. In the western part of Hamburg, Germany's largest port, a gigantic bridge was planned over the Elbe; to the east of it, in Altona, a Gau forum was to rise along the river with a party tower block of 250 metres and a public hall for 50,000 people. Similarly, in Linz on the Danube a great bridge over the river, construction projects along its south bank and, at right angles to them, a square for public functions surrounded by large buildings were planned. In Nuremberg, the area outside the city used for the annual Reich party rallies was expanded beyond the size required for its existing functions. A stadium for 400,000 people and the Luitpold Arena with an assembly area for 200,000 people were intended to provide a quite different setting for future party rallies than had the previous assembly area at the Zeppelin Field. In 1940 these five cities were politically canonized as 'Führer cities'. Partly through Hitler himself and partly through party functionaries this building frenzy spread to all large German cities, which could be declared 'renewal cities' on the basis of a law as of 1937. In 1941 there were at least forty-one such projects, most of them with a Gau forum of the party, a march-up area, and/or a broad street with correspondingly prestigious buildings, often intended for cultural institutions. In addition, planned towns were built in connection with armaments production, such as Wolfsburg (the city of the 'Strength through Joy' car), and Salzgitter (built for the smelting of domestic iron ore).

Very few of these projects were completed during the war, but many were started and, from 1937 onwards, their number increased: entire old city centres were ruthlessly gutted, torn down, levelled. In view of the general housing shortage, this did not strengthen social cohesion. At the same time, by order of the Führer, thousands of millions of Reichsmarks were diverted from rearmament, which in itself had priority. For Hitler, this urban redevelopment was actually intended for the next thousand years: 'Therefore, we deliberately exempt from criticism . . . the work to be performed for this purpose in coming years, and submit it to the judgement of the generations that will come after us' (1937). In this sense the plans presented to the public were intended to strengthen the German people's national self-confidence 'to satisfy legitimate requirements for their existence . . . by all [necessary] means' (1939). This was to be done primarily through armaments, which were used to prepare for war. But that was to remain a secret. The buildings were the visble part of the same process. They would not be constructed because of 'megalomania', but 'for the coldly calculated reason that only such imposing works can give a people the self-confidence . . . that their nation is the equal of any other, even America'. It was an urban architecture intended to promote the development of a mentality among the German population which would prepare them for future world domination, and was often not even functional. In spatial form, from the parade streets to the great halls and arenas, individual Germans would be made clearly aware of their absolute subordination to uniform thinking and acting, and also of their chance to participate in later national greatness. In many respects this reflected adolescent fantasies of omnipotence that had been raised, as it were, to the level of a state doctrine and which now were to be acted out.

Of course not every Gau leader who wanted to erect his own Gau forum with party buildings did so with the primary intention of promoting German world domination. Rather, Gau leaders were mainly interested in their own provincial prestige. And this occasionally made them objects of scorn even within their own ranks, as when the Gau leader of Mecklenburg, Schwede-Coburg, expressed his concern that the 'great ideas' were 'often misunderstood by the smallest "Führers and Artists" in pocket editions'. But the high costs in the present created a framework for a rite which was to be fully developed only in a vision of the future. This became clear above all at the party rallies held annually in Nuremberg under various titles ('Will', 'Freedom', 'Honour', 'Work', 'Greater Germany') until 1938. For 1939 a rally under the title 'Peace' was planned, and probably for the following year one with the title 'Victory'. At the rallies a different National Socialist formation marched up every day, from the Labour Service to the Hitler Youth and the SA. And the armed forces, too, participated. The formations were drawn up, roll-calls were taken in military style, parades were held, and flags were dedicated. But Hitler himself was always the centre of attention around which the activities of the formations were organized. He appeared at every assembly and made a speech or brief address, which was then declared to be a definitive guide for the future. And the rallies and military roll-calls were not limited to September in Nuremberg; there was an abundance of such events at other times and places in Nazi Germany.

The entire year was marked by new holidays which in many respects competed with, but were not able to replace, those of the Church year. Himmler, Darré, and Rosenberg all had the intention of presenting themselves as founders of a neo-heathen religion; but they were able to do this at most within their own spheres of activity. Official celebrations continued to be characterized to a considerable degree by the use of cultic elements of the most varied origins in addition to those of the Christian churches, all of them presented in such a way as to suggest, as it were, an inner salvation through the Führer. The National Socialist year began with the celebration of the 'Seizure of Power' (*Machtergreifung*) on 30 January, and continued in March with 'Hero Remembrance Day' (*Heldengedenktag*). This was followed by Hitler's birthday on 20 April, the Day of Labour (*Tag der Arbeit*) on 1 May, and

Mothers' Day and the summer solstice in June. The festival of thanks for the harvest (*Erntedankfest*) on the Bückeberg near Hameln at the beginning of October became a kind of agricultural annual party rally of the NSDAP. In addition to the party rally in Nuremberg in the autumn, the festival of 9 November commemorating the failed *putsch* of 1923, itself an attempt to blot out the disgrace of the revolution of 1918, was the high point of the National Socialist year. [. . .]

The efforts to establish a totalitarian state were never completely success-ful. Many of the appeals directed especially at German youth were narrow, specifically Nazi forms of ideas which had originated in youth organizations before the First World War. But it was several years before all other organiza-tions could be eliminated. Youthfulness and physical conditioning, above all in sports, but also through physical labour, were among the aims that helped make the word 'intellectuality' a disparaging term and caused the quality itself to be ridiculed. But in many respects the kindergartens of the National Socialist Public Welfare (*NS-Volkswohlfahrt* or NSV) were built upon the foun-dation of beginnings of pedagogical reforms in the 1920s, and had to compete with church establishments until 1940–1. In addition to the schools, the Hitler Youth and the Union of German Girls played important roles in the rearing of young people through youth centres and hostels, scouting games, and other leisure-time activities. These organizations competed both with parents and with schools, where more or less convinced National Socialists clashed with traditional teachers and with the content of their teaching. Because the schools could not be changed quickly enough, élite National Socialist schools were established. These were the National Political Education Institutes (*Nationalpolitische Erziehungsanstalten* or Napolas) under the direction of the SS, and the Adolf Hitler Schools of the NSDAP; both types were boarding schools that tried to attract pupils from a relatively broad social spectrum. For the subsequent education of select pupils there were the so-called Order Castles (*Ordensburgen*), which were located in scenic areas and established a new curriculum for the further ideological training of future party function-aries. It is doubtful whether, apart from the SA and the SS, these institutions were able to exercise as strong an influence in forming the consciousness of their pupils as Hitler claimed in his speech. It must be emphasized, however, that the Wehrmacht was legitimately incorporated into the National Socialist educational system, as it had been quick to revise its training guidelines to make them compatible with a fanatical National Socialism.

In this multi-dimensional matrix of National Socialist public space, the party year, and the biological-generational chain, one parameter had a decisive role: military orientation, subordination, and obedience to superiors, any superior and especially to Hitler personally. In its unconditionality this expressly included the readiness to give one's life for the national community when ordered to do so, especially in war.[1] The visible side of this was, of course, the active fighter, the soldier prepared to die. Of a total of 134 state funerals held in Germany between 1888 and 1989, seventy took place in the National Socialist period. Here the after-effects became evident of the deaths of millions of soldiers in the First World War, which in the 1920s had led to unprecedented efforts to bestow meaning on that catastrophe, and not only in Germany: the dead were declared to be, and then transfigured as, heroes who were to be emulated. Monuments were only one of the more conspicuous manifestations of this tendency. And among the German monuments, the Tannenberg Memorial in East Prussia, which provided the backdrop for the funeral of Hindenburg in 1934, was the most notable example. The cult of the dead was omnipresent, and previously canonized heroes were joined by specifically National Socialist martyrs. Even in the Weimar period a large monument was dedicated in Düsseldorf to Albert Schlageter, who had been shot for sabotage by the French during the occupation of the Ruhr in 1923. Horst Wessel was an SA man honoured because of his death after a fight with the members of the Communist Party in 1930; the song named after him became a second national anthem of the National Socialist state. Then there was Herbert Norkus, a member of the Hitler Youth who died in a similar brawl in 1932. The martyr cult with honours for the dead played a role in numerous National Socialist ceremonies, but nowhere more importantly than on 9 November, when the march of 1923 to the Feldherrenhalle in Munich was symbolically repeated and the National Socialists who had died then were, so to speak, resurrected when during the subsequent roll-call their names were called out individually over their coffins and the crowd responded by loudly shouting: 'Here!'. Radio coverage of the march was reminiscent of Christian religious processions with individual stations of the cross. The conclusion of the ceremony caused spectators and participants to think of resurrection and even salvation. Here, as elsewhere, the message was clear: only in a new, and as it were an expiatory war could fulfilment be found. Every training camp of the Hitler Youth had as its motto, 'We have been born to die for Germany.'[2] Everything was directed towards this aim, although such emotional conditioning to be heroes who could only reach their goal through death was incompatible with the official peace propaganda of the regime before September 1939, which itself was conducted with an eye to international opinion.

The test for the success of this indoctrination was the concrete danger of war. When a European war seemed imminent in the Sudeten crisis of September 1938, the German people showed themselves dismayed and displayed no readiness, not to mention enthusiasm, to go to war. In a secret speech to the press on 10 November 1938, Hitler was forced to take this reaction into account when he admitted how regrettable it had been that 'circumstances' had forced him to 'mouth a pacifist line' for years.[3] But it was not possible to create enthusiasm for a war. When the policy of extreme risk actually did unleash a war, in September 1939, the prevalent mood in Germany was one of anxiety; there was no war euphoria such as had marked the outbreak of hostilities in 1914. The memory of what a major war in the twentieth century could and would inevitably mean was still too strong. To die a hero had not become the joyfully accepted life's goal of most Germans. Interestingly enough, during the Second World War, which constantly provided new opportunities for funeral ceremonies for men who had died for Germany, the propaganda glorifying precisely that supposedly highest aim in life was reduced. Reality overtook myth. The experience of suffering caused by the deaths of millions of soldiers in the war made such heroic pathos appear increasingly hollow.

[*Nazi Germany 1933–1945: Faith and Annihilation* (London: Arnold, 1996), 111–16.]

Section E

National Socialism and German Society

INTRODUCTION

As with all individual aspects of the Third Reich, scholarship on the relationship of the regime to wider German society has reflected the evolution of broader frameworks of interpretation of the Nazi regime, changes in the relationship of post-war West Germany to its Nazi past, and shifts in historical method more generally. Initially, the image of an all-pervasive totalitarian regime dominating all areas of society and closing down all space for action outside of the regime's control precluded analysis of accommodation and dissent in everyday life, of participation, conformity, and opposition from different sectors of society. Initial studies of the conservative resistance to Hitler were as much indicative of a desire amongst an overwhelmingly conservative generation of historians to use the resistance as a means of relegitimizing elite conservative politics in the years following the Third Reich as of a dispassionate desire to analyse the conditions under which resistance could occur and the political motives underlying it. Indeed, scholarship on the relationship of both various social groups and various institutions to the regime has remained highly politicized and pressed into the service of broader contemporary agendas. Conservative scholars have tended to celebrate conservative resistance; scholars of more left-wing persuasion have focused on the much broader base of resistance amongst workers; historians of church opposition to Hitler who are close to the churches have often conflated attempts to preserve the institutional autonomy of the churches in the Third Reich with principled opposition to the regime and its racial policies as a whole.

During the 1960s, scholarly attention began to focus on broader popular resistance to Nazism, especially among the workers. Further, the emergence in the 1960s and 1970s of social history, 'history from below', and the history of 'everyday life', along with women's and gender history, enabled more nuanced discussion of the range of responses of different sectors of society to the regime—from resistance and opposition through dissent and non-conformity, through apathy and conformity, to consent, support, and active participation. Far from penetrating German society in its entirety, the regime appeared to succeed only partially in asserting its domination; many areas, it seemed, remained relatively immune to the attractions of Nazism; working-class and Catholic subcultures in particular, it seemed, remained at least partially intact. As the subtitles of some of the volumes of the 'Bavaria in the Third Reich' project of the 1970s implied, 'society' and 'regime' were often 'in conflict'.

More recently, however, scholars have tended to take a more sceptical view of the extent to which German society, or sectors of it, preserved its immunity from the Nazi state or remained impervious to its attractions. Manifestations of dissent on single issues could exist alongside fundamental support for the regime as a whole; rejection of one aspect of the system did not have to preclude participation in other, maybe more murderous aspects. In many ways, the key to understanding the stability of the regime's support might lie in recognizing the ability of the regime to accommodate limited expressions of dissent—even this most terroristic of fascist dictatorships negotiated its dominance over society and proved flexible in responding to popular opinion.

Where popular opinion is concerned, the overwhelming majority of Germans gave their consent to the regime until the middle of the war, and much of the underlying dynamism of the regime derived, according to the prevailing recent view, from its consensual and voluntarist underpinnings in German society. Moreover, broad sectors of society did not confine their role to offering plebiscitary backing for the regime. Tens and hundreds of thousands of 'ordinary Germans' became the active agents of its racially motivated killing campaigns. If we extend our definition of this to include the war on the eastern front, the figure rises to millions. As a social movement Nazism had mobilized the national, social, and ethnic resentments of whole sectors of society; as a regime, it co-opted whole sectors into the mass murder of those national, social, and ethnic groups against whom these resentments were directed.

Much recent work has attempted to illuminate the nature of popular participation in the crimes of the Third Reich. Although there is general consensus that a climate of ethnic suprematism pervading the regime and society as a whole was one important precondition, few scholars would accept the notion that ideological commitment was the sole, or even the prime, motive for many people's active collaboration in the crimes of the regime. Members of the SS were undoubtedly motivated by radical anti-Semitism. Their mentalities and actions also did much to foster the murderous 'occupation climate' in which a wide range of mass crimes was perpetrated. Yet SS men were not representative of German society as a whole, Jews were not the regime's only victims, and anti-Semitism in itself does not offer a satisfactory explanatory framework for the actions of ordinary people at the time. A mixture of anti-Semitism, more general racism, obedience to authority, socialization, acclimatization to brutality, peer pressure, and various other situational pressures was involved. Our abhorrence of the crimes of the Third Reich derives from even momentary consideration of the appalling suffering of the regime's millions of victims, Jewish and non-Jewish alike. Yet perhaps the most frightening lessons to be learned derive from consideration of the nature and motives of the perpetrators. For, under particular conditions, very ordinary people were co-opted into committing crimes of almost unimaginable proportions.

i Resistenz?

65 *Resistenz* and Resistance

> The 1970s witnessed the emergence of a more social history-orientated approach to the Third Reich, and with it a far more nuanced understanding of popular reactions to the regime. One of the most important projects to emerge was the multi-authored, multi-volume study of Bavaria during the Nazi period, coordinated by Martin Broszat. Analysing popular attitudes and behaviour during the period, the project detected a range of nonconformist or dissenting attitudes, manifesting themselves in a wide variety of everyday situations, which could not be characterized as 'Resistance' in the narrow sense, but which, taken together, suggested that there were many spheres of life and social milieux which the regime succeeded only partially in penetrating. For this they coined the term *Resistenz*. In this passage Broszat summarizes the findings of the project.

The perspectives pursued within the conceptual framework denoted by the term 'conflict' [. . .] led to an examination of resistance specifically from the perspective of its impact. To denote this, the medical term *Resistenz* has been used [. . .] *Resistenz*, in this context, means in general terms: effective warding off, delimitation, containment of the National Socialist regime or its claims, irrespective of who or which forces were involved or from what motives.

Such *Resistenz* could be grounded in the continued existence of relatively independent institutions (churches, bureaucracy, armed forces), in the assertion of ethical and religious norms, institutional and economic interests, or legal, spiritual, or artistic (among other) standards which ran counter to National Socialism; effective *Resistenz* could find its expression in active counteraction by individuals or groups (in the forbidden factory strike, in the criticisms of National Socialist measures from the pulpit), in civil disobedience (non-participation in National Socialist gatherings, refusal to give the Hitler salute, ignoring the ban on contact with Jews, prisoners of war, etc.), in the maintenance of communities of sentiment outside of the coordinated National Socialist organizations (in anti-Hitler Youth youth cliques, in church communities, in social gatherings of former members of the SPD, or suchlike), or purely in the preservation of anti-National Socialist principles and the immunity preserved thereby against National Socialist ideology and propaganda (rejection of anti-Semitism and racial ideology, pacifism, and suchlike). The only precondition for these different forms of attitude or reaction fulfilling the impact-centred concept of *Resistenz* is that they played an actual role in curtailing the impact of the National Socialist regime and National Socialist ideology. In this way defined, the—value-free—concept of *Resistenz* is on the one hand broader and on the other hand narrower than the value-loaded concept of 'Resistance' or 'Opposition' as emerges from perspectives based on the history of behaviour. It includes on the one hand manifestations of effective delimitation of the power of National Socialism, which were hardly, or not at all, politically motivated, conscious oppositional stances (for example, peasant resistance to particular plans or managerial interventions of the National Socialist Reich Food Estate organization); on the other hand it excludes the oppositional attitude which was only latent in the individual conscience but did not translate into action or communication with others, however 'ideal' it may have been.

The concept of *Resistenz* thus stands in clear contrast to those tendencies in research on the resistance which—by extensive exclusion of the actual impact of the resistance—concentrate primarily on the history of the motives and acts of resistance. In terms of the opening comments it also, however, opens up a substantial complementary and enhancing perspective on the treatment of and research into the subject.

In every socio-political system, even more so under a political regime such as that of National Socialism, what counts politically and historically above all is what was *done* and *effected*, much less what was merely *wanted* or *intended*. The historical failure of the active German resistance in the Third Reich does not dispense us from this assessment, but demands it of us again and again. If [. . .] it is made clear anew that active, fundamental resistance to the Third Reich remained in vain almost everywhere, but that on the other hand effective *Resistenz* can be located in a multitude of different political-social spheres of the German population, then this strikes us as a finding which in itself should give cause for reflection on the premisses of the concept of 'Resistance'.

The question is: should and can the legacy of the Resistance be confined to the futile martyrdom of people and groups who, despite the incredibly small chances of success, attempted to engage in active, illegal resistance to the regime? Is it not equally tragic that the many 'small' starting points for a more realistic partial opposition and *Resistenz*, which repeatedly offered themselves in the most diverse stages of development and spheres of policy of the National Socialist regime, were so little made use of? Should the historical legacy of the Resistance—also in respect of comparable challenges in the present and in the future—not be seen precisely here too, in the 'little manifestations' of civil courage, of feasible and effective *Resistenz*? We believe that the answer to this question is 'yes'. The significance in this context of the concept of *Resistenz*, focused as it is on the question of impact, consists in the fact that it offers insights into what ways it was actually possible to set limits to the regime's authority in the Third Reich. It also helps to avoid a demonization and monumentalization in historical perceptions of the Third Reich.

But the value-loaded concept of 'Resistance' or 'Opposition' which focuses above all on the subjective action (and not on its objective impact) gains a specific accentuation through the perspectives deployed by this project. With a perspective focusing on behavioural analysis the status of such 'opposition' is not measured exclusively or primarily by its motives or goals, but in relation to the real *situation* in which the opposition emerged, in relation to its greater or lesser difficulty or ease, and according to the extent of its individual or collective feasibility in the context. This means applying the same behavioural yardsticks to 'Resistance' as are used to measure 'opportunism' or 'fellow-travelling'. After all, the same could not be expected of different groups or individuals irrespective of their preconditions and their situation in the 'Third Reich', but rather more of those who in the National Socialist era—as officers, priests, and senior civil servants, for example—still had power, influence, social and institutional support, and were equipped with pre-National Socialist norms, and less from those who were isolated, powerless, young, or heavily dependent. Only in the context of all these co-determining circumstances in any given case can one construct a moral 'ranking' of opposition.

The classification of resistance according to behavioural criteria means, in addition, that the partial, not fundamental, character of opposition is not automatically excluded from the concept of 'Resistance'. Systematic analysis of the conflict zones of the Third Reich shows that partial opposition in connection with intermittent or partial affirmation of the regime and the coexistence of nonconformity and conformity were the rule. The aberrant and confused paths via which here and there individuals or groups came to an oppositional attitude and stance does not in itself diminish the quality of the opposition. Rather, the mixed forms of political behaviour, e.g. the braveness of an opponent who for a time had been a fellow-traveller, gain in human and historical profile through a close-up perspective on the real circumstances. The embedding of the concept of 'Resistance' in a general history of behavioural patterns also makes it clear that oppositional behaviour towards particular political-ideological demands of National Socialism was usually strongly co-determined by the defence of jurisdiction or interests and was often limited to this. A classic example of this is the opposition of the churches to the euthanasia campaign—which also affected church sanatoriums—in comparison to the only weak church opposition to the National Socialist persecution of the Jews [. . .] The embedding of the concept of Resistance in real historical situations illustrates that the moral dimension of an action, once that action becomes concrete, is usually also partial and interest-centred in equal measure. The ideal of opposition which is not delimited by such interests—as indispensable as it remains, for historians too—is in the final analysis centred around a metapolitical understanding of conscience and morality which mostly exceeds what one could reasonably demand.

['Resistenz und Widerstand', in Martin Broszat, Elke Fröhlich, and Anton Grossmann (eds.), *Bayern in der NS-Zeit*, 5 vols., vol. iv: *Herrschaft und Gesellschaft im Konflikt* (Munich: Oldenbourg, 1981), 697–9.]

KLAUS TENFELDE

66 The Social Bases of *Resistenz* and Resistance

Whilst the pioneering work of the 1970s and 1980s into patterns of dissent and nonconformity in everyday life played a major role in, for example, enabling scholars to think about the responses of various groups in society in more nuanced and differentiated ways, the notion of *Resistenz* was also criticized for encouraging too broad a definition of resistance. Further, as Klaus Tenfelde argues, one should not overestimate the extent to which *Resistenz* had a genuine political dimension in the sense that resistance did.

A very far-reaching change in perspectives is under way in the Federal Republic as a consequence of the adaptation to social historical methods, and primarily in the sphere of local and regional studies of the late period of the Weimar Republic and the so-called seizure of power. Early exceptions such as Günther Weisenborn's account of the 'silent revolt' aside,[1] studies of this type began with William S. Allen's study of Northeim[2]* and they increased in the 1970s, so that by now a very differentiated image has emerged of the forms and the process of the usurpation of power up until the stabilization of the regime on a local and regional level. Thanks are due not least to the recent emergence of the 'history of everyday life', which is also very widespread outside of the academic sphere, for giving substantial impulses to precisely this shift in research approach, within which larger undertakings such as the 'Bavaria in the National Socialist era' project of the Munich Institute for Contemporary History[3] in particular were a significant stimulus.† [. . .]

[A]t least one problematic characteristic should be pointed out, however: the tendency to concentrate on 'deviating' behaviour under the conditions of the dictatorial regime, within a broad spectrum ranging from mild signs of dissatisfaction to actual resistance. Whether in retrospect the Communist attempt at a general strike in rural Swabia in the period of the seizure of

---

* See extract 27 above. † See extract 65 above.

power is celebrated, while the long-since resigned or passive stance of the majority of the population is forgotten,[4] or whether attention in the prime years for the regime of 1936 to 1940 is focused exclusively on the few who thought or acted differently rather than on the consensual inclinations of the overwhelming majority of the population[5]—in each case there is a danger of significant distortions if the moral is sought among those few, with the unintended effect, as always, of exonerating the majority.

And further: the more comprehensively and impressively the spectrum of positions between accommodation and resistance is developed and the more our knowledge of different choices of behaviour in this period unfolds, the more our ability to reach a general judgement on the state of society could diminish, and along the way the question of guilt would be conjured out of existence. [. . .]

In the same way that the question of the causes of resistance always implies the next question, namely why resistance *did not* occur, similar can be said of *Resistenz*, and overall its prevalence in particular milieux cannot obscure the equally diverse forms of accommodation, but at best can enable judgements over the state of the milieu and the success of National Socialist attempts to penetrate it. Moreover, the limited actual political reach of various manifestations of *Resistenz* is easily visible: the fact that workers used their favourable position in the labour market during the economic boom and also grumbled when their daily living conditions were affected and encroached upon still does not enable us to form a judgement on their political stance overall and in particular on the impact of the foreign, domestic, and social policy attractions which the regime offered above all in the late 1930s.

There are further factors, which are very different for workers and peasants. Amongst the former the fatal political rifts of the years before 1933 were still highly present after 1933, as even the workers' leaders in exile were only occasionally able to overcome mutual party-political mistrust. The German 'class tradition' kept the German working class at a distance from the lower middle class before as after, and this distance may even have grown in the crisis and after 1933 as a consequence of the strong affiliation to National Socialism of the latter. One should not forget the shifts in the structure of employment which were associated with the economic upturn and above all armaments policy; in this connection an increasing upward mobility also had a disorientating effect above all when it was combined with political conformity. Finally, the growing influence of the National Socialist mass organizations, including the German Labour Front, should not be underestimated.

In the Bavarian countryside it was different. Here *Resistenz* signified more the desire to protect customary habits against the challenges of the regime than any political criticism; to the contrary, common political ground, for example in relation to National Socialist terror against the hated Left, probably predominated in the countryside.

Furthermore: *Resistenz* by and large remained an oral phenomenon; resistance demanded much more. Of course in many cases there was a sort of incremental shift of behaviour on the scale of nonconformity through to resistance, but one cannot, at least, describe the milieux described more closely above as a breeding ground. It is far more in the nature of a resistance tied to action that it is constituted on the basis of comprehensive political, but also moral, reflections; social conditions of formation are of a lesser significance. This is not true in every case. In the behaviour of priests of either confession it is difficult to distinguish between *Resistenz* and resistance; for them, not least because of surviving legal room for manœuvre, special conditions pertained. Seen from the perspective of the threat of punishment the distance between *Resistenz* and resistance also reduced during the war years. If previously someone who had expressed themselves 'improperly' in a guesthouse had got away with a mild sentence or, at worst, with 'protective custody', towards the end of the war repeated listening to enemy broadcasts could be punished by death. A more detailed study of the extent of punishments has yet to be undertaken. However, from the point of view of risk one can say that during the war *Resistenz* became resistance.

['Soziale Grundlagen von Resistenz und Widerstand', in Jürgen Schmädecke and Peter Steinbach (eds.), *Der Widerstand gegen den Nationalsozialismus: die deutsche Gesellschaft und der Widerstand gegen Hitler* (Munich: Piper, 1985), 799–800, 808–9.]

IAN KERSHAW

67   Resistance without the People?

In the following passage, Ian Kershaw questions whether manifestations of dissent—however widespread among various sectors of the population—had any real limiting effect on the ability of the regime to implement its murderous policies, and stresses the extent to which genuine resistance took place within a context of far broader popular support for the regime.

On the basis [of a] survey of various manifestations of dissent we can conclude that the regime's ability to function was hardly undermined by them, and that its 'will to power' was at best only temporarily and very partially limited. The extent of dissent is often astonishing, but its compatibility with a fundamental agreement with the main elements of National Socialist policy is even more astonishing. And for the functioning of the regime the large spheres of consensus were undoubtedly much more important than the [. . .]

areas of dissent. A far-reaching underlying consensus behind central elements of the National Socialist regime which—with the great exception of the former Left, of course—lasted until deep in the war was, further, able to neutralize dissent and to compensate for the rejection of particular aspects of National Socialism. The underlying consensus was rooted not only in an emotional concordance with fundamental aspects of National Socialist ideology, but also in the ability of the regime before the war to improve considerably the living standards of almost all sectors of the population in comparison to the period of the world economic crisis—or at least to raise hopes of an imminent improvement. Even when during the war the actual standards of living fell, this hope remained for a long time and only collapsed when the longed-for 'final victory' disappeared into the distance. The massive escalation of terror in the years 1944–5 was to no small extent a reaction of the regime to the fact that the underlying consensus had now almost dissolved, and that only a 'negative' consensus remained, which yearned for a quick end to the war.

Courageous opposition was mounted from within all sectors of the population, but especially from the working class, to National Socialism, which claimed thousands of deaths and unquantifiable arrests, torture, and suffering. Was it 'resistance without the people'? This rhetorical question can be interpreted in more than one way.

On a simple level the answer to the question is obvious. Even under authoritarian regimes with a less effective terror apparatus than that which the Nazis had, active resistance is always the preserve of a small majority of the population who are willing, if necessary, to risk their lives. The overthrow of such regimes is as a rule only possible through the participation of disillusioned groups within the leadership, namely the military. In view of the terroristic potential of the modern police state mass resistance is almost impossible from the start, as the KPD was soon forced to experience in the case of Germany. The mere presence of a ruthless repressive apparatus is usually sufficient to intimidate the mass of the population into not actively supporting the resistance.

On a second level the resistance was obviously not a 'resistance without the people' if one recognizes the fact that an essential contribution to the fundamental opposition to the National Socialist regime came not only from the social elites, but from many ordinary people, especially from working-class circles [. . .] The essential role of the organized—and in many cases very heroic—workers' opposition both from the SPD and, on a quite different scale and in other forms, from the KPD is by now completely beyond doubt and does not need to be specifically emphasized. Many other anonymous individuals and groups 'of the people' equally participated in the fundamental resistance to National Socialist tyranny. In this sense it was clearly not a 'resistance without the people.'

Viewed from a third perspective the answer to the question 'resistance without the people?' is different again. Not only did the resistance to Hitler act without the active mass support of the population, but, down to the end, large proportions of the population did not even passively support the resistance, but actually widely condemned it. In other countries—one only need think of Spain, Portugal, Greece, Argentina, and of other Latin American countries, and not least of Hungary, Czechoslovakia, and Poland more recently—there have actually been resistance movements which with the help of broad support from the mass of the population have overthrown authoritarian dictatorships and seriously threatened one-party states with rigorous repressive apparatuses. Perhaps this point would have been reached in Germany following a successful assassination attempt on Hitler. On the other hand it is thoroughly doubtful whether a successful coup would have found the support of the masses and whether the prospects for a government led by the assassins would have been so rosy, even in July 1944, following the heavy suffering of a long war. In any case Hitler's personal popularity appears—if only temporarily—to have risen again after 20 July 1944.[1] The fact cannot be denied: in comparison with many other authoritarian systems the National Socialist regime—or in any case essential elements of it—enjoyed a high degree of popularity until deep into the war, despite the many large spheres of dissent. The popularity was based on an underlying consensus which created a climate in which the resistance to Hitler, isolated from the start and essentially without support from the population, had to act honourably but, politically, as good as completely ineffectively. In this final but fundamental sense, the resistance to Hitler was indeed a 'resistance without the people'.

['Widerstand ohne Volk?', in Jürgen Schmädecke and Peter Steinbach (eds.), *Der Widerstand gegen den Nationalsozialismus: die deutsche Gesellschaft und der Widerstand gegen Hitler* (Munich: Piper, 1985), 793–5.]

KLAUS-MICHAEL MALLMANN AND GERHARD PAUL

68   *Resistenz* or Loyal Reluctance?

Klaus-Michael Mallmann and Gerhard Paul, co-authors of important work on patterns of popular accommodation and dissent in the Saarland during the Nazi period, have been among the most strident critics of the *Resistenz* concept. In this extract they relate their findings in the Saarland project to their rejection of the suitability of the term in connection with the Third Reich.

Contemporary historical research knows numerous cases of concepts creating red herrings but nonetheless finding their way into literature, schoolbooks,

and politicians' speeches and thereby leaving their mark on historical consciousness. One of those concepts which served more to obfuscate than to
enlighten was that of totalitarianism, which for decades defined our image of
National Socialism as that of a, to a large extent, contradiction-free, efficient,
omnipotent political system penetrating into all spheres of life, and which
only gradually is giving way to a more realistic picture. Similar can be said of
Ernst Fraenkel's concept of the 'dual state'* which was influential above all in
that part of research into National Socialism which was orientated towards
political science and which suggested the idea that alongside the genuinely
National Socialist arbitrary state there had been a state of law acting according to bourgeois norms.

In our view the concept of *Resistenz*, which has defined broad sections of
research into resistance since the early 1980s, belongs to this group, as it
reanimates the image of totalitarianism, paints an unrealistic and exculpatory
image of a broadly spread resistance to the Third Reich, internalizes the
overestimating, politicizing perspective of the National Socialist security
organs, and systematically suppresses the dimensions of consensus.[1] Further,
it is a concept with which historical politics can be pursued excellently. [. . .]

In many cases examination shows that that which elsewhere has been
celebrated as *Resistenz* existed merely as a mixture of unintentional polycratic
conflicts between National Socialist organizations, normal social conflictual
behaviour, the pious wishes of those in exile, and an exculpatory overinter-
pretation of dissent by post-war research. [. . .] [T]he National Socialist
regime certainly allowed the existence of zones of conflict; indeed it, first of
all, generated them through the promise of defined spheres of operation or
through inflationary social-revolutionary slogans, and also provided institutions for the resolution of crises and conflicts within the system, for example
the German Labour Front. The refusal to work Sunday shifts was, in this
sense, a completely normal act of social conflict, which neither in intent nor
impact set limits to the political system, but which even made use of the
existing National Socialist conflict management mechanisms and invoked the
promised 'factory community'—or what one took that to be.

Against this finding, the school of research which was hostage to the
concept of *Resistenz* achieved the historically distorting coup of reinterpreting the objective inability of the National Socialist regime to encompass all
spheres of life totally and to take control of the whole person into an ability
for disobedience, refusal, and opposition, and of making disputes within the
system into challenges from outside it. The background to this coup is a
simple and rigid model of society derived in the final analysis from the theory
of totalitarianism. Only from the perspective of a construct divorced from
reality, from that of a utopian ideal-type of 'total' domination, do all the

* See excerpt 41 above.

forms of nonconformity and dissent referred to under the concept of *Resistenz* appear as limitations on power;[2] they do not, however, from the perspective of a more social-historical orientated scholarship on National Socialism which also recognizes the polycratic disputes and structural conflicts. The model of a functioning totalitarian society adopted by Broszat—'a theoretical and practical absurdity' according to R. Mann[3]—underestimates not only the receptiveness and flexibility which characterizes regimes with totalitarian intentions too, but also ignores the objective existence of niches and conflict levels, in and on which contradictions and conflicts could also occur under the conditions of dictatorship.

In our examination the National Socialist regime proved itself to be far more elastic and capable of conflict than the rigid model of the regime used by the theory of totalitarianism hitherto supposed. The National Socialist rulers could live perfectly with insubordination, with purely superficial accommodation and conformity, with insidious criticism, even with refusals to work and with the 'crucifix struggle', as long as the consensus in political fundamental principles appeared secure and dissatisfaction, nonconformity, and partial opposition did not coalesce and organize. It would have had to fear the termination of this fundamental consensus and the transformation of partial opposition into political resistance. Against this, however, stood the successful isolation of the political resistance organizations and the over-whelmingly closed nature of the different social milieux inherited from the Weimar period. Despite their vocal attacks on 'grumblers and defeatists', against 'troublemakers in the factory community' and 'black agitants of the population', the political elite thus did not need to fear a threat to their domination from this direction.

Against the background of such a differentiated exercise of authority, the existence of spaces which were relatively free of domination is therefore to be regarded as highly ambivalent,[4] as autonomy and conflict did not *a priori*—as the 'Bavaria Project' suggested—have to be manifestations of *resistent* behaviour, but, precisely to the contrary, could be inherent within the system as preconditions for *Resistenz*. This in no way had to be the product of subjective capabilities of individuals, groups, and milieux, but could also be rooted in objective conditions. At the same time the limits of political-cultural hegemony did not remotely have to be restrictions to political power, as is claimed in the 'Bavaria Project'. Thus, for example, the expressions of disquiet among the German population registered everywhere in response to the concrete experience of the personal violence of the pogrom of 1938 tell us in themselves nothing about the actual extent of anti-Semitic propaganda, as the more discreetly proceeding extermination process of the Holocaust in the following years met altogether with secret acceptance. Expressions of aversion did not hinder the National Socialist extermination programme in the sense of *Resistenz*, but simply forced Hitler's extermination strategists, who showed themselves capable of learning here too, into a relatively unpublic process.

The extension of the concept of Resistance to forms of sporadic and ultimately inconsequential reluctance has thus been quite rightly criticized. We must agree with M. Prinz when he bemoans the fact that the introduction of the concept of *Resistenz*—in contrast to what Broszat himself intended—has not led to a revision of our image of the totalitarian character of the National Socialist regime fully penetrating everyday life, but that, quite the contrary, 'the often criticized totalitarianism theory has found its way back into the practices of historical research on National Socialism via the back door of research on *Resistenz*'[5]. [. . .]

The people living under the regime were as little free of contradictions as was National Socialism itself. The worker was not only a worker and the Catholic priest was not only a priest. Both were connected into multitudinous social networks and also contradictory in themselves. A contradictory stance towards the system could thus easily sit alongside consensus in other central fields of policy, in the same way as consensus in underlying questions of principle in no way ruled out protest in other fields. The *resistent* and immune personality, whom the brown ruling powers indeed will have feared, did not exist.[6] For example, the malicious gossip was in no way immunized against National Socialist ideology but could, for all his momentary irritations, be entirely a follower of the Third Reich. The worker who went on strike for his interests was also in no way immune to the social propaganda and to National Socialist racial doctrine, but, quite the opposite, often invoked precisely National Socialist calls for a 'better and more worthy life' and the propagandized 'factory community' against his class enemy, the employer, and thus found himself entirely in harmony with the brown elite. At most one can speak of a partial immunity in questions of church policy on the part of the observant Catholic rural community, whose *Resistenz*, however, often only consisted of the fact that they did not catch on to that which the brown masters in the metropolises expected of them.

Ultimately, from a social sciences perspective, the strength of the image of consistently *resistent* milieux adopted in numerous studies of resistance, especially as often supposed in the case of the Catholic and Social Democrat-orientated milieux, is doubtable. More likely, one can assume that over the space of twelve years it was hardly possible to preserve undamaged the substance of the identity of one's own milieu, and, further, that the Third Reich offered sufficient gratification for the Social Democratic worker for him to become successively reconciled to the dictatorship too. As we know precisely from experimental social psychology, the findings of which have hitherto been completely ignored by research on resistance, it is hardly likely that a purely superficially conformist attitude could be maintained in the long run against such a massive repressive and integrative pressure, without this having affected one's inner convictions.[7] *Resistenz*—it can be supposed—was thus not an unchanging permanent state, but more a sporadic and fragile behavioural pattern which was always capable of switching back into conformity.

These multiple gradations and combinations of rejection and accommodation, of consensus and dissent, the concrete motives of those concerned and the political impacts of their behaviour, can only be approached via an integrated methodological approach which combines structural history analysis with microanalytical case studies. One can only ascertain on an individual basis what caused someone to oppose the National Socialist regime and how the relationship of accommodation and aversion took concrete shape; and only the more far-reaching structural history approach may explain, to some extent, what impacts should be ascribed to the oppositional behaviour.

To find a more suitable expression for those patterns of behaviour hitherto categorized under the concept of *Resistenz* we would like to suggest the concept of 'loyal reluctance', which makes clear its conceptual difference from the concept of resistance and a proximity to the concept of loyalty, and which brings those entirely typical mixed forms of loyalty and resistant behaviour back to their ambivalent denominators. The concept also makes it clear that these forms of behaviour did not call into question the political and fundamental consensus, the (partial) loyalty underpinning the National Socialist regime; that it was an issue of forms of behaviour which at most caused the National Socialist regime peripheral trouble, but did not otherwise impinge upon its ability to function.

The numerous spheres of consensus were undoubtedly more important for the functioning of the National Socialist system than the fields in which loyal reluctance could emerge. Above all, however, this did not metamorphose into opposition and resistance activity. Even in the last months of the war—in complete contrast to the First World War—there was no mass termination of political loyalty. If the National Socialist claim to authority was seriously limited by anything at all, then above all it was by the internal, self-made conflicts in the National Socialist polycratic jungle. *Resistenz* with an impact was not brought about by malicious rumour-mongers, but by satraps and climbers competing for political influence within the apparatus of party and state. The biggest factor of *Resistenz* in the Third Reich was National Socialism itself. And one can hardly refer to that under the term 'resistance'.

['Resistenz oder loyale Widerwilligkeit? Anmerkungen zu einem umstrittenen Begriff', *Zeitschrift für Geschichtswissenschaft*, 41 (1993), 99, 113–16.]

ii Participation

ROBERT GELLATELY

69 **The Gestapo and Social Cooperation: The Example of Political Denunciation**

Contrary to popular perceptions at the time, and contrary to popular myth since, the Gestapo was, in numerical terms, very small. In a city such as Essen, for example, 43 Gestapo officers monitored a population of about 650,000. In order to be effective, the Gestapo had to rely on denunciation, which often came from the public, suggesting an 'informal social reinforcement of the terror system' (W. S. Allen). Drawing on research on the Gestapo case files in Würzburg begun by Reinhard Mann, Robert Gellately discusses the nature of political denunciation in National Socialist Germany and its significance.

The Gestapo had a reputation for brutality, and terror would seize individuals instructed by postcard to report to local Gestapo headquarters 'for the purpose of answering some questions.' Rumours about what went on in Gestapo cellars served to intensify the fear of being informed on or of being turned in on suspicion of the least deviation. However, it is also true that the Gestapo lacked the physical resources to execute surveillance of the vast majority of the population. How was it structurally possible, then, that the population could become terrorized? No doubt many other officials were also concerned with monitoring behaviour, and this too was well known to most Germans. But to suggest that the function of surveillance and control was performed almost exclusively by institutions that formed part of the so-called police state tends to place undue emphasis on coercion, force, or even open violence, and to regard the populace as essentially passive, apathetic, or just not involved. At least some degree of active participation of 'ordinary' citizens was required for the function of most policing or control organizations in Nazi Germany. [. . .] The enforcement of policy was constituted by what can be termed political denunciations, the volunteered provision of information by the population at large about instances of disapproved behaviour. [. . .]

Evidence in Würzburg and elsewhere suggests that in all likelihood most [. . .] categories contain instances of denunciations, though not all the accusations were lodged directly with the Gestapo. A case could commence when an individual merely dropped a hint sure to be overheard by some official or even a tell-tale neighbour. A classic example of the latter is offered in the story by Rolf Hochhuth, since turned into a film, *Eine Liebe in Deutschland*.[2] Beyond that, once in the grasp of the Gestapo, victims could easily incriminate themselves or others in the course of interrogation: and it is clear that on occasion chance played a role in the Gestapo's being made aware of some 'criminal' behaviour or other.

Though care must be taken with quantitative analysis of materials such as Gestapo case-files, especially regarding the sources that led to the opening of a case, it is clear that denunciations from the population were crucial to the functioning of the Gestapo. We know that 26 per cent of all cases began with an *identifiable* denunciation, and this must be taken as a minimum figure. Many of the other categories [. . .]—such as cases that began with information 'from Nazi organizations', 'other control organizations', 'communal and state authorities'—were also to a large degree dependent upon tips from citizens. With all due caution, it seems justified to suggest that denunciations from the population constituted the single most important cause for the initiation of proceedings of all kinds.

Put another way, these figures indicate that the regime's dreaded enforcer would have been seriously hampered without a considerable degree of public co-operation. This behaviour has hitherto been largely ignored or not fully understood. To ask whether this is evidence that the public was converted to Nazism, or that the Nazi message had actually become widely accepted— [. . .] is rather misconceived, because co-operation or collaboration was motivated by a whole range of considerations. The question of motives aside, denunciations from the population were the key link in the three-way interaction between the police, people, and policy in Nazi Germany. Popular participation by provision of information was one of the most important factors in making the terror system work. That conclusion suggests rethinking the notion of the Gestapo as an 'instrument of domination': if it was an instrument it was one which was constructed within German society and whose functioning was structurally dependent on the continuing co-operation of German citizens.[3] [. . .]

It is possible that some cases were sparked off by a tip from official sources, as when a Gestapo official merely wrote in the file that 'according to a confidentially disclosed report made to me today, it is alleged that the butcher Hans Drat remarked as follows', and so on.[4] Still, there would seem no reason for the dossier to be silent if the tip came from an official or even semi-official body. In all likelihood the source was 'from the population', but the full details of this side of the story remain hidden.[5]

The legal façade surrounding the 'seizure of power' no doubt paid dividends in that many law-abiding citizens, out of respect for the legal norms, simply complied and co-operated with the new regime. Because the take-over was not patently illegal, many could choose to ignore its revolutionary character, especially after the radicals were subdued following the purge in June 1934. The stoic acceptance, however, seems to have yielded to more positive attitudes. Hans Bernd Gisevius, a member of the Gestapo in 1933, later recalled that there was a new mood and a widespread (though far from unanimous) positive disposition towards the regime, especially in the efforts to put down the supposed Communist threat.[6] What struck him most forcefully was what he called 'individual *Gleichschaltung*', by which he meant a kind of willing self-integration into the new system.[7]

The terror system had both a formal side—embracing the whole range of institutional arrangements—and an informal side that worked in tandem with those arrangements. Much less has been written about the 'informal' politics in the Nazi dictatorship, but there is much evidence to suggest that existing informal power-structures underwent adjustments as many people began to bring their attitudes on all kinds of issues into line. People may have experienced anxieties, but there were other positive factors at work. [. . .]

The motives for offering information to the authorities ranged across the spectrum from base, selfish, personal, to lofty and 'idealistic'. The records project an image of the denouncers—who, not surprisingly, tended to come from the same milieu as those on whom they informed—as drawn largely from groups at the lower end of the social scale. This image is probably correct, but must be qualified lest these groups be judged too harshly. It needs to be borne in mind that upper-income groups and the nobility for the most part did not need to utilize the police, since they had other and more effective avenues through which to exercise social power. Moreover, the police, themselves largely drawn from the lower social orders, were more deferential in cases involving the nobility and the upper bourgeoisie, and pursued individuals from the lower end of the social hierarchy with greater alacrity. Even so, individuals from all social classes offered information to the police. The regime was bound to have second thoughts about this participation when, at times, it was inundated with charges, too many of which were careless or just plain false. But, despite some misgivings, it was felt better to have too much information and co-operation than too little.

[*The Gestapo and German Society: Enforcing Racial Policy 1933–1945* (Oxford: Oxford University Press, 1990), 129–30, 135–7, 158.]

CLAUDIA KOONZ

70   Mothers in the Fatherland

Claudia Koonz's argument that female no less than male consent and behaviour was essential in stabilizing and underpinning the Nazi regime unleashed an ongoing controversy among feminist historians.

> Whatever the merits of her argument, she successfully challenged
> what was in danger of becoming a comfortable orthodoxy for some
> feminist historians, namely that women should be seen purely as vic-
> tims of an essentially patriarchal system.

Because Nazi contempt for women was so blatant from the beginning, it
would be easy to assume that some ought not to share in the question of
German guilt. Perhaps women remained pure and powerless, repelled by the
racism, violence, and masculine élan of the Nazi Party. But did women really
remain immune to what Erich Fromm called 'the craving for submission and
lust for power' that had engulfed the nation? Voting statistics provide the
evidence. Thanks to electoral officials' curiosity about how women would
vote in the 1920s, German men were given gray ballots and women, white.
We don't have to estimate—we know that women nearly as strongly as men
supported the Nazis during the years of their spectacular rise to power
between 1930 and 1932.[1]

Women do not appear to have played a role in the Nazi movement before
1933 or the Nazi state thereafter because historians have not defined women's
support for Nazi Germany as a historical problem—i.e., a question that needs
explaining. After all, the image of politically inert women reinforces cher-
ished myths about motherhood. A fantasy of women untouched by their
historical setting feeds our own nostalgia for mothers who remain beyond
good and evil—preservers of love, charity, and peace, no matter what the
social or moral environment. Against the encroachments of the modern
state, we extol women who somehow keep the private beyond the reach of
the political. When 'feminine' ideals of love and charity flickered and were
extinguished in the Third Reich, we assume this occurred because of a masculine assault against women as victims of either force or hypnosis, or of
their own masochism. [. . .]

Every woman Nazi in Germany did not 'adore' a brute-hearted fascist. The
women who followed Hitler, like the men, did so from conviction, opportunism, and active choice. Far from being helpless or even innocent, women
made possible a murderous state in the name of concerns they defined as
motherly. The fact that women bore no responsibility for issuing orders from
Berlin does not obviate their complicity in carrying them out. Electoral statistics charted their enthusiasm, and Party propaganda depicts swooning
women as well as marching men. But women did more than faint and vote
for the only violently antifeminist party in Weimar politics. And they received
more than a 'boot in the face.'

What did this overtly misogynist movement offer to women? Nazi men
inadvertently gave women Nazis a unique opportunity because they cared so
little about the women in their ranks. Men allowed women considerable
latitude to interpret Hitler's ideas as they wished, recruit followers, write

their own rules, and raise funds. In other parties male leaders welcomed women officially, but then curtailed women leaders' independence and chastised them at the slightest sign of separatism. In the service of womanly ideals, Nazi women sometimes behaved in most un-'ladylike' ways: managing the funds they raised, marching, facing down hecklers, making soapbox speeches, and organizing mass meetings, marches, and rallies. While espousing women's special nature and a reactionary view of the family, these women never thought they would retreat to the household. True, they crusaded to take women out of politics, but they did so in order to open up other areas of public life to women. Before 1933 Nazi women viewed the world around them in pessimistic terms, actively working in the public but not the political arena to preserve their nostalgic vision of a world that never was.

What, then, did women do for the men who ignored them? Before 1933, they provided men with an ambience they took for granted, complementing the stridently masculine élan of the Nazi movement and cultivating a homey domestic sphere for Hitler's motley and marginal band. They gave men Nazis the feeling of belonging not just to a party but to a total subculture that prefigured the ideals of the Nazi state for which they fought. Women kept folk traditions alive, gave charity to poor Nazi families, cared for SA men, sewed brown shirts, and prepared food at rallies. While Nazi men preached race hate and virulent nationalism that threatened to destroy the morality upon which civilization rested, women's participation in the movement created an ersatz gloss of idealism. The image did not, of course, deceive the victims, but it helped Nazis to preserve their self-esteem and to continue their work under the illusion that they remained decent.

To a degree unique in Western history, Nazi doctrine created a society structured around 'natural' biological poles. In addition to serving specific needs of the state, this radical division vindicated a more general and thoroughgoing biological *Weltanschauung* based on race and sex as the immutable categories of human nature. The habit of taking psychological differences between men and women for granted reinforced assumptions about irrevocable divisions between Jew and 'Aryan.' In place of class, cultural, religious divisions, race and sex became the predominant social markers. To people disoriented by a stagnant economy, humiliated by military defeat, and confused by new social norms among the urban young, these social categories provided a sense of safety. The Jew and the New Woman, conservatives believed, had become too powerful in progressive Weimar society. The Nazi state drove both groups, as metaphors and as real individuals, out of the 'Aryan' man's world.

For women, belonging to the 'master race' opened the option of collaboration in the very Nazi state that exploited them, that denied them access to political status, deprived them of birth control, underpaid them as wage workers, indoctrinated their children, and finally took their sons and husbands to the front. The separation between masculine and feminine spheres, which followed logically and psychologically from Nazi leaders' misogyny, relegated women to their own space—both beneath and beyond the dominant world of men. The Nazi system rested on a female hierarchy as well as a male chain of command. Of course, women occupied a less exalted place in Nazi government than the men, and Reichsfrauenführerin Gertrud Scholtz-Klink, who stood at the pinnacle of the women's hierarchy, wielded less real power than, say, a male district chief or deputy minister. Standing at the apex of her own sphere, the woman leader minimized her lack of status vis-à-vis Nazi male leaders above her and instead directed her attention to the battalions of women under her command. As in wartime, women believed their sacrifices played a vital role in a greater cause. Scholtz-Klink saw herself as the chief of a lobby for women's concerns and as the leader of women missionaries who would bring Nazi doctrine 'home' to every family in the Reich. Far from remaining untouched by Nazi evil, women operated at its very center.

[*Mothers in the Fatherland: Women, the Family and Nazi Politics* (London: Jonathan Cape, 1987), 3–6.]

PAUL WEINDLING

71   Racial Hygiene and Professional Leadership

Paul Weindling's study of German medical culture since 1870 stresses the extent to which the German medical profession had adopted the notion of racial hygiene much prior to 1933, and that doctors' long-standing tendency to regard medicine in terms of service to state and nation rather than to sick individuals made it easy for the National Socialists to co-opt them into the service of the regime's racial policies; while there were tensions between technocratic-eugenicist and racial-biological anti-Semitic conceptions of social engineering, the points of similarity were sufficient, in a context which offered substantial professional advancement, to facilitate widespread collaboration.

Racism and anti-Semitism have often been depicted as simple and homogeneous categories. Yet there were many strands in their illiberal rejection of humanitarianism and tolerance. While Hitler's blend of Aryan glorification and violent anti-Semitism had great influence, other biological, medical and anthropological variants of racism influenced Nazi health and social policies, which were responses to social processes of urban and industrial growth, professionalization of health and welfare, and the emergence of a scientific technocracy. Racial concepts of public health were a means of social control and of promoting social integration in terms of both ideology and everyday habits. There resulted conflicting social interests, concepts and aims in the eugenics and racial hygiene movement, as well as rifts between scientific racial hygiene and anti-semitism. Racial hygiene had to undergo a series of transformations so that it could be adapted to Nazism. The long-term shift from the radicalism of the *Lebensreformer* and from liberal individualism to corporate and biologized social values made racial hygiene ripe for further metamorphosis. The term 'eugenics', associated with the welfare programme of the 1920s, was abandoned. The serologist Reche argued that racial hygiene should not degenerate into a welfare-oriented eugenics that promoted health without regard to racial origins.[1] A process of renegotiation and reformulation of racial hygiene was unleashed after 1933. The leaders of racial hygiene made pacts with their political masters by offering ideological racial programmes in such areas as health education and technical skills in racial classification and health promotion. The Nazis needed this support. As racial hygienists were influential in academic and professional spheres, they could mobilize doctors, nurses and other medical personnel to disseminate racial values. The Nazis needed the skills of anthropologists, demographers, psychiatrists and public health experts to identify and 'solve' the problems of the antisocial and the racially degenerate. Just as the Nazis had to compromise with other sectors of society such as the churches and the army, so a functioning, normal science was tolerated, even in spheres such as psychology and psychotherapy where the premises about the mind-body relations were individualistic and rationalist. But tensions persisted between scientists and the Nazi social system.[2]

The Nazi social system inherited a eugenics movement which was itself riven by conflicts. Competing power blocs and rival biological theories among the racial hygienists were overshadowed by power struggles among Nazi leadership groups. Scientific racial hygiene and public health were broken into splinter groups by rifts within Nazism. There was a growing rivalry between Nazi ideologists, seeking a populist type of national revival on the basis of widespread anti-Semitism, violence and propaganda and Nazi technocratic elites, especially among the SS and state officials whose elitist cadres deployed policing and scientific technologies. At the same time economic factors, war and territorial expansion, settlement and racial policies contributed to the further fragmentation and polarization of racial hygiene. In 1933 racial hygienists hoped that they would be given enlarged financial resources, and privileged social status. They would be dictators of social policy, moving from the position of advisors to executors of power. The fragmentary eugenic experiments of the Weimar Republic would be uniformly implemented throughout society. The spheres of health and race would be extended into the economic, financial and political dimensions. These hopes were the outcome of a fusion of authoritarian nationalism and scientific elitism. [. . .]

There was an affinity of intellectual structures of science with authoritarian politics. The two areas were linked by further developments of professionalization. Science-based professions hoped for corporate privileges from an authoritarian political structure. The liquidation of socialism was welcomed by those professions such as engineering which depended on an industrial up-swing. The nationalist stress on self-sufficiency offered opportunities for developing synthetic substitutes for oils, fibres and foodstuffs. The managing of the human resources of the nation could justify the medical profession's demands for exclusive privileges and an extension of powers. Nazism swept away the autonomy of sickness insurance funds and municipalities that threatened to develop socialized medicine. Practitioners expected that controls would be imposed on nature therapists and 'quackery'. The removal of Jewish practitioners would provide lucrative opportunities for practice, and relieve pressure in an overcrowded profession. Doctors found immense opportunities in the NSDAP, SS, army and industry in addition to private, hospital and insurance practice. The funding and scope for research in all these spheres was increased. Research and medical practice were often combined. In 1939 the military authorities welcomed the development that military medical officers were more frequently gaining the habilitation qualifications for lectureships.[3] Nazism boosted professional status, prestige and earning capacity.[4] It was hoped that racial hygiene would take a central role in placing medicine on a sound basis of nationalist values, and in enhancing professional powers. Medical students were to be inculcated with scientific principles of heredity and race. Medicine was to be transformed from being a liberal profession serving the individual patient to one in which the doctor would become the Führer of the people. He should supervise all aspects of family life such as diet and child care, and promote a reformed national lifestyle. Racial hygiene could thus advance professional powers and promote social integration.

Most accounts of Nazi medicine focus on the extreme forms of medical killing and concentration camp experiments that subjected human victims to extremes of cold, low pressure and sea water just as embryologists had subjected animal embryos to injury experiments during the 1890s. Little is known about daily medical practice, health conditions and the expectations of patients. Nazi eugenics is revealing of ultimate intentions and novel routines in a wide spectrum of medical and biological contexts. In certain respects expectations of the Nazi authorities were fulfilled. Racial values were given a privileged place in all aspects of education, NSDAP propaganda and policy-making. A series of racial laws had a strongly medical and hereditarian component. Public health was reorganized on a racial basis. The medical profession was purged of 'alien' Jewish and socialist elements, and given increased opportunities and powers. University chairs, research institutes and courses were established in racial hygiene. The German Racial Hygiene

Society began to expand under the direction of leading medical scientists and public health experts.

Yet there were many points of tension between eugenicists and racial ideologues. There were intellectual discrepancies between the Nazis' simple and popular glorification of a pure Aryan and German race, and anthropologists' views on the complex racial composition of the German population. Professionals and academics often found it difficult to accept the dictates of autodidact party ideologues. 'Unscientific' aspects of anti-semitism, as promoted by Nazi Jew-baiters such as Julius Streicher, could only be reconciled to objective science by subordination to the Führer, party and *Volk*. The Nazi system could not allow academics a privileged position unless they submitted to the controls of party political organizations such as the Racial Political Office of the NSDAP or SS. Factions within the party were hostile to antiquated academic privileges and promoted new forms of applied scientific research and practice.

A power struggle to control racial hygiene occurred. The rivalry was initially between the party allied to the Nazi Doctors' League, and public health officials allied to those racial hygienists advocating compulsory sterilization and segregation of the anti-social. By 1937 the SS emerged as a major force seeking to unify anti-semitism with the technocratic machinery of public health. The Nazi system of power was based on competing hierarchies which proliferated due to the Führer's divide and rule policy and because of the need to reconcile a diversity of social interests. Hitler was skilled in the manipulation of his entourage, their associated power blocs and public opinion. Moreover, there were elements of sheer anarchy in a system based on brute power rather than legitimate status or scientific excellence. As racial hygiene became caught up in Nazi power politics, its aims, institutions and active leadership were transformed.

The Nazis were able to play on inherent divisions within the racial hygiene movement, especially the tensions between those eugenicists, who were more state-and science-oriented, and the more radical right-wing party activists who were motivated by *völkisch* anti-semitism. There emerged two factions. One was party dominated. This consisted of ideologues such as Alfred Rosenberg and the Racial Political Office of Walter Gross (a protégé of Rudolf Hess), the National Socialist Welfare League (*NSV*), and the Nazi Doctors' League under Gerhard Wagner. They emphasized the role of the family doctor as fundamental in promoting primary health care. The alliance was held together by a high degree of ideological motivation to the party and to Aryan racial ideals, and benefited from the party infrastructure. The rival faction was more technocratic and elitist. This consisted of public health administrators, medical researchers, and the SS and its daughter racial organizations, the *Ahnenerbe* and *Lebensborn* which had racial hygienic programmes. Himmler emerged as the controlling power. He envisaged a German-dominated Europe, led by a Nordic elite. He advocated harsh policies of Germanization and elimination of other ethnic groups. These policies required medical expertise for sterilization, segregation, and mass killing, as well as for health-promoting and breeding policies. For their part, the scientists had fatal flaws in their beliefs. In many cases, the more scientific their outlook, the more politically naive they were. The more scientists tried to maintain authority and status, the more concessions had to be made to Nazism. The racial hygienists made a Faustian pact with Nazism. Its powerful forces and organizations had aims that went far beyond the racial hygienists' nationalism, and professionalized control over health care. Instead of leading a national revival to a healthy society, the racial hygienists became subordinate to forces leading to war and mass killings.

[*Health, Race and German Politics between National Unification and Nazism 1870–1945*
(Cambridge: Cambridge University Press, 1989), 493–7.]

MICHAEL H. KATER

72   The Problem of Motivation Reconsidered

Michael Kater's work also places emphasis on elements of continuity
from the pre-Nazi era; similarly, he emphasizes that even those doctors
who did not participate as actively as others still failed overwhelmingly
to condemn the murderous processes which they were helping to
facilitate. Here, he gives consideration to the factors motivating medical doctors to participate in the regime's racial policies.

Against the background of [. . .] impressive evidence of physicians' anti-Nazi attitudes, why did the majority of German doctors array themselves politic-ally with the Third Reich? Before probing more deeply the issue of motiv-ations, it must be stressed once more that hardly ever was a single moral action or the lack thereof black or white but that, instead, various shades of gray predominated. If some human motives were completely altruistic, others were crassly self-interested, and others were a mixture of both, with the proportions often changing. This qualifying rule would appear to apply not only in the case of supporters of the regime, but also in that of the saboteurs, or those medical professionals who may have passed as such. Who was to know then and who is to utter final judgment now upon what actually went on in the minds of people at that time? As one observant contemporary poignantly remarked at the end of 1943, when the war was considered by many to be all but lost, physicians in the Third Reich may have had more freedom of movement and expression than other citizens because even the tyrants were clinging to them for dear life[1]. Hence any concern or unrest doctors may have expressed must today be evaluated with more scrutiny than the valor, for example, of schoolteachers, who, as salaried state servants and invested models of authority for younger generations, would have chanced a great deal more in the event of open tumult.[2] Nor must it be forgotten that much the German doctors said and did may look like acts of political resistance in our time when in reality, given their unique position, matters of professional status and peer privilege could have been at stake. If it is true that Dr. Fritz Gietzelt's 1944 execution was delayed because prominent Leipzig physicians protested as a group, they may have done so for humanitarian reasons as much as for the sake of a collective egotism: to safeguard their professional pride and sense of corporate solidarity.[3]

A corollary would hold true for those physicians who served or joined the Nazi movement in any conceivable capacity. Certainly, not a small number of them did so for idealistic, politically motivated reasons: Dr. Kurt Klare, the Hitler disciple of long standing who soon was on Gerhard Wagner's payroll, or that anonymous young physician who in fall 1933 found occasion to propagandize 'Hitler and his tremendous movement' to colleagues in open letters of the party press.[4] Some listened to the regime's clarion call that doctors *must* be National Socialists and 'leaders of their people' that was issued to them incessantly.[5] But for many, plain necessity was the mainspring for political action. Young doctors hoping to start out with a panel fund practice appeared to have little choice: in the wake of the novel KVD* controls in 1933, they were driven to what may be termed an involuntary form of opportunism. For the KVD *required* every medical professional on its certification waiting lists to produce a spotless National Socialist record: registrants with Old Fighter laurels were to be given preference.[6]

Thus the cases of Dr. Herbert Volkmar and Dr. Hanna Donnerberg may stand for many others. Volkmar's candidacy for KVD installment was already filed with the Wiesbaden KVD chapter in November 1934 when an ailing older physician petitioned that Volkmar assume his fund practice. It was in Volkmar's favor that he had been an SA man since 1933 as well as a regular member of the NS-Ärztebund.[7] And a pristine Nazi reference was called for as late as 1938, when physicians were becoming scarce and were already being courted by the regime. Because the KVD divined that the forty-two-year-old Dr. Donnerberg of Rhenish Neuwied, previously a privately practicing professional, had shown insufficient commitment while attached to the Hitler Youth and had failed to make her mark 'in any other affiliate of the party', she was rated politically unreliable and her KVD certification was withheld. Donnerberg appealed the decision claiming that she had been libeled,

---

* KVD: *Kassenärztliche Vereinigung Deutschlands*: Association of German Health Insurance Doctors.

pointing to her excellent service record in the Nazi Women's League and the Labor Front, among other organizations. Her appeal was judged valid at higher KVD levels, after evidence showed the doctor to have been a faithful Nazi activist who had not, as charged, patronized Jewish stores as late as 1935. She was promptly instated.[8]

Moreover, in the early years of the regime, when many young doctors still were desperate for work, established Nazi practitioners would advertise full-time takeovers or part-time deputyships only for colleagues with a demonstrable party association.[9] The political factor was even more instrumental in the case of institutions such as municipal or private clinics seeking junior and senior staff.[10] Small wonder, then, if realistic job-hunters became expert at emphasizing their Nazi titles when they went soliciting for opportunities.[11] He wished to become a factory physician (*Betriebsarzt*), for the pay was not bad, wrote a neophyte doctor in November 1936. But would he be accepted, he wondered, because he lacked the preferred status of an Old Fighter of the movement.[12]

Doctors slated for employment by publicly administered institutions or by the government always had to endure an assiduous political screening that could take considerable time. Typical is the case of Dr. Hans Joachim Sewering, [. . .] Before he was to assume his posting as tuberculosis specialist in Schönbrunn in summer 1942, the Nazi Gauleitung, in accordance with requirements, was asked for a political bill of health. It responded that Sewering had joined the SS in 1933 and the NSDAP in 1934 and that he was currently on front-line duty. Still, the verdict was equivocal. 'Nothing detrimental is known,' it said in neat letter type, 'objections exist neither on political nor on social grounds.' The final comment was penciled in and potentially damaging: 'Until now he has shown no interest in the local party chapter and hence in the Nazi movement.' [. . .] This doctor's career progress was not impeded.[13]

Ways were known of using personal connections beyond nominal memberships and token affidavits that smacked of careerism bordering on ruthlessness, and these were in keeping with the scarcely hidden system of spoils and corruption that was a major dynamic of Nazi rule.[14] Thus a gynaecologist in Upper Bavarian Murnau did not hesitate to ask the local mayor for a lucrative hospital position because he was 'a party comrade of many years.'[15] But in another sense, these routines were reminiscent of channels of protection and influence characteristic of social structures more properly associated with pre-Nazi conventions, in particular the old-boy fraternity networks. This once again points up the curious marriage between reactionary interest-peddling and new political ambition, which bound, however tenuously, the traditional social elites to the new power brokers for the temporary expediency of both. Was Hans Pfundtner, secretary of state in the interior ministry and a confidant of Conti and Frick, not aware of this when he used his offices to curry favor on behalf of junior fraternity alumni, all physicians who were keen on quick advancement and promotion?[16]

There may, in fact, have existed several more dimensions to the political compromise of Third Reich physicians not easily interpreted today, for the pressures exerted by the Nazi movement were manifold, subtle, and complex, to the point of appearing not only confusing but paradoxical at times.[17] Amid general exhortations early in the regime for doctors to align themselves with the movement, what was one to make, for instance, of the public derision of Thuringian physicians by one of Wagner's functionaries, who exclaimed: 'In the world of politics, it is easy to coordinate yourself. All you have to do is to exchange your black tuxedo for a brown shirt and the matter is settled!'[18] If patients in the party were broadly encouraged to patronize the doctors of their regional Nazi Doctors' League chapter and if many doctors admittedly joined the NSDAP because 'it meant good business,' why were the movement's physicians still discriminated against at certain of the nation's clinics?[19] What of the post-World War II assurances of some that they approached the party 'because all the others were joining, without inner commitment,' and that of others that physicians were tricked into the movement with the bait of a party uniform but never the tenets of Nazism?[20] Was it not an anomaly that a known critic of the regime, upon attempting to leave the medical bureaucracy, was implored to enter the party as a guarantee of continuing employment, while another doctor, eager for NSDAP service and eventually in the pay of the police, was banned from the party's ranks because of his father's SPD past?[21] And did it fit together if some Nazi block warden pressured a doctor to sign up for the NSDAP when at the same time it was stressed that party members, after malpractice suits, would be more harshly dealt with than political abstainers?[22] [. . .]

[A] final, residual possibility must be considered. It would be that physicians entered the Nazi movement for the purpose of resisting the system from within: the classic 'Trojan Horse' theme said to have been enacted several times in the course of the Third Reich, as it was by Wolfram Sievers and Kurt Gerstein in the SS. But Sievers was a liar, and Gerstein very probably was deluding himself: the potential for such premeditated spying-cum-sabotage in any regime apparatus after 1933 was always diminutive.[23] Not one doctor is known to have joined a Nazi organization for the express purpose of countermanding the dictatorship,[24] or even of exerting a moderating influence, notwithstanding any assertions to the contrary.[25]

[*Doctors under Hitler* (Chapel Hill: University of North Carolina Press, 1989), 84–7.]

73   Death and Deliverance

> Michael Burleigh's humane and bleak work on the child and adult
> 'euthanasia' programme demonstrates convincingly that not only
> were broad sectors of the medical profession (including both doctors
> and nurses) complicit—for a variety of reasons—in the mass murder
> of many tens of thousands of mentally ill and mentally handicapped
> people, but that this was itself rooted in a broader 'moral climate' of
> consent or at least acquiescence, extending, most notably, to parents
> and relatives themselves.

As we all know, eugenic solutions to real, or perceived, social ills had widespread currency long before the Nazis came to power—and by no means exclusively in Germany. Being modern, 'progressive' and 'scientific', they were not bereft of devotees over the whole political spectrum. Just as many of the most innovative features of 'Weimar culture'—notably in painting—actually predate the First World War, so some of the most inhumane policies pursued by the Nazis had their origins in developments during the Weimar period. This was the case with discussions of the desirability of chucking overboard 'dead ballast' from the 'Ship of Fools' in the interests of enhanced national efficiency, which in Germany took on renewed saliency in the context of the multiple crises following the Versailles treaty. It was also the case with the initially optimistic brush between a reformed psychiatric sector and social problems whose scale had not been anticipated, and which hence engendered profound pessimism and the search for drastic rethinking of the viability of all expenditure in this area, with many psychiatrists calling for radical eugenic solutions and the killing of incurables. All of these developments predated the advent of a National Socialist government, and illustrate rather well the adverse sides of what the late Detlev Peukert called Weimar's experiment in classical modernity.

Although the advent of the National Socialist regime had very deleterious effects upon people living in asylums—i.e. conditions worsened, patients were compulsorily sterilised, and the regime's propaganda none too subtly disputed their human personality—the decision to kill people had complex origins. The so-called 'children's euthanasia' programme undoubtedly reflected the desire of some parents to rid themselves of the 'burden' represented by severely handicapped offspring, this being an element in the equation often conveniently overlooked by research on the subject. Some parents wanted to concentrate their flagging energies upon their other healthy children; others wanted to remove any 'taint' which might affect the purity of their family pedigree. These attitudes were hardly surprising, since they were largely in line with what limited opinion polls on these matters had revealed in the mid 1920s, polls which actually reveal parents anticipating the precise course of Nazi policy. Opinion-sounding undertaken by the SD (the SS security service) during the 'euthanasia' programme also reveals that people were far from unanimous in condemning these policies.

The 'euthanasia' programme for adults was very much bound up with clearing the decks in order to wage war. Hitler and his subordinates did not slither into it through contingent circumstances; nor did bureaucratic mechanisms assume a life of their own in the way that some historians imagine was the case with the 'Final Solution'. The 'euthanasia' programme was a carefully planned and covertly executed operation with precisely defined objectives. Those responsible believed in the necessity of what they were doing. Mentally and physically disabled people were killed to save money and resources, or to create physical space for ethnic German repatriates and/or civilian and military casualties, both in 'Aktion T-4' and through shootings carried out by the SS in Pomerania and Poland, and in the 'euthanasia' programme's various continuations. In other words, these policies reflected a non-medical agenda, even if some psychiatrists belatedly tried to give them some *ex post facto* medicalised rationalisation in order to defend their little beleaguered professional empires. The idea of 'modernising' psychiatric provision came to them after they had cold-bloodedly murdered tens of thousands of people, while recreating scenes of 'medieval' desolation in the asylums, with skeletal patients lying on straw or locked in vermin-infested bunkers.

Again, one has to bear in mind that most people affected had been placed in asylums by their families (state committals were exceptional, even under a regime which used inflationary definitions of insanity), and that there is little evidence of the latter exercising themselves to retrieve their relatives even when it was very obvious what fate was in store for them. Instead of concentrating upon well-known instances of individual outrage at these killings, historians might ask how far silent collusion facilitated the vast majority of them. One of the reasons this subject was so conspicuously neglected in postwar Germany is probably that its real secrets lie buried for ever in the consciences of many ordinary German families. The ways in which the state, and many members of the medical profession, systematically betrayed the trust of those who consigned their relatives to their care are unfortunately only part of the story. The gradual hardening of a particular moral climate— though this is admittedly a rather nebulous, albeit vital, analytical category— and the slow seepage of a post-Christian and illiberal ideology into the thoughts and actions of the generality are equally striking. Why did many plain people abandon concern for the 'weak', in favour of a vulgar Social Darwinist ideology which entailed a reversion to the laws of the farmyard or jungle? Did they imagine that they would always be on the side of the lions and wolves? Why did the rights of individuals collapse in front of such collectivist goals as the good of the economy, race or nation? What factors explain why some people were so susceptible to this ideology, and what explains those who rejected it? [. . .]

Many of the most devious and pernicious individuals [. . .] were 'ordinary' working-class people, e.g. agricultural labourers, builders, cooks or lorry-drivers, some of whom went on via the 'euthanasia' programme to command extermination camps. This is the story of a sort of social mobility from cook to camp commandant. There is also the matter of women perpetrators. This aspect of Nazism, the chance for bullies to lord it over others, tends to be neglected.

All societies have people supposedly professionally concerned with law and moral values, notably lawyers, judges and clerics, to spread the net no further. In this case, most of those people turned a blind eye towards—or worse, actively colluded in—these policies, as can be seen from the fact that half of the victims in the first phase of the 'euthanasia' programme came from ecclesiastical asylums. Down on the ground, in those asylums, a certain degree of haggling over the fate of individuals was permitted by the bureaucrats responsible for the policies, in order to promote collusive involvement, but also to cater for the element of human bad conscience. Protests from the churches came too late to be effective, were easily circumvented, and ran parallel with discussions between the Roman Catholic hierarchy and sections of the Protestant charitable network on the one side, and the regime on the other, about how the 'euthanasia' programme could be rendered more palatable to their sensitive consciences. I make no apologies for being dismissive of their so-well-documented agonising, and their high-level networking with men who were fundamentally contemptuous of them. It is a distortion of reality to highlight the odd individual, such as Bishop Galen, who—no doubt with great courage—decided to protest against these matters despite the possible deleterious consequences. Such individuals were not typical.

[*Death and Deliverance: 'Euthanasia' in Germany 1900–1945* (Cambridge: Cambridge University Press, 1994), 3–5.]

CHRISTOPHER BROWNING

74   Reflections on a Massacre

Not only the SS but also regular *Wehrmacht* and police units participated in the mass shootings of Jews in eastern Europe. Police Battalion 101 took part in one such mass shooting in the Polish town of Józefów in July 1942, at which at least 1,500 Jews were killed. The policemen had been given the choice not to participate in the shooting by their commanding officer, Major Trapp, earlier in the day. Despite this, the vast majority participated, at least initially.

Using the testimonies of participants gathered in the 1960s, Christopher Browning attempts to assess how 'ordinary men' chose to take part in mass murder.

At Józefów a mere dozen men out of nearly 500 had responded instinctively to Major Trapp's offer to step forward and excuse themselves from the impending mass murder. Why was the number of men who from the beginning declared themselves unwilling to shoot so small? In part, it was a matter of the suddenness. There was no forewarning or time to think, as the men were totally 'surprised' by the Józefów action.[1] Unless they were able to react to Trapp's offer on the spur of the moment, this first opportunity was lost.[2]

As important as the lack of time for reflection was the pressure for conformity—the basic identification of men in uniform with their comrades and the strong urge not to separate themselves from the group by stepping out. The battalion had only recently been brought up to full strength, and many of the men did not yet know each other well; the bonds of military comradeship were not yet fully developed. Nonetheless, the act of stepping out that morning in Józefów meant leaving one's comrades and admitting that one was 'too weak' or 'cowardly.' Who would have 'dared,' one policeman declared emphatically, to 'lose face' before the assembled troops.[3] 'If the question is posed to me why I shot with the others in the first place,' said another who subsequently asked to be excused after several rounds of killing, 'I must answer that no one wants to be thought a coward.' It was one thing to refuse at the beginning, he added, and quite another to try to shoot but not be able to continue.[4] Another policeman—more aware of what truly required courage—said quite simply, 'I was cowardly.'[5]

Most of the interrogated policemen denied that they had any choice. Faced with the testimony of others, many did not contest that Trapp had made the offer but claimed that they had not heard that part of the speech or could not remember it. A few policemen made the attempt to confront the question of choice but failed to find the words. It was a different time and place, as if they had been on another political planet, and the political values and vocabulary of the 1960s were useless in explaining the situation in which they had found themselves in 1942. Quite atypical in describing his state of mind that morning of July 13 was a policeman who admitted to killing as many as twenty Jews before quitting. 'I thought that I could master the situation and that without me the Jews were not going to escape their fate anyway . . . Truthfully I must say that at the time we didn't reflect about it at all. Only years later did any of us become truly conscious of what had happened then. . . . Only later did it first occur to me that had not been right.'[6]

In addition to the easy rationalization that not taking part in the shooting was not going to alter the fate of the Jews in any case, the policemen developed other justifications for their behavior. Perhaps the most astonishing rationalization of all was that of a thirty-five-year-old metalworker from Bremerhaven:

I made the effort, and it was possible for me, to shoot only children. It so happened that the mothers led the children by the hand. My neighbor then shot the mother and I shot the child that belonged to her, because I reasoned with myself that after all without its mother the child could not live any longer. It was supposed to be, so to speak, soothing to my conscience to release children unable to live without their mothers.[7]

The full weight of this statement, and the significance of the word choice of the former policeman, cannot be fully appreciated unless one knows that the German word for 'release' (*erlösen*) also means to 'redeem' or 'save' when used in a religious sense. The one who 'releases' is the *Erlöser*—the Savior or Redeemer!

In terms of motivation and consciousness, the most glaring omission in the interrogations is any discussion of anti-Semitism. For the most part the interrogators did not pursue this issue. Nor were the men, for understandable reasons as potential defendants, eager to volunteer any illuminating comments. With few exceptions the whole question of anti-Semitism is marked by silence. What is clear is that the men's concern for their standing in the eyes of their comrades was not matched by any sense of human ties with their victims. The Jews stood outside their circle of human obligation and responsibility. Such a polarization between 'us' and 'them,' between one's comrades and the enemy, is of course standard in war.

It would seem that even if the men of Reserve Police Battalion 101 had not consciously adopted the anti-Semitic doctrines of the regime, they had at least accepted the assimilation of the Jews into the image of the enemy. Major Trapp appealed to this generalized notion of the Jews as part of the enemy in his early-morning speech. The men should remember, when shooting Jewish women and children, that the enemy was killing German women and children by bombing Germany.

If only a dozen policemen stepped out at the beginning to extricate themselves from the impending mass murder, a much larger number either sought to evade the shooting by less conspicuous methods or asked to be released from the firing squads once the shooting had begun. How many policemen belonged to these categories cannot be ascertained with any certainty, but an estimate in the range of 10 to 20 percent of those actually assigned to the firing squads does not seem unreasonable. [One sergeant], for instance, admitted excusing as many as five from his squad of forty or fifty men. In [another] group, from which the greatest number of shooters was interrogated, we can identify six policemen who quit within four rounds and an entire squad of five to eight who were released considerably later. While the number of those who evaded or dropped out was thus not insignificant, it must not obscure the corollary that at least 80 percent of those called upon to shoot continued to do so until 1,500 Jews from Józefów had been killed.

Even twenty or twenty-five years later those who did quit shooting along the way overwhelmingly cited sheer physical revulsion against what they were doing as the prime motive but did not express any ethical or political principles behind this revulsion. Given the educational level of these reserve policemen, one should not expect a sophisticated articulation of abstract principles. The absence of such does not mean that their revulsion did not have its origins in the humane instincts that Nazism radically opposed and sought to overcome. But the men themselves did not seem to be conscious of the contradiction between their feelings and the essence of the regime they served. Being too weak to continue shooting, of course, posed problems for the 'productivity' and morale of the battalion, but it did not challenge basic police discipline or the authority of the regime in general. Indeed, Heinrich Himmler himself sanctioned the toleration of this kind of weakness in his notorious Posen speech of October 4, 1943, to the SS leadership. While exalting obedience as one of the key virtues of all SS men, he explicitly noted an exception, namely, 'one whose nerves are finished, one who is weak. Then one can say: Good, go take your pension'.[8]

Politically and ethically motivated opposition, explicitly identified by the policemen as such, was relatively rare. One man said he decisively rejected the Jewish measures of the Nazis because he was an active Communist Party member and thus rejected National Socialism in its entirety.[9] Another said he opposed the shooting of Jews because he had been a Social Democrat for many years.[10] A third said he was known to the Nazis as 'politically unreliable' and a 'grumbler' but gave no further political identity.[11] Several others grounded their attitude on opposition to the regime's anti-Semitism in particular. 'This attitude I already had earlier in Hamburg,' said one landscape gardener, 'because due to the Jewish measures already carried out in Hamburg I had lost the greater part of my business customers.'[12] Another policeman merely identified himself as 'a great friend of the Jews' without explaining further.[13]

The two men who explained their refusal to take part in the greatest detail both emphasized the fact that they were freer to act as they did because they had no careerist ambitions. One policeman accepted the possible disadvantages of his course of action 'because I was not a career policeman and also did not want to become one, but rather an independent skilled craftsman, and I had my business back home. . . . thus it was of no consequence that my police career would not prosper.'[14]

[*Ordinary Men: Reserve Police Battalion 101 and the Final Solution in Poland* (New York: Harper Perennial, 1992), 71–5.]

75   The Missing Years: German Workers, German Soldiers

> The recognition that the regular *Wehrmacht* was a crucial participant in
> the crimes of the National Socialist regime, especially on the eastern
> front, has had an important impact on the ways in which historians
> have approached broader issues of popular complicity in the barbar-
> ism of the regime. While, for example, social historians have tended to
> see workers as the social class most impervious to Nazism's popular
> appeal, scholars such as Omer Bartov have pointed out that this did
> not preclude the possibility of them participating in criminal acts
> under other guises—above all as soldiers themselves.

In recent years it has been convincingly shown that far from conforming to
the totalitarian image it strove to project, the 'Hitler State' was in fact made
up of a chaotic conglomeration of competing, overlapping, and often
superfluous institutions, with only the Führer, himself described by some
historians as a 'weak dictator' with limited powers, to divide and rule over
it.[1] Moreover, the Nazi ideal of establishing a so-called '*Volksgemeinschaft*' is
also said to have failed miserably, with German society, though submitting
to a terroristic police state, remaining riven by conflicting class interests.[2]
Similarly, while the 'Hitler Myth' retained its hold as a unifying concept for
a growing proportion of the German population until very late in the war,
the NSDAP, which in any case had never achieved even a simple majority,
lost much of its popularity in the early years following the 'seizure of
power.'[3]

The German working class is probably the most significant case in point as
regards the Nazi regime's failure—or unwillingness—to break down those
very class barriers against which the party had allegedly fought and whose
disappearance in an idyllic *Volksgemeinschaft* should have legitimized the
replacement of the Weimar Republic by a ruthless dictatorship. Extensive
research into this issue has indeed demonstrated that quite apart from outright resistance to the regime, mostly by former socialist and communist
activists, workers had shown a surprising degree of opposition to attempts by
the employers and the state to limit their gains, made following the rapid shift
in the 1930s from unemployment to manpower shortage as a result of massive
rearmament. The workers' struggle, involving an array of industrial actions
such as strikes, go-slows, frequent changes of work-places, and lowered
productivity, has been presented as a clear sign of the regime's failure to
create a totalitarian 'people's community,' based not just on fear and suppression, but also on acceptance of the new political system and creed. Social
structures inherited from pre-Nazi times are thus said to have persisted under
Hitler's rule and to have evolved gradually only after the fall of the Third

Reich, owing both to the terrible destruction of the war and the political upheavals which followed it.[4] Nevertheless, while on the one hand it may astonish us that there actually was such interest-group pressure from the working class under the Nazi dictatorship, on the other hand there is also room to inquire why this domestic tension rarely transformed itself into political resistance, and why the regime, though making a few temporary concessions to the workers (as it also did to the churches), does not seem to have been seriously threatened by the working class at any time, and could by and large pursue expansionist policies with no hindrance from within, indeed, with a great measure of support.[5]

Findings regarding industrial unrest in Germany in the late 1930s have significantly influenced views on some major issues of the period, such as the debate over the origins of the Second World War, the inquiry into the deeper causes and wider implications of the *Blitzkrieg* strategy, as well as the historical value of earlier theories of fascism and totalitarianism.[6] At the same time, it has also become necessary to define more precisely the meaning and applicability of such terms as 'resistance' and 'opposition,' both as regards the working class, and in the case of other groups hovering between collaboration and resistance, such as the churches, the military, and the traditional liberal-conservative elites.[7]

Yet precisely because of the centrality of this issue and the wide range of its implications, it may be of some interest to stress one of its aspects which does not seem to have received appropriate attention hitherto. The point is that in September 1939 Germany launched what turned out to be a world war, and although initially its people marched to battle without much enthusiasm, and its resources were not totally mobilized, as of winter 1941 Hitler's Reich found itself up to its neck in a vast military confrontation, fielding millions of soldiers, and straining both its physical and its mental capacities to the limit. Ultimately, the mass of Germany's population became involved in one way or another in the war, and a growing proportion of its men, young, middle-aged, and old, workers, bourgeois, and aristocrats, Nazis and former socialists and communists, were recruited and sent to the front, turning miraculously into Europe's toughest and most determined troops, mostly fighting with extraordinary cohesion almost until the bitter end. For throughout the war, combat morale in the *Wehrmacht* generally remained extremely high, mutinies were almost unknown, and an excellent system of manpower organization, draconian punishment, and extensive indoctrination combined to hold combat units tightly together, while a series of astonishing victories made it easier to withstand even greater defeats in the hope of fortune's wheel turning once more in Germany's favour.[8]

The question to be asked is thus, how did it come about that men who had been recruited from the mines and factories, who had demonstrated their capacity to oppose at least the social and economic policies of the regime, and some of whom may well have still remembered their former trade-union, SPD, or KPD affiliations, could within a matter of months be transformed into Hitler's tenacious, increasingly brutalized and fanaticized soldiers, spearheading his expanding Reich and executing or making possible the execution of his murderous policies? Indeed, what light does this shed on the greater or lesser susceptibility of various social strata to Nazism, on the extent, aims, and nature of opposition, on the degree to which it actually threatened the regime, and on the Third Reich's capacity to mobilize the mass of German society, 'Volksgemeinschaft' or not?

Put differently, it seems that we should clearly distinguish between the Nazi regime's evident failure to realize its proclaimed aim of establishing a 'Volksgemeinschaft' free of intersocial tensions, on the one hand, and the willingness of large sectors of the population to accept that same regime as the embodiment of the nation, and to sacrifice themselves for it at a time of war and crisis, on the other hand. [. . .]

While social historians have probed into civilian society, military historians have concerned themselves mainly with tactics, strategy and generals. Although it has of course long been recognized that in modern conscript armies the borderline between civilians and soldiers is extremely blurred, the army was treated as a separate institution, maintaining its own particular relationship with the state. If the social background of soldiers was considered at all, it was mainly that of the older, senior ranks, or of that tiny group of resisters, likewise quite highly placed in the military hierarchy.[9] Consequently, once conscripted, the social historians' protagonists were passed over to the military historians who, as far as the rank-and-file and junior officers were concerned, treated them as part of a vast, faceless mass of field-grey uniforms devoid of any civilian past. Conversely, once the war was over, those soldiers who had survived it were, so to speak, delivered back into the hands of the social historians, only to continue their civilian existence with very little reference to the fact that for years they had served as soldiers—just as in dust-jacket biographies, or in that recent film saga, *Heimat*, the workers too went off somewhere for a few years, and then some of them returned. What happened in between was a matter for soldiers' stories. [. . .]

It would [. . .] seem that by stressing the close connection between the Third Reich's civilian population and its soldiers, and by realizing that, though of course biased in favour of certain social and age (let alone gender and 'racial') categories, the *Wehrmacht* increasingly reflected the society from which its troops were recruited, our understanding of the soldiers' conduct, and more generally of conformity and opposition in Nazi Germany on the whole, can be substantially enhanced. From the point of view of the military, it appears that the army succeeded beyond all expectations in turning its millions of recruits into well-disciplined and highly motivated soldiers, whatever their social origins and political traditions. Quite apart from its policy of harsh punishments,[10] the *Wehrmacht* managed to persuade a high proportion of its men that, headed by 'the greatest *Feldherr* of all time,' they were fighting for the right 'cause' against an infernal host of political and biological enemies. Yet this could not have succeeded without first penetrating wide-ranging sectors of civilian society and indoctrinating soldiers-to-be into believing the central tenets of National Socialism. This process is of particular significance in the case of the working class, that social stratum said to have been most resistant to Nazi propaganda. For, examining what worker-soldiers thought, wrote, and carried out, one may well find it worthwhile to reconsider the nature and reasoning behind their opposition to the regime, and ask whether it actually stemmed from political/ideological, or rather from economic/interest-group motivation.

The [. . .] evidence [. . .] seems to suggest that Nazi ideas had indeed had an impact upon the German working class, and particularly upon the younger generation, as they had on German youth on the whole. This in no way means that those same workers did not hope to improve their economic condition, or protect those gains they had already made. But it does indicate that there was a large pool of nationalist phobias and racial prejudices among the working class on which the regime could draw, just as there is evidence of quite a powerful admiration for the Führer, whatever may have been thought of the party.[11] It is also quite likely that especially some of the younger men were attracted to the prospect of exchanging their dreary work-places for what seemed to be an invincible army, in which, moreover, owing mostly to the tremendous casualties, one could hope for relatively rapid promotion with diminishing consideration of social and educational qualifications, even if in reality this was not often the case.[12] The *Volksgemeinschaft* may well have turned out to be an illusion, but perhaps precisely because of that the longing for a real *Kampfgemeinschaft* actually increased, especially when facing, and initially smashing, enemies allegedly determined to destroy the Reich. Finally, it is also possible that particularly men stemming from the lower strata of German society felt a certain attraction to the idea of ruling over other peoples as the proud representatives of the Aryan '*Herrenvolk.*'

['The Missing Years: German Workers, German Soldiers', *German History*, 8/1 (1990), 49–52, 64–5.]

The Conditions for Genocide

> Michael Zimmermann's powerful study of the perpetrators of the
> genocide of the Sinti and Roma ('gypsies') offers a thoughtful analysis
> of the interaction between personal motives and mentalities, insti-
> tutional pressures, and the dynamism of the regime as a whole.

The NS annihilation of the gypsies was systematic murder which went
beyond massacre. It would hardly have been possible without the active and
effective participation of the administration and the police. Long before the
era of National Socialism, legislature and administrative system had subjected the gypsies in Germany to a discriminatory special legislation. Already
under the Empire and during the Weimar Republic, the administration and
the police had focused their attention towards 'deporting' those stigmatized
as 'gypsies' from town and village, and towards preventing their permanent
residence as far as possible. Once the political conditions had fundamentally
changed after 1933, it was not very far from that to the call for supposedly
more effective persecution measures. In fact it was not only the heads of the
criminal police but also the mayors, social service offices, chief constables,
district administrators, district offices, and district governors who demanded
concentration camp imprisonment or permanent expulsion in order to 'solve'
the 'gypsy problem' once and for all.

The deportation of gypsies into the *Generalgouvernement* in 1940, to Łódź in
1941, to Bialystok in 1942, and to Auschwitz-Birkenau in 1943 was greeted in
the administration and police to a large extent as a radical variant of traditional gypsy policy: at the same time, however, it was also trivialized as
essentially the continuation of this policy. These deportations were not only
referred to in police reports as 'resettlement', 'evacuation', and 'delivery':
they were also described in the records using the terms 'deportation' or
'transport'[1]—which long since had come to mean the compulsory escorting
by the police of itinerants from one location to the next, or quite generally
the moving on of gypsies.

There are many signs that indicate that such euphemisms could not completely appease the conscience. Records from the German occupation in the
Baltic show that those belonging to the administration of the civil occupation
withdrew from the 'gypsy policy' there and kept confused silence as they
found out about the murders of the security police, or they sought to rationalize the annihilation of the gypsies as an exception determined by the situation, as a limited 'special measure', necessitated by the proximity of the
front. Within the German Reich especially, traces can be found in the police
files of people recoiling when small children were to be brought to Auschwitz
by 'individual transport'. Nevertheless, these children were, ultimately,

deported too. The desire to make one's own area entirely or largely 'gypsy free', the principle of command and obedience in the police, and that of procedural obligation in the bureaucracy, as well as the both mentally exonerating and inhibition-reducing division of responsibilities,[2] combined in such a way that any resistance to deporting and murdering the Sinti and Roma remained shamefully limited.

Even the decisions to annihilate the gypsies were based in a certain way on institutionalized division of labour and separation of functions. This can be demonstrated for example with the genesis of the command to deport the Sinti and Roma to Auschwitz-Birkenau. A major prerequisite of this decision, which was murderous and denied the intention to murder at the same time, was the division of labour between the Reich Criminal Police Office and the Race Hygiene Research Office on one hand, and Auschwitz concentration camp on the other. Here too there was a division of responsibilities which both relieved the strain on those responsible and reduced their inhibitions. According to the decision of the Reich Criminal Police Office, those in the Birkenau gypsy concentration camp should no longer be allowed to leave it. However, the Criminal Police command and the racial hygienists advising them believed themselves not to be responsible for their imminent death, because, after all, in Auschwitz-Birkenau the camp commandant was responsible.

The concept on which the NS mass annihilation of the gypsies was based— not in the sense of an ultimate cause but of a necessary precondition—was not a specific product of the NS system. Modern racism, on which the murder was ideologically based, had already found approval in Germany before 1933 and not just on the *völkisch* Right.[3] It provided a discourse with the help of which the conventional projective defensive stance against Jews, gypsies, and other groups had been formed into a relatively closed and puta- tively scientifically sound framework. The racist view of society did not regard individuals, social classes, or a mankind considered as universally equal as the movers of history, but the 'races', who were divided biogenetically into 'superior' and 'inferior'. [. . .]

The extermination policy against Sinti and Roma, finally, throws new light on the historiographical debate between 'intentionalists' and 'structuralists' concerning the causes of the National Socialist genocide. The 'intentional- ists' postulated as its decisive cause an anti-Semitic murder programme that had been inherent in Hitler's 'world view'. However, the existence of such a programme fixed from the outset can just as little be proved for the Jews as, for instance, for the victims of the 'euthanasia' or for gypsy groups. The 'intentionalists' do not properly incorporate these into their considerations, associating genocide solely with anti-Semitism, although precisely they should explain why, for example, the gypsies, who were so irrelevant to Hitler's 'world view', were murdered. The focus of the 'intentionalists' on

Hitler does not do justice to the complex decision processes for mass extermination and to their implementation based on the division of labour. It also underestimates the modern system of terror which is actually just as moulded by the 'boundless drive of the servants of power' as by the 'overpowering, invulnerable master'.[4]

The 'structuralist' approach, which emphasizes the 'cumulative radicalization'[5] of National Socialist persecution and extermination brought about by the war, by competition within the NS polycracy, and by the political aporias and blind alleys brought about by the NS system itself, is better able to grasp the dynamics of mass extermination. It also underlines those explanatory factors which are not intentional in the narrower sense—factors such as careerism, obedience, subservience towards authority, group loyalties, economic interests, or the mental repression of murder. The more extreme version of 'structuralism', however, runs the risk now and then of letting the driving forces of the annihilation from a certain point onwards disappear behind a mechanistic image which could suggest an automatism of murder: 'once set fully in motion, the extermination of those unable to work developed a dynamic. The bureaucratic machinery built up by Eichmann and Heydrich functioned, as it were, automatically.'[6] Furthermore the 'structuralists', similarly in this respect to the 'intentionalists', regard as the core of the Hitlerist 'world view' the dictator's fanatical expressions of racial anti-Semitism:[7] the annihilation of the gypsies was therefore also barely considered by them.

Looking at the murder of the gypsies, both the Hitler-centrism of the 'intentionalist' approach and the inadequate consideration of murderous intentions in the structuralist approach appear to be problematic. The limitations of these approaches can perhaps be overcome if greater account is taken of those considerations—to be characterized, perhaps, as 'conceptualist'[8]—which regard modern racism as an ideological motor of the extermination policy, one whose effect was to remove inhibitions[9] precisely because of its supposed scientific character, and the Reich Security Main Office as its most powerful bearer. For the persecution of the gypsies, the Reich Criminal Police Office, and the Race Hygiene Research Office form that policing-scientific complex which transformed racist theory into the practice of persecution. The 'conceptualist' attempt at an interpretation thus underlines the importance of the racist model of society and of the institutions which have transplanted this concept of social policy into practice. It accentuates the intentions of mass annihilation without—unlike the 'intentionalists'—reducing this to the person of Hitler.

[*Rassenutopie und Genozid: die Nationalsozialistische 'Lösung der Zigeunerfrage'* (Hamburg: Christians, 1996), 376–80.]

Section F

The Impact of National Socialism

INTRODUCTION

Much careful scholarship in recent years has emphasized the extent to which National Socialism should be analysed within a broader continuum, stressing the need to examine social and cultural continuities running from the 1920s and early 1930s into the early years of the regime, and pointing to the impact of developments under National Socialism whose effects can be traced in the early post-war years. National Socialism did, indeed, emerge in the context of a modern industrial society and mobilized the potential of that society to pursue its goals; it is unsurprising, therefore, that certain aspects of it went with the grain of, and even accelerated, existing secular trends in specific spheres of society. For example, some scholars have argued that the absence of trade unions under National Socialism, and thus the lack of possibility of open collective working-class action, encouraged the emergence of an individualistic, upwardly mobile attitude amongst workers, who now sought advancement by exploiting their individual position within the labour market in a manner which prefigured the family-centred worker-as-consumer of the 1950s and 1960s. In the sphere of gender relations, moreover, some scholars have suggested that, beneath the rhetoric of separate spheres deployed by the regime, underlying processes of economic change accelerated by the armaments boom encouraged the further creation of 'feminized' work functions within the factory and thus the ongoing consolidation of gender inequalities within the workplace; similarly, the processes of bureaucratization under National Socialism may be seen to have encouraged the growth of white-collar functions 'suited to women', thus facilitating the further movement of women into certain, defined areas of the public sphere in a manner broadly consistent with long-term trends. Some have similarly suggested that a by-product of Nazi eugenics was the 'modernization' of ante- and post-natal care for women.

Whether or not one accepts that these and similar secular trends were accelerated as a by-product of National Socialism, it is important to emphasize that they were precisely this—a by-product. National Socialism was, above all, an attempt to construct an ideologically-inspired alternative modern utopia. Emphasizing the essential modernity of National Socialism is of value insofar as it enables us to recognize that it emerged in a society not

so radically different from our own, and that some of the policies and programmes in fields such as eugenics and euthanasia built upon ideas and
cultures which were very much visible in other societies at the time. However, if some secular trends were accelerated by the attempted realization of
this alternative utopia, they were very much the unintended, or accidental,
result of policies and practices pursued in the name of a radical programme
of racial engineering which meant that those policies were applied, above all,
on a selective basis. Improved ante-natal care may or may not have been
available to 'healthy' and 'superior' women; it was not available to those
women who were deemed to be socially or racially inferior and thus unfit to
breed. For these women, and for many men, brutal physical intervention in
their reproductive rights and capabilities was the consequence. For female
Soviet deported labourers during the war, 'ante- and post-natal care' often
simply meant enforced abortion. For those for whom this was not the case it
meant 60 hours per week of gruelling, exploitative factory labour on starvation rations until almost the moment of childbirth; the child would then
often die of malnutrition and lack of care, if it was not simply taken away and
murdered.

   Indeed, as the vision of the racially-engineered 'New Order' propelled the
regime into its radical imperialist aggression, brutal physical intervention was
superseded by a radical downwards spiral into mass murder. For ordinary,
'healthy' Germans the eugenicist vision of the regenerated nation foundered
on the realities of a war which left the country in ruins. Millions of German
soldiers were killed. Millions of German citizens suffered three years of a
bombing campaign which was unparalleled in its intensity and left Germany's cities in ruins. Some 12 million Germans became refugees or were
expelled from eastern Europe in violent acts of retribution by the Red Army
and the liberated populations. For millions of citizens of the occupied territories, the same vision of regeneration meant eradication. Millions suffered
the hardships, deprivation, and arbitrary brutality of occupation; millions
suffered the experience of forced labour under conditions which ranged from
at best extremely harsh to, in the case of those forced into building programmes under the SS, conditions which were intended to result in 'annihilation through labour'. Untold hundreds of thousands more experienced
similar, and often worse, fates in the sprawling network of concentration
camps which covered occupied Europe by the end of the war. The mass
murder of the Jews through arbitrary violence, forced labour, mass shootings, ghettoization, expulsion, and extermination in the death camps was the
climactic act of barbarism under a regime of murderous racism in the east
which also claimed the lives of millions of prisoners of war, and hundreds of
thousands of Sinti and Roma. Consideration of those secular trends which
were accelerated under National Socialism should not lead us to place those
aspects of the regime which were marginal at the centre of our understand-

ing; those aspects of the regime's impact which, taken together, were unique, should equally not be moved from the centre to the margins. At the centre of National Socialism was a regime of murderous racial annihilation—its impact is to be found in the appalling realization of these exterminatory ambitions.

77 The Third Reich and Society

> David Schoenbaum was one of the first scholars to recognize that, for all its atavistic rhetoric and the anti-modern elements of its ideology, developments under National Socialism in many ways went with the grain of longer-term secular changes. For Schoenbaum, this was a product of the fact that the regime represented a 'revolution of means and ends'—a revolution against bourgeois industrial society which mobilized bourgeois industrial society itself in its pursuit of the revolution. The resultant acceleration of secular trends inherent in industrial society, combined with the revolution of status engendered by National Socialism's radical egalitarianism, created the illusion of a classless society open to the talents, a transformation of objective and subjective reality which amounted, in Schoenbaum's view, to a 'social revolution'.

Franz Neumann's thesis that 'National Socialist social policy consists in the acceptance and strengthening of the prevailing class character of German society',[1] that the Third Reich represented, as before, the domination of the generals, the Junkers, and the industrialists with an admixture of Nazis, is a generally accurate reflection of the basic social situation, but doubly misleading. It is misleading in its suggestion of conscious purpose, its confusion of expediency with moral approval. It is still more misleading in its neglect of the dynamism characteristic of all Nazi policy, which revolutionized the role and influence of institutions and individuals with little reference to their size or titles.[2] What was involved was a revolution of class and a revolution of status at the same time. Two tendencies again interacted. On the one hand, the imperialist dynamics of the Third Reich, its eugenics and anti-intellectualism notwithstanding, sustained the position of the intellectual and the technician. National Socialism accelerated the already considerable mobility of German industrial society, creating at least an atmosphere of opportunity, and often enough, real evidence of it. Actual opportunity was limited in school and university, but neither of these was exactly a key institution in Nazi society. But it was real enough in the military, the economy, and even the civil service, the institutions that held Nazi society together.[3]

The status revolution, that accompanied this, was not a matter of elitism, even in the form of technocracy, but the triumph of egalitarianism, the reward and consummation of the *Volksbewegung* that had brought Hitler to power. The triumph of the down-and-out's, of the 'armed Bohemians' did not necessarily mean that they ruled the state, or in the special case of the SS, committed murder in a *Volksgemeinschaft* with princes and graduate lawyers. What it did mean was that they represented it, that a man without diploma, family, or independent economic position laid cornerstones, greeted foreign visitors at the station, shook the hands of graduates, and claimed the royal box at the theatre. This symbolic role represented real social opportunity for those who enjoyed it, opportunity that neither Weimar nor the Empire had offered them. [. . .]

National Socialism was to turn the clocks back, to make the German-speaking world safe for small business, small farmers, and small-towners. The goal was not only political but social revisionism, revision of the tyranny of big industry, big cities, big unions, big banks; and at the same time a revision of Versailles. But the simultaneous revision of Versailles and of the twentieth—not to say the nineteenth—century, *in* the twentieth century, was an attempt to square the circle. Revision of Versailles, in Nazi dimensions, involved at the very least the threat of force. But the threat of force in an industrial age presupposes industry, and there is, as Nazi society conclusively proved, no industry without an industrial society. [. . .]

In the context of both ideological mobilization and industrial recovery, every social group was integrated, almost overnight, into the new system. The immediate dissatisfactions were wiped out. The unemployed returned to work, the economic curve went up, the farm price index held firm. The new dissatisfactions, to the extent they were perceived at all, were rationalized and sublimated in a system whose very fluidity promised eventual solution to those with enough faith and hard enough elbows. Success promised more success, and war obviated the need for producing it. In the meanwhile, as a kind of advance payment on success, there were opportunities for the taking—by those with talent and those without it, those with education and those without it, those with money and whose without it.

The conflicts that might have arisen from extended reflection on the limits of such successes and the reality of such opportunities were resolved by the genuine conceptual difficulties the new situation presented. In the Third Reich, relative approximation of class and status came to an end. Discontent presupposes its recognition. The disillusion induced by one's awareness of his own importance or unimportance presupposes that one is aware of it—or at least is made aware of it by one's neighbors. This was next to impossible in the wonderland of Hitler Germany where there were no longer reliable indications of what was up and what was down. How important was a minister, a diplomat, a Party functionary, a Labor Front functionary, a Hitler Youth leader, a member of an Ordensburg? The question was unanswerable. [. . .]

Hitler's ministers like Papen's tended to be university graduates, doctors, high civil servants.[4] What did this say about Hitler's government compared with Papen's as a matter of class?

The answers depended on the observer. For the conservative observer, the old guard was the guarantor of continuity, of the historical state that demanded his confidence and his patriotism. For the radical observer, Hitler himself was the guarantor of change, of the new State that demanded his confidence and his patriotism. For even if the old guard was still on top,[5] Hitler himself, the corporal and 'building worker,' was at the very summit. In an economy primed in the meantime with armaments appropriations and building contracts, a society burgeoning with new offices and new opportunities, further reflection could be avoided where objective analysis was in any case impossible. In an extreme case—again the SS—members had the opportunity of humiliating doctors, professors, and judges while being led by doctors, professors, and judges. [. . .]

Objective social reality, the measurable statistical consequences of National Socialism, was the very opposite of what Hitler had presumably promised and what the majority of his followers had expected him to fulfill. In 1939 the cities were larger, not smaller; the concentration of capital greater than before; the rural population reduced, not increased; women not at the fireside but in the office and the factory; the inequality of income and property distribution more, not less conspicuous; industry's share of the gross national product up and agriculture's down, while industrial labor had it relatively good and small business increasingly bad. The East Elbian estates continued to be run by the gentry, the civil service by doctors and the Army by generals whose names began with 'von.' Not surprisingly, the history of the Third Reich is a story of frustration, cynicism, and resignation, the history of an apparently betrayed revolution whose one-time supporters, Otto Strasser, Rauschning, Feder, and Rosenberg, one after the other, denounced it as vehemently as its opponents.

Interpreted social reality, on the other hand, reflected a society united like no other in recent German history, a society of opportunities for young and old, classes and masses, a society that was New Deal and good old days at the same time. Like no world since 1914, it was a world of career civil servants and authoritarian paternalism, a world of national purpose and achievement where the Army was once again 'the school of the nation.' It was no less a world where officers and men ate the same meals and conversed 'as men to men'.[6]

[*Hitler's Social Revolution* (New York: Doubleday & Co., 1966; new edn. Norton & Co., 1980), 272–3, 275–6, 280–1, 282–3, 285–6.]

RALF DAHRENDORF

78   National Socialist Germany and the Social Revolution

Proceeding from an understanding of German history since the nineteenth century which drew heavily on old analyses of the supposed disjuncture between the 'modern', dynamic processes of industrialization and the survival of pre-industrial political structures—an understanding which informed much of the 'Special Path' thesis which was gaining currency at this time—Ralf Dahrendorf argued that National Socialism, in destroying the traditional social order and the existing particularist identities associated with it, was effectively enacting a delayed push into modernity. Dahrendorf's analysis was less empirically founded than Schoenbaum's; however, in giving more extensive treatment to the war, he was able to recognize that 'modernizing' impulses were as much a product of National Socialism's collapse as of its own policies.

Even in respect to the National Socialist seizure of power in 1933, historians speak of a revolution, a 'revolutionizing process' (Helmut Krausnick), a 'legal revolution' (Karl-Dietrich Bracher). What they mean is the rapid and firm transformation of the political constitution of the country. But the concept might prove adequate even if one considers the changes in German society that followed the political revolution. Here—to use Theodor Geiger's terms—not only the 'style' of an epoch, but the 'epoch' itself was transformed.

National Socialism completed for Germany the social revolution that was lost in the faultings of Imperial Germany and again held up by the contradictions of the Weimar Republic.

The substance of this revolution is modernity. Autonomous equality of opportunity for all men, which epitomizes modernity, does not, as we have seen, come about by itself. It is not a necessary consequence, or a condition, of industrialization. Moreover, wherever it did come about, at least the beginning of the process was violent. Entering the modern world proved painful for those involved everywhere. It required revolution and insecurity, uprooting and human sacrifice. The conclusion is hard to avoid that the road to modernity was not taken spontaneously and happily by men anywhere, that force was always required to make people embark on it. Only afterwards, if at all, did it find the agreement of men freed of the chains of minority. Breaking with the closed society hits people the harder, the later it occurs— harder in Germany than in England, harder in the new nations of our own time than in Germany. However, brutal as it was, the break with tradition and thus a strong push toward modernity was the substantive characteristic of the social revolution of National Socialism.

Even the intimation of a comparison between the National Socialist leadership clique and the Jacobins, or even the Bolsheviks, is bound to raise doubts and objections. While this will not allay such doubts, it should be added that the social revolution effected by National Socialism was an unintended, if inevitable result of its rule. It would clearly be wrong to say that Hitler set out to complete the revolution of modernity. On the contrary, his writings and speeches, indeed the entire cloudy National Socialist ideology seem to demand the recovery of the values of the past; the Nazis liked to appear Catonic where they were in fact radical innovators. For whatever their ideology, they were compelled to revolutionize society in order to stay in power.

The contradiction between the ideology and practice of National Socialism is as astonishing as it is understandable. It means, however, that the veil of ideology must not deceive us. As such, it was little more than an episode and in its substance a horrible mixture of all the half-truths of the time; but its social effects make the Nazi regime—quite apart from the consequences of the war it started—far more than an episode in German history. It gave German society an irreversible push, which exposed it to totalitarian dangers and opened it to liberal chances at the same time. [. . .]

Hitler could find a foundation and anchor for his rule only by demolishing parliamentary democracy. But he was well aware that this process of destruction required more than an enabling law or the outlawing of political parties; he had to remove what social realities there were behind these methods as well, but above all he had to attack the much more pronounced patterns that, while they did not support democracy, worked even more strongly against claims to total power. Total power presupposes the destruction of the power of all partial institutions, of all even faintly autonomous secondary centers. The revolution took its course along these lines.

The social basis of German authoritarianism, thus of the resistance of German society to modernity and liberalism, consisted in a structural syndrome that held people to the social ties in which they had found themselves without their doing and that prevented them from full participation. In Germany, the constitution of liberty was jeopardized by the institutionalized minority of its people. But—and this is not always seen—the claim to total power advanced by a political clique was necessarily jeopardized by such structures too. Authoritarian leaders find the chances and outlets for their peculiar mixture of benevolence and suppression in secondary centers without a claim to comprehensive influence. But for claims to total power even private virtues, and certainly the institutions springing from them, become a source of resistance. Just as the rulers of the new nations of our time have to break the tribal loyalties of their peoples in order to establish their power, the National Socialists had to break the traditional, and in effect anti-liberal, loyalties for region and religion, family and corporation, in order to realize their claim to total power. Hitler needed modernity, little as he liked it. [. . .]

What remains of the social revolution of National Socialism? If our thesis is correct, that is, if National Socialism was not an historical episode but the German revolution, it must have left its traces in the subsequent phase. This is indeed the case, although these traces are obscured by that other heritage of Nazi rule, which results from total defeat. The starting points of German social development after the war consisted first of all in a number of simple, if consequential facts. By war damage and war consequences Germany's economy was thrown back to an almost pre-industrial state. By the expulsion of millions of people from the eastern territories, economy and society in Germany were faced with extraordinary additional tasks. The disappearance of the entire National Socialist leadership elite made it necessary to form a new political class. The subdivision of the country into zones of occupation and the enmity of the occupation powers, which soon became apparent, imposed many additional limitations on the situation from which Germany took off. Even a sociologically informed account of German postwar development has to start with these initial conditions. [. . .]

German society remained illiberal in its structure and authoritarian in its constitution throughout the decades of industrialization. Although many of the bases of the absurd yet effective mixtures of old and new in the politics and society of Imperial Germany had gone in 1918, the Weimar Republic departed only very partially and anxiously from the old patterns. In times of crisis the nostalgia for past experiences grew. The mistaken alliance of conservative and National Socialist opponents of parliamentary democracy in 1933 was founded on this nostalgia; but soon after the seizure of power its false assumptions became clear. In order to maintain their power, the National Socialists had to turn against all traces of the social order that provided the basis for authoritarian rule. [. . .]

Despite the indescribable ruthlessness with which the process took place, they did not succeed wholly. There remained corners of tradition, sources of resistance and counterrevolution. But the push into modernity succeeded sufficiently to remove the social basis for future authoritarian governments along traditional German lines. National Socialism has finally abolished the German past as it was embodied in Imperial Germany. What came after it was free of the mortgage that burdened the Weimar Republic at its beginning, thanks to the suspended revolution. There could be no return from the revolution of National Socialist times.

[*Society and Democracy in Germany* (London: Weidenfeld & Nicolson, 1968), 402–4, 416–18.]

DETLEV PEUKERT
....

79 Brown Revolution?

Peukert, like Schoenbaum, was keen to stress the need to place developments under National Socialism within a broader continuum in order to assess the regime's social impact; unlike Schoenbaum, Peukert was sceptical about claims that the regime could have effected a 'social revolution' in such a short space of time. Moreover, Peukert was cautious about describing as 'modernizing' a regime which may well have accelerated various social trends but which also had a unique destructive side which Schoenbaum arguably did not take adequately into account. Seeking to accommodate both recognition of ongoing

secular trends within German society and the need to do justice to
National Socialism's racial barbarism, Peukert sought to discuss the
regime less in terms of its possible 'modernizing' effect than in terms
of its essential modernity, a modernity which contained pathological
and destructive potentials no less than emancipatory and progressive
ones.

The twelve years of the Third Reich form part of the longer material and
human continuity of industrial class society in Germany. Many long-term
trends within Germany—demographic, social-structural, economic—
continued through the epoch from 1933 to 1945, with short-term interruptions
but generally undisturbed. Furthermore, National Socialism unquestionably
absorbed elements of the authoritarian, militaristic and intellectually reactionary tradition in German history, while repudiating other traditions and other
elements.[1] On the other hand, these continuities were often not the mere
perpetuation by National Socialism of features that had already been present;
they were one-sided exaggerations, deformations or deflections of traditional
features, even though it took these distortions to make apparent just what
had been latent in the traditions all along. [. . .]

Did the ideological rigidities of the National Socialist policy for women,
then, simply founder on the realities of an industrialised economy? Did the
long-term trend towards modernisation covertly, but irresistibly, prevail? This
would be to put matters too crudely and to underrate the Nazis' policies on
women, the subtler versions of which were by no means hostile to female
industrial employment in all its forms and called, rather, for it to be restricted
to certain areas. In fact, the scheme of 'intrinsically female' types of work
played a considerable part in the long-term gender-based re-structuring of
the labour market. Women were designated to perform repetitive assembly-
line tasks because, according to ergonomic theorists, such work was particularly appropriate for them: having a dual role as workers and mothers,
women could find in child care, housework and family duties an emotional
compensation for the stresses of industrial monotony. In addition, women
were to gravitate, as expansions and contractions in the labour market dictated, between waged employment outside the home (especially before marriage) and domestic work within the family—or rather, to do two jobs during
booms and one during downturns. This was also the solution to the pressing
problem of retaining a fluctuating supply of labour without overloading the
social-security system with payments for unemployment and premature dis-
ability. The woman, if she was currently not employable, or was no longer
employable, was to be supported under the aegis of the family. The special
emphasis placed on women's familial role by Nazi propaganda, combined
with women's own adaptation to fluctuating and subordinate forms of
employment, thus gave rise during the Third Reich to a new, gender-based
division of labour that was in conformity with modern needs. [. . .]

The four years of rearmament-led boom before the outbreak of war are too short a period to yield a distinction between the intended results of Nazi policies and those developments that the Nazis merely put up with *faute de mieux*. David Schoenbaum's formulation, that National Socialism was reactionary in its goals but revolutionary in its methods, and that the longer-term effects of the regime were modernising by virtue of these revolutionary methods, sheds light on a partial aspect of the reality of the Third Reich. If, for example, we survey those business enterprises that were singled out for honour as 'model' National Socialist firms, we are struck, on the one hand, by attempts to perpetuate a certain paternalistic social tradition of entre-preneurship[2] but, on the other, by social and political measures which are part of a general tendency within the development of industrial societies: attempts to improve the working environment, holidays, and modern schemes of piece-work and incentive payments.[3] Ergonomic theories and policies in the Third Reich were a plain continuation of tendencies towards the rationalisation of production and the parallel 'modernisation' of indus-trial relations. They took their inspiration equally from 'Americanising' approaches centred around Henry Ford's social model of rationalised high productivity linked to high wages, and from the psycho-technological approaches of the German Institute for Technical Work Training designed to foster social partnership and the 'works community'.

On the other hand, the use of forced labour—foreigners, prisoners of war and inmates of concentration camps—and the establishment during the war of large numbers of forced-labour camps for German 'idlers' indicate that 'modern' achievement-orientated methods were only one facet of the National Socialist ethos of work: the other facet was the use of force against those who, for whatever reasons, were not to be motivated and integrated. Whereas modern liberal industrialised societies believe they can afford to tolerate the existence of marginal groups deviating from the prevailing social and employment norms, National Socialism set up a dual model of the way people were to be mobilised for work. It offered incentives for the achievement-minded, the 'talented' and those who through education or for other reasons were higher up the social scale; for the non-achievement-orientated at the bottom of the scale it prescribed forced labour, segregation and eventual annihilation.

The social reality of the Third Reich, then, involved these two aspects simultaneously: the dawning of the new achievement-orientated consumer society based on the nuclear family, upward mobility, mass media, leisure and an interventionist welfare state (though much of this still lay in the realms of propaganda and had not yet come into being); and the encroaching shadows cast by a project of social order based on racialist doctrines and terror. [. . .]

National Socialism can in no sense be described as out-and-out 'anti-modern'. It was often, indeed, precisely the profuse trappings of antiquated traditionalism or reactionary utopianism in Nazi ideology that served to make more acceptable in practical, social terms the modern technologies and structures they disguised. In addition, the opportunism of those in power and the internal logic of the drive for technological and economic war-readiness quickly swept aside the corporatist and other anti-modern experiments of the early period. [. . .]

National Socialism adapted readily to long-term trends towards modernisation. In terms of long-range socio-economic statistical data, the years of the Third Reich (or at least the years of peace up to 1939) show no divergence, either positive or negative, from the earlier course of development of industrial class society in Germany. As far as points of detail are concerned, the time-span involved is too short to validate any general claim that National Socialism was responsible for such comparatively small and inconsistent deviations from the longer-term trend as can be found. No particularly powerful new *thrust* towards modernisation can be inferred from the objective data available, although a continuation of the previously existing trend certainly can be. A different conclusion, on the other hand, seems indicated if we move from the hard data to the perceptible, if not statistically provable, shifts in values and changes in social behaviour. There are many indicators that National Socialism greatly loosened the previously firm hold of traditional social environments and systems of values and that, over and beyond its destructiveness, it contributed to the modernisation of everyday cultures. This applies, for instance, to the drive against traditional family-based education and in favour of egalitarianising peer-group work in youth organisations, exemplified in the Hitler Youth's slogan, 'Youth leads youth' and in the BDM's provision of non-domestic leisure activities for girls. At the same time, however, this selfsame example of the role of youth in the Third Reich shows how poor National Socialism was at detaching itself from long-outworn patterns and principles of socialisation and education, as a more modern trend towards the growth of youth sub-cultures spontaneously gave rise to gangs beyond the reach of state policies and, indeed, to forms of behaviour that ran contrary to the desired educational goal of the technically skilled yet soldierly 'warrior'. In this instance the shift in values, which was to be a decisive factor in the formation of the so-called 'sceptical' younger generation of the post-war period, was not a deliberate result or fortuitous by-product of Nazi policies, but was a bitterly combated counter-current. In short, the Nazis' positive drive towards modernisation was in many ways more short-winded than is commonly assumed. [. . .]

[T]he concept of the 'Brown revolution' does seem to be somewhat wide of the mark, even if, as many historians urge, we separate the concept of revolution from its customary association with progress and social innovation. Whatever concept of society historians may seek to distil from Hitler's inconsistent jumble of ideas, they must acknowledge that the competition between sources of authority that occurred once National Socialism was in power meant that all attempts at large-scale social reform broke down well short of their goal, ran aground in the shoals of polycracy, or were postponed until such time as 'final victory' had been won. The undoubtedly far-reaching, though not total, destruction of institutions, social environments and traditions that the National Socialists carried out is not of itself sufficient to warrant the term 'revolutionary' as long as it is unclear what functional equivalents might have arisen in their place. Many of the changes in outlook which led to the modern society of the 1950s thus took place through inadvertence, 'on the side', or even as a result of the population's refusal to fall in with what the Nazis had to offer and its retreat into 'normal' private life. Not least, it was in many instances only the war and its consequences that swept away for good those traditions and institutions which National Socialism had merely weakened (the large Junker estates east of the Elbe, for instance). It is only if the character of National Socialism is defined primarily in terms of its chaotic destructive and then self-destructive dynamism—i.e., if it is seen as the progressively more radicalised prolongation of the crisis of the 1920s into the war of the 1940s—that the great cataclysms of 1914–18, 1929–33 and 1939–45 can be construed as one single accelerating destructive process, and hence, in this sense, as a 'negative revolution'. But to do this would, in turn, be to erase from the analysis once again all the aspects of continuity in everyday life from the 1930s to the 1950s, all that was so fatally 'normal'; it would be to revert to the fiction of *Stunde Null*—'zero hour'—in 1945. The semantic games that have so often been played with the concept of revolution since the 1920s, then, are not of much help in providing a balanced historical assessment of the continuities and discontinuities within industrial class society in Germany.

[H]owever, the destructive dynamism of National Socialism and, in particular, its tendency to cloak the social and political inadequacies of its notions of *Volksgemeinschaft* by seeking out ever larger numbers of external enemies, reveals a long-term pathological dimension within modern industrial society itself: a dimension which was transfigured into the utopian vision of a racialist reconstitution of society and which found its apocalyptic fulfilment in the extermination camps.

[*Inside Nazi Germany: Conformity, Opposition and Racism in Everyday Life*, trans. R. Deveson (Harmondsworth: Penguin, 1987), 175, 178–83 (original Cologne: Bund-Verlag, 1982).]

JENS ALBER

80   National Socialism and Modernization

Jens Alber argues persuasively that developments during these years represented either no great departure from long-term trends, or short-term aberrations with few long-term structural consequences; either way, when compared with the dynamic processes of change associated with the post-war Federal Republic, Alber rejects the notion that the regime effected a social revolution in either Schoenbaum or Dahrendorf's sense of the phrase. This he attributes to National Socialism's inherent systemic inefficiencies, which left it unable to direct fundamental and systematic change to any effect.

Examination of some key indicators of the modernization process offers no evidence that the National Socialist era brought about a far-reaching break in continuity. In terms of both the substance and issues of method this can also hardly be expected, given the shortness of the period of time available to them. In methodological terms one has the problem that in many cases only sporadic data from two censuses in 1933 and 1939 are available. In terms of content, one can assume that a far-reaching remodelling of society demands more time than was available to the leaders of the Third Reich. This, objection, however, hits the advocates of the modernization thesis harder than their critics, in my view. Further, in the initial two decades of the Federal Republic the period of one decade was enough to foster in some areas faster and more far-reaching changes than the Hitler era. This will now be illustrated with some central characteristics of the modernization process.

The *speed of urbanization* was not accelerated above the long-term trend during the National Socialist era. The change in *occupational structure* shows the image of a reversion to trend after the short-term break caused by the economic crisis. Only with the Federal Republic did a radical change come, with a rapid reduction of the numbers employed in agriculture and a dynamic forging ahead of white-collar and public professions. Notable discontinuities can be seen in the National Socialist era in two areas, however: the *expansion of education* was stopped and cut back in a diversion from the path of modernization, and the *proportion of national income accounted for by taxation* rose sharply. The National Socialist tax regime may have mobilized resources to a hitherto unknown level, but still found itself in deficit to a growing extent, because it was unable to marry income and spending or its income structure with its spending structure as a result of its huge armaments exertions. [. . .]

The regime's success in *destroying traditional ties* and in constructing a national identity is hard to measure empirically. In order to test whether old particularist ties were successfully dissolved only a few broad indicators can be used. The proportion of marriages between members of the same confession was neither consistent during the National Socialist era nor did it sink below the long-term trend of development. Communications—one of the classic indicators of nation-formation—developed less quickly than in the early years of the Federal Republic.

We do know whether *familial ties* were strengthened or weakened. The

National Socialists attempted, indeed, to loosen divorce law, but divorce rates did not rise any faster than would conform to the long-term trend, and they developed in less dynamic fashion than during the Imperial period or under the Federal Republic. [. . .]

Contrary to long-term modernization trends *women* were confined to the cage of prescribed gender roles. Girls were pushed out of the institutes of higher education; the development of female employment conformed to the long-term trend before the Second World War. It thus remained clearly behind the extent of mobilization in England. Only in the Federal Republic did a substantially more dynamic increase in female participation in the labour market emerge. [. . .]

A summary of these empirical observations shows that the decisive push into modernity for German society occurred not during the National Socialist era but under the Federal Republic. As the National Socialist world collapsed and the free formation of intermediary groups became possible once more, the magic of the ideology of 'people's comrades' and the 'people's community', which was rooted in propaganda far more strongly than it was anchored in the social structure, dissolved too. [. . .]

It remains an indisputable fact that the National Socialists eliminated central characteristics of modernization—such as the political participation of citizens in free elections and the institutionalization of regulatory mechanisms for industrial conflict. With the destruction of the trade unions and other associations they took from the population reference groups which could have given validity to alternative modes of interpretation of the political and social order. With this grew the effectiveness of their propaganda and the chance to influence effectively the citizens' image of society for the duration of their rule.

Even under these conditions, however, because of the failure to create equality of people's life chances, the National Socialist regime saw itself repeatedly forced back into purely negative integration via the mobilization against 'enemies of the *Volk*' on the inside and war enemies on the outside. The idea that it was thereby able to generate permanently a hitherto incomplete national identity has yet to be convincingly proven. The continuity of political orientations under Weimar and Bonn shown by an analysis of the Federal elections of 1949 speaks against the idea of an effective destruction of traditional ties. Only the destruction of the National Socialist regime, the subsequent division of Germany—which relieved the social structure of the Federal Republic from some traditional burdens—and the integration of the Federal Republic into the cultural, economic, and defence community of the west created the bases for a successful modernization of the country which represents a radical break in continuity with the German past.

['Nationalsozialismus und Modernisierung', *Kölner Zeitschrift für Soziologie und Sozialpsychologie* (1989), 351–2, 355, 358.]

81 Persecution and Coordination

The Nazi seizure of power was accompanied by a massive wave of repression and persecution of political opponents, the main victims of which were the Communists. In this extract, Detlev Peukert illustrates the nature and extent of this process with examples from the Ruhr industrial area.

Immediately following the seizure of power the Hitler regime began to establish the fascist system: the reforming of the state apparatus into an even more effective instrument of repression and of state monopoly power, the campaign of destruction against the organizations of the working class, and the coordination of the bourgeois parties and associations. First of all the powers of the state executive were ruthlessly expanded (17 February 1933: Shooting Decree for the Police; 22 February: naming of SA and SS men as auxiliary police; 4 and 28 February: Emergency Decrees of the Reich President, which suspended the most important basic rights of the constitution). The culmination of this accumulation of emergency powers was the Enabling Act of 23 March in which all the parties of the Reichstag except for the Social Democrats and the Communists, who had just been driven into illegality, apparently legally transferred sole authority to the Hitler government. In the future the Reich government could even enact laws on its own which were not within the constitution. The subsequent abolition of the remaining democratic institutions, such as federalism, the division of powers etc. was only a logical consequence.

The persecution of the labour movement began with an unrestrained campaign of terror against the members and functionaries of the KPD and was already affecting Social Democrats and bourgeois democrats at the time of the Reichstag fire. Hitler's police had already acted against the KPD three days after the assumption of office and had occupied the Central Committee building in Berlin. Arbitrary arrests by SA troops, during which known workers' functionaries were abducted to SA barracks and tortured, personal acts of revenge, and sadistic excesses by Nazis against Communist and Social Democratic 'enemies' in working-class quarters were the order of the day. This terror, which had hitherto been thought impossible, was intended to break the workers' will to resist. Thus in Bochum, for example, several KPD leaders, among whom were the local section political leader Hans Schillach and the editor of the *Ruhr-Echo*, were beaten bloodily in SA barracks, dragged through the streets suffering from severe injuries, and were then thrown to the ground in busy squares and left lying helplessly, in order to cause paralysing fear among the Bochum population.[1] Courageous friends took in those who had been attacked and attempted to save them from renewed attack by the SA. When Hans Schillach was being sought by his persecutors he was hidden in an attic chamber in the Dutch consulate. There he was nursed to health with their knowledge and brought illegally to safety over the Dutch border. Despite the pain he had suffered Schillach returned to the Ruhr area after a few months, where he took over the political leadership of the Essen KPD.[2] Following the Reichstag fire, commented on by Nazi propaganda placards with 'The Reichstag in Flames! Crush Communism! Smash Social Democracy!', SA and police attacked the building of the KPD local leadership in Essen's Rottstrasse, arrested those present, and destroyed the printing press and editorial office of the *Ruhr-Echo* totally.[3] A thousand Communists were arrested immediately, and all those functionaries who had escaped were feverishly searched for. The card-files on the Left which the political police (1a) of the Weimar Republic had established served the Nazis well in this regard. Social Democrats were also victims of the wave of arrests. Thus in Essen after the communal elections of 14 March 1933 leading SPD parliamentarians were taken into 'protective custody'. On the night of 11 March SA troops occupied the main administration of the mineworkers' association in Bochum, destroyed the inner fixtures and fittings, and arrested the chairman of the trade union, the Social Democrat Fritz Husemann. Lawyers were arrested because, as in the case of Dr Levy from Essen, they had simply expressed doubt at the terror announcements of the Nazi press. Overall in the Ruhr area over 2,000 people had already been arrested by 2 March.[4] On 31 May 1933 the 'Higher Police Leader West, Special Commissar for the Reich Interior Ministry' based in Recklinghausen submitted a report on the arrests in the Rhine-Ruhr area from 14 to 28 May. According to this 2,830 people were arrested in these two weeks, among whom were 1,571 Communists and 1,128 Social Democrats; 4,862 people were held in 'protective custody' on 28 May 1933, including 4,780 Communists and 51 Social Democrats.[5] People awaited an uncertain fate in over-full prisons. [. . .] In the Essen prisons alone on 23 April approximately 500 people were in 'protective custody', not including those who had disappeared into the provisional concentration camps of the SA.[6] Such camps had been created, amongst others, in an old factory building in the Wuppertal 'Kemna', and in the mothballed 'Herkules' mine in Essen and 'Gibralter' mine in Bochum. Larger concentration camps for political prisoners, especially from the Ruhr area, emerged in Brauweiler near Cologne, in Kleve, and in the summer of 1933 in Börgermoor and Esterwegen in the Emsland.

On the day after the Reichstag elections of 5 March 1933 SA troops abducted over 100 Bochum functionaries of the SPD and KPD into the refectory of the Bochumer Verein steel plant, where they were brutally beaten in revenge for the high percentage of votes cast for the workers' parties.[7]

The terror claimed a heavy toll of lives among the workers. Albert Funk, for example, Reichstag deputy and popular functionary of the United German Mineworkers' Association, was taken after his arrest from the Dortmund Steinwache prison to the Recklinghausen police prison where after unceasing bloody interrogations his tormentors forced him to leap from the window with fatal consequences.[8]

On 9 June 1933 horrified Düsseldorfers found the bloody and beaten corpse of the railway worker Heinrich Kiepenheuer, who had paid with his life for spreading the truth about fascism, with signs painted by his murderers saying 'Communist—was selling *Freedom* yesterday' (the illegal organ of the Lower Rhenish KPD) and 'shot while escaping—ha ha!'[9] During the destruction of the trade unions on 2 May 1933 the four Duisburg functionaries of the ADGB* Emil Rentmeister, Michael Rodenstock, Johann Schlösser, and Julius Birk were abducted by the SA. Only on 21 April 1934 did walkers in the woods on the Oberlohberg near Dinslaken find their corpses in a pond.[10] The murder of the Essen Social Democrat Peter Burggraf is described by his brother: 'On 15 July 1933 the two brothers Peter and Johann Burggraf, who had been celebrating the birthday of the third brother, Heinrich, in Heidhausen, were walking past the school in the Kellerstrasse (since 14 May the "Adolf-Hitler-Barracks" of the National Socialist Labour Service had been housed there). Braying members of the Labour Service were lounging in the windows and throwing objects and bottles at passers-by. Peter Burggraf complained and was summoned by the young people to repeat his complaints inside the house. Peter Burggraf followed this unfortunate advice, entered the house and was beaten unconscious. When he could no longer move he was dragged by the feet into the cellar. His head hit on each of the 32 stairs. The heavily injured man remained lying in the cellar for another day until the neighbours called the police, as the injured man was crying from pain and whimpering. Having been taken to hospital Peter Burggraf died on 17 July 1933. The burial had the biggest attendance even seen'.[11]

The terror was even directed against conservative members of the Catholic Centre, such as for example against Heinrich Hirtsiefer, former Welfare Minister in the Prussian State Parliament, who on 11 September 1933 was forced by SA men to walk though the streets of Essen armed with an umbrella and the sign 'I am the starveling Hirtsiefer', while they mocked him.[12] A few days later he was abducted to the Börgermoor concentration camp.

[*Ruhrarbeiter gegen den Faschismus: Dokumentation über den Widerstand in Ruhrgebiet 1933–1945* (Frankfurt am Main: Röderberg, 1976), 43–6.]

* The German trade union federation.

82 The Concentration Camps as Part of the National Socialist System of Domination

> The concentration camp system grew from the initial 'wild' camps established largely spontaneously to deal with political opponents on the local level to encompass a massive network of camps all across Europe, which combined the roles of 're-education', persecution, and extermination with attempts to harness the labour of their inmates in the service of the National Socialist regime. By 1944–5 there were up to three-quarters of a million inmates in the concentration camps alone—not including those in the forced labour and extermination camps. Although, as Falk Pingel argues here, the economic aspect of the concentration camps grew in significance, their function remained overwhelmingly political.

The history of the concentration camps shows that despite the growth in importance of this institution, the SS remained bound by the general development of the regime and was obliged to adjust its own objectives in accordance with demands of senior authorities. The concentration camps were so much a part of the regime itself that their history can be divided to correspond with the periods of development within the history of National-Socialist rule as a whole. There were three such periods:[1]

(1) 1933–1936: the period of consolidation and stabilization of the executive within the National-Socialist state to which the concentration camps and their accompanying administrative organizations belonged. The creation of these camps can be traced to the implementation of one of the predominant authoritarian aims of National Socialism, namely the elimination of the workers' organizations (the German Communist Party, KPD: the Social-Democratic Party, SPD; and the trade unions). The structure and character of the camps was greatly affected by this struggle against these political-ideological opponents, and even the training given to the guards and other camp personnel was directed toward this aim. The prisoners were considered 'harmful to the people' (*Volksschädlinge*), in need of political re-education—insofar as they were considered 'educable' at all—by means of harsh treatment. If the SS considered prisoners 'incorrigible,' if they had occupied important posts in prohibited political organizations, or if they were Jews, they were slated for cruel and extreme torture.

(2) 1936/7–1941/2: during these years, the concentration-camp system experienced the repercussions of war preparations and its conduct. The Four-Year Plan led to the harnessing of the labor market to such an extent that for the first time economic considerations played a decisive role in the recruitment of new prisoners.

The concentration of all police functions in his person was exploited by Himmler, as chief of German Police, in order to further extend the concept of concentration-camp internment to those 'asocial' and 'criminal' elements—an objective he had failed to realize earlier. Concentration-camp internment was therefore possible in place of penitentiary, work-houses or prison sentences. The concentration camps also entered into competition with the penal administration of the judiciary, which remained outside the realm of political internment.

With the outbreak of war, stricter security was to be expected, and, in anticipation of this development, the concentration camps were expanded. Even so, the new facilities proved insufficient to accommodate the large numbers of new prisoners. The pogroms of 1938 and the intake of foreign prisoners from the conquered territories, especially from the East, led to catastrophic overcrowding of the camps and to disastrous conditions of accommodation for the prisoners. This state of affairs favored measures for mass extermination, which were put into practice soon after the beginning of the war, by means of starving Polish prisoners in Buchenwald, selections within the framework of 'euthanasia,' 'extermination through work' in Mauthausen, and the mass shooting of Soviet prisoners of war at the end of this period.[2] These measures, for the most part, did not start with the camp authorities, but were initiated outside the camps and then continued within their confines.

(3) 1942–1944/5: the turn of the war led to the concentration and reorganization of armament production and to an increase in the supply of forced labor, to which the prisoners were now systematically conscripted. The continuous intake of new prisoners was intended to expand the potential of the work force inside the camps. This was not an independent decision of the SS leadership: responsibility was borne jointly by Hitler, the Armaments Ministry under Albert Speer, and the Army Armament Office of the Armed Forces High Command under General Georg Thomas.[3] It was clear to these institutions that the continuation of essential weapon production could only be achieved if the flow of production and deployment of labor were more closely regulated. With the implementation of forced-labor conditions in the last phase of the National-Socialist regime, the concentration camps assumed an important role. The provision of a forced-labor supply did not, however, become the sole function of the camps. The original political and ideological objectives were retained even in view of the external and internal danger to National-Socialist rule.

At the beginning of the war against the Soviet Union, the National-Socialists instituted the systematic extermination of entire population groups. The army, SS and SD had to conduct this 'battle of the ideologies' with variable emphases. The camps of Auschwitz and Lublin-Majdanek, situated in occupied Polish territory, became the focus of the mass extermination of the

Jewish population. Here, in the most horrible manner, the demands of the National Socialists were turned into reality. Even in the face of defeat, and while forced to harness all their economic forces to enable the continuation of the war, the National Socialists did not renounce one of their most important objectives—the establishment of *Rassenherrschaft* (racial domination) in Europe. Even when it became clear that the material objectives of the war—the conquest of new territories—were unlikely to be realized, the National-Socialist leadership continued to pursue their ideological aims. The concentration camps had to serve these two objectives, for both—the ideological as well as the material objective—presupposed an apparatus of violence by which they could be realized. The SS maintained this double objective almost to the last moment: only with the beginning of the dismantling of the concentration camps themselves did the gassing of Jews cease. [. . .]

At the end of July 1933, there were almost 30,000 prisoners in 'protective custody' inside the Reich, but an even larger total number had been arrested by that time.[4] This date concluded the arrests that were directly connected with the dissolution and outlawing of the workers' organizations. From then on the intake of prisoners into the protective-custody camps decreased and remained fairly constant until the end of the first period (from 1934 until 1936 the number of concentration-camp prisoners was between 5,000 and 7,000; in 1933, approximately 5,000 prisoners were sent to Dachau; and in each of the following years about 2,000). With the average number of prisoners remaining constant, the number of deaths decreased (in Dachau from twenty-four mortalities in 1933 to ten in 1936). The terror, which was most severe at the time of the camps' establishment, was reflected in the death rate: of the twenty-four mortalities in Dachau in the year 1933, twelve died a violent death in April and May alone.[5] [. . .]

During the second period, new economic objectives and the new categories of prisoners led to a considerable rise in the number of prisoners: from approximately 7,000 at the beginning of 1937 to almost 25,000 at the beginning of the war. At the end of the second period, the number was close to 75,000. Prison conditions deteriorated rapidly, especially in the recently established camps, where the new categories of prisoners predominated and where the prisoners worked at forced labor mainly in quarries and camp construction work. Already in 1938, 10 percent of the average population of inmates at Buchenwald had died. As a result of the influx of Polish prisoners, who were treated with particular harshness, and because of temporary shortages of food and accommodation since the beginning of the war, the mortality rate rose to 20–30 percent and even higher. At this time Mauthausen had the highest mortality rate of all the camps. More than 8,000 prisoners died there during 1941. The mobilization of labor in prospect of a speedy victory and the perpetual overcrowding of the camps led to the complete exhaustion of the prisoners' strength, and even to their physical destruction. This applied in particular to severely persecuted political groups, such as the International Spanish Brigade, *Spanienkämpfer*, or to prisoners considered 'racially inferior,' like Jews and Poles.

The composition of the camp population reflected the crucial points of the persecution. Large groups of Jewish prisoners were first brought to the camps in 1938. For the Jews persecution had reached a new, threatening intensity. Until then they had suffered mostly social and economic discrimination. Now they were pursued by the police of the National-Socialist state with a ferocity unequalled even by that shown toward political opponents at the time that the government was making its bid for power. After the mass arrests that followed the attempt on the life of the German diplomat vom Rath in Paris, Jews were sent to the camps *en masse* in order to confiscate their fortunes and to force them to agree to emigrate.

From the beginning of the war, the largest influx was from Poland. In 1940, some 8,000 Polish prisoners were sent to Mauthausen alone. This was a result of the policy of resettlement (*Aussiedlung*), of racial ideology and of the battle against a relatively fast-developing resistance. As a rule, the only prisoners taken from the occupied countries of the West, including Czechoslovakia, were those who had been arrested during operations against acts of resistance. Here it was not a question of undifferentiated mass intake, as it had been in Poland. Once the preventive arrests of possible political opponents within the old Reich were completed at the end of 1939, the number of German prisoners, in comparison with foreign ones, rose only moderately. As a sufficiently large working force existed in the camps, most of the 'asocial' and 'criminal' prisoners were released for military service or were transferred to a place of work outside the camps.

The shift from 'asocial' and 'criminal' prisoners to Jews and prisoners from the occupied territories emphasizes the fact that, in the second period, the camps acquired new functions. State intervention in the labor market in order to fulfill the Four-Year Plan, intensified ideological persecution, and the conduct of the war significantly increased the number of prisoners in the camps and caused living conditions to deteriorate.

The years 1940 and 1941—when National Socialism spread across Europe by means of brute force and set out to put into practice its concepts of racial domination—constituted, at least for *the non-Jewish prisoners*, the most terrible years in the history of the concentration camps. The composition of the prison population was heterogeneous to an extreme, the conditions were subhuman, and any possibility of resistance, without the prospect of a speedy military defeat of the Nazi system, was slight.

Even though during this period the SS founded a number of its own enterprises in which the prisoners were put to work[6] the extermination action (*Vernichtungseinsatz*) prevented economic considerations from predominating within the SS. Preference was given to the political and ideological principles according to which the camps had been founded. As more and more prisoners considered 'congenitally inferior' were interned in the camps, these principles resulted in even more devastating consequences than during the first period. [. . .]

A change in orientation occurred only in the *third period*, when economic considerations slowly began to prevail and the concentration camp, with its labor potential, became increasingly integrated into the private sector of the economy. In the spring of 1942, the future adjustment of arrest operations in line with the requirements of the labor supply was prepared in discussions by the Nazi leadership. The reorganization of arms production also involved the SS. The two separate central offices, Finance and Buildings (*Finanzen und Bauten*) and Administration and Economy (*Verwaltung und Wirtschaft*), became the Economic and Administrative Main Office of the SS (*Wirtschafts-Verwaltungs-Hauptamt—SS-WVHA*). Supervision of the concentration camps was removed from the former SS Administration Main Office (*SS-Führungs-hauptamt*) and incorporated into the WVHA. The command and management of the WVHA now worked together with the Armaments Ministry, as well as with private and national concerns, in order to regulate the mobilization of prison labor. Thus, private institutions also gained insight into the living conditions of the prisoners, which they were actually in a position to influence through the mobilization of prison labor in their factories. Some factories took over the feeding and housing of prisoners (for which they were reimbursed by the SS) and therefore had a large share in the responsibility for their fate. I. G. Farben concluded an agreement of cooperation with the SS for the extension of the Auschwitz camp, and I. G. Farben factories were built in Monowitz.[7]

An increasing number of prisoners were now engaged as skilled labor in a central production sector. As the labor force had now gained in importance, in 1942–1943 the supervisory authorities in the camps tried to reduce the high mortality rate that had been the rule in preceding years. The measures they took for the improved maintenance of the prisoners indeed resulted in a distinct reduction of the mortality rate from the spring of 1943 until the autumn of 1944. Similar tendencies can also be observed in the treatment of prisoners of war and civilian forced laborers outside the camps.

['The Concentration Camps as Part of the National Socialist System of Domination', in *The Nazi Concentration Camps*, Proceedings of the Fourth Yad Vashem International Conference (Jerusalem: 1980), 3–8, 10–13.]

83 Racial Policy and Women's Policy

> Gisela Bock's work has explored, sometimes controversially, some of
> the links between National Socialism's racism and its sexism, particu-
> larly with respect to Nazi birth policy. Suggesting that the singularity
> of Nazi eugenics lies in its antinatalism rather than in its pronatalism,
> she argues that just as many women as men were among the victims
> of Nazi racism, that Nazi racism was shaped by gender, and that Nazi
> gender policy was primarily shaped by racism.

During the twelve years of National Socialist rule a minority of approximately 1 per cent of fertile women living in Germany in 1933 were sterilized;
an unknown proportion of those women deported to Germany or living in
the occupied areas were forced into an abortion and/or sterilization.
Although this only represented a minority, this policy was—as with racism
and racial policy overall—of significance for the entire female sex. For the
extent of the sterilization of women, of the violent and in so many ways
intrusive intervention into the female body, can be taken as an indicator for
that which National Socialism might impose, or believed itself able to
impose, on all women; the modest level of resistance which it experienced
here confirmed this assumption, at least partially.

Further, the boundary between minority and majority, between undesirable and desirable women, was entirely fluid. Its lack of definition was primarily a product of the sterilization diagnoses themselves, of the fact that
'here it is not so easy to draw the line between worthy and unworthy existences'.[1] Approximately 1 million people, i.e. a minority of 3 per cent of those
capable of begetting children, were registered for sterilization and thus categorized as 'suspicious'; many sterilizations were postponed until the period
following the 'final victory', and new categories of those to be sterilized were
planned. Further, not only sterilized women were affected by the prohibition
of their becoming mothers and by other consequences of sterilization, but
also hundreds of thousands of the non-sterilized: above all, the wives of
sterilized men, and women who were ('blood') relations of those sterilized.
Eugenicists hoped that, although outside the sterilization diagnoses 'a large
number of individuals remain whose reproduction is undesirable', these
would also gradually disappear: after all, such 'abnormal characters, who are
a burden on their own family and yet cannot be described as outright worth-
less', primarily came from just those families which fell under the Sterilization Law.* Scientists followed this logic to its conclusion: 'In the final analysis
the eugenicist is always in the position of the surgeon, who, with malignant

---

* Law for the Prevention of Hereditarily Diseased Offspring, 14 July 1933.

tumours, has to cut deep into the healthy material to be certain that the sick, degenerate element has been fully removed'.[2] [. . .]

If one attempts to summarize the eugenic 'solution of the woman question' as announced by Frick in 1933 and then consistently put into practice, one finds that the results contradict previous research. The pronatalist policy towards women represented nothing original, let alone specifically National Socialist; here they relied on measures which at most accentuated the traditional gender relationship in respect of childbirth, but did not fundamentally modify it. This also explains its modest impact, especially on women. Insofar as pronatalist policy was original, compared to the preceding epoch, it was not as a new valorization of childbirth, mothers, and mothering, but as a new cult of fatherdom, of its idealistic and above all material upwards revalorization. The cult of the mother was at best propaganda; the cult of the father was propaganda and politics. The cult of the father was, not least, the result of the male-specific dimension of racism, namely its cult of men and masculinity. This dimension was, moreover, imprinted with the '"Idée fixe" of racism' (Mosse), a both metaphorical and real fixation with procreation, with the procreator and the creation of the 'new man'; this characterized not only the cult of the father but also the policy of sterilization towards men. The majority of women remained what they had already been for a long time: mothers in the fatherland, albeit with the novum that feminine and motherly 'instincts' were castigated as a form of 'sentimental humanitarianism'.

The specific character, the historical novelty, and international singularity of National Socialist birth policy lay in its antinatalism. Pronatalism was at best propaganda; antinatalism was propaganda and politics. Antinatalism attained a temporal and fundamental priority, and of all the laws of importance and consequence for women the Sterilization Law acquired the status of establishing the 'primacy of the state in the field of life, marriage, and the family'. The specifically National Socialist birth policy, towards women too, was not, as is often assumed, '(ultra-)conservative', but was modern and made use of modern means. State and direct force was reserved for antinatalism alone; only for it was a state, professional, efficient apparatus staffed primarily by men established; its 'quantity' and 'quality' was regulated by the state. The women's and gender-historical dimension of National Socialist birth policy should therefore not be defined as pronatalism and the cult of the mother, but as antinatalism and the cult of the father and of men, combined with particular violence against a minority of women.

Never before had a state taken such comprehensive, effective, and violent measures to prevent births. The historical and international singularity of National Socialist antinatalism becomes even more apparent if one examines it in the light of the equally singular decline in the birth rate in Germany between 1930 and 1933. Occasionally politicians and academics attempted to estimate the number of births which had been hindered by sterilization. The

Reich Doctors' Leader complained in 1937, exaggerating obviously, of a loss of 5 million. According to the probability calculations of the 'empirical genetic prognoses' for the 'inferior', a shortfall of 1.6 million births can be adduced.[3] If such calculations are demographic nonsense, they were not so for contemporaries and can thus illustrate their significance even more. The promises of a 'positive eugenics' towards the 'German people', which some may have taken seriously, were redeemed with 'negative eugenics': 'regeneration' occurred through 'eradication'. In this the National Socialist realization of eugenic racism equated with that of anthropological racism. The 'Nordic idea', which as a 'positive goal' had promised an 'ideal state' for the 'German people', necessarily remained 'unclear and inconsequential'.[4] It showed consistency solely in the subjection and destruction of 'inferior' peoples. The self-glorification of the 'valuable' in both eugenic and anthropological racism showed itself to be that which it had always been in essence: disdain, discrimination, destruction of the 'alien race' and of the 'other' sex.

The priority of antinatalism revealed itself not only by virtue of the fact that it was state-managed and made use of state power, but through the fact that—as with racial policy overall—it was perhaps 'idealistic', but in no sense cheap. The necessary investments were all the more significant for the fact that they began in 1933, in the midst of economic crisis and mass poverty, and, moreover, three years before the granting of child subsidies, from which increases to the birth rate were promised. While pronatalist investments were made partly only in the form of loans and mostly were financed by the working population which was supposed to profit from them (unemployment insurance funds, Winter Aid),[5] expenditure on antinatalism was covered by tax revenue. [. . .]

In relation to women the core of National Socialist birth policy was thus its antinatalism. Further, 'racial mania' was also 'gender mania'. This is shown both in its cult of masculinity and in its attitude towards all women, and above all towards those women and men who became the objects of the myth of the 'threat' to the valuable by the 'inferior'. It saw and enforced 'differences' and 'polarity' between the sexes among the 'valuable'; among the 'inferior', it saw and enforced 'equality'—equal treatment through 'Special Treatment', through sterilization, forced labour, and murder. It reduced the 'inferior' in language and in theory, but above all in genderless fashion in the concentration camps, all the way to genocide as the undiscriminating destruction of the sexes, of the living and the 'coming' stock. It broke with the traditional definitions of the female sex, especially with those formulated by women, by placing it under the dictates of racism. It denied the 'other sex' the right to be 'different' without punishment in the same way as it denied 'alien' races this right. National Socialist birth policy was sexist, in that birth control, erstwhile domain of women, was nationalized; it was racist, in that it discriminated between 'valuable' and 'inferior' childbearers and births.

Sterilization-based racism became a vehicle for sexism, in that it decreed, defined, or implemented norms for the sexes and their relations which moulded sexuality and work and engendered violence; in that it forbade childbirth and becoming a mother; and in that it realized the blood- and murder-metaphors of 'sexual thinking' above all on the female sex. In the attempt to 'solve' social problems 'biologically', racial policy and women's policy merged into one.

[*Zwangssterilisation im Nationalsozialismus: Studien zur Rassenpolitik und Frauenpolitik* (Opladen: Westdeutscher Verlag, 1986), 456–7, 461–5.]

HANS-GEORG STÜMKE

84 The Persecution of Homosexuals in Nazi Germany

The Gestapo began collecting information on known or suspected homosexuals in 1934; in 1936 the Reich Central Office for the Combating of Homosexuality and Abortion was formed. The suffering of homosexual men was a product of ideological belief reinforced by widespread and deeply rooted social prejudice; the prevalence and durability of homophobic attitudes is shown by the fact that, after the war, the persecution of homosexuals during the 'Third Reich' was not deemed by the courts to have been a specifically 'Nazi' crime. Indeed, it took until 1969 for discriminatory legislation formulated during the National Socialist era to be removed from the West German statute books.

Both homosexuality and abortion signified the privatisation of sexuality and its products, thus flatly contradicting the *völkisch* view, whereby sexuality was construed in terms of collectivist biology. The decree that established the Reich Central Office made the connection explicit:

The considerable dangers which the relatively high number of abortions still being performed present for population policy and the health of the nation, and which constitute a grave infringement of the ideological fundamentals of National Socialism, as well as the homosexual activities of a not inconsiderable proportion of the population, which constitute a serious threat to young people, demands more effective measures against these national diseases than has hitherto been the case.

In other words, persecution of homosexuals was a product of 'population policy and national health', rather than as is sometimes claimed, a defensive psychological reaction on the part of a Nazi 'male state' whose homophobia was driven by anxieties about its members' own 'latent' homosexuality. [. . .]

In a quantitative sense, the years between 1936 and the outbreak of war were the high-point of persecution of homosexuals. In this period alone, almost one hundred thousand people were registered by the Gestapo. About a third of them were then investigated by the police, with every fourth person being successfully convicted in accordance with the amended version of Paragraph 175.*

Already in 1939, the Reich Central Office made a point of relaying the names of homosexuals of military age to the armed forces. Following the outbreak of war, when a large proportion of men 'capable of bearing arms' had been called up, persecution expanded within the military while the number of civilian arrests contracted. At the same time, persecution assumed a qualitatively different character. As early as 1935 the SS began demanding the death penalty for homosexuals. On 12 July 1940 Himmler ordered that 'in future all homosexuals who have seduced more than one partner are to be taken into police preventive custody following their release from prison'. Detention in a concentration camp was tantamount to a death sentence since the camps operated a programme of 'extermination through labour'. Homosexuals were also taken into preventive or protective custody throughout the Nazi period in order to protect the 'national community' from 'habitual and professional criminals', the 'asocial', 'community aliens' or 'parasites upon the people'. Already in 1933 the concentration camp at Hamburg-Fuhlsbüttel included a category designated homosexuals. On 15 November 1941 Hitler personally decreed the death penalty for homosexual members of the SS.

Although the SS managed to destroy a considerable proportion of records relating to concentration camps before the war ended, it is possible to find evidence for the presence of homosexuals in most of the camps. On the basis of an assessment of all of the available evidence, Rudiger Lautmann has estimated that about 10,000 men were forced to wear the degrading pink triangle in the camps, although 'it could have been 5,000 or 15,000'. Eugen Kogon, a political prisoner in Buchenwald until 1945, described their situation as 'deplorable'. Most of them simply died. They occupied the lowest rung in the prisoner hierarchy. In Buchenwald, according to Kogon, they made up the highest proportion of inmates transported to the extermination camps. According to R. Schnabel's eyewitness recollections of Dachau, the prisoners with the pink triangle 'never lived very long, and were rapidly and systematically eliminated by the SS'. A remarkable number of former political prisoners are in agreement that the SS treated homosexuals in a particularly brutal fashion. The writer Günther Weisenborn, who was sent to a concentration camp in 1942 on account of his activities in the Resistance, recalled that during his captivity he encountered 'many homosexuals who had been tortured', and that 'their sufferings were unspeakable; they were not sustained by any form of idea. They were absolutely defenceless and died rapidly because of this.'

The Nazis themselves were conscious that the terror they directed against

* Paragraph 175 of the German Criminal Code dealt with male homosexuality, which was a criminal offence.

homosexuals was ambivalent in character. Himmler himself remarked in 1936 that 'the great question of aberrant sexuality will never be regulated through policing'. In several scientific publications, the Nazi biologist and racial hyg- ienicist Theo Lang cautioned against propelling homosexuals into marriage and 'normal' forms of sexuality. He wrote that one had to consider that 'the failure of homosexuals to reproduce had to be viewed not simply from the perspective of a quantitative, but also a qualitative population policy'. Accord- ing to his theories, homosexuality was caused by chromosomatic disorders, from which he deduced 'that severe punishment and moral condemnation will drive homosexuals to at least attempt to marry and have children, or in other words [we will achieve] precisely the opposite of what harsh penalties are designed to prevent, namely the probable increase in the number of homosexuals in successive generations'.

These hypotheses reveal the fundamental dilemma the Nazis faced in combating homosexuality. As long as they were unable to satisfactorily answer the question 'What causes homosexuality?' the regime was effectively unable to embark upon a Final Solution in this area. Even if they succeeded in eliminating sections of the homosexual population, they would still be con- fronted with fresh generations of bisexuals and homosexuals. This made the situation of homosexuals rather different from that of other minorities per- secuted during the Third Reich, for example Jews or Sinti and Roma, who were murdered regardless of whether they were eight or eighty years old, and thus for whom genocide meant the end of any possibility of reproduc- tion. What connected the mostly Aryan homosexuals with these other groups, was that they were also categorised as being of 'lesser racial value' within the Nazis' programme of racial selective breeding. They shared this classification with those Aryan men and women who were compulsorily sterilised in order to inhibit their capacity to reproduce.

['From the "People's Consciousness of Right and Wrong" to "The Healthy Instincts of the Nation": The Persecution of Homosexuals in Nazi Germany', in Michael Burleigh (ed.), *Confronting the Nazi Past: New Debates on Modern German History* (London: Collins & Brown, 1996), 159, 162–4.]

DETLEV GARBE

85   Between Resistance and Martyrdom

The Jehovah's Witnesses, although a very small group numerically, experienced massive persecution under the Nazi regime, both for their unwavering commitment to their faith and for their mass conscien- tious objection to military service. As a highly marginal social group and religious community their suffering has rarely been acknowledged in mainstream post-war culture.

To the public, the Jehovah's Witnesses are mostly known only as people who ring the doorbell or sell *Watchtower* in the street. What is hardly known at all is that this comparatively small religious community was persecuted and repressed with relentless harshness in the Third Reich. Just a few months after the National Socialist 'seizure of power' a ban was placed on the Jehovah's Witnesses—the Christian community had taken this name in 1931: in Germany, however, the label 'Bible Students', or 'Serious Bible Students', an abbreviation of their official name, the 'International Bible Students', remained in use for a long time.[1] As those faithful to the doctrine of the Jehovah's Witnesses widely refused to submit to this ban they therefore found themselves in opposition to the National Socialist regime. They opposed its demands resolutely—for example, the prescribed 'Hitler greeting' and membership of obligatory National Socialist organizations—and as a result suffered in their thousands in prisons or concentration camps, or were persecuted as conscientious objectors by the National Socialist justice system for 'demoralization of the armed forces'; finally, following the outbreak of war they were also condemned to death in large numbers. [. . .]

In several ways the history of the Jehovah's Witnesses in the years 1933 to 1945 reveals peculiarities which are notable and in need of explanation:

- the Jehovah's Witnesses were the first religious community to be banned in the Third Reich.
- no other religious community refused or opposed in its entirety National Socialist coercion with comparable steadfastness.[2] The unity of the group and their sense of mission led to such a high degree of participation in resistance activities as can be matched only by the KPD in the first couple of years after the National Socialist 'seizure of power'[3] or by small political groups such as the International Socialist League of Struggle (ISK) or the KPD Opposition (KPO).[4]
- the courage of conviction and the (under the circumstances) recklessness of the numerically rather insignificant religious community occupied surprisingly large circles: at times, the highest legal, police, and SS organs were occupied with the 'Bible Students Question'.
- of all Christian communities the Jehovah's Witnesses were by far the most harshly and relentlessly persecuted under the National Socialist regime;[5] Hans Lilje, the long-standing state bishop of the Protestant state church of Hanover, considered in 1947 that 'no Christian community could remotely measure the number of its martyrs against theirs'.[6]
- the Jehovah's Witnesses were persecuted in the National Socialist era so intensely and vehemently that their fate has even been compared in historical writing with that of the Jews.[7]
- because of the indiscriminating persecution and the fact that it was

based solely on membership of this community the 'Bible Students', along with the 'Jews including so-called first-degree *Mischlinge*' and the 'gypsies after 8 December 1938', count as one of the so-called 'collective persecutees' according to compensation law.[8]

- they were—apart from the even much smaller group of Seventh-Day Adventists[9]—the only group who in their entirety espoused conscientious objection in the 'Third Reich' and also practised this for the most part: 'they can claim to be the only prominent group of conscientious objectors which existed in the Third Reich and which, further, existed openly and for reasons of conscience.'[10]

- in the concentration camps, in which the different categories of inmate were marked by the SS with different coloured triangles, the separate category of violet was used for the 'Bible Students', in addition to the 'politicals' (red), the 'criminals' (green), the 'asocials' (black), and the 'homosexuals' (pink). In this way a category was chosen which did not encompass all those who were persecuted by the National Socialists on account of their religiously motivated resistance (for priests usually had to wear the red triangle), but which existed purely and solely for the members of this philosophical community. The exclusive marking points to the in many respects special position of the Jehovah's Witnesses within the camp system: they formed a 'distinct category of prisoner, who were sociologically clearly distinguished from the others'.[11] In the eyes of many fellow inmates the 'Bible Students' were 'the most incredible community . . . within the concentration camps'.[12] [. . .]

For the main concentration camps the following figures can be adduced for the war period, which in each case represent the highest number of 'Bible Student'-inmates at one point and not the total number of 'International Bible Student'-inmates incarcerated there: Auschwitz (*c.* 150),[13] Buchenwald (477),[14] Dachau (*c.* 150),[15] Flossenburg (205),[16] Mauthausen (*c.* 150),[17] Neuengamme (*c.* 100),[18] Ravensbrück (*c.* 600),[19] Sachsenhausen (500–600),[20] and Wewelsburg (306).[21] Smaller numbers were incarcerated in the main concentration camps of Majdanek, Natzweiler, Stutthof, and Vught (Herzogenbusch).[22] On the basis of these individual figures—even if these figures do not include committals and death rates ('arrivals and departures')—it would appear possible to assume that overall a figure of 3,000 (or possible somewhat more) prisoners with the 'violet triangle' were incarcerated in the concentration camps, although this figure also includes the non-German 'Bible Students'. One can proceed fairly safely from the assumption, however, that the total number of foreign Jehovah's Witnesses in German concentration camps was less than 1,000.[23] [. . .] As far as is known, about 100 to 120 Jehovah's Witnesses died in Mauthausen, at least 37 in Neuengamme, and over 200 in Sachsenhausen.[24] Assuming that approximately 30 per cent of all 'Bible Student'-inmates were held captive in these three main camps, and taking into account the death rates derived elsewhere[25] (i.e. in relation to the overall number of 'Bible Student'-inmates) of 35 per cent, one may estimate that about 1,100 to 1,200 Jehovah's Witnesses died in the concentration camps. Again, these figures include the foreign 'Bible Student'-inmates. It is difficult to estimate their numbers; for the Austrian Jehovah's Witnesses a minimum figure of 94 and for the Dutch Jehovah's Witnesses a figure of 117 deaths in custody are established. As, however, a higher death rate above all for east European Jehovah's Witnesses must be assumed,[26] one may suspect that the figure for foreign victims can be estimated at 400. One would thus arrive at a figure of 700–800 German 'International Bible Student'-members who died in the concentration camps.[27] To these must be added those who died in judicial detention, those killed during Gestapo interrogations, and those who died as a direct consequence of their incarceration.[28] [. . .]

Of the 25,000 to 30,000 people who were members of the Jehovah's Witnesses' religious community in Germany 1933, approximately 10,000 were incarcerated for various lengths of time, of whom over 2,000 were sent to concentration camps. The number of deaths among German Jehovah's witnesses was around 1,200, of whom about 250 were executed, primarily on the basis of a court-martial judgement for conscientious objection. [. . .]

[*Zwischen Widerstand und Martyrium: die Zeugen Jehovas im Dritten Reich* (Munich: Oldenbourg, 1993), 9–13, 483–7.]

ULRICH HERBERT

86 Hitler's Foreign Workers

The conquest of Europe offered the National Socialist regime an enormous reservoir of labour in the occupied territories, from which millions of civilians were deported and put to work (alongside prisoners of war) in German agriculture and industry. Deployed in accordance with the ideological principles of the regime, the forced workers' experience was determined by their place in the National Socialist racial hierarchy. West European workers experienced substantial hardship; Polish, Soviet, and above all Jewish forced workers were put to work under barbaric and exploitative conditions which amounted to 'slave labour'. However, while 'slave labour' may evoke accurately the power relationships involved and the experience of a large proportion of the workers, such terminology does not capture the important fact that this system of labour was implemented in a modern, industrial society in a factory environment not so different from a contemporary shop-floor.

In the existing literature, there are, broadly speaking, two competing approaches to the interpretation of foreign labor deployment, both of which can be useful in eliciting facts and asking relevant questions. On the one hand, the employment of foreigners in the Third Reich is viewed as a continuation of 'normal' migrations of labor in Europe, and treated primarily as a problem in social engineering, while 'excesses' are seen as special cases due to the nature of the war. This is how Germans tend to remember foreigner deployment. On the other hand, the 'program of slave labor' is described as an unending process of humiliation, harassment, maltreatment and crime.

The truth is not located somewhere in the middle. Rather, the difficulty lies in combining the two approaches so as to shed light on the contradictory nature of National Socialist foreigner policy and on the life of the foreign workers in an exceptional situation that lasted for several years, but without blurring the contours.

Upon closer scrutiny, the deployment of foreign laborers in Nazi Germany reveals disgusting brutalities, today hardly imaginable in their cruelty and arbitrariness, creating the impression of a strange time in a strange land, far more remote than the 50 intervening years would suggest. On the other hand, workaday life in the factories, social interaction, even the daily routine, appear in many respects astonishingly familiar, and seem to be little different from the observable conditions and habits of life and work among foreign workers in Germany today. Only when the social reality of Nazi Germany is brought back from a seemingly remote and unreal past, to reveal a historical society that in many respects feels quite close, familiar, and in many ways similar to the observer's own, is it possible to grasp the true dimensions of the repression, terror and crimes perpetrated against the foreign laborers. From this one may being to understand what a social order built on racist principles really means in a modern society. [. . .]

The situation of the Polish agrarian workers in the first phase of the war was characterized by a slow change from the tradition of seasonal labor to forced labor, accelerated by the special regulations in criminal and social law for Polish workers introduced by the authorities, and by the radicalization of recruitment methods in the Generalgouvernement. However, it remains unclear how far and how quickly the repressive regulations on treatment of Poles were put into practice in rural areas. Complaints by SD offices suggest that the process was slower in those regions where there was a long-standing tradition of employing Polish agricultural workers than in areas where there was not. The political and personal debasement of the Poles was systematized after the campaign in France. The strict differentiation between Frenchmen, Poles and workers from 'friendly' countries did not necessarily make the actual situation of the Polish workers any worse, but it did render the discrimination explicit not only as far as the social conditions were concerned, but also when it came to the exemplary and brutal penalties, especially for so-called 'crimes of sexual intercourse,' which lay at the heart of the regime's racist political endeavors.

By contrast, the French civilian workers and POWs were subject to far less stringent regulations. They were housed in better appointed camps and received better food and wages. Reports on their high productivity and the constant complaints about excessively close contacts between the German population and the French workers indicate that the situation of many French civilian workers did not differ substantially from that of German workers living in workers' hostels.

At the end of 1941, a completely new situation arose, especially in factories and in the industrial towns, with the decision to push ahead with the deployment of Soviet workers. Although most of the Eastern workers arrived in Germany in good physical health, many of them were living below the minimum survival level after just a few weeks, just like Soviet POWs who had managed to survive the intentional starvation in the POW camps of the Wehrmacht in the East. Famine, epidemics, high mortality and merciless oppression characterized their existence after arrival in Germany. Not until 1942 were there slight improvements in the food situation, principally because many factories had started to provide additional rations for their Eastern workers. Even more than that of other foreigners, the fate of Soviet laborers depended on the camp they lived in, the factory they worked at, the job they had: living and working conditions differed enormously. A decisive factor for many was whether they were trained, and how. Although subject to discriminatory social legislation which was harsher and more extensive than for the Poles, they could nonetheless achieve at least the minimum for survival by upgrading their job skills.

Conditions in the individual plants and industries differed substantially. In plants with a high percentage of skilled workers, such as Krupp in Essen, a contradiction arose, deepening as the war went on, between differential and repressive regimentation, and the increasing integration of foreigners into the production cycle: fierce oppression and brutal penalties side by side with an array of ameliorations in the living and working conditions of the Eastern workers. By comparison, the situation of foreign workers in mining, especially Soviet deployees, was far more brutal and dangerous. Training programs to impart new skills were rarer here, performance and productivity correspondingly lower, maltreatment more frequent, and the number of deaths in mining, especially among Soviet POWs, was alarmingly high. This was a continuation of the war of extermination by other means, when other industries had already shifted to a program geared to increasing performance levels and improving working and living conditions.

In 1942, the differences in the living conditions of the different groups of foreigners in Germany were wider than ever. *Westarbeiter* and workers from 'friendly' countries enjoyed material conditions quite similar to those of

German workers. The main difference lay in the increasingly obvious coercive character of their stay in the Reich, the daily discriminations and the permanent threat from a harsh special penal code.

By contrast, the situation of workers from the East (and, from the summer of 1943, Italian internees) was characterized by poor diet, low wages, inadequate housing and clothing, excessively long hours, deficient medical care, cheating by German superiors, abuse and maltreatment, and high mortality. Although there were substantial differences depending on region and factory, the living conditions of the Eastern workers in particular, at this stage of the war, came very close to what the Nuremberg tribunal was to call 'slave labor.'

From 1943, however, the massive Allied air attacks on German cities quickly became the greatest single threat to the foreign workers. At the same time, efforts by the employers and the authorities since Stalingrad to bring about a lasting increase in productivity, especially that of Eastern workers, which encompassed efforts to improve their living and working conditions, were thwarted. In many localities, a paradoxical situation arose: the performance levels of the Soviet workers continued to rise while their living conditions deteriorated. Various factors were decisive here: more food for better performance, the widespread introduction of piecework wages, and the constant expansion of the plant-internal system of surveillance and punishment. Psychological elements were also involved: 'good work' as a way to express and maintain one's self-esteem and personal identity; resignation and compliance, seeing that an end to the war was nowhere in sight; and the hope of being left in peace if one did one's job. Finally, there were political aspects: loyalty to or liking for the Germans with whom one worked, and, among Soviet workers, the fear of revenge by the Red Army for suspected collaboration, or the lack of any personal perspective on the future after the Third Reich. The large number of Eastern workers unwilling to be repatriated after the war underscores, in retrospect, the importance of such fears.

In this connection, the especially high percentage of women among laborers from Poland and the Soviet Union (over 50 percent) also played a role. From 1943 onward, the female Eastern workers, who were mostly very young, were particularly sought after by industrial firms, because their performance was often outstanding, their wages especially low, and the protective measures for women in German social legislation did not apply to them. In contrast with their male workmates, they were also considered highly tractable. The German authorities had no fears that female Eastern workers would turn resistant or unruly. They were thus subject to a double oppression, as women and as Soviet workers, and had nothing to set against this except their performance.

The threat of forced abortion and sterilization placed them under additional massive pressure. The children of female Eastern workers had been singled out as an object of racial planning by the SS leadership. The horrible consequences of those plans became evident in the camps for foreign children during the second half of the war, and the deaths of hundreds of children of Eastern workers, many of which were never adequately explained, during its final phase.

Here, as in the liquidation of sick or handicapped Eastern workers in German hospitals and clinics, it was evident that the primacy of job performance did not mean that the regime had abandoned its racial principles. This also became clear to all foreign workers who, for whatever reason, had come to the attention of the security authorities. Conditions in many labor education camps were apparently little different from those in concentration camps, and it is impossible even to guess at the number of foreign workers murdered in such camps or while in police custody.

[*Fremdarbeiter: Politik und Praxis des 'Ausländer-Einsatzes' in der Kriegswirtschaft des Dritten Reiches* (Bonn: Verlag J.H.W. Dietz Nachf., 1985), trans. as *Hitler's Foreign Workers: Enforced Foreign Labour in Germany under the Third Reich* (Cambridge: Cambridge University Press, 1997), 382–3, 390–3.]

CHRISTIAN STREIT

87   Soviet Prisoners of War—Mass Deportation—Forced Workers

Operation 'Barbarossa' was conceived and embarked upon as an ideological war of destruction, and represented a type of warfare which was qualitatively different from that which occurred in western Europe. While the SS was at the forefront of implementing the regime's ideological goals in the east, the *Wehrmacht* also became deeply implicated—offering support and cooperation to the SS *Einsatzgruppen*, which killed over 2 million Jews, and causing the deaths of millions of Soviet prisoners of war. In this passage, Christian Streit discusses the fate of the Soviet prisoners of war at the hands of the *Wehrmacht*.

The sad fate of the German prisoners of war held in Soviet captivity is generally known in the Federal Republic. According to a commission of historians about 3,155,000 *Wehrmacht* soldiers fell into Soviet captivity; between 1,110,000 and 1,185,000 (35 to 38 per cent) died.[1]

The fate of the Soviet prisoners of war in German hands has remained—at least into the 1970s—hardly known. Around 5.7 million Red Army soldiers fell captive to the *Wehrmacht* between 22 June 1941 and the end of the war.[2] At the beginning of 1945 930,000 of these were still alive in the prisoner camps. A million at most had been released, mostly as 'volunteers' for *Wehrmacht* service. According to estimates of the Army High Command a further 500,000 had escaped or been liberated by the Red Army. The remaining 3.3

million (57 per cent) had died; almost 2 million had died by February 1942 alone.[3]

Five main causes led to the deaths of more than half the Soviet prisoners: hunger; completely inadequate accommodation; the manner of transportation, above all in 1941; inhumane treatment; finally, the murder of specific groups of prisoners.

Provision for the enormous number of prisoners indeed posed huge problems for the *Wehrmacht*, but this was not the cause of the mass deaths. The food resources of the east were one of the main goals of the war in the east. Their merciless exploitation was intended to maintain a 'peacelike' standard of nutrition for the German population and thus prevent any endangering of 'war morale'—November 1918 was a traumatic memory for both Hitler and his generals.

The ministerial civil servants, who were already planning this exploitation in detail months before the attack, were fully aware of the consequences. Through this, according to a discussion of the state secretaries of various ministries at the beginning of 1941, 'x millions of people will undoubtedly starve'.[4] This is to be seen in connection with the enormous plans being drawn up in the victorious euphoria of early 1941, which aimed at the most radical reordering of the population map of the European east. 'Many tens of millions of people' would 'become superfluous' in this process and 'die or emigrate to Siberia'.[5]

The expected prisoners of war had necessarily to be the first victims of this policy. The offices responsible were agreed from the outside that they should receive 'only the most necessary rations' and not be treated according to the usual international rules of warfare.[6] [. . .]

Right from the beginning the Soviet prisoners of war received completely inadequate rations.[7] Reports from the summer of 1941 mention daily rations such as '20g of millet and 100g bread or meat', or '100g millet without bread'—rations which represented less than a quarter of the minimum necessary for survival. The consequences soon became visible. Already in August 1941 it was known in the Armed Forces High Command that often only one-fifth of the prisoners in a transport arrived at the destination alive. At the beginning of August 1941 the OKW decreed standard ration levels of about 2,200 calories for working prisoners. The sources show, however, that these levels, which lay below the minimum for survival, were usually not reached. Reports from the summer and autumn of 1941 show that in many camps the desperate prisoners attempted to sate their hunger with leaves and grass.

In October 1941 the death rates rose radically.[8] The prisoners, completely exhausted by hunger and the exertions of marches of hundreds of kilometres, had nothing with which to resist the cold, infectious illnesses, and diseases born of hunger. They died, as one of the sources puts it, 'like flies'. In occupied Poland, for example, 54,000 deaths had been registered by 20

October 1941. In the following ten days alone, however, a further 45,690 prisoners died—almost 4,600 per day. Of the original 361,000 prisoners held there 310,000 died by April 1942, more than 85 per cent.

Despite this development the Army Quartermaster General, General Wagner—he later played an important role in the resistance—ordered a drastic reduction of rations for the front areas as late as 21 October 1941, which above all hit the already weakened prisoners who were not capable of work. In this Wagner was fulfilling a demand of Göring, who shortly before had once more emphasized the necessity of securing the 'morale' of the German population.[9]

The mass deaths reached their peak between October and December 1941. In December 46 per cent of the prisoners held in occupied Poland and in the Reich Commissariat in the Ukraine died, for example. The process was accelerated by the onset of winter, to which the prisoners were exposed with almost no protection. As only an absolute minimum of material and energy was to be used for the prisoners, pieces of land had simply been fenced off on troop training areas, in both the territory of the Reich and in occupied Poland, on which in each case tens of thousands of prisoners were to build their own highly primitive accommodation.[10] The commander in charge of prisoners of war in the *Generalgouvernement*, for example, who initially was to accommodate at least 500,000 prisoners, was only allocated 250 tonnes of barbed wire, along with chlorinated lime, cooking cauldrons, eating utensils, and tools, but neither barracks nor building materials. Only horse-drawn vehicles were available for transport. This led to the situation both there and in the territory of the Reich where prisoners were forced to vegetate into the winter in earth holes or mudhuts in the open air which they had dug themselves. By early 1942 the accommodation situation improved above all by virtue of the fact that the radically decimated number of prisoners found space in the shelters which by now had been finished.

Tens, if not hundreds, of thousands died in transit.[11] Down to the winter the majority of prisoners had to march for weeks to the camps. During this process tens of thousands of exhausted prisoners were shot on the spot. Individual troop leaders opposed this practice with indignant orders. However, such cases were repeatedly reported until the beginning of August 1942, even from the centres of cities such as Minsk and Smolensk. Further, there were troop leaders who were of a different view. In Field Marshal Reichenau's 6th Army it had been ordered that 'all flagging prisoners of war [are] to be shot'.

Insofar as prisoners were transported by rail, this occurred only in open wagons, on the order of the Army High Command. This not only limited the available transport capacity, but also brought enormous losses with the onset of winter. In the middle army rear area, for example, transport in closed wagons was only permitted on 22 November 1941, at which point there had been permanent frost for over three weeks. The concrete cause of this was that in one transport 1,000 prisoners—a fifth—had frozen to death. However, transportation in closed, unheated wagons meant no decisive improvement under the conditions of the Russian winter. According to a report of the beginning of December 1941 'between 25 and 70 per cent of the prisoners died during transport' in the Reich Commissariat in the East, also because for journeys of several days no food had been supplied.[12]

Above all in 1941 German soldiers must have had the impression that the life of Soviet people was worth nothing. This was not only because *Wehrmacht* propaganda also represented them as 'subhuman', it was above all the consequence of the orders of the military leadership.[13] The 'Court Martial Decree' of 13 May 1941 decreed that 'offences by enemy citizens' should not, as usual, by tried by court martial. Civilians engaging in active or passive resistance were to be 'mercilessly finished with', 'suspicious elements' to be shot on the orders of an officer. On the other hand crimes by German soldiers on Soviet citizens were not to be prosecuted if the perpetrator could prove political motives.[14] According to the Commissar Decree,[15] political commissars of the Red Army were to be shot upon capture. The *Wehrmacht* thereby became involved in the murder of political opponents for the first time. The army leadership was willing to support this policy. General Halder was of the view, as he noted in his War Diary, that 'in the East toughness means mildness in the future', and the army must 'also fight the ideological struggle through'.[16] [. . .]

['Sowjetische Kriegsgefangene—Massendeportation—Zwangsarbeiter', in Wolfgang Michalka (ed.), *Der Zweite Weltkrieg: Analysen, Grundzüge, Forschungsbilanz* (Munich: Piper, 1989), 747–50.]

LENI YAHIL

88 Killing Operations

The transition to systematic mass murder of Europe's Jews began with the invasion of the Soviet Union on 22 June 1941. Four SS *Einsatzgruppen* ('task squads') entered the Soviet Union behind the German armed forces and organized the mass shootings of Jews described in these passages by Leni Yahil. The experience of these killing campaigns, which quickly escalated in scope to the point where individual killing actions could claim many thousands of victims, led to the decision to embark upon the 'Final Solution'.

The millions of Jews with whom the Germans had come into contact in occupied Poland were now augmented by close to four million more in the newly occupied territories. They included more than two million in the

Soviet Union,[1] over a quarter of a million in the Baltic states, and a million in the areas that had formerly belonged to Poland. [. . .] In [. . .] Poland the Germans [had] failed to achieve the comprehensive solutions to which they had aspired. A large proportion of the Jewish community held fast despite persecution, overcrowding in the ghettos, and malnutrition; the process of natural mortality was less rapid than the Germans had hoped. Now they concluded that they could no longer rely on natural factors, and therefore had to do the job themselves, particularly since the plans for reservations in Poland and Madagascar had proved unworkable.

The vast area stretching from the Baltic Sea to the Black Sea was divided into four areas, with one Einsatzgruppe in each. They were known as groups A, B, C, and D, and each was commanded by an officer from the RSHA; each group was composed of several commando units, and most of their commanders were professional SS and Gestapo officers. Each of the Einsatzgruppen was attached to an army corps and, in accordance with prior agreement, acted in collaboration with it. As they advanced almost simultaneously with the fighting force, the speed of the military progress the first few months enabled the Einsatzgruppen to work swiftly.[2] The units moved systematically from place to place, assembling the Jews, conveying them outside towns and villages, and murdering them beside antitank trenches or pits dug especially for this purpose. The victims were ordered to strip and to stand in groups by the pit where they were shot by automatic weapons, the dead and dying falling into the mass graves. Sometimes the victims were even forced to lie down in the pit in neat lines, head to toe alternately, and there they were executed row by row by what the SS called the sardine method. Finally, the pits were covered with earth. Rivers of blood flowed and the earth sometimes heaved and trembled for days afterward.

The Order Police (ORPO) took part in the operations under the command of the Higher SS and Police Leaders (HSSPF) and their local collaborators. But, to the surprise even of the SS, the army cooperated of its own volition, and in certain areas army units played a very active role in mass murder. According to the preliminary planning, the local population was expected to collaborate. At first this method proved successful, but the readiness of the local population did not reach the dimensions the Germans had anticipated. More successful was the activation of local auxiliary police units under German command. The first wave of murders came to an end around the beginning of winter, and it is estimated that by then more than seven hundred thousand Jews had been murdered in these actions: at least four hundred thousand of them in Soviet Russia, close to two hundred thousand in the Baltic states, and the remainder in the areas that had belonged to Poland before the war.[3]

For propaganda purposes the Germans constantly claimed that the Jews were the main organizers of the partisan movement and hence must be exterminated, an argument that was first broached by Hitler at the planning session of July 16, 1941. Stalin had just called for partisan activity behind the enemy lines, and Hitler welcomed this statement as providing him with a pretext for German terror in the occupied areas. In fact, at this time the partisan movement was tiny and unorganized and did not constitute a real threat to the German army. The claim that it was being run by the Jews was certainly baseless. In many cases the mass murders were described as retaliation for the killing of German soldiers supposedly carried out by Jews, the ratio being 1: 100.

The commanding officer of Einsatzgruppe A, Franz W. Stahlecker, sent a detailed report on January 31, 1942, about activities in the Baltic countries and White Russia, covering the period from July 23 to October 15, 1941. According to this report the overall number murdered was 135,567. Among them, the known numbers of Jews killed are 80,311 in Lithuania, 30,025 in Latvia, 474 in Estonia, and 7,620 in White Russia; to this should be added 5,500 Jews killed in pogroms and 5,502 killed in the Tilsit (Sovetsk) sector and near the border with East Prussia. There were undoubtedly also an unknown number of Jews among the 3,387 'communists' and 748 mental patients mentioned in the report.[4]

According to a report submitted by Einsatzgruppe B, 45,467 were killed up to mid-November 1941, within its area of operation, that is, White Russia.[5] Owing to the slower advance of the army in the south, operations began there later. According to a report dated November 3, 1941, there were 80,000 Jews killed in the Ukraine, a large proportion of them (namely 34,000) in Kiev. The Kiev Operation—the Babi Yar slaughter—was one of the bloodiest and most notorious of all. The Einsatzgruppen units reached the city between September 19 and 25, 1941. At this time, Russian sappers set off two explosions, the second one destroying the German headquarters and a large part of the city center; 25,000 people were left homeless. In retaliation, the German authorities demanded resettlement of the Jews and called on them to assemble on September 29 for transfer. The 30,000 Jews who assembled were taken to the forest and slaughtered over the course of two days. According to the German report, 'there were no incidents.' It also emphasizes that 'thanks to the outstandingly efficient organization,' the Jews believed up to the last moment that they were being taken to their new homes. The local population—it is further reported—believed the story and were gratified by it. Only *post factum* did the truth emerge. The Germans boasted of having solved the housing problem by evacuating a suitable number of apartments—that is, by exterminating approximately 35,000 Jews.[6] Before the German occupation, 175,000 Jews had lived in the city; thus the victims accounted for only part of the Jewish community, which had comprised both local residents and refugees. A large percentage of these Jews had made their escape before the Germans arrived. Most of the victims were the old, the sick, and women and children who had been left behind.[7]

The Soviet evacuation of the Ukraine was more organized and workers, including Jews, were evacuated with their factories. Thus, for example, a report from Einsatzgruppe D, dated November 19, 1941, states that of the 100,000 Jews in Dnepropetrovsk, 70,000 fled before the Germans arrived; of those remaining, 1,000 were shot on the spot.[8]

Sometimes, economic considerations were brought up, as witness a report sent on December 2, 1941, by the representative of the Industrial Armaments Department of the Supreme Command (OKW) in the Ukraine to General Georg Thomas, who headed the department. The Jewish population of the Ukraine was mainly urban, the report explained, and often constituted more than 50 percent of the population of a town. These Jews 'carried out almost all the work in the skilled trades, and even provided part of the labor for small- and medium-sized industries.' The murder operations in the Ukraine were vaster in scope than anywhere else in the Soviet Union, but as the report states, 'no consideration was given to the interests of the economy.'[9]

Marshal Walther von Reichenau, supreme commander of the Sixth Army in the southern army corps, was one of the high-ranking officers who wholeheartedly supported National Socialism and Hitler personally. On October 10, 1941, he issued an order in which he noted that vague concepts were still rife as to how soldiers were to conduct themselves. 'The main objective of this campaign against the Jewish-Bolshevik system is to totally destroy the potential for power and to extirpate Asiatic influence on European cultural life.' He went on to explain that consequently German soldiers were faced with tasks above and beyond the conventional framework of conduct of warfare, 'The soldiers must fully understand the need for severe but just atonement of the Jewish subhumans.' There follows the customary argument that all partisan activities behind the front were organized by the Jews, and the soldiers were exhorted to refrain from treating the partisans as 'decent soldiers.' Only total cruelty could guarantee the safety of the army and ensure victory, 'Only thus can we carry out our historic task and once and for all liberate the German people from the Jewish-Asiatic danger'.[10]

Hitler was enthusiastic about the marshal's directive and ordered that it be distributed among all the army units; thus it also reached Field Marshal Erich von Manstein, the supreme commander of the Eleventh Army, which was operating in the Crimean Peninsula. At his trial before a British military tribunal in Hamburg, von Manstein claimed that he had known nothing of the extermination of Jews, notwithstanding the fact that he personally signed an order on November 20, 1941, reiterating von Reichenau's statement.[11]

[*The Holocaust: The Fate of European Jewry* (New York: Oxford University Press, 1990), 255–8.]

89 Children

The biological-racial determinism of National Socialist anti-Semitism meant that, once extermination had been decided upon, no Jew would be spared. Young or old, male or female, able-bodied or infirm—National Socialist ideology determined that no distinction be drawn. The survival prospects of young children were particularly low, as they had neither the physical stamina to survive the appalling conditions under which they were kept nor the independence or experience to attempt an escape. Raul Hilberg here describes the fate of Jewish children during the Holocaust.

The fate of the children may be charted in four consecutive situations. The first was the early regime of restrictions. The second was life in the ghetto. Then came selections for deportations or shootings. Finally children were killed.

There were comparatively fewer children in the Jewish community than in the surrounding non-Jewish population. The Jewish birthrate was declining more rapidly than that of non-Jews, and in Prussia, Austria, Bohemia-Moravia, Hungary, and Italy, it had fallen below the replacement level.[1] Nine months of anti-Jewish measures in German-controlled regions or in countries allied with Germany had the effect of depressing the rate even more. In areas where the process of pauperization and segregation took some time, not only infants but also small children were fewer. That is not to say that these children did not suffer.

During the phase of economic and social discrimination, the fortunes of children were those of their fathers and mothers. They lost space in housing when their parents were driven out of apartments, and their freedom of movement was reduced when all Jews were deprived of such freedom. They no longer had the old quantity or variety of food, when supplementary rations were cut or shopping hours shortened for Jews. They were specifically targeted as students in schools, somewhat analogously to adults dismissed from jobs. If they could not emigrate—and outside Germany and Austria the vast majority had no prospect of leaving—their lives were sober and somber. Like their elders, with whom they were trapped, they had little to look forward to and much to be anxious about.

In Eastern Europe, ghettoization, with its privations and constrictions, introduced a question of life and death. Here one may see a large magnification of death rates, with the smallest children suffering first and the most.

The most complete statistics for a larger ghetto come from Lodz, where the Jewish council prepared a detailed report for the period May 1940 to June 1942.[2] After the ghetto gates were closed on April 30, 1940, the Jewish population was 163,777. Tens of thousands of Jews were subsequently transported in from the countryside and from cities in Germany, Luxembourg, and Bohemia-Moravia, but this augmentation was outweighed by deaths and deportations. As of June 30, 1942, the count was only 102,546. The ghetto was wiped out in 1944.

In Lodz, as elsewhere, the birthrate of the Jewish population was plunging under German rule. From age distribution data in the report, it appears that during the 1930s, the average annual birthrates must have been around 16 per 1,000. The May–December 1940 rate was about 8 per 1,000 on an annual basis. The 1941 rate was 4 per 1,000.

At the beginning of the ghetto period in Lodz, disaster struck the infants. From May 1, 1940, to the end of 1941 there were 1,390 ghetto births. A total of 416 children died in this group during their first year of life by December 31, 1941. More than a third of these deaths were attributed to premature birth, and the following five of the identified causes were lung disease, diseases of the digestive system, food poisoning, malnutrition, and dysentery.

For the period May 1, 1940, to June 30, 1942, the total number of infants who died was 1,150, including 610 who had been born before the ghetto's formation, the 416 born in the ghetto whose death as infants occurred by the end of 1941, and 124 more ghetto born or newly arrived infants who died during the first half of 1942. So rapid was this attrition that 872 of these 1,150 children had already died in 1940.

The increasing mortality rate of children past infancy was roughly proportional to the steeply rising death rate of the adults. The report does not specify causes of death for children aged one to fourteen, but if premature births, heart disease, and diseases of old age are subtracted from a list compiled for the entire ghetto community, the major remaining causes were, in 1940, dysentery, lung diseases, and diseases of the digestive system, and in 1941 and 1942, tuberculosis and starvation. [. . .]

Rarely could adults escape from ghettos with children, although in the woods of Byelorussia there were some camps in which Jewish partisans tried to protect young families. A few attempts were also made to place children with gentile hosts. The following story is told in a judgment of a United States court. In the small town of Lisets (Lysiece), located in the Galician region and inhabited at the time by a mixed population of Ukrainians, Poles, and Jews, a Jewish physician managed to leave his small daughter with Polish friends before the Jewish community of Lisets was bodily transferred to the ghetto of Stanislawow. The little girl was passed on to a gentile Polish woman, Jadwiga Spilarewicz. When Mrs. Spilarewicz heard that a Polish family had been arrested for harboring Jews, she decided to take the child to Krakow and stopped in Lisets to obtain money from a relative for the trip. Two Ukrainian policemen immediately arrested her and she was held for several weeks. The child was also seized. One of the policemen, Bohdan

Kozij, was observed dragging her to the courtyard behind the police station. As the child was pleading to be spared, Kozij shot her at point-blank range. Her body was seen at the Jewish cemetery.[3]

Very few children could survive in camps. Of 4,918 children to age fifteen, who were deported to Auschwitz from Belgium, 53 came back.[4] Adolescents could sometimes pretend to be older. When Elie Wiesel arrived in Auschwitz, he was fifteen. A prisoner walked up to him to ask how old he was. Fifteen, was the reply. No, eighteen, the older prisoner corrected him. But he was fifteen, Wiesel said again. Not satisfied, the stranger told him to listen to his advice. When Wiesel was confronted by an SS officer who selected people for the gas chamber, he was asked about his age again. Eighteen, was the answer.[5]

In the pure death camps of Treblinka, Sobibor, Belzec, and Kulmhof, there was no chance for children at all. In Kulmhof, Simon Srebnik was thirteen. The German guards kept him as a mascot. When the camp was broken up, they shot him and left him for dead. He lived to tell his story.[6]

In areas where shooting operations were conducted, children were swept up as well. Only at the beginning, when men were selected did children remain with their mothers. It was a short reprieve.[7] After a while the remaining children became aware of what was happening. Dr. Peretz observed them in the Kaunas Ghetto playing grave digging, execution, and funeral.[8]

During the summer and fall of 1942, several hundred thousand Jews were massacred in the Volhynian-Podolian region. When the Germans entered a small ghetto and lined up its Jews, a little girl asked: 'Mother, why did you make me wear the Shabbat dress; we are being taken out to be shot.' The shooting site was on a hill about two miles away, and the mother, carrying the child, was forced to run this distance after a truck already filled with victims. Standing near the dugout half-filled with bodies, the child said: 'Mother, why are we waiting, let us run!' Some of the people who attempted to escape were caught immediately and shot on the spot. The mother stood there facing the grave. A German walked up to the woman and asked: 'Whom shall I shoot first?' When she did not answer, he tore her daughter from her hands. The child cried out and was killed.[9]

> [*Perpetrators, Victims, Bystanders: The Jewish Catastrophe 1933–1945* (New York: Harper Collins, 1992), 139–41, 147–9.]

FRANCISZEK PIPER

90   The Number of Victims

The largest of the extermination camps used in the genocide process was Auschwitz. Estimates as to how many people died there vary— given the nature of the killing process and the incomplete nature of the surviving evidence it will never be possible to arrive at exact figures. A broad consensus seems to have emerged that the *minimum* figure was approximately 1,100,000, of whom 90 per cent were Jews; the real figure may have been substantially higher.

In this extract, Franciszek Piper summarizes the findings of a recent attempt to document the number of Auschwitz victims.

The calculation method draws on all numerical data relating to the transports of persons deported to the camp, and to all reductions in prisoner population caused by transfers to other camps and by releases and escapes. By subtracting the latter figure from the former, one can obtain the number of persons who died in Auschwitz.

The Number Deported

Jews. Jews made up the largest group of deportees. Research findings in various countries served as the basis for a number of studies on the extermination of their Jewish nationals, including deportation of part of this group to Auschwitz. In France and Belgium, complete lists of names have been published, whereas in other countries, numerical totals have been prepared. The numbers of Jewish deportees add up to 1,100,000.

The breakdown in terms of individual countries is as follows: Hungary, 438,000,[1] Poland, 300,000,[2] France, 69,000,[3] Netherlands, 60,000,[4] Greece, 55,000,[5] Bohemia and Moravia (Theresienstadt), 46,000,[6] Slovakia, 27,000,[7] Belgium, 25,000,[8] Germany and Austria, 23,000,[9] Yugoslavia, 10,000,[10] Italy, 7,500,[11] Norway, 690,[12] concentration camps and other places, 34,000.[13] The approximate total is 1,095,190, which the author has rounded to 1,100,000. [. . .]

Poles. Gaps in source material permit only an approximation of the number of Poles deported to Auschwitz. Like other non-Jewish prisoners, Poles were assigned serial numbers. Therefore Polish prisoners can be counted among the 400,000 registered prisoners (with the exception of those not included in numerical registration). By deducting from that figure 205,000 registered Jewish prisoners,[14] 21,000 registered Gypsies, and 12,000 registered Soviet prisoners of war, one arrives at 162,000 prisoners comprising Poles and other nationalities, including 151,000 prisoners (not counting Jews) within the general (ordinary) serial camp category and 11,000 prisoners assigned the EH (reeducation) serial category comprising almost exclusively Poles.[15]

On the basis of transport lists that include 105,000 prisoners in the general category (without Jews) brought in from ten countries, it can be determined that 87,447, or 83.28 percent of all transports, came from Poland. Extrapolating that percent to the total of 151,000 prisoners produces, together with the EH category, a total of 137,000 registered Poles. In addition, at least 10,000 Poles were deported and subsequently put to death without having been registered,[16] including between 3,000 and 4,500 police prisoners. Thus the total number of Poles brought to the camp is estimated at 140,000 to 150,000.

Gypsies. Available evidence indicates that about 21,000 Gypsies were registered in the camp. Their names are listed in the camp's main book (*Hauptbuch*)[17] salvaged by prisoners. Most came from Germany, Austria, and the Protectorate of Bohemia and Moravia. In addition, about 1,700 nonregistered Gypsies were killed in the camp.[18] That adds up to a total of 23,000 Gypsies deported to Auschwitz.

Soviet prisoners of war. In the years 1941–44, some 12,000 Soviet POWs were registered and assigned serial numbers.[19] Other groups of POWs, not registered, were killed upon arrival in gas chambers or executed by shooting. Testimonies, accounts, and materials of the camp resistance movement allow one to estimate that there were at least 3,000 unregistered prisoners.[20] This means that at least 15,000 Soviet POWs ended up in the camp.

Other nationalities. The remaining 25,000 registered prisoners represented other nationalities, including Belorussians, Russians, Ukrainians, Lithuanians, Czechs, French, Yugoslavs, Germans, Austrians, and Italians. They were brought in groups ranging from a few prisoners to several thousand.[21]

In summary, from 1940 to 1945, at least 1,300,000 persons were deported to Auschwitz.

The Number Killed

Given the lack of camp documents, the only way to establish how many perished is by reconciling the increases and decreases in the number of prisoners at the camp. That can be accomplished by referring to camp and resistance-movement documents, lists of Auschwitz prisoners compiled after they arrived at other concentration camps, and other scattered sources of information.

Incomplete source material precludes the possibility of calculating all the numbers of transfers, releases, and escapes. Some prisoners may have been counted twice if, for example, a transport that carried prisoners from Auschwitz to an unknown destination was counted again in a list drawn up by another concentration camp. Even when calculations are made with all due care, faultless verification is not always possible.

According to two tables of information in the Auschwitz-Birkenau State Museum,[22] some 25,000 prisoners were transported from Auschwitz-Birkenau to other camps in the years 1940–43. A considerable discrepancy exists for the years 1944 and 1945. Therefore one must accept lists published by Andrzej Strzeleck,[23] that give a total of 187,820 persons, including registered prisoners and unregistered Jews from the transit camp in Birkenau. (According to Czech's *Kalendarium*, the latter category comprised about 25,000 persons.)[24]

To the number of prisoners who were transferred out of Auschwitz from 1940 to 1945 (212,820), one must add 1,500 released prisoners, 500 escapees, and 8,000 liberated inmates, for an estimated grand total of 222,820 prisoners who left the camp alive. However, many of these prisoners did not live to see the end of the war. Some perished en route to other camps, and many lost their lives in the last phase of the war. Former Auschwitz prisoners, for example, were among victims on the ship *Cap Arcona*, which was bombed one day before the end of the war.

Based on these calculations (1,300,000 deportees minus 200,000 survivors), at least 1,100,000 persons were killed or died in the camp. But if this number is regarded as a minimum estimate, what figure can we accept as a hypothetical ceiling?

Theoretically, any significant increase in the estimates can apply only to Jews, since in principle, prisoners of other nationalities were accounted for within the system of numerical registration. Even taking into account data contained in sources omitted from this analysis because of their dubious reliability, the number of unregistered Poles, Soviet POWs, and other prisoners could not have exceeded several tens of thousands.

If the aggregate losses sustained by the Jewish population are not changed, a hypothetical increase in the number of Jews killed in Auschwitz can occur only if one lowers the estimates of losses in other camps and extermination sites and adjusts the Auschwitz tally accordingly. [. . .]

['The Number of Victims', in Yisrael Gutman and Michael Berenbaum (eds.), *Anatomy of the Auschwitz Death Camp*. (Bloomington: Indiana University Press, 1994), 68–71.]

YITZHAK ARAD

91 Operation Reinhard

Operation Reinhard was the codename given by the Nazi regime to the programme to exterminate the Jews of the *Generalgouvernement* of Poland. From 1942 to 1943 1.7 million Jews were exterminated at Belzec, Sobibor, and Treblinka. Not only the Jews of the *Generalgouvernement*, but Jews from all over Europe perished in these camps. In these passages Yitzhak Arad summarizes the findings of his study of Operation Reinhard.

The largest single massacre action of the Holocaust, Operation Reinhard, which lasted twenty-one months, from March 1942 to November 1943, was carried out by, and accomplished according to the plans of, the Nazi extermination machine. It was an integral and substantial part of the overall plan for the 'Final Solution of the Jewish problem.'

The commanders of Operation Reinhard, Globocnik, Wirth, and the SS men subordinate to them, succeeded in creating an efficient yet simple system of mass extermination by using relatively scanty resources. In each of the death camps—in Belzec, in Sobibor, and in Treblinka—a limited number of 20 to 35 Germans were stationed for purposes of command and supervision, and about 90 to 130 Ukrainians were responsible for guard duties. All the physical work in the extermination process was imposed on 700 to 1,000 Jewish prisoners who were kept in each camp.

The layout and structure of the camps were adapted to serve the extermination system and procedure. They were relatively small and compact, which enabled permanent and strict control over the entire area and all activities in the camp. The material used to build the camps—lumber and bricks—and the means used for the extermination—a simple motor vehicle and ordinary petrol—were readily available in the immediate vicinity. Local workers and Jewish prisoners built the camps. All these elements made the entire operation independent of outside and distant factors. Anything needed for the smooth running of the extermination action could be procured in the surrounding areas within a short time. The killing system, as developed by Wirth, enabled the murder of tens of thousands of Jews every day in the three death camps under his jurisdiction.

The German authorities succeeded in keeping the erection of the camps and the activities there secret from the overwhelming majority of the victims throughout Operation Reinhard. Even when rumors or some information about Belzec and Treblinka, and, to a much lesser extent, about Sobibor, reached the Jews still left in the ghettos of the General Government, the people were reluctant to believe them. It was much easier to accept the Nazi ruse that the deportees were destined for labor camps somewhere 'in the East' where manpower was needed for wartime economic enterprises than to believe that innocent people were being sent to gas chambers. But even those who took the rumors about gas chambers and mass extermination seriously had no means of rescue for themselves and their families.

In the face of the hostility of substantial segments of the population and the indifference or neutrality of the majority of the local people, the chance to find refuge from deportation was practically nil. The Germans further influenced the non-Jewish population by using embedded anti-Semitic feelings, bribery, and threats to encourage the capture and surrender of Jews in hiding or those who were attempting to escape. The Germans were the beneficiaries of the 'non-interventionist' attitude of the local people, which kept them neutral and silent while their Jewish neighbors were dispatched to their death. This attitude, even if it was often motivated simply by fear of reprisals in case of extending help to Jews, contributed to the success of the Nazi extermination machine.

The Jewish people, in order to survive, were in need of active help from the local people in providing hiding places, food, and Aryan documents. This was forthcoming neither from the local Polish population nor from the Polish Underground. There were only a few exceptions to this general pattern of noninvolvement. The attitude of the majority of the Ukrainian population, which lived in the areas east of the camps, was even more hostile.

The Jews in the ghettos and in the camps were aware of the attitude of the local population and the slim chances of finding refuge among them. This, and the uncertainty of the destination and fate of the deportations, discouraged many from even considering escape. Nevertheless, many did try to escape during the deportations and from the trains. Very few survived.

The ruse continued even after the Jews arrived in the camps. Almost all of the victims went to the gas chambers believing that these were indeed baths. Secrecy, deception, and disguise on the one hand, and little chance for rescue or for hiding among the local population on the other hand, enabled the Nazis to keep their extermination machine running smoothly.

But those Jews who were selected for work in the camps and who were aware of what was going on there did not give up. Prisoners in Sobibor and Treblinka succeeded, despite the strict control and surveillance under which they were kept, in carrying out individual escapes and in staging an uprising accompanied by a mass escape. The uprisings ensured the survival of hundreds of prisoners and revealed the secrets of the death camps to the world. These survivors were the main witnesses at the Sobibor and Treblinka trials in the Federal Republic of Germany, as well as at other trials. The perpetrators did not succeed in their attempts to bury and burn the truth of the camps together with the victims.

While Nazi Germany succeeded in keeping the aim of the deportations and the existence of the death camps secret from their victims, they did not succeed in preventing the truth about Belzec, Sobibor, and Treblinka from reaching the governments in London and Washington. In the initial stages of Operation Reinhard, information was transferred by the Polish Underground to the Polish Government-in-Exile in London and through their channels to the governments of Great Britain and the United States. As time passed, and especially toward the end of 1942, more and more detailed and accurate information reached the free world. It can be assumed that such information also reached the government of the Soviet Union.

No action followed this information. No steps were taken to warn the victims, to call on the local population and Underground to help the victims, to bomb the railways, or even the camps, to disturb the smooth implementation of the deportations and extermination. The Jewish people were left to their fate.

The result was that 1.7 million innocent Jewish people were murdered by the Nazis in Operation Reinhard.

The silence that prevailed in the fields of Belzec, Sobibor, and Treblinka after the dismantling of the camps did not last long. While the Germans still controlled the area, and, to a greater extent, immediately after the liberation, in the summer of 1944, shameful scenes occurred on the sites of the former death camps. Rumors spread among the local population in the areas close to the camps, and even in more distant places, that not all the bodies had been burned and that some of the victims had been buried with their clothes without having undergone a search. The informants claimed that in the seams and folds of the garments were hidden money, gold, and diamonds; there were also gold teeth that had not been removed. It was further said that the Jews who had been prisoners in the camps had buried great treasures. This was more than enough to bring farmers swarming all over the sites of the former death camps, digging and searching.

Rachel Auerbach, who visited Treblinka on November 7, 1945, as part of a delegation of the Polish State Committee for the Investigation of Nazi War Crimes on Polish Soil, described what she saw:

Masses of all kinds of pilferers and robbers with spades and shovels in their hands were there digging and searching and raking and straining the sand. They removed decaying limbs from the dust [and] bones and garbage that were thrown there. Would they not come upon even one hard coin or at least one gold tooth? They even dragged shells and blind bombs there, those hyenas and jackals in the disguise of man. They placed several together, set them off, and giant pits were dug in the desecrated ground saturated by the blood and the ashes of burned Jews . . .

Scenes of this kind also took place in the fields of Belzec and Sobibor. The search for treasures continued. The area was dug up again and again, and each section of the land was checked thoroughly by local people and people from afar who tried their luck. These acts ceased only when the Polish government decided to turn the camp areas into national memorial sites. These memorials bear witness to the tragedies and massacres that were carried out on these sites and will remain for generations a mark of shame and disgrace, a reminder of the brutality and inhumanity that were the essence of Nazi Germany, and a warning to all peoples of the deadly dangers of racism and hatred.

[*Belzec, Sobibor, Treblinka: The Operation Reinhard Death Camps* (Bloomington: Indiana University Press, 1987), 377–80.]

FRANK GOLCZEWSKI

92   Poland

Up to 90 per cent of Polish Jewry was murdered by the National Socialist regime. In the following piece, Frank Golczewski discusses the problems of arriving at reliable figures; as importantly, he emphasizes the extent to which Jewish life in Poland was effectively destroyed.

Reference to the census average of 3,350,000 Jews in 1939 leaves one, through a simple process of subtraction (without taking into account the relevant territorial expansion of the state), with a figure of c.3,000,000 murdered Polish Jews. Hilberg,[1] Krakowski,[2] and Gilbert[3] arrive at this figure. It would appear, however, to be too high. This is even more the case for the first estimates after the war, which went as far as 3,271,000.[4] In a first scholarly attempt Reitlinger assumed a range of variation between 2,350,000 and 2,600,000, emphasizing however that these were only 'approximate estimates'.[5] We are more inclined to subtract the 300,000 returnees from those who fell under German power prior to 1941. Gerald Fleming[6] and Czeslaw Madajczyk[7] also assume 2,770,000 Polish Jewish victims. As the latter assumes 110,000 Polish Jews in Displaced Person camps in the rest of Europe and, following Reitlinger, reaches a figure of a further c.500,000 in the USSR, Madajczyk assumes 890,000 Polish Jewish survivors.[8] [. . .] The addition of realistic lowest figures for the Polish-Jewish victims of the extermination centres is:

Chelmno (first phase)	215,000
Sobibór	80,000
Belzec	390,000
Treblinka	974,000[9]
Auschwitz	300,000
Majdanek	50,000
Chelmno (second phase)	10,000
	2,019,000

Madajczyk ascribes 2,000,000 victims to these centres. He also, however, estimates approximately 700,000 further deaths in ghettos, in labour camps, and as a consequence of direct murder (task squads, executions, arbitrary violence in 1939).[10] Hitherto it has appeared impossible to substantiate firmly this last figure.

Taking the population deficit and the sum of the minimum figures for proven murders the stated figure of 2,700,000 can, however, be regarded as realistic, with the proviso that it is more likely to need revision upwards rather than downwards.

The damage done to the Jewish population is only partially indicated, however, by reference to the murders committed by the German National Socialists. Polish Jewry was dealt a fatal blow as a living human community. The process of demographic renewal was dramatically interrupted. The unnatural living conditions of the Polish Jews can be seen as one reason why the birth figures fell drastically and soon reached a level approaching zero. The deviation of the birth rates from the normal situation prevented the normal regeneration of European Jewry after the Second World War down to the present day—the survivors, of whom not all were capable of having children after their experience of suffering and medical experiments, comprised an aged population; Poland is no exception here.

Taking everything into account, the figure of 300,000 survivors appears realistic in relation to those Jews living within the borders of the Polish state after 1945. But life for these people was also far from secure thereafter. The initial post-war years in Poland were formed by civil war, political power struggles, and the attempts to overcome the consequences of the war. And yet there was no cessation of anti-Semitism in the liberated country. Not a few Poles had profited materially by the German persecution of the Jews, and were attempting to secure their property. 'Gold-diggers' flooded into the camp locations and dug for valuables hidden by the inmates.[11] Abstruse accusations of ritual murder revived, and assumptions within right-wing circles of an identity of interest between Jews and Communists poisoned the atmosphere. As a result of the Polish civil war, but also of the Cracow pogrom of 11 August 1945 and that of Kielce of 4 July 1946 (c.40 dead), along with numerous other cases, which among other things involved the return of housing given to the Poles by the National Socialists, Jews met with violent deaths in Poland once more.[12]

The rest were expelled in the subsequent decades. An orderly emigration to Israel[13] or to other emigration states (USA, Australia) was possible for some years after the Second World War. After 1957 some Jews could leave Poland as part of the process of reuniting German families which had been agreed with the Federal Republic of Germany. Almost all the remaining Polish Jews were driven out of the country in the 1968 'anti-Zionist' (in reality, in Poland, anti-Semitic) smear campaign. About 5,000 remained, the overwhelming majority of whom were sick and old people, so that the day can be foreseen when Poland is a state without citizens of Jewish origin.

['Polen', in W. Benz (ed.), *Dimensionen des Völkermords: Die Zahl der jüdischen Opfer des Nationalsozialismus* (Munich: Oldenbourg, 1991), 494–7.]

MICHAEL BURLEIGH AND WOLFGANG WIPPERMANN

93   The Persecution of Sinti and Roma

One of the least well-known and at the same time most comprehensive acts of destruction on the part of the National Socialist regime was the genocide of the Sinti and Roma, which has consistently been overshadowed by the much larger genocide of the Jews. Up to 500,000 Sinti and Roma may have been killed in the Holocaust.

Throughout Germany in the Nazi period, both the citizenry and local authorities took it upon themselves to remove Sinti and Roma from private land, depositing them in *ad hoc* camps which gradually assumed coercive characteristics. For example, in Berlin prior to the 1936 Olympic Games, the authorities quite illegally rounded up about 600 Sinti and Roma, corralling them on an insalubrious wasteland near a sewage dump and a cemetery at Marzahn, a site which was particularly offensive to a people hyper-sensitive about cleanliness.[1] The justification for this measure was that the Sinti and Roma might sully the clean image of the Olympic host city. Many of them succumbed to diseases. Thereafter, the Berlin welfare authorities unsuccessfully tried to regularise this anomaly of their own making (while offloading the attendant costs of medical care) by pressing for the site's reclassification as a concentration camp. This practice would be emulated in several other German towns. [. . .]

A conference on racial policy organised by Heydrich took place in Berlin on 21 September 1939, which may have decided upon a 'Final Solution' of the 'Gypsy Question'.[2] According to the scant minutes which have survived, four issues were decided: the concentration of Jews in towns; their relocation to Poland; the removal of 30,000 'Gypsies' to Poland; and the systematic deportation of Jews from German incorporated territories using goods trains. An express letter sent by the Reich Main Security Office on 17 October 1939 to its local agents mentioned that the 'Gypsy Question will shortly be regulated throughout the territory of the Reich'.[3] Thenceforth, Sinti and Roma were confined to designated sites and encampments. Those who attempted to leave were sent to concentration camps. Many Sinti and Roma were actually in camps already, on account of activities deemed to be 'criminal' or 'asocial'.[4] Many Sinti and Roma were taken into 'protective custody' during the large-scale round-up of the 'asocial' in 1938.[5] In October 1939 they were joined by 'soothsayers', whom Himmler regarded as a potential threat to national morale.[6] In June 1940 the Reich Security Main Office forbade the release of Sinti and Roma serving determinate concentration camp or regular prison sentences.[7] At about this time, Adolf Eichmann made the recommendation that the 'Gypsy Question' be solved simultaneously with the 'Jewish Question' by appending 'three or four trucks' of Sinti and Roma to the trains taking Jews from Vienna to the Generalgouvernement.[8] In fact, matters did not run so smoothly, although some 2,500 Sinti and Roma were deported to Poland from the western areas of the Reich between April and May 1940 as an alleged 'security threat'.[9] A few of them managed to survive on the loose as entertainers or musicians. Most of them either simply starved to death or were used by the SS as forced labour. Those who fell sick were shot. Some 80 per cent of those deported from Hamburg alone failed to return alive. Plans to follow up these modest numbers with the wholesale deportation of Germany's 30,000 Sinti and Roma met with the opposition of Hans Frank, Hitler's satrap in occupied Poland,[10] although 5,000 were deported from the Burgenland to the Łódź ghetto, to be subsequently gassed in Chelmno in January 1942. Major deportations of Sinti and Roma were halted so as to give priority to the deportation of Jews, whose homes were needed for ethnic German repatriates. For once, an itinerant way of life reprieved the Sinti and Roma from persecution. This meant that the earlier short-term policy of corralling them in *ad hoc* camps became a long-term affair. Conditions in camps like Marzahn, and Lackenbach and Salzburg in Austria, were atrocious.[11] Those held in Lackenbach were subjected to beatings, solitary confinement, dietary deprivation, heavy manual labour, and such indignities as the shaving of their heads. The authorities' response to epidemic disease was: 'Massive loss of life in the restricted area only interests us in so far as it represents a threat to the non-Gypsy population'.[12] In the case of camps in towns or near villages, matters were made worse by the constant complaints from people living or working in their proximity that the Sinti and Roma were 'spies' or a threat to the morals of the local population. Complaints made by 'national comrades' were then used by local authorities to demand the Sinti and Roma's deportation. The Criminal Police responded by saying that a final decision in this case was pending.

As in the case of the Jews, the invasion of the Soviet Union marked the transition from persecution to extermination. SS Einsatzgruppen and units of the regular army and police began shooting Sinti and Roma in Russia, Poland, and the Balkans.[13] Possibly as many as 250,000 Sinti and Roma died in these actions, which were legitimised with the old prejudice that the victims were 'spies'.

Differences of opinion at the highest levels of government account for the final equivocations in the resolution of the 'Gypsy Question'. Himmler, encouraged by his SS 'Ancestral Heritage' organisation, wanted to keep a few token clans of pure Sinti, Roma and Bohemian Lalleri alive on a reservation, as a form of ethnic curiosity.[14] This scheme was opposed by Martin Bormann—as the spokesman of both Hitler and the ordinary NSDAP membership—notwithstanding the very small number of people Himmler intended to keep alive. Himmler signed the order despatching Germany's Sinti and Roma to Auschwitz on 16 December 1942.[15] The 'Final Solution' of the 'Gypsy Question' had begun. The order sending Sinti and Roma to Auschwitz mentioned categories of exempt persons, which were ignored by Himmler's Criminal Police subordinates who carried out the deportations.

[*The Racial State: Germany 1933–1945* (Cambridge: Cambridge University Press, 1991), 117–18, 121–5.]

Section G

The Legacy of National Socialism

INTRODUCTION

Nazism's impact did not cease with the total defeat of the regime in 1945. As a consequence of National Socialist war, occupation, terror and genocide there were millions of 'Displaced Persons' all over Europe. First, there were the survivors of forced labour, ghettos, concentration camps, and extermination camps—most, but not all, of whom wished to return home; there were millions of refugees, above all those who had been expelled from their homes as or shortly after the Red Army liberated central and eastern Europe; in addition, there were millions of prisoners of war, evacuees, and homeless who had to be returned to their homes and housed. The huge physical destruction wrought by the land war and by air raids was such that in the west overcoming this situation took a full fifteen years; in parts of eastern Europe it took much longer.

As the Cold War set in and economies first stabilized and then boomed, some memories of Nazism were perpetuated while others were suppressed. In West Germany, the 1950s witnessed the emergence of a culture in which ordinary Germans came to regard themselves as having been the main victims of the regime and the war. Thousands of local memorials were established to the victims of allied air raids, to German soldiers missing in action or held as prisoners of war, and to those who had suffered expulsion from the east. The fate of the Jews, not to mention the many other groups who had suffered as racial or political persecutees, received no such recognition. Although the Federal government under Chancellor Adenauer agreed to pay restitution to Israel in 1952, this and similar gestures were always motivated as much by calculation as by contrition—for example, by the desire to facilitate West Germany's integration into the west—and were often opposed by broad currents of popular opinion. Further, although 95 per cent of Nazism's victims had been foreign, only 5 per cent of the compensation paid by the West German government to those who had suffered as a result of Nazism went to non-Germans.

In East Germany, the official doctrine of 'anti-fascism' used to legitimize the fledgling Communist Republic also led to the swift marginalization of the Jews in official discussions of the Nazi past. Celebration of the Communist resistance to Nazism, embodied most famously in the Buchenwald memorial, went hand in hand with a successive downplaying of the Jews as passive and increasingly deracialized 'victims of fascism'. The Cold War context in which post-war engagement with the legacies of Nazism occurred meant that the German Democratic Republic never made any restitution payments to Israel, with whom it did not establish diplomatic relations prior to 1989, and moves in the 1980s to reach accommodation with American-based Jewish groups were motivated not least by the declining East German state's desire to gain 'most favoured nation' status from the USA. Official constructions of the Nazi regime as the 'dictatorship of monopoly capitalism' meant that the German Democratic Republic could claim to have dealt fully and finally with Nazism by having nationalized all industry; the implied exoneration of ordinary workers and peasants did not, however, lead the Communist elites to feel that they could trust ordinary East Germans with democratic rights after 1945.

Far from being a period of silence, the 1950s was a period in which the Nazi past had a profound immediacy. Debates over the amnestying of former Nazis, the payment of compensation and restitution, West German rearmament, and the suspension of the statute of limitations took place in an environment in which the physical scars on the landscape provided daily reminders of the recent past. However, the 1950s witnessed in the Federal Republic a rapid scaling down of judicial prosecution of Nazi crimes, the widespread amnestying of those who were deemed to have committed only minor offences, and the reintegration of most former perpetrators and participants into society. Although the immediate process of denazification was harsher in the Soviet zone, this pattern also established itself in the East German Republic, as the regime similarly connived in the fostering of the myth of the guilty Nazi leadership and the innocent mass of the population.

For some in the west, this reintegration was a necessary precondition for the stabilization of West German democracy. For others, such a generous policy of rehabilitation meant that hundreds of thousands of people in bureaucracy, administration, business, and the judiciary were not punished adequately, if at all; many critical voices spoke of a 'renazification' of public life and of a 'restoration' which would inevitably have a strong retarding effect on the formation of a liberal, democratic political culture. Such critical voices gained a more favourable audience in the 1960s, when a series of events and cultural shifts contributed to bringing the issue of unpunished pasts to the fore. In 1958, the trial in Ulm of members of one of the *Einsatz-gruppen* which had operated in the Soviet Union was instrumental in raising awareness that many perpetrators had yet to face justice. The 1961 Eichmann Trial in Jerusalem and the Frankfurt Auschwitz Trial were among the many subsequent high-profile trials to reinforce this, while the electoral gains of the far Right in 1966 ensured the renewed topicality of fascism in contemporary life.

As the culture of popular self-pity gave way to a more critical attitude to the Nazi past, the victim mentality of West German society was superseded by a climate in which the real victims of Nazism's racial and political persecution began to receive more recognition. The Holocaust began to move to the centre of both popular and academic discussions of the Nazi past; the easing of east–west relations and the subsiding of the virulent anti-Communism of the 1950s and early 1960s helped to create a climate in which victim groups such as Soviet prisoners of war or forced labourers could be given more proper treatment. The 1970s and 1980s witnessed a substantial broadening of public discussion of the Nazi past in which a more differentiated understanding of both the nature of the perpetrators and the experience of the victims began to emerge. The 1980s were also, however, characterized by neo-conservative attempts to consign the Nazi past to history and to relativize the crimes of the regime by suggesting that they had been a natural response to the threat of Communism or by comparing them to those of other genocidal regimes. Most famously, the ineptitude of President Reagan and Chancellor Kohl's behaviour over their visit to the Bitburg war cemetery became the prelude to the rancorous 'historians' dispute' of 1986/7, which centred around the contested significance of the Nazi past for the identity of the Federal Republic.

Arguments about national past and political identity were of necessity radically reframed by the reunification of Germany in 1989/90. In some ways, the reunification of Germany had a positive effect on discussion of the Nazi past, liberating it from the ideologically loaded framework of the Cold War. On the other hand, it might also be said merely to have substituted one political and cultural moment for another, leading for example to the renewed assertion of a more affirmative national history from some quarters, and engendering a culture of post-Cold War triumphalism which fed not least back into histories of the early Federal Republic and its supposed success in coming to terms with the past compared to East Germany. The past remains as contested in Germany now as it ever was. Ongoing controversies suggest that in some ways it is becoming more present as it recedes into the temporal distance. The 1990s have witnessed public arguments over the role of big business, banks, and insurance companies in the Holocaust; they have witnessed popular debates on the role of ordinary Germans as perpetrators, culminating in the famous 'Goldhagen controversy'; they have witnessed related conflicts over the 'crimes of the *Wehrmacht*' stimulated by a controversial touring exhibition on the subject; they have also witnessed a protracted debate over whether and how to memorialize the Holocaust in the 'new' capital, Berlin. Such disputes provide a telling prism through which contemporary German society and culture can be observed. Whether these conflicts and the memories they stir remain as immediate in the future as they are now, whether they are the product of a particular transitional moment as the generation which experienced Nazism first-hand rapidly dies out, or whether they start to recede as the history of the Third Reich is no longer 'this century's history' but that of the last, remains to be seen.

i Confronting the Past

PETER STEINBACH

94 **On the Engagement with National Socialist Violent Crimes in the Federal Republic of Germany**

In the following passages, Peter Steinbach discusses the ways in which public opinion in the 1950s militated against the successful prosecution of perpetrators of crimes committed during the National Socialist era.

Although during the years of National Socialist rule the Germans had become eyewitnesses to the defamation, repression, ghettoization, and persecution of political opponents, of minorities defined as 'unworthy', and of Jews, they appeared initially after the liberation from National Socialism to have been surprised by the extent and nature of the mass shootings and by the almost unquantifiable system of industrial-style murder in extermination camps. The worst rumours, the broadcasts of allied radio stations, and allied leaflets were surpassed by the reality. No one could be in any doubt that the National Socialists had not only prosecuted a war against the rest of the world, but also a 'war against the Jews'.[1] The war aim of destroying European Jewry, the 'Final Solution', was pursued all the more vehemently by them the more the military 'final victory' was in doubt. The allies had already announced during the war that the violent crimes of the National Socialists would be punished; directly following the occupation of the Reich preparations were begun for large-scale trials, which at the least had the following goals:

- to punish a 'criminal elite' in accordance with international law and in a manner which set standards;
- to create a basis for an orderly denazification which was not arbitrary and which conformed to legal norms;
- to spread knowledge of the criminal character of National Socialism, in order to prevent the emergence of legends which would burden the future and thus hinder the process of democratization.

The Nuremberg Trial of 1945–6, which took place with the participation of all the allies, and the subsequent Nuremberg trials were able to achieve some of these goals. In particular, they illuminated in a manner which is still accepted today the fact and the extent of the crimes of National Socialism.

'Crimes against humanity' referred to all those acts which today still are judged according to paragraph 211 of the Criminal Code (Murder), and which mostly constituted large criminal case bodies because they made many participants from all levels of the decision-making process (from 'desk perpetrators' through organizers down to those doing the shooting) into murderers and accomplices to murder. The main case bodies of National Socialist crimes were made known at Nuremberg and in part also became the objects of the so-called subsequent trials. However, the prosecution of National Socialist misdeeds by the (western) allies ceased comparatively quickly at the end of the 1940s, National Socialist perpetrators were amnestied, and the will to enlighten and to prosecute appeared to wane. This was connected in part to the experiences of many Germans of denazification, whereby clearly their will but also their ability to differentiate and to distinguish criminal from political guilt disappeared. Many felt persecuted and pardoned themselves and all the other denazified people, war criminals, and National Socialist violent criminals at the same time.[2] The conceptual differentiation between different types of incrimination only established itself later and must be mentioned as an important precondition for the judicial punishment by German courts since the late 1950s. In addition to the exculpatory self-pity of many Germans there were the attempts to set the guilt of the Germans against the alleged wrongs and behaviour of the victors. The excesses of Soviet soldiers, deportations, the bombing of civilians and of cities of no importance to the war effort (Dresden, Würzburg, among others, in the last months of the war), expulsion, and internment were juxtaposed to the Germans' crimes in the political discussions of pub regulars. From the practice of balancing out there followed an equation of war crimes and National Socialist crimes—with the result that unambiguous acts of murder were hardly regarded and condemned by society as such, but rather threatened to sink into general oblivion: in the general consciousness of former soldiers war crimes were always taken relatively easily for granted.

Neither were the developments in international politics conducive to an unsparing punishment of National Socialist crimes. The emergence of the Cold War led on the allied and on the German side to an increasingly lax denazification process and to the imposition of trivial punishments; in this process the difficult denazification cases were initially to be left to the end, to facilitate an exact investigation of the offences. In the context of the debate over rearmament a wide-scale amnesty of war criminals was pushed for, especially on the part of the Germans. This demand may not have been met in every respect by the western allies—thus even in 1951 the death penalty was carried out on condemned *Einsatzgruppen* leaders—but nonetheless they did not ignore it and released many of the highest war criminals, who because they could not be convicted twice for the same act often—not always!—remained unpunished thereafter.[3] In the 1950s thus—with the exception perhaps of the euthanasia proceedings and of the National Socialist crimes against political dissidents and the Jews within the Reich—all political signals pointed in the direction of a general amnesty. R. M. Kempner, one of the best-informed people on this set of problems, even spoke of a highly effective 'mercy lobby',[4] which was strengthened not least by the constitutionally guaranteed re-employment obligation in favour of German civil servants (paragraph 131 of the Basic Law). In the 1950s the will and the ability to punish in court National Socialist crimes seemed to have waned widely; only the return of the German prisoners of war from the Soviet Union brought new information about crimes which had been elaborately kept secret by the National Socialists but which had been recognized clearly as crimes by their puppets. In this sense the silence of many in the 1950s reflected their clear awareness of having committed crimes.[5]

To offer a summarizing judgement on the 1950s, the fact that their end brought with it a new increase in the will to investigate and to punish seems almost like a political miracle. The German parties could hardly become a motor of this development—apart from the SPD, in whose ranks were many resistance fighters. After all, after 1945 the parties had the task, among other things, of integrating into the political system of the Federal Republic many of the incriminated people, many of the fellow-travellers, and also ordinary party members.[6] This task was fulfilled by many of the small middle-class parties. We cannot criticize this development in the abstract, as every political or social upheaval gives rise to the problem of reintegration; however, the question arises of the cost of integrating the fellow-travellers and the committed, even incorrigible, National Socialists, who may even have incurred criminal guilt. As individual social and professional groups were deemed to be particularly incriminated and self-righteous—one thinks for example of senior judges, of doctors, of civil servants or officers—the question of their particular guilt came up repeatedly, but in part the impression also arose that the punishment of their crimes—such as the judicial mass murder under the People's Court or the murder of the mentally ill under the co-responsibility of the doctors—was not being pursued resolutely. This impression emerged above all in that sector of the public which in the 1950s too demanded the unrelenting prosecution of National Socialist perpetrators; among the great majority, however, there was a widespread wish to draw a line under the past. It may correspond to the laws of democracy if the politicians orientate themselves by the views of the majority—but it is then all the more surprising that the judicial prosecution of National Socialist crimes did not grind to a complete halt under the influence of public opinion as manifested in opinion polls.

['Zur Auseinandersetzung mit nationalsozialistischen Gewaltverbrechen in der Bundesrepublik Deutschland', *Geschichte in Wissenschaft und Unterricht* (1984/2), 65–8.]

95 Post-war Society and National Socialism: Memory, Amnesia, Defensiveness

> Awareness of central aspects of National Socialism was repressed by broad sectors of the population after 1945; other central aspects reproduced themselves, in different ways, in post-war attitudes and culture. Both processes shaped public and private memories of the Third Reich and were central in the consolidation of exculpatory responses to it, as Wolfgang Benz analyses here.

The collapse of the National Socialist regime was followed by a phase of public memory and mental working through of what had happened. From 1945 on, this found its expression on a literary level in numerous published memoirs from the persecuted and the resistance[1] along with a contemplative literature by authors from Romano Guardini to Alfred Weber.[2] Above all (up till 1948) numerous cultural and political journals devoted themselves to the problem of the spiritual overcoming of National Socialism.[3] This was—quite unintentionally—counteracted by the efforts of the occupation forces, above all of the Americans, to use educational means to confront the Germans with the atrocities which they had committed, through, for example, enforced visits to the concentration camps and, in general, through the machinery of denazification. The strong engagement of the military government and the everyday experience of powerlessness on the part of German offices led to amnesia, to a distancing from that which had occurred, which could be compensated for by the achievements of reconstruction. The sizeable and early success of reconstruction intensified into defensiveness, as existing structures such as anti-Semitism, anti-Communism, and the feeling of having been forced into the position of loser again (loss of capacity for self-determination and of the unity of the nation) combined with immediate guilt and traditional inferiority complexes.

In large sectors of German post-war society the willingness to maintain memory was then buried by defensive mechanisms, which were kept up with slogans such as the 'collective guilt theory' or 're-education', with covering memories (Dresden, allied war crimes, expulsion of the Germans from eastern central Europe), or with political scare slogans (Soviet imperialism, American economic penetration). [. . .]

The findings of the anti-Semitism survey of the autumn of 1949* can be summarized as follows: that most Germans retained the old prejudices; that

---

* One of a number of surveys on German public opinion carried out by the US military government.

behind occasional expressions of regret and commitments to restitution there was little understanding or insight; that defensiveness and reservedness dominated. On the way to a democratic society the Germans, if one is to believe the results of opinion polls, had invested little effort in gaining knowledge and understanding of the impact of one of the most central points of the National Socialist programme, namely the consequences of the translation of anti-Semitism into political practice and destruction.

Another ideological tradition was carried forward even more strongly, one which, in contrast to anti-Semitism, could also be expressed openly—and with profit: anti-Communism. Indeed, the strict rejection of Communism formed a central element of the founding consensus behind the Federal Republic and was perhaps the most important part of the West Germans' state doctrine. The fact that anti-Semitism and anti-Bolshevism had been two similar and interrelated components of Nazi ideology was quickly forgotten after 1945. The anti-Semitic part was separated off and repressed; the anti-Communist sentiment could be deployed all the better for this. Of course many Germans experienced extensive feelings of shame and guilt, but these were eased in traditional fashion. People's own suffering—the flood of refugees, everyday life under the occupation, homelessness, hunger, housing shortages—was foremost and acted to divert attention.

The 'Displaced Persons', who were housed in barracks, were of foreign origin, mostly actually spoke Yiddish (which German Jews had never done), and who naturally initially were mostly treated better by the allies on account of their suffering, were regarded just as unsympathetically by the average German as victims of the Nazi regime as those who had been liberated from the concentration camps as anti-fascist,[4] since people had a guilty conscience with respect to them. People sought consolation in the rebuilding of the physical damage, and soon most accustomed themselves to thinking of this as a form of restitution, and it was not long then before pride in German hard work and superiority flourished once more.

Consolation was not only found in the euphoria of reconstruction, however. The assumption that war, and participation in it, were necessary means for the successful pursuit of national aspirations made it easier after 1945 for many to dismiss and excuse the atrocious and shameful acts of the National Socialist regime. The phrase 'it was war, after all' helped (and helps) many to repress or at least to trivialize the facts of the persecution of the Jews, the extermination camps, the murder of Soviet prisoners of war in contravention of international law, and other *genuine and historically singular* National Socialist atrocities. Such an argument rests not only, however, on the fatal assumption that war is in itself necessary or unavoidable, but also on the illusion that this war had been one of excessive dimension but still, so to speak, a normal and necessary war. The Second World War was not such a war, as it consisted not only of conquest or defence, of the expansion of German territory and the acquisition of resources: the National Socialist regime intended the destruction, eradication, and enslavement of entire peoples; it intended the implementation of an inhumane ideology with all means. The evidence for this does not need to be expounded here. The key words: the task squads of the SS, who murdered innocent and defenceless civilians in their hundreds of thousands because they were Jewish or were deemed to be 'political commissars' of the Red Army; the preconceived deaths of over 3 million Soviet prisoners of war; the campaign of annihilation against the Polish intelligentsia; the policies of 'Germanization' in the east. The Second World War was the actual and ultimate embodiment of National Socialist policy.

At the same time, however, this war could also naively be understood as the defence of the Fatherland against external enemies. And in this manner it came to fulfil a particular function in the repression of the past: memory of the war survived to cover the crimes of the regime and one's own guilt in them—for the unaware or knowing majority and for the minority who had participated actively. The Second World War acquired the function of normalizing the National Socialist regime in memory; at the same time, however, this memory helped to separate the regime off from the German people, as through this one could distinguish retrospectively between the brave soldiers on the front and their helpers in the homeland, who did their duty in the defence of German soil, German culture, of themselves and their families— they were the good side—and the functionaries of National Socialism, the party bosses, the SS—they were the criminals.[5]

The fact that the boundary between good and bad was not so easy to draw is easier to recognize with hindsight than it was for those affected at the time. For everyone who had welcomed Hitler's diplomatic and military successes, because they regarded this as underlining their patriotism, without meaning that they were Nazis, could subjectively claim the feeling and status of innocence. This was no less true for domestic politics. Most people had not murdered, had not appropriated the property of others, had not held captive, tortured, deported, or exterminated people on grounds of their religion, origin, or political conviction. Of course, most people had known of the atrocities of the regime, but on the one hand this was not punishable by law, and on the other many felt morally compromised and chastized simply because of this knowledge, which accounts for the long-persisting collective insistence that no one had known anything.

['Nachkriegsgesellschaft und Nationalsozialismus: Erinnerung, Amnesie, Abwehr', in *Erinnern oder Verweigern*, Dachauer Hefte 6 (Dachau: Verlag Dachauer Hafte, 1990), 13, 19–21.]

The question of amnestying past crimes, of releasing imprisoned war criminals or former Nazis, and of reintegrating such 'victims of denazification' (as they were widely and sympathetically regarded in West Germany) into society and professional life was central to the domestic political agenda of the 1950s. A broad political consensus existed between the Christian Democrats and SPD on the policy of amnesty and reintegration. Cold War exigencies aside, as Norbert Frei argues, this was largely due the fact that both major parties had to appeal for votes in a fledgling democracy whose population, only ten years earlier, would have voted overwhelmingly for Hitler, and who now refused to accept the reality of the enormity of the crimes committed by and under the regime, especially in the east.

The amnesties for National Socialist perpetrators, the reintegration of the 'victims of the purges', the release of the war criminals, and, not least, the depoliticization of the civil service as a result of its material corruption through the Law on Paragraph 131 produced effects far beyond the circle of those who benefited directly. Together they also served to satisfy collective emotional needs of a society which had undergone a singular political and moral catastrophe in the 1940s, the memory of which concealed deeply disruptive experiences of social disintegration thereafter. Here—and not only in the structurally, politically, and communicatively tangible asymmetry between the majority of fellow-travellers and the minority of victims—were obviously also important reasons for the widespread silence, and indeed consent, with which the latter accompanied this process of inner pacification. This was at the cost of living memory. The question of how far the former victims suffered as a result of this ossification and ritualization is an open one and perhaps cannot be answered at a general level; it is quite clear, however, that the concomitant political deactualization of remembrance made life easier for the former fellow-travellers.

The desire to draw a strong line under the decade of chaos—in which were also included with little differentiation the post-war years, during which time even the Social Democrat Adolf Arndt saw 'traces of a civil war'—and to face the hoped-for better future was firmly fixed in the minds of the Germans at the beginning of the 1950s. Included within this, as an element of the oft-noted increased desire for security of the 'Adenauer era', was the desire for self-rehabilitation: a society which could register the first successes of economic and political reconstruction, but which had still to wait both for recognition from the controlling powers and its neighbours, and for the return of state sovereignty, more or less 'excused' itself. In this sense the excessive desire for peace and integration also reflected a normality which was withheld from 'outside' but impatiently yearned for within.

Maybe in this sense it is not going too far to see in the notorious demands for integration and amnesty also the substitute expressions of a politically debased but still virulent nationalism which Adenauer had practically forbidden the Germans. The fact is that the old nationalist sentiments and forces thrived in few fields as much as in that of the 'politics of the past'—and that the Chancellor, focused on a quick and firm binding of the 'core' German state to the west, often appeared as a lone voice preaching reason and moderacy in pursuit of his central goal. [. . .]

In such an atmosphere of willing silence concerning the National Socialist past of individuals, conflicts over individuals such as Globke, which occurred occasionally but which were in no sense systematically instrumentalized, were really only the exception that proved the rule. Driven by the debate over war criminals, an interpretation of the National Socialist era gained currency which did not deny the fact of the acts of which people were accused, but which increasingly subsumed these within the 'horrors of modern warfare', with the activities of partisans or with the 'turmoil of war' in general, and which transplanted them to nebulous locations 'in the east' in which real Germans as perpetrators were almost impossible now to imagine. Even an *Einsatzgruppen* leader who had originally been condemned to death and who had been proven to have committed mass murder could, under such circumstances, be seen again primarily as a former academic pupil or the son of a Württemberg notable and reckon on the advocacy of a Carlo Schmid or Theodor Heuss. Top industrialists or civil servants who had been condemned at Nuremberg, such as Ernst von Weizsäcker, profited from such '(social-) neighbourly' or 'collegial' help to a far greater extent, even.

In summary, one must conclude that by the middle of the 1950s a general attitude had established itself that saw the responsibility for the crimes of the Third Reich as solely that of Hitler and a small clique of 'major war criminals', while ascribing to the Germans as a whole the status of politically 'misled' people who, as a result of the war and its consequences, had themselves even been turned into victims. The millions of former soldiers had to be allowed to retain the possibility of seeing a meaning in their deployment, at the expense of historical truth. The war was thus followed by a struggle for memory: the question of the fundamentally criminal character of the German aggression, of its barbarism and sheer madness from the outset, posed so clearly at Nuremberg—and, for foreign opinion, answered quite clearly—was repressed. Here are to be found the causes of the obstinate insistence on an interpretation which placed the Second World War in a continuum with the First World War and which—partly out of innocence, partly intentionally and knowingly—claimed for the Second World War a normality which the singular crimes of the Germans could not claim.

If the fragility of this interpretative framework did not really become a problem until well into the 1960s then this was a product of the soon-emergent 'hyperstability' (Richard Löwenthal) of the young Federal Republic, which was based not least on the achievements of 'policy towards the past'. The careful shift which began around 1959–60—above all initially in the field of the scandalously neglected judicial engagement with the National Socialist past and the not less scandalous continuities in personnel within the judiciary—was, as with so much in the Adenauer era, mainly induced from outside: by Israel, which, as the land of the victims, searched for those perpetrators living abroad untroubled by the German authorities, and which apprehended Adolf Eichmann in Argentina in the spring of 1960; by the eastern bloc states, who were now, as even the worst crimes were threatening to fall under the statue of limitations, presenting documents and former victims of the mad German pursuit of 'living space in the East'; above all, however, by the GDR, which had attempted with much conspiratorial effort since the middle of the 1950s to use the facts and problems of the 'unmastered past' in order to destabilize the Federal Republic.

The emergence from the 'long 1950s' in terms of the 'politics of the past' now gradually set in, but it needed further generational shifts before a fundamental change could occur with the beginnings of the students' movement. In place of those interpretations inspired by the theory of totalitarianism, in which the Third Reich appeared as an alien regime which had effectively forced itself on Germany from outside with a small number of 'collaborators' and an army of harmless fellow-travellers, there emerged a growing awareness of the dimensions of the crimes of the 'Final Solution' and a critical examination of the social bases of National Socialism, of its leading groups, and of the complicity of those functional elites which were present again after 1945. It must be emphasized, however, that this development towards a serious public confrontation of National Socialism was preceded by a phase of great mildness towards individuals, which in some sense itself created the basis for a more open engagement with the past: the phase of the 'politics of the past' whose political errors and moral failings lastingly shaped the cultural climate of the Federal Republic.

[*Vergangenheitspolitik: die Anfänge der Bundesrepublik und die NS-Vergangenheit*
(Munich: C. H. Beck, 1996), 401–2, 405–6.]

LUTZ NIETHAMMER

97 The Fellow-Travellers' Factory

Lutz Niethammer's pioneering study of denazification in Bavaria, which originally appeared in 1972, showed how the Americans' understanding of Nazism as a personal quality led them to privilege a person-centred approach over structural reform; once in the control of German authorities, the emphasis quickly shifted from punishment to rehabilitation, with the bulk of the 'ordinary party comrades' being acquitted as fellow-travellers (*Mitläufer*).

In retrospect denazification is regarded by many West Germans as that process by which any share of responsibility on their part for fascism in Germany and for its consequences was more than dealt with, and namely in a discriminatory and corrupt fashion. This is true in that, with the exception of particular criminals who had been personally involved in mass murder in the Third Reich, hardly anyone was officially accused and punished for having been a member of a National Socialist organization or having otherwise—for example through having occupied a powerful position in society—facilitated the establishment or functioning of fascist dictatorship in Germany. This is further true in that denazification represented, in its impenetrable motives and consequences, a temporary period of discrimination, and that its implementation offered numerous opportunities for corruption. Nonetheless, this widely held opinion is in essence false. It neglects to mention that under denazification purging and rehabilitation merged into one and the same process; that the discrimination which the American purging policy of 1945 represented for members of National Socialist organizations in powerful positions in society was almost totally abandoned by the tribunals; and that corruption in the tribunals came above all from the accused or worked in their favour.

Denazification drove above all a large part of the middle classes and public sector employees into a defensive attitude immediately following the Third Reich and impeded impulses towards an active political reorientation of the mass of former Nazi followers; rather, it strengthened their inclinations to adapt themselves to whatever regime was in power, as long as this enables private success without public conflict. As the measure of a liberal occupation dictatorship which had got bogged down it also paralysed autochthonous alternatives to fascism, insofar as on the Right it undermined the beginnings of an authoritarian system of law and order and in that on the Left it took the wind out of the sails of anti-fascist structural reform aiming at social restructuring. Even before the dramatic intensification of the Cold War, American-style denazification created, under the pretext of radical measures against National Socialism, the social bases for integration into the west. These contributed to overcoming the deep-seated social crisis following the collapse of fascism through stabilizing interventions on the part of the occupation authorities which favoured substantial continuities in the social order and the unhindered establishment of liberal parliamentary institutions. At the same time, however, denazification demanded a reduction in scope of these liberal ambitions. For, in the process of dampening down authoritarian and socialist alternatives to fascism, the regaining of public confidence in the rule of law had to be postponed, while among large groups interest in political participation could not be awakened.

Such consequences were not, however, the product of the realization of long-held plans, but emerged step by step through a complex process of interaction between very diverse interests and conceptions on the part of the occupation authorities and of the Germans, and between them. Only a concrete, detailed examination of these forces and their interaction can contribute to explaining a process in which a gigantic intended purge metamorphosed into a no less monstrous rehabilitation campaign and suppressed the possibility of a public working through of the experience of fascism. [. . .]

The conditions which denazification in the western zones created for society under the Federal Republic do not consist of a substantial transformation of the social structure. Here its consequences were confined to a declining small proportion of the population (the National Socialist political leadership); beyond that, they represented a temporary period of fear for those affected rather than a lasting social reality. In contrast to the direct consequences of the war, which were characterized by their socially arbitrary distribution among the population and thus overwhelmingly affected the socially weaker, the temporary social effects of denazification—which were with few exceptions reversed by the judgements of the tribunals—clearly had their main impact on the middle class, both among the independent middle class and the 'service class' i.e. the public sector.

The temporary exclusion of the mass of the bourgeois middle classes, who were waiting to be rehabilitated by the tribunals, misled many Social Democrats and other progressives into a euphoric belief in the possibilities of more wide-scale reform and initially gave them a dominant public role. As, however, the exceptional circumstances of collapse, whose difficult material conditions initially encouraged pragmatic reconstruction and the postponement of reform, began to give way to an unreformed normalization of living conditions and to the beginnings of a new economic upturn, the denazified also returned, 'fellow-traveller pass' in their pocket, back to positions in which they had never really been replaced, believing that they had been wronged and that chaos would rule without them. If progressives understood this to be a restoration, they failed to recognize that freedom of disposition at the so-called 'zero hour' was above all in the hand of the occupation powers.

The basic experience of those affected by denazification was the threat to their social status by repressive acts of the occupation powers in the field of personnel policy, the period of waiting during a period of general need and abnormality caused by the ban on employment, and rehabilitation by a quasi-punishment which—and this was something positive for those affected—branded them as a political opportunist and penalized them with a symbolic fine. This occurred in 1947–8 at just the right time to enable them to participate from the beginning in the consolidation of socio-economic relations and to profit from it. For some of those affected professional reintegration was delayed by the period of unemployment which followed the currency reform, but this did not distinguish them from other sectors of the population, including the tribunal personnel. From the beginning of the 1950s, however, the 'fellow-travellers' were also reintegrated into public service without social discrimination.

The risk of political engagement which was made clear by denazification may have disadvantaged the bourgeois parties in the establishment of their mass membership organizations. However, one cannot trace the political-organizational inactivity and the prioritizing of the work and family sphere on the part of the bourgeois middle class too directly back to denazification, for, as the overwhelming majority of those affected by the tribunals attempted to make clear at their hearings—and their representation does not contradict the social history of fascist organizations before and after 1945—their membership of the party did not denote political engagement in the narrow sense of the word, but rather above all social protest and conformity without political commitment (which was concealed by surrogates such as faithfulness, the movement, dressing up in uniform, etc.), which, of course, was structurally adequate behaviour for the National Socialist regime. In as much as precisely this 'passive' engagement of the bourgeois middle classes, which had made the fascist system possible in the first place, along with the technical-professional fulfilment of functions by the elites, were accepted by the tribunals as normal behaviour and were rewarded with classification as a 'fellow-traveller' or with an amnesty, the lack of active democracy and the corresponding authoritarian predispositions, which have often been noted as key characteristics of the first fifteen years of the Federal Republic, were confirmed rather than caused by the denazification process.

On the other hand, the cadres of active NS functionaries were eliminated not by denazification, but by the defeat of fascism, and thus by the self-invalidation in the eyes of its followers of a legitimacy based on inner stability and external expansion. And, in this sense too, the purges legitimized rather than confirmed historical developments. The ever-recurring and ever-failing embittered attempts of middle- and high-ranking NS functionaries to reconstitute the NS support base in the Federal Republic only showed their lack of historical-political insight. They failed to see that this mainly middle-class support base was not bound to the NS leadership in 'firm loyalty', but regarded it with as much reservation and concern for peace, order, and personal success as they now did the parliamentary constitutional state under the FRG, only that now, under changed conditions, and on the basis of their experiences in the Third Reich, they recognized pluralism and the rule of law as better guarantors of their interests than fascist adventurers.

[*Die Mitläuferfabrik: die Entnazifizierung am Beispiel Bayerns*
(Bonn: Verlag J. H. W. Dietz Nachf., 1982), 653–4, 664–6.]

CLEMENS VOLLNHALS

98 Denazification

Clemens Vollnhals' assessment of the impact of denazification is representative of a generally critical attitude of most German scholars to the process.

If the judicial settling of accounts—beginning with the main trial before the International Military Tribunal in Nuremberg[1]—was by its nature focused on the past, then in the case of denazification the motive of general retribution and that of general prevention were directly linked. Did the change of political system and the removal from power of the old leadership caste make for an adequate break with the National Socialist past? Or was it not far more the case that the eradication of Nazism would falter halfway as long as the millions of former party members remained in high office and honour? If denazification was primarily to facilitate the replacement of elites as part of a limited political purge, then the main focus had to be on the occupation of a broadly defined set of key positions in politics, administration, economy, and cultural life with reliable democrats. Or should it, in the spirit of retribution, punish by dismissal all those who had participated in the National Socialist dictatorship as party members, in whatever form that had been?

This question had to be answered in the actual practice of occupation. As the victorious allied powers could not agree on a common definition of aims and procedures, each of them followed their own line. [. . .]

This fact alone necessarily undermined its moral legitimacy, the more circumstances returned to normality. The impression of a more or less arbitrary purging policy intensified inevitably as even within occupation zones procedures varied from state to state and underwent multiple revisions, as was the case to varying extents in the British, French, or Soviet zones.

Of the western powers the American occupation authority was the toughest. It had conceived denazification as a 'personnel-centred solution of the anti-fascism question'[2] and raised it to a central element of its occupation policy. The British and French pursued a substantially more pragmatic line and prioritized administrative efficiency and reconstruction from the start. Denazification in the Soviet zone followed a completely different direction. Here it was instrumentalized in the implementation of the Communist consolidation of power. [. . .]

The success or failure of denazification can neither be measured solely by the yardstick of dismissal figures or the rigorousness of the purging apparatus, nor separated from the political goals which were being pursued through a political purge of personnel. Precisely the example of the Soviet zone of occupation shows that denazification and the democratization of German society were not necessarily linked processes.

The political and social rehabilitation of the army of millions of former NSDAP members was unavoidable after a certain interim period. As Egon Kogon formulated it drastically in his much cited essay 'The Right to Political Error' in 1947, one could 'only kill them or win them over; world history shows us that enemies should never be treated in any other way. (And how many genuine enemies there are among these millions!)'[3] In practice the tribunals followed this maxim and pursued a generous policy of rehabilitation, which regularly privileged clemency over justice. The reintegration of former National Socialists had effectively been completed by the end of 1948. [. . .]

This process, perceived anxiously by critical contemporaries as a 'renazification', restored extensively bureaucratic continuity in the western zones and contributed substantially to the efficiency of the administration and the economy. However questionable their pasts and their personal integrity on an individual basis, the reappointed people did not engage in neo-Nazi activities but submitted themselves loyally to the *normative* demands of the democratic new beginning.

A closer examination also shows, of course, that the willingness to pursue a process of purging was only present to a very limited extent in post-war society, and that the small minority of committed opponents of National Socialism was far too weak to become the vanguard of a comprehensive process of self-purging. The network of collegial, social, and familial obligation and consideration formed a highly effective barrier which caused the purging desires of the tribunals to fade into nothing. Generously distributed and often false exonerating references, the so-called *Persilscheine*, mostly testified that the person concerned had only joined the NSDAP out of opportunism and had harmed nobody. The local 'fabric of neighbourhood and friendship'[4] exerted a real pressure in favour of rehabilitation. Anyone who despite this still gave incriminating evidence and even maintained it in the tribunal process was soon cast as a denouncer and was excluded from the company of decent citizens as a social troublemaker. Refusal to bear witness and indifference soon characterized the atmosphere, insofar as it was not a matter of the local National Socialist leadership, feared denouncers, or corrupt party officials. Former National Socialists enjoyed the most extensive advocacy from Protestant church leaders, who from the beginning denounced denazification as a great injustice.[5] [. . .]

The generous policy of rehabilitation made it easier for millions of former National Socialists, both the chastened and the more unrepentant, to identify with the new state. The formation of a democracy based on consensus demanded integration and could not be established on the basis of the exclusion of large sectors of the population. In the early 1950s many opponents of National Socialism felt increasingly pushed onto the defensive by the 'relentless return of yesterday's men'.[6] What was problematic was less the highly varied but overall nonetheless successful integration process than primarily the lack of sensitivity in referring to the National Socialist past. Thus it would have reflected well on the young Federal Republic if high and top offices in politics, administration, and the judiciary had been reserved exclusively for people whose pasts demanded no embarrassed justification. Such a signal of high political symbolism would have underlined effectively the undoubted break with the National Socialist past which occurred on the normative level. The heaviest legacy of the process of repression which soon set in is represented, however, by the fact that in the 1950s the judicial prosecution of National Socialist crimes also practically came to a standstill.[7] The victims of the National Socialist dictatorship could only register this with powerless indignation or silent resignation. Critical engagement with the National Socialist past did not re-emerge in German society on a broad basis until the early 1960s.[8]

['Entnazifizierung: politische Säuberung unter alliierter Herrschaft', in Hans-Erich Volkmann (ed.), *Ende des Dritten Reiches—Ende des Zweiten Weltkriegs: eine perspektivische Rückschau* (Munich: Piper, 1995), 371–2, 386–9.]

HERMANN LANGBEIN

99   In the Name of the German People

Hermann Langbein (b. 1912, Vienna) was incarcerated in numerous National Socialist camps, including Dachau, Neuengamme, and Auschwitz, on account of his Communist activities; after the war, he was secretary of the International Auschwitz Committee and an important activist on behalf of survivors of National Socialist atrocities.

He also played an important role in attempts to bring former Nazi criminals to justice. Here, in a 1963 discussion of the limping progress made thus far, he discusses the impact of the 1958 Ulm *Einsatzgruppen* Trial, which achieved wide publicity and marked a turning point in attitudes, and the subsequent decision to establish the *Zentrale Stelle der Landesjustizverwaltungen* (Central Office of the State Justice Authorities), which was given the task of coordinating legal action against Nazi criminals.

The conscience cannot be deceived. The passage of time and the rapid recovery caused the wounds which had caused such pain slowly to scar over. A new generation grew up which was untainted and asked questions without inhibition. This development—which surprised many—became obvious when the publication of Anne Frank's diary in 1955 left such a lasting impression. Previously people flinched sensitively when this subject—the suffering caused to innocent people by National Socialism—was mentioned. People did not want to listen. Now people read, went to the theatre, discussed. The slogan of the 'unconfronted past' became fashionable.

In this atmosphere the Ulm *Einsatzgruppen* trial, which in the spring and summer of 1958 examined extensive murder campaigns in Lithuania and in which ten accused, among whom were six SS leaders, were put on trial, aroused strong public interest. The well-known journalist Ernst Müller-Meiningen describes it as a haunting trial. Witnesses described how the innocent victims—men, women, the elderly, children—were herded together like animals for the slaughter, and forced to dig their own graves while being beaten and abused; and how then on the orders of the SS men they were mercilessly shot. The process was so terrible that even Heinrich Himmler, who had been the 'guest of honour' at an especially well-organized execution, was made to feel ill and ordered the use of gas for subsequent mass murders. This journalist's assertion that this first large trial was actually an arbitrary product of an arbitrary judicial process, 'as thousands of murderers still live undisturbed among us', caused unease.[1] The legal proceedings in Kiel against Clauberg, the unbelievably impertinent sterilization doctor who had placed an advertisement for a secretary to continue his 'scientific work', also aroused further interest, even if the death of the accused meant that he did not come to trial.* Immediately prior to Ulm the unimaginably sadistic rages of SS-*Hauptscharführer* Walter Sommer in the Buchenwald bunker, which occupied a court in Bayreuth, had a much greater resonance than similar previous trials. The great significance of the Ulm proceedings, which mark the beginning of a new phase in the activities of the German judicial system, also lies in the fact that the preparation of the documentation by the public

---

* Clauberg was tried in Kiel in August 1957 for undertaking sterilization experiments on female Jews and gypsies in Auschwitz and Ravensbrück 1942–4.

prosecutors was excellent. Thus the court did not just get a general impression of individual episodes. The organizational system of mass murder was presented. One had to recognize that this was not a matter of a crass isolated case, but of a well-conceived, bureaucratically planned organization of murder of unimaginable extent.

The justice minister of Baden-Württemberg, Dr Wolfgang Hausmann, has summarized the impact of the trial thus: 'The Ulm *Einsatzgruppen* trial, particularly, forced one to recognize that unfortunately numerous crimes have yet to be punished.'[2] Witnesses who had entered the courtroom as respected citizens in influential positions were arrested there under strong suspicion of having taken part in the mass murders.

Press, radio, and television discussed the trial and its lessons very extensively. Once more, the great responsibility which the media also have to bear in this field became apparent. A representative of the young generation— Gert Kalow—writes: 'A German who, after the Ulm trial, denies the events of the catastrophe is not a free man but a slave of his past. He obstructs his own view of the current situation and will spend the rest of his life in a sulk.'[3] Another journalist takes issue with those who polemicize against such trials: 'Honest and dishonest people demand in a loud voice in response to the recent trials: An end to these things, now, thirteen years after the end of the war! In reality, however—apart from the numerous allied trials, of the generals through to the industrialists, which often came close to being representative show trials and trials by example, and apart also from a 'denazification' process which failed for being too generalized—actually nothing at all systematic has been undertaken against the criminals of that time. Books such as Kogon's *SS-State* were ignored, at least by the German justice system.[4] The courageous bi-weekly journal *Gegenwart* energetically demands: 'One cannot undo the terrible crimes, but, if one seriously wishes, one can deal with the accomplices to murder as the criminal code allows.' And unbiased members of the judiciary are explicitly demanded for this job: 'If we are only now learning in such detail as in the Ulm trial of much which occurred at that time then we are right to ask if there was—and still is—here and there within the justice authorities a notable lack of interest in pursuing such criminal acts.'[5]

These quotes should not give the impression that the German press was united in offering such an opinion. But it was still the first time that such an opinion was consistently presented in the serious German press. Public opinion outside of Germany has already often drawn attention to these things. The moral pressure thereby exerted was not without impact. It was particularly significant, however, that the German voices demanding action from the justice system did not only awkwardly base their argument on the embarrassing question 'what will foreign countries say otherwise?'

This mood also found expression in the Federal parliament. Deputy Jahn characterized it thus: 'for some months there has been a justified and ever-growing concern among the public over certain aspects of our legal system, over judgements and other court decisions, which cannot be mistaken and on which in our view neither the Federal parliament nor the Federal government can remain silent.'[6] [. . .]

Naturally the activities of the justice authorities are complicated by the fact that many functionaries in the justice system and in the police were similarly active in such functions during the National Socialist dictatorship. In how many cases did an officer of the police or legal system have to proceed against a culprit who was previously known to him as a colleague or friend? Drastic individual cases, from which one cannot of course generalize, lead further still.

Many members of the criminal police did their service after 1933 with the Gestapo and incurred guilt. After 1945 they returned to their old jobs. The *Einsatzgruppen*, who had been charged with carrying out mass murders of Jews, Russians, and gypsies in the east, had mostly been comprised of such officers. I have details of the current careers of 133 people who were or are being tried for their participation in such crimes. Forty-eight of them were re-employed with the police until their arrest, or in individual cases elsewhere in the service of the state. Up until his arrest Georg Heuser, the former *SS-Hauptsturmführer* who was condemned to fifteen years in prison in Koblenz for his leading participatory role in the mass murder of at least 31,400 Jews, was head of the state criminal police agency in Rheinland-Pfalz. The German press reported that following his arrest his colleagues sent him a bouquet of flowers in his prison cell in Koblenz.[7] The chief criminal police superintendent of the state criminal police agency of Hanover, the former *SS-Hauptsturmführer* Bodo Struck, was condemned to four years' imprisonment in Berlin for being an accessory to the murder of 5,450 people. Alfred Krumbach held a leading position in the Office for the Protection of the Constitution. He is now serving a four-and-a-half year prison sentence for having been an accessory to mass murder in 827 cases. His colleague, the former *SS-Sturmbannführer* Wilhelm Döring, has appealed against his sentence—six years' imprisonment for being an accomplice to mass murder in 600 cases. Up until his arrest he was head of the criminal police in Siegburg. Immediately after the war he had gone 'underground'. In September 1953 he was reappointed to the criminal police. Clearly such a late application was not taken there as grounds for examining Döring's past. He was quickly promoted to criminal police superintendent. And the head of the Gießen protection police, Hans Hoffmann, was condemned to three and a half years' imprisonment in the first instance. Recently the head of the criminal police in Flensburg was arrested on suspicion of having participated in war crimes, as was his colleague in Ludwigshafen and the deputy head in Frankenthal. [. . .]

In cases against groups of defendants the courts are generally also confronted with the following difficulty: he who participated directly in the extermination campaigns—he who fired the gun, drove the gas van, or threw the poisoned gas into the chambers—is easier to convict than he under whose command entire extermination campaigns took place. The 'small fish' cannot persuade the court that he had not known what happened to the victims. Many of the 'big fish', however—they are often referred to as 'desk perpetrators'—try to excuse themselves in this way. One can understand that every accused criminal tries to deny his guilt or to diminish it. This places a very serious obligation on the courts, however. No amount of lying can help him who can be proven to have fired the gun. Can he who can be proved to have directed the victims to the place where they were murdered be believed when he says that he did not know what fate awaited them there? In cases of doubt the court is obliged to decide in favour of the accused. But must not every judge make every effort to exclude all reasonable doubt in the cases of such insidious responsibility of a 'big fish'? A man such as the former SS-*Hauptscharführer* Otto Hunsche, who for over three years was head of a division of Eichmann's department, which, as is well known, was primarily occupied with the organization of the mass murder of Jews and gypsies, cannot be believed when he asserts that he had not known what happened to the victims in Auschwitz; that he had believed that everyone who was deported there was put to work. Is it just that only he who can be proven to have poured Zyklon-B into the gas chambers of Auschwitz is deemed to be a perpetrator? The former SS-*Sturmbannführer* Martin Fellenz, who had been chief-of-staff and adjutant to the all-powerful SS and Police Leader in Cracow, was regarded at the time as 'privy to secrets'. Despite this the Flensburg court believed that 'he may possibly have known nothing'.

The Council of the Protestant Church of Germany has also offered important words on this: 'The principle of personal responsibility of each person of sound mind, including those in senior positions of responsibility who have the powers of command over other authorized people, must be retained as indispensable.'[8]

One can understand the chairman of the Bonn court who in the summing up of the trial of the SS troop of the extermination camp of Chelmno said: 'everything, absolutely everything has been demanded of us in the reaching of this verdict.' And one can understand him when he expresses regret that the leaders had betrayed and sold out their subordinates and had avoided conviction by making false assertions while now—according to his observations—everything was being dumped on the back of the 'little man'. For the heavy responsibility of a court also lies in the need not to allow these leaders—who are often of a higher degree of intelligence and mostly have experienced solicitors—to wriggle out of their higher responsibility through cheap lies.

[*Im Namen des deutschen Volkes: Zwischenbilanz der Prozesse wegen nationalsozialistischer Verbrechen* (Vienna: Europa Verlag, 1963), 35–7, 41–2, 48.]

100 National Socialist Extermination Camps as Reflected in German Trials

> General problems of lack of evidence combined with the legal obligation to prove individual guilt for specific murders (proving membership of a group which had carried out mass murder collectively was not enough) made securing convictions of former Nazi criminals extremely difficult in the early years after the war. This was especially the case given that judges were often insufficiently informed of the broader historical context in which these occurred. Adalbert Rückerl, who headed the *Zentrale Stelle der Landesjustizverwaltungen* from 1966, discusses some of the problems involved in this extract.

A complex problem [. . .] is raised by the question, which is occasionally put, of whether, and if so to what extent, courts and public prosecutors should engage in historical research in the context of their legal remit to prosecute criminal acts. Historians rightly emphasize that history cannot be written solely on the basis of court judgements, because judicial arguments have to be focused above everything else on the person of the accused and his actions in relation to the facts of the case. On the other hand, they in no way mistake the benefits which historical research could draw from the results of the work of those justice authorities engaged in the relevant investigations. The head of the Institute for Contemporary History in Munich, Professor Broszat, draws attention in this connection

to the results of judicial investigations and processes which by their critical usage of all relevant documents have considerably enriched knowledge of these processes. Often chided for their cautious judgements, which in cases of doubt pleaded for the accused or for an open verdict, the justice system of the Federal Republic, with its extensive investigative apparatus, which has been active for many years, has, precisely in the area of the extermination camps, contributed much more to explaining this complex of National Socialist crimes than historians would have been able to do.[1]

Some critics, however, have been unable to agree with this praise by historians of the judicial system. They would prefer to see public prosecutors and courts confining themselves to bringing behind bars those criminals who have stolen other people's possessions or who have induced errors through false pretences and thus damaged the property of another. They allow the judicial system to prosecute bank robbers, kidnappers, and taxi murderers, and not a few tirelessly demand the reintroduction of the death penalty in this context. The same critics, however, see the need to recommend to the judges and state prosecutors that they keep out of everything which has anything to do with politics, war, history, and above all with events from the time of the so-called 'Third Reich'. And it cannot be denied that some judges and state prosecutors would be only too pleased to follow this recommendation. The indisputable fact that many criminal lawyers do their best to avoid being used in the prosecuting of National Socialist crimes is primarily to be explained by the fact that this activity is, more than any other, exposed to strong, emotionally driven criticism from all sides. Occasionally the reason for this resistant attitude is also to be found in a type of insecurity in the face of a problem which hardly ever surfaced in everyday criminal procedures but which has gained in significance in the so-called NS trials. The chairman of the court in the first Auschwitz Trial, Senate President Dr Hofmeyer, put it thus: 'In these trials of NS violent crimes one must be clear if the subject of the proceedings or the issue of the trial is merely the guilt of the accused, and thus personal, individual guilt, or if the events as a whole should move to the fore in the proceedings.'[2] In other words—should it leave out practically everything which is not directly related to the person of the accused and his actions? Hofmeyer himself gives an apparently very pragmatic answer to this question: 'The criminal procedure code gives a clear answer to this question, and the court cannot be appointed to provide historical documentation and thus to anticipate historical writing. If the trials are thus divested of all those things, historically interesting as they undoubtedly are, it should be possible to reduce the difficulties of these trials.'

But even this judge, who was rightly praised on all sides for his proven knowledge of the subject and for his supreme direction of the proceedings in the Auschwitz Trial, is unable—and probably unwilling, given the singularity of each individual case—to prescribe when and how far one can dispense with the clarification of the historical background in an NS trial, without the court failing in its duty to enlighten. The Auschwitz Trial was—intentionally or not—the 'historical trial' par excellence. The court and the prosecutors were able patiently and precisely to shake the objective contents out of the witness statements, and thus to free them from emotional and political-propagandistic embellishment; they cited documentary evidence in the relevant context in each case and were thus above all able to correct some of those eyewitness descriptions which claimed to hold true on a general level but which themselves were based on having been able to see only a part of the overall process.

In the context of the imminent renewed extension of the statute of limitations for National Socialist violent crimes in 1969 the word 'criminal by association' was used time and time again to describe persons prosecuted by the judiciary in the NS trials who did not conform to the 'perpetrator type' of the violent criminal of the 'conventional sort'. The regular usage of this concept was obviously intended as a call both to the politicians and to those judges and prosecutors involved in the relevant proceedings, to take more notice of the political and social 'web' in which the accused had mostly got entangled without their own doing. Such a call to the judiciary was unnecessary, however. The courts and prosecutors had already been making vigorous efforts for years in the NS trials—sometimes at a cost which appeared excessive to the superficial observer—to clarify the background against which the crimes of which the defendant was accused have to be seen. The sole motive for this was to broaden the depth of understanding for the judgement of the extent of individual guilt. These efforts found their obvious manifestation in the ever-growing length of the proceedings—inasmuch as they were caused in part by the increasing difficulties of proof—and in the ever-expanding size of the written court judgements.[3] Compared to the judgements of the earlier years the result was clearly a stronger differentiation of guilty verdicts and punishments, which often, but in no way regularly, worked in favour of the defendants.

It is undoubtedly not the task of the judiciary to engage in historical research or to provide historical documentation. Where, however, this task falls to it in pursuit of the clarification of circumstances relevant to a criminal offence and the assessment of individual guilt, it should not timidly define its boundaries too narrowly.

This demand is justifiable also purely in connection with the aim of punishment, no matter what one sees the purpose of this as being for NS criminals. It goes without saying that both the modern conception of punishment, that of resocialization, improvement, and education, and the purpose of deterrence of the perpetrator personally against committing further crimes have no more purpose for defendants in the NS trials, whose average age is between 60 and 70. Whether in the case of NS criminals atonement is to be seen as the purpose of punishment is doubtable, given that in recent years a lack of any willingness to atone has regularly been discernible. If, however, one wishes to define atonement as the purpose of punishment, the court then has to explain clearly to the accused for what it is he has to atone; it has to make clear to what extent society contributed to the emergence of the crimes of National Socialism, and what beyond that is to be attributed to the accused as personal guilt, to be atoned for by him. The same is true for the—equally not uncontentious—punishment of retribution. Here too the court must demonstrate convincingly where the boundary lies between the responsibility of society and the actions for which the perpetrator alone is responsible, which have to be paid for. If, after all, one proceeds—in the broadest sense of the word—from the punishment motive of general deterrence in order to protect the rule of law, it then becomes essential—because of the intended effect on the community—to explain the relationship between the behaviour of society and the actions of the perpetrator.

[*NS-Vernichtungslager im Spiegel deutscher Strafprozesse: Belzec, Sobibor, Treblinka, Chelmno* (Munich: Deutscher Taschenbuchverlag, 1977), 16–19.]

CHARLES S. MAIER

101 **Bitburg History**

> Reflecting on the debates surrounding the Bitburg controversy, Charles Maier suggests that they reflected a broader agenda which was seeking to shift the boundaries of acceptability in public discussion of and attitudes to the National Socialist past. The misrepresentation of the past articulated in the alleged service of reconciliation was thus linked to an intellectual culture in which the *Historikerstreit* itself occurred a year or so later.

Begin, where historical memory so often starts, with the dead. In this case just a handful of dead, whose honoring at the German military cemetery at Bitburg raised questions about the millions of dead left by the most recent German Reich and, finally, by the adversaries who combined to defeat it. At Bitburg, it will be recalled, Ronald Reagan was scheduled to lay a wreath as part of the fortieth-anniversary celebrations of V-E Day. The visit was intended as a ritual of reconciliation; it ended as catharsis manqué. It failed as ceremonial because it mobilized contrary impulses about history. Memory escaped from the control of its normal custodians—politicians who sought to play on it, and academics who lived by analyzing it—and became an unpredictable force as powerful, say, as economic discontent. The unquiet graves of the Palatinate awoke recriminations that caught up the vast audiences of the evening news in the United States and the Federal Republic, not to mention the official spokesmen for governments, veterans' and Jewish organizations, and the other constituencies crystallized around the traumatic events of the Third Reich and World War II.

Real history, painful memory, took its revenge for mismanaged pageantry. [. . .]

Two levels of rhetoric characterized the Bitburg debate and the other statements commemorating the end of the European war. On the one hand, written speeches on both sides demonstrated acute concern for moral responsibility and for preserving a decent respect to the past. The Berlin address by the Federal Republic's president, Richard von Weizsäcker, was perhaps the noblest statement.[1] Weizsäcker has been especially eloquent on these themes, perhaps because he had the painful task of coming to terms with the role of his own father—indeed of defending him before the Allied tribunal at Nuremberg in 1946. Ernst von Weizsäcker was not a party member but nonetheless served the Third Reich as chief permanent official (*Staatssekretär*) at the Foreign Office from 1938 to 1943. The son has had four decades to reflect on the nature of that collaboration. On several occasions, most notably on the fortieth anniversary of the Reich's surrender, he eloquently recognized that Germans must always remind themselves of the Nazi past, that it continued to be a national responsibility, even if most current Germans were too young to have had even a remote role in putting Hitler into power or supporting him. Chancellor Kohl also delivered a sensitive statement at Bergen-Belsen that sanctioned no West German moral evasiveness. 'Germany under the National Socialist regime filled the world with fear and horror. That era of slaughter, indeed of genocide, is the darkest, most painful chapter in German history. One of our country's paramount tasks is to inform people of those occurrences and keep alive an awareness of the full extent of this historical burden'.[2] But many statements were more evasive. (President Reagan's notion that the SS boys buried at Bitburg were equally victims with those attacked by the Nazi state represented one response, to be echoed later by Ernst Nolte's view that Claude Lanzmann's film *Shoah* revealed it was probable that the SS camp crews 'could also have been victims in their way'.[3] Or they reflected a sense that too much breast-beating was abject and counterproductive. Thus in May 1986, a year after Bitburg, the American ambassador, Richard Burt, told a German-American historical conference at Nuremberg that West Germany should not harp on the Nazi past but should think positively about postwar achievements: long, sustained, and well-distributed economic growth, a stable and open democracy, and international reliability.[4] His words only sanctioned what many had thought on both sides of the Atlantic. One did not have to be an aging German war veteran or unrepentant party comrade, grousing at a beer-hall table, to believe that *Mea Culpa* was unbecoming as a national motto. Bitburg, in short, became a sacrament of resentment, not of reconciliation.

This mangled ceremonial certainly did not unleash the historical controversy now under way. But it revealed a change in attitude—not a thinking about the unthinkable, but a debate over the hitherto undebatable. Certainly scholars cannot deplore that fact alone. Neither genuine questions nor good-faith answers should be placed off limits. [. . .]

I use the term *Bitburg history* to refer to a multiple muddying of moral categories and historical agents. [. . .] Let the concept frankly stand as an ideal type of historical approach characterized by several assumptions.

First, as typified by President Reagan's effort at sympathy, Bitburg history unites oppressors and victims, Nazi perpetrators of violence with those who were struck down by it, in a common dialectic. [. . .] It confuses the formal, logical dependence of victim and victimizer (there can by definition exist no perpetrator without a victim), with a shared responsibility for the wrong committed. As Primo Levi has written, both victim and perpetrator seek to deny the memory of the crime: 'we are confronted with a paradoxical analogy between the victim and the perpetrator . . . but the offender, and only he, has set and triggered it, and if he has come to suffer from his deed, it is just that he suffers; whereas it is an iniquity that the victim also suffers, as indeed he or she suffers, even after many years.'[5]

Second, Bitburg history finds it difficult to pin down any notions of collective responsibility. Admittedly the latter notion is one of the most problematic concepts for ethics or history. It is hard enough to assign individual responsibility, which is one of the thorniest issues, say, for judges, biographers, and others who must confront personal action. Individual responsibility has emerged as an especially difficult concept to apply to agents of bureaucracies or military hierarchies. Obviously it preoccupied Europeans especially as they debated the appropriateness of postwar judicial sanctions and purges against collaborators.[6] It intervened as a problem in weighing the appropriateness of the Bitburg site as one for public commemoration. But it is still a somewhat different issue from that of the degree to which West Germany as a national society accepts responsibility for the Nazi past, and for how long it must acknowledge such responsibility. In what sense does collective responsibility exist? [. . .] The tentative and brief response, I would suggest for the moment, is that insofar as a collection of people wishes to claim existence as a society or nation, it must thereby accept existence as a community through time, hence must acknowledge that acts committed by earlier agents still bind or burden the contemporary community. This holds for revolutionary regimes as well.

Insofar as past acts were acknowledged as injurious, this level of responsibility stipulates that whatever reparation is still possible must be attempted. West German leaders have accepted that responsibility, not with consistently good grace, but to a major degree. Nor does this responsibility have a time limit. Responsibility for a burdened past can justifiably become less preoccupying as other experiences are added to the national legacy. The remoter descendants of those originally victimized have a more diluted claim to compensation. But like the half life of radioactive material, there is no point at which responsibility simply goes away. [. . .]

Finally, Bitburg history—again, an ideal type—has a third component. It suggests that the particular edge of Nazi crimes is less cutting given the general record of twentieth-century massacre and murder. Auschwitz may have been horrendous, but consider the atomic bombings of Hiroshima and Nagasaki; the conventional bombings of Hamburg, Dresden, and Tokyo; the Stalinist massacres of so-called kulaks, Crimean Tatars, Ukrainian farmers, blind folksingers, and old Bolsheviks. Recall the Turkish genocide of the Armenians, the Khmer Rouge's slaughter of fellow Cambodians. Are the Germans just getting worse marks because they mechanized the process?

because gas has an aura of horror that bullets and bombs do not?[7] This issue is critical for the historian, for it raises the legitimacy of comparison, a tool he or she can never really renounce but can evidently abuse.

Thus Bitburg cast into relief fundamental questions about historical judgment. Judgment is obviously problematic, for it calls upon more than reasoning alone. It is an activity of mind and conscience, never entirely to be liberated from subjectivity, but crucial for aesthetics, for ethics, for politics, and consequently for history. Bitburg confused the possibilities for judgment along three dimensions. Once again it raised questions about individual responsibility for murderous acts. It revealed persisting disagreement over the degree to which a national community might be held responsible. And it opened the question of whether National Socialist Germany was itself so special a case in the annals of mass murder. By their inability to discriminate reconciliation from revisionism, the participants at Bitburg helped dissolve the inhibitions of historical discourse in Germany.

[*The Unmasterable Past: History, Holocaust and German National Identity* (Cambridge, Mass.: Harvard University Press, 1988), 9–16.]

RAUL HILBERG

102   Bitburg as Symbol

The nature of the controversy over Bitburg was itself replete with ironies which revealed the problematic and distorted memory of National Socialism. Amidst all the controversy over the Waffen-SS graves, for example, no one questioned the appropriateness of a visit to the military cemetery itself, despite the deep complicity of the regular *Wehrmacht* in the worst atrocities of the regime. As Hilberg argues here, this itself was symptomatic of the extent to which the Second World War was being remembered as a 'normal' war, a war qualitatively little different from the First World War, and the extent to which the peculiar atrocities associated with it were being filtered out of public memory.

When the Western leaders met in 1984, they celebrated the anniversary of the landings in Normandy without Kohl. Deeply stung, Kohl received small consolation from a ceremony with French president Mitterand at a Verdun cemetery of the First World War. For the Germans of the 1980s, the resurrection of 1914–18 was not the right commemoration, and the holding of hands by the two men at Verdun lent itself to caricature. Kohl needed a more powerful presence, on German soil, at a place symbolizing the *Second* World War. The man to be invited for this purpose was the genuine head of the Western world, the president of the United States, and the site of his visit was to be a typical German military cemetery near the town of Bitburg. About two thousand fallen soldiers of the Third Reich lay buried there. Interspersed among these graves were those of forty-seven or so SS men. [. . .]

An American president, standing amid the buried German soldiers and SS men, was to place a wreath to commemorate them all without distinction. Was this to be an act of total redemption of Nazi Germany? Had the survivors' testimony not been heard? Had the captured documents of Adolf Hitler's Reich been overlooked? Had the message failed? Under President Carter, the Congress had established a United States Holocaust Memorial Council. Elie Wiesel was serving as its chairman. President Reagan had personally received the council in the White House during his first term. Was he now negating its mission? Was he playing politics with memory?

A key element in the debate was the cluster of SS graves at Bitburg, and everything seemed ultimately to depend on the measure of their significance. The history of U.S. policy toward postwar Germany had been an attempt to whittle down the size of the Nazi problem, to diminish the ranks of those who were to be held accountable for the Nazi regime. The beginning was the rejection of 'collective guilt.' The next step was a judicial division of organized German society into two segments, one of which was to be left largely undisturbed, while the other was to be pursued further. The first group included the vast majority of the judges, generals, diplomats, civil servants, industrialists, and bankers, only a handful of whom stood trial for an activity deemed contrary to the old laws of war or the new law of aggression. The second group consisted of power centers that were found by the Nuremberg International Military Tribunal to have had a criminal purpose. If a member of such a hierarchy had joined or remained in it voluntarily with knowledge of its character, he had committed a crime. One of these criminal organizations was the leadership corps of the Nazi Party; another was the Gestapo and Security Service; the third comprised all SS men, except draftees who were given no choice and who had committed no crimes. Eventually, the SS in particular remained in the public eye as the hard core of Nazism. Eichmann was an SS officer, Mengele belonged to the SS, and many others, known and unknown, were part of it. SS men were at the forefront of the shootings of hundreds of thousands of Jews in occupied Eastern Europe, and SS men were implicated in the killing of millions in the camps. As of 1985, there was still a Central Office for Investigation of National Socialist Crimes in West Germany, gathering evidence against SS men and party stalwarts for prosecutions in West German courts. At the same time, there was an Office of Special Investigations in the U.S. Department of Justice, charged with instituting proceedings for denaturalization and deportation of individuals, from the Baltic area, the Ukraine, and elsewhere, who had served as willing accomplices of the German SS and Police in lethal operations against Jews, Gypsies, and others. In this manner, the notion of culpability for inexcusable offenses, no matter what the date of their commission, was still being upheld by West Germany and by the United States in tangible legal actions. With the advent of Bitburg, however, a psychological reversal was in the offing. The president's wreath seemed to cover the entire history of the Third Reich with a nebulous collective innocence.

Aggravating the situation were all of the circumstances leading to the decision. President Reagan announced at first that he would not visit a concentration camp, lest he 'reawaken the memories and so forth, and the passions of the time.'¹ After protests were voiced about Bitburg, he decided to go to a camp after all, but when he announced the additional visit to Bergen-Belsen, he antagonized the protesters even more, for now he was going from the mass graves of Jews to the headstones of SS men, explaining that both were victims. [. . .]

The deepest psychological conflict between the Germans and the Jews had become a contest of public relations in which only simple, visible cues could matter. Few newspapers and fewer television programs could cope with the complexity of the issue. No one approached the question of the German army. Here was a cemetery in which most of the fallen had been soldiers. Was it 'contaminated' only because of the relative handful of SS men buried alongside these men? Would the controversy have been prevented altogether if the choice had been a 'pure' military burial ground? The Germans had certainly spent years trying to conjure up an image of the Wehrmacht, which was the name of the armed forces during the Third Reich, as a military organization like other armed forces fighting for its homeland. [. . .]

In truth, the separation of the military from the SS in terms of the soldierly professionalism of the one and the ideological fanaticism of the other has always been strained. The German army played a heavy role in Adolf Hitler's Germany, and it cannot be detached from the Nazi regime, because it was an integral part of it. Americans have not been well informed and the press has not been explicit about such topics as the fate of Soviet prisoners of war in the transit camps (Dulags) and main camps (Stalags) of the German military. By the end of the war, well over two million Red Army men in German army custody were dead of starvation and exposure.² By the same token, the general public is not aware of the multiple functions performed by uniformed members of the German armed forces in the destruction of the Jews. [. . .]

The German army was not the only reversible symbol at Bitburg. An effort was made to transform the Second World War, to make it look like the First. The strategy was a mirror image of the Mitterand–Kohl meeting at Verdun in 1984, where the French government had substituted the First World War for the Second. The French, of course, had good reasons for centering attention on the older battlefield, if only because there they could console not only Kohl but also themselves. France had suffered five times as many casualties in 1914–18 as in 1939–45, and their dead in the Second World War included Vichy troops who had battled the British in Syria, Alsatians drafted into the German army, and ideological French collaborators in formations fighting on the German side to the bitter end. Bitburg presented more subtle problems. Not only were tripods for television cameras banned, lest an SS grave be glimpsed by viewers, but an air of timelessness was to be introduced, a blending of the wars, a walk across the ages. At the side of an American president in his mid-seventies stood an American general who was even older. During the wordless ceremony, a German bugler played 'Ich hatt' einen Kameraden' (I had a comrade), a song that predated the Nazi regime. An American television audience could see nothing wrong in this scene, and Germans could be reminded of an earlier history, the period before 1933, to which no shame was attached, or for which at least no exclusive responsibility had to be taken.[3]

The complexities of history are buried in books and journals. Collective memories are highly selective and often embrace only a partial past in the form of nostalgia. How much time will pass before a future generation in Germany will have difficulty distinguishing between the two wars that occurred twenty years apart in the first half of the century?

['Bitburg as Symbol', in Geoffrey Hartman (ed.), *Bitburg in Moral and Political Perspective* (Bloomington: Indiana University Press, 1986), 16–17, 18–19, 21, 23.]

GEOFF ELEY

103   Nazism, Politics, and the Image of the Past

Writing from an engaged position to the left of the liberal and Social Democrat-aligned protagonists of the *Historikerstreit*, Geoff Eley argues that the dispute represented a new phase in an ongoing contestation of the right to shape the dominant public image of the German past, a contest which derives its vigour from the politicized nature of scholarship on the German past and its close relationship to contemporary political discourses. The conservative positions advanced in the dispute, Eley contends, represent a new attempt by the Right, in the wake of the *Tendenzwende*, to recentre historical discourse on issues of nationhood and national identity.

The interpretation of modern German history has become so vested with larger meanings—has been so heavily overdetermined by more general intellectual, moral and political considerations—that more nuanced or intermediate positions are extraordinarily hard to defend. How one positions oneself in particular debates is invariably tantamount to a larger statement of principle, because taking a position on the origins of Nazism means simultaneously placing oneself in a present-related discourse about the bases of legitimacy in contemporary Germany. There remains a sense in which general matters of value and commitment, politics and public responsibility, pedagogy and personal intellectual orientation—one's *erkenntnisleitende Interessen*, in the talismanic phrase of the 1970s—are much closer to the surface than elsewhere.

This has been shown once again, in a controversy that raged from the summer of 1986 to the West German elections of January 1987, and has lasted less frenetically right down to the present. [. . .]

At one level, the *Historikerstreit* (as the affair became known) is only the most recent installment in a continuing debate about how the German past is to be addressed for public pedagogical purposes. But it also reflects a particular moment in West German intellectual and political life, in which questions of national identity have returned to the centre of public discussion. Most obviously, this is linked to the much-vaunted *Tendenzwende*, the conservative turn of German intellectual life since 1977. The return of the C.D.U./C.S.U. to government in 1982–3 has also shifted the terms of public discourse more decisively, and encouraged a less inhibited airing of views on the right. Certain conservative historians have definitely taken this as an opportunity for advancing a particular image of the German past. In effect, the controversy stirred up by Nolte freezes this important moment of historiographical flux. [. . .]

The fuss is about the image of the past. We can see this by tracing the changing boundaries of the acceptable in West German treatments of National Socialism since 1945. Immediately after the war, for instance, all parts of the political spectrum 'contained vocal dissenting minorities which were resolutely anti-Nazi and either pacifist, anti-capitalist or libertarian-democratic in outlook', and which seemed momentarily capable of exercising a major influence on the political culture of the emerging state.[1] In fact the policies of the Allied occupying administrations combined with the origins of the Cold War and the dynamic of indigenous restoration to stifle those developments, and the 'democratic-progressive elements were defeated around a number of important post-war debates'—the debate over *Mitbestimmung* (co-determination in industry) in 1950–2, the campaign against rearmament in 1950–5, the struggle against nuclear arms in 1957–8 and the protracted opposition to the Emergency Laws (1958–68). Thus 'these basic debates failed to establish within the existing party structures any institutional space for dissenting socialist, left-nationalist, pacifist, and left-libertarian forces which could have questioned the FRG's defining principles'.[2] Instead they shaped a new extra-parliamentary milieu which, while banished to the margins of the system, allowed a small but vocal democratic intelligentsia to maintain an unsettling critique of the official culture. This was the context in which the A.P.O. (extra-parliamentary opposition) and the student movement of the mid-1960s started to emerge, which generated the first frontal challenge to the normative ideology of the C.D.U.-state. This was a traumatic time for conservatives: the general assault on established authority, the reform of the universities, the confrontational style of student politics and the exuberance of the counter-culture conjoined with the S.P.D.'s advance in the political arena to produce a profound dislocation in the existing intellectual culture. The launching of the *Ostpolitik*—the bitterly contested normalization of the Federal Republic's relations with the Democratic Republic and the other socialist countries by the Brandt-Scheel administration of 1969–74—completed the polarization of opinion.

For West German historians these changes were accompanied by several specific developments, which likewise reverberated dramatically in the wider public arena. One was the famous 'fascism debate' conducted in a variety of settings, the most important of which was undoubtedly the new Marxist journal *Das Argument*. Convening a variety of theoretical perspectives, this discussion transformed perceptions of National Socialism for a younger student generation, and simultaneously initiated a broader public interrogation of the Nazi experience.[3] Concurrently, the Fischer Controversy overturned the established interpretations of an earlier period and connected the fascism discussion to a larger argument about authoritarian continuities with the eras of Bismarck and Wilhelm II. In the polarized atmosphere of the later 1960s, given the troubling rise of neo-Nazism in the form of the N.P.D., much of this intellectual energy was also harnessed to the analysis and indictment of 'fascist' potentials in the present.[4] For the first time, in all of these ways, the German public was being forced—very successfully for a time—to 'come to terms with the past'. Moreover, given the simultaneous breakthrough to social-history and social-science methodology, a number of political, cultural and more specifically historiographical developments were now running in the same direction, to produce a powerful unity of commitments—an anti-fascist critique of the Federal Republic's political culture, the demand that Germany acknowledge its historic responsibility for the crimes of Nazism at home and abroad, a democratic critique of the university, and the demand for new types of history.

As it turned out, this unity held together rather briefly. It lasted, perhaps, until the climax of the *Ostpolitik* in 1972–3, during which the exponents of progressive history publicly affirmed the relationship of the eastern treaties to the principled reckoning with the past their scholarship was meant to advance.[5] But if the *Ostpolitik* unified progressive opinion, another process was already fragmenting it: namely, the degeneration of certain elements of the extra-parliamentary left into terrorism, and the concomitant recourse of the authorities to repression. This new polarization was driven above all by the activities of the Red Army Fraction (otherwise known as the Baader-Meinhoff group), which were at their peak during 1972–4, and by the general strengthening of the state's police powers in response, most notably through the system of ideological surveillance known as the *Berufsverbot*, which established criteria of political reliability for public employees. Thus just as the commitments of the new liberal-cum-social democratic public were gathering momentum, an accumulation of contradictions with the more radical left started to slow them down. The tightening of legitimate discourse against Marxism, however heterodox, not only fractured any broader front of progressive opinion, but also engendered new oppositions which compromised the integrity of the moderate viewpoints. The effects in education were particularly clear, as the radicalization of student demands for university reform and new proposals for curriculum change in the schools soon outflanked the thinking of the younger professorial generation. Within history as such the fronts also divided, with certain groupings turning away from the social science history of the previous decade to explore instead alternative possibilities in cultural anthropology, ethnography, oral history and latter-day Marxism.[6] The cuts in higher education and the contraction of the university job-market in history also coincided with these developments.

This potted history is necessary for an understanding of the conservative *Tendenzwende* of the later 1970s, which at one level was clearly an ideological rejoinder to the radicalism of the previous decade. We should not exaggerate the speed or success of this right-wing offensive. If anything, the late 1970s still indicated the *limits* on any attempt to close the books on Nazism and open a new nationalist account—the Filbinger affair in 1978 in which the C.D.U. premier of Baden-Württemberg was forced from office by his Nazi past, the extension of the statute of limitations on Nazi war crimes in 1979 (which coincided with the showing and reception of the television series *Holocaust*) and the debacle of the Strauss C.D.U./C.S.U. chancellor candidature in 1980 would all be good examples.[7] On the other hand, the revival of interest in the national question certainly gave the intellectual right some much-needed leverage. For our own purposes, this has also involved an important reconfiguration of the intellectual-political discourse around German history. [. . .]

In 1977 a major exhibition had been mounted in Stuttgart on the culture of the Staufen period (1150–1250), whose success suggested a large reservoir of public fascination with the national past. In addition, unlike another symptom of popular interest—the so-called 'Hitler wave' of the earlier 1970s—this had the advantage of being further removed from the dangerous issues of the twentieth century.[8] During the last decade, in fact, an interest in cultural representations of the past has developed—'museumism', as one observer has dubbed it—going far beyond the main earlier initiative in this area, the Reichstag exhibition 'Questions on German History', which opened in 1971.[9] By far the most prestigious instance was the Prussia exhibition in West Berlin in August-November 1981 ('Prussia: Attempt at a Balance'), the most recent and extravagant the 750th anniversary of Berlin in 1987.[10] Much of the activity has been fuelled by anniversaries. The Reichstag exhibition had itself been prompted by the centenary of German unification, and the fiftieth anniversary of the Nazi seizure of power in 1983 also attracted massive attention.[11] And here we rejoin the Bitburg scenario. For since the 1983 elections a new purpose has infused the officially sponsored activity. In particular, plans are proceeding for two permanent national museums, a Museum of German History in West Berlin and a similar 'House of History of the Federal Republic' in Bonn. [. . .]

At this point in the public discussion, which largely coincided with the return of the C.D.U./C.S.U. to government, there was a definite shift from a rather open-ended reflection on the changing meanings of the national tradition, without any obvious political charge (as in the Berlin Historical Commission conference), to a more pointed emphasis on the problem of German *identity* in the present.[12]

This is what lies behind the ruminations of a Hillgruber and the more extensive politicking of a Stürmer, and lends an extra topicality to the ideas of Nolte, whose idiosyncratic pronouncements about Marxism, Communism and fascism had otherwise enjoyed a longer provenance without drawing the kind of controversy Habermas now set out to provoke. It is this larger ideological conjuncture that the *Historikerstreit* connotes.

['Nazism, Politics and the Image of the Past: Thoughts on the West German
Historikerstreit', *Past and Present*, 121 (1988), 172, 178, 186–9, 192–3.)

PETER BALDWIN

104   The *Historikerstreit* in Context

> Peter Baldwin, although agreeing with Geoff Eley that the *Historikerstreit* reflected issues which were rooted in the West German present rather than the Nazi past, is inclined to see a more complex and shifting set of alignments at play than that which a simple Left–Right political division would suggest; like Eley, he takes the virulence of the discussion—although in itself often unedifying—as positive evidence that the National Socialist era continues to occupy a prominent place in contemporary public consciousness.

The immediate conflict identified two groups. One side suggested that the Nazi regime, although reprehensible, had been far from unique when seen in the broader perspective of the twentieth century. This group claimed that the time had come to assimilate historically the dictatorship within an extended continuity of German development so that it no longer remained as an insurmountable barrier to the past, distorting national self-identity, and preventing contemporary West Germans from appreciating the positive aspects of the Federal Republic's Weimar and Imperial antecedents. The other side included those historians who argued that such integration and relativization represented an unvarnished nationalist attempt to gloss over the horrors of the Nazi period and to glorify the Imperial tradition whose peculiarities and weaknesses, as inherited by Weimar, had played a crucial role in allowing Hitler to power.

At this level, the dispute took place along fairly direct political lines, with those arguing for a nationalist position based on a relativization of the Nazi past being scholars associated with the Christian Democrats, while their opponents tended to be members of the Social Democratic or at least Liberal camp. Nevertheless, this simple polarity does not do justice to the complexity of the themes intertwined with the *Historikerstreit*. Along with this particular dispute, other issues of contention have also affected the various stances assumed during the course of intellectual jousting. Several ongoing debates prompted by various aspects of German history have intersected with the *Historikerstreit* to produce a welter of possible and sometimes cross-cutting positions. [. . .]

More overarchingly, it is clear that singularity and comparison, relativization and normalization can be sought or accomplished for different purposes and different ends, from Left as from Right, as accusation and as excuse. There is little inherent in these various approaches that determines the ideological spin put on them. The question is not methodological in a narrow sense, but political. As with so many debates that have political overtones, the important thing is less what is said than why. Comparison of the Nazi system both with other contemporaneous regimes and with the German past can serve different aims. The Left relativizes and compares with the past to show continuities, to draw Bismarck into Hitler's maelstrom; it compares with other countries to argue that all bourgeois regimes contain such inherently dangerous potentialities. The Right compares to show similarities with other nations and periods, to dilute the bestialities of the Nazi period in an unpleasant but mutually shared heritage. A singularizing approach, for its part, can be intended either to keep the memory of the Holocaust sacred or to isolate the genocide as an aberration. [. . .]

The *Historikerstreit* came as but one element in a broader political dispute over questions of national identity and the role of the Nazi past in the democratic present. An important aspect of the wider context of the *Historikerstreit* was Chancellor Kohl's attempt to draw a line under the Hitler era, exemplified in the Bitburg affair and in the speech held during his 1984 visit to Israel in which he insisted that 'the grace of late birth' had absolved his generation of direct implication in the horrors of German history. The disputes given vent at about the same time over the proposed construction of two historical museums in Bonn and Berlin and the nature of the presentation their exhibitions should strive for were yet further examples of similar concerns. Falling on such well-marled soil, the initial spores of the *Historiker-streit* quickly grew into a squabble of prize proportions.

The *Historikerstreit* is, from this perspective, an outcome of the larger political shift in a conservative direction that Germany has undergone along with other European nations and the United States—what is known as the *Wende*, which, beginning here in the late 1970s, was cemented with the formation of the Christian Democratic-Liberal coalition government in 1982. In the broadest sense, the controversy has been political, not intellectual or scholarly.[1] At heart, the debate has revolved around the nature of the Federal Republic's historical and therefore national identity, its self-understanding. Should Germany, as Franz Joseph Strauss, the late Bavarian Christian Socialist leader, demanded during the 1987 election campaign, 'emerge from the dismal Third Reich and become a normal nation again'.[2] Nolte and his allies have accused scholars to the left-of-center of starting the debate in dismay at the political and intellectual shift rightwards, in response to their inability to continue dictating the historical agenda.[3] These historians have, in turn, attacked conservatives for fostering a form of guilt-free nationalism that is no longer possible for a post-Nazi Germany. [. . .]

The *Historikerstreit* is not without a broader significance. The most important theme that it raises concerns the inevitability of a new coming to terms with Germany's recent past, for Germans and for others alike. As the Nazi regime recedes into historical view, as the accretions of the postwar period multiply to fill the retrospective foreground, it is unavoidable that the emotional and moral thrust of the Hitler era be dulled, that the perspectives of the victim and the participant cede pride of place to those of the observer and the descendant. As the two halves of the former Reich unify, Germans will search for a degree of historical normalcy, a present less freighted with the past, than has been possible until now. The Nazi era and its horrors will not change, the past will not be rewritten. Despite all understandably concerned alarm, that sort of revisionism has never found any sure foothold. But the perspective on the Hitler era will evolve. As the historical distance on Nazism lengthens and as interpretations grow more sophisticated, it is foreseeable that the regime and the Holocaust will be placed in increasingly broad contexts, ones that will—superficially at least—serve to dilute their specificity and partially to historicize them. And yet, as the *Historikerstreit* has shown, there is no automatic process by which the past recedes, by which the scaring memories of contemporaries become the footnotes of dispassionate scholarship. When and how an event becomes History is a political decision.

One thing, however, seems clear. The fears of Jews and others among the regime's victims, the hopes—in turn—among the most conservative Germans and their foreign allies, that the Nazi era will at some point be subsumed without trace into a seamless continuity of the past, that it will become a diminishing blip on larger secular oscillations, that its bestialities will disappear at the vanishing point in the *longue durée* of historical retrospective—these fears are baseless, these hopes are in vain. There is no historical statute of limitations after which a 'normal' perspective will set in once again. The question is not when will Nazism finally be viewed as part of history as usual, for that day is unlikely ever to come, but how will this period, with all its anguish and inexplicability, be situated within our collective memory. How the history of this era will be written is the issue over which the dispute has been fought, a question that will continue to prompt controversy. Given the eventual inevitability of a distancing of perspective, the *Historikerstreit* and especially its polemical edge, the swath it has cut outside the academy, should not be feared as a foretaste of how the unprecedented will be normalized, the barbaric domesticated. Instead, the debate should be welcomed as evidence that Nazism and its horrors are far from having been swallowed up by forgetfulness.

['The *Historikerstreit* in Context', in Peter Baldwin (ed.), *Reworking the Past: Hitler, the Holocaust and the Historians' Debate* (Boston: Beacon Press, 1990), 10–11, 20–1, 27–30.]

JAMES E. YOUNG

105   Germany: The Ambiguity of Memory

Even the need to commemorate the victims of the Holocaust and National Socialist brutality has been, and still is, disputed in Germany. The difficult search for an adequate medium to articulate memories reflects the ambivalence of German memory itself. Memorials, and monuments even more, traditionally act as legitimizing devices celebrating national achievements; as James E. Young discusses here, this creates particular problems for a nation seeking to commemorate the millions of victims of its own acts in the past.

[N]o one takes their memorials more seriously than the Germans. Competitions are held almost monthly across the 'Fatherland' for new memorials against war and fascism, or for peace; or to mark a site of destruction, deportation, or a missing synagogue; or to remember a lost Jewish community. Students devote their summers to concentration camp archaeology at Neuengamme, excavating artifacts from another, crueler age. Or they take up hammer and nails to rebuild a synagogue in Essen, or to build a monument at the site of Dachau's former satellite camp at Landsberg. Brigades of young Germans once again report dutifully to Auschwitz, where they repair delapidated exhibition halls, tend shrubs around the barracks, and hoe weeds from the no-man's-land between formerly electrified fences. No less industrious than the generations preceding them, German teenagers now work as hard at constructing memorials as their parents did in rebuilding the country after the war, as their grandparents did in building the Third Reich itself.

Nonetheless, Holocaust memorial work in Germany today remains a tortured, self-reflective, even paralyzing preoccupation. Every monument, at every turn, is endlessly scrutinized, explicated, and debated. Artistic, ethical, and historical questions occupy design juries to an extent unknown in other countries. In a Sisyphian replay, memory is strenuously rolled nearly to the top of consciousness only to clatter back down in arguments and political bickering, whence it starts all over again. Germany's ongoing memorial work simultaneously displaces and constitutes the object of memory. Though some, like the Greens, might see such absorption in the process of memorial building as an evasion of memory, it may also be true that the surest engagement with memory lies in its perpetual irresolution. In fact, the best

German memorial to the Fascist era and its victims may not be a single memorial at all—but simply the never-to-be-resolved debate over which kind of memory to preserve, how to do it, in whose name, and to what end.

Given the state-sponsored monument's traditional function as self-aggrandizing locus for national memory, the ambiguity of German memory comes as no surprise. After all, while the victors of history have long erected monuments to their triumphs and victims have built memorials to their martyrdom, only rarely does a nation call upon itself to remember the victims of crimes it has perpetrated. Where are the national monuments to the genocide of American Indians, to the millions of Africans enslaved and murdered, to the Russian kulaks and peasants starved to death by the millions? They barely exist.[1]

What then of Germany, a nation justly forced to remember the suffering and devastation it once caused in the name of its people? How does a state incorporate its crimes against others into its national memorial landscape? How does a state recite, much less commemorate, the litany of its misdeeds, making them part of its reason for being? Under what memorial aegis, whose rules, does a nation remember its own barbarity? Where is the tradition for memorial mea culpa, when combined remembrance and self-indictment seem so hopelessly at odds? Unlike state-sponsored memorials built by victimized nations and peoples to themselves in Poland and Israel, those in Germany are necessarily those of the persecutor remembering its victims. In the face of this necessary breach in the conventional 'memorial code,' it is little wonder that German national memory remains so torn and convoluted: it is that of a nation tortured by its conflicted desire to build a new and just state on the bedrock memory of its horrendous crimes.

Germany's struggle with memory of its Nazi past is reflected in nearly every aspect of its national being: from its deliberations over the government's return to Berlin to its ambivalence over a single national holiday; from the meticulously conceived museums on the former sites of concentration camps to a new generation of artists' repudiation of monumental forms, still redolent of Nazi art. [. . .]

Even the search for a 'national day,' a day intended to unify Germans in memorial reflections on their past, churns up more angst than pride. While some in Germany would pinpoint the moment of their national rebirth at Null-Stunde (Zero Hour) on 8 May 1945, many others are loath to turn the day of their unconditional capitulation into a national holiday. A few have suggested 20 July, the day in 1944 of the Wehrmacht officers' unsuccessful attempt on Hitler's life; but again, this would have commemorated an attempted coup of German leaders against their own in wartime, a patriotic contradiction. As became all too clear, in fact, any day finally chosen would have to compete with the only day on the calendar to have acquired truly national proportions over the course of the twentieth century in Germany:

an antiday, the unspoken holiday around which great events continue to cluster in spite of itself—November 9.

On this day in 1918, Kaiser Wilhelm II abdicated his throne, marking the beginning of the Weimar Republic. With this day of the Reich's dissolution in mind, Adolf Hitler attempted to anoint himself leader on 9 November 1923 in his failed Munich beerhall putsch. In partial homage to that event, Kristallnacht was launched on the eve of 9 November 1938. During the war itself, the Nazi leadership saved its victory speeches for 9 November, as if to blot out Hitler's earlier ignominy. And, as if mystically drawn by the great negative gravity of this day fifty years after Germany invaded Poland, Germans broke through the Berlin Wall on 9 November 1989, leading to the reunification of their country less than a year later. If there were ever a single national day around which practically all of Germany's twentieth-century history might be organized, this is it.

Precisely because of its terrible load, of course, the ninth of November will remain only a phantom national day. Germany's national day has been set for 3 October, after the day in 1990 when East and West Germany (symbolizing East and West Europe) officially became one nation again. It will be a new day, unencumbered by the past, to commemorate yet another beginning, which will turn the period between 1945 and 1989 into a gestatory interregnum, a rehabilitative sentence served before Germany could be reborn again, whole. At the first parliamentary meeting of the reunified Germany, on 3 October 1990, Chancellor Helmut Kohl called a moment's silence to remember all the victims of events leading up to and issuing from Germany's division: the victims of nazism, communism, and the Berlin Wall. On the one hand, this moment reminded Germans that they had internalized remembrance of the Holocaust to such a degree that it had become, in Dan Diner's words, the actual—if unwritten—constitution of the Federal Republic.[2] At the same time, however, by uniting memory of its own martyrs with those it once victimized, making all victims the center of its first nationally shared memorial moment, Germany also attempted a qualified return to more traditional patterns of national remembrance, to what has been called a normalization of the past.[3]

For a nation's impulse to memorialize its own crimes is difficult to sustain and is almost always imposed as a certain kind of penance from without. When memory and penance are linked, however, what happens when the greatest burden of penance—Germany's division—is removed? It is likely that without the wall as a punitive reminder, Germany will become a little more like other nations: its national institutions will recall primarily its own martyrs and triumphs. These include civilian victims of Allied bombings, dutiful soldiers killed on the front, and members of the wartime resistance to Hitler. One wonders whether the whole new Germany will become more like its former western part, forever trying to overcome memory. Or whether the new Germany will become a little more like the former eastern sector, absorbed in the future, having already officially mastered the past. Finally, even Germany's nearly obsessive preoccupation with memory itself may be partly displaced by the reunification process, submerged by its sheer costs. As was the case immediately after the war, the arts of memory, monuments, and museums may even seem a little luxurious in the face of national reconstruction.

[*The Texture of Memory: Holocaust Memorials and Meaning* (New Haven: Yale University Press, 1993), 17–26.]

LUTZ NIETHAMMER

106   Jews and Russians in the Memory of the Germans

Lutz Niethammer draws on the experience of collecting and interpreting self-narrated biographies through the practice of oral history to compare German memories of National Socialist anti-Semitism in the post-war Federal Republic and in the former Democratic Republic. He emphasizes how narrative of private testimony is structured in accordance with the dominant ideological frameworks and cultural responses of each post-war state respectively, with private memories being written and rewritten under the influence of public and state-sanctioned discourses in each case.

Overall, in the self-narrated life stories of older Germans, Jews rarely appear in the period before the war, and discrimination against them before the autumn of 1938 is almost never mentioned. If Jews are mentioned, it is usually as employers, as traders, or as providers of services (e.g. doctors). In West Germany a Jewish employer, doctor, or neighbour seems to me to have remained in the active memory or to be recallable through prompting more often; overall, the social distance to the Jews appears to have been less in parts of the middle class than in the rest of society. Personally held anti-Semitic attitudes are remembered by people in east and west who were adult at the time—as far as I can see—only if people still retain them today and wish to express them, which is rare on both sides, but which does occur. Such anti-Semitism is always ideologically coloured and makes no reference to personal experiences with Jews. In both parts of Germany the question of whether people had dealings with Jews is answered most commonly by broad sectors of the population with the mention of Jewish businesses and warehouses in their own town and the memory that the family had shopped in Jewish shops, which is mostly more-or-less explicitly taken as evidence that people had not been anti-Semitic; mostly, however, they also add that in particular the clothing shops concerned had been comparatively cheap or had given more favourable credit, and that the Jewish shopkeeper, who is usually remembered as having been particularly accommodating, had as his business motto: 'It's quantity that matters!' [. . .]

Almost all Germans in east and west who lived through it remember, however, having seen the destruction of Jewish businesses, the plundering, and the burning synagogues after the so-called *Reichskristallnacht* with their own eyes. Many who had heard about the destruction went into town in order to see it. Almost all declare that they had rejected the pogrom, very often referring to its disruptiveness. In no instance do people remember their own participation in the pogrom or having exploited it for enrichment; at the same time, hardly anyone remembers having helped its victims or even any form of contact. Middle-class people occasionally mention having helped emigrating Jews by taking over their possessions. But almost every German remembers passers-by who were marked out in the street as Jews by the yellow star. Occasionally (more in the west) this is also reported of Jewish personal acquaintances, mostly with the observation that they themselves had avoided the establishment of contact. The early war years, again, are dominated by the stereotype which holds true for all Germany, that one day those Jews remaining in one's surroundings were just 'gone', that one did not know where they had gone, and that one did not give it a second thought.

Most older Germans resist giving an answer to the question of whether they knew anything about the destruction of the Jews—the concentration camps. The great majority denies it. While this is simply untrue in relation to concentration camps as such, it is less clear in relation to the systematic murder of the Jews. A minority, however, which appears to me to be larger in the east and in which in each case people who were then children are strongly represented, tell of rumours at the time that something terrible was happening to Jews in the east, and of jokes about 'Jew soap', of soldiers on leave who hinted at unimaginable atrocities against Jews, or of their own observations of ghettos and camps in Poland and the treatment of their inmates. The few who speak of their own such observations, who mostly, in the DDR as well, appear to have been active Christians and in a few cases left-wing dissidents, also emphasize that they could have talked to nobody about it—not even in their own family; occasionally fear of denunciation is added as an explanation.

Most emphasize, however, that they first heard about the Holocaust, or about other NS crimes, only after the war. In the DDR it is mostly the early education which gets emphasized. Thus, for example, the news of the Nuremberg Tribunals or the anti-fascist Defa-films, such as *Professor Mamlock*, are remembered, which subsequently dissolve in markedly vague fashion into the recognition of the anti-fascist and above all the Communist resistance and into memories, for example, of visits to the Buchenwald memorial, both of which of course have only little to do with the fate of the Jews. The Jews are no longer a socially significant group in the DDR. Since the wave of anti-Semitism which spread through eastern Europe during Stalin's last year the DDR has registered practically no returners, even though its leadership prevented the worst effects in its area at that time. Relations with Israel have been blocked right up until most recently, and the Jewish state was denounced in the media as fascistic on a daily basis. There is no official philo-Semitism, but an economic class-based explanation of fascism, according to which Jews too were murdered through work, or by other means, in the interests of capitalism.

As the Communist resistance is retrospectively grossly exaggerated and seeks adherents, the problem of the consensus behind the NS regime and the atomization of a society dominated by totalitarian rule is not of political consequence. Most are thus not dissociated from comradely support of the victims, but are liberated from the question of personal guilt. This manifests itself in the DDR in mostly less spontaneous, colder, more stereotyped memories of Jews, but on the other hand in less forced reflections upon guilt. At the same time one should not exaggerate such differences of degree, which are more conspicuous in the collective memory of the DDR than in private memories, as this memory is linked via the western media to West German elements of discourse and these have other themes and another rhythm. Anyone who wishes to become aware does so and poses the questions to himself and his friends. He who does not, however, is not forced by official anti-fascism to do so.

In the west a slower, but in the long term in this respect more thorough process of activating memory seems to have occurred. This took a long time in the post-war period: the concentration of Jewish Displaced Persons in Upper Bavaria met, after Auschwitz, with indifference and, in cases of conflict, with an unbroken latent anti-Semitic attitude within the population, among whom according to opinion polls surviving fascist sympathies after 1945 receded only at the same rate as the economic miracle legitimized democracy. When leading politicians in the early period of the Republic decided for moral, diplomatic, and trade reasons to pay financial reparations to Jewish survivors and to Israel, the initial strong, if not insurmountable resistance came not from the people but from within the political class itself. The fact that so-called compensation was pushed through had, in the long term, above all the consequence for the historical education of the West German public that the question of German guilt towards the Jews was no longer tabu. Only then could the struggle for memory begin.[1] [. . .]

In the end, the linking of historical learning to personal memories has its limits, which become more impermeable the stronger these memories are anchored in the collective memory. Foreign Jews, i.e. over 95 per cent of the victims of the Holocaust, are practically absent from the Germans' memories

in both east and west.[2] Most never met them. Auschwitz is not only unbelievably abstract for them in the sense that the factory-style asphyxiation or
murder of whole peoples by other means exceeds all imagination and had
not been threatened in even the most critical modernist utopias, but also in
the sense that the victims in their mass were as a rule totally unknown in the
society which is burdened with responsibility for their deaths, and were not
even included in the negative communicative relationship of a military
struggle.[3]

There are two main exceptions to this: one consists of encounters with
those Jews who were deported but who were not gassed, but rather who
were shipped to the Reich to work in the armaments industry, especially in
the last year of the war, and of whom a sizeable proportion survived—
although of course a small and declining percentage of the entirety of the
European Jews included in the so-called 'Final Solution'. Even apart from the
limited nature of their own knowledge and apart from the ban on contact
with German workers and also language problems, they could hardly
become the messengers of the truth of the genocide of the Jews for the
German conscience: as one of the smaller groupings they were subsumed
into the polymorphic mass of foreign workers in the final crisis of the Third
Reich and, where they were registered, they were probably more likely to
have been taken as a sign that Jews did after all still exist after their disappearance from German everyday life.

The other exception to this unconnectedness was of course those who
were charged with the registration, ghettoization, deportation, and the
destruction of the victims—namely, but not exclusively, members of the SS.
Insofar as they had returned to post-war German society they attempted to
conceal their experiences, which society first attempted to interrogate out of
them in the concentration camp trials following the Eichmann Trial. It was
precisely through the dominating attempts of the perpetrators to refuse their
testimony or to trivialize in the unavoidable court reconstructions of the
destruction process that the few initial perpetrator testimonies, such as, for
example, that of the Auschwitz-commandant Höss, spread in the collective
memory in a diffuse manner which led precisely sensitive younger Germans
to see a suspect in almost every older person and a potential perpetrator in
everyone. Historically, however, this diffusion, which is of fundamental significance for the moral reflexes of our society, only gives the appearance of
having made the abstraction of Auschwitz more concrete. [. . .]

['Juden und Russen im Gedächtnis der Deutschen', in Walter H. Pehle (ed.), *Der historische
Ort des Nationalsozialismus* (Frankfurt: Fischer, 1990), 119–24.]

107 A War Against Memory?

As Isabel Wollaston suggests, even variations in the terminology we use to signify the National Socialist genocide of the Jews betray different basic assumptions about its nature and its place in history and memory.

The 1980s and 1990s have been marked by a series of fiftieth anniversaries relating to Nazism, World War II, and the Holocaust. For example, 1985: the Nuremberg Laws; 1988: the *Anschluss*, Munich, *Kristallnacht*; 1989: the outbreak of World War II; 1990: the Battle of Britain; 1991: the invasion of the Soviet Union, Pearl Harbour; 1992: the Wannsee Conference, El Alamein; 1993: the Warsaw Ghetto Uprising; 1994: D-Day, the Warsaw Rising; 1995: the liberation of Auschwitz, Dresden, VE-Day, Hiroshima and Nagasaki, the end of World War II. Such anniversaries are observed with varying degrees of solemnity and public interest. Few of them are immune to controversy. In Britain, for instance, heated debates have surrounded the unveiling of a statue to Bomber Harris, the initial plans for commemorating D-Day, and the 'twinning' of Coventry and Dresden in ceremonies remembering the effects of saturation bombing.[1]

The diverse reactions to the ceremonies commemorating the fiftieth anniversary of the liberation of Auschwitz serve in many ways to illustrate the 'memory-ignited rage' that simmers close beneath the surface of any attempt to remember these events.[2] Such 'rage' is all too often triggered by anniversaries, as these serve to highlight the extent to which various individuals and groups have different, and often conflicting, memories of the same events. Auschwitz, for many the ultimate symbol of the Holocaust, also serves as the ultimate symbol of the conflict generated by remembrance of these events. Hence the conclusion reached by Neal Ascherson:

The truth about Auschwitz is that there can never be consensus about the use of its ruins. It has too many symbolisms for too many different, and sometimes mutually suspicious, groups of people . . . But this inner discord, which can never fully be overcome, is what Auschwitz and its memory is all about.[3]

Inevitably, the memory of events is multi-layered, and often fractured. How they are remembered is influenced by the age, gender, nationality and political or religious affiliations of the individual or group remembering. Memory is further coloured by the circumstances of those remembering, both in the past (for example, whether they experienced occupation, served in the armed forces, were a member of the resistance, or an inmate in a concentration camp or death camp) and in the present. Such differences in perspective are reflected, in part, by the choice of terms such as 'the Second World War', 'the Great Patriotic War', '*Hitlerzeit*', and 'the Holocaust'. [. . .]

While there is consensus concerning the need to remember the Holocaust, there is widespread, often vehement disagreement over what should be remembered, by whom, and for what purpose. Particularly controversial is the question of what forms of remembrance are appropriate, and what significance should be attached to the Holocaust in relation to other aspects of Jewish culture, history, and belief. Current disagreement over something as seemingly basic as an appropriate name serves as a fitting symbol of the complexity of contemporary perceptions of these events. [. . .]

It is an obvious, although often overlooked, truism that the Holocaust is not one event, but rather 'a generalization that unites a variety of discrete events under one rubric'.⁴ As such, 'Holocaust', and terms like it, tend to dissolve many distinct events and experiences into one. The very act of naming thus inevitably entails a degree of simplification. For this reason, it is often suggested that no one word or label is sufficient to describe these events. However, recurrent debates over appropriate nomenclature would seem to imply that some names are more appropriate than others. In the words of Dominic LaCapra, we are entering 'an area where there are no easy, uninvolved, or purely objective choices'.⁵ Yet such choices have to be made, for the range of possibilities is seemingly endless: 'Holocaust', 'holocaust', 'Shoah', 'Hurban', 'the Tremendum', 'the Event', 'the Kingdom of Night', 'l'univers concentrationnaire', 'the Lager', 'KZ-Zeit', 'genocide', 'the destruction of the European Jews', 'extermination', 'the Final Solution' . . . are but a few examples.

As James Young notes, 'The names we assign this period automatically figure and contextualize events, locating them within the continua of particular historical, literary and interpretive traditions'.⁶ As suggested above, it is for precisely this reason that some remain adamant that we should resist the temptation to impose any name upon these events. If to name is to place certain experiences within a particular narrative or interpretive framework, then it can also serve to domesticate or conventionalize the inexpressible. According to Amos Oz, 'all these words attempt to bypass, to soften, to prettify, or to place everything into one known familiar historic pattern'.⁷ Yet, even if Oz is correct, to be remembered events have to be thought about and spoken about. To name is to remember, however partially or provisionally. Each of the above names 'remembers' in a way that signifies the adoption (consciously or unconsciously) of a particular discourse, with attendant implications that may be ethical, historical, philosophical, political, rhetorical, or theological.

By way of example, to speak of 'Hurban' or 'l'univers concentrationnaire' is to adopt the discourse of the victims, whereas to speak of 'extermination' or 'the Final Solution' is to adopt the language of Nazi bureaucracy. To speak of 'Hurban' is to contextualize events within the continuum of Jewish history and belief, whereas 'Shoah' and 'Holocaust' were both coined, in part, to suggest a rupture within that continuum. To capitalize 'Holocaust' is to assert the uniqueness of these events; to refuse to do so is to distance oneself from such an assertion. The situation is complicated further by the changing, often multiple meanings of particular terms. Today, the adoption of 'Shoah' generally signifies the rejection of any attribution of religious meanings to these events, although a number of biblical usages of the term carry associations of a disaster sent by God.[8]

'Holocaust', arguably more than any other, is both a term that can be understood in a variety of ways, and one that is frequently accused of misrepresenting the reality it purports to express. On the one hand it is a term that belongs to the discourse of victims; on the other it is the term 'currently most widely employed'.[9] Etymologically, 'Holocaust' is problematic for many because of its sacrificial overtones, suggestive of a 'burnt offering'. Yet, for others, the significance of the term lies in its awe-ful connotations and its associations with fire. However, as Elie Wiesel, one of the term's earliest advocates, points out, such associations are often lost in the transition from survivor discourse to popular culture.[10] The prevalent popular usage of the term serves to routinize its meaning; a process which in itself often counteracts any sacrificial connotations. Finally, 'Holocaust' tends to be the term favoured by those engaged, consciously or unconsciously, in the mythologization of these events.

[A War against Memory? The Future of Holocaust Remembrance (London: SPCK, 1996), 1–3.]

Notes

Extract 8

ERICH FROMM: *The Psychology of Nazism*

1. Cf. to this whole chapter and specifically to the rôle of the lower middle class, Harold D. Lasswell's illuminating paper on 'The Psychology of Hitlerism' in the *Political Quarterly*, Vol. IV, 1933, Macmillan & Co., London, p. 374, and F. L. Schuman's *Hitler and the Nazi Dictatorship*, Hale, London, 1936.
2. Schuman, *op. cit.*, p. 104.

Extract 13

HANS-ULRICH WEHLER: *The German Empire 1871–1918*

1. H. Rosenberg, *Probleme der deutschen Sozialgeschichte* (Frankfurt am Main, 1969), 7–49.
2. P. Kielmansegg, 'Von den Schwierigkeiten, deutsche Geschichte zu schreiben', *Merkur*, 276 (1971), 366–79.

Extract 14

JÜRGEN KOCKA: *The Causes of National Socialism*

1. M. Horkheimer, 'Die Juden in Europa', *Zeitschrift für Sozialforschung*, 8 (1939), 115–37 (116).
2. For example in the influential paperback R. Kühnl, *Formen bürgerlicher Herrschaft: Liberalismus-Faschismus* (Reinbek, 1971). Cf. as overviews of the theoretical discussion: W. Wippermann, *Faschismustheorien* (Darmstadt, 2nd edn. 1975); A. Kuhn, *Das faschistische Herrschaftssystem und die moderne Gesellschaft* (Hamburg, 1973); R. Saage, *Faschismustheorien* (Munich, 1976). A very good discussion is H. A. Winkler, 'Die neue Linke und der Faschismus: zur Kritik neomarxistischer Theorien über den Nationalsozialismus', in id., *Revolution, Staat, Faschismus* (Göttingen, 1978), 65–117. Cf. also E. Hennig, *Bürgerliche Gesellschaft und Faschismus in Deutschland* (Frankfurt, 1977).
3. As is well known, the conflict over the question of how the deficit in the state unemployment insurance arising out of the crisis was to be covered was the cause of the collapse of the Great Coalition, on which the government of Hermann Müller was based. It resigned on 27 March 1930. The German People's Party (DVP) which also represented the interests of industry wanted to retain the previous insurance contribution of 3.5% for employers and 3.5% for employees: the SPD, linked closely with the trade unions, called for an increase to 4%. No compromise was reached. Thus the parliamentary system ceased to function. For the presidential cabinets which now followed under Heinrich Brüning (from 30 Mar. 1930), Franz von Papen (from 1 June 1932), and Kurt von Schleicher (from 3 Dec. 1932) could no longer rely on parliamentary majorities, but governed with

the authority of the German president. The Reichstag tolerated this. It was too much at loggerheads to be able to reach agreement on a policy supported by the majority. Cf. K D. Bracher, *Die deutsche Diktatur: Entstehung, Struktur, Folgen des Nationalismus* (Cologne, 1969), 185–218.

4. Cf. M. Broszat, *Der Staat Hitlers* (Munich, 1969); D. Petzina, *Autarkiepolitik im Dritten Reich* (Stuttgart, 1968); T. W. Mason, 'Der Primat der Politik: Politik und Wirtschaft im Nationalsozialismus', *Das Argument*, 41 (1966), 473–94; id., 'Primat der Industrie?', *Das Argument*, 47 (1968), 193–209. On the outbreak of war see W. Deist et al., *Ursachen und Voraussetzungen der deutschen Kriegspolitik* (Stuttgart, 1979); W. Benz and H. Graml (eds.), *'Sommer 1939': die Großmächte und der europäische Krieg*, (Stuttgart, 1979); U. D. Adam, *Judenpolitik im Dritten Reich* (Düsseldorf, 1972).

5. Cf. as an introduction chs. I and II of D. Schoenbaum, *Die braune Revolution: eine Sozialgeschichte des Dritten Reiches 1933–1939* (Cologne, 1968).

6. Regarding the 'old middle class' cf. [. . .] H. A. Winkler, *Mittelstand, Demokratie und Nationalsozialismus* (Cologne, 1972). On white-collar workers: J. Kocka, *Angestellte zwischen Faschismus und Demokratie: zur politischen Sozialgeschichte der Angestellten: USA 1890–1940 im internationalen Vergleich* (Göttingen, 1977), 49–57 (overview of the state of research on the political social history of the German white-collar workers up to 1933). Published after that: H. Speier, *Die Angestellten vor dem Nationalsozialismus: ein Beitrag zum Verständnis der deutschen Sozialstruktur 1918–1933* (Göttingen, 1977) (currently the best synthesis); H.-J. Priamus, *Angestellte und Demokratie: die nationalliberale Angestelltenbewegung in der Weimarer Republik* (Stuttgart, 1980).

7. Cf. re this interpretation generally, E. Bloch, *Erbschaft dieser Zeit* (1935; expanded new edn. Frankfurt, 1962), 104–42; repr. E. Nolte (ed.), *Theorien über den Faschismus* (Cologne, 1967), 182–204; R. Dahrendorf, *Gesellschaft und Demokratie in Deutschland* (Munich, 1965); see also Th. Nipperdey, 'Probleme der Modernisierung in Deutschland', *Saeculum*, 30 (1979), 292–303.

8. Cf. generally and with numerous literature references Winkler, 'Die "neue Linke" und der Faschismus', particularly 74–83; H. Rosenberg, 'Die Pseudodemokratisierung der Rittergutsbesitzerklasse', in id., *Probleme der deutschen Sozialgeschichte* (Frankfurt, 1969), 7–50; H.-J. Puhle, *Von der Agrarkrise zum Präfaschismus* (Wiesbaden, 1972); biased, but with important material; B. Buchte, *Die Junker und die Weimarer Republik* (Berlin, 1959); on the employers and capitalists [. . .] see also H. A. Winkler, 'Unternehmerverbände zwischen Ständeideologie und Nationalsozialismus', in id., *Liberalismus*, 175–94; M. Schneider, *Unternehmer und Demokratie; die freien Gewerkschaften in der unternehmerischen Ideologie der Jahre 1910–1933* (Bonn, 1975). Cf., on the culture and intellectual historical components of the problems addressed here, F. Stern, *Kulturpessimismus als politische Gefahr: eine Analyse nationale Ideologie in Deutschland* (Bern, 1963); K. Sontheimer, *Antidemokratisches Denken in der Weimarer Republik: die politischen Ideen des deutschen Nationalismus zwischen 1918 and 1933* (2nd edn., Munich, 1968).

Extract 15

GEOFF ELEY: *What Produces Fascism: Pre-industrial Traditions or a Crisis of Capitalism?*

1. See the following: F. Zipfel, 'Gestapo and the SD: A Sociographic Profile of the Organisers of Terror', in S. U. Larsen, B. Hagtvet, and J. P. Myklebust (eds.), *Who were the Fascists? Social Roots of European Fascism* (Bergen, 1980), 301–11; G. C. Boehnert, 'The Jurists in the SS Führerkorps, 1925–1939', in G. Hirschfeld and L. Kettenacker (eds.), *Der Führerstaat: Mythos und Realität* (Stuttgart, 1981), 361–74; Tim Mason, 'Zur Entstehung des Gesetzes zur Ordnung der nationalen Arbeit: ein Versuch über das Verhältnis "archäischer" und "moderner" Momente in der neuesten deutschen Geschichte', in H. Mommsen, D. Petzina, and B. Weisbrod (eds.), *Industrielles System und politische Entwicklung in der Weimarer Republik* (Düsseldorf, 1974), 322–51; K.-H. Ludwig, *Technik und Ingenieure im Dritten Reich (Düsseldorf, 1976)*; A. D. Beyerchen, *Scientists under Hitler: Politics and the Physics Community in the Third Reich* (New Haven, 1978). See also K.-J. Müller, 'French Fascism and Modernisation', *Journal of Contemporary History*, 11 (Oct. 1976), 75–108.

2. [This argument] owes much to E. Laclau, 'Fascism and Ideology', in *Politics and Ideology in Marxist Theory* (London, 1977), 81–142.

3. R. Fraser, 'The Spanish Civil War', in R. Samuel (ed.), *People's History and Socialist Theory* (London, 1981), 197.

4. J. Kocka, *White-Collar Workers in America 1890–1940. A Social-Political History in International Perspective* (London, 1980), 252.

5. The phrase comes from the penultimate section of Abraham's final chapter, 'Towards the Extra-systemic Solution', in D. Abrahams, *The Collapse of the Weimar Republic: Political Economy and Crisis* (Princeton, 1981), 313–18.

6. Here I am abstracting from a number of recent works, which are separated by numerous specific differences and whose authors may not share the particular formulations I have chosen. See, in particular: B. Weisbrod, *Schwerindustrie in der Weimarer Republik: industrielle Interessenpolitik zwischen Stabilisierung und Krise* (Wuppertal, 1978) and 'Economic Power and Political Stability Reconsidered: Heavy Industry in Weimar Germany', *Social History*, 4 (May 1979), 241–63; Abraham, *Collapse of the Weimar Republic*; D. Stegmann, 'Kapitalismus und Faschismus 1929–34: Thesen und Materialen', in H. G. Backhaus (ed.), *Gesellschaft: Beiträge zur Marxschen Theorie* (Frankfurt am Main, 1976), vi. 14–75; C. D. Crohn, 'Autoritärer Kapitalismus: Wirtschaftskonzeptionen im Übergang von der Weimarer Republik zum Nationalsozialismus', in D. Stegmann, B.-J. Wendt, and P.-C. Witt (eds.), *Industrielle Gesellschaft und politisches System* (Bonn, 1978), 113–29; Charles S. Maier's summing up at the 1974 Bochum conference on the Weimar Republic, in Mommsen, Petzina, and Weisbrod (eds.), *Industrielles System und politische Entwicklung*, 950 ff.

7. See W. Luthardt (ed.), *Sozialdemokratische Arbeiterbewegung und Weimarer Republik: Materialien zur gesellschaftlichen Entwicklung 1927–1933*, 2 vols. (Frankfurt am Main, 1978).

Extract 16

DIETER GROH: *The Special Path of German History: Myth or Reality?*

1. David Blackbourn and Geoff Eley, *Mythen deutscher Geschichtsschreibung: die gescheiterte bürgerliche Revolution von 1848* (Berlin, 1981), 56 ff.
2. See the last pages of my article 'Reflections on the Making of the German Working Class', *Social History*, 8 (1983), 391–7.
3. *Merkur*, 35 (1981), 483.

Extract 18

JEREMY NOAKES: *The Nazi Party in Lower Saxony*

1. For example in Brunswick see Roloff, *Bürgertum und Nationalsozialismus 1930–1933* (Hanover, 1961), pp. 42–3. The DDP however remained outside.
2. The party always made great propaganda out of the funeral services and deaths of its 'martyrs'.
3. See R. Dahrendorf, *Gesellschaft und Demokratie in Deutschland* (Munich, 1965), 432 ff.
4. e.g. an article in the *Niedersächsische Beobachter* of 4 May 1929, maintained that 'the rebuilding of Germany is not the task of the generation whose best representatives were already by 1914 formed and completed personalities. All the acts and measures of these politicians and leaders become reactionary at the decisive moment. As the generation of the 30-year-olds, in other words, those who were formed by war, revolution, and the post-war period without ever being able to become torpid or to age seriously, enters politics, the contrast to the pre-war generation will become sharper.'
5. S. Neumann, *Die deutschen Parteien. Wesen und Wandel nach dem Kriege* (Berlin, 1932), pp. 100 ff. Rohe describes the opposition of the SPD functionaries to the attempts to transform its propaganda style after 1930 in *Das Reichsbanner Schwarz-Rot-Gold. Ein Beitrag zur Geschichte und Struktur der politischen Kampfverbände zur Zeit der Weimarer Republik* (Düsseldorf, 1966), p. 409.
6. For a discussion of the chiliastic features of the Nazi movement, see T. Heuss, *Hitler's Weg* (1932; repr. Stuttgart, 1968), pp. 166 ff. and N. Cohn, *The Pursuit of the Millennium* (London, 1962), pp. 307 ff.

Extract 20

ROGER GRIFFIN: *The Rise of German Fascism*

1. K. Sontheimer, *Antidemokratisches Denken in der Weimarer Republik* (Munich, 1968), 288.
2. D. Mühlberger, 'Germany', in D. Mühlberger (ed.), *The Social Basis of European Fascist Movements* (London, 1987); D. Mühlberger, *Hitler's Followers: Studies in the Sociology of the Nazi Movement* (London, 1991).
3. K. Vondung, *Magic und Manipulation: ideologischer Kult und politischer Religion des Nationalsozialismus* (Göttingen, 1971); K. Vondung, 'Spiritual Revolution and Magic: Speculation and Political Action in National Socialism', *Modern Age*, 23/4 (1979).

Extract 23

HANS MOMMSEN: *The National Socialist Seizure of Power and German Society*

1. Cf. Michael Schneider, *Unternehmer und Demokratie: die freien Gewerkschaften in der unternehmerischen Ideologie in den Jahren 1918–1933* (Bonn, 1975); Bernd Weisbrod, *Schwerindustrie in der Weimarer Republik: Interessenpolitik zwischen Stabilisierung und Krise* (Wuppertal, 1978), 472 ff.
2. *Deutchlands Erneuerung*, 16/3 (Mar. 1932), 181.
3. Cf. Oswald Spengler, *Preußentum und Sozialismus* (Munich, 1920), 12 ff.; Horst Möller, 'Die nationalsozialistische Machtergreifung: Konterrevolution oder Revolution?', *VfZ* 31 (1983), 25–51 does not, remarkably, go into this issue although he is concerned to reproduce contemporary discussions of the subject of revolution.
4. Cf. Reinhard Neebe, *Großindustrie, Staat und NSDAP 1930–1933* (Göttingen, 1981), 160 ff.
5. Cf. Kurt Koszyk, 'Paul Reusch und die "Münchner Neueste Nachrichten"', *VfZ* 20 (1972), 75–103.
6. Henry A. Turner, 'The Ruhrlade, Secret Cabinet of Heavy Industry in the Weimar Republic', *Central European History*, 3 (1970), 195–228.
7. See Neebe, *Großindustrie, Staat und NSDAP*, 145 ff.
8. See above all Heinrich-August Winkler, 'Mittelstandsbewegung oder Volkspartei? Zur sozialen Basis der NSDAP', in W. Schieder (ed.), *Faschismus als soziale Bewegung: Deutschland und Italien im Vergleich* (2nd edn., Göttingen, 1983), 102 ff.
9. Cf. Andreas Dorpalen, 'SPD und KPD in der Endphase der Weimarer Republik', *VfZ* 31 (1983), 105 ff.

Extract 24

RICHARD BESSEL: *Why Did the Weimar Republic Collapse?*

1. Gerald D. Feldman, 'Economic and Social Problems of the German Demobilisation, 1918–19', *Journal of Modern History*, 47 (1975); Carl-Ludwig Holtfrerich, *The German Inflation 1914–18: Causes and Effects in International Perspectives* (Berlin and New York, 1986), p. 129; Harold James, *The German Slump. Politics and Economics 1924–1936* (Oxford, 1986), pp. 41–2.
2. Heinz Haller, 'Die Rolle der Staatsfinanzen für den Inflationsprozess', in Deutsche Bundesbank (ed.), *Währung und Wirtschaft in Deutschland 1876–1975* (Frankfurt/Main, 1976), pp. 140–1. Quoted in Holtfrerich, *The German Inflation*, p. 137.
3. See Holtfrerich, *The German Inflation*, pp. 124–5.
4. See Holtfrerich, *The German Inflation*, p. 317.
5. See the, still rather tentative, discussion in Richard Bessel and David Englander, 'Up from the Trenches: Some Recent Writing on the Soldiers of the Great War', *European Studies Review*, 11 (1981), pp. 387–95.

Extract 26

IAN KERSHAW: *30 January 1933*

1. That a combination of crisis symptoms was decisive for the collapse of Weimar is especially emphasized by Detlev J. Peukert, *Die Weimarer Republik: Krisenjahre der klassischen Moderne* (Frankfurt am Main, 1987), 269 ff.

2. See Richard Bessel, '1933: A Failed Counter-Revolution', in E. E. Rice (ed.), *Revolution and Counter-Revolution* (Oxford, 1991), 109–27. Bessel refers to Richard Löwenthal's definition of counter-revolution in M. Broszat et al., *Deutschlands Weg in die Diktatur* (Berlin, 1983): 'A counter-revolution is an attempt to turn back the wheel of history and to restore a system which had already once been in existence. The attempt at counter-revolution was that of Papen and Hindenburg, not that of the Nazis' (95).

3. *Regensburger Anzeiger*, 31 Jan. 1933.

4. The transformation of power relationships within the 'power cartel' is the subject of the analysis of Peter Hüttenberger, 'Nationalsozialistische Polykratie', *Geschichte und Gesellschaft*, 2 (1976), 480–508.

5. See Bessel, ('1933'), 120–1.

6. Klaus-Jürgen Müller, *Armee, Politik und Gesellschaft in Deutschland 1933–1945* (Paderborn, 1979), 44 ff.

7. See André Gorz, *Farewell to the Working Class* (London, 1972), 58–63.

Extract 27

WILLIAM SHERIDAN ALLEN: *The Nazi Seizure of Power*

1. For a comparative example see Ernst-August Roloff, *Bürgertum und National-Sozialismus: Braunschweigs Weg ins Dritte Reich* (Hanover, 1961).

Extract 28

ZDENEK ZOFKA: *The Growth of National Socialism in the Countryside*

1. The significance of the party programme for the winning over of broad sectors of the electorate is often overestimated. See, for example, Heinrich August Winkler, *Mittelstand, Demokratie und Nationalsozialismus: die politische Entwicklung von Handwerk und Kleinhandel in der Weimarer Republik* (Cologne, 1972), 160; cf. also the critique by Annette Leppert-Fögen: 'Der Mittelstandssozialismus der NSDAP', *Frankfurter Hefte*, 29 (1974), 656–66, (663). In my view the overestimation of the significance of written party programmes for voting decisions is rooted in a misjudgement of the political culture of the Weimar Republic. Party programmes may have played some role in the winning of individual opinion formers, but even here their influence should not be overemphasized.

2. Cf. for example Jeremy Noakes, *The Nazi Party in Lower Saxony 1921–1933* (Oxford, 1971), 128: 'The party sent members into committee meetings.' In general much significance (in terms of electoral support) is attributed to the National Socialist infiltration of the interest-group organizations. Cf. e.g. Winkler, *Mittelstand*, 167 ff.; Hans Mommsen, 'Zur Verschränkung traditioneller und faschistischer Führungsgruppen in Deutschland beim Übergang von der Bewegungs- zur Systemphase', in Wolfgang Schieder (ed.), *Faschismus als soziale Bewegung, Deutschland und Italien in Vergleich* (Hamburg, 1976), 157–82 (166); Horst Gies, 'NSDAP und landwirtschaftliche Organisationen in der Endphase der Weimarer Republik', *Vierteljahrshefte für Zeitgeschichte*, 15 (1967), 341–76 (376). The overestimation of these processes (or in part also the uncritical use of the term 'infiltration') is certainly connected to National Socialist propaganda at the higher level ('Into the

Reich Agrarian League!'; 'Into the factories!'). On the other hand this is not to say that these infiltration processes (e.g. of the Reich Agrarian League) were not necessarily of enormous significance on other levels and in other regions.

3. Neither did the winning of National Socialist majorities in the interest organizations, in order to install National Socialist chairmen or be able to proclaim resolutions or electoral slogans in favour of the Nazis, play any role in our area (cf. Claus-Dieter Kohn und Dirk Stegmann, 'Kleingewerbe und National-sozialismus in einer agrarisch-mittelständischen Region: das Beispiel Lüneberg 1930–1939, *Archiv für Sozialgeschichte*, 17 (1977), 41–91, 63 ff.). The conversion of respected, 'proven' opinion leaders made its impact even without the formal decisions of the organizations they led.

4. Mommsen, 'Zur Verschränkung traditioneller', 166.

Extract 29

RUDY KOSHAR: *Toward the Mass Party*

1. Comparison of percentages of individuals receiving different types of unemployment compensation in Marburg and all German cities of 20,000–50,000 inhabitants, 1930–2:

	Insurance	Crisis support	Welfare	Total
Marburg	25.1	17.9	57.0	100.0 (N = 2,888)
All cities of 20,000–50,000	31.0	25.0	44.0	100.0 (N = 1,055,693)

Sources: 'Arbeitslose und Arbeitslosenhilfe 1930 und 1931', *Statistisches Jahrbuch Deutscher Städte* (SJDS), 27 (1932), 310–20; 'Arbeitslose und Arbeitslosenhilfe 1932', *SJDS* 28 (1933), 543–9; and 'Arbeitslose und Arbeitslosenhilfe 1934', *Statistisches Jahresbuch Deutscher Gemeinde*, 29 (1934), 416–21. On Reich benefits for needy Marburg pensioners see *Oberhessische Zeitung* (OZ), 4 Sept. 1930. See also *OZ* 13 Jan. 1919; 19 Mar. 1921; 11 Feb. 1922; *Hessisches Tagesblatt*, 29 Oct., 9 and 18 Dec. 1925; on Polish labour see Landrat to Regierungspräsident Kassel, 5 Jan. 1928 in Hessisches Staatsarchiv Marburg 180, La Mbg, 3807; see also *OZ* 14 Feb. 1928; *HT* 30 Apr. 1928; *OZ* 7 Sept. 1931; 'Hauptübersicht: Aufbau der Bevölkerung, der Finanzen und der Wirtschaft,' in *SJDG* 30 (1935) 1–27.

2. The Landrat had emphasized the 'misery of the farmers' in early 1928 and simultaneously stressed the long-term aspects of such problems as labour shortages in the countryside. See Landrat to Regierungspräsident Kassel, 5 and 12 Jan. 1928, in HSAM 180, La Mbg, 3807.

3. An NSDStB advertisement before the 1931 AMSt campaign hardly reflected a predominant concern for economic hardship: 'We demand the exclusion of foreign races from German universities; only Germans as educators of German youth; doing away with the Versailles Treaty and war guilt lies; a secure future; the intellectual and material strengthening of Germans' capabilities to defend

themselves militarily; a chair for military science at each German university; the awakening of Germans' consciousness about folk characteristics; a chair for the study of hereditary and racial teachings at all German universities; the purposive use of all elements of German culture (the press, theater, art, literature and radio) in the struggle for folk-national interests; the struggle of the German student for the German worker! We demand: the unification of the worker of the head and worker of the hand, the national and social liberation of the German people in a true folk community. That's what it's all about in the struggle at the university. German student, do you want what we want? Then vote for the NSDStB list, list 3!' (*Hessische Volkswacht*, 4/5 July 1931).

4. The organizations were Schaumburgia, Chattia, Saxnot, Normannia, and Akademischer Turnerbund. In addition, the NSDStB assumed that it could count on the support of another forty fraternity students who were not activists but were loyal to the party. See von Eltz to NSDStB *Propagandaabteilung*, c. Aug. 1928, Archiv der Universitätsbibliothek Würzburg/Archiv der ehemaligen Reichsstudentenführung und des NSDStB, UWAR II/A 10.

5. Gilde Saxnot invited Student League member Werner Gaul to speak at an open house in the summer of 1929. During that semester, Arminia and the Akademischer Turnbund also invited NSDStB speakers to discussion evenings and informal talks. Due to von Eltz's friendship with Stahlhelm students, the NSDStB and Stahlhelm student group marched together at the 1929 Bismarck Day ceremonies; see letters from von Eltz to Reich NSDStB, 5 June and 22 July 1929, AUWAR II/A 10. For the contact organizations, see Anselm Faust, *Der Nationalsozialistische Deutsche Studentenbund: Studenten und Nationalsozialismus in der Weimarer Republik*, 2 vols. (Düsseldorf, 1976), ii. 29–35.

6. For Wißner, see interview with Bauer, 1 Apr. 1977; Verein für Leibesübungen 1860, *Festschrift zum 90. Stiftungsfest des VfL 1860 Marburg* (Marburg, 1950), 17; *Marburger Einwohnerbuch* (1925), 36; and Marburg NSDAP membership list (with membership numbers) n.d. in HSAM 327/1, 5488; for Schweinsberger, see NSDAP membership list n.d in HSAM 321/1, 5488; *OZ* 9 Nov. 1929; and minutes of 5 Oct. 1931 Kreishandwerkerbund meeting, Amtsgericht Kreis Marburg, Vereinsregister, 74; for Hübner, see HSAM 305a, Acc. 1954/16, 45; report from Landjägerpost Sterzhausen to Landrat on 15 Nov. 1930 NSDAP meeting (at which Hübner appears for the first time as a Nazi assembly leader) in HSAM 180, LA Mbg, 2917; and Hübner, 'Korporationsstudent und Nationalsozialismus', in HV 4/5 July 1931.

Extract 30

ODED HEILBRONNER: *The Abandoned Regulars' Table*

1. Some examples of association chairmen who stood in local elections: K.R., Triberg, was chairman of the local gymnastics association 1860 (*Triberger Bote*, 10 Dec. 1931); H.S. Schonach, was chairman of the local singing club 'Sängerkreis' (*TB* 2 Dec. 1930); the entire committee of this association stood in the local 'citizens' association'; cf. Minutes Book of the male choral association, Schonach (in private possession of the current association chairman).

2. Alternative views are expressed in Z. Zofka, *Die Ausbreitung des Nationalsozialismus*

auf dem Lande (Munich, 1979), 37, 81; W. Kaschuba and C. Lipp, *Dörfliches Überleben* (Tübingen, 1982), 267; R. Koshar, *Social Life, Local Politics and Nazism: Marburg 1880–1935* (Chapel Hill, NC, 1986), ch. 5; M. Kieserling, *Faschisierung and gesellschaftlicher Wandel: Mikroanalyse eines nordhessischen Kreises 1928–1939* (Wiesbaden, 1991), 121 ff.

3. *Donaubote*, 26 July 1932, 17 Feb. 1932 ('Letters from the central Black Forest'); M. Hildebrand (ed.), *Haslach im Kinzigtal* (Haslach, 1978), 27–9.

4. The priest of Lahr compared the gymnastics association with the local Nazi party in discussion of the question of whether uniforms could be worn in church. Erzbischöflichesarchiv Freiburg B2/NS1, 4 July 1931.

5. R. Hamilton, *Who Voted for Hitler* (Princeton, 1982), ch. 12 and 13; W. S. Allen, *The Nazi Seizure of Power* (New York, 1984), 144; J. Noakes, *The Nazi Party in Lower Saxony* (Oxford, 1971), 211; G. Pridham, *The Nazi Movement in Bavaria 1923–1933* (London, 1973), 110 ff.; Zofka, *Ausbreitung*, 100; I. Kershaw, *The Hitler Myth: Image and Reality in the Third Reich* (Oxford, 1989), 37–43; H.-U. Thamer, *Verführung und Gewalt: Führerideologie und Parteiorganisation der NSDAP (1919–1933)* (Düsseldorf, 1972), ch. 5; G. Paul, *Aufstand der Bilder: die NS Propaganda vor 1933* (Bonn, 1991).

6. Some of the most important studies of Catholic society in rural areas before 1933 are Zofka, *Ausbreitung*; Kaschuba and Lipp, *Überleben*; D. Kaufmann, *Katholisches Milieu in Münster 1928–1933* (Düsseldorf, 1984); R. Möhler, *German Peasants and Agrarian Politics 1914–1924: The Rhineland and Westphalia* (Chapel Hill, NC, 1986). Notable is the important study by G. Plum, *Gesellschaftsstruktur und politisches Bewußtsein in einer katholischen Region 1928–1933: Untersuchung am Beispiel des Regierungsbezirks Aachen* (Stuttgart, 1972); see also the relevant chapter in G. Pridham, *The Nazi Movement in Bavaria* (London, 1973); also K. Holmes, 'The NSDAP and the Crisis of Agrarian Conservatism in Lower Bavaria', diss. Georgetown University, 1982.

7. *Donaubote*, 26 July 1932 ('Citizen, be on your guard').

8. Staatsarchiv Freiburg, BZ Neustadt—245/184. 25 Jan. 1932 Joostal-Titisee.

Extract 31

WOLFRAM PYTA: *Protestant Rural Milieu and National Socialism Prior to 1933*

1. The author attempts to portray the interaction of the rural Protestant social milieu and the world of politics in his *Habilitation* work: *Dorfgemeinschaft and Parteipolitik 1918–1933: die Verschränkung von Milieu und Parteien in den protestantischen Landgebieten Deutschlands in der Weimarer Republik* (Düsseldorf, 1995). The ideas in this essay on village social milieu and rural policy-making are based on the said *Habilitation*, for which reason detailed individual refererences are dispensed with here.

2. Karl Rohe has aptly described it thus: 'that politics is more or less understood as an extension of normal social affairs', in Karl Rohe, 'Zur Typologie politischer Kulturen in westlichen Demokratien', in Heinz Dollinger, Horst Gründer, and Alwin Hanschmidt (eds.), *Weltpolitik—Europagedanke—Regionalismus* (Münster, 1982), 581–96 (588).

3. On regional variations in agricultural structure cf. the informative study by

Heinrich Becker, *Handlungsspielräume der Agrarpolitik in der Weimarer Republik zwischen 1923 und 1929* (Stuttgart, 1990), esp. 53–61.

4. The hitherto most thorough regional study of the National Socialists' penetration of the countryside also draws attention to this: Zdenek Zofka, *Die Ausbreitung des Nationalsozialismus auf dem Lande* (Munich, 1979), esp. 343–9.

Extract 37

ERNST GOTTSCHLING: *The Fascist State: The German Example*

1. Georgi Dimitroff, 'Die Offensive des Faschismus und die Aufgaben der Kommunistischen Internationale im Kampf für die Arbeiterklasse gegen den Faschismus', in *VII Weltkongress der Kommunistische Internationale* (Berlin, 1975), 94.
2. W. I. Lenin, 'Über eine Karikatur auf den Marxismus und über den "imperialistischen Ökonomismus"', in Lenin, *Werke*, vol. xxiii (Berlin, 1964), 34.
3. Martin Broszat, *Der Staat Hitlers* (Munich, 1969), 339.

Extract 38

ERNST FRAENKEL: *The Dual State*

1. This was a consequence of Dr Schacht's policy.
2. Hamburger (Hanseatisches) Oberlandesgericht, 4 May 1937 (*Hanseatische Rechts- und Gerichtszeitung* (1937), 216.
3. Ibid.
4. Er nennt's Vernunft und braucht's allein,
   Nur tierischer als jedes Tier zu sein.
   (Goethe, *Faust*).

Extract 39

FRANZ NEUMANN: *Behemoth*

1. Ernst Fraenkel, *The Dual State* (New York, 1941).
2. Reinhard Höhn, *Die Wandlung im staatsrechtlichen Denken* (Hamburg, 1934).
3. Gottfried Neesse, *Führergewalt* (Tübingen, 1940).
4. Roger Diener, 'Reichsproblem und Hegemonie,' *Deutsches Recht* (1939), 551–66.
5. Neesse, *Führergewalt*, 54.
6. 'Der Reichsbegriff im Völkerrecht', *Deutsches Recht* (1939), 341–4.

Extract 40

TIM MASON: *The Primacy of Politics*

1. Thus Gerhard Schulz in K.-D. Bracher, W. Sauer, and G. Schulz, *Die nationalsozialistische Machtergreifung* (Cologne, 1960), part 2, ch. v; also Ingeborg Esenwein-Rothe, *Die Wirtschaftsverbände von 1933 bis 1945* (Berlin, 1965) and David Schoenbaum, *Hitler's Social Revolution* (New York, 1966). The controversy about totalitarianism rests on similar postulates. The only exceptions are Arthur Schweitzer, *Big Business in the Third Reich* (Bloomington, Ind., 1964), Dieter Petzina, *Autarkiepolitik im Dritten Reich* (Stuttgart, 1968), and Berenice A. Carroll, *Design for Total War* (The Hague, 1968).

2. Quoted after Dietrich Eichholtz, 'Probleme einer Wirtschaftsgeschichte des Faschismus in Deutschland', *Jahrbuch für Wirtschaftsgeschichte* (1963), 3. 103. This essay brings about important refinements to the Marxist-Leninist concept of fascism and one awaits with interest the author's book on the German war economy 1939–45; but he still writes of 'the tasks allotted by finance capital to its fascism'. For a critical review of East German historiography see B. Blanke, R. Reiche, and J. Werth, 'Die Faschismus-Theorie der DDR', *Das Argument—Berliner Hefte für Probleme der Gesellschaft*, 33 (May 1965).

3. The New Deal in the USA, the Popular Front of 1936 in France, and the Labour government of 1945 in Britain represented a different kind of variation from the norm—their limited reforms tended to strengthen the existing social order, the needs of which they understood better than the respective ruling classes.

4. So great was the shortage of foreign exchange that considerable quantities of weapons and machine tools for their production were exported.

5. For the crisis see Arthur Schweitzer, 'The Foreign Exchange Crisis of 1936', *Zeitschrift für die gesamte Staatswissenschaft* (1962). The autarchy programme needed time, and the continued acceleration of rearmament was in fact only made possible by the unforeseeable revival of international trade during 1937.

6. Hardly any of the production goals of the Four Year Plan were in fact reached, but the achievement was considerable in relation to the narrow margin of German reserves in September 1939—full figures in Petzina, *Autarkiepolitik*, 182.

7. Cf. T.W. Mason, 'Some Origins of the Second World War', *Past and Present*, 29 (1964).

8. Bundesarchiv Koblenz, R43 II/528; R41 I/174; WiIF5, 560/1 and 560/2; R22 Gr. 5/1206.

9. The quarterly reports on the economy of Berlin 1938–9 give a good picture of the process (Bundesarchiv Koblenz, R41/155–6). The role of the cartels in the 1930s has not yet been properly studied.

10. On the trend towards concentration in industry, see the reports on the economy of Berlin (n. 9 above). Dr Karl Krauch of IG Farben was in charge of chemical production under the Four Year Plan; 30 per cent of his staff in this office came from IG Farben (Petzina, *Autarkiepolitik*, 123).

11. Cf. Alan Milward, *The German Economy at War* (London, 1965), ch. 4.

Extract 41

PETER HAYES: *The Nazi Empire 1938–1944*

1. See Klaus Hildebrand, 'Innenpolitische Antriebskräfte der nationalsozialistischen Aussenpolitik,' in H.-U. Wehler (ed.), *Sozialgeschichte Heute* (Göttingen, 1974), p. 658; and Jost Dülffer, 'Zum "decision-making process" in der deutschen Aussenpolitik 1933–39,' in Manfred Funke (ed.), *Hitler, Deutschland und die Mächte* (Düsseldorf, 1976), pp. 202–3. On the inability of private industry to promote a peaceful foreign policy, see Bernd Martin, 'Friedens-Planungen der multinationalen Grossindustrie (1932–1940) als politische Krisenstrategie,' *G & G*, 2 (1976), pp. 66–88 especially the concluding remarks.

2. For examples of such writing, see David Abraham, *The Collapse of the Weimar Republic* (Princeton, N. J., 1981); and the works of Hans-Erich Volkmann, notably 'Das aussenwirtschaftliche Programm der NSDAP, 1930–1933' *AfS*. 17 (1977),

pp. 251–74; 'Die NS-Wirtschaft in Vorbereitung des Krieges,' in W. Deist and M. Messerschmidt (eds.), *Ursachen und Voraussetzungen der deutschen Kriegspolitik* (Stuttgart, 1979), pp. 177–368; and 'Politik, Wirtschaft, und Rüstung unter dem Nationalsozialismus,' in M. Funke (ed.), *Hitler, Deutschland und die Mächte*, pp. 269–91. But compare R. J. Overy, 'Hitler's War and the German Economy: A Reinterpretation,' *EHR*, 35 (1982), pp. 279–80; and idem, *Goering: the 'Iron Man'* (Boston, 1984), pp. 111–12.

3. See Timothy W. Mason, 'Innere Krise und Angriffskrieg 1938/39,' in F. Forstmeier and H.-E. Volkmann (eds.), *Wirtschaft und Rüstung am Vorabend des Zweiten Weltkriegs* (Düsseldorf, 1975), pp. 158–88; and Jost Dülffer, 'Der Beginn des Krieges 1939: Hitler, die innere Krise und das Mächtesystem,' *G & G*, 2 (1976), pp. 443–70.

4. On heavy industry, compare Michael Geyer, 'Zum Einfluss der nationalsozialistischen Rüstungspolitik auf das Ruhrgebiet,' *RVB*, 45 (1981), pp. 241–50, and John R. Gillingham, *Industry and Politics in the Third Reich* (New York, 1985), pp. 50–111.

5. Overy, *Goering*, p. 89.

6. Josiah DuBois, *The Devil's Chemists* (Boston, 1952), especially pp. x, 11; Dietrich Eichholtz, *Geschichte der deutschen Kriegswirtschaft 1939–1945*, Bd. 1: 1939–41 (East Berlin, 1969); Hans Radandt, *Fall 6: Ausgewählte Dokumente und Urteil des IG-Farben-Prozesses* (East Berlin, 1970); R. Sasuly, *IG Farben* (New York, 1947); Janis Schmelzer, *Unternehmen Südost* (Wolfen, 1966); John Boylan, *Sequel to the Apocalypse* (New York, 1942).

7. Eichholtz, *Geschichte*, vol. I, pp. 149–52; Tim Mason, 'The Primacy of Politics,' in H. A. Turner (ed.), *Nazism and the Third Reich* (New York, 1972), p. 192.

8. In August 1940, IG estimated the value of its property losses and reparations payments under the Versailles treaty at 203 million marks; NI-11252/93, IG's New Order plan, 3.VIII.40, p. 10. The fear of destruction was hardly fanciful. In the victor nations of World War I, where the memory of the Little IG's role in poison gas deployment was kept alive by reprintings of Victor Lefebure's *The Riddle of the Rhine* (New York, 1923), IG was the subject of persistent attacks. On German sensitivity to this, see BA Koblenz, ZSg 127, Bd. 825, 'Stimmungmache gegen deutsche Chemie,' *Die chemische Industrie*, 4.IV.37.

9. See, for example, NI-4954, Affidavit by F. Ehrmann, 13.III.47, *NMT*, vol. 7, pp. 1487–8; NI-7121/55, RWM to Verm. W., 5.VII.39; NI-7124/55, reply of 7.VII.39.

10. The best short guide to Nazi intentions in each of the conquered territories is Lothar Gruchmann, *Nationalsozialistiche Grossraumordnung* (Stuttgart 1962), pp. 76–101. I am adopting here a modified version of the distinction among occupied areas to be found in Otfried Ulshöfer, *Einflussnahme auf Wirtschaftsunternehmungen in den besetzten Nord-, West- und Südosteuropäischen Ländern während des Zweiten Weltkriegs* (Tübingen, 1958), pp. 16–17. That IG observed this distinction is clear from NI-8454/70, Legal Position and Legal Organization of the Occupied Territories, 2.X.40.

11. This is the title of chap. 5 in Borkin, *Crime and Punishment*. Significantly, Borkin's entire discussion contains only one indication of the size of the companies involved, a misleading remark concerning the French Etablissements Kuhlmann.

12. On the nitrogen industry, see Oster II/36, O. Dobias to Oster, 29.I.47; II/38, Statement of M. W. Holtropp, 20.III.48; Bütefisch VII/87, Affidavit by G. Lelong, 26.II.48; Oster II/49, Statement by B. Eriksen, 28.I.47. For other representative

examples, see Bayer 13/25, 7th meeting of the Southeast Europe Committee, XII.39, and Bayer 64/9, Weber-Andreä and Heider to Soda- und Aetzkalien Ost GmbH, 10.XI.42.

13. See among many relevant publications, Gruchmann, *Grossraumordnung*; Alan Milward, *The New Order and the French Economy* (London, 1970), pp. 33–4, 42–3, 72, 146–80; and Alexander Dallin, *German Rule in Russia 1941–1945* (London, 1957), chaps. 15 and 18.

Extract 42

HANS MOMMSEN: *The Civil Service in the Third Reich*

1. Cf. on this the important work by Wolfgang Runge: *Politik und Beamtentum im Parteienstaat: die Demokratisierung der politischen Beamten in Preußen zwischen 1918 und 1933*, Industrielle Welt (5) (Stuttgart, 1965), 237 ff.

2. On the *Generalgouvernement* see Martin Broszat, *Nationalsozialistische Polenpolitik 1939–1945*, Schriftenreihe der Vierteljahrshefte für Zeitgeschichte 2 (Stuttgart, 1961); on France see Eberhard Jäckel, *Frankreich in Hitlers Europa* (Stuttgart, 1966).

3. See the general comments in K.-D. Bracher, *Die Auflösung der Weimarer Republik: eine Studie zum Problem des Machtverfalls in der Demokratie* (3rd edn. Villingen, 1960), 730 ff., and K. D. Bracher, W. Sauer, and G. Schulz, *Nationalsozialistische Machtergreifung: Studien zur Errichtung des totalitären Herrschaftssystems in Deutschland 1933/34* (Cologne, 1960), 50 ff., 167 ff.

4. Cf. Waldemar Besson, *Württemberg und die deutsche Staatskrise 1928–1933* (Stuttgart, 1959), 354 ff.

5. A characteristic example of this is a conversation between representatives of the Prussian Civil Servants' Association and *Ministerialdirektor* Dr Landfried of the Prussian State Ministry on 24 Feb. 1933, in which the Civil Servants' Association spoke in favour of the preservation of the professional civil service and of the protection of civil servants' rights, but conceded 'that in times such as these the special needs of the state were not unrecognized' (Geheimes Staatsarchiv Berlin-Dahlem, Stiftung Preußischer Kulturbesitz, Rep. 90, No. 613).

6. NG-1296, 4; cf. Aufgabenkreis und Verantwortlicheit des Staatssekretärs der Reichskanzlei Dr Wilhelm Kritzinger, in *Gutachten des Instituts für Zeitgeschichte*, ii (Stuttgart, 1966), 376 ff.

7. Cf. ibid 377; characteristic of this are the private papers of Bernhard Lösener: 'Als Rassereferent im Reichsministerium des Innern', *Vierteljahrshefte für Zeitgeschichte*, 9 (1961), 264 ff.

8. Cf. the exaggerated, but pertinent, critique of Goerdeler in the memorandum *Der Weg*, in W. Ritter von Schramm (ed.), *Beck und Goerdeler: Gemeinschaftsdokumente für den Frieden 1941–1944* (Munich, 1965), 198, and Hans Mommsen, 'Gesellschaftsbild und Verfassungspläne des deutschen Widerstands', in H. Buchheim and W. Schmitthenner (eds.), *Der deutsche Widerstand des 20. Juli* (Cologne, 1966).

9. Cf. also on this Alan S. Milward, *Die deutsche Kriegswirtschaft 1939–1945* (Stuttgart, 1966).

10. *Gutachten des Instituts für Zeitgeschichte*, ii. 377.

Extract 43

JANE CAPLAN: *State Formation and Political Representation in Nazi Germany*

1. Hans Mommsen, *Beamtentum in Dritten Reich* (Stuttgart, 1966), 13.
2. This is discussed in my essay, 'Bureaucracy, Politics and the National Socialist State', in P. Stachura (ed.), *The Shaping of the Nazi State* (London, 1978), 234–56.
3. This point was made long ago by F. Neumann, in *Behemoth: The Structure and Practice of National Socialism* (London, 1942), 72–3.

Extract 44

DIETER REBENTISCH AND KARL TEPPE: *Administration versus Human Leadership*

1. Cf. Hans Mommsen, 'Zur Verschränkung traditioneller und faschistischer Führungsgruppen in Deutschland beim Übergang von der Bewegungs- zur Systemphase', in Wolfgang Schieder (ed.), *Faschismus als soziale Bewegung* (Hamburg, 1976), 157–81.
2. Thus for example Christoph Dipper, 'Der deutsche Widerstand und die Juden', *Geschichte und Gesellschaft*, 9 (1983), 375.
3. Cf. Hans Mommsen, 'Die Stellung der Beamtenschaft in Reich, Ländern und Gemeinden', *Vierteljahrshefte für Zeitgeschichte*, 21 (1973), 151–65; Rudolf Morsey, 'Beamtenschaft und Verwaltung zwischen Republik und "Neuem Staat"', in K. D. Erdmann and Hagen Schulze (eds.), *Weimar: Selbstpreisgabe einer Demokratie* (Düsseldorf, 1980).
4. Martin Broszat, *Der Staat Hitlers: Grundlegung und Entwicklung seiner inneren Verfassung* (Munich, 8th edn., 1979), 381, 433.
5. Individual historical studies of the majority of the Reich ministries and of the politically most important supreme Reich authorities have been absent up till now. Insofar as such depictions exist at all they are often narrowly focused special studies in periodicals, in collective volumes, and, particularly, in ministerial anniversary publications. Meanwhile, the biographical literature on the Reich ministers of the National Socialist period is characterized by the fact that they focus on the political profile and the political activities of the departmental heads and only rarely, or not at all, consider their bureaucratic-administrative qualities and achievements or weaknesses and failings. In view of these deficits contemporary publications still have a certain value: Hans Pfundtner (ed.), *Dr Wilhelm Frick und sein Ministerium* (Munich, 1937); Franz Albrecht Medicus, *Das Reichsministerium des Innern* (Berlin, 1940); J. von Schönfeldt, *Die allgemeine und innere Verwaltung* (Berlin, 1943); F. Sauer, *Das Reichsjustizministerium* (Berlin, 1939). More recent works are often dominated by the legal situation; as in the section on the labour administration in Andreas Kranig, *Lockung und Zwang: zur Arbeitsverfassung im Dritten Reich* (Stuttgart, 1983), 149–89. Very informative and full of insight, by contrast, is Willi A. Boelcke, *Die deutsche Wirtschaft 1930–1945: Interna des Reichswirtschaftsministeriums* (Düsseldorf, 1983).
6. See in addition to Lutz Graf Schwerin von Krosigk, *Memoiren* (Stuttgart, 1977), 161 ff. Fritz Blaich, 'Die Grundzüge nationalsozialistischer Steuerpolitik und ihre Verwirklichung', in Friedrich Wilhelm Henning (ed.), *Probleme der nationalsozialistischen Wirtschaftspolitik* (Berlin, 1976).

Extract 45

KLAUS-JÜRGEN MÜLLER: *The Army and the Third Reich*

1. The armed forces' role in the consolidation of the regime has been thoroughly described in W. Sauer, 'Die Mobilmachung der Gewalt', in K.-D. Bracher, W. Sauer, and G. Schulz, *Die nationalsozialistische Machtergreifung: Studien zur Entwicklung des totalitären Herrschaftssystems in Deutschland 1933–34* (2nd edn., Cologne, 1962).

2. On the Fritsch–Blomberg crisis see Harald C. Deutsch, *Hitler and his Generals: The Hidden Crisis, January–June 1938* (Minneapolis, 1974) and the relevant chapter in K.-J. Müller, *Das Heer und Hitler: Armee und nationalsozialistisches Regime 1933–1940* (Stuttgart, 1969). On Beck's resignation see K.-J. Müller, *General Ludwig Beck: Studien und Dokumente zur politischen Vorstellungswelt und beruflichen Tätigkeit des Generalstabschefs 1933–1938* (Boppard, 1979), ch. VI.

3. Harold D. Lasswell, 'The Garrison State', *American Journal of Sociology*, 46 (1941); id., 'The Garrison State Hypothesis today', in S. P. Huntingdon (ed.), *Changing Patterns of Military Politics* (New York, 1962). See also A. Lüdtke, 'Militärstaat und Festungspraxis', in Volker R. Berghahn (ed.), *Militarismus*, Neue Wissenschaftliche Bibliothek 83 (Cologne, 1975).

4. David Schoenbaum, *Hitler's Social Revolution* (New York, 1966, 1968) and in a similar vein Ralf Dahrendorf, *Gesellschaft und Demokratie in Deutschland* (Munich, 1971). This question has recently been treated from a specific viewpoint in a work rich in both substance and thought: Timothy W. Mason, *Arbeiterklasse und Volksgemeinschaft: Dokumente und Materialien zur deutschen Arbeiterpolitik 1936–1939* (Opladen, 1975).

Extract 46

WILHELM DEIST: *The* Gleichschaltung *of the Armed Forces*

1. Commanders' conference of 3 Feb. 1933. Cf. Thilo Vogelsang, 'Neue Dokumente zur Geschichte der Reichswehr 1930–1933', *Vierteljahrshefte für Zeitgeschichte*, 2 (1934)m 397–436 (433).

2. Institut für Zeitgeschichte Archives, Ed. 1, vol. 1, Liebmann's record of the commanders' conference of 1 Mar. 1933.

3. On Blomberg's attitude towards Hitler and the Nazi movement cf. K-J. Müller, *Das Heer und Hitler: Armee und nationalsozialistisches Regime 1933–1940*, Beiträge zur Militär- und Kriegsgeschichte 10 (Stuttgart, 1969), 49 ff., 61 ff.; also the inadequate analysis in Matthew Cooper, *The German Army 1933–1945: Its Political and Moral Failure* (London, 1978), 20 ff.

4. Manfred Messerschmidt, *Die Wehrmacht im NS-Staat: Zeit der Indoktrination* (Hamburg, 1969), i and *passim*.

5. Müller, *Das Heer und Hitler*, 67.

6. Ibid. 71 ff. Blomberg thus created an essential precondition for the penetration process defined by Hüttenberger: Peter Hüttenberger, 'Nationalsozialistische Polykratie', *Geschichte und Gesellschaft* 2/4 (1976), 417–42 (427).

7. Müller, *Das Heer und Hitler*, 68, 78.

8. Müller *Das Heer und Hitler*, 134 ff.; Michael Salewski, 'Die bewaffnete Macht im Dritten Reich 1933–1939', in *Wehrmacht und Nationalsozialismus 1933–1939*,

Handbuch zur Deutschen Militärgeschichte 1648–1939, 7 (Munich, 1978), 13–287 (51, 81 ff.); cf. Blomberg's announcement at the ministerial conference on 1 Aug. 1934, in *Die Regierung Hitler*, ed. Karl-Heinz Minuth, pt. 1 (1933/34), 2 vols., Akten der Reichskanzlei: Regierung Hitler 1933–1938 (Boppard, 1983), ii., No. 382, p. 385.

9. Blomberg at a commanders' conference on 12 Jan. 1935; cf. Müller, *Das Heer und Hitler*, 167.

10. Heinz Höhne, *The Order of the Death's Head* (London, 1969), 439 ff.; Müller, *Das Heer und Hitler*, 147–8.

Extract 47

MANFRED MESSERSCHMIDT: *The* Wehrmacht *in the National Socialist State*

1. Bundesarchiv-Militärarchiv, II L 51/7, sheets 122 ff.; and M. Messerschmidt and U. von Gersdorff (eds.), *Offiziere im Bild von Dokumenten aus Drei Jahrhunderten*, Beiträge zur Militär- und Kriegsgeschichte 6 (1964), Doc. 97, 255 ff.

2. *Militär-Wochenblatt*, 18 Aug. 1933. The News-sheet of the Naval Officers' Association used this article, which appeared particularly important to it. See 17 (1933), 234 ff.

3. M. Messerschmidt, *Die Wehrmacht im NS-Staat: Zeit der Indoktrination* (Hamburg, 1969), 38 ff.

4. W. Sauer, 'Die Mobilmachung der Gewalt', in Karl-Dietrich Bracher, Wolfgang Sauer, and Gerhard Schulz, *Die nationalsozialistische Machtergreifung: Studien zur Errichtung des totalitären Herrschaftssystems in Deutschland 1933–1934* (Cologne, 1962), 717.

5. Reich Citizenship Law and Law for the Protection of German Blood and German Honour, both 15 Sept. 1935, Reichsgesetzblatt I, 1146 ff., and the relevant decrees of 14 Nov. and subsequently.

6. Issue 16 and Issue 18.

7. Max Domarus, *Hitler: Reden und Proklamationen 1932–1945*, vol. ii/1 (Munich, 1965), 1058.

8. (1939) 5, ed. Armed Forces High Command, Interior Department.

Extract 48

LOTHAR GRUCHMANN: *Justice in the Third Reich*

1. This is well put in G. Radbruch, 'Des Reichsjustizministeriums Ruhm und Erde', *Süddeutsche Juristenzeitung* (1948), 60.

2. Cf. Führer decree on Special Plenipotentiary Powers of the Reich Ministry of Justice of 20 Aug. 1942 (RGBl.I, 535).

Extract 49

RALPH ANGERMUND: *Jews on Trial*

1. See for example the comments of H. Frank at the Congress of German Lawyers in Oct. 1933 in *Deutsche Justiz* (1933), 268 ff.

2. Thus for example the Law of the Reich President for the Prevention of Malicious Attacks on the Government of National Uprising of 21 Mar. 1933, *Reichsgesetzblatt*

(1933), I. 135, and the Law for the Prevention of Political Violence of 4 Apr. 1933, *Reichsgesetzblatt* (1933), I. 162.

3. *Reichsgesetzblatt* (1933), I. 295–302.

4. W. Hempfner, *Die nationalsozialistische Staatsauffassung in der Rechtssprechung des Preußischen Oberverwaltungsgerichts* (Berlin, 1974). National Socialist legal specialists criticized this practice, furthermore, as 'patching things over'.

5. Thus amongst other things Matzke, 'Die Anfechtung der Rassenmischehe nach geltendem Recht', *Juristische Wochenschrift* (1934), 2593–601 (2598), H. Henkel, *Die Unabhängigkeit des Richters in ihrem neuen Sinngehalt* (Hamburg, 1934), 17f.

6. See amongst other things R. Freisler, 'Richter und Gesetz', *Deutsche Justiz* (1933), 694 ff.; H. Franzen, *Richter und Gesetz* (Hamburg, 1935); H. Lange, *Die Entwicklung des bürgerlichen Rechts seit 1933* (Tübingen, 1941).

7. See on the other hand B. Rüthers, *Entartetes Recht: Rechtslehren und Kronjuristen im Dritten Reich* (Munich, 1988), 432 ff.; for criticism of the usefulness of the concept of 'spirit of the age' see, however, id., 'Zeitgeist und Recht?' *Zeitschrift für Rechtspolitik* (1988), 283 ff.

8. See also W. Hofer, 'Stufen der Judenverfolgung im Dritten Reich 1933–1939', in H. A. Strauss and N. Kampe (eds.), *Antisemitismus: von der Judenfeindschaft zum Holocaust* (Bonn, 1985), 172–85 (178 ff.).

9. *Reichsgesetzblatt* (1935), I. 1146. The judgements based on this law have been written about on numerous occasions (e.g. Lothar Gruchmann, 'Blutschutzgesetz und Justiz', *Aus Politik und Zeitgeschichte*, 48, 30 Nov. 1985 and *Vierteljahrshefte für Zeitgeschichte* (1983), 418 ff.; D. Majer, *Fremdvölkische im Dritten Reich: ein Beitrag zur nationalsozialistischen Rechtssetzung und Rechtspraxis in Verwaltung und Justiz unter besonderer Berücksichtigung der eingegliederten Ostgebiete und des Generalgouvernements* (Boppard am Rhein, 1981). As a result only some individual judgements, in which the social dimensions of 'miscegenation' become clear, will be analysed.

10. Thus H. Robinsohn, *Justiz als politische Verfolgung: die Rechtssprechung in 'Rassenschandefällen' beim Landgericht Hamburg 1936–1943* (Stuttgart, 1977), 133.

11. Ibid.

12. Robinsohn, *Justiz*, esp. 135 ff.; a similar development can be seen in the special courts of the Supreme Court district of Cologne.

13. Anti-Semitic attitudes and behavioural patterns were in general stronger in younger generations. See, for example, I. Kershaw, 'German Popular Opinion and the "Jewish Question" 1939–1943: Some Further Reflections', in A. Paucker et al. (eds.), *Die Juden im nationalsozialistischen Deutschland* (Tübingen, 1986), 365–86. Of the probationers appointed between 1933 and 1936, 99 per cent are supposed to have been members of the NSDAP, of whom the majority were 'old party comrades'. (F. Neumann, *Behemoth: Struktur und Praxis des Nationalsozialismus 1933–1944* (1st edn. 1942; Cologne, 1977), 442.)

14. *Deutschland–Berichte der Sozialdemokratischer Partei Deutschlands (Sopade) 1934–1940* (Salzhausen: Verlag Petra Nettelbeck, 1980), v. 193.

15. Cf. Robinsohn, *Justiz*, 135f.

Extract 50

ROBERT KOEHL: *Feudal Aspects of National Socialism*

1. 'When our opponents say "It is easy for you, you are a dictator"—we answer them, "No, gentlemen, you are wrong; there is no single dictator, but ten thousand, each in his own place"' (Adolf Hitler in a speech, April 8, 1933, cited in Fritz Nova, *The National Socialist Führerprinzip and its Background in German Thought* (Philadelphia, 1943), p. 4).

2. For an oath demanded by Seyss-Inquart, see *Hitlers Tischgespräche* (Bonn, 1951), p. 243. The oath of personal loyalty to Hitler of February 1934, was exacted precisely because Hitler did not have patriarchal authority; such an oath was also a visible repudiation of *Rechtstaat* loyalty to the office (E. Vermeil, *The Third Reich* (New York, 1955), p. 304).

3. Hitler speaks of 'die Fehler des ewigen Reglementierens' as specifically a German exaggeration of modern bureaucracy. Both in the relations of Berlin with the provinces and of Germans with foreign races the maximum of freedom was to be observed. Not totalitarianism, but its opposite, feudal decentralization, was the goal. *Hitlers Tischgespräche*, pp. 110–111, 116–118. Cf. Max Weber's contrast of feudal and patriarchal dominion. *Wirtschaft und Gesellschaft*, it (Tübingen, 1956). 751.

4. Cf. the slogan 'Gebt mir vier Jahre!' (Give me four years!) used in the years 1933–1936 to win public confidence. See also Nova, *Führerprinzip*, pp. 31–33; Vermeil, *Third Reich*, pp. 301–302.

5. For example, 'Osaf' Pfeffer-Salomon: K. Heiden, *Der Führer* (Boston, 1944), pp. 350, 742; *Gauleiter* Josef Wagner of Silesia: testimony of SS General Bach-Zelewski, U.S. Military Tribunal case 8, transcript, p. 383; *Gauleiter* Streicher of Franconia (reluctantly!): *Hitler's Secret Conversations 1941–1944* (New York, 1953), pp. 126–127.

6. e.g., the case of Martin Luther in the Foreign Office: Erich Kordt, *Wahn und Wirklichkeit* (Stuttgart, 1948), p. 373, n. 1. On Darré: affidavits of Aufsess and von Hannecken, U.S. Military Tribunal case 11, Darré defense book I; on Ley: Franz Neumann, *Behemoth* (London, 1944), pp. 619–621; on Rosenberg: *The Memoirs of Alfred Rosenberg*, ed. S. Lang and E. von Scheak (New York, 1949), pp. 282–289; on Hans Frank: NO 2202, case 8, prosecution document book V-A.

7. E. K. Bramstedt, *Dictatorship and Political Police* (London, 1945), p. 98; NO 2676, case 8, prosecution document book XIV–A; NO 3078, case 8, pros. doc. bk. II-B.

8. Darré and Frank both attempted to play off Himmler and Göring against each other in this fashion: NG 1759, case 11, pros. doc. bk. 104; 2233 PS, *Trials of War Criminals*, IV, 889–891. Dietrich was attached dependently to Goebbels, Seyss-Inquart to Göring, and von Schirach to Hess.

9. Hans B. Gisevius, *Bis zum bitteren Ende* (Hamburg, 1947), I, 121–123, 138–139, 155 ff. Otto Strasser, *Die deutsche Bartholomäusnacht* (6th ed., Zürich, 1935), pp. 17–33, 47 ff., 73–81. Cf. Walter Görlitz and Herbett Quint, *Adolf Hitler* (Stuttgart, 1952), pp. 629–631.

10. Rosenberg, *Memoirs*, p. 231.

11. *Tischgespräche*, pp. 250, 252, 254. Cf. Neumann, *Behemoth*, p. 535; Vermeil, *Third Reich*, p. 299.

12. A characteristic stage in the development of feudal offices is the assignment of

tasks by the leader to table-companions and household employees. Precisely this stage was reached in 1945 in Hitler Germany, especially in the Führer-Bunker. Furthermore, whether guilty or innocent, Göring and Himmler were accused in April 1945 by Hitler of that fatal feudal disease: *frondieren*. Each absented himself from the court, in a suspiciously distant corner of the kingdom.

Extract 52

PETER DIEHL-THIELE: *Party and State in the Third Reich*

1. From 12 May 1941: Bormann's Party Chancellery.
2. Hans Mommsen, *Beamtentum im Dritten Reich* (Stuttgart, 1966), 31.
3. By the 'party'—in contradistinction to the 'movement'—is meant always the corps of functionaries of the NSDAP. In the literature published on this subject during the Third Reich the term 'Party' usually has a dual meaning, since for ideological reasons the unity of the movement's formations was always supposed to be stressed. Carl Johanny referred to the party in our more narrow sense, however, when he wrote in 1936 that '"Party and State" is the central problem of contemporary German domestic policy.' Quite rightly he described the resolution of this situation as a precondition for the creation—striven for in vain by the Reich Ministry of the Interior—of a new Reich constitution (C. Johanny, 'Partei und Staat', diss., Wüzburg, 1936).
4. Along with the general and domestic administration it was primarily the legal system and the judiciary on which the 'pressure' of the NSDAP, and, in the case of the judiciary, especially that of the SS too, was concentrated. The pressures of conscience emerge most clearly among those judges who, against their own better judgement, had to punish those who (in the eyes of the regime) were 'political criminals' with excessive severity in the knowledge that they would otherwise fall prey to the executioner, in the form of an SS commando. See, for example, the comments of Hitler during his table-talk on 7 June 1942 (Percy Schramm (ed.), *Hitlers Tischgespräche im Führerhauptquartier 1941 bis 1942* (Stuttgart, 1963), 392).
5. Nonetheless, the party made the absurd demand that even railway officials should be political activists, for example (cf. letter of Bormann to Dörpmüller of 3 Apr. 1940, reprinted in Mommsen, *Beamtentum*, 196).
6. According to the view of the Reich Minister of the Interior this hostile state of affairs already existed in Mar. 1934. Cf. Rep. 320, No. 441, 183 ff.
7. Cf. *Mein Kampf*, 501.

Extract 54

PETER HÜTTENBERGER: *National Socialist Polycracy*

1. The expression 'pact' is to be understood here in a metaphorical sense, since general contractual agreements in the legal sense did not of course occur. It is an issue far more of evolving discussions, judgements of the situation, and considerations, as for example the actions of Hitler during the establishment of the DAF in 1933–4 show.
2. The expression 'big business' is chosen intentionally. On the one hand, this

excludes medium-sized industry, and on the other hand it indicates that it relates not only to the industrial interest associations, but also to the nexus of large-scale factory managements and their links to the leading positions of the organizations of the private sector. This does not yet imply which individual people, plants, and associations are meant, since this question cannot be confidently answered as long as the internal decision-making processes of the large companies are not known. Big business is not identical with 'economics' in the sense of the Mason/Czichon controversy. On the economy of the Third Reich in general see F. Blaich, 'Wirtschaftspolitik und Wirtschaftsverfassung im Dritten Reich', *Aus Politik und Zeitgeschichte*, 8 (1971), 3–18; R. Erbe, *Die nationalsozialistische Wirtschaftspolitik 1933 bis 1939 im Lichte der modernen Theorie* (Zurich, 1956); W. Fischer, *Deutsche Wirtschaftspolitik 1918–1945* (Opladen, 1968); A. Schweitzer, *Big Business in the Third Reich* (Bloomington, Ind., 1964); I. Esenwein-Rothe, *Die Wirtschaftsverbände von 1933 bis 1945* (Berlin, 1965); D. Petzina, *Grundrisse der deutschen Wirtschaftsgeschichte 1918–1945* (Stuttgart, 1973).

3. E. N. Peterson's view that the Third Reich can be described in terms of the dualism of party and state does not conform to the reality of it. The state–party conflict belongs to the subordinate level of conflict situations. As a rigid explanatory model it is useless from the start: E. N. Peterson, *The Limits of Hitler's Power* (Princeton, 1969). This question naturally engaged students of constitutional law in the Third Reich a great deal, since the terminology of traditional German constitutional theory no longer applied to the Third Reich. Numerous attempts were undertaken to approach this with the help of artificial contructions. However, the mass of the surviving literature should not lead to false conclusions. Cf. for example G. Neesse, 'Das Verhältnis von Partei und Staat nach fünf Jahren nationalsozialistische Reichsführung', *Verwaltungsarchiv*, 43 (1938), 9–46; C. Schmitt, 'Staat, Bewegung, Volk: die Dreigliederung der politischen Einheit', in *Der deutsche Staat der Gegenwart*, vol. i (Hamburg, 1933); W. Stuckart, 'Partei und Reich', *Deutsches Recht*, 5 (1935), 352–86; E. R. Huber, 'Partei, Staat, Volk', *Deutsches Recht*, 5 (1935), 309–12; W. Merk, *Der Staatsgedanke im Dritten Reich* (Stuttgart, 1935).

4. Hitler's policy of accommodation and compromise towards industry and the *Reichswehr* compelled precisely the NSDAP with an immanent imperative not only to control the administration and associational life, but also to 'coordinate' them, i.e to see them in social-political terms as usable spoils. In this an internal competition situation was inevitably created. Notable, for example, is the competitive behaviour between Stahlhelm or PO members and the SA for the distribution of jobs.

5. H. Krausnick, 'Der 30. Juni 1934: Bedeutung, Hintergründe, Verlauf', *Aus Politik und Zeitgeschichte*, 30 June 1954; K.-J. Müller, 'Reichswehr und 'Röhm-Affäre', *Militärgeschichtliche Mitteilungen*, 1 (1968), 107–44; H. Bennecke, 'Die Reichswehr und der 'Röhm-Putsch', in *Politische Studien*, ii (Munich, 1964). PO is the abbreviation for 'Political Organization'.

6. O. Geigenmüller, *Die politische Schutzhaft im nationalsozialistischen Deutschland* (Würzburg, 1937).

7. H. G. Pridat-Guzatis, *Berufständisches Strafrecht* (Berlin, 1937).

Extract 55

TIM MASON: *Intention and Explanation*

1. See Klaus Hildebrand, 'Monokratic oder Polykratie? Hitlers Herrschaft und das Dritte Reich', in Gerhard Hirschfeld and Lothar Kettenacker (eds.), *The 'Führer State': Myth and Reality. Studies on the Politics and Structure of the Third Reich* (Stuttgart 1981), pp. 17–29.

2. Contrast on this point the emphasis which Martin Broszat does allow to agency in 'Soziale Motivation und Führer-Bindung des Nationalsozialismus', *Vierteljahrshefte für Zeitgeschichte*, vol. 18, no. 4 (1970), pp. 329–65, with the full-blown functionalism of Ludolf Herbst ('Die Krise des nationalsozialistischen Regimes am Vorabend des Zweiten Weltkrieges und die forcierte Aufrüstung', *Vierteljahrshefte für Zeitgeschichte*, vol. 26, no. 3 (1978), pp. 347–92) in which the subsystems have taken over from the people.

3. These points have been repeatedly emphasized by Hans Mommsen, 'National Socialism. Continuity and Change', in Walter Laqueur (ed.), *Fascism: A Reader's Guide* (Harmondsworth 1976), pp. 179–210.

4. Joachim Radkau, 'Entscheidungsprozesse und Entscheidungdefizite in der deutschen Aussenwirtschaftspolitik 1933–1940', *Geschichte und Gesellschaft*, vol. 2, no. 1 (1976), pp. 33–65, makes a first, stimulating but empirically unsatisfactory attempt to ask questions of this kind.

Extract 56

MICHAEL GEYER: *The State in National Socialist Germany*

1. See Edgar Loening, 'Der Staat (allgemeine Staatslehre),' *Handwörterbuch der Staatswissenschaften*, 2d ed., 8 vols. (Jena: Gustav Fischer, 1906). 6:907–40; Adolf Wagner. 'Der Staat in nationalökonomischer Sicht,' ibid., 6:940–51; Richard Thoma. 'Staat (allgemeine Staatslehre).' ibid., 4th ed., 8 vols. (Jena: Gustav Fischer, 1926). 7:724–56; Adolf Wagner and Franz Oppenheimer, 'Staat in nationalökonomischer Sicht.' ibid., 7:737–79. Peter Koslowski, *Gesellschaft und Staat. Ein unvermeidlicher Dualismus* (Stuttgart: Klett-Cotta. 1981).

2. In one or the other form this remains one of the basic assumptions even in recent work that has shown the fragility of boundaries between state and society and the fluctuations within the sphere of the state. Compare the contributions in Gerhard Hirschfeld and Lothar Kettenacker, eds., *The 'Führer-State': Myth and Reality: Studies on the Structure and Politics of the Third Reich* (Stuttgart: Klett-Cotta, 1981).

3. This process has been described by Hans Mommsen, *Beamtentum in Dritten Reich* (Stuttgart: Deutsche Verlagsanstalt, 1966); Martin Broszat, *The Hitler State: The Foundation and Development of the Internal Structure of the Third Reich* (London: Longman, 1981); Jane Caplan, 'Civil Service Support for National Socialism: An Evaluation,' in *The 'Führer-State'*, ed. Hirschfeld and Kettenacker, pp. 167–90.

4. Peter Hüttenberger, *Die Gauleiter: Studien zum Wandel des Machtgefüges in der NSDAP* (Stuttgart: Deutsche Verlagsanstalt, 1969); Shlomo Aronson, 'Heydrich und die Anfänge der SD und der Gestapo', (Ph.D. diss., Berlin, 1967).

5. Jane Caplan. 'Theories of Fascism: Nicos Poulantzas as Historian', *History Workshop*, 3 (Spring 1977), p. 90.

6. Hans Mommsen, 'Hitlers Stellung im nationalsozialistischen Herrschafts system', in *The 'Führer-State'*. ed. Hirschfeld and Kettenacker, pp. 23–40. and his 'Die innere Struktur des nationalsozialistischen Herrschaftssystems,' *Politische Bildung*, 5 (1972): 37–52.

Extract 57

IAN KERSHAW: *Working towards the Führer*

1. See Martin Broszat, *Der Staat Hitlers* (thereafter Broszat, *Staat*) (Munich: dtv, 1969), esp. chs. 8–9.
2. The internal government of Germany during the war has now been systematic-ally examined by Dieter Rebentisch, *Führerstaat und Verwaltung im Zweiten Weltkrieg* (Stuttgart, 1989).
3. Louis D. Lochner ed., *Goebbels Tagebücher aus den Jahren 1942–43* (Zürich: Atlantis Verlag, 1948), 241, 274, 296.
4. Albert Speer, *Erinnerungen* (Frankfurt am Main/Berlin: Propyläen Verlag, 1969), 270.
5. See Broszat, *Staat*, ch. 8.
6. The recently discovered, formerly missing, parts of Goebbels' diaries make explicitly clear Hitler's role in approving the most radical measures both as regards to pogrom itself and its aftermath. See the extracts published in *Der Spiegel*, No. 29 (1992), 126–8; an abbreviated version of the diary entry for 10 Nov. 1938 is available in Ralf Georg Reuth (ed.), *Joseph Goebbels: Tagebücher* (Munich: Piper, 1992), iii, 1281–2.
7. I have attempted to present the evidence in my study *The 'Hitler Myth': Image and Reality in the Third Reich* (Oxford: Oxford University Press, 1987).
8. For an excellent study of how the medical profession exploited the opportunities offered to National Socialism, see Michael H. Kater. *Doctors under Hitler* (Chapel Hill/London: University of North Carolina Press, 1989).
9. Martin Broszat, 'Soziale Motivation und Führer-Bindung des Nationalsozialis-mus', *Vierteljahrshefte für Zeitgeschichte*, Vol. 18 (1970), 405.
10. See Franz Neumann, *Behemoth: The Structure and Practice of National Socialism* (London: Victor Gollancz, 1942).

Extract 58

ERNST BLOCH: *Inventory of Revolutionary Appearance*

1. The ceremonial opening session of the new Reichstag in the Garrison church in Potsdam, a shrine of Prussian imperialism. The chosen date for initiating the Third Reich was also symbolic, since 21 March was the day on which Bismarck had opened the new Reichstag of the Second Reich in 1871.
2. An anti-semitic Nazi propaganda newspaper acquired by the party in 1920. It was turned into a daily paper in 1923.
3. Horst Wessel, 1907–30, an SA leader who was made into a Nazi martyr. The 'Horst Wessel Lied' (1933) was a Nazi anthem, written by Horst Wessel to an old music-hall tune.
4. The signing of dictated peace terms by the Germans in November 1918 in a French railway carriage in the forest of Compiègne.

5. Goebbels deliberately plagiarized Eisenstein's techniques when he assumed the role of film director for several Nazi propaganda films during the thirties and the Second World War.

Extract 59

KLAUS VONDUNG: *Magic and Manipulation*

1. *Vorschläge der Reichspropagandaleitung zur nationalsozialistischen Feiergestaltung,* 1/16 (1935).
2. Ibid.
3. 'Thingplätze für Freilichttheater und festliche Kundgebungen', in the special issue of the journal *Bauamt und Gemeindebau* (Hanover, n.d.); cited from Joseph Wulf, *Theater und Film im Dritten Reich* (Gütersloh, 1964), 166.

Extract 60

ANSON G. RABINBACH: *The Aesthetics of Production in the Third Reich*

1. 'Eine der schönsten Aufgaben des neuen Deutschlands; Dr. Ley vor dem Mitarbeitern und Referenten des Amtes', *Schönheit der Arbeit*, 1/6 (October 1936), 265.
2. Ibid.
3. Albert Speer, 'Schönheit der Arbeit—Fragen der Betriebsgestaltung', *Schönheit der Arbeit 1934–1936* (Berlin 1936), 198.
4. Karl Kretschmer, ' "Schönheit der Arbeit"—ein Weg zum deutschen Sozialismus!,' *Wege zur neuen Sozialpolitik. Arbeitstagung der Deutschen Arbeitsfront vom 16. bis 21. Dezember 1935* (Berlin, 1936), 180.
5. Anatol von Hubbenet (ed.), *Das Taschenbuch Schönheit der Arbeit* (Berlin 1938), 17.
6. Tim Mason, 'Zur Entsthung des Gesetzes zur Ordnung der nationalen Arbeit, vom 20. Januar 1934: Ein Versuch über das Verhältnis 'archaischer' und 'moderner' Momente in der neuesten deutschen Geschichte' in Hans Mommsen and others (ed.), *Industrielles System und politische Entwicklung in der Weimarer Republik*, (Düsseldorf 1974), 325–27. See also Tim Mason, 'Labour in the Third Reich 1933–1939' in *Past and Present*, 33 (April 1966), 113–16.
7. Arthur Schweitzer, *Big Business in the Third Reich* (Bloomington, 1964), 381.
8. Tim Mason, 'The Primacy of Politics—Politics and Economics in National Socialist Germany', in S. J. Woolf (ed.), *The Nature of Fascism* (London, 1968), 171.
9. Herbert Steinwarz, 'Schönheit der Arbeit' im Kriege und Frieden (Berlin, 1941), *Beleuchtung in den Betrieben und ihre Verdunkelung* (Berlin 1939).
10. Otto Marrenbach, *Fundamente des Sieges: die Gesamtarbeit der deutschen Arbeitsfront von 1933 bis 1940* (Berlin, 1940), 325.
11. Ernst Bloch, *Vom Hasard zur Katastrophe: politische Aufsätze 1934–1939* (Frankfurt am Main, 1971), 47.
12. Henry Ashby Turner Jr.'s definition of fascism as 'utopian anti-Modernism' does not consider the actualities of fascist modernism in both practice and ideology. See Henry Ashby Turner Jr., 'Fascism and Modernization' in *World Politics*, Vol. 24 (July 1972), 555.
13. 'Drei Freundinnen erleben ihren Arbeitstag', *Schönheit der Arbeit*, op. cit., vol. 1, no. 1, (May 1936), 8.

Extract 61

<small>HANS DIETER SCHÄFER:</small> *Split Consciousness*

1. D. Peukert, in *Aus Politik und Zeitgeschichte* (14 July 1979), 22–46 (33); on the unequal wages situation see D. Schoenbaum, *Die braune Revolution: eine Sozialgeschichte des Dritten Reiches* (Cologne, 1968), 136 ff.; R. Grunberger, *Das zwölfjährige Reich: der deutsche Alltag unter Hitler* (Vienna, 1972), 198 ff.
2. *Deutschlandberichte der Sozialdemokratischen Partei Deutschlands (SOPADE) 1934–1940*, ed. Klaus Behnken (Salzhausen, 1980), June 1939, 746.
3. Grunberger, *Das zwölfjährige Reich*, 210; Schoenbaum, *Die braune Revolution*, 143 ff.
4. Grunberger, *Das zwölfjährige Reich*, 214.
5. Bayerisches Hauptstaatsarchiv, Poster Collection.
6. Werner Maser, *Adolf Hitler: Legende, Mythos und Wirklichkeit* (Munich, 1971), 206. See also Ferry Porsche, 'Geburtsort Garage: wie ich die Entwicklung des VW mitlerlebte', *Auto Motor Sport*, 9 (6 May 1981), 15–17, and there the suggestion that Hitler had demanded the Volkswagen as early as the Automobile Exhibition of 1934. On the basis of a 'Memorandum concerning the construction of a German Volkswagen' Porsche received—despite the protest of the automobile industry—100,000 Marks to develop a first prototype, 'which left the garage of our family home in Stuttgart . . . in Autumn 1935'. One year later Porsche visited the River Rouge Ford Factory near Detroit and a General Motors factory for Hitler, as 'I am to build a factory for 500,000 cars a year. There is still no example of this in Europe.'
7. Henry Picker, *Hitlers Tischgespräche im Führerhauptquartier* (3rd fully revised and expanded new edn., Stuttgart, 1976); cf. also Ferdinand Porsche, 'Erste Vorstudie zum Volkswagen 1934: Volkswagen KdF Limousine 1937–8', in *Die dreißiger Jahre: Schauplatz Deutschland* (Munich, 1977), 186, pictures, 240–1 (Exhibition Catalogue of the House of Art, Munich).
8. 'Volkswagen fahren durch Berlin: die zur Besichtigung in Berliner Betrieben bestimmte, aus 6 Wagen bestehende Volkswagenkolonne machte am Dienstag eine Rundfahrt durch die Straßen Berlins', *Deutsche Automobilzeitung*, 54 (11 Feb. 1939), *Berliner Rundschau*.
9. 'Die technischen Leistungen und Phänomene werden zu Leistungen und "Markenzeichen" des Regimes,' in Johannes Beck et al. (eds.), *Terror und Hoffnung in Deutschland 1933–1945: Leben im Faschismus* (Reinbek, 1980), 139.
10. Heinrich Hauser, 'Deutschlands Motorisierung: Nachwort zur Berliner Autoschau', *Die Tat*, 26 (1934/5), 2. 928.
11. In 1930 in the USA 23 million people drove cars, in Germany 500,000; by 1938/9 the number of car owners in the German Reich had trebled.
12. E. Günther Gründel, *Die Sendung der jungen Generation: Versuch einer umfassenden revolutionären Sinndeutung der Krise* (Munich, 1932), 140 ff.
13. Peter Suhrkamp, 'Rasse', *Neue Rundschau*, 54 (1933), 2. 203.

Extract 62

<small>PETER REICHEL:</small> *The 'Seductive Surface' of the Third Reich*

1. See Berthold Hinz, 'Disparität und Diffusion: Kriterien einer "Ästhetik" des Nationalsozialismus', *kritische berichte*, 17/2 (1989), 111 ff.

2. Thus Hitler in his speech on cultural policy at the Reich party rally of 1935, cited ibid.

3. See Arne Fryksen, 'Hitlers Reden zur Kultur: kunstpolitische Taktik oder Ideologie?', in *Probleme deutscher Zeitgeschichte*, Studies in International History 3 (Stockholm, 1974), 235 ff.

4. Hinz, 'Disparität', 111.

5. Ralf Schnell, 'Die Zerstörung der Historie: Versuch über die Ideologiegeschichte faschistischer Ästhetik', in Ralf Schnell (ed.), *Kunst und Kultur im deutschen Faschismus* (Stuttgart, 1978).

6. Gert Selle, *Design-Geschichte in Deutschland* (Cologne, 1987), 240.

Extract 63

ALF LÜDTKE: *The Honour of Labour: Industrial Workers and the Power of Symbols under National Socialism*

1. Walter Benjamin, 'Das Kunstwerk im Zeitalter seiner technischen Reproduzierbarkeit,' *Gesammelte Schriften*, Vol. I, No. 2. (Frankfurt, 1974), pp. 471–509, p. 506.

2. On this theme, see Rainer Stommer, *Die inszenierte Volksgemeinschaft. Die 'Thing-Bewegung' im Dritten Reich* (Marburg, 1985), p. 91, p. 93 f.

3. Eberhard Heuel, *Der Umworbene Stand. Die ideologische Integration der Arbeiter im Nationalsozialismus* (Frankfurt/Main, New York, 1989), p. 409 ff.; see also Artur Axmann, *Der Reichsberufswettkampf* (Berlin, 1938).

4. See Josef Winschuh, *Industrievolk an der Ruhr* (Oldenburg/Berlin, 1935); Peter Schirmbeck, *Adel der Arbeit. Der Arbeiter in der Kunst der NS-Zeit* (Marburg, 1984); see Krupp, *Zeitschrift der Kruppschen Betriebsgemeinschaft*, from issue 26 (1933/4); for example, issue 30 (1938/9), p. 161 ff., p. 273; see also the text and picture book by Heinrich Hauser, *Opel, ein deutsches Tor zur Welt* (Frankfurt, 1937) and Hauser, *Im Kraftfeld von Rüsselsheim* (München, 1940); see also Thomas Lange, 'Literatur des technokratischen Bewusstseins,' *Lili: Zeitschrift für Literaturwissenschaft und Linguistik*, No. 40, 1989, pp. 52–81, p. 61ff; see the photographic illustrations in Axmann, *Reichsberufswettkampf*, after pp. 168, 232, 321, 344; only word-pictures, which attempt to be all the more 'poetic,' can be found in Heinz Kindermann (ed.), *Ruf der Arbeit* (Berlin, 1942).

Extract 64

JOST DÜLFFER: *The Matrix of Totalitarian Imagery: Public Space, the National Socialist Year, and the Generational Cycle*

1. Jay W. Baird, *To Die for Germany* (Bloomington, Ind., 1990); Volker Ackermann, *Nationale Totenfeiern in Deutschland von Wilhelm I. bis Franz Josef Strauss: eine Studie zur politischen Semiotik* (Stuttgart, 1990); Sabine Behrenbeck, *Der Kult um die toten Helden im Nationalsozialismus: Nationalsozialistische Mythen, Riten und Symbole* (Vierow, 1995).

2. Peter Stachura, 'Das Dritte Reich und Jugenderziehung: Die Rolle der Hitler Jugend 1933–1939', in Manfred Heinemann (ed.), *Erziehung und Schulung im Dritten Reich* (Stuttgart, 1976), i. 90–112 (99).

3. Wolfgang Michalka (ed.), *Das Dritte Reich*, 2 vols. (Munich, 1985), i. 261–2.

Extract 66

KLAUS TENFELDE: *The Social Bases of* Resistenz *and Resistance*

1. Günther Weisenborn, *Der lautlose Aufstand: Bericht über die Widerstandsbewegung des deutschen Volkes 1933–1945* (repr. Frankfurt am Main, 1974).
2. William Sheridan Allen, *Das haben wir nicht gewollt! Die nationalsozialistische Machtergreifung in einer Kleinstadt 1930–1935* (Gütersloh, 1966).
3. *Bayern in der NS-Zeit*, i: *Soziale Lage und politisches Verhalten der Bevölkerung im Spiegel vertraulicher Berichte*, ed. Martin Broszat, Elke Fröhlich, and Falk Wiesmann; ii: *Herrschaft und Gesellschaft in Konflikt*, part A, ed. Martin Broszat and Elke Fröhlich; iii and iv: *Herrschaft und Gesellschaft in Konflikt*, parts B and C, ed. Martin Broszat, Elke Fröhlich, and Anton Grossmann; v: *Die Parteien KPD, SPD, BVP in Verfolgung und Widerstand*, ed. Martin Broszat and Hartmut Mehringer; vi: *Die Herausforderung des Einzelnen: Geschichten über Widerstand und Verfolgung*, ed. Martin Broszat and Elke Fröhlich (Munich, 1977–83). For further publications cf. the report by Werner Müller, 'Opposition und Widerstand gegen die nationalsozialistische Herrschaft im Alltag', *Internationale wissenschaftliche Korrespondenz zur Geschichte der deutschen Arbeiterbewegung*, 20 (1984), 35–44.
4. Cf. Hans-J. Althaus et al., *Da ist nirgends nichts gewesen außer hier: das 'rote Mössingen' im Generalstreik gegen Hitler. Geschichte eines schwäbischen Arbeiterdorfes* (Berlin, 1982), 9 ff.
5. With the right emphasis Detlev Peukert, *Volksgenossen und Gemeinschaftsfremde: Anpassung, Ausmerze und Aufbegehren unter dem Nationalsozialismus* (Cologne, 1982), 78–93 and *passim*.

Extract 67

IAN KERSHAW: *Resistance without the People?*

1. M. Steinert, *Hitlers Krieg und die Deutschen* (Düsseldorf, 1970), 469–90; Ian Kershaw, *Der Hitler-Mythos; Volksmeinung und Propaganda im Dritten Reich* (Stuttgart, 1980), 186 ff.; Ortwin Buchbender and Reinhold Sterz (eds.), *Das andere Gesicht des Krieges: deutsche Feldpostbriefe 1939–1945* (Munich, 1982), 20 ff., 141 ff.

Extract 68

KLAUS-MICHAEL MALLMANN AND GERHARD PAUL: Resistenz *or Loyal Reluctance?*

1. M. Broszat, 'Resistenz und Widerstand: eine Zwischenbilanz des Forschungsprojekts', in M. Broszat, E. Fröhlich, and A. Grossmann (eds.), *Bayern in der NS-Zeit*, vol. iv (Munich 1981), 698. The concept of 'organized' or 'passive *Resistenz*' has also been used by Karl Mammach (*Widerstand 1933–1939* (Cologne, 1984), 291, 188) albeit with other connotations. In modern fashion, Mammach understands by this a form of productivity strike or go-slow.
2. E. Köhler, 'Die langsame Verspießerung der Zeitgeschichte: Martin Broszat und der Widerstand', *Freibeuter*, 36 (1988), 59 ff.
3. R. Mann, 'Was wissen wir vom Widerstand? Datenqualität, Dunkelfeld und Forschungsartefakte', in R. Mann, *Protest und Kontrolle im Dritten Reich: Nationalsozialistische Herrschaft im Alltag einer rheinischen Großstadt* (Frankfurt am Main, 1987), 324.

4. Cf. G. Botz, 'Methoden- und Theorieprobleme der historischen Widerstandsforschung', in H. Konrad and W. Neugebauer (eds.), *Arbeiterbewegung—Faschismus—Nationalbewußtsein* (Vienna, 1983).

5. M. Prinz, 'Der Nationalsozialismus: eine braune Revolution?', in M. Hettling (ed.), *Revolution in Deutschland? 1789–1989* (Göttingen, 1991).

6. Cf. E. Fromm, *Arbeiter und Angestellte am Vorabend des Dritten Reiches: eine sozialpsychologische Untersuchung* (Stuttgart, 1990); this work, based on a questionnaire of the Frankfurt Institute for Social Research from the years 1929–30, was first published posthumously, as the exiled heads of the Institute—according to H. Marcuse in 1979—did not want to arouse the impression 'that German workers had always been despite or indeed precisely because of their socialist attitude at heart fascist' (42).

7. Cf. for example S. Milgram, *Das Milgram-Experiment: zur Gehorsamsbereitschaft gegenüber Autorität* (Reinbek, 1982); S. E. Asch, 'Änderung und Verzerrung von Urteilen unter Gruppen-Druck', in M. Irle (ed.), *Texte aus der experimentellen Sozialpsychologie* (Neuwied, 1969); as a summary R. Peukert, *Konformität: Erscheinungsformen—Ursachen—Wirkungen* (Stuttgart, 1975).

Extract 69

ROBERT GELLATELY: *The Gestapo and Social Cooperation: The Example of Political Denunciation*

1. W. S. Allen, *The Nazi Seizure of Power: The Experience of a Single German Town 1922–1935* (rev. edn., New York, 1984), 189, suggested that 'the Gestapo became extraordinarily efficient by reason of rumours and fears'.

2. Rolf Hochhuth, *Eine Liebe in Deutschland* (Reinbek bei Hamburg, 1980), esp. 115 ff.

3. See D. Peukert, *Die KPD im Widerstand: Verfolgung und Untergrundarbeit an Rhein und Ruhr 1933 bis 1945* (Wuppertal, 1980), 116 ff. I discuss the use of such words as 'instruments' to refer to the terror in my 'Terror System, Racial Persecution and Resistance in Nazi Germany: Remarks on the Historiography', *German Studies Review*.

4. Hauptstaatsarchiv Düsseldorf, Gestapo 17,922 (Düsseldorf, Sept. 1939).

5. See Staatsarchiv Würzburg, Gestapo 753, for one of the rare denunciations from the SD. The denouncer was married, Protestant, and not a party member.

6. Hans-Bernd Gisevius, *To the Bitter End*, trans. R. and C. Winstone (London, 1948), 101–2.

7. Ibid. 105.

Extract 70

CLAUDIA KOONZ: *Mothers in the Fatherland*

1. It should be noted that after the first national elections, constitutional challenges ended the separate ballots in many states. Gabrielle Bremme, *Die politische Rolle der Frau in Deutschland* (Göttingen: Van den Hoeck and Ruprecht, 1956), 76, and Richard Hamilton, *Who Voted for Hitler* (Princeton: Princeton University Press, 1983), 60–61, note 46 on 512–513, and 360–393; Thomas Childers, *The Nazi Voter* (Chapel Hill: University of North Carolina Press, 1983), 188–189 and 259–260.

Michael Kater, *The Nazi Party. A Social Profile of Members and Leaders, 1919–1945* (Cambridge: Harvard University Press, 1983), 147–153.

Extract 71

PAUL WEINDLING: *Racial Hygiene and Professional Leadership*

1. K. Saller, *Die Rassenlehre des Nationalsozialismus in Wissenschaft und Propaganda* (Darmstadt, 1961), p. 61.
2. U. Geuter, *Die Professionalisierung der Psychologie im Nationalsozialismus* (Frankfurt-am-Main, 1984); G. Cocks, *Psychotherapy in the Third Reich: The Göring Institute* (New York and Oxford, 1985).
3. BA Militärarchiv Freiburg 420/480 Heeressanitätsinspektion, 10 June 1939.
4. S. Leibfried and F. Tennstedt, *Berufsverbote und Sozialpolitik, 1933: die Auswirkungen der nationalsozialistischen Machtergreifung auf die Krankenkassenverwaltung und die Kassenärzte* (Bremen, 1981), pp. 2–18.

Extract 72

MICHAEL H. KATER: *The Problem of Motivation Reconsidered*

1. This was said with a glance at the great surgeon Ferdinand Sauerbruch, whose own antiregime stance has been acknowledged in the earlier postwar literature, but, in view of more recent analyses, is now very doubtful. See entry for November 6, 1943, in Ursula von Kardorff, *Berliner Aufzeichnungen: aus den Jahren 1942 bis 1945* (3rd edn., Munich, 1962), p. 75.
2. The situation of teachers is sketched in Michael H. Kater, 'Hitlerjugend und Schule im Dritten Reich,' *Historische Zeitschrift* 228 (1979): 572–623 and idem, 'Die deutsche Elternschaft im nationalsozialistischen Erziehungssystem: ein Beitrag zur Sozialgeschichte der Familie,' *Vierteljahrschrift für Sozial- und Wirtschaftsgeschichte* 67 (1980): 484–512.
3. The protest is recorded as a fact by Kurt Kühn, 'Deutsche Mediziner im Kampf gegen den Faschismus: dargestellt an Lebensbildern antifaschistischer Ärzte,' in Kurt Kühn (ed.), *Ärzte an der Seite der Arbeiterklasse: Beiträge zur Geschichte des Bündnisses der deutschen Arbeiterklasse mit der medizinischen Intelligenz* (Berlin, 1973), p. 232, but alluded to merely as a possibility in Karl-Peter Werle, 'Formen des Widerstandes deutscher Ärzte 1933 bis 1945' (diss., Kiel, 1974), p. 37.
4. Klare to Dr. B. Scheidegg, March 31 1933, in Kurt Klare, *Briefe von Gestern für Morgen: Gedanken eines Arztes zur Zeitenwende* (Stuttgart, 1934), p. 71; 'Der Leser hat das Wort,' in *Ziel und Weg* 3 (1933): 546.
5. Quotation from Arthur Gütt, 'Der deutsche Arzt im Dritten Reich,' *Ziel und Weg* 3 (1933): 81. Also in this vein see *Ziel und Weg* 5 (1935): 139; Kurt Blome, 'Die Neuordnung der ärztlichen Fortbildung,' *Deutsches Ärzteblatt* 66 (1936): 3; Gerhard Wagner, 'Die Reichsärzteordnung, ein Instrument nationalsozialistischer Gesundheitspolitik,' *Ziel und Weg* 6 (1936): 3; Dietrich Amende, 'Arzt und Nationalsozialismus, Idealismus und Glaube,' *Ziel und Weg* 7 (1937): 56–7; Dr. Hellmann, 'Besonderheiten der ärztlichen Landpraxis,' *Ziel und Weg* 7 (1937): 369–70; and Otto Dittmann's remarks in *Ziel und Weg* 8 (1938): 108–9.
6. This last provision is mentioned by Wilhelm Ackermann, 'Der ärztliche

Nachwuchs zwischen Weltkrieg und nationalsozialistischer Erhebung' (diss., Cologne, 1940), p. 135.

7. Althen to Wortmann, [Wiesbaden], November 9, 1934, HHSAW, 483/3159.

8. Dr. Ideler and Dr. Sonnenberg, 'In der Streitsache der praktischen Ärztin Dr. med. Hanna Donnerberg,' [Berlin, September 30, 1938], UK, 130. 118. 02/4. On this general principle see Dieter Rebentisch, 'Die "politische Beurteilung" als Herrschaftsinstrument der NSDAP,' in Detlev Peukert and Jürgen Reulecke (eds.), *Die Reihen fast geschlossen: Beiträge zur Geschichte des Alltags unterm National-sozialismus* (Wuppertal, 1981), esp. p. 114.

9. See the typical advertisements in *Ziel und Weg* 3 (1933): 101, 173, 273.

10. Examples in ibid., pp. 205, 274, 311–12. Sometimes Nazi movement affiliation was circumscribed, through the use of the expression 'the national attitude' (*die nationale Einstellung*), as in a Berlin ad of August 19, 1933, a facsimile of which is in Käte Frankenthal, *Der dreifache Fluch: Jüdin, Intellektuelle, Sozialistin: Lebenserin-nerungen einer Ärztin in Deutschland und im Exil*, ed. Kathleen M. Pearle and Stephan Leibfried (Frankfurt am Main, 1981), p. 195.

11. *Ziel und Weg* 3 (1933): 28, 101, 173–74, 205, 273, 311, 353.

12. 'Willi' to 'Hans,' Ruhrort, November 10, 1936, BA, R 561/83.

13. Quotation from NSDAP-Gauleitung München-Oberbayern to Steinbrecher, Munich, June 26 and August 13, 1942, BDC, PK Sewering. Also see the positive party verdict on Dr. H. O. (Starnberg) in Ortsgruppenleiter Munich to NSDAP Kreisleitung, Munich, January 18, 1937, SAM, NSDAP/28 (SA). For the government, see case Dr. B. (1936–41) in Reich interior minister, memorandum, Berlin, December 1941, BA, R 18/2958.

14. See my remarks in Michael H. Kater, *The Nazi Party: A Social Profile of Members and Leaders, 1919–1945* (Cambridge, Mass., 1983), pp. 207–12, 223–28.

15. Dr. A. E. to Wust, Murnau, July 7, 1933, SAM, NSDAP/84.

16. Cases of Drs. Hu., Hü., N., and R. (1935–43) in BA, R 18/5576. Under Himmler as new interior minister, Pfundtner was isolated at his post in November 1943 (Erich Stockhorst, *Fünftausend Köpfe: wer war (wer im Dritten Reich* (Velbert, 1967), p. 323).

17. On the general difficulty of gauging multifaceted motivations for intraparty behavior, see Kater, *Nazi Party*, pp. 157–9.

18. Walter Gross, 'Von der politischen zur geistigen Revolution,' *Deutsches Ärzteblatt* 64 (1934): 822. Also idem, 'Hütet die Flamme!,' *Ziel und Weg* 3 (1933), 115. Less acerbic but no less serious is the chastising of fair-weather Nazi colleagues by Wilhelm Josenhans in *Ziel und Weg* 3 (1933): 157.

19. Quotation ascribed to Stolberg Dr. Theodor Kerten, as in Saul K. Padover, *Experiment in Germany: The Story of an American Intelligence Officer* (New York, 1946), p. 97. Further see Althen to HJ, Bann 80, [Wiesbaden], October 5, 1934, HHSAW, 483/3159; *Ziel und Weg* 5 (1935): 337.

20. Quotation according to Alice Platen-Hallermund, *Die Tötung Geisteskranker in Deutschland* (Frankfurt am Main, 1948), p. 100; also see Theodor Brugsch, *Arzt seit fünf Jahrzehnten* (2nd edn., Berlin, 1958), pp. 292–3.

21. Hermann Radetzky's testimony in Günter Albrecht and Wolfgang Hartwig (eds.), *Ärzte: Erinnerungen, Erlebnisse, Bekenntnisse* (3rd edn., Berlin, 1973), p. 219; case of Dr. Adolf Sotier in Friedrichs to Hauptamt Ordnungspolizei, Berlin, July 22, 1940, BDC, PÄ Sotier. Also see the case of Dr. Wilhelm Hagen, *Auftrag und*

Wirklichkeit: Sozialarzt im 20. Jahrhundert (Munich-Gräfelfing, 1978), p. 146, who says he joined the party to protect himself as a formerly committed Social Democrat.

22. Peter Bamm (Dr. Curt Emmrich), *Eines Menschen Zeit: Memoiren eines Überheblichen* (Munich, 1980), p. 149; Franz Berger, 'Einzelheiten zur Berufsgerichtsbarkeit', *Deutsches Ärzteblatt* 69 (1939): 82.

23. For the case of Sievers, see Michael H. Kater, *Das 'Ahnenerbe' der SS 1935–1945: ein Beitrag zur Kulturpolitik des Dritten Reiches* (Stuttgart, 1974), pp. 313–38; for that of Gerstein, see Saul Friedländer, *Kurt Gerstein oder die Zwiespältigkeit des Guten* (Gütersloh, 1968).

24. Rudolf Neubert's statement to that effect rings hollow: *Mein Arztleben: Erinnerungen* (Rudolstadt, 1974), p. 87. His was the role of the picture-book opportunist: SPD-aligned in the Weimar Republic, a nominal Nazi in the Third Reich, and a communist fellow traveler in the post-1945 DDR.

25. As was claimed by several Nazi euthanasia doctors after World War II, according to Platen-Hallermund, *Tötung*, p. 122; and Ernst Klee, *'Euthanasie' im NS-Staat: die 'Vernichtung lebensunwerten Lebens'* (2nd edn., Frankfurt am Main, 1983), p. 273.

Extract 74

CHRISTOPHER BROWNING: *Reflections on a Massacre*

[HW stands for 'Investigation and Trial of Hoffmann, Wohlauf and others, Office of the State Prosecutor, Hamburg, 141 Js 1957/62'.

G stands for 'Investigation of G. and others, Office of the State Prosecutor, Hamburg, 141 Js 128/65'.

IMT stands for 'Trials of the Major War Criminals before the International Military Tribunal, 42 Vols.']

1. Heinz B., HW 4413; Kurt D., HW 4339.

2. In her analysis of Polish rescuers, Nechama Tec also notes that the initial decision to help Jews was impulsive and instinctive, not the result of prolonged reflection and calculation. *When Light Pierced the Darkness: Christian Rescue of Jews in Nazi-Occupied Poland* (New York, 1986), 188.

3. Anton B., HW 2693.

4. Bruno D., HW 2535, 2992.

5. August W., HW 4592.

6. Erwin G., HW 1640, 2505, 4344.

7. Friedrich M., HW 1708.

8. *IMT* 29: 151 (1919-PS).

9. Karl G., HW 2194.

10. Hans Pz., HW 3938.

11. Hero B., HW 890.

12. Arthur S., HW 1165.

13. Hermann W., HW 1947.

14. Gustav M., G 169–70.

Extract 75

OMER BARTOV: *The Missing Years: German Workers, German Soldiers*

1. H. Mommsen, 'National Socialism: continuity and change,' in W. Laqueur (ed.), *Fascism; A Reader's Guide* (Harmondsworth, 1979), pp. 151–92; E. N. Peterson, *The Limits of Hitler's Power* (Princeton, N.J., 1969).

2. T. Mason, *Sozialpolitik im Dritten Reich* (Opladen, 1977); S. Salter, 'Class harmony or class conflict?' in J. Noakes (ed.), *Government, Party and People in Nazi Germany* (Exeter, 1980), pp. 76–97.

3. I. Kershaw, *The 'Hitler Myth'* (Oxford, 1987); and id., *Popular Opinion and Political Dissent in the Third Reich* (Oxford, 1983).

4. T. Mason, 'The workers' opposition in Nazi Germany,' *History Workshop Journal*, Vol. 11, 1981, 120–37; I. Kershaw, *The Nazi Dictatorship* (London, 1985), p. 143. The opposite view in R. Dahrendorf, *Society and Democracy in Germany* (London, 1968); D. Schoenbaum, *Hitler's Social Revolution* (London, 1966).

5. This question is in fact posed by Mason himself in his 'Workers' opposition.'

6. T. Mason, 'The primacy of politics,' in H. A. Turner (ed.), *Nazism and the Third Reich* (New York, 1972), pp. 175–200; and id., 'Some origins of the Second World War', in E. M. Robertson (ed.), *The Origins of the Second World War* (5th edn., London, 1979), pp. 105–35; A. Milward, 'Fascism and the economy,' in Laqueur, *Fascism*, pp. 409–53; a different view in R. J. Overy, 'Hitler's war and the German economy,' *Economic History Review*, Vol. 35, 1982, pp. 272–91. Also, see Institut für Zeitgeschichte (ed.), *Totalitarismus and Faschismus* (Munich, 1980).

7. Mason, 'Workers' opposition'; Kershaw, *Dictatorship* pp. 14 (n. 38 for further literature), 34. See also, e.g., H. Graml et al., *The German Resistance to Hitler* (London, 1970); K.-J. Müller, *Armee, Politik und Gesellschaft in Deutschland, 1933–45* (Paderborn, 1979); J. Conway, *The Nazi Persecution of the Churches, 1933–1945* (London, 1968); K. Kwiet and H. Eschwege, *Selbstbehauptung und Widerstand* (Hamburg, 1984).

8. Emphasis on indoctrination in O. Bartov, *The Eastern Front, 1941–45* (London, 1985); and M. Messerschmidt, *Die Wehrmacht im NS-Staat* (Hamburg, 1969). Outline of disciplinary measures in M. Messerschmidt, 'German military law in the Second World War', in W. Deist (ed.), *The German Military in the Age of Total War* (Leamington Spa and New Hampshire, 1985), pp. 323–35.

9. See, e.g., on the army as an institution, K.-J. Müller, *Das Heer und Hitler* (Stuttgart, 1969); R. J. O'Neill, *The German Army and the Nazi Party, 1933–39* (London, 1966). On senior ranks and resisters, K.-J. Müller, *General Ludwig Beck* (Boppard am Rhein, 1980); J. Kramarz, Stauffenberg (Frankfurt/M., 1965). Some initial work on junior officers in Bartov, *Eastern Front*, pp. 40–67; I. Welcker et al., Qualifikation zum Offizier? (Frankfurt/M., 1982); D. Bald, *Der deutsche Offizier* (Munich, 1982).

10. See n. 8 above. A good example in *The Goebbels Diaries: The Last Days*, ed. H. Trevor-Roper (2nd edn., London, 1979), p. 80.

11. Kershaw, 'Hitler Myth,' pp. 65–6, 71, 86–7, 90–3, 126–8, 132, 215.

12. On changes in promotion policy, see G. Papke, 'Offizierkorps und Anciennität', in H. Meier-Welcker (ed.), *Untersuchungen zur Geschichte des Offizierkorps* (Stuttgart, 1962), pp. 177–206.

Extract 76

MICHAEL ZIMMERMANN: *The Conditions for Genocide*

1. Hauptstaatsarchiv Wiesbaden 407/863, Kriminalpolizeistelle Darmstadt, 27 May 1940, with enclosure 8 on the deportation of Sinti and Roma from south-west Germany to the *Generalgouvernement*; here the terms 'resettlement', 'evacuation', 'transport', 'deportation'; Generallandesarchiv Karlsruhe 364/Zug.1975/3 II, Fasc. 24, Polizei Station Oberschefflenz, 28 Mar. 1943, J. No. 378, with the terms 'transport', 'delivered', and 'journey'.

2. Herbert Jaeger, 'Arbeitsteilige Täterschaft: kriminologische Perspektiven auf den Holocaust', in Hanna Loewy (ed.), *Holocaust: die Grenzen des Verstehens. Eine Debatte über die Besetzung der Geschichte* (Reinbek, 1982), 160–5.

3. See the overview, which also brings in other countries, of Peter Weingart, Jürgen Kroll, and Kurt Bayertz, *Rasse, Blut und Gene: Geschichte der Eugenik und Rassehygiene in Deutschland* (Frankfurt am Main, 1992).

4. Wolfgang Sofsky, *Die Ordnung des Terrors: das Konzentrationlager* (Frankfurt am Main, 1993), 318.

5. Hans Mommsen, in Institut für Zeitgeschichte (ed.), *Totalitarismus und Faschismus: eine wissenschaftliche und politische Begriffskontroverse* (Munich, 1980), 18–27; Hans Mommsen, 'Hitlers Stellung im nationalsozialistischen Herrschaftssystem', in Gerhard Hirschfeld and Lothar Kettenacker (eds.), *Der Führerstaat: Mythos und Realität* (Stuttgart, 1981), 43–69.

6. Hans Mommsen, 'Die Realisierung des Utopischen: Die "Endlösung der Judenfrage" im Dritten Reich', in Wolfgang Wippermann (ed.), *Kontroversen um Hitler* (Frankfurt am Main, 1986), 248–98.

7. Mommsen, 'Hitlers Stellung', 63.

8. The notion of 'conceptualism' [Konzeptualismus] would offer the possibility of making connections to Foucault's theory of discourse, in which discursive concept, institutional power, and the exclusion of social groups are discussed in relation to one another.

9. For reference to the moral inhibition-reducing effect of this discourse, which surfaces under the guise of scholarship, I thank Lutz Niethammer. The mass extermination could then be rationalized by the murderers as the execution of generally valid scientific knowledge and 'laws'.

Extract 77

DAVID SCHOENBAUM: *The Third Reich and Society*

1. Franz Neumann, *Behemoth*, New York, 1942, p. 367.

2. Irrespective of their striking similarities, a striking difference between Hitlerism and Stalinism is the near absence of purges in the former. The purge of June 1934 is remarkable as an exception. Failure or differences of opinion with Hitler led not to show trials, exile or execution, but at worst to private life in the case of Schacht or the Nazi version of an old Bolshevik like Feder; in the case of others, Frank, Rosenberg or Goering, it led to continued or even augmented titles and honors. At the same time, it seemed a characteristic of both states that actual influence could well be in inverse proportion to size—though the Labor Front might again be an exception. Thus, in the Third Reich, Party influence declined

as the Party increased, and in the SS, as total membership grew, power was continually concentrated in one subdivision after another. Cf. Hannah Arendt, *The Origins of Totalitarianism*, New York, 1958, p. 403; Karl O. Paetel, 'Geschichte und Soziologie der SS, *Vierteljahrshefte für Zeitgeschichte, 1954, pp. 1ff.*

3. Cf. William Shirer, *Berlin Diary*, London, 1941, p. 218. 'Did a mike interview with General Ernst Udet tonight . . . Udet . . . is something of a phenomenon. A professional pilot, who only a few years ago was so broke he toured America as a stunt flier, performing often in a full dress suit and a top hat, he is now responsible for the designing and production of Germany's war planes. Though he never had any business experience, he has proved a genius at his job, . . . I could not help thinking tonight that a man like Udet would never be entrusted with such a job in America. He would be considered "lacking in business experience." Also, businessmen, if they knew of his somewhat bohemian life, would hesitate to trust him with responsibility. And yet in this crazy Nazi system he has done a phenomenal job.' Udet, the hero of Carl Zuckmayer's 1946 play *'Des Teufels General,'* later committed suicide in despair with Hitler's policies.

4. Nor were Nazis with doctorates, even the most aggressively egalitarian of them like Ley and Goebbels, inhibited about appearing in public with their titles.

5. According to a typical contemporary joke, 'NSBO = Noch sind die Bonzen oben.' ['The bigwigs are still on top'.]

6. Cf. Shirer, op. cit., pp. 213, 345.

Extract 79

DETLEV PEUKERT: *Brown Revolution?*

1. On continuity, see: T. Nipperdey, in M. Stürmer (ed.), *Die Weimarer Republik: Belagerte Civitas* (Königstern, 1980), E. Nolte, *Three Faces of Fascism*, (New York, 1960).

2. Wolfgang Schäfer (ed.), *Eure Bänder rollen, nur wenn wir es wollen! Arbeiterleben und Gewerkschaftsbewegung in Südniedersachsen,* IG Chemie-Verwaltungsstelle Hann. (Münden, 1979), especially pp. 113 ff. and 163 ff.; cf. Jürgen Reulecke, 'Die Fahne mit dem goldenen Zahnrad: der "Leistungskampf" der deutschen Betriebe 1937–1939', in Detlev Peukert and Jürgen Reulecke (eds.), *Die Reihen fast geschlossen: Beiträger zur Geschichte des Alltags unterm Nationalsozialismus* (Wuppertal 1981), pp. 245–72.

3. References to continuities with the pre-1933 and post-1945 periods are in, e.g.: Wolfgang Strohmeyer, 'Der "Arbeitskreis für Arbeitsstudien". Ein Beitrag zur Strategie der Gewerkschaften nach 1945', *Jahrbuch Arbeiterbewegung*, vol. 6, Frankfurt, 1978, pp. 44–77; Peter Hinrichs and Lothar Peter, *Industrieller Friede? Arbeitswissenschaft, Rationalisierung und Arbeiterbewegung in der Weimarer Republik,* (Cologne, 1976); Peter Hinrichs, *Um die Seele des Arbeiters*, Cologne, 1981. Waltraut Bergmann et al, *Soziologie im Faschismus 1933–1945* (Cologne, 1986). Cf. also: Ludolf Herbst, 'Die Mobilmachung der Wirtschaft 1938/39 als Problem des nationalsozialistischen Herrschaftssystems', in Wolfgang Benz and Hermann Graml (eds.), *Sommer 1939* (Stuttgart, 1979), pp. 62–106.

Extract 81

DETLEV PEUKERT: *Persecution and Coordination*

1. Letter of Karl Adolphs of 23 Mar. 1974, VVN-Archive, Düsseldorf; interview with Christine Schröder, Bochum (D. Peukert), 13 Jan. 1975.
2. Ibid.
3. Lehnert, 'Der blutige Rosenmontag: Folgen des Reichstagsbrandes auch in Essen zu spüren': series of articles in the *Neue Ruhr-Zeitung*, Essen, 27 Feb. to 20 Mar. 1958.
4. Ibid.; catalogue on 'Bergarbeiter' (Bochum, 1969); H.-J. Steinberg, *Widerstand und Verfolgung in Essen 1933–1945* (Bonn, 1973), 43.
5. Central Party Archive, Institute of Marxism-Leninism of the Central Committee of the SED (IML/ZPA), Berlin, St3/74.
6. *Essener Lokalpost*, 23 Apr. 1933.
7. Interview with Fritz Rische, Düsseldorf (D. Peukert), 22 Oct. 1974; interview with Christine Schröder, Bochum (D. Peukert), 13 Feb. 1974; interview with Konrad Buchner, Bochum (D. Peukert), 19 Feb. 1975.
8. *Deutsche Widerstandskämpfer, 1933–1945: Biographien und Briefe* (Berlin, 1970), i. 280.
9. Düsseldorf Murder Statistics, 1933, *Die Tat* (Frankfurt am Main [14/36], 7 Sept. 1963; two police photos of the victim were published in Peter Altmann, Heinz Brüdigam, Barbara Mausbach-Bromberger, and Max Oppenheimer, *Der deutsche antifaschistischer Widerstand 1933–1945; in Bildern und Dokumenten* (Frankfurt am Main, 1975),
10. IML/ZPA, St3/764.
11. Report of Heinrich Burggraf, VVN Essen.
12. *Nationalzeitung*, Essen, 12 Sept. 1933.

Extract 82

FALK PINGEL: *The Concentration Camps as Part of the National Socialist System of Domination*

1. I have developed this in further detail in my book: *Häftlinge unter SS-Herrschaft, Widerstand, Selbstbehauptung und Vernichtung im Konzentrationslager* (Hamburg, 1978).
2. See in detail: *Buchenwald-Mahnung und Verpflichtung* (Berlin (GDR), 1961), pp. 110 ff., 144 if.; Friedrich K. Kaul, *Die Psychiatrie im Strudel der 'Euthanasie'* (Frankfurt a.M., 1979), pp. 102 ff.; Christian Streit, *Keine Kameraden—Die Wehrmacht und die sowjetischen Kriegsgefangenen 1941–1945* (Stuttgart, 1978). Hans Marsalek. *Die Geschichte des Konzentrationslagers Mauthausen* (Vienna, 1974).
3. Willi A. Boeleke, *Deutschlands Rüstung im Zweiten Weltkrieg. Hitlers Konferenzen mit Albert Speer 1942–1945*, (Frankfurt a.M., 1969); Joseph Billig, *Les camps de concentration dans l'economie du Reich hitlerien*, (Paris, 1973).
4. *Studien zur Geschichte der Konzentrationslager*, Stuttgart, 1970; Martin Broszat, 'The Concentration Camps 1933–45,' in Helmut Krausnick et al., *Anatomy of the SS State* (London, 1968), p. 406.
5. Pingel, *op. cit.*, pp. 50 ff.: Günther Kimmel, 'Das Konzentrationslager, Dachau— Eine Studie zu dem nationalsozialistischen Gewaltverbrechen,' *Bayern in der NS-Zeit*, Martin Broszat, Elke Fröhlich, Falk Wiesemann (eds.), Vol. I (Munich, 1977), p. 359.

6. Enno Georg, *Die wirtschaftlichen Unternehmungen des SS*, (Stuttgart, 1963); Lotte Zumpe, 'Die Textilbetriebe der SS im Konzentrationslager Ravensbrücks,' *Jahrbuch für Wirtschaftsgeschichte*, Vol. I, 1969, pp. 11–40.

7. For further elaboration of the subject, see Pingel, *op. cit.*, pp. 291ff.; see also Franciszek Piper, 'Die Sklavenarbeit der Häftlinge,' *Ausgewählte Probleme aus der Geschichte des KL Auschwitz*, (Auschwitz, 1978), pp. 59–80; *Auschwitz—Nazi Extermination Camp*, (Warsaw, 1978).

Extract 83

GISELA BOCK: *Racial Policy and Women's Policy*

1. G. Deile, 'Die erbbiologische Bewertung des Hilfsschulskindes', *Zeitschrift für Gesundheitsverwaltung und Gesundheitsfürsorge*, 4 (1933), 528–35 (534).

2. Theodor Mollison, 'Rassenkunde und Rassenhygiene', in Ernst Rüdin (ed.), *Erblehre und Rassenhygiene im völkischen Staat* (Munich, 1934), 34–48 (34f.); Frithjof Hager, *Der gegenwärtige Stand der Sterilisierung minderwertiger in Deutschland* (Diss. med., Kiel, 1934), 18.

3. Of these a million were 'inferior'. Such a calculation can be found for example in Walter Kreienberg, *Die Auswirkungen des G.V.e.N. an dem Krankenbestand der Psychiatrischen und Nervenklinik Erlangen* (diss. med., Erlangen, 1937), 21f.; cf. also Brigitte Burgschweiger, *Humangenetische und anthropologische Arbeiten (Dissertationen) in der medizinischen Fakultät der Universität Erlangen in den Jahren 1933–1945* (diss. med., Erlangen, 1970), 60–2.

4. Patrick von zur Mühlen, *Rassenideologien* (Berlin, 1977), 243f.; similarly Kurt Novick, *'Euthanasie' und Sterilisierung im Dritten Reich* (Göttingen, 1980), 66ff.; cf. also Geoffrey G. Field, 'Nordic Racism', *Journal of the History of Ideas*, 38 (1977), 523–40, esp. 536ff.; Fritz Reuter, *Aufartung durch Ausmerzung* (Berlin, 1936). That National Socialism also signified an 'attack on the family' in other ways is shown, for example, by Barbara Beuys, *Familienleben in Deutschland* (Reinbek, 1980), 472–91.

5. Cf. Dorothee Klinksiek, *Die Frau im NS-Staat* (Stuttgart, 1982), 89; Tim Mason, 'Zur Lage der Frauen in Deutschland 1930–1940', *Gesellschaft*, 6 (Frankfurt am Main, 1976), 118–93 (144); Bundesarchiv Koblenz, R 43 II/400, fos. 216–21 ('Transformation of Unemployment Insurance Contributions into Contributions to the Reich Family Fund).

Extract 85

DETLEV GARBE: *Between Resistance and Martyrdom*

1 The terms 'Bible Students' and 'Jehovah's Witnesses' refer to the religious group as a whole and to individual members, whereby for the time after 1931 the terms are used interchangeably. This is justified insofar as the old term 'Bible Students' continued to be used by the public, the Nazi persecution organs, and the believers themselves. The name International Bible Students' Association (IBV) refers to the community of believers and to the organizational form of the Bible Students (Jehovah's Witnesses). 'Watch Tower Bible and Tract Society' (WTB) refers to the legal title and publishing body of the Jehovah's Witnesses and is

used to refer to both the position of the American overall leadership and the German branch leadership of the religious community.

2. In his study of the 'Dual State' which first appeared in New York in 1941, Ernst Fraenkel, the former head of the German Metalworkers' Association, ascribed a general validity beyond the narrow circle of the religious groups to this assertion: 'The members of this sect, whose pacifism allows no compromises and whose honouring of Jehovah incorporates the denial of all worldly authority, represent the prototype of a community living according to absolute natural laws. None of the illegal groups rejects National Socialism in a more uncompromising fashion than this obstinate group. (Ernst Fraenkel, *Der Doppelstaat: Recht und Justiz im Dritten Reich* (new edn., Frankfurt am Main, 1984), 147.)

3. Of the approximately 300,000 registered members of the KPD in 1932 *c.* 60,000 were arrested and interned in prisons or concentration camps in 1933/4 (cf. Hermann Weber, 'Die Ambivalenz der kommunistischen Widerstandsstrategie bis zur "Brüsseler Parteikonferenz"', in Jürgen Schmädecke and Peter Steinbach (eds.), *Der Widerstand gegen den Nationalsozialismus: die deutsche Gesellschaft und der Widerstand gegen Hitler* (Munich, 1985), 73–85 (79). On the basis of the available documentation on the resistance circle of the west German KPD Detlev Peukert has estimated that the 'number of Communists involved at some point in the illegal organizations [was] more than a quarter, and probably between a third and a half of all members at the end of 1932/beginning of 1933 (D. Peukert, *Die KPD im Widerstand: Verfolgung und Untergrundarbeit an Rhein und Ruhr 1933–1945* (Wuppertal, 1980), 166.

4. On participation in the resistance activities of left-wing splinter groups cf. Jan Foitzik, *Zwischen den Fronten: zur Politik, Organisation und Funktion linker politischer Kleinorganisationen im Widerstand 1933 bis 1939/40 unter besonderer Berücksichtigung des Exils* (Bonn, 1986), esp. 241 ff. Jan Foitzik proceeds from the assumption that in the middle of the 1930s approximately half of the membership of the left-wing splinter organizations (total membership in 1933: 22,000) were still active in the resistance. An almost identical set of figures can be confirmed for the IBV, also in terms of proportions.

5. Cf. John S. Conway, *Die Nationalsozialistische Kirchenpolitik 1933 bis 1945: Ihre Ziele, Widersprüche und Fehlschläge* (Munich, 1939), 212; Detlev Garbe, '"Gott mehr gehorchen als den Menschen": neuzeitliche Christenverfolgung im Nationalsozialistischen Hamburg', in Projektgruppe für die vergessenen Opfer des NS-Regimes (ed.), *Verachtet—Verfolgt—Vernichtet* (2nd edn., Hamburg, 1988), 179–219 (180).

6. Hans Lilje, *Im finstern Tal* (Nuremberg, 1947), 59.

7. This comparison is drawn, for example, by Philip Friedman, *Das andere Deutschland: die Kirchen*, issue 2 (Berlin, 1960), 23; Reiner W. Kühl, 'Widerstand im Dritten Reich: die ernsten Bibelforscher in Friedrichstadt', *Unterhaltung für Friedrichstadt und die angränzende Gegend: Mitteilungsblatt der Gesellschaft für Friedrichstädter Stadtgeschichte*, 27 (1985), 165–90 (165); Friedrich Zipfel, *Kirchenkampf in Deutschland 1933–1945: Religionsverfolgung und Selbstbehauptung der Kirchen in der nationalsozialistischen Zeit* (Berlin, 1965), 203.

8. Cf. Proceedings of the Bundestag, appendices, vol. 341 (Bonn, 1986), 10/6287, 11 (Report of the Federal Government on Compensation and Restitution for

National Socialist Crimes of 31 Oct. 1986). The question of whether the Bible Students were to be counted among those persecuted groups whom the National Socialist regime had 'intended to exclude from the cultural or economic life of Germany' in their entirety (section 51 para. 4, Federal Compensation Law) was disputed in compensation and restitution law for many years. Cf. *Rechtssprechung zum Wiedergutmachungsrecht*, 9 (1958) 29, Bundesgerichthof IV ZB 154/57, Judgement of 9 Oct. 1957; Blessing-Ehrig-Wilden, *Bundesentschädigungsgesetze. Kommentar* (3rd, expanded edn., rev. Hans-Georg Ehrig and Hans Wilden, Munich, 1960), 483; Walter Schwarz, *Rückerstattung nach den Gesetzen der Allierten Mächte* (Munich, 1974), 130 ff.

9. Cf. Hans Fleschutz, *Und folget ihrem Glauben nach! Gedenkbuch für die Blutzeugen der Siebenten-Tags-Adventisten Reformationsbewegung: Zeugnisse der Treue und Standhaftigkeit aus Deutschlands dunklen Tagen*, ed. International Missionary Association of the Seventh-Day-Adventist Reform Movement (Jagsthausen, n.d. [1967]).

10. Lilje, *Im finstern Tal*, 59. With the exception of foreigners who were to be forced into the German armed forces (citizens of Alsace and Lorraine, Luxembourgers, Poles from section 3 of the German *Volksliste*) Jehovah's Witnesses represented by far the largest group of conscientious objectors in the Third Reich (cf. 365–8). In treatments of conscientious objection in the Third Reich they are often neglected or 'forgotten', however. For example, in a television report broadcast in 1987 by the ARD first programme on the Protestant pacifist Hermann Stöhr, it was stated that next to Stöhr only 'seven Catholics, one Quaker, and seven Adventists' paid for their conscientious objection with their life. The narrator called this a 'thin balance-sheet for the religion of love' (*Mein Gewissen sagt nein. Hermann Stöhr: Kriegsdienstverweigerer im Dritten Reich. Ein Film von Martin Graff*, Südwestfunk Baden-Baden, 1987).

11. Michael Kater, 'Die ernsten Bibelforscher im Dritten Reich', *Vierteljahrshefte für Zeitgeschichte*, 17 (1968), 181–218 (208). Kater rightly points out that this fact has been paid little attention by research hitherto.

12. Heinrich Christian Meier, *So war es: das Leben im KZ-Neuengamme* (Hamburg, 1946), 31.

13. Figure for 1944: cf. Hermann Langbein, *Menschen in Auschwitz* (Frankfurt am Main, 1980), 280; Hermann Langbein, *Nicht wie die Schafe zur Schlachtbank: Widerstand in den Nationalsozialistischen Konzentrationslagern 1938–1945* (Frankfurt am Main, 1980), 189; Wachtturm Bibel und Traktat Gesellschaft (ed.), *Jehovas Zeugen in Gottes Vorhaben* (Wiesbaden, 1960), 169.

14. Figure for 1938; cf. Bundesarchiv Koblenz, NS 4 Bu/Vorl. 137, roll call 1 Nov. 1938; Eugen Kogon, *Der SS-Staat: das System der deutschen Konzentrationslager* (11th edn., Munich, 1983), 49; Moritz Zahnwetzer, *KZ-Buchenwald: Erlebnisbericht* (Kassel, 1946), 27.

15. Figure for 1939; cf. Matthias Lex, Affidavit under Oath, Trials of the Major War Criminals, vol. 31, 300, Document 2928-PS; Hans Maršálek, *Die Geschichte des Konzentrationslagers Mauthausen: Dokumentation*, ed. Österreichischer Lagergemeinschaft Mauthausen (2nd edn. Vienna, 1980).

16. BA NS 4 Fl/15, overview of the available beds and numbers of inmates of 18 July 1942.

17. The following figures show how problematic the establishment of statistical

figures is. During the entire time of its existence over 250 Jehovah's Witnesses were interned overall in Mauthausen. In the following years, following the transfer of 144 German and Austrian Bible Students from the temporarily closed KZ Dachau on 29 Sept. 1939 (of whom more than 60 were murdered in the following year) the numbers fell considerably. On 1 Dec. 1943 the number of Bible Student inmates was just 22. Following transfers the number rose towards the end of the war to approximately the level of 1939. On 31 Mar. 1945 104 Bible Students were registered; among the female inmates of Mauthausen there were 43 Bible Students on 31 Mar. 1945. Figures according to Maršálek, *Mauthausen*, 273 ff.; Falk Pingel, *Häftlinge unter SS-Herrschaft: Widerstand, Selbstbehauptung und Vernichtung im Konzentrationslager* (Hamburg, 1978), 302 n. 182; Sybil Milton, 'Deutsche und deutsch-jüdische Frauen als Verfolgte des NS-Staates', in Wolfgang Benz and Barbara Distel (eds.), *Frauen: Verfolgung und Widerstand*, Dachauer Hefte 3, (Dachau, 1987), 3–20 (10); Federal Ministry of the Interior, Öffentliches Denkmal und Museum Mauthausen, letter of 22 Feb. 1985 and 18 June 1986.

18. Figure for 1941.

19. Figure for 1940; cf. Margarete Buber-Neumann, *Als Gefangene bei Stalin und Hitler. eine Welt im Dunkel* (Stuttgart, 1958), 244; *Jehovas Zeugen in Gottes Vorhaben*, 168. Not included are the '300 young Russian Jonadabe [as yet unbaptized, newly converted believers] who learned the truth even in the camp' named in the latter source.

20. Figure for 1939; cf. *Erwachet!*, 8 Apr. 1939, 14; *Todeslager Sachsenhausen: eine Dokumentationsbericht vom Sachsenhausener Prozess* (Berlin, 1948), 42.

21. Figure for 1941; cf. Karl Hüser, *Wewelsburg 1933–1945: Kult-und Terrorstätte der SS* (Paderborn, 1982), 81, 91.

22. Figures for Majdanek: Jósef Marszalek, *Majdanek: Geschichte und Wirklichkeit des Vernichtungslagers* (licensed edn., Reinbek bei Hamburg, 1982), 81; for Natzweiler/Schirmeck: *Der Wachtturm*, 15 Nov. 1980, 5–10, 21–3; testimony of Egon Knöller, 30 Apr. 1983; for Stutthof: *Der Wachtturm*, 1 Mar. 1987, 21–4; VVN Hamburg, Committee Documents N3; BA Z Sg 134/28 [. . .] for Vught: *Der Wachtturm*, 15 Nov. 1980, 5–10; testimony of Johan Wildschut, 25 June 1986.

23. There is no evidence in the KZ-documents for Kater's assumption that 'in the wake of National Socialism's campaign of conquest thousands of foreign Bible Students were captured in their homelands and subsequently shipped to KZ camps' (Kater, 'Bibelforscher', 208). Pingel has referred to this too, noting correctly that 'in all camps during the war there were small groups of primarily German inmates' (Pingel, *Häftlinge*, 262 n. 99).

24. Cf. *Todeslager Sachsenhausen*, 43.

25. The mortality rate of 35 per cent is derived in a study of Lautmann, Grikschat, and Schmidt from the evaluation of data on 751 Bible Student inmates from different concentration camps. For Mauthausen the mortality rates lie well above 50 per cent, a reflection of the even harsher conditions predominating there (see 319 n. 19). An above-average percentage rate can be assumed for Sachsenhausen and Flossenbürg. Otherwise the rates conform to those adduced by Lautmann, Grikschat, and Schmidt. In the case of the KZ at Wewelsburg the rate was substantially lower, due to the exceptional circumstances there—of the 306 Bible Students held captive there 19 died (cf. Hüser, *Wewelsburg*, 81).

26. Those Jehovah's Witnesses from east European countries who in addition to their religious persecution also experienced racial persecution were exposed to even worse conditions in comparison to their German and west European co-religionists. When conditions for the latter improved from 1942 onwards, the former benefited from this only indirectly (gifts of food from their co-religionists); their allocation to harsher work commandos generally continued (cf. Maršálek, *Mauthausen*, 274).

27. The number of Bible Students who died in women's concentration camps has been estimated at 120 (cf. VVN/BdA Kreis Freiburg (ed.), *Verfolgung, Widerstand, Neubeginn in Freiburg 1933–1945: eine Dokumentation* (Freiburg am Breisgau, 1989), 160.

28. *Jahrbuch der Zeugen Jehovas* (1974), 212.

Extract 87

CHRISTIAN STREIT: *Soviet Prisoners of War—Mass Deportation—Forced Workers*

1. Kurt W. Böhme, *Die deutschen Kriegsgefangenen in sowjetischer Hand: eine Bilanz* (Munich, 1966) (*Zur Geschichte der deutschen Kriegsgefangenen des Zweiten Weltkrieges*, vol. vii), 151 and corrections sheet.

2. According to a list of the Department *Fremde Heere Ost* of 20 Feb. 1945 (situation on 31 Jan. 1945) the total number of Soviet prisoners of war was 5,734,528 (Bundesarchiv-Militärarchiv Freiburg [BA-MA], H3/728). A list of the *Feldwirtschaftsamt* of the OKW of 20 Jan. 1945 gives as an estimate of the OKW/Head of the Prisoner of War Department for Dec. 1944 the figure of 5.6 million (BA-MA WiVI.82); Joachim Hoffmann, 'Die Kriegsführung aus der Sicht der Sowjetunion', in *Das deutsche Reich und der Zweite Weltkrieg* (Stuttgart, 1983), gives with reference to unreferenced unknown documents a total figure of 'exactly 5,245,882'; Alfred Streim, *Die Behandlung sowjetischer Kriegsgefangener im 'Fall Barbarossa'; Eine Dokumentation* (Heidelberg, 1981), 224, uses a list of the POW Department of the OKW of 1 May 1944 in which a figure of 5,163,381 is given. Neither author gives any reason for not using the above-named sources.

3. For calculations see Christian Streit, *Keine Kameraden: die Wehrmacht und die Sowjetischen Kriegsgefangenen 1941–1945* Studien zur Zeitgeschichte 13 (2nd edn. Stuttgart, 1980) 128ff. 244–66. The figure of 3.3 million is to be seen as an approximation. Even a notionally accurate figure for the number of victims is impossible to give because of the fragmentary surviving evidence. It should be noted that the relevant state and military offices were at pains from the outset to prevent the creation of statistical data on these prisoners, in order to destroy the traces of these mass deaths (ibid. 129 ff.). Proceeding from the lower total figure Streim, *Behandlung*, 246, calculates the number of victims at '*at least* 2,530,00' (Streim's emphasis). Hoffmann, 'Kriegsführung', 730, gives 'about 2 million', a figure which stands in clear contradiction to the sources. The apologetic work by Hans Roschmann, *Gutachten zur Behandlung und zu den Verlusten sowjetischer Kriegsgefangener in deutscher Hand* (Ingolstadt, 1982), is not acceptable as a scholarly work. By repeatedly subtracting the same factors Roschmann gets the number of victims down to 1,680,000.

4. Memorandum, 2 May 1941, Nuremberg document 2718-PS, IMT vol. 31,84.

5. Economic Guidelines of the Agriculture Group in the Economic Staff East, 23 May 1941, Nuremberg document 126-EC, IMT vol. 36, 144 ff.

6. Streit, *Keine Kameraden*, 67–79.

7. On the feeding of the Soviet POWs cf. ibid. 137–62.

8. On the development of mortality rates 1941–2 see ibid. 130–7.

9. Ibid. 23 f. 224 ff.

10. On this and the following see ibid. 171–7.

11. On the following see ibid. 162–71. The evidence for the Reichenau's order is in a report of a colleague of Chief of the *Abwehr* Canaris from the end of Oct. 1941: NOKW-3147.

12. Streit, *Keine Kameraden*, 166.

13. On the subject of the 'criminal orders' raised here see ibid. 28–61; Helmut Krausnick, 'Kommissarbefehl und "Gerichtsbarkeitserlaß Barbarossa" in neuer Sicht', *Vierteljahrshefte für Zeitgeschichte*, 25 (1977), 682–738; Jürgen Förster, 'Das Unternehmen Barbarossa als Eroberungs- und Vernichtungskrieg', in *Das deutsche Reich und der Zweite Weltkrieg*, iv. 413–77.

14. Text printed in Gerd R. Ueberschär and Wolfram Wette (eds.), *'Unternehmen Barbarossa': der deutsche Überfall auf die Sowjetunion 1941* (Paderborn, 1984), 305–8. Cf. also the binding interpretation of the army leadership by the General for Special Purposes of the Army Supreme Command, ibid. 337 f.

15. Text in ibid. 313 f.

16. Franz Halder, *Kriegstagebuch: tägliche Aufzeichnungen des Chefs des Generalstabs des Heeres 1939–1942* ed. Hans-Adolf-Jacobsen, vol. ii (Stuttgart, 1963), 337 and 299 (30 Mar. 1941 and 6 May 1941).

Extract 88

LENI YAHIL: *Killing Operations*

DOH: Documents on the Holocaust: Selected Sources on the Destruction of the Jews of Germany and Austria, Poland, and the Soviet Union, ed. Y. Arad, Y. Gutman, and A. Margaliot (Jerusalem, 1981).

TWC: Trials of War Criminals: before the International Military Tribunal, 42 vols. (Nuremberg, 1947–9).

NCA: Nazi Conspiracy and Aggression: Office of the United States, Chief of Counsel for Prosecution of Axis Criminality, 11 vols. (Washington: United States Government Printing Office, 1946–7).

IMT: International Military Tribunal.

1. Wila Orbach, 'The Destruction of the Jews in the Nazi-Occupied Territories of the USSR,' *Soviet Jewish Affairs*, 6, no. 2 (1976), pp. 14–51. The number of Jews killed in the Ukraine, 1,533,000; Byelorussia, 375,000; Crimea, 50,000; other areas, 200,000—the total, 2,158,000.

2. See Raul Hilberg, *The Destruction of the European Jews* (Chicago, 1961), pp. 188f. On cooperation between the *Einsatzgruppen* and the army, see Helmuth Krausnick, *Hitlers Einsatzgruppen: Die Truppen des Weltanschauungskrieges 1938–1942* (Frankfurt, 1985), passim.

3. It is difficult to arrive at an exact overall reckoning of the number of these victims.

4. *TWC*, 4, L-180, pp. 154–70; *DOH*, pp. 389–93. For a detailed description see Hans-Henrich Wilhelm, 'Die Einsatzgruppe A der Sicherheitspolizei und des SD 1941/42: Eine exemplarische Studie,' in Helmut Krausnick and Hans-Heinrich Wilhelm, *Die Truppe des Weltanschauungskrieges: Die Einsatzgruppen der Sicherheitspolizei und des SD 1938–1942* (Stuttgart, 1981).

5. Einsatzgruppen-Report USSR, no. 133, November 14, 1941: *TWC*, 4, NO-2825, 170–74.

6. Einsatzgruppen-Report no. 106: NO-3140 and report no. 128: *TWC*, 4, NO-3157, 146–54.

7. Orbach, 'Destruction of the Jews,' p. 16.

8. Einsatzgruppen-Report no. 135: *TWC*, 4, NO-2832, p. 181.

9. *NCA*, 5, PS-3257, pp. 994–97. Also see part of this report in *DOH*, pp. 417–19.

10. *IMT*, 35, pp. 84–86. On this order and that of Manstein (see pp. 475, 504 ff.), see Yehuda L. Wallach, 'Feldmarschall Erich von Manstein und die deutsche Judenausrottung in Russland,' in *Jahrbuch des Instituts für deutsche Geschichte* (Tel Aviv, 1975), vol. 4, pp. 457–72.

11. Wallach, 'Feldmarschall Erich von Manstein . . . '; Gerald Reitlinger, *The Final Solution: The Attempt to Exterminate the Jews of Europe, 1939–1945*, 2d rev. ed. (London, 1968), pp. 210–12.

Extract 89

RAUL HILBERG: *Children*

1. See Arthur Ruppin, *The Jews in the Modern World* (London, 1934), pp. 100–102.

2. Statistical report in the YIVO Institute, Lodz Ghetto Collection No. 58.

3. *United States v. Bohdan Kozij*, 540 F. Supp. 25 (1982).

4. Klarsfeld and M. Steinberg, *Mémorial de la déportation des Juifs de Belgique.* (Brussels and New York, 1982).

5. Elie Wiesel, *Night* (New York: 1969), pp. 40–42.

6. Claude Lanzmann, *Shoah* (New York, 1985), pp. 3–5, 96, 103–105.

7. Report by Standartenführer (Colonel) Karl Jäger, December 1, 1941, Institut für Zeitgeschichte, Munich, Fb 85/2.

8. Testimony by Dr. Peretz, May 4, 1961, Eichmann trial transcipt, sess 28 p. Nn1.

9. Testimony of the mother, Mrs. Rivka Yosselevska, May 8, 1961, Eichmann trial transcript, sess. 30, pp. L1–N1. Mrs. Yosselevska, wounded, crawled out of the pit. Small children, also wounded, escaped from the grave as well but, not knowing where to go, were rounded up and shot.

Extract 90

FRANCISZEK PIPER: *The Number of Victims*

1. R. L. Braham, *The Destruction of Hungarian Jewry* (New York, 1963), pp. 443, 522. The figure of 437,402 Hungarian Jews, cited by Braham, should be supplemented by two transports of Hungarian Jews from the Kistarcsa camp, on August 13, 1944 (at least 131 persons) and October 18, 1944 (152 persons). See also D. Czech, *Kalendarium der Ereignisse im Konzentrationslager Auschwitz-Birkenau 1939–1945* (Reinbek bei Hamburg, 1989), pp. 848, 911.

2. Czech, *Kalendarium der Ereignisse*, passim; M. Gilbert, *Atlas of the Holocaust* (London, 1982/o, passim.

3. S. Klarsfeld, *Memorial to the Jews Deported from France 1942–1944* (New York, 1983).

4. *Documenten van de Jodenvervolging in Nederland 1940–1944* (Amsterdam, 1965), pp. 115–20.

5. D. Czech, 'Deportation und Vernichtung der Griechischen Juden im KL Auschwitz,' *Hefte von Auschwitz*, 11 (1970), p. 537.

6. H. G. Adler, *Theresienstadt 1941–1945* (Tübingen, 1955), pp. 50, 688–94; Lagus, *Josef Polak: Mesto nad mrizemi* (Prague, 1964).

7. R. Hilberg, *The Destruction of the European Jews* (London, 1961), pp. 458–73. See also Moreshet Archives, Giv'at Haviva, Israel, call no. D.1. 5705.

8. S. Klarsfeld, *Maxime Steinberg: Memorial de la déportation des Juifs de Belgique* (Brussels, 1982).

9. *Juden unterm Hakenkreuz: Verfolgung und Ausrottung der deutschen Juden 1933–1945* (Berlin, 1973); *Gedenkbuch: Opfern der Verfolgung der Juden under der nationalsozialistischen Gewaltherrschaft in Deutschland 1933–1945* (Koblenz, 1986); K. M. Kempner, 'Die Ermordung von 35,000 Berliner Juden,' in *Gegenwart in Ruckblick: Festgabe für die Jüdische Gemeinde zu Berlin 25 Jahre nach dem Neubeginn* (Heidelberg, 1970), pp. 184–88.

10. J. Romano and L. Kadelburg. 'The Third Reich: Initiator, Organizer and Executant of Anti-Jewish Measures and Genocide in Yugoslavia,' in *The Third Reich and Yugoslavia 1933–1945* (Belgrade, 1977), pp. 684, 690; E. le Chene, 'Yugoslavs in Nazi Concentration Camps,' in ibid.; Czech, *Kalendarium*, pp. 280, 284, 287, 290, 488, 493.

11. *Ebrei in Italia: Deportatione, resistenza, giuntina* (Florence, 1975), table-deportatione degli Ebrei dall Italia.

12. L. Poliakoff and J. Wulf, *Das Dritte Reich und die Juden: Dokumente und Aufsätze* (Berlin-Grunewald, 1961), p. 140: *Dokumentensammlung über 'Die Deportierung der Juden aus Norwegen nach Auschwitz'* (Ramat Gan, 1963), pp. 1–52; Czech, *Kalendarium*, pp. 347–427 Auschwitz-Birkenau State Museum (ASAM): D-RF-3/121/ transport 32.

13. Czech, *Kalendarium*, passim.

14. This number tallies the data relating to the RSHA transports (about 200,000 persons) as well as other transports.

15. The highest serial number in the EH (reeducation) category was assigned to an unknown prisoner who died in Czechoslovakia during the evacuation of the camp; ASAM, Mat 1207.

16. Determined mainly on the basis of records of the resistance movement and depositions by former prisoners.

17. The highest serial number entered into the Hauptbuch of the Gypsies is 10,094; ASAM, D-AuII-3/1/2. The highest number assigned to a Gypsy woman— 10,888—was entered in the book of block 22B in the women's camp; ASAM, D-AuI-3/1, p. 87.

18. ASAM, Depositions, file 123, card 58, account by a former prisoner, Tadeusz Joachimowski.

19. The highest number assigned to a Soviet POW to be found in documents preserved in ASAM is 11,964 (Yakushel); ASAM, D-AuII-3a/1134. In addition, several

numbers were assigned to two prisoners each. According to J. Brandhuber, this double assignation occurred also in the AU series (with a total of 177 serial numbers); see Brandhuber, 'Die sowjetischen Kriegsgefangenen in Konzentrationslager Auschwitz,' *Hefte von Auschwitz* 4 (1961), p. 45.

20. Brandhuber, p. 45, lists four such groups of prisoners, numbering over 1,800 persons. According to a Sonderkommando prisoner, 10 to 15 prisoners were executed weekly by shooting at the crematoria ovens in Auschwitz, and even more were shot in Birkenau. These figures warrant a conclusion that in two years, more than 1,000 POWs were put to death in this fashion. See *Amidst a Nightmare of Crime*: Notes of Prisoners of Sondercommando Found at Auschwitz. (Oswiecim, 1973), p. 44.

21. At the present state of research, we are unable to break down this figure precisely into national categories. For example, among the 39,159 preserved campphotos, we find, in addition to Poles, Jews, and Gypsies, 4,760 photographs of Germans, 2,465 of Czechs, 1,578 of Russians (not POWs), 797 of Yugoslavs, 654 of French, 548 of Ukrainians, nine of Dutch, two of Danes, two of Romanians, two of Spaniards, and one of a Lithuanian.

22. The list, compiled by L. Krysta, comprises some 182,000 transferred prisoners; a similar list, prepared by St Iwaszko, has 225,000. These figures require verification. ASAM, Collection, file 100.

23. A. Strzelecki, *Ewakuacja, Likwidacja i wyzolenie KL Auschwitz* (Oswiecim, 1982), tables, pp. 248–318.

24. This number is an approximation, since sources do not always indicate whether a given transport comprised registered or unregistered prisoners.

Extract 92

FRANK GOLCZEWSKI: *Poland*

1. Raul Hilberg, *Die Vernichtung der europäischen Juden: die Gesamtgeschichte des Holocaust* (Berlin, 1982), 812.

2. Schmuel Krakowski, 'Avedot Yehudei Polin baShoa', in *Dapim icheker tkufat HaShoa*, 2 (Tel Aviv, 1982/3), 232.

3. Martin Gilbert, *Die Endlösung* (Frankfurt am Main, 1984), 244. A little lower is the figure of 2,900,000 given by Jacob Lestschinsky, *Crisis, Catastrophe and Survival: A Jewish Balance Sheet 1914–1948* (New York, 1948), 60, in which no more exact sources are given, however.

4. Cf. Gerald Reitlinger, *Die Endlösung* (Berlin, 1956), 573: the source here is an Anglo-American estimate from 1946.

5. Ibid. 573; Reitlinger's own estimate.

6. Gerald Fleming, *Hitler und die Endlösung* (Wiesbaden, 1982), 207.

7. Czeslaw Madajczyk, *Polityka III Rzeszy w okupowanej Polsce*, 2 vols. (Warsaw, 1970), ii, 328.

8. Ibid. The necessary figure of c.3,500,000 as the initial Jewish population is arrived at by Madajczyk by increasing the figures in the census by the number of so-called 'racial Jews' according to the National Socialist definition, who could be of Christian confession and Polish tongue at the same time.

9. Unusually we feel able to take a higher figure here than that of Wolfgang

Scheffler, whose number (900,000) Wolfgang Benz uses in the introduction to this volume. For one, the 'celebration' of the millionth prisoner is something notable; further, the arising discrepancy is not so great that significant differences would occur. On the other hand, this illustrates on what vague indicators quantitative assertions are based.

10. Madajczyk, *Polityka*, ii. 328.

11. On Treblinka cf. Alexander Donat, *The Death Camp Treblinka* (New York, 1979), 265. On the anomalous nature of the demographic structure of the Polish Jews cf. Michal Grynberg, 'Struktura spoleczna repatriantów oraz szacunek liczby ludności zydowskiej w Polsce w pierwszych latach po II wojnie światowej', *Folks-Sztyme* 29/27 (1974).

12. Cf. Yisrael Gutman and Schmuel Krakowski, *Unequal Victims* (New York, 1986), 370. The figure of 353 deaths seems to be safe (Julius H. Schoeps, 'Unbequeme Erinnerungen', *Die Zeit*, 42 (9 Oct. 1987), 23. Gilbert, *Endlösung*, 241, gives a figure of 1,000 victims. In May 1945 a resolution of the state council of activists of the PPR (Polish Workers' Party) within the Jewish milieu stated: 'The council condemns completely the criminal activities of reactionary elements of the NSZ, who are continuing the excesses of Hitler towards the rescued Jewish population and who are even murdering Jewish women and children' (after B. Mark, 'Do dziejów odrdzenia osiedla zydowskiego w Polsce po II wojnie światowej', *Biuletyn Zydowskiego Instytutu Hiistorycznego* (1964), 51, 15. Cf. also S.L. Schneiderman, *Between Fear and Hope* (New York, 1947); Bernhard Goldstein, *Die Sterne sind Zeugen* (Hamburg, 1950), 287.

13. Between 1946 and 1948 17,000 Jews arrived in Palestine; between 1948 and 1951 a further 106,000 came to Israel (Malcolm Proudfoot, *European Refugees 1939–1952* (London, 1957), 356, 359).

Extract 93

MICHAEL BURLEIGH AND WOLFGANG WIPPERMANN: *The Persecution of Sinti and Roma*

1. For a detailed account see Ute Brucker-Boroujerdi, Wolfgang Wippermann, 'Gutachten über den Zwangscharakter des "Zigeunerlagers" Berlin-Marzahn in der NS-Zeit' (MS, Freie Universität, Berlin, 1988), and their 'Nationalsozialistische Zwangslager in Berlin III. Das "Zigeunerlager" Marzahn', in Wolfgang Ribbe (ed.), *Berlin-Forschungen II* (Berlin, 1987), pp. 189–201; Wippermann, 'Das "Zigeunerlager" Berlin-Marzahn 1936–1945', *Pogrom: Zeitschrift für bedrohte Völker*, 18 (1987), pp. 77–80.

2. Unfortunately the detailed minutes of this meeting have not been found. For what was discussed see Ritter's letter to the DFB dated 15 June 1940, BA R 73/14.005, and the testimony of Adolf Würth in B. Müller-Hill, *Murderous Science. Elimination by Scientific Selection of Jews, Gypsies, and Others, Germany 1933–1945* (Oxford, 1988), p. 145.

3. 'Schnellbrief des Reichssicherheitshauptamtes vom 17. Oktober 1939 an die Staatlichen Kriminalpolizei Leitstellen, betr. "Zigeunererfassung"', Erlasssammlung des Reichskriminalpolizeiamtes—Vorbeugende Verbrechensbekämpfung, Institut für Zeitgeschichte, Munich, Dc 17.02, reprinted in W. Wipperman, *Das Leben in Frankfurt zur NS-Zeit* (Frankfurt am Main, 1986), Vol. 1, pp. 80f.

4. On the 'Zigeunerlager' in Frankfurt see Wippermann, *Das Leben in Frankfurt*, Vol. 2, pp. 28 ff. On the camp at Marzahn, see Brucker Boroujerdi, Wippermann, 'Nationalsozialistische Zwangslager in Berlin III'; for the 'Zigeunerlager' at Lackenbach see Erika Thurner, *Nationalsozialismus und Zigeuner in Österreich* (Salzburg, 1983).

5. See Hans Buchheim, 'Die Aktion "Arbeitsscheu Reich"', *Gutachten des Instituts für Zeitgeschichte*, 2 (Munich, 1966), pp. 196–201; Wolfgang Ayass, '"Ein Gebot nationaler Arbeitsdisziplin". Die Aktion "Arbeitsscheu Reich" 1938', *Beiträge zur nationalsozialistischen Gesundheits-und Sozialpolitik*, 6 (Berlin, 1988), pp. 43–74.

6. 'Schnellbrief des Reichssicherheitshauptamtes vom 20. November 1939'. Erlasssammlung des Reichskriminalpolizeiamtes—Vorbeugende Verbrechensbekämpfung, Institut für Zeitgeschichte, Munich, Dc 17.02.

7. 'Schnellbrief des Reichssicherheitshauptamtes vom 18. Juni 1940, betr. "Haftprüfung der gemäss Erlass vom 1. Juni 1938 festgenommenen Personen"', Erlasssammlung des Reichskriminalpolizeiamtes—Vorbeugende Verbrechensbekämpfung, Institut für Zeitgeschichte, Munich Dc 17.02.

8. See Donald Kenrick, Grattan Puxon, *Sinti und Roma. Die Vernichtung eines Volkes im NS-Staat* (Göttingen, 1981), p. 67.

9. For a detailed discussion of the deportations see Wippermann, *Das Leben in Frankfurt*, Vol. 2, pp. 82 ff. See also M. Zimmermann, *Verfolgt, vertrieben, vernichtet. Die nationalsozialistische Vernichtungspolitik gegen Sinti und Roma* (Essen, 1989), pp. 43 ff.

10. 'Protokoll der Besprechung Heydrichs mit Seyss-Inquart und anderen SS-und Polizeiführern am 30. Januar 1940', *Nürnberger Dokumente* No. 5322, reprinted in Kurt Pätzold (ed.), *Verfolgung, Vertreibung, Vernichtung: Dokumente des faschistischen Antisemitismus 1933 bis 1942* (Leipzig, 1983), pp. 258f. See also Zimmermann, *Verfolgt, vertrieben, vernichtet*, p. 48.

11. See note 1 above.

12. Michael Zimmermann, 'Von der Diskriminierung zum "Familienlager" Auschwitz. Die nationalsozialistische Zigeunerverfolgung', *Dachauer Hefte*, 5 (1989), p. 103.

13. See for example 'Bericht des Kommandeurs der 281. Sicherungsdivision vom 23. Juni 1942 über die Erschiessung von 127 Zigeunern in Nororschew durch die geheime Feldpolizei', *Nürnberger Dokumente* NOKW 2072, also *Nürnberger Dokumente* NOKW 2535, 2022, 802 and 1486; 'Schreiben der 339. Infanterie Division an die Befehlshaber rückwärtigen Heeres-Gebiet Mitte vom. 5. November 1941', *Bundesarchiv Militärarchiv Freiburg* RH 26–339/5. For detailed accounts see Kenrick, Puxon, *Sinti und Roma*, pp. 93 ff.; Helmut Krausnick, *Die Truppen des Weltanschauungskrieges 1938–1942* (Frankfurt am Main, 1985), pp. 135 ff.; Raul Hilberg, *Die Vernichtung der europäischen Juden. Die Gesamtgeschichte des Holocaust* (Berlin, 1982), pp. 197 ff.; Martin Gilbert, *Atlas of the Holocaust* (London, 1988).

14. 'Schreiben des Reichssicherheitshauptamtes vom 13. Oktober 1942, betr. "Zigeunerhäuptlinge", Erlasssammlung des Reichskriminalpolizeiamtes—Vorbeugende Verbrechensbekämpfung', *Institut für Zeitgeschichte*, Munich, Dc 17.02, reprinted in Wippermann, *Das Leben in Frankfurt*, Vol. 1, pp. 106f. See also Michael H. Kater, *Das 'Ahnenerbe' der SS 1935–1945. Ein Beitrag zur Kulturpolitik des Dritten Reiches* (Stuttgart, 1974), pp. 206f.; Thurner, *Nationalsozialismus und Zigeuner in Österreich*, pp. 143f.

15. The decree has not been found. See however 'Schnellbrief des Reichssicherheits-hauptamtes vom 29. Januar 1943 betr. "Einweisung von Zigeunermischlingen Ròm-Zigeunern und balkanischen Zigeunern in ein Konzentrationslager"', Erlasssammlung des Reichskriminalpolizeiamtes-Vorbeugende Verbrechensbe-kämpfung, *Institut für Zeitgeschichte*, Munich, Dc 17.02, reprinted in Wippermann, *Das Leben in Frankfurt*, 1, pp. 109–14.

Extract 94

PETER STEINBACH: *On the Engagement with National Socialist Violent Crimes in the Federal Republic of Germany*

1. L. S. Dawidowicz, *Der Krieg gegen die Juden 1933–1945* (Munich, 1979); M. Broszat, 'Hitler und die Genesis der "Endlösung"', *Vierteljahrshefte für Zeitgeschichte*, 25/4 (1977), 739 ff.
2. J. Fürstenau, *Entnazifizierung: ein Kapitel deutscher Nachkriegspolitik* (Neuwied, 1969).
3. This granting of clemency on the part of the allies provides the most important explanation for the phrase 'the big ones get let off and the little ones get hanged'.
4. R. M. Kempner in 'Kolloquium über die Bedeutung der Nürnberger Prozesse für die NS-Verbrecherprozesse', in P. Schneider and H. J. Meyer (eds.), *Rechtliche und politische Aspekte der NS-Verbrecherprozesse* (Mainz, 1968), 14 ff.
5. On the sense of right and wrong of the perpetrators see the still exhaustive H. Jäger, *Verbrechen unter totalitärer Herrschaft: Studien zur nationalsozialistischen Gewaltkriminalität* (Olten, 1967; now in paperback: Frankfurt am Main, 1982).
6. On the thesis of the unavoidable integration after 1945 of the generation which had become 'incriminated' and even 'guilty' cf. H. Lübbe, '"Es ist nichts ver-gessen, aber einiges ausgeheilt": der Nationalsozialismus im Bewußtsein der deutschen Gegenwart', *Frankfurter Allgemeine Zeitung*, 19 (24 Jan. 1983), 9.

Extract 95

WOLFGANG BENZ: *Post-war Society and National Socialism: Memory, Amnesia, Defensiveness*

1. Important examples: Eugen Kogon, *Der SS-Staat* (Munich, 1946); Wolfgang Langhorn, *Die Moorsoldaten* (Munich, 1946); Nico Rost, *Goethe in Dachau* (Munich, 1949); Ernst Wiechert, *Der Totenwald* (Munich, 1946); Günther Weisenborn, *Memorial* (Berlin, 1948); Fabian von Schlabrendorff, *Offiziere gegen Hitler* (Zürich, 1946).
2. Romano Guardini, *Die Waage des Daseins* (Tübingen, 1946); Friedrich Meinecke, *Die deutsche Katastrophe* (Wiesbaden, 1946); Max Picard, *Hitler in uns selbst* (Erlen-bach, 1946); Alfred Weber, *Abschied von der bisherigen Geschichte* (Hamburg, 1946).
3. To name but a few examples: *Frankfurter Hefte; Deutsche Rundschau; Die Gegen-wart; Das Goldene Tor; Der Ruf; Ost und West; Die Wandlung.* For a summary see Thomas Koebner, 'Die Schuldfrage: Vergangenheitsverweigerung und Lebens-lügen in der Diskussion 1945–1949', in T. Koebner, G. Sautermeister, and S. Schneider (eds.), *Deutschland nach Hitler* (Opladen, 1987), 301–29.
4. Compare the images presented from the area surrounding Bergen-Belsen in

Rainer Schulze (ed.), *Unruhige Zeiten: Erlebnisberichte aus dem Landkreis Celle 1945–1949* (Munich, 1990).

5. Compare the results of the project initiated by Lutz Niethammer on 'Lebensgeschichte und Sozialkultur im Ruhrgebiet 1930–1960', which have been published in three volumes: *Die Jahre weiss man nicht, wo man die heute hinsetzen soll* (Berlin, 1983); *Hinterher merkt man daß es richtig war, daß es schiefgegangen ist* (Berlin, 1983); *Wir kriegen jetzt andere Zeiten* (Berlin, 1985).

Extract 98

CLEMENS VOLLNHALS: *Denazification*

1. Cf. amongst others Bradley F. Smith, *Der Jahrhundert-Prozeß: die Motive der Richter von Nürnberg. Anatomie einer Urteilsfindung* (Frankfurt am Main, 1977); M. Hirsch et al. (eds.), *Politik als Verbrechen: 40 Jahre 'Nürnberger Prozesse'* (Hamburg, 1986); Frank M. Buscher, *The US War Crimes Trial Program in Germany 1945–1955* (New York, 1989).

2. Lutz Niethammer, *Entnazifizierung in Bayern: Säuberung und Rehabilitierung unter amerikanischer Besatzung* (Frankfurt, 1972), 18. New edition entitled: *Die Mitläuferfabrik: die Entnazifizierung am Beispiel Bayerns* (Berlin, 1982).

3. *Frankfurter Hefte*, 2 (1947), 655 (emphasis in original).

4. Hans Woller, *Gesellschaft und Politik in der Amerikanischen Besatzungszone: die Region Ansbach and Fürth* (Munich, 1986), 147.

5. Clemens Vollnhals, *Evangelische Kirche und Entnazifizierung 1945–1949: die Last der Nationalsozialistischen Vergangenheit* (Munich, 1989); id., 'Die Hypothek des Nationalprotestantismus: Entnazifizierung und Strafverfolgung von NS-Verbrechen nach 1945', *Geschichte und Gesellschaft*, 18 (1992), 51–69.

6. Eugen Kogon, 'Beinahe mit dem Rücken zur Wand', *Frankfurter Hefte*, 9 (1954), 641–5. Cf. also Peter Merz, *Und das wurde nicht ihr Staat: Erfahrungen emigrierter Schriftsteller mit Westdeutschland* (Munich, 1985).

7. Cf. Martin Broszat, 'Siegerjustiz oder strafrechtlicher "Selbstreinigung"? Aspekte der Vergangenheitsbewältigung der deutschen Justiz während der Besatzungszeit 1945–1949', *Vierteljahshefte für Zeitgeschichte*, 29 (1981), 477–544; Peter Steinbach, *Nationalsozialistische Gewaltverbrechen: die Diskussion in der deutschen Öffentlichkeit nach 1945* (Berlin, 1981); Albert Rückerl, *NS-Verbrechen vor Gericht: Versuch einer Vergangenheitsbewältigung* (2nd edn., Heidelberg, 1984).

8. Clemens Vollnhals, 'Zwischen Verdrängung und Aufklärung: die Auseinandersetzung mit dem Holocaust in der frühen Bundesrepublik', in Ursula Büttner (ed.), *Die Deutschen und die Judenverfolgung im Dritten Reich* (Hamburg, 1992), 357–92.

Extract 99

HERMANN LANGBEIN: *In the Name of the German People*

1. Ernst Müller-Meiningen in the *Süddeutsche Zeitung*, Munich, 30–1 Aug. 1958.

2. Justice Minister for Baden-Württemberg Dr Wolfgang Haussmann, at a press conference in Stuttgart on 29 Mar. 1961.

3. Gert Kalow in the article 'Aug' im Auge mit unserer Geschichte', *Frankfurter Allgemeine Zeitung*, 3 Dec. 1958.

4. *Süddeutsche Zeitung*, Munich, 30–1 Aug. 1958.
5. From 'Die Gehilfen' – appeared in *Gegenwart* 138, 6 Sept. 1958.
6. Member of the Bundestag Jahn (SPD, Marburg) in the Bundestag debate on 22 Jan. 1959.
7. *Die Zeit*, Hamburg, 8 June 1962.
8. Statement of the Council of the Protestant Churches of Germany at the Synod in Bethel, *Frankfurter Neue Presse*, 16 Mar, 1963.

Extract 100

ADALBERT RÜCKERL: *National Socialist Extermination Camps as Reflected in German Trials*

1. Martin Broszat, 'Zur Kritik der Publizistik des antisemitischen Rechtsextremismus', in *Aus Politik und Zeitgeschichte*, Beilage 19/76 zur Wochenzeitung *Das Parlament*, 8 May 1976, also in *Vierteljahrshefte für Zeitgeschichte*, 2 (1976).
2. Hans Hofmeyer, 'Prozeßrechtliche Probleme und praktische Schwierigkeiten bei der Durchführung der Prozesse', in *Probleme der Verfolgung und Ahndung von nationalsozialistischen Gewaltverbrechen* (Munich, 1967).
3. In 1951 the main proceedings in the first trial of a member of the German personnel of the extermination camp Treblinka held in a court in the Federal Republic of Germany lasted for a mere three days (Stadtarchiv Frankfurt an Main: 55 KsI/50). The accused was sentenced to lifelong imprisonment. In the entire twenty-one pages of the written court judgement the representation—or rather: the fleeting mention—of the historical backround of the deed was confined to a few lines. The main proceedings in a case against a further ten German members of the camp personnel of Treblinka in 1964, by contrast, took nearly eleven months (Stadtarchiv Düsseldorf: 8 I Ks2/64). The court imposed custodial sentences of between life and four years. The written court judgements run to 673 pages; of these, 39 detail the historical background.

Extract 101

CHARLES S. MAIER: *Bitburg History*

1. Speech by Richard von Weizsäcker, May 8, 1945, in *Verhandlungen des Bundestages*; translated in Geoffrey H. Hartman (ed.), *Bitburg in Moral and Political Perspective* (Bloomington, Ind., 1986), pp. 262–273.
2. Address by Helmut Kohl during the ceremony marking the fortieth anniversary of the liberation of the concentration camps, April 21, 1985; distributed in English on April 22 by the German Information Center, *Statements & Speeches*, 7, no. 11 (New York, 1985); also in Hartman, *Bitburg*, pp. 244–50.
3. Ernst Nolte, 'Vergangenheit, die nicht vergehen will' [A past that will not pass away], *Frankfurter Allgemeine Zeitung* (cited hereafter as *FAZ*), June 6, 1986.
4. Speech by Richard Burt, May 23, 1986, cited by Hans Mommsen, 'Suche nach der "verlorenen Geschichte"? Bemerkungen zum historischen Selbstverständnis der Bundesrepublik' [Search for a 'Lost History'? Comments on the historical self-conceptualization of the Federal Republic], *Merkur*, 40 (1986), 864–874.
5. Primo Levi, 'The Memory of Offense,' in Hartman, *Bitburg*, pp. 130–137.

6. The most interesting debates took place among the French. For the most ruthless position see Maurice Merleau-Ponty, *Humanism and Terror*, trans. John O'Neill (Boston: Beacon, 1960), who came close to arguing that whoever lost a political struggle could not protest the penalties that followed. To take part in a historical or political movement was to recognize that defeat was tantamount to accepting guilt. 'We don't judge, we choose sides,' says Henri in Simone de Beauvoir's fictional dramatization *The Mandarins*, trans. L. M. Friedman (London:-Fontana, 1960), p. 144. See also Albert Camus's *The Fall*, trans. Justin O'Brien (New York: Knopf, 1958) for a later effort to think the matter through.

7. To suggest, as does Joachim Fest, that the use of poison gas (the insecticide Zyklon B even more than carbon monoxide) merely reflected a barbarous efficiency obscures part of its horror. Mass execution by gas relieved the psychological pressure on SS machine-gunners (see Christopher R. Browning, 'The Development and Production of the Nazi Gas Van,' in Christopher R. Browning, *Fateful Months: Essays in the Emergence of the Final Solution* (New York, Holmes & Meier, 1985), pp. 57–67. But gas also evoked a persisting fascination with delousing and killing vermin, images of which recur in German newsreels that show Polish, Russian, and Jewish prisoners being happily disinfected.

Extract 102

RAUL HILBERG: *Bitburg as Symbol*

1. Text of news conference held on March 21, 1985, *New York Times*, March 22, 1985.
2. On the treatment of Soviet prisoners of war, see Christian F. Streit, *Keine Kameraden* (Stuttgart: Deutsche Verlags-Austalt, 1978). In a speech at Bergen-Belsen on April 21, 1985, Chancellor Kohl mentioned the dead Soviet prisoners, but without any reference to the German army. Test of address in German Information Center. *Statements and Speeches*, vol. VII, no. 11, April 22, 1985.
3. In fact, the legacy of the old days was not devoid of problems. The most controversial book in postwar Germany was not any treatment of the Nazi regime, but a heavy monograph about World War I: Fritz Fischer's *Der Griff nach der Weltmacht* (The grab for world power), translated into English and published in America under the more sedate title *Germany's Aims in the First World War* (New York: Norton, 1967). Fischer discovered records of the German Foreign Office of 1914, showing some German eagerness for war at that time. The Weimar period is similarily problematical. In 1922, Chancellor Josef Wirth summarized his 'eastern program' in a conversation with Count Brockdorff-Rantzau, saying 'Poland has to be finished off.' Herbert Helbig. *Die Träger der Rapallo-Politik* (Göttingen: Vandenhoeck & Ruprecht, 1958), pp. 118–20. Gordon H. Mueller, 'Rapallo Reexamined: A New Look at Germany's Military Collaboration with Russia in 1922. *Military Affairs*, October 1976, pp. 109–17. Rapallo was in several respects a precursor of the secret German-Soviet protocol of August 1939.

Extract 103

GEOFF ELEY: *Nazism, Politics, and the Image of the Past*

1. Michal Bodemann, 'The Green Party and the New Nationalism in the Federal

Republic of Germany', in *Socialist Register, 1985/86* (London, 1986), 139, following the argument of Karl-Werner Brandt, Detlef Büsser and Dieter Rucht, *Aufbruch in eine andere Gesellschaft: neue soziale Bewegungen in der Bundesrepublik* (2nd edn., Frankfurt, 1986).

2. Bodemann, 'Green Party'. 139f. See also Michael Schneider, *Demokratie in Gefaln? Der Konflikt um die Notstandsgesetze: Sozialdemokratie, Gewerkschaften und untellektueller Protest, 1958–1968* (Bonn, 1986).

3. The relevant issues of *Das Argument* were: nos. 30 (1964), 32 (1965), 33 (1965), 41 (1966), 47 (1968), 58 (1970).

4. The emblematic text that brought the historical and political arguments together was Imanuel Geiss and Volker Ullrich (eds.), *15 Millionen beleidigte Deutsche oder Woher kommt die GDU? Beitrage zur Kontinuitat der burgerlichen Parteien* (Reinbek bei Hamburg, 1970).

5. For a good example of the public engagement of these years, and of the breadth of progressive sentiment, see the public declaration supporting the eastern treaties, signed by 204 senior historians and political scientists, which defined the *Ostpolitik* as an essential aspect of coming to terms with the Nazi past. The declaration was published by Karl Dietrich Erdmann with some other materials in *Geschichte in Wissenschaft und Unterricht*, 23 (1972), 353–63, as the occasion for launching his own attack on it. It is worth nothing that, while neither Nolte nor Hillgruber nor Hildebrand signed this declaration, Stürmer did.

6. In educational policy the political lines were confused by SPD *Land* governments' efforts at subsuming history into social studies in a reformed school curriculum, which produced protracted conflicts, notably in Hesse. See, for instance, Hans-Ulrich Wehler, 'Folgen Sozialliberale antiquierten Aversionen gegen die Geschichte?', in Landesverband Nordrhein-Westfalischer Geschichtslehrer (ed.), *Informationen zum 34. Deutschen Historikertag in Minister* (n.p., 1982), 3–12. For recent debates in social history, Georg Iggers (ed.), *The Social History of Politics: Critical Perspectives in West German Historical Writing since 1945* (Leamington Spa, 1985), introduction, 10 ff.: Eve Rosenhaft, 'History, Anthropology and the Study of Everyday Life'. *Comp. Studies in Soc. and Hist.*, 29 (1987), 99–105; Hans Medick, 'Missionaries in the Row Boat'? Ethnological Ways of Knowing as a Challenge to Social History', ibid. 76–98.

7. Much of the evidence presented in the *New German Critique* dossier on the reception of *Holocaust* can be read in this way: *New German Critique*, 19 (winter 1980), 3–136. See also Hans Mommsen, 'The Burden of the Past', in J. Habermas (ed.), *Observations on 'The Spiritual Situation of the Age': Contemporary German Perspectives* (Cambridge, Mass.: MIT Press, 1984) 263–81.

8. See *Die Zeit der Staufer: Geschichte. Kunst, Kultus, Katalog der Ausstellung* (Stuttgart, 1977). For the Hitler wave, see Eva Kolinsky, *Parties, Opposition and Society in West Germany* (New York, 1984), pp. 272–5: Saul Friedlander. *Reflections on Nazism: An Essay on Kitsch and Death* (New York, 1984). So far, the fiasco of the forged. 'Hitler Diaries' has been the climax of this process: see the fascinating account in Robert Harris, *Selling Hitler* (Harmondsworth, 1986).

9. See *Questions on German History: Ideas, Forces, Decisions from 1800 to the Present: Historical Exhibition in the Berlin Reichstag Catalogue*, 2nd updated edn. (Bonn, 1984). The term Museumismus was used by the architect, Bruno Schindler, in a

dossier published by the Greens on the museum question: see Bruno Schindler, 'Einige Anmerkungen zu der Vorstellung gegenüber dem alten Reichstag ein Museum für deutsche Geschichte zu errichten'. in Die Grünen (eds.), *Wider die Entsorgung der deutschen Geschichte: Streitschrift gegen die geplanten Museen in Berlin (W) und Bonn* (Bonn, 1986), pp 28–30.

10. For the Prussia exhibition, see Manfred Schlenke, Peter Brandt, H. Kuhn, A. Marquardt and H. Rathsack (eds.), *Preussen: Versuch einer Bilanz: Ausstellung Berlin, 1981*, 5 vols. (Reinbek bei Hamburg, 1981); and the critical report by Christine Lattek, *History Workshop JL.*, no. 13 (spring 1982), pp. 174–80.

11. For an indication of this activity, see Martin Broszat *et al.*, *Deutschlands Weg in die Diktatur: International Konferenz zur nationalsozialistischen Machtübernahme* (Berlin, 1983); Michalka (ed.), *Nationalsozialistische Machtergreifung.* (Paderborn, 1984).

12. For instance, contrast the terms of Otto Busch and James J. Sheehan (eds.), *Die Rolle der Nation in der deutschen Geschichte und Gegenwart* (Berlin, 1985) with those of Klaus Hildebrand (ed.), *Wem gehört die deutsche Geschichte?* (Cologne, 1987). For another pluralist volume on the eve of the more politicized discourse after the change of government in 1982–3, Werner Weidenfeld (ed.), *Die Identität der Deutschen* (Munich, 1983). Renata Fritsch-Bournazel, *Confronting the German Question: Germans on the East–West Divide* (Oxford, 1988; original German edn. 1986) is a straightforward introduction to the overall context.

Extract 104

PETER BALDWIN: *The Historikerstreit in Context*

1. One of the main points made by Hans-Ulrich Wehler in *Entsorgung der deutschen Vergangenheit? Ein polemischer Essay zum 'Historikerstreit'* (Munich, 1988).

2. Quoted in Anson Rabinbach, 'German Historians Debate the Nazi Past: A Dress Rehearsal for a New German Nationalism?' *Dissent* (Spring 1988): 192.

3. See for example, Imanuel Geiss, *Die Habermas-Kontroverse: Ein deutscher Streit* (Berlin, 1988), which examines the debate from a relatively moderate right-of-center position.

Extract 105

JAMES E. YOUNG: *Germany: The Ambiguity of Memory*

1. In the rare event when a state does commemorate its crimes, it is nearly always at the behest of formerly victimized citizens. The memorial unveiled on 30 Oct. 1990 in Moscow, for example, to 'the millions of victims of a totalitarian regime' was instigated by a group calling itself 'Memorial,' composed of scholars, cultural figures, dissidents, and former victims of Stalin's terror.

Likewise, a new monument by Maya Lin to the civil rights movement in Montgomery, Alabama—inscribed with the names of those who died for the cause—was commissioned and constructed by the Southern Poverty Law Center there, which had chronicled and prosecuted civil rights cases. In neither the Soviet nor American case did the state initiate the monument, but in both instances representatives of the state later endorsed these memorials—a move by which both current governments sought to create an official distance between themselves and past, guilty regimes.

2. Cited in Elizabeth Domansky, 'How to Remember What to Remember: Jenninger's Speech,' paper given at a conference at Northwestern University entitled 'Lessons and Legacies of the Holocaust,' November 1989, p. 2.

3. In fact, what both sides of the *Historikerstreit* (Historians' Debate) in Germany seem to have in common is the resistance to remembering the Third Reich solely in the image of Auschwitz. The vociferous response inside Germany and out to Ernst Nolte's infamous charge that 'certain interests,' especially those of the persecuted (i.e., the Jews), kept Auschwitz in view only to sustain their privileged status among the nations, led to his revised explanation of the killings: that the Nazis committed 'Asiatic deeds' only in fear of the deeds to be perpetrated upon the Germans by the Asiatics themselves. In 'Vergangenheit die nicht vergehen will,' his essay in the *Frankfurter Allgemeine Zeitung* (6 June 1986) that ignited the Historians' Debate in Germany, Nolte wrote: 'Did not the National Socialists, did not Hitler perhaps commit an "Asiatic" deed only because they regarded themselves and those like them as potential or real victims of an "Asiatic deed"? Was not the Gulag Archipelago more original than Auschwitz? Was not the "class murder" of the Bolsheviks the logical and factual prius of the "racial murder" of the National Socialists?' See also Nolte, 'Between Myth and Revisionism: The Third Reich in the Perspective of the 1980s;' in H. W. Koch, (ed.), *Aspects of the Third Reich* (New York and London, 1985), 17–38.

Though Martin Broszat was one of many who argued forcefully and eloquently against this revisionist critique, he also suggested that it would behove all historians not to view the Third Reich solely through the lens of Auschwitz, that a historical normalization is necessary if we are ever to grasp the entire significance of Hitler's time. In his view, the hegemony of Holocaust memory had begun to bury the rest of Hitler's social and political crimes, losing them to further inquiry and understanding. See Broszat, 'Plädoyer für eine Historisierung des Nationalsozialismus,' *Merkur 39* (May 1986): 373–85.

Extract 106

LUTZ NIETHAMMER: *Jews and Russians in the Memory of the Germans*

1. While, for example, in the so-called Stuttgart Declaration of the Protestant Church of 1945, a pioneering achievement of historical-moral sensibility in West Germany, brought about by international opportunity, the dimension of the Jewish Holocaust still does not appear at all.

2. The only exceptions to this are the memoirs of a comparatively small number of former soldiers, stationed above all in Poland, and who in their perceptions—e.g. as active Christians—had become less morally indifferent than the mass of their comrades.

3. For Germans, the forcefulness of Raul Hilberg's and Claude Lanzmann's initial attempts to document the Holocaust lie precisely in the fact that, in their representation of the railway transports clattering through the whole of Europe to the extermination centres, they undermine and destroy the unimaginability of the victims and even the process of destruction itself.

Extract 107

ISABEL WOLLASTON: *A War against Memory?*

1. For a more detailed discussion of such controversies, see: P. Clough, 'Now Dresden's Horror is Recalled' (*Sunday Times* 29.1.95); J. Ezard, 'The Firestorm Rages On' (*Guardian* 18.5.92); R. Harris, 'The Big Difference between "Butcher" Harris and a Nazi' (*Sunday Times* 31.5.92); I. Katz, 'A Good Night's Work' (*Guardian* 26.7.94); R. Littlejohn, 'Don't Ask Me to Say Sorry for the Dresden Bombing' (*Daily Mail* 10.2.95); J. Taylor, 'Monuments to Massacre' (*New Statesman and Society* 22.5.92), pp. 31–2.
2. J. E. Young, 'The Future of Auschwitz' (*Tikkun* 1992, 7:6), pp. 31–3, p. 77. For more detail on the controversy generated by the commemoration of the fiftieth anniversary of Auschwitz, see: I. Buruma, 'The Misleading Mystique of Mass Extermination' (*Spectator* 28.1.95), pp. 9–11; J. Jackson, 'Return to Auschwitz' (*Time* 6.2.95), pp. 18–19; A. Nagorski, 'A Tortured Legacy' (*Newsweek* 16.1.95), pp. 24–5; *The Tablet* 4.2.95, p. 157.
3. N. Ascherson, 'Remains of the Abomination' (*Independent on Sunday Review*, 22.1.95), pp. 12–16, pp. 15–16.
4. G. Kren, 'The Holocaust as History' in A. Rosenberg and G. Myers (eds.), *Echoes from the Holocaust* (Philadelphia: Temple University Press, 1988), pp. 3–50, p. 4.
5. D. LaCapra, 'Representing the Holocaust' in S. Friedlander (ed.), *Probing the Limits of Representation* (Cambridge: Harvard University Press, 1992), note 4, p. 357.
6. J. E. Young, *Writing and Rewriting the Holocaust* (Bloomington: Indiana University Press, 1988), p. 85.
7. A. Oz, *The Slopes of Lebanon* (Vintage, 1991), p. 159. See also: P. Lopate, 'Resistance to the Holocaust' (*Tikkun*, 1989, 4:3), p. 55; J. Neusner, *The Jewish War against the Jews* (New York: KTAV, 1994), pp. 51–2; and E. Wiesel, in P. de Saint-Cheron and E. Wiesel, *Evil and Exile* (Notre Dame: University of Notre Dame Press, 1990), p. 38.
8. U. Tal, 'On the Study of Holocaust and Genocide: Excursus on Hermeneutical Aspects of the Term *Sho'ah*' (*Yad Vashem Studies* 1979, 13), pp. 7–52, pp. 46–52.
9. E. Fackenheim, 'Holocaust' in A. Cohen and P. Mendes-Flohr (eds.), *Contemporary Jewish Religious Thought* (New York: Free Press, 1988), pp. 399–408, p. 399.
10. Etymologically, 'Holocaust' derives from the Greek translation of *ola* (Gen. 22.1; 1 Sam. 7.9). For Wiesel, the term had a number of advantages: (a) it alluded to the *Akedah*, the Binding of Isaac; (b) it emphasized 'the mystical, religious texture of the tragedy'; (c) 'this catastrophe was redolent of fire above all else . . . What does "Holocaust" mean? Total offering by fire'; (d) 'the term also implies total catastrophe'. (de Saint-Cheron and Wiesel, *Evil and Exile*, p. 39). Today, Wiesel argues that 'Holocaust' has been misused, even corrupted: 'It has been so trivialized and commercialized. These days it's used to refer to just about anything.' As a result, he now prefers the term 'Hurban' (see *Evil and Exile*, pp. 39 and 88).

   For a critique of 'Holocaust', see Z. Garber and B. Zuckerman, 'Why Do We Call the Holocaust "the Holocaust"?' (*Modern Judaism* May 1989), pp. 197–211.

Further Reading

Texts which have been used in the body of this reader have not been referred to again in these suggestions for further reading, which are intended to complement those texts cited in each section.

GENERAL

The best introduction to the history of the Third Reich is the four-volume reader of primary sources edited by Geoffrey Pridham and Jeremy Noakes, with an excellent commentary by Jeremy Noakes linking the texts:

NOAKES, JEREMY (ed.), *Nazism 1919–1945*, iv: *The German Home Front in World War II* (Exeter: Exeter University Press, 1998).

PRIDHAM, GEOFFREY, and NOAKES, JEREMY (eds.), *Nazism 1919–1945*, Volume 1: *The Rise to Power, 1919–1934* (Exeter: Exeter University Press, 1983).

—— —— (eds.), *Nazism 1919–1945*, ii: *State, Economy, Society 1933–1939* (Exeter: Exeter University Press, 1984).

—— —— (eds.), *Nazism 1919–1945*, iii: *Foreign Policy, War and Racial Extermination* (Exeter: Exeter University Press, 1988).

Of the many general accounts, historiographical surveys, and biographies of Hitler available the following are particularly useful:

AYÇOBERRY, PIERRE, *The Nazi Question: An Essay on the Interpretation of National Socialism (1922–1975)* (London: Routledge & Kegan Paul, 1981).

BESSEL, RICHARD (ed.), *Fascist Italy and Nazi Germany: Comparisons and Contrasts* (Cambridge: Cambridge University Press, 1996).

BRACHER, KARL-DIETRICH, *The German Dictatorship: The Origins, Structure and Effects of National Socialism* (New York: Praeger Publishers, 1970).

BULLOCK, ALAN, *Hitler: A Study in Tyranny* (New York: Harper & Row, rev. edn. 1962).

CHILDERS, THOMAS, and CAPLAN, JANE, (eds.), *Reevaluating the Third Reich* (New York: Holmes & Meier, 1993).

FEST, JOACHIM, *The Face of the Third Reich* (London: Penguin, 1972).

—— *Hitler* (London: Weidenfeld & Nicolson, 1974).

FREI, NORBERT, *National Socialist Rule in Germany: The Führer State 1933–1945* (Oxford: Blackwell, 1993).

HILDEBRAND, KLAUS, *The Third Reich* (London: Allen & Unwin, 1984).

KERSHAW, IAN, *Hitler* (London: Longman, 1991).

—— *The Nazi Dictatorship: Problems and Perspectives of Interpretation* (London: Arnold, 3rd edn. 1993).

—— *Hitler 1889–1936: Hubris* (London: Allen Lane, 1998).

STACKELBERG, RODERICK, *Hitler's Germany: An Interpretative History* (London: Routledge, 1999).

THE RISE OF NATIONAL SOCIALISM

BARANOWKSI, SHELLEY, *The Sanctity of Rural Life: Nobility, Protestantism and Nazism in Weimar Prussia* (Oxford: Oxford University Press, 1995).

BESSEL, RICHARD, *Germany after the First World War* (Oxford: Clarendon Press, 1993).

—— *Political Violence and the Rise of Nazism: The Stormtroopers in Eastern Germany 1925–1934* (New Haven: Yale University Press, 1984).

BROSZAT, MARTIN, *Hitler and the Collapse of Weimar Germany* (Leamington Spa: Berg, 1987).

CHICKERING, R., *We Men who feel most German. A Cultural Study of the Pan-German League* (London: George Allen & Unwin, 1984).

CHILDERS, THOMAS, *The Nazi Voter: The Social Foundations of Fascism in Germany 1919–1933* (Chapel Hill: University of North Carolina Press, 1983).

ELEY, GEOFF, *Reshaping the Right: Radical Nationalism and Political Change after Bismarck* (New Haven: Yale University Press, 1980).

—— *From Unification to Nazism: Reinterpreting the Nazi Past* (London: Allen & Unwin, 1986).

EVANS, RICHARD J., *Rethinking German History: Nineteenth Century Germany and the Origins of the Third Reich* (London: Unwin Hyman, 1987).

FEUCHTWANGER, EDGAR, *From Weimar to Hitler: Germany 1918–1933* (Basingstoke: Macmillan, 1993).

HAMILTON, RICHARD F., *Who Voted for Hitler?* (Princeton: Princeton University Press, 1982).

HERF, JEFFREY, *Reactionary Modernism: Technology, Culture and Politics in Weimar and the Third Reich* (Cambridge: Cambridge University Press, 1984).

KATER, MICHAEL, *The Nazi Party: A Social Profile of Members and Leaders 1919–1945* (Oxford: Blackwell, 1983).

MOMMSEN, HANS, *The Rise and Fall of Weimar Democracy* (Chapel Hill: University of North Carolina Press, 1996).

MÜHLBERGER, DETLEV, *Hitler's Followers: Studies in the Sociology of the Nazi Movement* (London: Routledge, 1991).

PRIDHAM, GEOFFREY, *Hitler's Rise to Power. The Nazi Movement in Bavaria 1923–1933* (London: Hart-Davis, 1973).

TURNER, HENRY ASHBY, *German Big Business and the Rise of Hitler* (New York: Oxford University Press, 1985).

—— *Hitler's Thirty Days to Power: January 1933* (London: Bloomsbury, 1996).

THE NATURE OF THE NATIONAL SOCIALIST REGIME

BARKAI, AVRAHAM, *Nazi Economics: Ideology, Theory and Policy* (Oxford: Berg, 1990).

BEETHAM, DAVID (ed.), *Marxists in the Face of Fascism* (Manchester: Manchester University Press, 1983).

BULLOCK, ALAN, *Hitler: A Study in Tyranny* (New York: Harper & Row, rev. edn. 1962).

CARR, WILLIAM, *Arms, Autarky and Aggression: A Study in German Foreign Policy, 1933–1939* (London: Edward Arnold, 2nd edn. 1979).

DEIST, W., *The Wehrmacht and German Rearmament* (Basingstoke: Macmillan, 1981).

—— (ed.), *The German Military in the Age of Total War* (Leamington Spa: Berg, 1985).

FINNEY, PATRICK (ed.), *The Origins of the Second World War* (London: Arnold, 1997).

GILLINGHAM, JOHN R., *Industry and Politics in the Third Reich* (Stuttgart: F. Steiner Verlag, 1985).

GREGOR, N., *Daimler-Benz in the Third Reich* (New Haven: Yale University Press, 1998).

HIRSCHFELD, G., and KETTENACKER, L. (eds.), *The Führer State: Myth and Reality* (Stuttgart: Klett-Cotta, 1981).

JÄCKEL, EBERHARD, *Hitler's Weltanschauung: A Blueprint for Power* (Middleton, Conn.: Wesleyan University Press, 1972).

KERSHAW, IAN, and LEWIN, MOSHE (eds.), *Stalinism and Nazism: Dictatorships in Comparison* (Cambridge: Cambridge University Press, 1997).

KOCH, H. W. (ed.), *Aspects of the Third Reich* (London: Macmillan, 1985).

KRAUSNICK, HELMUT, et al., *Anatomy of the SS State* (St Albans: Paladin, 1968).

LAQUEUR, WALTER, *Fascism: A Reader's Guide* (Harmondsworth: Penguin, 1979).

MOMMSEN, HANS, *From Weimar to Auschwitz* (Cambridge: Polity Press, 1991).

MÜLLER, INGO, *Hitler's Justice: The Courts of the Third Reich* (Cambridge, Mass: Harvard University Press, 1991).

NOAKES, J. (ed.), *Government, Party and People in Nazi Germany* (Exeter: Exeter University Press, 1980).

ORLOW, DIETRICH, *The History of the Nazi Party, 1919–1933* (Pittsburgh: University of Pittsburgh Press, 1969).

—— *The History of the Nazi Party, 1933–1945* (Pittsburgh: University of Pittsburgh Press, 1973).

OVERY, RICHARD J., *War and Economy in the Third Reich* (Oxford: Clarendon Press, 1994).

PETERSON, EDWARD N., *The Limits of Hitler's Power* (Princeton: Princeton University Press, 1969).

SCHLEUNES, KARL, *The Twisted Road to Auschwitz: Nazi Policy towards the Jews 1933–1939* (Urbana: University of Illinois Press, 1970).

SEATON, A., *The German Army 1933–1945* (London: Weidenfeld & Nicolson, 1982).

SOFSKY, WOLFGANG, *The Order of Terror: The Concentration Camp* (Princeton: Princeton University Press, 1997).

STACHURA, P. (ed.), *The Shaping of the Nazi State* (London: Croom Helm, 1978).

STERN, J. P., *Hitler, the Führer and the People* (Hassocks: Harvester Press, 1975).

WEINBERG, GERHARD, *The Foreign Policy of Hitler's Germany: Diplomatic Revolution in Europe, 1933–6* (Chicago: University of Chicago Press, 1970).

—— *The Foreign Policy of Hitler's Germany: Starting World War II, 1937–1939* (Chicago: University of Chicago Press, 1980).

—— *Germany, Hitler and World War II: Essays in Modern German History and World History* (New York: Cambridge University Press, 1995).

ZIEGLER, HERBERT F., *Nazi Germany's New Aristocracy: The SS Leadership, 1925–1939* (Princeton: Princeton University Press, 1989).

THE 'SEDUCTIVE SURFACE' OF NATIONAL SOCIALISM

ADAM, PETER, *The Art of the Third Reich* (London: Thames & Hudson, 1992).

ADES, DAWN, et al. (eds.), *Art and Power: Europe under the Dictators 1930–1945* (London: Thames & Hudson, 1995).

BURDEN, H. T., *The Nuremberg Party Rallies 1923–1939* (London: Pall Mall Press, 1967).

LEISER, E., *Nazi Cinema* (London: Secker & Warburg, 1974).

PETROPOLOUS, JONATHAN, *Art as Politics in the Third Reich* (Chapel Hill: University of North Carolina Press, 1996).

RENTSCHLER, ERIC, *The Ministry of Illusion: Nazi Feature Films and their Afterlife* (Cambridge, Mass.: Harvard University Press, 1996).

SCHULTE-SASSE, LINDA, *Entertaining the Third Reich: Illusions of Wholeness in Nazi Cinema* (Durham, NC.: Duke University Press, 1996).

STEINWEIS, ALAN, *Art, Ideology and Economics in Nazi Germany: The Reich Chambers of Music, Theatre and the Visual Arts* (Chapel Hill: University of North Carolina Press, 1993).

WELCH, DAVID (ed.), *Nazi Propaganda: The Power and the Limitations* (London: Croom Helm, 1983).

—— *The Third Reich: Politics and Propaganda* (London: Routledge, 1993).

—— *Propaganda and the German Cinema* (Oxford: Clarendon Press, 1983).

NATIONAL SOCIALISM AND GERMAN SOCIETY

BANKIER, DAVID, *The Germans and the Final Solution: Public Opinion under Nazism* (Oxford: Blackwell, 1992).

BESSEL, RICHARD (ed.), *Life in the Third Reich* (Oxford: Oxford University Press, 1987).

BEYERCHEN, ALAN D., *Scientists under Hitler: Politics and the Physics Community in the Third Reich* (New Haven: Yale University Press, 1977).

CARSTEN, FRANCIS L., *The German Workers and the Nazis* (Aldershot: Scolar, 1995).

CREW, DAVID (ed.), *Nazism and German Society 1933–1945* (London: Routledge, 1994).

KERSHAW, IAN, *The 'Hitler Myth': Image and Reality in the Third Reich* (Oxford: Oxford University Press, 1987).

—— *Popular Opinion and Political Dissent in the Third Reich: Bavaria 1933–1939* (Oxford: Clarendon Press, 1983).

LARGE, DAVID CLAY (ed.), *Contending with Hitler: Varieties of German Resistance in the Third Reich* (Cambridge: Cambridge University Press, 1991).

LIFTON, ROBERT JAY, *The Nazi Doctors: Medical Killing and the Psychology of Genocide* (Basingstoke: Macmillan, 1986).

MASON, TIMOTHY W., *Nazism, Fascism and the Working Class* (Cambridge: Cambridge University Press, 1995).

—— *Social Policy in the Third Reich: The Working Class and the 'National Community' 1918–1939* (Oxford: Berg, 1993).

MÜLLER-HILL, BENNO, *Murderous Science: Elimination by Scientific Selection of Jews, Gypsies and Others: Germany, 1933–1945* (Oxford: Oxford University Press, 1988).

NICOSIA, FRANCIS, and STOKES, LAWRENCE, *Germans against Nazism: Nonconformity, Opposition and Resistance in Everyday Life* (New York: Berg, 1990).

PINE, LISA, *Nazi Family Policy, 1933–1945* (Oxford: Berg, 1997).

STEINERT, MARLIS, *Hitler's War and the Germans: Public Mood and Attitude during the Second World War* (Düsseldorf: Econ Verlag, 1978).

STEPHENSON, JILL, *Women in Nazi Society* (London: Croom Helm, 1975).

THE IMPACT OF NATIONAL SOCIALISM

ALY, GÖTZ, CHROUST, PETER and POSS, CHRISTIAN, *Cleansing the Fatherland: Nazi Medicine and Racial Hygiene* (Baltimore: Johns Hopkins University Press, 1994).

BARTOV, OMER, *The Eastern Front 1941–1945: German Troops and the Barbarisation of Warfare* (Basingstoke: Macmillan, 1985).

—— *Hitler's Army: Soldiers, Nazis and War in the Third Reich* (New York: Oxford University Press, 1992).

BAUER, YEHUDA, *The Holocaust in Historical Perspective* (London: Sheldon Press, 1978).

BRIDENTHAL, RENATE, et al. (eds.), *When Biology became Destiny: Women in Weimar and Nazi Germany* (New York: Monthly Review Press, 1984).

BURLEIGH, MICHAEL, *Ethics and Extermination: Reflections on Nazi Genocide* (Cambridge: Cambridge University Press, 1997).

CESARANI, DAVID (ed.), *The Final Solution: Origins and Implementation* (London: Routledge, 1984).

DALLIN, A., *German Rule in Russia 1941–1945: A Study in Occupation Policies* (London: Macmillan, 2nd edn. 1981).

FRIEDLAENDER, HENRY, *The Origins of Nazi Genocide: From Euthanasia to the Final Solution* (Chapel Hill: University of North Carolina Press, 1995).

—— and Milton, S. (eds.), *The Holocaust: Ideology, Bureaucracy and Genocide* (New York: Krans International, 1980).

FRIEDLAENDER, SAUL, *Nazi Germany and the Jews, i: The Years of Persecution 1933–1939* (New York: HarperCollins, 1997).

GROSS, J. T., *Polish Society under German Occupation: The Generalgouvernement 1939–1944* (Princeton: Princeton University Press, 1979).

HAYES, PETER (ed.), *Lessons and Legacies: The Meaning of the Holocaust in a Changing World* (Evanston, Ill.: Northwestern University Press, 1991).

HILBERG, RAUL, *The Destruction of the European Jews* (Chicago: University of Chicago Press, 1961).

HIRSCHFELD, G., *The Policies of Genocide: Jews and Soviet Prisoners of War in Nazi Germany* (London: Allien & Unwin, 1986).

KOEHL, R., *RKFDV: German Resettlement and Population Policy 1939–1945* (Cambridge, Mass.: Harvard University Press, 1957).

MARRUS, MICHAEL, *The Holocaust in History* (Harmandsworth: Penguin, 1987).

PROCTOR, ROBERT N., *Racial Hygiene: Medicine under the Nazis* (Cambridge, Mass.: Harvard University Press, 1988).

THE LEGACY OF NATIONAL SOCIALISM

ALTER, REINHARD and MONTEATH, PETER (eds.), *Rewriting the German Past: History and Identity in the New Germany* (New York: Humanities Press, 1997).

ASCHHEIM, STEPHEN E., *Culture and Catastrophe: German and Jewish Confrontations with National Socialism and Other Crises* (London: Macmillan, 1996).

BERGMANN, WERNER, and ERB, RAINER, *Antisemitism in Germany: The Post-Nazi Epoch since 1945* (New Brunswick, NJ: Rutgers University Press, 1997).

BRENNER, MICHAEL, *After the Holocaust: Rebuilding Jewish Life in Postwar Germany* (Princeton: Princeton University Press, 1987).

BURUMA, IAN, *The Wages of Guilt: Memories of War in Germany and Japan* (New York: Vintage, 1994).

EVANS, RICHARD J., *In Hitler's Shadow: West German Historians and the Attempt to Escape from the Nazi Past* (New York: Tauris, 1989).

FRIEDLAENDER, SAUL, *Memory, History and the Extermination of the Jews in Europe* (Bloomington: Indiana University Press, 1993).

FULBROOK, MARY, *German National Identity after the Holocaust* (Oxford: Polity, 1999).

HARTMAN, GEOFFREY, *Bitburg in Moral and Political Perspective* (Bloomington: Indiana University Press, 1986).

HERF, JEFFREY, *Divided Memory: The Nazi Past in the Two Germanys* (Cambridge, Mass.: Harvard University Press, 1997).

KURTHEN, HERMANN, BERGMANN, WERNER, and ERB, RAINER (eds.), *Antisemitism and Xenophobia in Germany after Unification* (Oxford: Oxford University Press, 1997).

LaCAPRA, DOMINIC, *History and Memory after Auschwitz* (Ithaca, NY: Cornell University Press, 1998).

NOVICK, PETER, *The Holocaust in American Life* (Boston: Houghton Mifflin, 1999).

STERN, FRANK, *The Whitewashing of the Yellow Badge: Antisemitism and Philosemitism in Postwar Germany* (Oxford: Pergamon, 1992).

TIMM, ANGELIKA, *Jewish Claims against East Germany: Moral Obligations and Practical Policy* (Budapest: Central European University Press, 1997).

YOUNG, JAMES E., (ed.), *The Art of Memory: Holocaust Memorials in History* (New York: Prestel, 1994).

Acknowledgements

Alber, Jens, 'Nationalsozialismus und Modernisierung', *Kölner Zeitschrift für Soziologie und Sozialpsychologie* (1989).

Allen, William Sheridan, *The Nazi Seizure of Power* (London: Eyre & Spottiswood, 1966).

Angermund, Ralph, *Deutsche Richterschaft 1919–1945* (Frankfurt am Main: Fischer, 1990), © 1990 Fischer Taschenbuch Verlag GmbH, Frankfurt am Main, reprinted by permission of Fischer Taschenbuch Verlag GmbH.

Arad, Yitzhak, *Belzec, Sobibor, Treblinka. The Operation Reinhard Death Camps* (Bloomington, Ind.: Indiana University Press, 1987).

Arendt, Hannah, *Origins of Totalitarianism* (London: Secker & Warburg, 1958), © Harcourt Brace Inc. San Diego.

Baldwin, Peter, 'The *Historikerstreit* in Context', in Peter Baldwin (ed.), *Reworking the Past: Hitler, the Holocaust and the Historians' Debate* (Boston: Beacon Press, 1990).

Bartov, Omer, 'The Missing Years: German Workers, German Soldiers', *German History*, 8/1 (1990) (London: Arnold Publishers Ltd., 1990).

Benz, Wolfgang, 'Nachkriegsgesellschaft und Nationalsozialismus: Erinnerung, Amnesie, Abwehr', in *Erinnern oder Verweigern*, Dachauer Hefte 6 (Dachau: Verlag Dachauer Hefte, 1990), reprinted by permission of the author.

Bessel, Richard, 'Why Did the Weimar Republic Collapse?' in Ian Kershaw (ed.), *Weimar: Why Did German Democracy Fail?* (London: Weidenfeld & Nicolson, 1990).

Bloch, Ernst, 'Inventory of Revolutionary Appearance', in *Heritage of our Times* (Cambridge: Polity Press, 1991).

Bock, Gisela, *Zwangssterilisation im Nationalsozialismus: Studien zur Rassenpolitik und Frauenpolitik* (Opladen: Westdeutscher Verlag, 1986), reprinted by permission of the author.

Bracher, Karl-Dietrich, 'Stufen der Machtergreifung', in K.-D. Bracher, W. Sauer, and G. Schulz, *Die nationalsozialistische Machtergreifung: Studien zur Errichtung des Totalitären Herrschaftssystems in Deutschland 1933/4* (Cologne: 2nd edn. Westdeutscher Verlag, 1962), reprinted by permission of the author.

Bracher, Karl-Dietrich, 'Totalitarianism as Concept and Reality', in *Turning Points in Modern Times: Essays in German and European History* by Karl-Dietrich Bracher, (Cambridge, Mass.: Harvard University Press, 1995), © 1995 by the President and Fellows of Harvard College, reprinted by permission of the publisher.

Broszat, Martin, 'Soziale Motivation und Führerbindung des Nationalsozialismus',

Vierteljahrshefte für Zeitgeschichte, 18 (1970), reprinted by permission of R. Oldenbourg Verlag.

Broszat, Martin, 'Resistenz und Widerstand', in Martin Broszat, Elke Fröhlich, and Anton Grossmann (eds.), *Bayern in der NS-Zeit*, iv: *Herrschaft und Gesellschaft im Konflikt* (Munich: Oldenbourg, 1981), reprinted by permission of R. Oldenbourg Verlag.

Broszat, Martin, *The Hitler State* (London: Longman, 1980).

Browning, Christopher, *Ordinary Men: Reserve Police Battalion 101 and the Final Solution in Poland* (New York: Harper Perennial, 1992).

Burleigh, Michael, *Death and Deliverance: 'Euthanasia' in Germany 1900–1945* (Cambridge: Cambridge University Press, 1989).

Burleigh, Michael, and Wippermann, Wolfgang, *The Racial State: Germany 1933–1945* (Cambridge: Cambridge University Press, 1991).

Caplan, Jane, *Government without Administration* (Oxford: Oxford University Press, 1988), reprinted by courtesy of Oxford University Press.

Dahrendorf, Ralf, *Society and Democracy in Germany* (Weidenfeld & Nicolson, 1968), © Piper Verlag.

Deist, Wilhelm, 'The Rearmament of the Wehrmacht', from Militärgeschichtliches Forschungsamt (ed.), *Germany and the Second World War* (Oxford: Clarendon Press, 1990).

Diehl-Thiele, Peter, *Partei und Staat im Dritten Reich: Untersuchungen zum Verhältnis zwischen NSDAP und allgemeiner innerer Staatsverwaltung 1933–1945* (Munich: C. H. Beck, 1971), reprinted by permission of Verlag C. H. Beck.

Dülffer, Jost, *Nazi Germany 1933–1945: Faith and Annihilation* (London: Arnold Publishers, 1996).

Eley, Geoff, 'What Produces Fascism: Pre-industrial Traditions or a Crisis of Capitalism?', in *From Unification to Nazism* (London: Allen & Unwin, 1986), courtesy of Routledge.

Eley, Geoff, 'Nazism, Politics and the Image of the Past: Thoughts on the West German *Historikerstreit*', *Past and Present* (1988).

Falter, Jürgen, *Hitlers Wähler* (Munich: C. H. Beck, 1991), reprinted by permission of Verlag C. H. Beck.

Fraenkel, Ernst, *The Dual State* (Oxford: Oxford University Press, 1941), reprinted by courtesy of Oxford University Press.

Frei, Norbert, *Vergangenheitspolitik: die Anfänge der Bundesrepublik und die NS-Vergangenheit* (Munich: C. H. Beck, 1996).

Fromm, Erich, *The Fear of Freedom* (London: Routledge, and New York: Holt Rinehart, 1942).

Garbe, Detlev, *Zwischen Widerstand und Martyrium: die Zeugen Jehovas im Dritten Reich* (Munich: Oldenbourg, 1993), reprinted by permission of R. Oldenbourg Verlag.

Gellately, Robert, *The Gestapo and German Society: Enforcing Racial Policy 1933–1945* (Oxford: Oxford University Press, 1990), reprinted by courtesy of Oxford University Press.

Gerlich, Fritz, in *Prophetien wider das Dritte Reich: aus den Schriften des Dr. Fritz Gerlich und des Paters Ingbert Naab*, ed. Dr Johannes Steiner (Munich: Verlag Dr Schnell & Dr Steiner, 1946), reprinted by permission of Verlag Schnell & Steiner.

Geyer, Michael, 'The State in National Socialist Germany', in C. Bright and S. Harding (eds.), *State-Making and Social Movements: Essays in History and Theory* (Ann Arbor: University of Michigan Press, 1984).

Golczewski, Frank, 'Polen', in W. Benz (ed.), *Dimensionen des Völkermords: die Zahl der Jüdischen Opfer des Nationalsozialismus* (Munich: Oldenbourg, 1991), reprinted by permission of R. Oldenbourg Verlag.

Gottschling, Ernst, 'Der faschistische Staat: das deutsche Beispiel', in Dietrich Eichholtz and Kurt Gossweiler (eds.), *Faschismusforschung: Positionen, Probleme, Polemik* (Berlin: Akademie Verlag, 1980), reprinted by permission of Akademie Verlag.

Griffin, Roger, *The Nature of Fascism* (London: Routledge, 1991).

Groh, Dieter, 'Le "Sonderweg" de l'histoire allemande: mythe ou réalité', *Annales* 5 (1983), reprinted by permission of Armand Colin.

Gruchmann, Lothar, *Justiz im Dritten Reich 1933–1940: Anpassung und Unterwerfung in der Ära Gürtner* (Munich: Oldenbourg, 1990), reprinted by permission of R. Oldenbourg Verlag.

Hayes, Carlton J. H. 'The Novelty of Totalitarianism', *Proceedings of the American Philosophical Society* (1940).

Hayes, Peter, *Industry and Ideology*: IG *Farben in the Nazi Era* (Cambridge: Cambridge University Press, 1987).

Heilbronner, Oded, 'Der verlassene Stammtisch; vom Verfall der bürgerlichen Infrastruktur und der Aufstieg der NSDAP am Beispiel der Region Schwarzwald', *Geschichte und Gesellschaft*, 19 (1993).

Herbert, Ulrich, *Hitler's Foreign Workers: Enforced Foreign Labour in Germany under the Third Reich* (Cambridge: Cambridge University Press, 1997).

Heuss, Theodor, *Hitlers Weg* (1932), copyright Theodor Heuss Archive, Stuttgart, reprinted with the permission of Deutsche Verlags-Anstalt Stuttgart.

Hilberg, Raul, *Perpetrators, Victims, Bystanders: The Jewish Catastrophe 1933–1945* (New York: Harper Collins, 1992), © Raul Hilberg, reprinted by permission of Harper Collins Publishers, Inc.

Hilberg, Raul, 'Bitburg as Symbol', in Geoffrey Hartman (ed.), *Bitburg in Moral and Political Perspective* (Bloomington: Indiana University Press, 1986).

Hüttenberger, Peter, 'Nationalsozialistische Polykratie', *Geschichte und Gesellschaft*, 2 (1976).

Kater, Michael H, *Doctors under Hitler* (Chapel Hill: University of North Carolina

Press, 1989), © 1990 by the University of North Carolina Press, used by permission of the publisher.

Kautsky, Karl, 'Einige Ursachen und Wirkungen des deutschen Nationalsozialismus', *Der Kampf: sozialdemokratische Monatschrift*, 26/6 (June 1933).

Kershaw, Ian, 'Der 30. Januar 1933: Ausweg aus der Krise und Anfang des Staatsverfalls', in H. A. Winkler (ed.), *Die deutsche Staatskrise 1930–1933* (Munich: Oldenbourg, 1993), reprinted by permission of R. Oldenbourg Verlag.

Kershaw, Ian, 'Widerstand ohne Volk?', in Jürgen Schmädecke and Peter Steinbach (eds.), *Der Widerstand gegen den Nationalsozialismus: die deutsche Gesellschaft und der Widerstand gegen Hitler* (Munich Piper, 1985), reprinted by permission of the author.

Kershaw, Ian, 'Working towards the Führer: Reflections on the Nature of Hitler's Dictatorship', *Contemporary European History*, 2(1993) (Cambridge: Cambridge University Press, 1993).

Kleist-Schmenzin, Ewald von, 'Der Nationalsozialismus', in Anton Kaes, Martin Jay, and Ed Dimendberg (eds.), *The Weimar Republic Sourcebook* (Berkeley and Los Angeles: University of California Press, 1994), © 1994 The Regents of the University of California.

Kocka, Jürgen, 'Ursachen des Nationalsozialismus', *Aus Politik und Zeitgeschichte* (June 1980).

Koehl, Robert, 'Feudal Aspects of National Socialism', *American Political Science Review*, 54 (1960), reprinted by permission of American Political Science Association.

Koonz, Claudia, *Mothers in the Fatherland* (London: Jonathan Cape, 1987), © Abner Stein, London.

Koshar, Rudy, *Social Life, Local Politics and Nazism: Marburg 1880–1935*, (Chapel Hill: University of North Carolina Press, 1986), © 1986 by the University of North Carolina Press, used by permission of the publisher.

Langbein, Hermann, *Im Namen des deutschen Volkes: Zwischenbilanz der Prozesse wegen nationalsozialistischer Verbrechen* (Vienna: Europa Verlag, 1963), reprinted by permission of Loisi Langbein.

Laski, Harold, *Reflections on the Revolution of our Time* (London: Allen & Unwin, 1941), courtesy of Routledge.

Lüdtke, Alf, 'The Honour of Labour: Industrial Workers and the Power of Symbols under National Socialism', in D. Crew (ed.), *Nazism and German Society 1933–1945* (London: Routledge, 1994).

Maier, Charles S., *The Unmasterable Past* (Cambridge, Mass.: Harvard University Press, 1988).

Mallmann, Klaus-Michael and Paul, Gerhard, 'Resistenz oder loyale Widerwilligkeit? Anmerkungen zu einem umstrittenen Begriff', *Zeitschrift für Geschichtswissenschaft*, 41 (1993).

Mann, Thomas, 'Deutsche Ansprache: ein Appell an die Vernunft' (Frankfurt am Main: S. Fischer, 1930), all rights with S. Fischer Verlag GmbH, Frankfurt am Main, reprinted by permission of S. Fischer Verlag.

448 ACKNOWLEDGEMENTS

Mason, Tim, 'The Primacy of Politics', *Das Argument* (1966).

Mason, Tim, 'Intention and Explanation: A Current Controversy about the Interpretation of National Socialism', in T. W. Mason, *Nazism, Fascism and the Working Class* (Cambridge: Cambridge University Press, 1996).

Messerschmidt, Manfred, 'Die Wehrmacht im NS-Staat', in K.-D. Bracher, M. Funke, and H.-A. Jacobsen (eds.), *Deutschland 1933–1945: neue Studien zur nationalsozialistischen Herrschaft* (2nd edn. Düsseldorf: Droste Verlag, 1993), reprinted by permission of Droste Verlag.

Mierendorff, Carl, 'Überwindung des Nationalsozialismus', *Sozialistische Monatshefte* (Mar. 1931).

Mommsen, Hans, *Beamtentum im Dritten Reich* (Stuttgart: Deutsche Verlags-Anstalt, 1966).

Mommsen, Hans, 'Der Nationalsozialismus: kumulative Radikalisierung und Selbstzerstörung des Regimes', in *Meyers Enzyklopaedisches Lexikon* (Mannheim: Lexikonverlag, 1976).

Mommsen, Hans, 'Die nationalsozialistische Machtergreifung und die deutsche Gesellschaft', in Wolfgang Michalka (ed.), *Die nationalsozialistische Machtergreifung* (Paderborn: Ferdinand Schöningh, 1984), reprinted by permission of Verlag Schöningh.

Müller, Klaus-Jürgen, *The Army, Politics and Society in Germany* (Manchester: Manchester University Press, 1987).

Naab, Ingbert, 'Das Dritte Reich ist da!', *Der Gerade Weg* (19 June 1932), reprinted in *Prophetien wider das Dritte Reich: aus den Schriften des Dr. Fritz Gerlich und des Paters Ingbert Naab*, ed. Dr Johannes Steiner (Munich: Verlag Dr Schnell & Dr Steiner, 1946), reprinted by permission of Verlag Schnell & Steiner.

Neumann, Franz, *Behemoth: The Structure and Practice of National Socialism* (San Francisco: Harper & Row, 1966), © Hippocrene Books, New York.

Niethammer, Lutz, *Die Mitläuferfabrik: die Entnazifizierung am Beispiel Bayerns* (Bonn: 1982 Verlag J. H. W. Dietz Nachfolger), © Verlag J. H. W. Dietz Nachfolger GmbH Bonn 1982, reprinted by permission of Verlag J. H. W. Dietz Nachfolger.

Niethammer, Lutz, 'Juden und Russen im Gedächtnis der Deutschen', in Walter H. Pehle (ed.), *Der historische Ort des Nationalsozialismus* (Frankfurt: Fischer, 1990), © 1990 Fischer Taschenbuch Verlag GmbH, Frankfurt am Main, reprinted by permission of Fischer Taschenbuch Verlag GmbH.

Noakes, Jeremy, *The Nazi Party in Lower Saxony 1921–1933* (Oxford: Oxford University Press, 1971), reprinted by courtesy of Oxford University Press.

Paterna E, et al., *Deutschland 1933–1939* (East Berlin: Verlag der Wissenschaften, 1969).

Peukert, Detlev, *Ruhrarbeiter gegen den Faschismus: Dokumentation über den Widerstand im Ruhrgebiet 1933–1945* (Frankfurt am Main: Röderberg, 1976).

Peukert, Detlev, *The Weimar Republic: The Crisis of Classical Modernity* (London: Penguin Books Ltd., 1991).

Peukert, Detlev, *Inside Nazi Germany* (London: Penguin Books Ltd., 1987).

Pingel, Falk, 'The Concentration Camps as Part of the National Socialist System of Domination', in *The Nazi Concentration Camps*, Proceedings of the Fourth Yad Vashem International Conference (Jerusalem, 1980).

Piper, Franciszek, 'The Number of Victims', in Yisrael Gutman and Michael Berenbaum (eds.), *Anatomy of the Auschwitz Death Camp* (Bloomington: Indiana University Press, 1994).

Pyta, Wolfram, 'Ländlich-evangelisches Milieu und Nationalsozialismus bis 1933', in H. Moeller et al. (eds.), *Nationalsozialismus in der Region* (Munich: Oldenbourg, 1996), reprinted by permission of R. Oldenbourg Verlag.

Rabinbach, Anson G., 'The Aesthetics of Production in the Third Reich', *Journal of Contemporary History*, 11 (1976), reprinted by permission of Sage Publications Ltd.

Rauschning, Hermann, *Germany's Revolution of Destruction* (London: Heinemann Educational Publishers, 1939).

Rebentisch, Dieter and Teppe, Karl (eds.), *Verwaltung contra Menschenführung im Staat Hitlers* (Göttingen: Vandenhoeck & Rupprecht, 1987).

Reichel, Peter, *Der schöne Schein des Dritten Reiches: Faszination und Gewalt des Faschismus* (Munich: Carl Hanser-Verlag, 1991), reprinted by permission of Carl Hanser Verlag.

Rückerl, Adalbert, (ed.), *NS-Vernichtungslager im Spiegel deutscher Strafprozesse: Belzec, Sobibor, Treblinka, Chelmno* (Munich: dtv, 1977), © 1977 Deutscher Taschenbuch Verlag, Munich, Germany, reprinted by permission of Deutscher Taschenbuch Verlag.

Schäfer, Hans Dieter, *Das gespaltene Bewusstsein: deutsche Kultur und Lebenswirklichkeit 1933–1945* (Munich: Carl Hanser Verlag, 1981), reprinted by permission of Carl Hanser Verlag.

Schoenbaum, David, *Hitler's Social Revolution* (New York: Doubleday, 1966), © 1966 by David Schoenbaum, used by permission of Doubleday, a division of Random House, Inc.

Steinbach, Peter, 'Zur Auseinandersetzung mit nationalsozialistischen Gewaltverbrechen in der Bundersrepublik Deutschland', *Geschichte in Wissenschaft und Unterricht* (1984/2), reprinted by permission of the author.

Streit, Christian, 'Sowjetische Kriegsgefangene—Massendeportation—Zwangsarbeiter', in Wolfgang Michalka (ed.), *Der Zweite Weltkrieg: Analysen. Grundzüge. Forschungsbilanz* (Munich: Piper Verlag, 1989).

Stümke, Hans-Georg, 'From the "Peoples' Consciousness of Right and Wrong" to "The Healthy Instincts of the Nation": The Persecution of Homosexuals in Nazi Germany', in Michael Burleigh (ed.), *Confronting the Nazi Past: New Debates on Modern German History* (London: Collins & Brown, 1996).

Tenfelde, Klaus, 'Soziale Grundlagen von Resistenz und Widerstand', in Jürgen Schmädecke and Peter Steinbach (eds.), *Der Widerstand gegen den Nationalsozialismus: die deutsche Gesellschaft und der Widerstand gegen Hitler* (Munich: Piper, 1985).

Toller, Ernst, 'Zur deutschen Situation (1932)', in *Gesammelte Werke*, i: *Kritische Schriften, Reden und Reportagen* (Munich: Carl Hanser Verlag, 1978), reprinted by permission of Carl Hanser Verlag.

Tyrell, Albrecht, 'Die NSDAP als Partei und Bewegung: Strategie und Taktik der Machtergreifung', in Volker Rittberger (ed.), *1933: wie die Republik der Diktatur erlag* (Stuttgart: Kohlhammer, 1983), reprinted by permission of the author.

Ulbricht, Walter, *Der faschistische deutsche Imperialismus* (East Berlin: Dietz, 1956), reprinted by permission of Karl Dietz Verlag Berlin.

Vollnhals, Clemens, 'Entnazifizierung: politische Säuberung unter alliierter Herrschaft', in Hans-Erich Volkmann (ed.), *Ende des Dritten Reiches—Ende des Zweiten Weltkriegs: eine perspektivische Rückschau* (Munich: Piper Verlag, 1995).

Vondung, Klaus, *Magic und Manipulation: ideologischer Kult und politische Religion des Nationalsozialismus* (Göttingen: Vandenhoeck & Rupprecht, 1971).

Wehler, Hans-Ulrich, *The German Empire 1871–1918* (Oxford: Oxford University Press, 1985), reprinted by courtesy of Oxford University Press.

Weindling, Paul, *Health, Race and German Politics between National Unification and Nazism 1870–1945* (Cambridge: Cambridge University Press, 1989).

Wild, Alfons, *Hitler und das Christentum* (Augsburg: Verlag Kaas & Grabherr, 1931).

Wollaston, Isabel, *A War against Memory? The Future of Holocaust Remembrance* (London: SPCK, 1996).

Yahil, Leni, *The Holocaust. The Fate of European Jewry* (Oxford: Oxford University Press, 1990).

Young, James, E., *The Texture of Memory: Holocaust Memorials and Meaning* (New Haven: Yale University Press, 1993).

Zimmermann, Michael, *Rassenutopie und Genozid. Die Nationalsozialistische 'Lösung der Zigeunerfrage'.* (Hamburg: Christians Verlag, 1996), reprinted by permission of Christians/Druckerei & Verlag.

Zofka, Zdenek, *Die Ausbreitung des Nationalsozialismus auf dem Lande: eine regionale Fallstudie zur politischen Einstellung der Landbevölkerung in der Zeit des Aufstiegs und der Machtergreifung der NSDAP 1928–1936* (Munich: Neue Schriftenreihe des Stadtarchivs. München, 1979), reprinted by permission of the author.

Index